VR Developer Gems

VR Developer Gems

Edited by
William R. Sherman

CRC Press
Taylor & Francis Group
Boca Raton London New York

CRC Press is an imprint of the
Taylor & Francis Group, an **informa** business

AN A K PETERS BOOK

CRC Press
Taylor & Francis Group
6000 Broken Sound Parkway NW, Suite 300
Boca Raton, FL 33487-2742

First issued in hardback 2019
First issued in paperback 2022

ISBN 13: 978-1-138-03012-1 (hbk)
ISBN 13: 978-1-03-247549-3 (pbk)
ISBN 13: 978-1-315-15776-4 (ebk)

DOI: 10.1201/b21598

Library of Congress Cataloging-in-Publication Data

Names: Sherman, William R., author.
Title: VR programing gems / William R. Sherman.
Other titles: Virtual reality programming gems
Description: Boca Raton : Taylor & Francis, a CRC title, part of the Taylor & Francis
imprint, a member of the Taylor & Francis Group, the academic division of T&F
Informa, plc, 2019. | Includes bibliographical references.
Identifiers: LCCN 2018056231 | ISBN 9781138030121 (hardback : acid-free paper)
Subjects: LCSH: Virtual reality—Computer programs.
Classification: LCC QA76.9.C65 S48 2019 | DDC 006.8—dc23
LC record available at https://lccn.loc.gov/2018056231

Visit the Taylor & Francis Web site at
http://www.taylorandfrancis.com

and the CRC Press Web site at
http://www.crcpress.com

Contents

Section III   Interaction

Section IV   Agents & Avatars

Section V   Third Person POV Cameras

Section VI   Virtual Worlds

Section VII   Advanced Rendering for VR

Section VIII   Perception for Immersion

Section IX   DIY VR Hardware

Section X   Building the Infrastructure of VR

Preface

Wow! As my co-author Alan Craig and I state in our book *Understanding Virtual Reality, second edition*, virtual reality (VR), a technology-driven medium that has been making steady progress for literally half a century, has, *all of a sudden*, become an overnight success.

Surely however, over the entire course of those 50 years, a lot of good work has been done and shared throughout the (then) relatively small VR community. I (and I'm sure others) have felt for some time that we need a Gems-style book to help not just that community but also help all the new enthusiasts joining in. Because of other book projects hanging over me, it took some time before I felt comfortable pulling the trigger on a "Gems" book—though as it happens, the rapid growth of the VR community sufficiently compelled me to disregard sanity and initiate this book even before that other project was complete. And so, with the help of Rick Adams at Taylor and Francis, I embarked on this effort to collect useful contributions in bite-sized morsels of wisdom to share with that growing community.

As with other "Gems" series, the goal with this volume is to provide concepts and code that can help old and new practitioners to do something new or bring a new approach to current and future projects. *VR Developer Gems* probably has a more even balance between concepts and code than many of the other series of this type. For readers looking primarily for code, there is plenty of that, but we hope that all readers will find the value in knowing more about the audience of VR experiences, both from the approach of human perception along with their expectations of the medium and how those expectations change as the medium and the audience matures.

Chapter Roundup

The most important consideration for a gems collection book is who the contributors should be and what topics they can address. My goal was to find authors who were experts in many different areas as well as from different eras of VR development. Furthermore, I had hoped to get contributions from all seven continents (including work done in Antarctica). Not all my recruiting efforts were successful, often the timing of competing deadlines was a factor—and while I didn't quite get all the continents this time, there is a pretty good mix of authors and topics.

I also worked to have a broad composition of software tool representations, but the book has somewhat of a Unity bias. This was not intentional but more of a consequence that there is an imbalance in Unity usage within the VR research community, which is thus reflected here.

On the people side, a good portion of the contributors have been working in the field of VR for half of the medium's 50 years of evolution. Many other contributors have perhaps been working for only a decade or so, and a few are up and coming toolsmiths, applications developers, and theorists.

For this volume, contributions were solicited from existing VR-related email lists (including my own personal list of VR colleagues), plus I reached out to individuals recommended to me by those who learned of the project through one channel or another. And finally, I invited contributions based on interesting VR projects that I encountered while doing my own VR research—did I mention I happened to be writing another book at the time.

Once all the contributions were confirmed, I divided and ordered them into ten categories to help our readers quickly find chapters of immediate interest. Obviously for a "gems" book, readers are not expected to engage with each chapter in the order presented, but given a list of topics, they (you) might be able to quickly find related topics that might be immediately beneficial and then by considering the other chapter section groupings will find themselves (yourself) intrigued by what else might be hidden in the mix.

Time Value of Knowledge

Progress in the medium of VR continues to accelerate, which means, we now enjoy improvements to hardware, software development tools, and most importantly, highly polished experiences faster than can be absorbed. While this keeps us all on our toes, it also has the unfortunate consequence of dating and moving onto other fashions of what's presently hot in the VR developer community. This consequence can affect different topics/chapters of this book at different rates. Of course overall the principles of good development don't change and neither do basic graphical transformations, but sometimes the programming interface used evolves in such a way that our code no longer matches the new interface.

In some chapters, the choice was made to provide algorithms in pseudo-code that the reader can then transpose into their own preferred development environment. In other cases, code examples are for a specific development environment. In these cases, however, the code has been commented to a point where a developer using another system (or an evolved version of the same system) can still apply the principles presented to their own work.

I'll mention some of the editorial oversight later, but code comments was one place where I tried to ensure consistency among the chapters. Indeed, one of my longstanding personal programming principles has been the insistence of highly (and well) commented code. (As an undergraduate student, I was taught in one of my first classes on artificial intelligence that the primary reader of any code you write will be a human.) And I found that often the particular human reading those comments would be me. Undoubtedly, more often than not, comments I wrote years before would help me know what I was thinking at the time I was developing whatever code I was now reevaluating. So I know firsthand the value of good commenting habits.

Quirks of Editorship

In the prefaces of my other book-scale publishing efforts, I (and my co-author) speak of our "quirks of authorship." Well in this effort I have a different role. Certainly not all the authors are going to write in the same style, and I had no intent to coax style uniformity. However, I did attempt to have this book present a fairly consistent usage of terminology, while not wanting to be overly heavy-handed in forcing my particular quirks on the authors (perhaps with one exception).

And that exception is my one "forbidden" term: *immersive virtual reality*. (A phrase you will not see again here and should exclude from your thoughts!) Why do I eschew that term? Well, I contend that the use of **that term** implies that there would also be non-immersive VR—but "physical immersion" is a key element of VR, perhaps the primary element. Thus, there cannot be, and therefore, I don't want to imply the existence of, a non-immersive form of VR. So to avoid that implication, I avoid-like-the-plaque the use of **that term**.

There are other terminology expressions which I encourage, though don't 100% mandate, such as preferring the use of the word "*travel*" when talking about moving around a space and saving "*navigation*" for when movement is combined with wayfinding.

Another terminology issue I have is with the term "*position*," which I find to be ambiguous in that it can mean anything from a 1-D point on a number line to a point in 3-D coordinate space, to the rotational setting of a knob, to telling someone not to move any of their body parts—"hold that position." Therefore, my tendency is to use "*location*" for a point in N-space (1-D, 2-D, 3-D) and "*orientation*" for a sequence of rotations about given axes. When using "*position*," I prefer to then qualify what usage is being indicated, such as 6-degree-of-freedom (DOF) position (which means both location and orientation and is the type of value returned by a "6-DOF position tracker"). (And I contend that most people also subconsciously believe that to be the case even if in their writings they treat "position" to only mean "location." In fact, I believe I can demonstrate that they subconsciously believe that but only in person and only when they don't know that I'm demonstrating that.) But alas, my influence is limited and most game engines use "position" to specifically refer to "location in 3D coordinates."

One last terminology consideration is, as with my other books, I prefer the use of singular them/their as genderless pronouns, and I point to Shakespeare and Austin as trendsetters in that regard.

In Unity C# the "this" operator refers to the object to which a script has been attached. However in most Unity C# code you will not notice many uses of "this" because for many of the common uses of "this" such as referring to the object's "transform" value Unity assumes the intent is "this.transform". As this book is designed as a pedagogical resource, I prefer to avoid the "implicit this" and make it explicit. Thus you may notice a greater preponderance of "this" operators in the Unity code herein.

One final quirk (not counting extensive comments mentioned in the previous section), or perhaps this is more of a pet-peeve of mine, is the use of numeric citations. Many academic papers use numeric superscripts to call out reference citations, but as I read those papers, I find it annoying to have hold my place and interrupt my reading to search at the back of the paper/chapter/book to see who is being cited. Thus, for the chapters herein, I have imposed my preference for citations that indicate author(s) and year directly within the prose.

Acknowledgments

All published books are a team effort, and a book with contributed chapters even more so. My first thanks go to Rick Adams and his team at Taylor & Francis, including Jessica Vega and Jennifer Stair as well as Kritheka and the rest of the production team at codeMantra. Rick and I had been discussing the possibility of my doing a programming-oriented book on VR for a few years before we decided 1) I was too busy to write an entire new book by myself and 2) the VR programming paradigm had shifted considerably from VR-specific libraries that interface with OpenGL—though I still do work in that sphere from time to time, as required. So in 2015, Rick and I agreed that a gems-style book was a good solution to those two considerations. And thus, our journey began.

Next I would like to thank my long-time colleagues John Stone and Dan Coming, with whom I've worked and continue to work on various VR-related projects. John and Dan both provided encouragement for pursuing the gems-style book and provided advice in chapter recruitment and selection.

Obviously all the contributing authors provide the most important value that this book provides, and I thank them profusely for agreeing to contribute and then following through not just with a first draft but with my multiple requests for changes and clarifications that, for some, may have bordered on the obsessive. I also owe my thanks to all the contributors for their patience as this book took 18 months or so longer than I anticipated for it to make it to the shelf. I take full responsibility for that, from my crazy conceit that I could juggle this at the same time as working on another big book project as well as teaching and all my other responsibilities.

I also would like to thank the VR community at large. It doesn't seem that long ago that I was a newbie myself participating in a community of experts who were always willing to share their knowledge with anyone joining the community and in particular with a couple of youngish researchers from a fairly nascent VR facility at a supercomputing center in the Midwest who audaciously thought they were ready to write a book on VR (back in 1994). Of particular note are the IEEE VR and SIGGRAPH communities where ideas and demonstrations of VR were great places to connect and learn.

Speaking of supercomputing centers, I was blessed with the opportunity to start my career at a premiere (in conversation I might argue *the* premiere—at least at the time) supercomputer center—the National Center for Supercomputing Applications (NCSA) where I was able to expand my knowledge of computer graphics and then VR as part of The Visualization Group. From there my thanks go to the people at the Desert Research Institute who entrusted me with a brand new Vis and VR team. And finally to another great visualization team at another amazing supercomputing organization—the Advanced Visualization Lab at Indiana University. I've been privileged to not just have time and access to the best equipment but also great people with whom to collaborate. And of course, one of those people is Alan Craig with whom I've been co-authoring articles and then books on VR and during that time travelling the world visiting VR facilities near and far to gather as much information as possible from all the wonderful researchers and practitioners at those labs—and then debate each other on the best way to communicate what we learned.

Of course, I also owe a debt of gratitude to my wife Sheryl and the rest of our family that allow me to spend evenings and weekends working on this and other VR projects!

A Look to the Future

As noted at the outset of the preface, I had hoped to include many more authors and many more topics in this volume. In particular, I'd like to see more inclusion of the Unreal Engine for VR development, along with more Unity implementations. Ideally, if there is a favorable outcome for this book, there will be a favorable outlook for additional volumes in this series.

Possible future volumes would not necessarily have the same chapter section groupings, but neither will sections from this volume be excluded. And perhaps we'll get that contribution from Antarctica among other new domains.

Editor

William R. Sherman is a member of the Indiana University Advanced Visualization Lab, where he leads efforts in scientific visualization and VR. He also teaches undergraduate and graduate courses on VR and visualization, which he has done for two decades, including at the University of Nevada, Reno (UNR) and before that, at the University of Illinois at Urbana–Champaign (UIUC).

Previously he founded the Center for Advanced Visualization, Computation, and Modeling (CAVCaM) at the Desert Research Institute (DRI), where he led the VR and visualization efforts, including overseeing the installation of a FLEX CAVE-style VR system as well as a six-sided CAVE system. Prior to DRI, he led the VR effort at the NCSA at UIUC, working with the Electronic Visualization Lab to install and operate the second CAVE VR system—at NCSA in 1994.

He has authored several book chapters and papers on the topics of scientific visualization and VR and has organized and led "bootcamps" on immersive visualization in collaboration with the Idaho National Laboratory and Kitware, Inc. Sherman is the architect of the *FreeVR* VR integration library. He has attended every single IEEE Virtual Reality Conference since 1995 and was chair of the 2008 Conference in Reno Nevada. Even prior to consumer availability of VR, Sherman had the opportunity to visit and participate in a plethora of VR experiences at more than 100 VR research and development labs throughout the world. And he is the co-author of the books: *Understanding Virtual Reality, Developing Virtual Reality Applications*, and *Understanding Virtual Reality, second edition*.

List of Contributors

Mahdi Azmandian
University of Southern California
Los Angeles, California

Felipe Bacim
Apple, Inc.
Cupertino, California

Amy C. Banić
University of Wyoming
Laramie, Wyoming

Christoph W. Borst
University of Louisiana at Lafayette
Lafayette, Louisiana

Doug A. Bowman
Center for Human-Computer Interaction,
    Virginia Tech
Blacksburg, Virginia

Nicholas Brunhart-Lupo
National Renewable Energy Laboratory
Golden, Colorado

Andrew Cordar
University of Florida
Gainesville, Florida

Maxime Cordeil
Faculty of Information Technology
Monash University
Melbourne, Victoria, Australia

Andrew Cunningham
School of Information Technology and
    Mathematical Sciences
 University of South Australia
Adelaide, South Australia, Australia

Margaret Dolinsky
Indiana University
Bloomington, Indiana

Jason Drummond
University College London
Bloomsbury, London

Chauncey E. Frend
Indiana University (IUPUI)
Indianapolis, Indiana

Luis Diego González-Zúñiga
Samsung Research
Staines, UK

Kenny Gruchalla
National Renewable Energy Laboratory
Golden, Colorado
and
University of Colorado at Boulder
Boulder, Colorado

Andrew Guagliardo
University of Hawai'i at Mānoa
Honolulu, Hawaii

Yao Heng
University of Florida
Gainesville, Florida

Elliot Hunt
University of Wyoming
Laramie, Wyoming

Bret Jackson
Macalester College
Saint Paul, Minnesota

Kyle Johnsen
University of Georgia
Athens, Georgia

J. Adam Jones
University of Mississippi
Oxford, Mississippi

Daniel F. Keefe
University of Minnesota
Minneapolis, Minnesota

Rajiv Khadka
University of Wyoming
Laramie, Wyoming

Robert Kooima
Chicago, Illinois

Regis Kopper
Duke University
Durham, North Carolina

Marc Erich Latoschik
University of Würzburg
Würzburg, Germany

Jason Leigh
University of Hawai'i at Mānoa
Honolulu, Hawaii

Benjamin Lok
University of Florida
Gainesville, Florida

Peter O'Shaughnessy
John Lewis Partnership
Bracknell, UK

Shawn Patton
Principal Game Designer at Schell Games
Pittsburgh, Pennsylvania

Kevin Ponto
University of Wisconsin
Madison, Wisconsin

Bernie Roehl
Virtual Escapes Inc.
Waterloo, Ontario, Canada

Evan Suma Rosenberg
University of Minnesota
Minneapolis, Minnesota

Daniel Roth
University of Würzburg
Würzburg, Germany

Rebecca Rouse
Rensselaer Polytechnic Institute
Troy, New York

William R. Sherman
Indiana University
Bloomington, Indiana

Richard Skarbez
La Trobe University
Melbourne, Victoria

Booker Smith
Purdue University
West Lafayette, Indiana

Jan-Philipp Stauffert
University of Würzburg
Würzburg, Germany

Anthony Steed
University College London
Bloomsbury, London

Frank Steinicke
University of Hamburg
Hamburg, Germany

John E. Stone
University of Illinois at
    Urbana-Champaign
Urbana, Illinois

Ainsley Sutherland
MIT Comparative Media Studies
Cambridge, Massachusetts

Fatemeh Tavassoli
University of Florida
Gainesville, Florida

Russell M. Taylor II
ReliaSolve LLC
Pittsboro, North Carolina

Deniz Tortum
MIT Comparative Media Studies
Cambridge, Massachusetts

Ross Tredinnick
University of Wisconsin
Madison, Wisconsin

Kees Van Kooten
NVIDIA
Santa Clara, California

Mingqian Wang
University College London
Bloomsbury, London

Lee Wasilenko
VR Dev School Inc.
and
Orange Bridge Studios Inc.
Nelson, British Columbia

Rene Weller
University of Bremen
Bremen, Germany

David Whittinghill
Purdue University
West Lafayette, Indiana

Mary C. Whitton
University of North Carolina at Chapel
    Hill
Chapel Hill, North Carolina

Jeffrey Wood
University of Florida
Gainesville, Florida

Jason W. Woodworth
University of Louisiana at Lafayette
Lafayette, Louisiana

Rhys Yahata
University of Southern California
Los Angeles, California

Ming-Der Yang
National Chung Hsing University
Taichung, Taiwan

Gabriel Zachmann
University of Bremen
Bremen, Germany

SECTION I
The Medium of VR

The content may be everyday or fantastical. It may be to learn how to accomplish a task, or become more familiar with the workings of a molecule.

We indicated at the outset that physical immersion is one of the things that makes VR interesting—it is also a key ingredient that distinguishes VR from other media. Our definition of VR also integrates the notion of immersion, but in that case focuses on a different aspect of immersion—mental immersion. Immersion can thus be partitioned into two concepts: physical immersion and mental immersion.

Mental immersion is imagining oneself in another place or situation. Physical immersion is having the ability to (bodily) interact in a place or situation. For virtual reality we might say:

- *Mental Immersion:* when the **mind** engages a world as though it were real.
- *Physical Immersion:* when the **body** engages a world as though it were real.

Physical and mental immersion are thus not the same thing, though the two can certainly go hand-in-hand. Importantly, while mental immersion is often important to a VR experience, we can also attain mental immersion from many other media. Therefore, mental immersion is not a unique aspect of virtual reality.

One way in which the two forms of immersion are intertwined (and indeed this might also be possible for other media) is through physiological responses—responses such as increases in heart rate, perspiration, and perhaps rate of breathing. If one's heart starts beating rapidly from an experience through a medium, does that not also imply that their body is engaged in the world? Okay, yes, it is the brain (the mind) that is controlling those bodily functions, but then the brain is part of the body! So perhaps the demarcation of what is and is not physical immersion is a little blurry.

In any event, the medium of VR does require that the virtual world be presented from a physical perspective that matches their body movement, in particular their head.

1.2.2 What's in a Name?

We have a pretty solid definition of what it is, but this medium we now call virtual reality has not always gone by that name. It wasn't until 1989 when the expression *virtual reality* was coined and popularized by the founder of VPL, one of the first companies to market this technology: Jaron Lanier. Funded through contracts with NASA, Lanier's company, VPL, developed a head-mounted display and a glove-input device for NASA, which were also made available for purchase by research labs around the world. These products, the VPL Eye-phones and the VPL Data-glove, were perhaps the first time research teams could explore virtual reality without having to also develop the technology itself.

Prior to the coining of *virtual reality*, the medium was often referred to as "Virtual Environments" or "Immersive Environments." Going back to the original VR system from Ivan Sutherland's lab (in Harvard and then moved to the University of Utah), the system was simply known simply as the "Head Mounted Display." The more interesting name was assigned to one of the tracking technologies: "The Sword of Damocles." *The Sword of Damocles* referred specifically to the mechanical tracking system that was mounted to and extended from the ceiling—hanging over the participant reminiscent of the fabled sword.

Before Sutherland's system, there were flight simulators to train pilots on various aspects of flight, but to that point (and not for another few years), these simulators did not use digital computers to simulate the virtual world, and thus they fall outside our particular definition of virtual reality. However, modern flight (and ship and railroading) simulators do fall within our definition, and in general can be considered a specific form of virtual reality.

1.3 To What End?

Knowing what VR is, and having a name to refer to it, while important, do not get to the heart of why we should pursue this medium. We need to address the question: what can we do with it? Or more importantly, why should we make use of this medium over another, perhaps easier to wield, medium?

Observing the current VR landscape, one could be forgiven for mistaking it as being all about games and gaming. And perhaps for some (or most) users it is! Certainly the gaming market plays a major role in the medium, particularly by serving as a catalyst that has made VR affordable. However, that's not how the medium was first envisioned, and indeed there are many other established "genres" of VR experiences.

Yet, being a catalyst for affordability isn't necessarily the only contribution of entertainment VR experiences—people who learn how to interact within such virtual worlds become accustomed to the interface, and can jump right in when it comes to some other (e.g. scientific, business, etc.) uses of VR.

So, if not just for fun, how else might VR be employed?

- If we can put researchers, designers, etc. into a world where some object exists (future automobile, future building, future wing design), then what can they learn by visiting that world? If they learn that there is a mistake in that future car or wing design, they can come back to present reality and make corrections.
- If a new worker needs to become familiar with machines they are not accustomed to operating, can we send them to a world where mistakes are not catastrophic (or even mildly detrimental), and have them return to our reality now familiar with those machines?
- If a museum-goer has not personally suffered a brain injury, can we send them to a world where they can get a small taste of the inner, unseen, impairment of a person who does suffer ailments from injury or disease, and then return a little wiser?
- If a patient visits a world where something playful and snowy is occurring, can we keep their mind away from the reality of painful treatments as they undergo them?
- If another patient wants to inure themself (under the guidance of a therapist) of some psychological handicap or traumatic memory, can we help them do so in a safe place, and at a measured pace.
- If someone has to learn how to make quick decisions in particular scenarios that may arise as they execute a mission, can we put them in representative situations where decisions are made, and where that experience can be relived and reevaluated afterward? (Of course, in this case, the first widespread use of what we can consider VR—flight simulation—has done this for decades. Now though this has been extended to friend/foe room evacuation missions and even sports.)

- If a biologist wants to shrink themself and fly around molecular structures to gain insights on how water moves through a membrane pore, or how chlorophyll converts sunlight into energy, we can make it so. And they can share that world with collaborators and students (Figure 1.1).
- If a student wants to explore ancient Rome (Figure 1.2), or Harlem in the Roaring 20 s, by "walking" the streets themself, or perhaps led by a guide with information about the sights and sounds of the era, they can do so without leaving their home, or dorm.
- If a documentarian wants to capture events in a visually and sonically all-encompassing way, such that it can be presented back in as realistic a form as possible, then they can provide the means for others to have a partial first-person experience of that event.

Figure 1.1

The *VMD* molecular visualization tool has both desktop and VR interfaces. Here VMD is run in a CAVE-like system, allowing the primary user to walk around, while allowing other viewers to come along for the ride. (Image courtesy of Chauncey Frend.)

Figure 1.2

In this *Rome Reborn* application for educating participants about the statue of Maxentius, icons indicate where audio recordings with information about the Basilica and statue can be activated. (Image courtesy of Frischer Consulting, Inc.)

- If a geologist wants to prepare the team for a research trip to the field—perhaps many thousands of miles away—and would like them to have at least some nominal familiarity with the region, perhaps they can go on a virtual reconnaissance trip first. Or maybe any tourist who plans to visit modern Rome in the near future!
- If a designer wants to work free-form in three dimensions, they might engage with a 3D painting tool, or a tool with 3D shapes that can be placed and manipulated, perhaps adding visual or vocal annotations for later visits to the world either by themself or collaborators or clients.
- And yes, if someone does want a challenge where they find themself in a world with fantastical weapons accompanied by companions to battle a hoard of foes... well they can do that too.

Obviously there are enormous possibilities of how one can make use of the medium of VR. And in each of the instances listed above there are many different scenarios expanding the potential exponentially. Indeed, many of these propositions have already been explored—some for decades [Craig et al., 2009].

1.3.1 Early Experimentation

In his paper and talk on "*The Ultimate Display*," computer graphics pioneer Ivan Sutherland succinctly expressed many of these notions even before he and his colleagues developed the first VR system with a computer-generated virtual world [Sutherland, 1965]. Thus once Sutherland's team did develop the first HMD driven by computer simulation [Sutherland, 1968], those first VR virtual worlds were far too simple to accomplish any of the concepts listed above. Indeed, other than the real-time perspective rendering, these worlds were not very interesting at all.

Yet these worlds, or at least the conceptualization of The Ultimate Display with these working demonstrations were enough to spark the imagination in others who recognized that eventually the technology would be sufficient to create such worlds, and they set out to move the technology forward, and along the way explore the effectiveness of this nascent medium. Among those that recognized the medium's potential were Fred Brooks and Scott Fisher.

Fred Brooks, as chair of the new Department of Computer Science at the University of North Carolina at Chapel Hill (UNC-CH), was enthralled by the possibilities of what was to later be named virtual reality. One of the first projects for exploring the utility of the medium for scientific advancement was the GROPE project [Brooks et al., 1990]. GROPE was both a tool for researching molecular dynamics, and also a system by which the performance of the researchers could be measured. In their paper, Brooks and colleagues report four key conclusions about the utility of such an interface:

- Adding haptics to a visual display improves "*perception and understanding both of force fields and of world models populated with impenetrable objects.*"
- Adding a haptics feedback interface to the tool seems to improve performance by about two-fold (yet they seemed to be expecting a better improvement).
- Researchers (chemists) were able to use the system to quickly arrive at what (unbeknownst to them) were good, even optimal, docking positions of a drug into an active site of a protein molecule.

- Researchers (chemists) found that they had a much higher understanding of "*the details of the receptor site and its force fields, and of why a particular drug docks well or poorly.*"

They also made the (accurate) prediction that "*entertainment, not scientific visualization, will drive and pace the technology*" [Brooks et al., 1990].

Beyond academia, one organization with a need for good tools for science and engineering research and development was the U.S. space agency, NASA. Beginning in the mid-1980s (again before VR was the term), Scott Fisher formed the VIrtual Environment Workstation (VIEW) lab to do as the title implied—explore the technology and content creation of virtual environments, with a focal point on what would come to be called virtual reality [Fisher et al., 1988] (Figure 1.3). At the time they had to build or contract companies to prototype and build the interface hardware required for VR. Specifically, they built their own head-based viewing displays in-house, and contracted to VPL for "datagloves" (a glove input device that provides hand and finger pose tracking).

After some time exploring the display and rendering technology, the team also began looking at applications relevant to NASA's mission. One application in particular that came about from this work was the *Virtual Windtunnel* (VWT) [Bryson and Levit, 1992]. The VWT project was shared between a handful of organizations, mostly within NASA, but also some academic institutions, including Brown University, where they began work on how to best design the user interface.

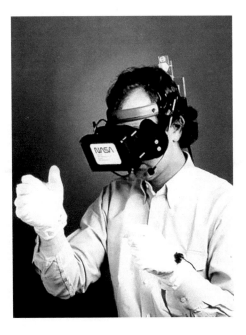

Figure 1.3

In the NASA VIEW program commercial HMDs were not yet available, so NASA often built their own units (here the second version), and also commissioned contractors to construct units. (Image courtesy of NASA / S.S. Fisher, W. Sisler, 1986.)

1.3.2 Early Commercial Success

Before becoming viable, virtual reality had to be explored, and we've seen a couple of those explorations. Eventually, the technology reached a point where researchers, technologists, and business-minded people would explore how this technology could be financially profitable.

Flight simulation was the early commercial success, and already had a large pool of consumers able to pay the costs of what was then pretty expensive equipment. Of course, this enterprise was well before the concept was looked upon as virtual reality, and to a large degree used technologies different from the typical head-tracking that was becoming common in the growing field. At the time it was labeled "out-the-window simulation," which today we might consider a particular genre of VR. And so this success is different than some of the other attempts at income-earning VR.

In the mid 1990s, research studies demonstrated the profitable (in a patient-healing sense of profit) use of VR for exposure treatment for psychological afflictions, beginning with the treatment of phobias. Specifically, collaborators at Emory University and Georgia Tech teamed up [Rothbaum et al., 1996], and after the research success created the company Virtually Better Inc. to package hardware and software for purchase by clinicians for the treatment of various phobias directly in the doctor's office—whereas the typical phobia exposure therapy would often involve traveling to various sites where the fear can be experienced in the real world—a small step at a time.

Later, in addition to phobia exposure, Virtually Better also explored the treatment of Post Traumatic Stress Disorder (PTSD) with clinicians guiding treatments through an interface control board. This has also been further researched by collaborators with military units, which during times of conflict often have an abundance of patients (Figure 1.4).

For people in every-day experiences there have also been opportunities to experience VR at various public-venue installations. The first notable foray into public-VR came from the company W-Industries. They created the Virtuality arcade-VR system—a system using personal-computer capacity systems for computation and graphics, and an internally

Figure 1.4

In the *Bravemind* program realistic events from a war zone are recreated to help guide soldiers suffering from PTSD to recovery (through the aid of a clinician). (Image courtesy of Skip Rizzo, USC-ICT.)

designed HMD along with position-tracked controllers and the sitting or standing kiosks for the players (Figure 1.5).

The initial push was to place groupings of two or four units in standard video arcades of the era (early 1990s), where multiple people could compete in a shared virtual world, starting with the "classic" *Dactyl Nightmare*. The problem is that unlike most of the game machines in an arcade (which don't require an employee's constant attention), VR experiences require considerable explanation, and then also supervision while the game is taking place—otherwise either the participant might damage something, or not know what to do and have a terrible experience. This extra personnel expense, combined with the more expensive gaming units, as well as larger floor space requirements made these systems an unsustainable investment for most arcades—though at the beginning, the novelty may have brought some new customers, it just wasn't enough to cover the expenses.

Another business model attempted with the Virtuality systems was to have an extended experience that would require return visits. The *Legend Quest* experience was thus developed to provide a VR role-playing style game, years before it would be popular as a desktop gaming genre. In *Legend Quest*, players explore a Dungeons & Dragons style world and battle skeletons and giant spiders and wolves, etc, as well as finding treasure and equipment that they can use to further their quest. By promoting the experience as something people would return to with a consistent group of friends to continue their quests, they looked to create an on-going audience.

And while certainly this was breakthrough technology at the consumer-access level, and there was considerable interest for a time, it simply was before its time. Virtuality was first released in 1990, and by 1997 the company was filing for bankruptcy.

Another foray into VR for public consumption was entered by the Walt Disney companies. At first, there was a single VR experience that was made available as a "limited release" at the Epcot Center in Orlando Florida. Indeed, this release was also a means for

Figure 1.5

In the *Legend Quest* experience (a Dungeons & Dragons styled quest game for multiple players using the Virtuality arcade-VR system), participants face creatures as they go out on quests to find treasures in the virtual world. (Images courtesy of Virtuality Group PLC.)

the Disney VR creative team to test what worked best with the general population as far as VR was concerned. For example, the VR pods that were deployed had ergonomics similar to a motorcycle, and indeed could be tilted from side to side. However it was found that this "feature" was a detriment to the experience for too many people, so it was disabled, and the seats were set to be immobile, which is how they were ultimately deployed in the "wider" release [Pausch et al., 1996].

One modern business model for location-based VR entertainment (i.e. public venue) is to have multiplayer mission-based experiences, often using widely recognized intellectual property such as from the *Ghostbusters* and *Star Wars* film series. The VOID group has developed this model, deploying experience venues in several cities world-wide. To make these venues attract audiences, they go beyond what can be experienced in the home, providing on-body tactile effects for multiple players along with technologies such as $30' \times 30'$ physical tracked walking space, passive haptics, and 4D effects (e.g. misters, wind, heat, smell). But there are also those pursuing a business model of VR arcades, where people can pay an hourly rate to use consumer VR systems, but with the added benefit of a large library of software they would otherwise have to purchase. Plus a VR arcade will have helpers who know how to operate the system and be able to help them get started with the experiences—and perhaps recommend experiences. Also, the reduced hardware costs, and indeed software that is more cost effective—either because it has become easier to develop, or because it is being sold at mass-market costs. On top of all that, the public audience is now much more amenable to virtual reality, and generally more comfortable with higher-technology interfaces.

1.3.3 Reaping the Rewards of VR

So there is certainly fun to be had from VR, and there are plenty of entertainment opportunities available. Indeed, in the modern era of VR (post January 2016), VR for entertainment dwarfs the other uses of VR, whereas in the past, VR was almost exclusively used for scientific, business, and military purposes. Now all non-gaming uses of VR have essentially become the "noise" in the VR economy. Even so, the use of VR in the non-gaming areas has also increased, but it is just more difficult to notice. So there are still many uses of VR that can be profitable.

The profits obtained by VR are not necessarily financial rewards. So in what ways can VR profit us?

- **Intellectually (Scientifically)**: VR can help reveal interrelationships within datasets that might otherwise be hard to find.
- **Educationally**: VR can bring students to places (including abstract places) that let them explore worlds and tinker with the relationships between concepts and become better informed through personal experience.
- **Experientially**: VR can provide the means to practice a skill in a circumstance more closely resembling the actual activity—except perhaps more safely, and with better statistical analysis of their performance over time. In some cases, they might prepare for a particular operation (be it medical or combat or whatever). Another experiential benefit comes from the narrative offshoot style of VR ("cinematic-VR"), which provides a means of fictional and journalistic narratives that put the viewer in the scene, even if their only interaction is in how they turn their head.

- **Healthily**: In addition to better training and preparation by medical personnel, and better medical devices and pharmaceuticals through scientific explorations, we have already found how VR can serve to improve the mental health of patients with particular maladies.
- **Creatively**: VR can assist in creative pursuits both on the design and design review side of things, and in the fine arts, and sometimes even the performing arts.
- and of course: **Financially**: When VR can help prevent a bad design, or lead more quickly to a revelation about a medical issue, or avoid drilling where there is no oil, that savings in time and materials is savings in money. Or perhaps some future application may provide the tools for doing direct financial analysis and/or business process assays.

To reiterate, gaming and entertainment now dominate the landscape of immersive experiences, with the "serious" applications only being a fraction of the available applications—perhaps even a seemingly insignificant amount. Yet the pool of "serious" applications continues to grow, and there are also many new tools for the building of custom applications—custom applications that can be easily shared with others now more likely to have compatible hardware configurations.

1.4 Design Choices

Not surprisingly, the design of VR experiences has shifted dramatically due to the rise of consumer VR systems. Both on the hardware front, but also in world creation software that has made it easier to jump in and start creating virtual worlds. In a short overview chapter we can only touch upon the basics. For an in-depth look at design choices, I un-humbly refer to my book-long exploration of VR [Sherman and Craig, 2018].

1.4.1 Designing for the Hardware

In the past there was very little consistency between VR systems (perhaps other than a small cadre of CAVE installations that shared software through a user community). In many other cases, software was written in-house, and generally that's where it stayed. For software that was shared between sites with non-homogeneous hardware, the software would thus need to be able to handle a wide variety of configurations, and certainly that software did exist, but few of these tools were installed in more than a handful of facilities [Bierbaum et al., 2001; Kreylos, 2008; Sherman et al., 2013].

In the past a major consideration for the development of a new VR experience was what hardware it should be designed for: CAVE vs. HMD; one hand or two; track finger movements, or use buttons and joysticks; and whether to track other parts of the body. Of course in many instances these decisions were made at the time of establishing the research lab which, once it chose a CAVE or an HMD, that is the hardware all their software would target from that point forward.

With the advent of consumer VR systems, most include an HMD with two hand controllers—or on the lower end of the scale (i.e. phone holders to convert a phone into an HMD with a built-in computer). For a time, these may be independent consumer bases, and certainly differences will remain—the computing power of a phone will likely always be less than a desktop, and the phone interface controllers will probably be simpler than a full HMD system (though in this case perhaps at some point both will simply track a user's hand directly). But for now, they are different, and most full HMD systems will have two full 6-DOF controllers (location and orientation) whereas the phone systems may have one 3-DOF controller (orientation only).

1.4.2 Designing with Modern Software

Creators are now developing to a much larger user base, and even when creating applications for use in-house, lower hardware costs allow for several teams and users within their organization able to be equipped to make use of the tool. Certainly the big boon for development has been the inclusion of VR interface features into popular game development systems—aka "game engines"—such as Unity and Unreal (both of which are featured in various chapters in this book).

In addition to providing a platform that can be easier to quickly begin creating a virtual world, game engines can also now abstract the type of VR device to the point where developers are less concerned about specific hardware interface devices, and more concerned with how body movements (gestures) can be melded with physical controls such as buttons and joysticks to provide an intuitive user interface.

Because game engines have become so widely used, and simplify application creation for HMD VR systems, other developers have likewise created the means to link at least one of the popular game engines (Unity) with CAVE-style VR displays. (For example, see the gem in Chapter 4 [Tredinnick and Ponto, 2019]).

1.4.3 Designing the Virtual World

The design of virtual worlds for virtual reality interfaces is of course a very important component of the resultant experience. Indeed, it is sufficiently important that a few paragraphs in an introductory chapter on developing VR is unsuitable for attempting to provide advice on what works and what should be avoided. However, we can convey some broad choices that designers will need to address from the outset (and other chapters in this book will provide further advice).

Probably the first choice a VR experience designer will consider is how to represent the world. And the first question for that representation is whether the world should be verisimilar or not. Verisimilar, which means appearing to be real, is often thought of as a good thing, and in many cases, such as providing a simulation experience for training, realism is especially important. But the look of reality is not necessarily important in other cases, and that can go either direction: less real, or hyper-real/fantastical.

Representations that are less real can serve the tasks of visualization and data inquiry well. In cases such as exploring a relationship graph there aren't even any real-world corollaries to make verisimilar a possibility. The same is true in the case of molecular visualizations, once you get smaller than the wavelength of visible light. But scientists have constructed representations that have become familiar to the point that we accept them as being true (even though to a degree there are certainly some aspects that are misrepresentations of reality).

We could consider the other end of the spectrum then to be fantastical worlds where things look somewhat realistic, but go beyond what we know to be possible in our planet Earth existence. We might encounter these representations in worlds designed to entertain us either as an interactive game, or as an experiential narrative (360-movie / Cinematic-VR).

Thus broadly speaking we can see this as three steps in semblance to our reality:

- utilitarian
- verisimilar
- fantastical

1.4.4 Designing the Interface to the World

For the user interface to the world, we might again divide interface styles into realistic and non-realistic. And again considering tools for exploring data or exploring designs (perhaps the look of a new shoe), we might have a utilitarian interface that instead of having to physically walk through the space, we can fly or spring through the world around us. Indeed, verisimilar means of travel can become rather tedious when viewing a building that has been designed for a client to inspect: does one have to walk up all the stairs and all the way down the hall just to look at the corner office?

The two primary aspects of an experience that require user interaction involve their movement through the world and their ability to manipulate objects within the world. For example, does the user make a fist grabbing gesture to take hold of an object? Or perhaps they can point at the object from a distance and pull a trigger that "grabs" the object while it is well beyond their physical reach. In considering both travel and manipulation, we might find where the two overlap. For example, one might use the grab action on a virtual steering wheel object in the virtual world, which in turn affects movement through the world. Alternately, the world itself may be thought of as an object which can be grabbed!

1.4.4.1 Navigation: Travel + Wayfinding

Once again, for training simulations, the verisimilar course would generally be the best, though within reason, if physical walking isn't an impactful part of the training, then perhaps a means of jumping or flying through the space can be acceptable, but then maybe the hand-world interface should be more realistic.

Flying around unrealistically might be an appropriate travel interface both for utilitarian types of experiences (e.g. molecular visualization) and for fantastical experiences. Perhaps the exact same interface operations will be good in either instance. Although flying in the fantastical world might require flapping of the arms, or at least making a Superman flying pose.

Again, travel and object manipulation might present overlapping design options. Specifically, as alluded to above, one might consider the world to be an object when designing the means to move through the world. From the user's perspective: the question is what is being moved? Me, or the world? And perhaps—though not sufficiently studied— if you consider the world to be an object that you are moving as you are remain still, your brain might then not consider the vestibular perception of non-motion to be a mismatch with your visual perception (which would be beneficial in reducing sim-sickness).

Of course, the most realistic form of travel is the physical movement of the user's own body—physical locomotion. Though certainly most adults generally have enough experience in the control of vehicles (or perhaps even mounted animals) that enables these forms to be treated as methods of travel that match their everyday experience.

Otherwise, a common form of travel in VR is simply to point in the desired direction of movement and away you go. A newer solution, made popular by companies selling VR to consumers, has been the point-teleport (or what I call "tele-hop") method of travel. By avoiding continuous virtual movement it is thought to reduce the likelihood of sim-sickness. This form of travel is operated ether by pointing at the floor to where you want to hop, or pointing upward with a parabolic arc emanating from your hand/controller and where it arcs back downward contacting a flat surface, that's where you'll jump when you release the activation. (In some cases the direction you face when you land can be a rotational offset controlled either by a wrist rotation or a valuator input.)

Another choice available to VR experience designers is to take the available physical movement space and make it seem larger than the reality. These techniques work by fooling the user either into thinking they are walking straight when in fact they are walking in a circular arc (*redirected walking* [Razzaque et al., 2001]), or by altering the world behind their back causing them to exit a space with the outside world rotated from how it was when they entered the space (*impossible spaces* [Suma et al., 2011]). A small game that demonstrates the impossible spaces is the "Unseen Diplomacy" experience (Figure 1.6), which has users moving down corridors and crawling through ducts, and as they do, the outer world is altered in order to always keep the user within the physical walking space. The notion of redirected walking is discussed in some detail in Chapters 27 and 28 of this book [Steinicke, 2019; Azmandian et al., 2019].

One other aspect of moving through a virtual world is the concept of wayfinding. We can think of wayfinding as being the flip-side of travel, whereby the two operations together (wayfinding + travel) comprise the complete operation of navigation. Navigation then is moving through the world with a purposeful destination and consciously working to arrive at the right place.

Features that can be designed into a virtual world to assist with wayfinding include things such as large, distinguishable landmarks, signs that point the way toward particular points of interest, and maps, which might be static maps, or GPS-style maps that show where you are located within the world.

Figure 1.6

In *Unseen Diplomacy*, the virtual world is generated such that users are always turned back to remain within the trackable bounds of the real world.

1.4.4.2 Object Interaction

Another important consideration for the interaction design of a VR experience is how the user(s) can interact with objects. We have already alluded to two forms of interaction—making a fist when in contact with an object to initiate a grab operation is the first; the other form is the telekinetic reach style where the user might shoot a ray from one of their hands, and when that ray hits an object that is not just part of the background scenery, then it can be grabbed with an activation trigger. The user might then be able to summon the object to their proximity, or manipulate it remotely by twisting it or flying it across the room and placing it.

At the top level, we speak of four classifications for how manipulations can be actioned by the user:

- **Direct user control**: gestured actions performed by the user that mimic a real-world interaction;
- **Physical control**: using a physical device that the user touches to control an element of the virtual world;
- **Virtual control**: using virtual objects (those within the world itself) to control another element of the virtual world; and
- **Agent control**: giving commands (typically vocally) to an entity within the virtual world to have it perform the manipulation.

The verisimilar approach is of course to use the *direct user control* approach as it is defined as mimicking reality. Of course, as with the other design choices, strict fidelity to reality is not always the best (or most appropriate) selection. Yet that does not mean direct user control should always be avoided. Sometimes the *physical control* method is problematic for the reason that it is too easy for the developer to map button presses or joystick movements to actions in the world, which is convenient for them to program, but can often be non-intuitive and thus hard to remember for the users. *Virtual controls* have the issue that because they exist only in the virtual world, another control method is required to manipulate the virtual controls! Perhaps there is a virtual lever within the virtual world, and the participant operates that lever with direct user control—i.e. they reach for the knob at the end of the lever, make a fist, and move the lever up (Figure 1.7). The *agent control* method requires a means of communicating with the agent. Modern speech recognition solves half of this problem, but the system must then parse the meaning from the word sequence.

And the other ingredient of manipulating the virtual world is how the world is programmed to respond to the actions. With modern game engines, a common method is to apply simulated physics to the objects in the world that the user can interact with, and just allow the realistic object interactions proceed unscripted. Again, this verisimilar method might be good in some situations, but not the best solution in others. For example in our molecular viewer, we might want to properly calculate bonding forces between the molecules, but not have "realistic" gravity which causes the molecules to fall to the ground—we'd rather have them remain floating in space for the user to choose their own preferred view.

1.5 In Closing

So there it is, a quick introduction to virtual reality, and how as designers of immersive experiences there are first and foremost, many avenues for which VR can be applied and

Figure 1.7

In *Titanic VR*, there are virtual controls that are operated using the physical hand controller to "grab" the joystick to manipulate the controls of the submersible the participant is virtually riding. This experience also permits direct physical inputs using the circular touchpads on the controllers as an alternate means of affecting the submersible operations.

be useful, and while we might all enjoy being entertained, we should continue to explore that plethora of directions this medium can be taken. And when designing experiences in these varying fields, design for the task at hand. You might even use the same software—the same game engine—when working on your molecular viewer, but you can employ different features of that software to provide an interface appropriate to the task.

The rest of this book provides a wide variety of tips, techniques, concepts, and simply things to think about when creating immersive experiences, and so read through the ones that seem to apply to your immediate goals, and then skim the rest.

Let's get out there and create the best virtual reality experiences we can.

References

[Azmandian et al., 2019]

Azmandian, Mahdi, Rhys Yahata, and Evan Suma-Rosenberg (2019). Exploring large environments with redirected walking. In Sherman, W. R., editor, *VR Developer Gems*, Chapter 28. Boca Raton, FL: A K Peters/CRC Press.

[Bierbaum et al., 2001]

Bierbaum, Allen, Christopher Just, Patrick Hartling, Kevin Meinert, Albert Baker, and Carolina Cruz-Neira (2001). VR juggler: A virtual platform for virtual reality application development. In *Proceedings of the IEEE Virtual Reality 2001 Conference*, Yokohama, Japan: IEEE, pages 89–96.

[Brooks et al., 1990]

Brooks, Jr., Fred. P., Ming Ouh-Young, James J. Batter, and P. Jerome Kilpatrick (1990). Project grope GROPE—Haptic displays for scientific visualization. *SIGGRAPH Computer Graphics,* Dallas, TX, 24(4):177–185.

[Bryson and Levit, 1992]

Bryson, Steve and Creon Levit (1992). The virtual wind tunnel. *IEEE Computer Graphics and Applications*, 12(4):25–34.

[Craig et al. 2009]

Craig, Alan B., William R. Sherman, and Jeffrey D. Will (2009) *Developing Virtual Reality Applications*. Burlington, MA: Morgan Kaufmann Publishers.

[Fisher et al., 1988]

Fisher, Scott, Elizabeth M. Wenzel, C. Coler, and Michael W. McGreevy (1988). Virtual environment interface workstations. In *Proceedings of the Human Factors Society 32nd Annual Meeting*, Santa Monica, CA, pages 91–95.

[Kreylos, 2008]

Kreylos, Oliver (2008). Environment-independent VR development. In *International Symposium on Visual Computing (ISVC)*, Las Vegas, NV: Springer, pages 901–912.

[McLuhan, 1964]

McLuhan, Marshall (1964). *Understanding Media: The Extensions of Man*. New York, Toronto: McGraw-Hill.

[Pausch et al., 1996]

Pausch, Randy, Jon Snoddy, Robert Taylor, Scott Watson, and Eric Haseltine (1996). Disney's Aladdin: first steps toward storytelling in virtual reality. In *SIGGRAPH '96, Proceedings of the 23rd Annual Conference on Computer Graphics and Interactive Techniques*, New Orleans, LA: ACM, pages 193–203.

[Razzaque et al., 2001]

Razzaque, Sharif, Zac Kohn, and Mary Whitton (2001). Redirected Walking: Technical Report TR01–007. Technical report, University of North Carolina at Chapel Hill, Chapel Hill, NC.

[Rothbaum et al., 1996]

Rothbaum, Barbara Olasov, Larry Hodges, Benjamin A. Watson, G. Drew Kessler, and Dan Opdyke (1996). Virtual reality exposure therapy in the treatment of fear of flying: A case report. *Behaviour Research and Therapy*, 34(5–6):477–481.

[Sherman et al., 2013]

Sherman, William. R., Daniel Coming, and Simon Su (2013). FreeVR: Honoring the past, looking to the future. In *Proceedings of the Engineering Reality of Virtual Reality 2013*, San Francisco, CA: International Society for Optics and Photonics (SPIE), volume 8649, pages 864–906.

[Sherman and Craig, 2018]

Sherman, William. R. and Alan B. Craig (2018). *Understanding Virtual Reality: Interface, Application, and Design*, Second Edition. Cambridge, MA: Elsevier.

[Steinicke, 2019]

Steinicke, Frank (2019). Misperception of self-motion and its compensation in virtual reality. In Sherman, W. R., editor, *VR Developer Gems*, Chapter 27. Boca Raton, FL: A K Peters/CRC Press.

[Suma et al., 2011]

Suma, Evan A., Seth Clark, Samantha Finkelstein, Zachary Wartell, David Krum, and Mark Bolas (2011). Leveraging change blindness for redirection in virtual environments. In *Proceedings of the IEEE Virtual Reality 2011 Conference*, Singapore, pages 159–166.

[Sutherland, 1965]

Sutherland, Ivan. E. (1965). The ultimate display. In *Proceedings of 3rd International Federation for Information Processing (IFIP) Congress*, New York, NY, pages 506–508.

[Sutherland, 1968]

Sutherland, Ivan. E. (1968). A head-mounted three dimentional display. In *Proceedings of 4th International Federation for Information Processing (IFIP) Congress*, Edinburgh, UK, pages 757–764.

[Tredinnick and Ponto, 2019]

Tredinnick, Ross and Kevin Ponto (2019). UniCAVE: A distributed rendering system for Unity3D. In Sherman, W. R., editor, *VR Developer Gems*, Chapter 4. Boca Raton, FL: A K Peters/CRC Press.

2

VR and Media of Attraction
Design Lessons from History

Rebecca Rouse
Rensselaer Polytechnic Institute

2.1 Introducing Media of Attraction

Designers working with emerging media today, such as virtual reality (VR), may have much in common with other early practitioners working with new technologies from years past. Design practice changes in significant ways as a medium undergoes the economic, cultural, and technological processes of institutionalization. Pioneering VR designers today, for example, likely have more in common in terms of challenges faced, techniques used, and solutions implemented with the pioneering designers of old media, than they will with mainstream designers who work with VR if it becomes as institutionalized as Hollywood film or commercial videogames. This chapter presents a theoretical and historical framework for understanding the work of practitioners at the forefront as designers of *media of attraction*. This cross-historical perspective can not only give us new insights about how to design work with emerging media, but also encourage us to rethink some central debates in the field, including how we might value and understand our own work today. What would Georges Méliès, or Alice Guy Blaché, or any other of these early adventurers in the new media of years past, have created with VR? The media of attraction concept looks back to earlier innovators to gain inspiration and insight for our own practice with technologies like VR, and future media yet to emerge.

What are media of attraction? This concept is inspired by film scholarship on what is known as Cinema of Attraction. Beginning in the late 1970s and early 1980s a group of film scholars [Gunning 1986, 2003; Musser 1990, 1994; Abel 1993; Gaudreault 2011] came to realize the way early film had been understood was misguided. Early cinema had previously been looked at through the lens of contemporary film and characterized as an 'infant' cinema, not quite worthy of scholarly investigation. Historicized from a standpoint of medium centricity (a way of thinking that is a hallmark of Modernism) the development narrative had been constructed to center on the most talented practitioners uncovering or discovering the essential characteristics inherent to film. These discoveries then allowed the film medium to develop to its natural and fullest potential, starting in silence and black and white, then progressing to sound, and then color, large formats, 3D, the digital, and beyond.

This way of thinking had some problems. The early cinema works were devalued as primitive, and as a result they had not been studied closely. In addition, the surrounding ancillary cultural and economic practices that were a part of early film had not been studied either. And the role of these cultural and economic forces in the development of film as an institutionalized form (as we know it today) had not been closely examined, because the myth of medium centric development served as a totalizing explanation. Unsurprisingly, the neat periodization of film history related above has since been debunked [Abel and Altman 2001; McMahan 2002]. It turns out the innovation and development processes for film were much messier and more circular—a process certainly familiar to those working with emerging technologies today.

In the late 1970s and early 1980s when this group of film scholars and historians dug more deeply, they found that early work on film was so different from the later institutionalized form, they needed a new word to describe it. They coined the term Cinema of Attraction to describe films made around the world from the 1890s to about 1907–1908, when the film institutionalizing process began to take off with more speed. This change occurred thanks to developments like the formation of Thomas Edison's Motion Picture Patents Company (MPPC) in 1908. (Edison's MPPC began to conglomerate independent producers and impose standards in the burgeoning industry, as well as introduce costly litigation for patent infringement, and generally narrow the field, making entry into the industry more difficult for newcomers.) But why did the film scholars choose the term *attraction* to describe these early works? Their thesis is that these early works exhibit a remarkable range of qualities, making it difficult to gather them all under one term, but they all share the quality of attraction. This means that for the spectator, these film experiences all include an aspect of wonder or astonishment at the capability of the film technology itself. In addition, early films were often exhibited as attractions, at World's Fairs and Expositions, as a part of vaudeville shows, and in other explicitly performative venues like the Musée Grévin in Paris, alongside magic shows and other illusions and spectacles.

Beyond the exhibition venues, there were many significant differences between Cinema of Attraction films and the later institutionalized films we know today. To begin with, the pioneering filmmakers had no word for their role. This was before the term 'director' was developed, and as a result they were called all sorts of names including presenter of views, operator, moving photographer, and kinematographer, and often unnamed and uncredited (credits did not regularly appear in the earliest films, and there was no copyright process for scripts until 1912). There was no streamlined distribution network in the beginning years, and so films were exhibited in other venues such as fairs and vaudeville houses. In addition, the director did not do the editing; this was the job of the presenter.

The person responsible for exhibiting a collection of films at a venue would be the one to decide in what order the short films would be shown, whether to make any cuts, and whether to add sound such as live musicians, a film narrator (a live performer who would accompany projection), or even live actors staged behind the projection screen voicing dialogue.

This ecosystem surrounding early film presentation points to another unique quality for Cinema of Attraction—it often lacked narrative self-sufficiency. Supporting technologies and techniques (and people) were needed to help the audience make sense of the experience. This may sound familiar to designers working with new technologies today. The experience for today's users is rarely as seamless as some technology developers or the popular press might have us believe. Often, good old-fashioned, human interaction and performance is key to bringing users in and out of the experience, for troubleshooting, and for explaining or teaching users how to engage the technology.

The case of early sound in film is a good example to further illustrate this often circular, messy, and fascinating history of technology development. Contrary to what many of us may remember from history class, *The Jazz Singer* (1927) was not the first sound film. As Alison McMahan has so brilliantly articulated, a closer look at the historical development of sound in film "rewrites periodization" of film history [McMahan 2002, p. 45]. By 1902, Gaumont, a major French filmmaking company, was making sound films (with hundreds produced between 1902 and the early 19-teens—see Figure 2.1.) But even earlier, the technology had been demonstrated by three different companies at the 1900 Paris Universal Exposition. Before that, the German filmmaker Oskar Messter began work with sound film in 1896, and still earlier, Edison's *Dickson Experimental Sound Film* was developed in 1894.

Figure 2.1

Film still from Alice Guy Blaché's *Tourne une Phonoscène* (1905). Alice Guy Blaché directs a sound film at Gaumont, in one of the first "backstage" films. This film depicts Blaché at work in the Gaumont studio in Paris with the Chronophone 'sound-on-disc' technology.

It must be noted, the technologies used to create these early sound film experiences were not the same as the famous *The Jazz Singer* feature length 'talkie' in 1927. Later films used a different sound synchronization technology, with optical synchronization, meaning the sound was photographically recorded onto the side of the image film strip. These later sound films also used more advanced technologies for amplification. The earlier films used 'sound-on disc' recording technologies like the phonograph, along with mechanical synchronization techniques to play the phonograph record and film images together, and compressed air systems for amplification of sound. The earlier systems were difficult to develop for, and often glitchy in performance. But they were nevertheless widespread and enjoyed by the film-going public. So the silent film era was not so silent after all. McMahan has gone on to develop a compelling argument for the public expectation and understanding that even those films shown without synchronized sound in the early years were understood by audiences as *supposed* to have sound. McMahan also demonstrates that early film practitioners had sound in mind as they wrote and directed these early projects, using sound (voiced or not) to advance dramatic narrative, create atmosphere, for comic effect, and so forth.

Looking at the incredibly complex and fascinating history of early sound film with its multiplicity of approaches, technologies, and techniques reveals a messiness (and creative flexibility) that may seem more familiar to those of us working with new technologies today, and less like the polished technologies, codified team structures, and streamlined processes of Hollywood. If we accept there is not much connection between Cinema of Attraction and cinema in its contemporary institutionalized form, then can we find an interesting relationship between Cinema of Attraction and other media in attraction phases, such as radio, television, and even VR today? If emerging media works today could be understood as part of a larger, cross-historical category of media of attraction, instead of naïve or embryonic forms of some forthcoming standardized form, we might open up new ways of understanding this type of work and how it should be valued. Some of the dominant rhetorics about innovation, standardization, and seamlessness might be reframed, and we could have a new perspective on what constitutes progress in the field. To further explore this idea, I suggest a set of characteristics or qualities that define media of attraction, based on both historical research as well as my own experiences as a mixed reality designer working with emerging technologies over the past 12 years.

Thinking in this cross-historical manner can allow a kind of genealogical approach to emerge, looking at technologies and creative practice across time periods (Figure 2.2). Take for example Winsor McKay's *Gertie the Dinosaur* (1914) [Canemaker 2005]. Being aware of the surrounding cultural and economic forces at work to produce this kind of media artifact mean it is no longer just an example of "early animation" that is primitive compared to contemporary works by Disney and Pixar, but that it has all sorts of interesting connections with other practices, both from before (such as animal shows and chalk talks) and after (like Mixed Reality).

In summary, media of attraction can be understood as encompassing great variety and exuberant divergence in creative strategies across time and technologies, but with four central characteristics in common across this multiplicity: media of attraction are *Unassimilated, Interdisciplinary, Seamed,* and *Participatory.*

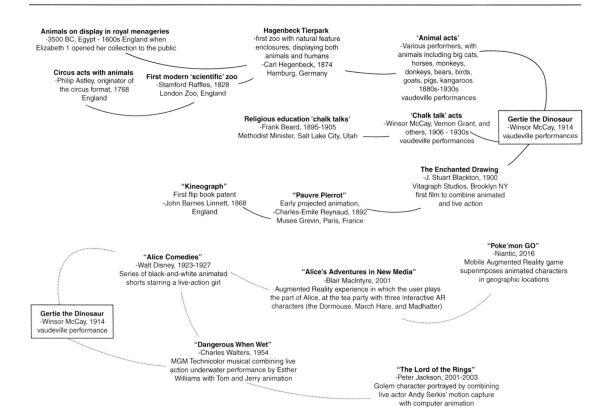

Figure 2.2

Towards a visual representation for the genealogy of media of attraction artifacts, highlighting historical and aesthetic connections, with *Gertie the Dinosaur* as an example. The top tree, with solid line connections, displays historical influences on the artifact; the bottom tree displays later descendants.

2.1.1 Characteristic 1: Media of Attraction are Unassimilated

Unassimilated here refers to a set of related qualities that undergird media of attraction. These media are not yet institutionalized, meaning they retain a sense of novelty for audiences, and have no formal, codified training for practitioners. They also lack a formalized means of criticism, having no 'language' or standard set of aesthetic/formal characteristics established as best practices. A valuable outcome of these qualities of unassimilation is the opportunity to develop a wide range of custom-made artifacts, unfettered by the conventions of production and reception seen in established media. On the other hand, the unassimilated qualities of media of attraction also lead to some detrimental outcomes—most notably difficulty in distributing work, and lack of archiving.

2.1.2 Characteristic 2: Media of Attraction are Interdisciplinary

Media of attraction draw on multiple art forms and techniques, and necessitate the application of a variety of skills and approaches. They usually require complex teams to support this mode of production. Interdisciplinary teams not only result in particular challenges, but also have the potential for synergy, leading to a rich multiplicity of forms and functions, and an enigmatic quality not seen as often in fully institutionalized forms or those created by a solo producer.

2.1.3 Characteristic 3: Media of Attraction are Seamed

Contrary to the rhetoric and even outright hype of popular press that often surrounds media of attraction, the artifacts themselves do not exhibit a seamless quality. Instead, edges show, and the patchwork of ways in which multiple forms of representation come together are not hidden. Sometimes, this manifests as a lack of narrative 'self-sufficiency,' meaning ancillary structures, technologies, and techniques are needed for the audience member to make sense of the experience. As discussed in Sherman and Craig's paper on Literacy in Virtual Reality, the VR user is "about as literate as a beginning reader […] often, we need an expert to guide us through the meanings of elements we don't yet comprehend—typically a person involved in the creation of the application" [Sherman and Craig 1995, p. 39]. However, this exposure of seams can also be leveraged for the pleasure of mediation, enhancing the user experience, by making the user aware of the technology itself, and enabling a double sense of wonder at both the mastery of the designers, and the technological illusion itself. Of course, this is not always achieved; seams also have the potential to confuse and frustrate users.

2.1.4 Characteristic 4: Media of Attraction are Participatory

Media of attraction artifacts all reach out to their audiences to engage in a direct way. This engagement stretches along a continuum, from direct address soliciting audience responses in performance contexts like vaudeville theaters, to interactive mechanical and digital systems that require user input to run. Tensions are developed between attraction, narrative, participation or interactivity, and seamedness, however, these tensions can prove to be productive.

Across all four of these characteristics, a vast variety of aesthetic, structural, and narrative choices are available to media of attraction practitioners. By definition, these choices have not yet been narrowed (or closed off) at this stage of the medium's development. This array of choices is nevertheless all inextricably bound up with the particular challenges, limits, and affordances of the technology at hand—all of which the creators are (at times quite painfully) aware. Still, there is an exciting promise for the designer working at the frontier of a media of attraction: the possibility to mine these four characteristics for exploration of the widest variety of approaches, to support creativity, and to value bespoke, novel solutions. More in-depth discussion of each of these characteristics can be found in recent publications [Rouse 2016; Rouse, Chang, & Ruzanka 2017]. These characteristics can also be observed in early VR work, surveyed in *Developing Virtual Reality Applications* [Craig et al. 2009]

2.2 Historical Examples

To further illustrate the media of attraction concept, a variety of examples across time periods are presented. Instead of revisiting well-trodden ground and discussing works by those already considered major designers in the history books, designers and examples discussed less often are highlighted, as they have much to offer in terms of insight and inspiration.

2.2.1 Robert Barker and Panoramania

The panorama, first patented by Irish military landscape painter Robert Barker in 1787, has been discussed by several theorists as pre-cinematic or pre-VR [Grau 2003; Griffiths 2008]. Georges Méliès himself even noted a connection between the panorama and film in his fascinating 1907 treatise on the art of filmmaking, "Kinematographic Views" [Méliès 1907]. Méliès discusses the need for absolute precision in backdrop and set painting for film, recommending filmmakers seek out painters with panorama painting experience, because of their skill in creating not only detailed, perspectively correct painting on flat and curved surfaces, but also their ability to incorporate physical three-dimensional objects into the panorama exhibition space, in what might be understood as a relative of today's Mixed Reality. The panorama is an interesting example to examine from a media of attraction perspective at a macro level, not focusing on the work of a particular designer, but looking at the technology's trajectory in overview. To understand the panorama's story, it helps to understand the particulars of how these immersive illusions were designed and developed. Even with advances in linear perspective painting and drawing techniques in the late 1700s, it was no easy task to produce these large-scale, meticulously painted immersive illusions.

Stephen Oettermann's excellent study of the history of the panorama goes into great detail about the necessary process and techniques required to develop these works [Oettermann and Schneider 1997]. The first step was to scout a location, which needed to provide a high central point from which one could have a clear view of the surrounding landscape. Then, a 360° sketch was made to scale while on site. Next, the canvas needed to be prepared and mounted in a cylindrical frame. This created a complication for drawing perspective correctly, because there were two curvatures that needed to be accounted for, both the cylindrical curvature of the canvas that creates the panorama's surrounding circle as well as the curvature of the canvas bowing inward, produced as a result of stretching the fabric on its frame.

The next step was to apply the outlines of the sketch. This step was difficult as well, because the artists who worked on drawing the outlines were positioned so close to the canvas, which was quite large, that it was not possible for them to draw in perspective correctly. Therefore, another artist acted as a guide, positioned in the center of the panorama. The guide would use a long pointer with a charcoal attached on the end to mark corrections for the artists working close to the canvas. After the outline of the sketch was completed, paint was applied. Lighting and architecture also needed to be considered, and in 1793, 6 years after Robert Barker filed his panorama patent, the first panorama rotunda was designed and built explicitly for the purpose of showcasing panorama paintings in London's Leicester Square (see Figure 2.3). The rotunda was designed to maximize the illusion of the panorama, by first plunging the visitor into darkness at the entrance to the rotunda, then leading them up a darkened walkway or stairs to the large, dimly lit exhibition space where vellum was stretched over a skylight above. The skylight allowed for variations in light, such as from passing clouds, to create the most realistic and dynamic impression possible.

The panorama was a wild success, fortuitously timed to coincide with Europe's industrial revolution and new middle class. A visit to the panorama was as much a chance to see its wonders as it was to be seen by others in society. It was an event. Following Barker's

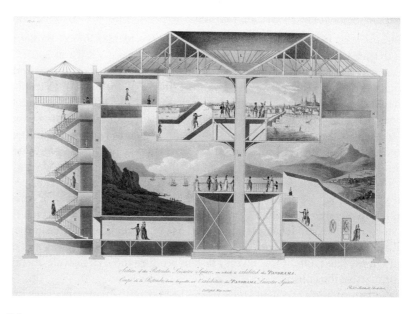

Figure 2.3

The drawing's caption reads, "Section of the Rotunda, Leicester Square, in which is exhibited the PANORAMA. Published May 15, 1801. Robert Mitchell, Architect."

innovation, a "Panoramania" swept across Europe and the UK throughout the late 18th and early 19th centuries, drawing millions of visitors to specially built rotundas [Hyde 1988]. Panoramas even went on tour to other rotundas, which was no easy feat due to a lack of standard dimensions for canvasses and rotundas. Additional innovations were added to the panorama to increase the immersive and performative effects: three-dimensional elements like clay figures; effects such as sound, wind, and smoke; a live performer acting as a narrator or guide; souvenirs in the form of miniature panoramas; scrolling panorama toys; moving panoramas that simulated journeys or were used in theatre productions or 'dioramas,' and even panorama 'rides.'

Of these panorama rides, both the Cineorama and the Mareorama sound particularly spectacular in the few accounts that detail their existence, meticulously researched in Errki Huhtamo's work on the topic. Both the Cineorama and the Mareorama (in French: Maerorama) were exhibited at the 1900 Exhibition Universelle in Paris. The Cineorama was the first film panorama, and was designed to represent a hot-air balloon flight. Spectators climbed into a viewing platform that resembled a hot air balloon based with a large balloon base tethered above, and then panoramic footage from a balloon ascent and descent were shown on all sides, giving the feeling of flight. While the Cineorama was hugely successful, the other complex panorama ride at the 1900 exhibition was less so. The Mareorama simulated a Mediterranean Sea voyage. Visitors climbed aboard a steam ship platform that pitched and rolled, with side-scrolling painted panoramas evoking forward movement. Fans produced ocean breezes, lighting effects simulated day, night, and a lightning storm, actual seaweed and tar added to the atmosphere, and actors played the part of deckhands and locals from ports at stops along the journey. However, like many experiences developed in research labs today that simultaneously push the envelope of creativity and technical capability, the Mareorama never worked reliably, and hosted very few visitors [Huhtamo 2013].

Despite these innovations, such as the use of large-scale film projection and scrolling panoramas in motion, the basic, painted panorama remained a popular and reliable favorite. As discussed in Oetermann's history of the form, they can be understood as an early visual mass medium, and were so popular there were even miniature panoramas to take home from the experience—intricately detailed guides to the panoramas known as "souvenir programs" (see Figure 2.4). As the panorama's popularity continued to increase throughout the 1800s, the inclusion of innovations such as movement and narration became more widespread. *Banvard's Mississippi River Journey* (1852) was a good example of a theatrical version of the panorama experience. Audiences sat in a darkened auditorium, watched a side-scrolling painted panorama on stage, accompanied by dynamic

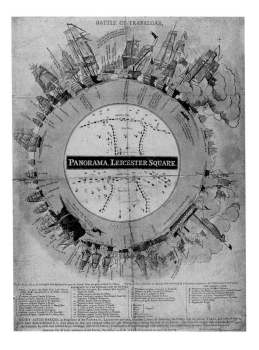

Figure 2.4

This detailed guide illustrates the Battle of Trafalgar panorama displayed at the Leicester Square rotunda in 1806 by Robert Barker's son, Henry, who clearly felt some anxiety about inheriting the business after his father had recently died. Visitors are provided with numbered positions with "Reference to the English Line of Battle" as well as "The Enemy Line." The lower caption reads: "HENRY ASTON BARKER, as Proprietor of the PANORAMA, LEISTER-SQUARE, takes the Liberty of informing the Public, that the various Views and other Subjects which have been exhibited in it, were taken by him, and painted under his sole Management, during the Life of his Father. He therefore hopes, that the same Attention to give Satisfaction, by strict and faithful Representation, will entitle him to a Continuance of that Patronage with which the Panorama has for so many Years been honored. Open from Ten till Dusk—Admittance to each Painting, One Shilling—N. B. [Latin nota bene, which means "note well."] A Person always attends to explain the Painting."

narration from John Banvard, the painter himself. These performances were several hours long, with the panorama scrolling slowly horizontally in real time, to simulate the experience of leisurely boating down the Mississippi river in person. This version of the panorama experience begins to sound pre-cinematic indeed, with an audience seated together in the dark, watching a real-time representation of a river journey, narrated by a charismatic performer.

This experience is perhaps not so different from many of the first immersive large-format films, such as Cinerama's *Windjammer* (1958), which chronicles a 17,000 mile Norwegian schooner trip, and the early IMAX film, *The Greatest Places* (1998), which includes a segment navigating the Amazon River, as well as a selection of other spectacular and hard-to-reach geographies, and we can even see some connections with elements of early experiments in 360-VR films such as the New York Times' *The Displaced* (2015). Across all of these variations in the panoramic form, it is striking to note the similarities clustered around the four media of attraction characteristics. As an unassimilated novelty, the panorama was consistently exhibited as a attraction, with no formalized training for its designers, and no codified form of critique to evaluate its formal and aesthetic qualities. In terms of interdisciplinarity, the panorama grew to pull from a multitude of sources including landscape painting, architecture, sculpture, engineering, and theatre. As a participatory medium, the panorama called out to its visitors to enter, be enveloped, and explore on foot in the rotunda-based format.

As for the panorama's seams, these were evident in a variety of ways including angles or views where the mechanisms of illusion were readily perceptible. An example of this might be in a panorama that includes not only the painted, cylindrical image, but also physical objects. Some panoramas included clay figures in the foreground, closer to the visitors' viewing platform, to extend the illusion. Some of these clay figures would be split in half, at the border of the canvas, with the rear half of the figure portrayed by two-dimensional panting, and the half of the figure in the foreground created in three-dimensional clay projecting into the space. This kind of literal seam, down the middle of a figure, could become perceptible if lighting conditions were less than ideal, for example. Other seams include the use of guides or maps to instruct users how one ought to move through the space to follow the historical narratives presented, and live performers acting as guides or re-enactors. It is easy to imagine visitors' mixed experiences in complex historical battle panoramas, which were probably the most common genre represented, as the experience vacillated between enjoyment and wonder at the spectacle of the immersive view, and confusion or even frustration at how to follow points of action along the spatialized narrative, identify historical figures, locations, and so forth.

Yet despite the panorama medium's incredible popularity as a durable crowd-pleaser for over a century, it never quite reached an institutionalized state, and remained an attraction diffused across theatre, fairs and expositions, and spectacular rotundas, with no centralized distribution network and no production standards, never quite becoming integrated, codified, and commonplace. It is interesting to note that despite its popularity and reach, the form essentially remained a media of attraction, operating culturally more like a theme park than film, radio, television, or videogames. It would be a fascinating project to further investigate the cultural and economic forces that combined to produce this outcome, as the destiny of VR in terms of cultural positioning is speculated about today.

Another commonality across the panorama's iterations bears mentioning: the stories that were told seem to fall into particular categories: historic battles (reflecting the military background of the landscape painters like Robert Barker who pioneered the form); faraway places or virtual travel; and the display of new technologies such as railroads, steamships, and hot air balloons. Notably, fiction was not represented. This marks another contrast with the coming form of film. While the earliest films were dominated by 'actualities' or proto-documentaries, the first pioneers, including Georges Méliès, Edwin S. Porter, and Alice Guy Blaché (who is discussed below), were major innovators of the development of the fiction form for film. Media theorist Marie Laure Ryan has articulated the question of 'fit,' in terms of a medium finding what type of narrative it can present most compellingly, as the crucial factor in terms of determining a medium's entertainment capacity, and cultural staying power [Ryan 2004, p. 356]. It is possible that one contributing factor to the panorama's decline was its lack of engagement with fictional narratives.

2.2.2 The Films of Alice Guy Blaché

Alice Guy Blaché's story intersects with the panorama through her visit to the 1900 Exhibition Universelle in Paris. She was awarded the *Diplôme de collaboratrice* or Award to Collaborator for her exhibiting her film work at the fair, and while there is no proof of her visiting the Cineorama or Mareorama, it is highly likely she was at least aware of the attractions. Blaché's employer, the Gaumont photography and film company, had recently acquired the rights to an early sound film technology, improved upon it, and added projection capabilities and sound amplification. Blaché worked as an office manager for Gaumont, and was tasked with creating many films for the company, including promotional films to demonstrate the new sound and projection system, dubbed the Chronophone. Sound was recorded first, using a phonograph, then performers were filmed lip-synching. The synchronization and sound amplification aspects of the system were still glitchy, but sufficiently impressive that when exhibited at the 1900 Exposition, Gaumont was awarded the Grand Prix [Abel 1998, p. 11]. And it was at this same fair that Blaché came across the art exhibition by James Tissot of his biblical paintings. She purchased a copy of the Tissot Bible for herself, and went on to use the artwork in the volume as the blueprint for one of her most elaborate and lengthy early films, *La Vie du Christ* in 1906, much in the way later filmmakers used storyboards—although this was well before that practice was established [Blaché 1986, pp. 45–46].

Although Alice Guy Blaché may not be quite the household name of early film history that Georges Méliès and Edwin S. Porter are, throughout her career as a director, writer, producer (and even performer) in early film from 1896 to 1920, she worked on over 1,000 films. While other early film pioneers like the Lumière brothers made no films after 1905, and Méliès and Porter left the industry in 1913 as it moved full-throttle into institutionalization, Blaché persisted, adapted, and continued to produce innovative and successful work. Where the panorama provides an interesting example of a medium of attraction that never transformed into an institutionalized media form, film provides a counterpoint. Blaché's 24-year film career is a particularly interesting corpus, given the span her work bridges from film's Cinema of Attraction beginnings through the birth of Hollywood, and her own practice led her from Paris, to New Jersey and New York (the first US film hub), and then on to California.

Blaché's filmography boasts representative works from every genre imaginable, including actuality films (precursors to documentary), musicals (phonoscènes), slapstick comedy, religious drama, social satire, melodrama, and romance. Her contributions to the development of the fiction film or story film are landmark, along with her contemporaries Méliès, Porter, and the Lumières. (This group were all aware of each others' works, and even borrowed to the point of remaking each others' films.) Blaché is also credited with major contributions to the discipline of film acting; her studio was famous for the giant banner that read "Be Natural!" hung behind the camera, facing the performers.

The incredible range of experimentation that is a hallmark of the media of attraction phase can be seen across Blaché's early films. From the single year of 1906, for example, looking across just four of the scores of films she created that year, we see an incredible variety, from documentary, to social satire, to religious epic, and slapstick comedy (see Figure 2.5). *Le ballon dirigible "La Patrie"* falls into the documentary category, and chronicles the launch of a large airship built by the French military. The ship backs out of its hangar, is released from its moorings, and floats off, fading into an increasingly cloudy sky. (The feeling of mystique created by the fade at the end of the film is enhanced by the ship's ill-fated history; a year after the film was shot the ship was lost after becoming unmoored, drifting over Wales and Ireland, and then out to sea, never to be recovered.). *La Patrie* also contributes to long-standing, fascinating sub-genre of films about ballooning, including films shot from balloons by photographer-balloonists such as Félix Nadar, and the creators of the Cineorama at the Paris Exhibition Universelle in 1900. Nadar's colorful memoirs on the subject, recently translated into English, are an excellent resource [Nadar 1900].

Created in the same year as *La Patrie,* Blaché's *La glu* (1906) presents a slapstick comedy centered on a young boy who finds that all sorts of mischief can be achieved with a large pot of curiously strong glue. The boy paints a bench and steps with the mixture, and manages to trap an unsuspecting pair of ladies, as well as the good Samaritans who would try to help them get loose, before becoming trapped himself at the end with the large glue pot stuck to his own bottom, in a gesture of comedic justice.

Also in 1906, *Les resultants du feminisme* showcases yet another genre for Blaché; social satire. This film explores the feared results of the suffrage movement—complete gender role reversals. In the film, male actors exhibit stereotypically female behaviors, ironing clothes, fussing about hats and other accessories, tending to children, and shyly fending off unwanted sexual advances. The female actors portray stereotypical male behaviors, smoking pipes, relaxing in coffee shops, pawing the 'girls' in the film, and refusing to acknowledge their parentage of children born out of wedlock! The result is not only comedic, but also a sly commentary on the essentially performative nature of gender, even more remarkable for this nuance given its date decades before contemporary gender studies scholarship on the subject of performativity by Judith Butler and others.

And finally, from the same year, *La vie du Christ* is an epic religious drama, bringing the illustrations from the Tissot Bible to life. This film is incredibly long and complex for the time, running at nearly 33 min, with a cast of over 300 extras. Across all four of these films (which are available to watch on YouTube.com) we see Blaché's exuberant experimentation with the plasticity of the film form, special effects like cuts and superimpositions, a variety of acting styles, and a range of storytelling techniques. In contrast, by the late teens, as film began to leave the media of attraction phase for institutionalization, Blaché's

Figure 2.5

(From top) Stills from three of Alice Guy Blaché's 1906 films. *La Glu*: An unsuspecting couple become stuck to their steps. *Les Resultants du Feminisme*: Men perform stereotypically female tasks, ironing and sewing, while the woman puts her feet up to relax. *La Vie du Christ*: Scene depicting the last supper.

work continued to be successful and interesting, however a narrower focus had settled in, emphasizing melodrama and romance. The market also skewed towards the presentation of feature films, which of course took longer to produce, perhaps also limiting experimentation. The benefit of this narrower focus was of course the ability to specialize and refine.

2.2.3 Muriel Cooper's Information Landscapes

Moving to the more recent past, Muriel Cooper's work with the Visible Language Workshop at the MIT Media Lab provides another fascinating example of media of attraction. As discussed in research from David Reinfurt and Robert Wiesenberger, Cooper's lab worked at the forefront of interactive graphics and hypertext, producing the landmark *Information Landscapes* project, presented at TED in 1994 [Reinfurt 2007; Reinfurt and Wiesenberger 2017]. Cooper's innovative early interactive 3D work opened up questions about interaction design we still wrestle with today, particularly in 3D environments like VR.

Cooper began her career in print graphic design, and early on showed an interest in innovating forms and pushing boundaries. Her methods were heavily inspired by the Bauhaus workshop traditions, and she was the designer of the iconic MIT Press colophon logo.

During her time as the design director of the press from 1967 to 1974, she developed a series of processes and systems to revitalize the press. Integrating a new IBM Electric typewriter, Cooper was able to circumnavigate the usually lengthy back-and-forth between press and professional typesetter to generate drafts. Cooper also experimented with the print form, including a flip book in the margins of one of her publications, and showcasing another by creating a filmed stop-motion animation of its pages.

Although her background was in art and design, it was clear she had a penchant for technology and experimentation. This thread continued and developed further in her work, as she began to offer a course at MIT, "Messages and Means," in collaboration with fellow designer and technologist Ron MacNeil. In this hands-on workshop course, students explored printing technologies, graphic and information design. The space occupied by this wildly popular course was known as the Visible Language Workshop (VLW). When Nicholas Negroponte founded the MIT Media Lab in 1985, he invited Cooper and MacNeil to bring the VLW to the Media Lab as one of the initial seven research foci.

Relocating to the Media Lab positioned Cooper ideally to integrate 'cast-offs' from the other research centers in the lab (slightly outdated hardware or software the other researchers had finished with, but was still significantly advanced in terms of what was commercially available.) Digital printing, large-format Polaroid photography, image transmission through the emerging internet, and experiments with real-time interactive 3D graphics and typographic space were all part of the work developed in the VLW. This last research project, titled *Information Landscapes,* was presented publicly shortly before Cooper's untimely death in 1994. Information Landscapes was an interactive 3D textual universe, providing novel ways of displaying data relationships and navigating text. Concepts about transparency, blur, and scale were explored in terms of usability in the new graphic space, and innovative solutions developed that we now take for granted in interaction design.

Cooper was prescient not only in her cutting-edge design work, but also in the questions she asked. In a talk she gave at the Walker Art Center in 1987, she addressed subjects including the links between physical and digital design artifacts, toolkits, and processes; presented a vision of the future as ubiquitous computing well before the term was coined; questioned the ethics of copying and collaboration in the digital and internet age; discussed the role of the computer as an interdisciplinary change agent, breaking down traditional academic categories; and positioned the core role of graphics as the interface for accessing information like big data in the digital age [Cooper 1987].

Quoted on the Art Director's Club page inducting Cooper into their Hall of Fame, Cooper stated in 1994 shortly before her death: "When you start talking about design in relation to computers, you're not just talking about how information appears on the screen, you're talking about how it's designed into the architecture of the machine and of the language. You have different capabilities, different constraints and variables than you have in any other medium, and nobody even knows what they are yet" [Art Directors Club 2004]. Cooper was acknowledging the open field in computing and information design at the time as a media of attraction.

2.3 Connecting to Design Practice

What can a media of attraction approach offer designers in VR today? First, a different outlook than is often expressed. By understanding the unique value of works created in media of attraction phases, we might not wish standardization upon ourselves quite so fervently. When emerging media solidify into "platforms," they become less flexible in many ways. The embedded politics of system become entrenched, audience expectations calcify, and a developed market demands certain production qualities and viewpoints. Platforms and systems are not the only elements of institutionalized media with embedded politics. An established media's 'language' is also political at core, in terms of what is chosen and highlighted, how values are communicated, and what is left out or even invisible. By embracing a media of attraction approach as designers of new media today, we might more consciously value the multiplicity we are in, and work to better catalogue and archive the rich variety of artifacts we generate, and the design processes with which we experiment.

In addition, a set of prescriptive principles can be suggested, based on the four central qualities of media of attraction as unassimilated, interdisciplinary, seamed, and participatory:

- *Unassimilated media must be carefully archived.* We need an archive of attraction, that values the rich multiplicity found in these types of artifacts. We need a way of representing genealogical relationships between related forms, and must pay careful attention to the voice of the designer, which has often been lost in the case of historical media of attraction.
- *Interdisciplinary media require interdisciplinary teams,* and therefore careful attention to the process of team building. There is a wealth of literature of the topic of teamwork, but research on performing arts teams may be most relevant for other expressive domains.
- *Seamed media are best approached through seamful design tactics* that seek to exploit these rough edges. Seams in media of attraction may not only be caused by technical limitations, but also by issues related to these media's lack of assimilation, such as lack of conventions or audience expectations. A seamful design approach identifies the areas of dissonance, and incorporates them into the design as affordances or opportunities for creative interaction.

- *As participatory media, media of attraction need to be designed to support emergent interpretations.* User behavior with media of attraction is often highly unpredictable, given the unassimilated nature of the technologies and techniques in play. To accommodate this, and develop the naïve user's creativity as an asset, designers should work to strike a balance between providing opportunities for emergent interactions to develop, and careful consideration of how to provide proper constraints to ensure a meaningful experience.

Finally, in the design process, media of attraction exercises could be developed to further strengthen design techniques in line with the media of attraction tradition. Many emerging media claim to incorporate all previous media. This has been claimed about film, radio, television, the computer, and is certainly claimed about VR as well, at least in the popular press and trade publications. A historically-centered media of attraction ideation exercise could help practitioners more actively and meaningfully engage with playful remediations, by suggesting a design concept be sketched out for a variety of 'dead' media. For example, a concept to create an educational VR application to tell the story of your town's history during the contentious midcentury urban renewal/historic preservation era could be sketched out for the panorama, the stereoscope, flip book, chronophone, and radio before moving to the VR platform. These 'dead' media versions may provide alternate forms of storytelling, modes of representation, and sensory engagements that might not be as easily excavated working in the digital medium alone.

In conclusion, the media of attraction design approach suggested here should be developed into a more nuanced and complete framework, created in collaboration with the larger community, and based on continuing historical research across time periods and technologies such as early radio, television, and videogames. The aim is to produce a design vocabulary that is generative and specific, but ultimately values the multiplicity at the core of media of attraction. Instead of thinking of progress in VR (or whatever media of attraction emerges in the post-VR landscape) as the narrowing toward best practices that exploit unique affordances, and eventual canonization as an institutionalized medium, we could re-imagine progress as the continued great exploration of the widest variety of approaches.

References

[Abel 1993]

Abel, Richard (1993) *French Film Theory and Criticism: A History/Anthology: Volume 1: 1907–1929*. Princeton, NJ: Princeton University Press.

[Abel 1998]

Abel, Richard (1998) *The Ciné Goes to Town: French Cinema, 1896–1914, Updated and Expanded Edition*. Berkeley, Los Angeles, and London: University of California Press.

[Abel and Altman 2001]

Abel, Richard, and Rick R. Altman, Eds. (2001) *The Sounds of Early Cinema*. Bloomington and Indianapolis, IN: Indiana University Press.

[Blaché 1986]

Blaché, Alice Guy, Trans: Roberta Blaché and Simone Blaché, Ed: Slide, Anthony (1986) *The Memoirs of Alice Guy Blaché*. Lanham, MD and Kent, England: Scarecrow Press, Inc.

[Canemaker 2005]

Canemaker, John (2005) *Winsor McKay: His Life and Art*. New York: Harry Abrams.

[Cooper 1987]

Cooper, Muriel (1987) Art and technology in the information age. *Insights Design Lecture Series*. Minneapolis MN: Walker Art Center.

[Craig et al. 2009]

Craig, Alan B., William R. Sherman, and Jeffrey D. Will (2009) *Developing Virtual Reality Applications*. Burlington, MA: Morgan Kaufmann Publishers.

[Gaudreault 2011]

Gaudreault, André (2011) *Film and Attraction: From Kinematography to Cinema*. Chicago, IL: University of Illinois Press.

[Grau 2003]

Grau, Oliver (2003) *Virtual Art: From Illusion to Immersion*. Cambridge, MA: MIT Press.

[Griffiths 2008]

Griffiths, Alison (2008) *Shivers Down Your Spine: Cinema, Museums, and the Immersive View*. New York: Columbia University Press.

[Gunning 1986]

Gunning, Tom (1986) The cinema of attraction: Early film, its spectator and the avant-garde. *Wide Angle*, 8 3–4, pp. 63–70.

[Gunning 2003]

Gunning, Tom (2003) Re-newing old technologies: Astonishment, second nature, and the uncanny in technology from the previous turn-of-the-century. In: Thorburn, D., and Jenkins, H. (Eds.). *Rethinking Media Change: The Aesthetics of Transition*. Cambridge, MA: MIT Press, pp. 39–60.

[Huhtamo 2013]

Huhtamo, Erkki (2013) *Illusions in Motion: Media Archeology of the Moving Panorama and Related Spectacles*. Cambridge, MA: MIT Press.

[Hyde 1988]

Hyde, Ralph (1988) *Panoramania! The Art and Entertainment of the All-Embracing View*. London: Trefoil Publications.

[McMahan 2002]

McMahan, Alison (2002) *Alice Guy Blaché: Lost Visionary of the Cinema*. New York and London: Continuum International Publishing Group, Inc.

[Méliès 1907]

Méliès, Georges (1907) Kinematographic views. In: Gaudreault, A. (Ed.). *Film and Attraction: From Kinematography to Cinema*. Chicago, IL: University of Illinois Press.

[Art Directors Club 2004]

Muriel Cooper (2004) *adcglobal.org*. Art directors club hall of fame biography. http://adcglobal.org/hall-of-fame/muriel-cooper/

[Musser 1990]

Musser, Charles (1990) *The Emergence of Cinema: The American Screen to 1907*. New York: Scribners.

[Musser 1994]

Musser, Charles (1994) Rethinking early cinema: Cinema of attractions and narrativity. *Yale Journal of Criticism*, 7 2, pp. 203–232.

[Nadar 1900]

Nadar, Félix (1900) *When I was a Photographer*. Trans: Eduardo Cadava and Liana Theodoratou. Cambridge, MA: MIT Press, 2015.

[Oettermann and Schneider 1997]

Oettermann, Stephan, and Deborah Lucas Schneider (1997) *The Panorama: History of a Mass Medium*. New York: Zone Books.

[Reinfurt 2007]

Reinfurt, David (2007) *This Stands as a Sketch for the Future: Muriel Cooper and the Visible Language Workshop*. Cambridge, MA: Center for Advanced Visual Studies, MIT.

[Reinfurt and Wiesenberger 2017]

Reinfurt, David, and Robert Wiesenberger (2017) *Muriel Cooper at MIT, 1954–1994*. Cambridge, MA: MIT Press.

[Rouse 2016]

Rouse, Rebecca (2016) Media of attraction: A media archeology approach to panoramas, kinematography, mixed reality and beyond. In: Nack, F., and Gordon, A. S. (Eds.). *Interactive Storytelling: Lecture Notes in Computer Science 100045*. Berlin, Germany: Springer Press International, pp. 97–107.

[Rouse et al. 2017]

Rouse, Rebecca, Benjamin, Chang, and Silvia Ruzanka (2017) Diving into the multiplicity: Liberating your design process from a convention-centered approach. In *Proceedings of the IEEE Virtual Reality Conference*, Los Angeles, CA, pp. 429–430.

[Ryan 2004]

Ryan, Marie-Laure (2004) Will new media produce new narratives? In: Ryan, M. (Ed.). *Narrative Across Media*. Lincoln, NE: University of Nebraska Press, pp. 337–359.

[Sherman and Craig 1995]

Sherman, William R., and Alan B. Craig (1995) Literacy in virtual reality: A new medium. *ACM SIGGRAPH Computer Graphics*, 29 4, pp. 37–42.

SECTION II
VR with Game Engines

3

Getting Started with SteamVR and Unity

Lee Wasilenko
VR Dev School Inc.
Orange Bridge Studios Inc.

Experience with general purpose game engines such as Unity are quickly becoming a requirement for anyone looking to create virtual reality (VR) experiences. In addition to having skill with a particular game engine there are also many VR specific SDK's and API's out there for each VR hardware set. Valve has attempted to take some of the complexity out of supporting multiple VR platforms by publishing its OpenVR API which provides developers with a common software API across multiple VR hardware platforms. Valve has also published the SteamVR Unity Plugin which is a set of tools that allows developers to access OpenVR device functionality easily in Unity and simplifies common VR experience requirements such as hand interactions and locomotion.

In this chapter we look at how to get started creating cross platform VR experiences using Unity and the SteamVR Unity Plugin. We will look at how to create a VR scene, how to interact with objects, and how to use teleportation as means of locomotion.

This chapter has been created using Unity 2017.1.0p5, SteamVR Unity Plugin 1.2.2 and an HTC Vive, and later tested with Unity 2017.3.1f1sg and SteamVR Plugin 2.0.1. The Oculus Rift with Touch as well as later versions of Unity and SteamVR should function similarly. You must have Steam and the SteamVR Runtime installed as well.

3.1 SteamVR Unity Plugin Overview

The SteamVR Unity Plugin is a collection of assets provided by Valve to make creating VR experiences using Unity on OpenVR devices as simple as possible. Most importantly, the package contains VR camera rig prefabs and scripts which give developers access to tracked devices, such as HMD's and motion controllers, and low level SteamVR system events.

In addition, Valve has included code for the Interaction System; a lightweight and flexible system for interacting with game objects and managing the context specific behavior of tracked VR devices by sending messages based on Hover and Attached states to interactable game objects.

3.2 How to Import the SteamVR Unity Plugin

We're going to get the SteamVR Unity Plugin from the Unity Asset Store, so open up a new Unity project and then click on *Window* in the menu bar to open the drop down and then select *Asset Store*. In the search field enter 'SteamVR Plugin' and look for the result from Valve Corporation (Figure 3.1).

Select this result and then click on *Import* to bring the contents into your project. After the import you will be prompted to accept the Recommended Project Settings. Click *Accept All* to allow those changes. As of version 2.0 of the SteamVR Plugin it will also provide a window of how to configure the inputs—choosing the defaults is fine.

Figure 3.1

SteamVR Plugin from the Unity Asset Store.

3.3 Create a Very Simple SteamVR Scene in Unity

Let's start exploring the SteamVR package by creating a simple scene. First, select Assets/Create/Scene from the menu bar and call it **SteamVR_Intro**. Your scene will appear under the Assets folder in the Project panel. Double-click to open the scene if it is not already open.

Let's create a platform to stand on by adding a plane to our scene. Right-click on the Hierarchy panel and select 3D Object/Plane. A 10 × 10 plane centered at the origin in our scene will be created. Select the plane in the hierarchy and rename it **Floor** in the inspector.

Now we need a VR camera rig for our scene. Delete the default **MainCamera** in the Hierarchy pane and then expand the Assets/SteamVR/Prefabs folder in the Project pane. Select the *[CameraRig]* prefab and drag it over to the Hierarchy pane to place it in the scene at the origin. You'll see the play area boundary wireframe appear in your scene (Figure 3.2).

Expanding the **[CameraRig]** (now in the hierarchy) reveals three subcomponents, including the **Camera (head)** object and two controllers—**Controller (left)** and **Controller (right)**. If you expand the **Camera (head)** object, you will reveal the **Camera (eye)** and **Camera (ears)** objects (Figure 3.3).

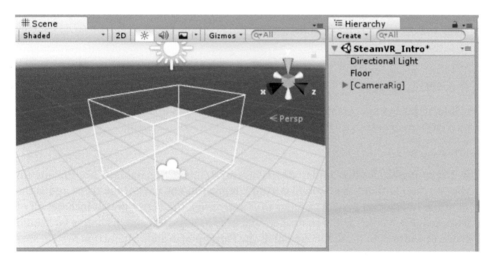

Figure 3.2

A basic SteamVR scene.

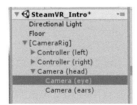

Figure 3.3

Here is the **[CameraRig]** object with the **Camera (head)** expanded and the eye selected.

Figure 3.4

Make sure all SteamVR device icons are green (pictured are the icons for the standard HTC Vive).

You're just about ready to run your VR scene. Make sure the SteamVR Runtime is running and that all of the device icons are green (Figure 3.4). You can start the SteamVR Runtime by clicking on the VR button in the menu bar of the Steam application. Once SteamVR is loaded and ready all you need to do is click on the *Play* button or press CTRL-P (CMD-P on OS/X) in Unity to enter Play mode and then put on your headset. You should now be looking around in your first SteamVR scene!

3.4 Interaction System

Now that you've got a VR scene up and running you'll probably want to add a few objects and start playing with them. Luckily Valve has included an Interaction System with SteamVR that will allow you to perform simple interactions quickly and easily.

The Interaction System included with SteamVR was the basis for the mini-games included with Valve's *The Lab* VR demo, so if you're familiar with *The Lab* you will recognize some of options available to you in the Interaction System. All of the code, prefabs and other assets for the Interaction System can be found under Assets/SteamVR/InteractionSystem.

3.5 Core Components of the Interaction System

The Interaction System contains a number of objects for you to use in your own code. Here are seven components that are at the heart of the Interaction System.

3.5.1 Player

The *Player* prefab, located under Assets/SteamVR/InteractionSystem/Core/Prefabs (in earlier versions without the "Core/" portion), represents the user in the scene and is the core of the Interaction System. Similar to *[CameraRig]*, the *Player* prefab includes all of the tracked objects such as the controllers and head as well as the main camera and audio listener. In addition to those fundamentals the *Player* prefab adds Interaction System specific scripts such as the *Hand* script. To get started with the Interaction System simply delete the existing *[CameraRig]* from your scene and drag in the *Player* prefab.

With the *Player* prefab, you can do some testing when an HMD display isn't handy by going into "2D Debug" mode, which allows you to use the standard WASD keys to move around (Figure 3.5). The "2D Debug" mode is automatically enabled when no VR system is found, or it can be activated with a toggle.

3.5.2 Hand

While the *Player* prefab forms the core of the Interaction System, the Hand class is the real workhorse. This class is attached to each controller and forms the basis of interaction with other objects in the scene. The Hand class checks the objects it is hovering over for

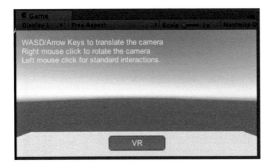

Figure 3.5

The *Player* prefab provides a "2D Debug" (i.e. non-VR) mode that allows developers to do testing without the need for an HMD. The toggle button on the bottom resumes VR mode when available.

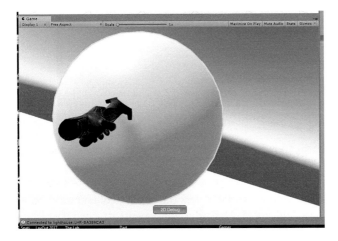

Figure 3.6

When a controller of the *Player* prefab interacts with other objects in the scene that are set as "Interactable", the object is highlighted with a silhouette. (Also note that in versions of the SteamVR Plugin 2.0 and later the *Player* prefab adds a hand model to the controllers, as shown.)

an Interactable component and sends them messages based on the current hover state (Figure 3.6).

3.5.3 Interactable

While there's not very much code in the Interactable class, it serves as an important identifier in the Interaction System and allows a reference to the Hand to be obtained. Adding this component to any game object with a collider will allow the Hand to recognize the object as interactable (Figure 3.7). When you touch an object with the Interactable component attached, but no other interaction extensions, you will be able to see the controller

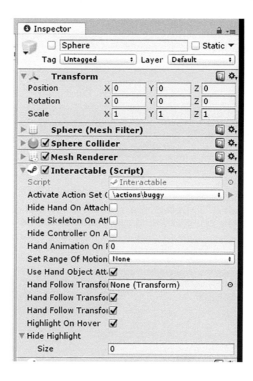

Figure 3.7

This inspector panel shows a basic Sphere object with the "Interactable" script added, including many new options in version 2.0 of the SteamVR Plugin.

outline appear when your controller enters the object's collider and you will feel a haptic bump. You will need additional behavioral components attached if you wish to expand the interaction. See for example *Throwable* below.

3.5.4 Throwable

Adding this script component to an object will allow the user to pick up the object and throw it. The object will attach to the hand when the trigger button is pressed (Figure 3.8). When the trigger button is released the throwable is detached from the hand and the hand's velocity is transferred to the object. This script requires the Interactable script as well as a rigid body and the *VelocityEstimator* script. Since these requirements are hard-coded into the script via the [RequireComponent] tag, Unity will go ahead and add them for you if they are not already present.

3.5.5 LinearDrive

This class allows you to create objects with defined linear paths to be moved only along those paths. For example, you can use it to create levers or sliding drawers that only trans-mit the hand's motion along a defined linear path between the start position transform and end position transform. To map between the points, create an empty **GameObject** for the *StartPosition* and *EndPosition* each and then drag them into the matching slots in the Inspector (Figure 3.9). The public Linear Mapping variable will be updated at runtime to reflect how far along the *LinearDrive* is between the *StartPosition* and the *EndPosition*. (The *LinearMapping* script is created and attached to the *LinearDrive* at run time if it doesn't already exist.)

(a) (b)

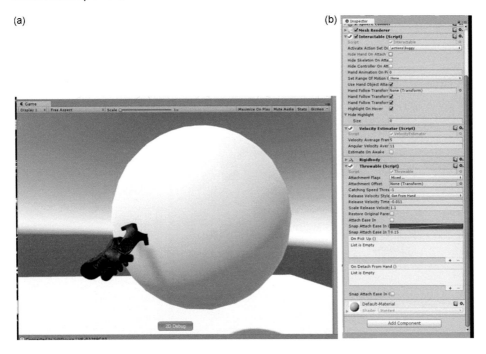

Figure 3.8

(a) Here the user grabs and is about to throw the large sphere. (b) Adding the "Throwable" script also adds a Rigidbody to the object along with the "Velocity Estimator" script.

(a) (b) (c)

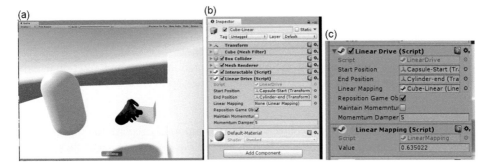

Figure 3.9

(a) Here the user grabs the cube and can slide it between the capsule and cylinder. (b) The "Linear Drive" script includes fields to specify the two ends along with the object may slide. (Often the ends would be invisible game objects, but here we have chosen visible objects for demonstration.) (c) While running, a "Linear Mapping" script is added and shows the percentage distance of the cube from the capsule to the cylinder ("*Value*").

(a)

(b)

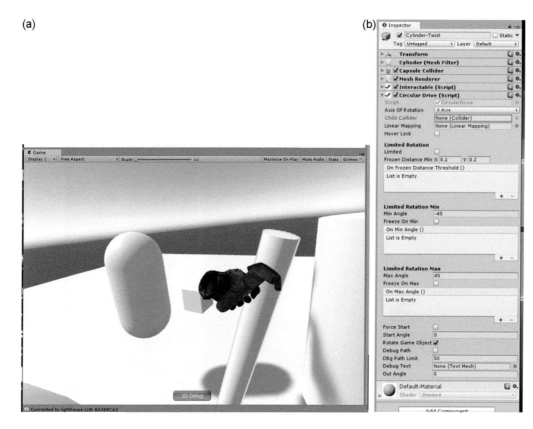

Figure 3.10

(a) Here the user grabs and rotates a bar. The bar can only be rotated about it's X-axis.
(b) The CircularDrive script has many options, however in this example we have left them all as the default, including the axis of rotation.

3.5.6 CircularDrive

The CircularDrive limits an object's motion to rotation about one rotational axis. This component is useful for creating interactable wheels, spinners and dials (Figure 3.10).

3.5.7 ItemPackages

An ItemPackage is a collection of objects that will temporarily replace the functionality of the hand. A good example of this is the longbow in *The Lab*. When a user picks up the longbow one hand is replaced with the bow while the other hand is replaced by the arrow. While holding the *Longbow* ItemPackage the functionality of the hand is replaced by the behaviour of the longbow. ItemPackages are useful for creating tools which have context sensitive behaviour when attached to the hand (Figure 3.11).

To use an ItemPackage in your scene you will need to create prefabs for the one or two items you want to attach to the hands and then give the ItemPackage references to those

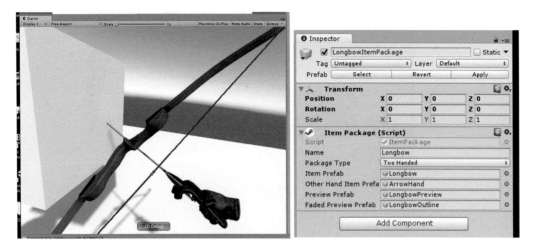

Figure 3.11

The SteamVR Plugin provides a Longbow ItemPackage as an example. In this sample scene the user clicks on the cube at which point their primary hand is mapped to the "Item Prefab" (here the Longbow), and the "Other Hand Item Prefab" is the ArrowHand. The "*LongbowItemPackage*" is itself a prefab that is assigned to the spawning object—in this scene the cube.

prefabs. Then you will make your ItemPackage a prefab and create an *ItemPackageSpawner* and give the *ItemPackageSpawner* a reference to the ItemPackage prefab.

3.6 Interaction System Example Scene

Valve has helpfully included an example scene with the Interaction System which shows off much of the functionality included with the package. You can find the scene under Assets/SteamVR/InteractionSystem/Samples/Interaction_Example (in previous editions there was a "Scenes/" folder between "Samples/" and "Interaction_Example").

Explore each exhibit in the scene in VR and then have a look at each component in the Unity Inspector pane to get a better idea of how each part of the Interaction System combines to form a series of interesting interactions with a few simple building blocks (Figure 3.12).

3.7 Using the Interaction System to Throw a Ball

Let's have a look at how we can leverage the Interaction System to create a throwable ball.

1. Open the SteamVR_Intro scene we created earlier and delete the [**CameraRig**] object if you haven't already.
2. Drag the *Player* prefab from Assets/SteamVR/InteractionSystem/Prefabs into the Hierarchy pane to create a copy of the prefab at the origin (if you haven't already).

Figure 3.12

A view of the Interaction System demonstration scene which shows how several of the interaction scripts available in the SteamVR Plugin work.

3. Right-click in the Hierarchy and select 3D Object/Sphere to create a sphere.
4. Select the **Sphere** in the Hierarchy.
5. Set the Transform's (X, Y, Z) Position to (0, 0.1, 0) in the Inspector.
6. Set the Transform's (X, Y, Z) Scale to (0.2, 0.2, 0.2) in the Inspector.
7. Click *Add Component* and add the *Throwable* script as a component.

Note that Unity automatically added an Interactable component to the **Sphere** because *Interactable* is a required component of *Throwable (similarly for the RigidBody and Velocity Estimator components)*.

Now click *Play* or press CTRL+P to start Play mode and put on your HMD. When the controller highlights to indicate it is hovering over the **Sphere** you should be able to pick it up by pressing and holding the trigger button. Release the trigger button to throw the sphere.

3.8 Adding New Behavior to Button Presses

Using the interaction system to add behavior on button presses is very straightforward. All SteamVR device button presses are handled in the *SteamVR_Controller* class. You can get a reference to the *SteamVR_Controller* device through the *Hand* and you get a reference to the *Hand* through the *Interactable* attached to the game object. Let's add some behavior to our **Sphere** so interacting with it changes the functionality of the hand it is currently attached to.

Create a new C# script on the **Sphere** by selecting it in the Hierarchy and then clicking *Add Component* in the Inspector. Select *New Script,* name the script *SphereBehaviour* and then enter the text in Listing 3.1.

Listing 3.1. Adding simple behavior to controller buttons.

```
using UnityEngine;
using Valve.VR.InteractionSystem;

[RequireComponent(typeof(Interactable))]
public class SphereBehaviour : MonoBehaviour
{

    private Hand hand;

    // Get a reference to the Hand through the OnAttachedToHand event in Interactable
    private void OnAttachedToHand(Hand attachedHand)
    {
        Debug.Log("Attached to Hand");
        hand = attachedHand;
    }

    // Remove the reference when the object is detached from the Hand
    private void OnDetachedFromHand(Hand attachedHand)
    {
        Debug.Log("Detached from Hand");
        hand = null;
    }

    void Update()
    {
        // Check if object is attached to a Hand
        if (hand != null) {
            // Use the SteamVR_Controller reference to check for a button press
            if (hand.controller.GetPressDown(SteamVR_Controller.ButtonMask.Touchpad)) {
                // Do something when attached and button pressed
                Debug.Log("Touchpad Pressed Down");
            }
        }
    }
}
```

Save the script and hit *Play* in Unity to see this script in action.

1. Pick up the **Sphere** by holding down the Trigger button and you will see the message "Attached to Hand" printed out in the Console pane.
2. Click the Touchpad button on the top of the controller to see the "Touchpad Pressed Down" message in the Console.
3. Finally, release the Trigger button to see the "Detached from Hand" message appear in the Console.

The *Throwable* behavior is already using the Trigger button so we looked for a click on the Touchpad. If you do not have any action assigned to the Trigger button on your object and want to use the Trigger instead of the Touchpad for your action, you can simplify the code above by using hand.GetStandardInteractionButtonDown() instead of hand.controller.GetPressDown(SteamVR_Controller.ButtonMask.Touchpad).

In general, in SteamVR you can access all of the button states on your controller by getting a reference to the underlying SteamVR_Controller.Device, using the desired

'Get*Action*' method and passing in the `SteamVR_Controller.ButtonMask` for the button you are interested in polling. For the Vive you have the following options for `ButtonMask`:

- `System`
- `ApplicationMenu`
- `Grip`
- `Touchpad`
- `Trigger`

3.9 Teleporting

The SteamVR Interaction System code also includes the teleportation system used for locomotion in *The Lab*. You can easily add this system to your scene to start moving around.

The Teleportation system has three basic components: Teleporting, TeleportPoint, and TeleportArea.

3.9.1 Teleporting

The *Teleporting* prefab found under Assets/SteamVR/InteractionSystem/Teleport/Prefabs contains all of the code needed to add teleportation to your scene. The teleportation system is fairly complicated and contains many components but most of the logic is contained in the *Teleport* script. Luckily the *Teleporting* prefab has everything we need ready to go. Simply drag this prefab into your scene to get started.

3.9.2 TeleportPoint

The *TeleportPoint* prefab represents one point where the player can teleport to. The player will be teleported to the center of this point regardless of exactly where the arc was pointed. Place one of these prefabs when you want to have more precise control over where the player will end up (Figure 3.13).

To add TeleportPoint to the SteamVR_Intro scene follow these steps:

1. Drag the *Teleporting* prefab into the Hierarchy.
2. Drag the *TeleportPoint* prefab into the Hierarchy.
3. Select the **TeleportPoint** object in the Hierarchy and use the Move tool to place it somewhere in the scene. Keep it on top of the **Floor** plane by making sure that its Transform's Y-value stays at zero or above.
4. Click *Play* and put on your HMD.
5. Press and hold the Touchpad button to bring up the teleport arc and reveal available **TeleportPoints**.
6. Point the arc at the **TeleportPoint** and release the Touchpad button to be teleported to the center of the **TeleportPoint**.

3.9.3 TeleportArea

The *TeleportArea* script allows the player to teleport to any mesh this script is attached to as long as that mesh also has a collider attached. The player will be teleported to the exact point on the mesh where the arc was pointed (Figure 3.14).

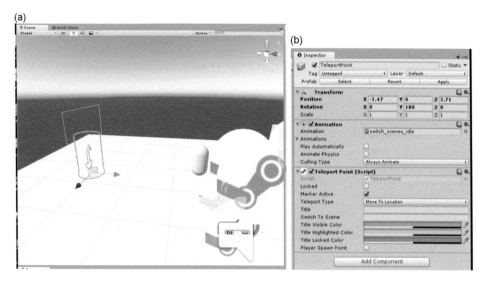

Figure 3.13

(a) A point to which the user can teleport is shown with an arrow pointing to the location on the floor. (b) The "TeleportPoint" script allows the colors of the teleport marker to be set, and automatically includes the Animation component for the indicator (e.g. the arrow) to move up and down.

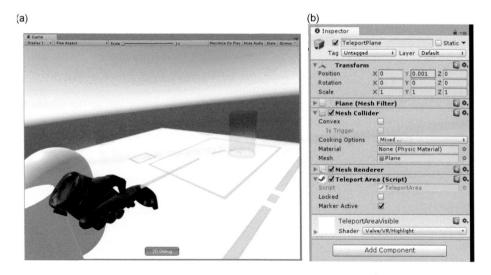

Figure 3.14

(a) For the TeleportArea script, a rectangular area is shown on the teleport surface which represents the area of movement as configured for the system—with the particular point where the user will land represented by the translucent cylinder. (b) The TeleportArea script is added to a plane mesh in the game world (called "TeleportPlane").

To add a TeleportArea to the SteamVR_Intro scene follow these steps:

1. Drag the *Teleporting* prefab into the Hierarchy if it's not already in the scene.
2. Right-click on the **Floor** plane in the Hierarchy.
3. Select 3D Object/Plane to create a new plane as a child of the original **Floor** plane in our scene.
4. Rename the new child plane **TeleportPlane**.
5. Select **TeleportPlane** in the Hierarchy.
6. Set the Y-value of **TeleportPlane**'s Transform to 0.001 so that it is floating 1 mm above **Floor**.
7. Click *Add Component* in the Inspector and add a *TeleportArea* script to **TeleportPlane**.
8. Click *Play* and put on your HMD.
9. Press and hold the Touchpad button to bring up the teleport arc and reveal the **TeleportPlane**.
10. Point the arc anywhere on **TeleportPlane** and release the Touchpad button to be teleported to that location.

3.10 Where to Go from Here

In this chapter we've gone over the basics of starting a VR project using Unity and the SteamVR Unity Plugin. By using the Interaction System as a basis for adding behaviour and the Teleport system for locomotion you've got the building blocks you need to create a wide variety of compelling VR experiences.

When you're ready to dig deeper into the SteamVR Unity Plugin you can start by exploring the rest of code that is included in the package. In addition to finding this code on the Unity Asset Store, as we have in this chapter, you can find the latest version of OpenVR and the SteamVR Unity Plugin at Valve's public GitHub repository [SteamVR GitHub].

For general questions and help with SteamVR you can go to the SteamVR section of the Steam Community Forums [SteamVR Forums].

For more developer and hardware focused support you can go to the SteamVR Developer Hardware Community Forums [SteamVR Hardware Forums].

Finally, if you're looking for more tutorials and VR how-to's as well as in-depth VR and AR courses checkout my website, VR Dev School [VR Dev School] at http://learn.vrdev.school/.

References

[SteamVR Forums]

SteamVR Forums. SteamVR https://steamcommunity.com/app/250820/discussions/

[SteamVR Hardware Forums]

SteamVR Hardware Forums. SteamVR Developer Hardware https://steamcommunity.com/app/358720/discussions/

[SteamVR GitHub]

SteamVR GitHub. https://github.com/ValveSoftware/steamvr_unity_plugin/tree/master/Assets/SteamVR

[VR Dev School]

VR Dev School. http://learn.vrdev.school/

UniCAVE

A Distributed Rendering System for Unity3D

Ross Tredinnick and Kevin Ponto
University of Wisconsin

4.1 Introduction

Recently, Unity3D has become a top choice content authoring tool for virtual reality (VR) development. VR systems have traditionally come in two forms: head-mounted display systems (HMDs), in which the displays are affixed to the user's forehead, and CAVE systems, in which the display system surrounds the user [Cruz-Neira et al., 1993]. While the hardware and software environments for HMD systems have become somewhat standardized, CAVE systems tend to be unique, with display technology, screen positions, and environment size varying considerably from system to system. Unity3D provides excellent support for consumer market HMDs such as the Oculus Rift and HTC Vive; however, support for non head-mounted VR display systems such as CAVEs and tiled display walls [Ponto et al., 2015] has been limited. A commercially available effort towards solving this problem exists [Kuntz, 2015]; however, no open source solution to the problem exists, thus inhibiting widespread adoption of Unity3D for non head-mounted systems. The complications from driving such systems include distributing rendering content, supporting stereoscopic rendering, and interfacing with tracking technologies. This chapter introduces UniCAVE, a free Unity3D plugin, which provides support for these types of distributed VR rendering systems. Some basic familiarity with Unity3D is expected and will aid in successfully adapting the plugin on an immersive non head-mounted VR display system.

4.2 The UniCAVE Plugin

The UniCAVE plugin works on immersive display systems driven by either a single machine or a cluster. Cluster-based immersive display systems distribute rendering, tracking, and processing across many machines, thus creating another layer of challenges to operate with these systems. While subsequent sections of this chapter will focus on the challenges of running Unity3D seamlessly across a distributed, immersive projection VR environment, all introduced solutions also apply to single machine environments.

4.2.1 Configuration

Methods for configuring CAVE systems have traditionally relied on input files, often configured through text. This method can make initial configuration and debugging quite difficult. Visual configuration mechanisms have shown great promise [Kuntz, 2015]; however, these systems have utilized their own proprietary graphical user interface to produce standard configuration files, thus requiring the additional step of learning the GUI tool to create correct configuration files as well as potentially learning a new configuration file format.

The UniCAVE plugin attempts to solve these configuration issues by allowing users to make use of the Unity3D editing environment to configure an immersive projection setup. This approach has several advantages compared to what is traditionally utilized. First, assuming some basic prior experience with Unity3D, the Unity3D editor presents a familiar user interface, allowing users to potentially configure their environment more rapidly. Second, hierarchical transformations can be applied to the entire display system. This enables operations such as scaling all projection surfaces to be accomplished through parent transformation. Finally, display system setups can be parented to game objects, enabling the dynamic movement of the viewing position based on game-level interaction.

4.2.2 Architecture

The overarching challenge when adapting a game engine such as Unity3D to a non head-mounted VR display system is to maintain display synchronization, that is to maintain a seamless (optionally) head-tracked, stereoscopic image across displays connected to one or more PCs via distributed rendering. Raffin et al. [2006] highlight various techniques for synchronizing a display cluster. Following Raffin's terminology: UniCAVE falls into a Sort-First data parallelism scheme with static partitioning of the scene. In this scheme, each machine in a cluster renders scene objects that are visible within its frustum, and the final image is the side-by-side composition of the various display images. Data distribution occurs from a single head node to other machines in the cluster. UniCAVE accomplishes data distribution through a combination of Unity3D networking techniques that allow the sharing of camera transformations, user input, randomization seeds, and time step information. Details on the networking setup of UniCAVE is covered in Section 4.4. Prior to covering the networking component of UniCAVE, it is first necessary to understand how UniCAVE is setup and the differences in how rendering is performed within the plugin.

In order to accomplish the distributed rendering necessary to seamlessly render and synchronize a display cluster using Unity3D, the UniCAVE plugin extends the existing Unity3D editor and engine functionality. UniCAVE can be downloaded as a unitypackage file [Tredinnick et al., 2017] and extracted into any Unity3D scene as shown in Figure 4.1.

The UniCAVE unitypackage consists of several prefab objects that have a similar structure. An example prefab that works with a six-sided CAVE system using one head node and six rendering nodes is shown in Figure 4.2. Each prefab contains two main object types within the hierarchy, a series of objects that represent the physical display system

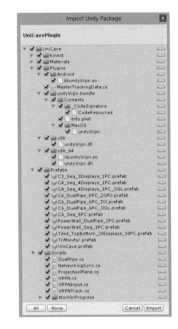

Figure 4.1

Importing the UniCAVE unitypackage.

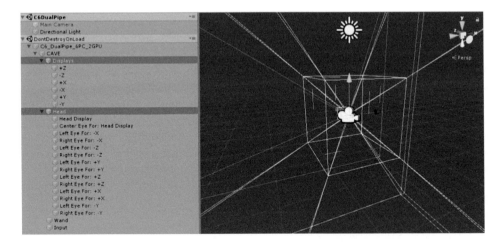

Figure 4.2

UniCAVE configuration for a six-sided CAVE System within the Unity3D editor. The system hierarchy is displayed on the tab on the left.

projection surfaces (*Displays*) and a series of cameras that perform the rendering onto the projection surfaces (*Head*). For systems that have 6-degree-of-freedom (6-DOF) tracking input devices, two additional objects (*Wand, Input*) exist in the prefab hierarchy to enable correct tracking of an input device. UniCAVE uses a previously developed plugin for interfacing with the VRPN open-source virtual reality input system to handle a variety of input devices [Redig, 2014; Taylor et al., 2001].

Listing 4.1. Code snippet for calculating camera transformations within UniCAVE.

```
// plane is the quad object associated with the cameras
//    and set via the Unity editor
// eyeOffset should be the offset from the tracking device
//    to the eye in tracker space.
// trackedRotation is the Tracker Rotation object that
//    tracks head orientation via VRPN.
void CalcMVP(Camera eye, GameObject plane, Vector3 eyeOffset,
               Quaternion trackerRotation,
               Camera. StereoscopicEye e)
{
        Vector3 pll, plr, pur;
        //  camera holder's position is tracked via VRPN
        //   (this assumes it is immediately above this object)
        Vector3 trackedHead = this.transform.parent.position;
        Mesh m = plane.GetComponent<MeshFilter>().mesh;
        pll = plane.transform.TransformPoint(m.vertices[0]);
        plr = plane.transform.TransformPoint(m.vertices[2]);
        pur = plane.transform.TransformPoint(m.vertices[3]);
        // we want cameras to be oriented the same as the
        //   plane we're projecting onto
        this.transform.rotation = plane.transform.rotation;
        Vector3 eyePos = trackedHead + (trackerRotation * eyeOffset);
        eye.transform.position = eyePos;
        // set both below to handle native / non-native stereo
        eye.projectionMatrix = asymProj(pll, plr, pur, eyePos, eye);
        eye.SetStereoProjectionMatrix(e, eye.projectionMatrix);
}
```

Under the *Head* game object, a number of game objects containing Unity3D camera objects exist per machine: one for monoscopic rendering; or two for stereoscopic rendering. Under the *Displays* game object, a number of game objects representing physical projection surfaces exist. A key UniCAVE script is the "*PhysicalDisplay.cs*" script on child game objects of *Displays*. This script associates the one or two cameras with the physical surface dimensions via an asymmetric perspective projection matrix calculation. A snippet of the setup for this calculation is shown in Listing 4.1. Details about the asymmetric perspective projection calculation are discussed below in Section 4.2.3.

4.2.3 Camera Projections

Typical perspective projection matrices, as calculated within OpenGL and DirectX, assume a user is centered relative to the display and not moving. This generally makes sense, as graphics applications are developed assuming the user is operating the application with

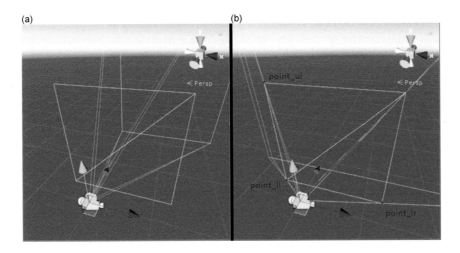

Figure 4.3

The Unity3D quad representing the display surface is outlined in green. (a) Shows the standard camera projection, while (b) shows the camera with the asymmetric projection.

their view centered on the monitor and without any sort of 6-degree-of-freedom (6-DOF) tracking system. For CAVE or tiled display systems that incorporate head tracking, a view of the scene must be rendered with perspective according to where the user is physically located relative to the display surface. UniCAVE handles this by allowing a user to define their physical display setup via Unity3D quad objects and then ties the asymmetric projection specifically to a quad via the Unity script in Listing 4.2 as adopted from Kooima [2019]. An example of the effect of the above script on a camera's projection in Unity3D versus a normal perspective projection is shown in Figure 4.3.

4.2.4 Networking

An important principle for distributed rendering involves the coordination of events between systems. Raffin and Soares highlight various techniques for synchronizing a display cluster [Raffin et al., 2006]. Put simply, many cluster-based systems aim to have the same actions happen at the same time while distributing viewpoints between nodes.

Key components within Unity3D that UniCAVE uses for accomplishing distributed rendering are Unity3D's NetworkManager and NetworkIdentity components together with the NetworkBehaviour class. Game objects that need distribution require a NetworkIdentity component, which is automatically created if a script that inherits from NetworkBehaviour is attached to the game object. A NetworkManager component must be used to instantiate a connection between a server and clients, this is currently done within the *NetworkInitialization.cs* script. Following the data distribution concept of passing information from a head node to slaves as discussed in Raffin et al. [2006], UniCAVE assumes one machine serves as a head node, and thus the server, while other machines act as slaves, thus clients. The *NetworkInitialization* script's `HeadMachine` variable defines the machine name within the cluster that acts as the server. Network initialization is performed in the *NetworkInitialization.cs* script via the `NetworkManager.StartServer` Unity3D function, called on the head node machine, while a `NetworkManager.`

StartClient function call connects the slaves to the head node. A precaution must be made while starting up multiple executables and initializing the network, as there is no guarantee that the head node has initialized the server prior to slave nodes attempting to connect to it. To address this circumstance, UniCAVE checks the Unity3D asynchronous callback function, `void OnFailedToConnect(NetworkConnectio nError error)` that will occur after issuing an unacknowledged `NetworkManager. StartClient` function call. When a connection fails, the client machines wait two seconds and then attempt to reconnect. This repeats until a successful connection is made or a predetermined number of attempts occurs and a failure state is reached.

Listing 4.2. Unity C# code snippet calculating projection matrix for an asymmetric perspective projection from an eye point to the corners of a quad.

```
// point_ll, point_lr, point_ul are lower left, lower right,
//    and upper left points defining projection quad
Matrix4x4 asymProj(Vector3 point_ll, Vector3 point_lr,
                   Vector3 point_ul, Vector3 eyePos, Camera cam)
{
       Vector3 right = (point_lr - point_ll).normalized;
       Vector3 up = (point_ul - point_ll).normalized;
       Vector3 normal = Vector3.Cross(vr, vu).normalized;
       // compute screen corner vectors from eye
       Vector3 v_ll = point_ll - eyePos;
       Vector3 v_lr = point_lr - eyePos;
       Vector3 v_ur = point_ur - eyePos;
       // find the distance from the eye to screen plane
       //    any point works here, v_ll chosen arbitrarily
       float d = Vector3.Dot(v_ll, normal);
       // calculate and set matrix values
       float n = cam.nearClipPlane;
       float f = cam.farClipPlane;
       float l = Vector3.Dot(right, v_ll) * n / d;
       float r = Vector3.Dot(right, v_lr) * n / d;
       float b = Vector3.Dot(up, v_ll) * n / d;
       float t = Vector3.Dot(up, v_ur)* n / d;
       Matrix4x4 mat = Matrix4x4::zero;
       mat[0 ,0] = 2.0f * n / (r - l);
       mat[0 ,2] = (r + l)/ (r - l);
       mat[1 ,1] = 2.0f * n / (t - b);
       mat[1 ,2] = (t + b)/ (t - b);
       mat[2 ,2] = -(f + n) / (f - n);
       mat[2 ,3] = (-2.0f * f * n) / (f - n);
       mat[3 ,2] = -1.0f;
       return mat;
}
```

The NetworkIdentity component and NetworkBehaviour class serves to keep certain variables and components of a game object synchronized across a network. Certain Unity3D networking components, such as NetworkTransform and NetworkAnimator (both which inherit from NetworkBehaviour), can synchronize components such as transforms and animators across a network. Within the UniCAVE hierarchy, NetworkIdentity components exist on the *Head* object to synchronize positional camera tracking, the *Wand* object for synchronizing a tracked input device, and the parent object of the UniCAVE prefab (e.g. *CAVE* in Figure 4.2), for synchronizing user navigation. A script on two objects

(*Head* and *Wand*) called *VRPNTrack*.cs handles the interfacing with VRPN and sets the object transform position (location) and/or orientation (depending on whether the "Track Position" and/or "Track Rotation" check boxes are on or off in the Unity3D inspector) from a VRPN enabled tracking system. This script also derives from NetworkBehaviour so that tracking information can be synchronized, which can be done via a NetworkTransform component. One note, a NetworkTransform component has only a maximum send rate of 29 frames per second, and in a real-time VR system, the update rate, and thus network send rate would at least be 60 frames per second. Due to this limitation, UniCAVE explicitly synchronizes head tracking information using RPC calls as this allows for a greater send rate of the head node tracking information. This occurs in the *UCNetwork.cs* script, which is attached to the parent object in the hierarchy (e.g. *CAVE* in Figure 4.2).

4.2.5 Timing

The overall system must stay synchronized to guarantee a seamless projection display. This helps subsystems such as Animation, Physics, and Particles stay synchronized across nodes. Maintaining a consistent timing across nodes becomes particularly challenging in Unity3D, as we cannot directly set a common frame time amongst nodes via an exposed class variable (although this can be done for the physics update loop via the Unity3D's variable `Time.fixedDeltaTime`). To work around this problem, UniCAVE uses an exposed variable `Time.timeScale` to adjust the time scale of the engine—`timeScale` is typically used for effects such as slow-motion.

The UniCAVE plugin uses the `Time.timeScale` variable to synchronize nodes within a cluster by monitoring the relative game time of the master and slave nodes. When the game time of a slave node is ahead of the master node, the plugin slows down the slave node slightly for a few frames, and likewise if the slave node is behind the master node, the plugin speeds up the time scale of the slave node. This concept is handled via the following equation:

$$\text{timeScale} = \frac{\left(\left(M_t - S_t\right) + \Delta_{sync}\right)}{\Delta_{sync}}$$

Δ_{sync} is a tunable parameter which controls the rate at which timeScale is adjusted. M_t is the time since start of application on the master node, while S_t is the time-scaled game time of a slave node. Setting Δ_{sync} at a rate too frequent or infrequent can cause irregularities in performance. In practice, the authors found that syncing the time every tenth of a second maintains smooth synchronization between nodes. This equation has shown to synchronize animations across a six-sided CAVE system and aid in synchronizing other sub-systems that rely on engine time. If timing is slightly off, users would notice that images at seams in the display are not perfectly seamless, so tweaking the Sync Time (Δ_{sync}) value in the *UCNetwork.cs* script may help.

4.2.6 Random Numbers

Random number generation within a display cluster must guarantee that all machines initiate their random number generators with the same seed number in order to guarantee matching numbers across nodes. UniCAVE achieves this by sending the random number seed generated by the head node to all slave nodes within the cluster, whereby the slave nodes then use that seed to initialize their respective random number generators using the Unity3D function `Unity.Random.InitState(int seed)`. Similar to synchronizing head node transformations, UniCAVE makes use of networking RPC function calls to send the data from head node to slave nodes. See the UniCAVE source for an example and Unity3D's documentation networking RPC calls for further information.

4.3 Challenges

While the UniCAVE plugin provides support for many of the features needed for a distributed rendering environment, certain challenges still remain. These challenges include: input, multiple displays, stereo, multiple GPUs, and underlying software changes.

4.3.1 Input

Input serves as a challenge when trying to create a distributed rendering system within Unity3D due to limitations in how Unity3D provides access to a project's input definitions. UniCAVE supports basic input via interfacing with VRPN and furthermore supports basic distribution of the input across a cluster. Ideally, one would be able to tap into Unity's input processing system by taking advantage of such functions as `Unity.Input.GetKeyDown` and call it once with the expectation that it would run across the cluster. We can see how this does not work in a cluster by considering input from a keyboard. Keyboard and other direct inputs do not work on a clustered Unity3D system because they are only attached to one machine, and the user, probably situated at the head node, could press a key, but the script running and calling the `GetKeyDown` function would only detect a key press on the head node, not the other machines in a cluster. A potential solution to this would be to be able to "inject" input events into the Unity engine; however, this is currently not an exposed feature within the Unity scripting engine. Input events can only be detected rather than injected. UniCAVE provides basic support for sending keyboard input across the cluster by checking whether the `Input.inputString` variable has a length greater than zero, and, if so, it sends the string from head node to slave nodes. A user of the plugin could then custom script an action dependent on the value of the string sent across the network.

Currently, UniCAVE handles VRPN wand button presses by detecting a wand button press on the head node and then disguising these values within a Unity transform object, which is synchronized via a NetworkTransform component and therefore sent across the cluster automatically. Slave machines check the values of this transform to see if they are non-zero, and, if so, perform some sort of action (such as changing the color of a material within the model). Currently, analog input from a wand navigates the user within the scene by adjusting the transform of the UniCAVE parent prefab object on the head node. The *Wand.cs* script provides some options (such as navigation speed and limiting vertical movement) for customizing the default navigation technique. The adjustments made to the transform of this prefab synchronize across a cluster via RPC calls, allowing basic user navigation within a scene. Overall, the current solution for input is far from ideal, and the UniCAVE authors are seeking and working out ways for improving the current clustered input solution.

4.3.2 Multiple Displays

There are certain nuanced differences in Unity3D when attempting to use multiple displays for DirectX vs. OpenGL executable builds and between operating systems. Currently, Unity3D (Version 5.5) does not support multiple displays when building with OpenGL on Windows. However, it does support multiple displays when building OpenGL on Linux. DirectX executable builds support multiple displays, with the caveat that additional displays must be explicitly activated. In UniCAVE, an extra display will be activated if the user toggles on the "Use Specific Display" checkbox and specifies a display index on the *PhysicalDisplay* script. This will automatically adjust any created camera object's target display to the specified index, i.e. "Display 2" instead of "Display 1" if the index is set to 1 instead of 0. Some of the pre-packaged prefabs within UniCAVE are configured to work with multiple displays, particularly prefabs meant to be built with DirectX.

In the case of using OpenGL on Windows, multiple displays are handled as a single window spread over them with camera viewports dividing the window into separate parts. In this situation, all cameras target "Display 1" but then the Viewport Rect values are modified. A summary example of these differences is shown in Figure 4.4. UniCAVE comes pre-packaged with example prefabs to handle the OpenGL for Windows case.

4.3.3 Stereo

The UniCAVE plugin provides support for different stereo techniques. Techniques such as quad-buffered stereo, side-by-side stereo, or split-screen stereo are configured by way of setting up the correct camera and viewport configurations in the Unity3D editor. For quad-buffered stereo, which often requires setting an underlying operating system stereo flag for the window, UniCAVE offers particular options depending on the version of Unity3D. Prior to Version 5.1, Unity3D provided no support for quad-buffered active stereo. To support OpenGL quad-buffered stereo in this case, the UniCAVE plugin provides a stereo injection technique by way of GLIntercept [Trebilco, 2013]. The plugin works by counting how many glClear calls are made on a bound frame buffer that returns true for a `glGetBooleanv(GL_STEREO)` call. The `GL_STEREO` check ensures that the counter only increments for the main rendering window, instead of frame buffer objects for off-screen rendering, as they return `false` for this check.

The release of Version 5.1 of Unity3D added a player settings option titled "virtual reality supported." When checking this box, a list of VR-supported devices can be chosen. This was largely added for support of commercially-available HMDs such as the Oculus Rift and HTC Vive. One option, titled *"Stereo Display (non-head mounted),"* provides support for quad-buffered stereo. One caveat of using this option is that Unity3D's underlying engine follows a stereo rendering path, and, prior to Version 5.4.2, it would simply use an automatically computed version of the projection matrix, which, in the case of immersive projection display systems (e.g. a CAVE), might be wrong due to the matrix's lack of support for head tracking and correct asymmetric projection. With the release of Unity3D 5.4.2, the function `Camera.SetStereoProjectionMatrix` can be used to set a custom projection matrix, thus allowing asymmetric perspective projection matrices as described in this chapter to be assigned in conjunction with enabling the *"Stereo Display (non-head mounted)"* option.

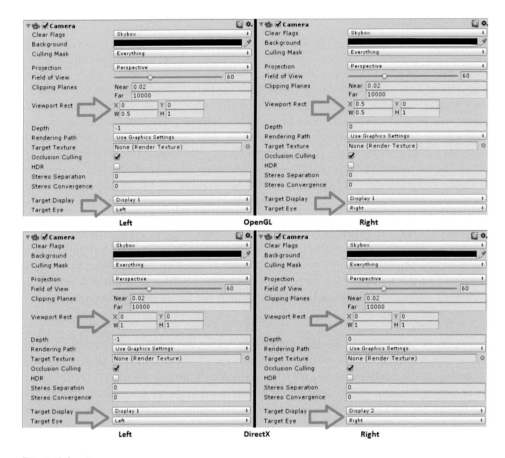

Figure 4.4

Comparing handling of multiple displays between OpenGL and DirectX builds. In this example, two displays are used for stereo rendering where a single eye is assigned to each display.

4.3.4 Multiple GPUs

A note for users of systems with multiple GPUs, Unity3D contains a hidden "-gpu #" executable command line argument. Enabling this argument can benefit systems with multi-GPU setups, although adjustments to application launching might be required. For example, a prefab that would have used multiple displays might now, instead, render to a single display, but more than one instantiation of the application could be launched with the "-gpu #" command line argument with a value matching the index of the GPU driving the corresponding portion of the OS desktop. The Unity.Display.SetParams function can be used to move and resize the application window to match the portion of the OS desktop being driven by a GPU. The authors have successfully enabled this on a dual GPU immersive display setup, seeing nearly double frame rate speeds in most applications.

4.3.5 Underlying Software Changes

As Unity3D is a continuing, developing software tool, features are continuously being added and also periodically removed. This evolution means that more efficient methods of utilizing the Unity3D infrastructure for distributed display systems might be possible in the future. On the other hand, the methods described in this chapter might become unsupported in future versions of Unity3D software. This problem is well described by O'Leary et al. [2017] in the case of VR support for the Visualization Toolkit (VTK). While the hope would be that someday the features of this plugin become integrated into the Unity3D core software infrastructure, the UniCAVE plugin provides support for these types of systems in the interim.

4.4 Conclusion

UniCAVE is an on-going project that has a website at *https://unicave.discovery.wisc.edu* and a GitHub repository at *https://github.com/livingenvironmentslab/UniCAVE*. The website contains documentation for the plugin as well as a step-by-step guide on how to create your own prefab for an immersive projection system. (As of this publication, support for Unity version 2018 can be found in the GitHub repository.) The UniCAVE team encourages those who create such prefabs to contribute them to the active repository, so that others with similar configurations might use your prefab to avoid "reinventing the wheel."

References

[Cruz-Neira et al., 1993]

Cruz-Neira, Carolina, Daniel J. Sandin, and Thomas A. DeFanti (1993). Surround-screen projection-based virtual reality: The design and implementation of the CAVE. In *Proceedings of the 20th Annual Conference on Computer Graphics and Interactive Techniques*, Anaheim, CA: ACM, August 1–6, pages 135–142.

[Kooima, 2019]

Kooima, Robert (2019). Perspective projection for VR. In Sherman, W. R., editor, *VR Developer Gems*, Chapter 33. Boca Raton, FL: A K Peters/CRC Press.

[Kuntz, 2015]

Kuntz, Sébastien (2015). MiddleVR a generic VR toolbox. In *Proceedings of 2015 IEEE Virtual Reality (VR)*, Arles, France, March 23–27, pages 391–392.

[O'Leary et al., 2017]

O'Leary, Patrick, Sankhesh Jhaveri, Aashish Chaudhary, William Sherman, Ken Martin, David Lonie, Eric Whiting, James Money, and Sandy McKenzie (2017). Enhancements to VTK enabling scientific visualization in immersive environments. In *Proceedings of Virtual Reality (VR)*, Los Angeles, CA: IEEE, March 18–22, pages 186–194.

[Ponto et al., 2015]

Ponto, Kevin, Joe Kohlmann, and Ross Tredinnick. (2015). DSCVR: Designing a commodity hybrid virtual reality system. *Virtual Reality*, 19(1):57–70.

[Raffin et al., 2006]

Raffin, Bruno, Luciano Soares, Tao Ni, Robert Ball, Greg S. Schmidt, Mark A. Livingston, Oliver G. Staadt, and Richard May (2006). PC clusters for virtual reality. In *Proceedings of IEEE Virtual Reality Conference (VR 2006)*, Alexandria, VA: IEEE, March 25–29, pages 215–222.

[Redig, 2014]

Redig, Scott (github: "Laremere") (2014). *Simple VRPN wrapper for Unity*. https://github.com/Laremere/unityVRPN

[Taylor et al., 2001]

Taylor II, Russell M., Thomas C. Hudson, Adam Seeger, Hans Weber, Jeffrey Juliano, and Aron T. Helser (2001). VRPN: A device-independent, network-transparent VR peripheral system. In *Proceedings of the ACM Symposium on Virtual Reality Software and Technology*, Banff, AB: ACM, November 15–17, pages 55–61.

[Trebilco, 2013]

Trebilco, Damian (2013). GLIntercept-OpenGL function call interceptor/logger. https://github.com/dtrebilco/glintercept

[Tredinnick et al., 2017]

Tredinnick, Ross, Brady Boettcher, Sam Solovy, Simon Smith, and Kevin Ponto (2017). UniCAVE github repository. https://github.com/livingenvironmentslab/unicave

5

Using the Kinect for Head-Tracked Perspective and Pointing in Stationary VR Displays

Jason W. Woodworth and Christoph W. Borst
University of Louisiana at Lafayette

5.1 Introduction

This chapter shows how to use the Microsoft Kinect sensor V2 to track body parts and how to set up a stationary (non-headset) virtual reality (VR) display with head-tracked perspective and pointing. Topics include how to set up the virtual camera perspective, how to render stereoscopic imagery in side-by-side stereo format, how to get started with the Kinect to obtain body part positions, and how to use the Kinect data to move the virtual cameras and an interaction wand. We illustrate these concepts using Unity 2018.3 scripts, a Kinect 2 sensor with the Windows adapter, and a 3D TV with side-by-side stereoscopic capabilities (Figure 5.1). The code will be comprehensible to most Unity or VR developers, and we recommend that readers know the basics of matrix transformations and coordinate spaces.

5.2 Kinect

The Kinect sensor is a low-cost depth camera that measures color and depth of points in its view. It uses this information and decision trees to classify points into specific body parts,

Figure 5.1

An example of the final Perspective TV application. The user does not need to wear any tracking devices; tracking is handled with the Kinect. Note the Kinect clamped on the TV's stand to keep it near the TV.

and then it fits a skeleton to these body parts. While marketed mainly as an input device for video games, the Kinect has been used for many other types of applications, such as environment sensing for robots and body tracking for "serious" VR applications. With the Kinect V2, your application will be able to detect the positions of 26 different joints on up to six people within its view, plus detect some basic body state information, analyze facial expressions, and more.

5.3 Working with the Kinect SDK

5.3.1 Getting the SDK

The Kinect For Windows SDK 2.0 and associated Unity add-on packages can be downloaded from the Microsoft Kinect Developer website [Microsoft 2019]. There are three Unity packages included: the standard Kinect assets used for tracking body joints, assets for tracking face movement and expressions, and assets for using gesture recognition. This chapter will only consider the standard body joint package.

In addition to the Unity packages, example scripts and a scene included under *Kinect View* folder give a starting example for reading Kinect joint data and visualizing the body. The scripts *BodySourceManager.cs* and *BodySourceView.cs* are of particular interest. Examining these scripts is recommended, as this chapter will build from these when describing how to track joint positions.

5.3.2 Kinect SDK Components

The Kinect SDK contains many classes and scripts. We will briefly explain the purpose and contents of the classes most important to this chapter.

BodyFrame and **BodyFrameReader**: The information captured by the Kinect is given to the developer through three major objects: a color frame, a depth frame, and a body frame. The color and depth frames report information from the Kinect's color and depth cameras, respectively, while the body frame reports information about the bodies the Kinect has identified. The latest body frame can be grabbed from the body frame reader. Once a frame is grabbed, you can pull body information as an array of Body objects.

Body: The body object contains all information about a single body the Kinect has identified. Most interestingly, it contains information about the different joints in the body in a collection called "Joints" that maps a **JointType** to the actual **Joint** object. It also contains some other basic information, like hand state, whether the person is wearing glasses, and whether their eyes are open are closed. Each Body contains a unique tracking ID, and should be referenced through it.

Joint and **JointType**: For each body, the Kinect tracks the local positions of 26 "joints," primarily those that connect two body segments such as the elbows or knees. However, the Kinect API uses the name "joints" more generally, also referring to segment endpoints such as the head position. The **JointType** class is a simple enumeration of all of the joints the Kinect is tracking. Examine this class to get an idea for what parts of the body you can track.

5.4 Motivating Application: Head Tracked VR with Pointer

Traditional stationary (non-headset) VR displays, such as projection displays or desktop "fish tank" displays, make the virtual world feel real in part by naturally changing the perspective as the viewer's head moves. This is required for an accurate perspective 3D geometry, making the screen or monitor analogous to a window into the 3D virtual world—where the view changes when looking from different locations. This changing perspective provides a powerful depth cue with head motion. Even with monoscopic displays, the motion can provide a sense of 3D space, especially when viewed with a single eye or through a video camera (see the Johnny Lee YouTube video for a popular example [Lee 2007]). In contrast, standard 3D movie or desktop game systems usually lack head tracking and are rendered based on a particular fixed viewer position—correct only from a static "sweet spot." Due to the proliferation of consumer-grade trackers, such as the Kinect, it is now affordable to provide a head-tracked VR experience with a standard 3D monitor or TV.

5.4.1 Unity Object Overview

The approach for building the head-tracked display in Unity relies on a few in-game objects and scripts, organized as follows and shown in Figure 5.2:

- A top-level base object (a Unity empty GameObject), which we have called "**Perspective TV**," holds the other components, grouping them, and allowing them to be moved as a collection.
- A "quad" (four vertex polygon) scaled to represent the viewable monitor size (width in x, height in y), is parented to the "**Perspective TV**" object and should have the same origin and orientation as the "**Perspective TV**" base. This representation of

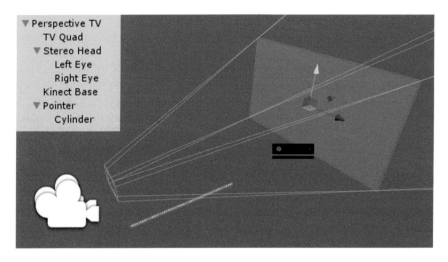

Figure 5.2

All Unity objects under the Perspective TV hierarchy.

your monitor will be used to compute the projections. Making this an in-game object allows easy changes to the monitor size and helps show whether projections are working (in Unity's editor).

- An object that we call "**Kinect Base**" represents the Kinect and contains the script that retrieves joint positions. Its position (location) and rotation (if any) in relation to the TV Quad should be made to match how the real Kinect is placed relative to the real monitor. For simplicity, we suggest starting with the Kinect placed in the same orientation as the monitor (no rotation) and placed just above or below the monitor.

- A "**Head**" object represents the position of the user's head. The position will be set based on Kinect tracking. The head should be oriented (rotated) the same way as the TV, matching how users typically view the TV. Note that if you extend tracking to include head orientation, perspective would be incrementally improved by applying head rotation, allowing the location of each eye to be determined more precisely.

- A camera or set of cameras acts as a surrogate for the eyes. Each camera has a script configuring the perspective view. The camera objects should be children of the head object to follow the head and remain oriented the same way as the head and TV. Note that if you extend tracking to include head orientation, the eye objects should be scripted to rotate into alignment with the TV, rather than matching head alignment, to satisfy requirements for the perspective matrix construction.

- A wand pointer will be used for pointing at scene objects for interaction. The wand uses a thin cylinder and has a script that defines the pointing direction based on certain joint positions.

5.4.2 Camera Projection Matrix for an Off-Axis Eye

A virtual camera's frustum is the volume that it sees. The frustum contents get projected onto the viewing screen. This frustum can be described by a common 6-parameter model shown in Figure 5.3. This defines the volume in terms of distances, or coordinates, along

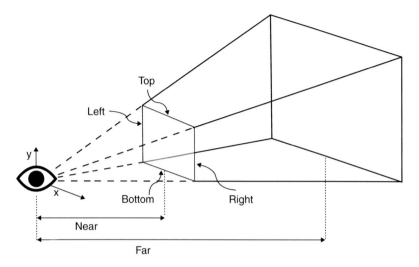

Figure 5.3

A common 6-parameter camera model that defines a perspective frustum. Left, right, top, and bottom define the distances from the camera, along principal axes, to the front window edges.

principal axes of a coordinate system centered on the camera (eye). A slice through the pyramid at distance *near* from the camera defines a virtual viewing window that ranges from *left* to *right* in eye X coordinates and *bottom* to *top* in eye Y coordinates. This X axis points toward the screen's (eye's) right, and Y points up.

The six frustum parameters can be converted into a projection matrix as part of camera configuration for graphics rendering. A script from the Unity documentation on the *Camera.projectionMatrix* variable shows exactly how to convert the parameters into a projection matrix. The relevant code can be seen in Listing 5.1.

Listing 5.1. Taken from Unity developer documentation for the Camera class (version 2018.3) **[Unity 2019]**.

```
// Set a Unity camera projection matrix with custom values
Matrix4x4 PerspectiveOffCenter(float left, float right, float bottom, float top, float near,
float far) {
    float x = 2.0f * near / (right - left);
    float y = 2.0f * near / (top - bottom);
    float a = (right + left) / (right - left);
    float b = (top + bottom) / (top - bottom);
    float c = -(far + near) / (far - near);
    float d = -(2.0f * far * near) / (far - near);
    float e = -1.0f;
    Matrix4x4 mat = new Matrix4x4();
    mat[0, 0] = x;
    mat[0, 1] = 0;
    mat[0, 2] = a;
    mat[0, 3] = 0;
    mat[1, 0] = 0;
    mat[1, 1] = y;
```

```
mat[1, 2] = b;
mat[1, 3] = 0;
mat[2, 0] = 0;
mat[2, 1] = 0;
mat[2, 2] = c;
mat[2, 3] = d;
mat[3, 0] = 0;
mat[3, 1] = 0;
mat[3, 2] = e;
mat[3, 3] = 0;
return mat;
}
```

To create a head-tracked perspective window, we set up a frustum that matches the pyramid defined by the real eye and the real viewing surface (monitor). We first measure the dimensions of the real screen, and the algorithm uses these to calculate monitor extents along principal axes of the eye (or screen, because eye and screen coordinate systems are aligned for the 6-parameter model). Consider an eye that is off-center from the monitor as shown in Figure 5.4, with the monitor and eye both represented in the eye's coordinate system:

$$left = \text{monPos.x} - (W/2.0)$$
$$right = \text{left} + W$$
$$top = \text{monPos.y} + (H/2.0)$$
$$bottom = \text{top} - H$$
$$near = \text{monPos.z}$$

The frustum from these calculated parameters has a front "window," or pyramid slice, matching the monitor size and distance from the eye. It also would set up the camera's

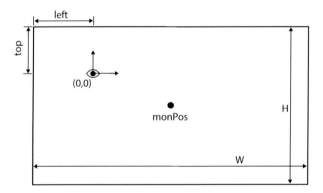

Figure 5.4

The monitor and eye. The monPos is the position of the center of the monitor and it will be computed in the eye-attached coordinate system (so, it holds the center's distances from the eye). W and H are the monitor's width and height, respectively. Left and top are the distances from the eye to the left and top sides of the monitor.

     5. Using the Kinect for Head-Tracked Perspective and Pointing in Stationary VR Displays

near plane to this eye distance, but that is not usually desired, because objects closer to the eye than the near plane will not render. However, we want a 3D view that allows object to "pop out" some distance in front of the screen. To enable the application to show objects closer than the screen surface, we separate the near plane from the monitor distance by scaling all parameters by $s = near/monPos.Z$, where *near* is now an arbitrary desired near plane distance (such as the Unity camera default value). Scaling all the parameters together like this preserves field of view (angles in the pyramid) but moves the slices defining the visible depth range. The *near* and *far* values can then be set as desired.

The final camera parameter values are:

> *near* = (as selected by developer, typically a small value)
> $s = near/\text{monPos.Z}$
> *left* = (monPos.x–W/2.0) * s
> *right* = left + (W * s)
> *top* = (monPos.y + H/2.0) * s
> *bottom* = top–(H * s)

We now create a script—we'll call it *PerspectiveCamera.cs*—that can be placed on the camera to give it the desired frustum. It will need a reference to the monitor quad (rectangle), described earlier, to convey the monitor's size. Note the script uses Unity's "**LateUpdate()**" instead of "**Update()**", to ensure the camera setup runs after the head position is set (otherwise, the perspective could be computed using the head position from a prior frame). The script is shown in Listing 5.2:

Listing 5.2. PerspectiveCamera.cs: set an off-axis view based on the location of an eye.

```
// PerspectiveCamera.cs
public Transform _monitor;
private Camera _cam; // Reference should be set in Start

void LateUpdate() {
    // Get the monitor's position in the eye/camera's coordinate system
    Vector3 monPos = this.transform.InverseTransformPoint(_monitor.transform.position);

    // Define width and height from the monitor quad.
    float H = _monitor.localScale.y;
    float W = _monitor.localScale.x;
    float s = _cam.nearClipPlane / monPos.z;

    float left = (monPos.x - W / 2.0) * s;
    float right = left + (W * s);
    float top = (monPos.y + H / 2.0) * s;
    float bottom = top - (H * s);
    float near = _cam.nearClipPlane;
    float far = _cam.farClipPlane;

    // The PerspectiveOffCenter function from Listing 5.1 should be included in this script.
    _cam.projectionMatrix = PerspectiveOffCenter(left, right, bottom, top, near, far);
}
```

In Unity, you can tag this script to execute in edit mode to more easily see its effects. As you move the camera around, its frustum edges should continue to run through the defined monitor quad's corners. If you build a room behind the quad, then you will see your view of the room change as the camera moves.

5.4.3 Side-by-Side Stereoscopic 3D

We next set up a two-camera rig for stereoscopic rendering. Note that Unity has a built-in stereo rendering capability with rendering speedups, but it does not currently have sufficient parameters to reproduce the required viewing geometry for head-tracked stationary displays—it doesn't handle arbitrary head/eye positions relative to the screen.

Many stereoscopic 3D consumer displays support a "side-by-side" image format. This format places the left and right eye images on each corresponding half of a single input image, and the device then separates the two halves back into left and right images. For example, for 3D TVs with battery-powered shutter glasses, two half-size images are stretched across the entire screen when in 3D mode, and the TV alternatingly shows these left and right images in sync with LCD shutters in the 3D glasses. Some passive 3D TVs use alternating lines for left and right views, with light from these lines being polarized in different ways to be separated by polarizing lenses on the glasses. In Unity, side-by-side rendering can be done using two cameras, one for each eye, that are separated by the distance between the viewer's eyes, also known as the interpupillary distance or IPD.

To set up a stereo pair of cameras in Unity, create an empty GameObject representing the head and create two cameras as child objects. These two camera objects, the left and right eyes, should be offset along the head x direction by half of the IPD per eye/direction, to create a total separation of IPD. In some cases, y and z offsets may also need to be applied for more accuracy, if there is substantial distance from the eyes to where the Kinect places the head joint. Each camera should have its viewport width reduced to a value of 0.5 to cover only half the screen. The viewport representing the right eye should be moved to cover the right half of the screen by setting the X value to 0.5, as shown in Figure 5.5. Each camera should then have the *PerspectiveCamera.cs* script placed on it, to set the proper perspective frustum. Each camera (eye) will then produce slightly different images from the other, as seen in Figure 5.6.

A screen-centered (on-axis) head position using the monitor's 3D mode should produce an accurate perspective window when your head's distance from the screen matches the virtual camera's distance from the monitor quad.

Note that certain TV features such as motion smoothing or noise reduction can introduce visual lag. We suggest disabling such features and enabling any special lag-reducing "game modes" when available.

5.4.4 Adding Head Tracking

5.4.4.1 Retrieving Joint Positions

The *KinectView* main scene from Microsoft's Unity package gives valuable insight into how Kinect data can be accessed. The first step is to create a manager to access and store all Kinect Body data. The script *BodySourceManager.cs* included with the Unity package can be reused for this. Its purpose is to collect Body instances from the KinectSensor class's

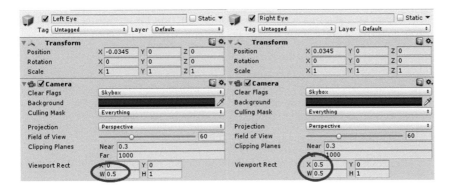

Figure 5.5

Camera viewport and transform settings for the left and right eyes, using an IPD of 0.69.

Figure 5.6

An example of side-by-side half-width images for left and right eyes.

BodyFrameReader, putting the body information into an array to be read from the class we will create.

The second main step is to create the script that then reads joint data. The *BodySourceView.cs* script effectively finds all joints for all bodies tracked by the Kinect. We need to ensure that our 3D application consistently tracks the head of a single tracked body—it is only possible to provide consistent correct 3D for a single person. We will call our script that does this *TrackBodies.cs*.

A first step in creating this script is to create a function for retrieving a desired joint's position from a single known body. Such a function is defined in Listing 5.3.

Listing 5.3. Excerpt from "TrackBodies.cs": function to extract the proper joint position data relative to the Kinect.

```
// from TrackBodies.cs
private Vector3 GetJointLocalPosition(Kinect.Body body, Kinect.JointType jt) {
    //Note that because Joint is ambiguous between the default Unity Joint class
    //  and the Kinect Joint, the full namespace will need to be spelled out
    Windows.Kinect.Joint joint = body.Joints[jt];
    return new Vector3(joint.Position.X, joint.Position.Y, joint.Position.Z);
}
```

As indicated by the name of the function (*GetJointLocalPosition*), it returns the *local* position of the specified joint. Here, local refers to the right-handed coordinate system that the Kinect uses to report positions—reported in meters with respect to its base. For example, if the Kinect reports the head joint at (1, .7, 3), the user's head is 1 m to the right of the Kinect (viewed from the front), .7 m above, and 3 m away from it. Note that mapping the coordinate to a corresponding Unity object's space can involve negating the z coordinate to convert to Unity's left-handed convention.

Local coordinates are sufficient for particular applications. For example, some applications only need to know the distance to a user, or what body pose gesture is made. However, if your application needs to know the joint's position relative to an object in the world (e.g., testing foot collision with a soccer ball), you typically convert the position into a world-referenced position. Generally, *TrackBodies.cs* is added to a GameObject that can be considered the Kinect base and is positioned in the virtual world as needed. A joint's world-referenced position can be found by transforming the local Kinect-reported position as shown in Listing 5.4. Note the z negation to switch from right-handed to left-handed conventions.

Listing 5.4. Excerpt from "TrackBodies.cs": function to extract joint position data relative to the world coordinates.

```
// from TrackBodies.cs
private Vector3 GetJointWorldPosition(Kinect.Body body, Kinect.JointType jt) {
    Windows.Kinect.Joint joint = body.Joints[jt];
    return this.transform.TransformPoint(new Vector3(joint.Position.X, joint.Position.Y,
                                         -joint.Position.Z);
}
```

Position tracking can be demonstrated by making the script track the head of a user in view. This involves adding code to the script's Update loop in fashion similar to Microsoft's *BodySourceView.cs* script. The code is shown in Listing 5.5—without standard null checks:

```
// from TrackBodies.cs
public BodySourceManger _bodyManager;
private Dictionary<ulong, GameObject> _heads; // Map body IDs to a created head object

void Update() {
  Kinect.Body[] bodyData = _bodyManager.GetData();
  // Collect unique IDs for each tracked body.
  List<ulong> trackedIDs = new List<ulong>();
  foreach (var body in bodyData) {
    if (body.isTracked)
        trackedIDs.Add(body.trackingId);
  }
  // Go through the IDs in the head dictionary to remove heads that are not tracked
  foreach (var ID in _heads.Keys) {
    if (!trackedIDs.Contains(ID)) {
        Destroy(_Heads[ID]);
        _heads.remove(ID);
    }
  }

  // Update the positions of heads for each body.
  UpdateTracking(bodyData);
}

private void UpdateTracking(Kinect.Body[] bodyData) {
  // For each body, update the head position
  // If there's a new body, create a new head
  foreach (var body in bodyData) {
    if (body.isTracked) {
        if (!_heads.ContainsKey(body.trackingId)) {
            // Create some basic gameobject and put it in _heads map
            CreateHead(body.TrackingId);
        }
        // Update position of that GameObject
        _heads[body.trackingId].transform.position =
          GetJointWorldPosition(body, Kinect.JointType.Head);
    }
  }
}
```

With this script, any person entering the Kinect's field of view will spawn an object that follows along the head's tracked position in the game. If a person leaves the view, then the object tracking their head will be destroyed. Because the position is being transformed by the Kinect Base object's transform, you can move the Kinect Base object around and the tracked heads will follow.

5.4.4.2 Tracking a Single User

Our application requires that only a single user's head data be read and maintained for consistent 3D. *TrackBodies.cs* can read the position of a joint from any single known body, but how do we keep track of which one should be read? The solution is simple: because the Kinect maintains a single unique ID for each body in view, we keep track of a desired ID and only read the head joint of the body associated with it. To that end, we modify *TrackBodies.cs* as shown in Listing 5.6:

Listing 5.6. TrackBodies.cs: changes the previous TrackBodies script to track a single user; needed to give consistent 3D. The user is arbitrarily defined, But the FindNewBody function can optionally be enhanced to pick a user in view with greater specification.

```
// from TrackBodies.cs
private ulong _singleUserId;
private Kinect.Body _singleUserBody = null;
private int bodiesPresent = 0;

private void UpdateTracking(Kinect.Body[] bodyData) {
    // Ensure there is a tracked body, otherwise return
    int bodiesPresent = 0;
    foreach (var body in bodyData)
        if (body.IsTracked) bodiesPresent++;
    if (bodiesPresent == 0) {
        _singleUserBody = null;
        return;
    }

    // If the current body being tracked isn't in our known bodies, pick a new one
    // This occurs when the application first starts or the tracked user walks out of view
    if (!_heads.ContainsKey(_singleUserId)) {
        _singleUserBody = FindNewBody(bodyData);
        _singleUserId = _singleUserBody.TrackingId;
        CreateHead(_singleUserId);
    }

    // Update head position
    _heads[_singleUserId].transform.position =
        GetJointWorldPosition(_singleUserBody, Kinect.JointType.Head);
}

private Kinect.Body FindNewBody(Kinect.Body[] bodyData) {
    foreach (var body in bodyData) {
        // Kinect does not always put a valid body in the first slot of bodyData
        // We need to go through the array and pick the first valid one.
        if (body.TrackingId == 0) continue;
        return body;
    }
    return null;
}
```

The *FindNewBody* function is simplistic, and only finds the first valid body the Kinect sees in no particular order, but could be changed to find the closest user, a user making a particular gesture, etc. This script allows access to a single consistent body that can then be tracked from external scripts through a simple function such as in Listing 5.7.

Listing 5.7. From TrackBodies.cs: allows for external scripts to access the position data for a single user. For example, the perspective camera will use it to track the single user's head position.

```
// GetUserJointWorldPosition() allows external scripts to access position data for the single
//   tracked user
public Vector3 GetUserJointWorldPosition(Kinect.JointType jt) {
    if (_singleUserBody != null)
        return GetJointWorldPosition(_singleUserBody, jt);
```

5. Using the Kinect for Head-Tracked Perspective and Pointing in Stationary VR Displays

```
    else
        return this.transform.position; // If nobody in view, just return a generic value
}
```

5.4.4.3 Linking Head Position and Perspective Camera

Finally, we make head position tracked for the perspective cameras to give the viewer an accurate 3D perspective. The code, shown in Listing 5.8, can be added to the Update function of a new script we'll call *FollowHead.cs*, which can then be placed on the head object.

Listing 5.8. Excerpt from FollowHead.cs: moves the attached GameObject to follow the tracked head position. Attaching this to the head object will create the desired perspective 3D effect.

```
Vector3 headPose = TrackBodies.instance.GetUserJointWorldPosition(Kinect.JointType.Head);
this.transform.position = headPose;
```

5.4.5 Adding a Pointer for Interaction

Just looking at a scene through a perspective window can be interesting, but being able to interact with the scene is critical to making engaging VR applications. One common way to interact in VR is through a wand or pointer ray. These are typically defined by a tracked controller with some kind of button to trigger interaction. But, it is possible, with the Kinect's body tracking, to use the viewer's pointing direction and hand gesture information to define a wand and trigger.

The wand avatar can be a long thin cylinder (large local Y scale). Rotate the cylinder around the X axis by 90° and parent it to an empty GameObject placed at the end of the cylinder, as in Figure 5.7. This creates a more convenient wand coordinate system for the following code and allows you to affect wand length by adjusting the parent's local Z scale. The user's pointing direction can be defined as the normalized vector between two joints on the user's arm, such as the elbow and wrist. To point the wand in that direction, we'll create a script called *Pointer.cs* in the Wand parent object, shown in Listing 5.9.

Figure 5.7

Example of a pointer wand. The given transform is for the inner cylinder.

Listing 5.9. Excerpt from Pointer.cs: Update() loop to move the pointer wand. Using the example joints, the wand will be placed on the user's right wrist, and will point in the direction defined by the vector from their elbow to their wrist.

```
// from Pointer.cs
public Kinect.JointType pointingFrom = Kinect.JointType.ElbowRight;
public Kinect.JointType pointingTo = Kinect.JointType.WristRight;

void Update() {
    Vector3 pfPose = TrackBodies.instance.GetUserJointWorldPosition(pointingFrom);
    Vector3 ptPose = TrackBodies.instance.GetUserJointWorldPosition(pointingTo);
    Vector3 pointingDir = (ptPose - pfPose).normalized;
    // Point the wand in the proper direction and place it on the "pointing to" joint
    this.transform.rotation = Quaternion.LookRotation(pointingDir);
    this.transform.position = ptPose;
}
```

We use the elbow-to-wrist direction as our default pointing direction because using palm and finger joints can give jittery results. Developers can try other combinations to identify what works with their application and Kinect placement.

In addition to joint positions, the Kinect gives some other information about tracked body part states. This includes the state of the user's hands, with possible states being open, closed, and lasso (referring to a state in which the user holds two fingers up). We use the closed state of the non-pointing hand (left in this example) to trigger interaction. There is a tradeoff between using the pointing hand to trigger, which may be more intuitive, and using the non-pointing hand, which may reduce side-effect motion or jitter of the pointing hand. We add the code in Listing 5.10 to *TrackBodies.cs* to retrieve hand state:

Listing 5.10. Excerpt from TrackBodies.cs: allows external scripts to access the left hand state of the single user.

```
Public Kinect.HandState GetSingleUserHandState() {
    return _singleUserBody.HandLeftState;
}
```

The *Pointer.cs* script can then be updated to detect interaction through the code in Listing 5.11:

Listing 5.11. Excerpt from Pointer.cs: detects if the user has closed their left hand, and calls some interact function.

```
if (TrackBodies.instance.GetSingleUserHandState() == Kinect.HandState.Closed) {
    Interact();
}
```

The Interact function can then be defined in a way that is appropriate for your application. Common interactions include selecting or picking up an object that the wand is intersecting, or teleporting to an indicated area in the scene. For example, to activate an object the wand is touching, you could find the object either with a raycast from the base of the wand or by checking collisions with the wand. If this finds an object, you could send a message using Unity's *GameObject.SendMessage()* function, telling it to run the proper activation code. Many other interactions and implementation methods are possible.

5.4.6 Tips for Good 3D Scenes

The placement of objects becomes significantly more important when considering 3D. The scene will look dull if all objects are exclusively placed far from the user. Objects will "pop out" at the user when they are closer (between the screen and the eye) and the stereo effect is also stronger for closer objects. But, note that objects very close to the eye can be difficult to view. If your application permits movement throughout the world, then you should expect the viewer to move close to things, creating more dynamic views.

High contrast features can increase ghosting (bleeding of one eye's image into the other), which varies for different types of glasses. For example, a bright white line on a black background is a worst case, and such features should be avoided if possible. Setting the background color to something neutral can help.

The scale of objects also becomes more important when designing for VR. With an effective perspective view, the scale of scene objects should appear equal to its designed value; 1 meter in the virtual world should appear to be 1 meter to the viewer. It is possible to change this by scaling the configuration of the TV/monitor to make the scene appear smaller, or down to make it appear larger. This involves scaling the values of H and W when computing the perspective matrix, and scaling the Head position by the same ratio. All required scaling can be achieved by simply scaling the Perspective TV root object of the configuration by some uniform value.

5.5 Conclusion

This chapter presented a method for creating a low-cost stationary VR display using a Kinect V2 sensor and a 3D TV. With this combination of hardware, the user will not have to wear any tracking devices. Completing the exercises in this chapter lays the groundwork for creating interactive VR applications with access to other tracking information from the Kinect. The perspective viewing concepts are similar to those used in many VR systems.

Acknowledgment

Part of this material is based upon work supported by the National Science Foundation under Grant No. 1451833.

References

[Lee 2007]

Lee, Johnny (2007, December 21). Head Tracking for Desktop VR Displays using the Wii Remote [Video File]. Retrieved from https://youtu.be/Jd3-eiid-Uw

[Microsoft 2019]

Microsoft (2019). Developing with Kinect for Windows. Retrieved from https://developer.microsoft.com/en-us/windows/kinect/develop

[Unity 2019]

Unity (2019). Camera.projectionMatrix. Retrieved from https://docs.unity3d.com/2018.3/Documentation/ScriptReference/Camera-projectionMatrix.html

6

The Vehicle Pattern for Simplifying Cross-Platform Virtual Reality Development

Anthony Steed
University College London

6.1 Overview

There is now a diverse range of consumer virtual reality hardware. Unfortunately, this diverse hardware comes with a diverse variety of tools, platforms, environments, and plugins for development. Developers may need to get their hands on many bits of equipment to test their applications in order to support a variety of platforms. Users are increasingly using a variety of add-on devices for which custom code may be required (e.g., a walking platform or a glove). Larger developers who want to support the main consumer systems can afford the time to create custom user interfaces for each platform. However, smaller developers, or professional users who want to support their own custom systems, may struggle to maintain large codebases with lots of optionality for different hardware.

While there are efforts to support device abstraction such as Open Source Virtual Reality [OSVR, 2017], and OpenXR [Khronos Group Inc., 2017], these address relatively low-level device abstractions. Their aim is to isolate APIs for specific devices so that application code doesn't need to know the specifics of, say, which tracking devices are attached. These efforts allow, or will allow, the user to switch hardware, as long as that hardware roughly matches in functionality. To the application, it might not matter exactly what head-mounted display (HMD) is attached to the computer, or which tracking system is used. However, the application still needs to make decisions about how to implement interactions between the user and the environment, and with these device abstractions the application author might need to support various different cases such as whether or not the hand-held controllers have analogue joysticks, support finger gestures, etc.

For many application developers who want to support a variety of hardware, coding to each platform is repetitive and error prone. Each application must be developed for each platform, with its different devices and its different potential ways of interacting with the user. High-level toolkits may help (e.g. Vrui [Kreylos, 2008] or VRTK [The Stonefox, 2017]), but these do not directly address the problem of making the application as portable as possible.

We note that the building of virtual reality applications involves writing two main types of code: environment-specific code that implements behaviors (interaction styles) for the application, and code that deals with input devices and implements locomotion and object manipulation. The latter code is often quite generic. It is commonly re-used between applications and might be itself quite complex. The former is often much more specific to the application, or even a specific asset within the application. It might itself be commonly reused (e.g., code for opening and closing doors), but this code doesn't need to depend on the specific details of the virtual reality interface.

Thus, we propose the *Vehicle Pattern*, which is an interface and set of conventions that try to separate these code concerns so that applications can be ported very quickly between hardware platforms or customized to support uncommon hardware. We use the term "vehicle" because this conveys the idea that the user needs an interface to travel and interact over long distances. In addition, this was the term used for a similar concept in an experimental virtual reality system called DIVE [Frécon and Stenius, 1998; Frécon et al., 2001]. The term "pattern" is used across many areas of design to refer to solutions to design problems that are generic and re-useable. Many readers may have come across the term in the context of software design patterns [Gamma et al., 1995] but the concept is quite general and has been applied broadly to the design of human-computer interfaces (e.g. [Seffah, 2010]).

6.2 Vehicle Pattern

6.2.1 Design

The main idea behind the Vehicle Pattern is to make as few dependencies between environment-specific code and interaction code as possible. We illustrate the pattern by an implementation in Unity, though we have found that similar principles using different implementation strategies are useful on other platforms.

First, we can examine how the user interaction code and environment-specific code are inter-connected. Unity uses a scene graph abstraction, where a tree structure is formed from objects called *GameObjects*. Each GameObject of the scene graph has one or more instances of *Components*. Each Component type represents a type of functionality such as 3D transformations, visual and audio rendering, meshes, collision volumes, etc. The developer extends the functionality of the scene graph by writing scripts that compile to create new types of Components that can then be added to GameObjects.

There are explicit and implicit mechanisms by which the functions of different GameObjects become inter-connected. Explicit mechanisms include Components holding references to other Components or GameObjects. It is very common for a script Component to have a public variable which is a reference to another GameObject. The developer can assign this reference within the Unity development environment by dragging a GameObject to this variable. This makes a tight connection between the two. It is also common for scripts to look up other components and game objects based on name, type, tags or layers (see the Unity documentation for description of these). Sometimes the script will look these up dynamically, and sometimes they are looked up once and then considered constant. These types of explicit connections cause problems when scene-graphs are rearranged.

There are various implicit mechanisms that create relationships between objects. Proximity between objects might cause collision events in the scene, objects might interact through ray-casting, or objects might even cause visual effects such as shadowing. We describe the impact of some of these in the following sections.

6.2.2 Vehicle and Zone

The main part of the pattern is to create two isolated sub-graphs in the scene named *Vehicle* and *Zone*. It is not strictly necessary to create two separate graphs, but it makes the different roles of the two sub-graphs very obvious and it facilitates easy deletion and replacement of the Vehicle (Figure 6.1). The Vehicle contains GameObjects that isolate the device-specific and interaction-specific code. The Zone is the environment-specific code. These two sub-graphs interact implicitly: the renderers in the Vehicle will "see" the Zone objects, the collision volumes in both will interact, and physics engine will consider both sets of objects ensemble. However, we want to minimize explicit code interactions between the two or at least provide a specific point of code interaction.

If we have set up the Vehicle correctly, then it should be interchangeable for any other Vehicle. In our demonstration in Unity, the Vehicles are relatively straightforward: they provide for locomotion about the environment, selection of objects and grabbing of objects. We will discuss two example Vehicles that we use commonly in our own testing: one that supports the HTC Vive and one that supports interaction with the mouse and keyboard. We want to support the latter not only because it is a still a common control system, but also because during iterative development is it often convenient not to have to put on an HMD and step away from the desk in order to do a quick test. We have commonly had two or more Vehicles embedded in the Unity scene, but with all but one disabled, so that the developer can very rapidly switch between platforms.

We discuss implementation specific details in Section 6.2.5, but first we describe how scripts in the Vehicle and Zone can interact.

6.2.3 VehicleMaster Singleton

Many behaviors are initiated by input from the user. In standard Unity design, scripts have various callback functions that respond to different events. These callbacks include a

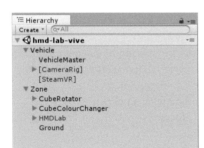

Figure 6.1

A fragment of a screen capture of the Unity Editor showing an example scene comprising a Vehicle and a Zone.

function called once a frame (*Update*), but also functions on collision between objects (e.g. *OnTriggerEnter*), amongst others. We would like to enable a similarly simple programming model. We also want to allow the support of functions that go the other way, where objects in the scene change the vehicle behaviour. This is not discussed in this chapter, but is an easy extension (see online materials).

We achieve these goals by adding a singleton class that represents the Vehicle's functionality. The following code from the *VehicleMaster* class shows the creation of singleton class. A singleton class is a common software design pattern: exactly one of these objects is created at run-time, and this single object can be found by a static reference at run-time.

Listing 6.1. Part of the VehicleMaster class showing the implementation of a singleton.

```
// VehicleMaster is the main interface class between the Vehicle and Zone
public class VehicleMaster : MonoBehaviour {
    private static VehicleMaster instance;
    // Construct
    private VehicleMaster() { }
    // Instance
    public static VehicleMaster Instance {
        get {
            if (instance == null)
                instance = GameObject.FindObjectOfType (typeof(VehicleMaster))
                        as VehicleMaster;
            return instance;
        }
    }
}
```

In the Listing 6.1 code, the `get` function represents the accessor on the public static `Instance` variable. Another script can then just access the variable `VehicleMaster.Instance` to point to the singleton object. Thus, later we will see lines of code such as the following (Listing 6.2):

Listing 6.2. Registering a callback delegate with the VehicleMaster singleton.

```
VehicleMaster.Instance.OnGrabStartThis += OnTouchOrGrab;
```

where a script on an object under the Zone sub-graph uses this singleton to register a callback.

6.2.4 Event Delegates

The main function of the singleton is to provide a single point for registering functions to be called by user interaction. The goal is to hide any device-specific or device-ensemble configuration from the Zone. We introduce four generic events that objects can register for:

- *TouchStart*: the user reaches out and makes contact with an object
- *TouchEnd*: the user stops touching a touchable object
- *GrabStart*: the user grabs and tries to manipulate an object
- *GrabEnd*: the user drops an object that they were able to grab

6. The Vehicle Pattern for Simplifying Cross-Platform Virtual Reality Development

Of these, the intentions GrabStart/GrabEnd are obvious: the user wants to pick up a scene object and will drop it later. Touch is less obvious. It makes sense with a device with tracked input: some proxy of the user's hand or fingers collides with the object. It is not immediately obvious with a mouse and keyboard or a rotation only device with a single button such as Google Cardboard- and Daydream-based devices. However, we think the meaning can be clear. The "user is reaching out" has an analogy to clicking on something with a mouse, or dwelling on a fixed target in the case of head gaze-based interaction. These types of interaction are very common in virtual reality systems and they are logically different to grabbing an object, which is usually triggered by holding a button.

We added a negotiation step, where the Vehicle essentially asks whether the object can be touched or grabbed. We also support a script registering interest in interactions with just its own GameObject, or in any attempt to touch or grab an object. This can support behaviors specific to a particular object (see the example in Section 6.2.6 of a cube that changes color when picked up), or are general to any interaction (e.g., playing a sound when an object is dropped).

The following code excerpt (Listing 6.3) shows the implementation of `DoTouchStart`, which is the function a vehicle implementation would call inside *VehicleMaster* when it wishes to announce that the user has started to touch an object. The function takes not only the target of the touch, but also the object that touched it. At the moment, this source object is vehicle implementation dependent, but as discussed later, a future implementation may try to implement an abstract avatar representation so that the receiving script can tell which body part touched the object.

Listing 6.3. A fragment from the VehicleMaster implementation showing how the touch event is processed.

```
// Event Handling :
//
//    Touch events
public delegate bool OnTouchStartEvent(GameObject target, GameObject source);
public event OnTouchStartEvent OnTouchStartAny;
public event OnTouchStartEvent OnTouchStartThis;
// DoTouchStart() method calls delegate functions to notify them that the vehicle
//    implementation is attempting to grab the object.
//    returns true when it succesfully grabs the object; false when the grab fails.
public bool DoTouchStart(GameObject target, GameObject source) {
    // Trigger those delegates that registered for all callbacks
    if (OnTouchStartAny != null && OnTouchStartAny.GetInvocationList () != null &&
            OnTouchStartAny.GetInvocationList().Length > 0) {
        OnTouchStartAny (target, source);
    }
    // Trigger those delegates that registered for their individual callback
    if (OnTouchStartThis != null && OnTouchStartThis. GetInvocationList () != null &&
            OnTouchStartThis.GetInvocationList().Length > 0) {
        System.Delegate[] handlers = OnTouchStartThis.GetInvocationList();
        bool success = true;
        foreach (var item in handlers) {
            MonoBehaviour interestedObject = (MonoBehaviour)(item.Target);
            if (interestedObject.gameObject.Equals(target)) {
                object[] parameters = new object[] { target, source };
                success &= (bool)item.Method.Invoke(interestedObject, parameters);
            }
```

```
        }
        return success;
    }
    return true;
}
```

The code uses the C# event and delegate mechanism. An external script will define a function of type `OnTouchStartEvent`. Note that the external script can register on two types of events: `OnTouchStartAny` or `OnTouchStartThis`.

Within the `OnTouchStartEvent` function, there are two main blocks of code. The first calls the delegate functions of all the scripts that have registered interest in any object being touched. The second block checks that the target object matches the script that the delegate is registered to (through the cast to `MonoBehaviour` which is the base class for all script components). Note that the invocation of the delegate (`item.Method.Invoke`) returns a boolean. This is then combined with any other flags from other delegates to return to the vehicle implementation a success or failure. For example, the vehicle should stop any response to touching this object. This is useful for ignoring objects that cannot currently be touched.

6.2.5 Vehicle Implementations

We have developed various vehicles for different platforms. We have various custom virtual reality systems in the lab, so our vehicles tend to be quite specific. However, we illustrate the principles with two simple vehicles, one for keyboard and mouse, and one for the HTC Vive. We list short excerpts from the vehicle implementations as these are simple variants of example code.

6.2.5.1 Vive Vehicle

The Vive vehicle is based on the standard SteamVR Unity plugin. Our vehicle is based on code from an online tutorial that we have used in student projects [de Kerckhove, 2017].

We start with the default scene graph for a SteamVR application. This adds GameObjects for the camera system, the camera and the two main controllers. To each of the controllers we add a small sphere collider and set it to be a collision trigger. In a script attached to each controller we then add a script (`ViveController.cs`). The following code (Listing 6.4) shows how touch is then implemented very easily, based on the collider on the controller game object hitting other colliders in the scene. `OnTriggerEnter` is a standard Unity callback from the collision system.

Listing 6.4. Part of the Vive Vehicle implementation showing how the touch event is implemented.

```
// Use the Unity OnTriggerEnter() method to implementation implement touch for
// the Vive Vehicle.
public void OnTriggerEnter(Collider other) {
    if (!VehicleMaster.Instance.DoTouchStart(other.gameObject, this.gameObject)) {
        return;
    }
    SetCollidingObject(other);
}
```

6. The Vehicle Pattern for Simplifying Cross-Platform Virtual Reality Development

Note that the call through to `DoTouchStart` function can be rejected, indicating that this object is not touchable. See the online material for the detail of implementation of touch ending, and grabbing.

This demonstration implements locomotion through a simple teleport technique. This involves an implicit interaction between the Vehicle and Zone, which is that the teleport technique can only effect travel to points on objects in a layer labeled "Ground." However, this is a simple constraint to enforce, and we can use the same labeled objects in the Mouse and Keyboard Vehicle.

6.2.5.2 Mouse and Keyboard Vehicle

This demonstration is based on Unity's Standard Asset package. It modifies two scripts: `RigidbodyFirstPersonController` and `DragRigidbody`.

The first-person locomotion controller has been modified with a simple switch between moving mode and manipulation mode, and some code that we don't discuss in this chapter that constrains the walkable region to the same region that the Vive vehicle's teleport functionality can reach.

We illustrate the grabbing functionality in the following excerpt (Listing 6.5). When the user presses a mouse button, a ray is cast into the scene. The object that is hit should have a `RigidBody` component. We then call through the *VehicleMaster* to check whether the object can be picked up or not (`VehicleMaster.Instance.DoGrabStart`).

Listing 6.5. Part of the Update function for the Mouse and Keyboard vehicle that uses the Unity Physics Engine to send a ray attached to the mouse into the screen.

```
// We need to actually hit an object (if not then return)
RaycastHit hit = new RaycastHit();
if (!Physics.Raycast(mainCamera.ScreenPointToRay(Input.mousePosition).origin,
                     mainCamera.ScreenPointToRay(Input.mousePosition).direction,
                     out hit, 100, Physics.DefaultRaycastLayers)
    return;

// We need to hit an object that's a rigidbody (otherwise return)
if (!hit.rigidbody)
    return;

// We need a rigidbody that's earmarked as grabbable (otherwise return)
if (!VehicleMaster.Instance.DoGrabStart(hit.rigidbody.gameObject, this.gameObject))
    return;

// At this point we know that hit.rigidbody is an object we can grab
// (see online material for the rest of the vehicle implementation)
```

See the online materials for the rest of the implementation of this example vehicle.

6.2.6 Demonstrations

A very simple demonstration is shown in Figure 6.2. This is a distilled version of a basic environment we use in various experiments at UCL where the user is sat in a virtual version of the lab where they are physically sat. The online materials include a second simple demonstration which is a recreation of the virtual pit demonstration [Usoh et al., 1999]; this is a common demonstration that we use with new users of virtual reality.

Figure 6.2

A simple scene modelled on one of our labs at UCL. The left cube is not manipulable and will spin when the user attempts to interact with it. The right cube is being held by the user and is changing color.

There are two interactive objects in this environment that illustrate the main principles of the Vehicle Pattern. We show the whole scripts to emphasize how similar these are to standard script structures. The first interactive object is the cube on the left of the table in Figure 6.2. (It is called CubeRotator in the scene graph in Figure 6.1). In Listing 6.6 you can see how the delegate is registered with the lines in the Awake callback. Note that the OnTouchOrGrab function rejects the touch or grab and then starts a co-routine to spin the object.

Listing 6.6. The BoxSpin class spins the object when it is grabbed.

```
// BoxSpin.cs
// A behaviour that causes an object to spin when the object is grabbed.
public class BoxSpin : MonoBehaviour {
   private bool moving;

   // register the OnTouchOrGrab script (delegate) to OTST & OGST
   void Awake() {
      moving = false;
      VehicleMaster.Instance.OnTouchStartThis += OnTouchOrGrab;
      VehicleMaster.Instance.OnGrabStartThis += OnTouchOrGrab;
   }

   bool OnTouchOrGrab(GameObject source, GameObject target) {
      if (!moving) {
         StartCoroutine("MoveAndWait");
      }
      return false; // Reject the touch event
   }

   // A coroutine that rotates "this" object once
   IEnumerator MoveAndWait() {
      float angle = 0;
      moving = true;
      while (angle <= 360.0) {
         this.transform.eulerAngles = new Vector3(0, angle, 0);
         angle = angle + 3.0f;
         yield return new WaitForFixedUpdate();
      }
      this. transform.eulerAngles = new Vector3(0, 0, 0);
      StopCoroutine("MoveAndWait");
      moving = false;
   }
}
```

The code for the second box is very similar (see Listing 6.7). It registers two different delegates, `OnGrabStart` and `OnGrabEnd`. The former accepts the grab event and thus the vehicle is now free to manipulate the object. It also starts to change the color of the object. The color changing is stopped when the latter delegate is called, remaining as the last randomly selected colour.

Listing 6.7. The ColourChange class behaviours causes an object to change colour repeatedly when held.

```
// ColourChange.cs
// The ColourChange behaviour causes an object to change colour repeatedly
//       when the user is holding the object.
public class ColourChange : MonoBehaviour {
    private bool changing;
    Renderer rend;          // Store "this" object's renderer component

    // When "game" starts (world is initialized)
    void Awake() {
        rend = this.GetComponent<Renderer>();
        changing = false;
        VehicleMaster.Instance.OnGrabStartThis += OnGrabStart;
        VehicleMaster.Instance.OnGrabEndThis += OnGrabEnd;
    }

    // While "this" object is grabbed change colour.
    bool OnGrabStart(GameObject source, GameObject target) {
        if (!changing) {
            StartCoroutine("ChangeColour");
        }
        return true; // Accept the Grab event
    }

    // Disable the colour change when the grab is ended
    bool OnGrabEnd(GameObject source, GameObject target) {
        if (changing) {
            StopCoroutine("ChangeColour");
            changing = false;
        }
        return true;
    }

    // Change colour of "this" object for every .5 seconds until the co-routine is cancelled.
    IEnumerator ChangeColour() {
        changing = true;
        while (true) {
            rend.material.SetColor("_Color", new Color(Random.Range(0F, 1F),
                Random.Range(0F, 1F), Random.Range(0F, 1F)));
            yield return new WaitForSeconds(0.5f);
        }
    }
}
```

6.3 Discussion

6.3.1 Constraints and Limitations

The separation between Vehicle and Zone relies on several implicit assumptions. For example: a natural human scale of objects; an understanding that the Vehicle will not create collision volumes that are too large and that the camera will move at a certain range of speeds (so that collision detection works), etc. The Vehicle Pattern as described is sufficient for basic applications that do not have highly specialized needs for interaction. The pattern is easy to extend to fit specific needs, and we continue to develop our example implementation.

For example, an obvious extension would be to develop a standard representation of the user's avatar so that environment-specific interaction could start to address the avatar's representation. This would usefully include scene graph objects that components can discover which indicate the user's head position, hand positions, standing position, etc., so that even environment-specific scripts can reference them. For example, a script might want to animate an avatar so that it looks at a user. It would also be useful to have a more refined collision volume associated with the user so that fine-scale collision detection can be done. For a Vehicle based on a mouse and keyboard, or other interface without full 3D tracking, some of these avatar object positions would need to be hypothesized based on the camera position and user interaction.

When we get to the area of dynamic user interfaces that construct visual representations inside the scene such as menus, the decisions become more difficult. The separation of touch and grab works in many situations, but there is currently no fallback for an environment behavior that is triggered by a specific button on a controller. If this was needed the programmer would have to customize the Vehicle itself. However, in our opinion abstractions such as the Vehicle can be extended to cover a very wide range of application needs.

The Vehicle Pattern doesn't deal with porting of visual and audio assets between different platforms. Some platforms are significantly less powerful than others. When producing a game in Unity it is common to simplify assets for low-end platforms and keep different versions of scenes. How assets can be managed in real-time to support low-end platforms remains a research question.

6.3.2 Related Work

The Vehicle Pattern is strongly influenced by prior work in the area that uses similar principles. In particular models of web-browsing where the user has a lot of control over their web browser's behavior. Although a lot of functionality is fixed, users can customize their web browser with various extensions. Presently, most VR development is not supporting this type of customizability for the user. Our Vehicle Pattern highlights the fact that by having developers begin the development process with device abstractions, interaction techniques are no longer customizable by the end user. The Vehicle Pattern is part of a skeleton implementation by the author, called *Yther*, that proposes one type of solution to this dilemma [Steed, 2015].

Previous efforts to support a broad range of 3D interfaces have acknowledged similar problems. The VRML97 and then X3D standards [VRML, 1997; X3D, 2013] had specific methods to support device independence. For example, the NavigationInfo node had a recommended type of locomotion, such as "Walk" or "Fly" that the browser should support. In addition, manipulation of objects was done in a way that could imply motion constraints. For example, the PlaneSensor node supported objects that could be dragged along a surface. It was up to the VRML or X3D browser to determine how to implement the dragging within the user interface.

Our pattern is most strongly related to the vehicle concept from an older research platform called DIVE [Frécon and Stenius, 1998; Frécon et al., 2001]. This was browser-centric in the sense that scenes were developed independent of user interaction specification, and each user installed and ran a browser that could implement interaction in various ways. In fact, the browsers themselves were highly customizable (they were written in the TCL language), so a browser could dynamically switch its interaction style, or in the DIVE terminology switch "Vehicle." The system was event-based, with decoupled message passing between the browser and in-scene objects. Some of message types are similar to the delegate types we propose: they included *grasp*, *select* and *move* events. They also included various events for multi-user interaction, and other application-level events such as loading of sub-scenes. Although we have previously argued for asynchronous message passing as a mechanism to decouple user-interaction and environment-specific code, delegate-based calling seems more appropriate in modern platforms where latency is paramount [Steed, 2008]. Asynchronous message passing has its advantages, but especially in Unity there are significant downsides. For example, developers often rely on knowing the rough ordering or lack of ordering of different functions (e.g., callbacks from different internal functions such as fixed-update callbacks, the order of script evaluation in a scene graph, .Net 2.0 yield functionality, etc.), which can match poorly with asynchronous message-passing.

6.4 Conclusions

The excitement around consumer virtual reality, and the ready availability of a variety of new devices means that there are great opportunities to develop new user interfaces. Unfortunately, there is a dearth of high-level toolkits that simplify support for a range of devices. While development environments such as Unity or Unreal Engine enable development for many devices, porting code between different devices, or ensembles of devices, is tricky.

In this chapter we have described the Vehicle Pattern, which attempts to separate the concerns of programming support for user-interaction on devices, from virtual environment-specific behavior. This pattern has proved very useful in our lab, where students may want to develop on one machine, but quickly deploy to another that supports a specific hardware configuration. While the skeleton implementation is simple, we hope that it can be useful for others as is. We also hope that the principles can help inform future toolkits so that some conventions, or even standards, can emerge that alleviate some of the need for the developer to consider which virtual reality systems their content may run on.

References

[de Kerckhove, 2017]

de Kerckhove, Eric Van (2017). HTC Vive Tutorial for Unity. https://raywenderlich. com/149239/htc-vive-tutorial-unity/. (accessed July 1, 2017).

[Frécon et al., 2001]

Frécon, Emmanuel, Gareth Smith, Anthony Steed, Mårten Stenius, and Olov Ståhl (2001). An overview of the COVEN platform. *Presence: Teleoperators and Virtual Environments*, 10(1):109–127.

[Frécon and Stenius, 1998]

Frécon, Emmanuel, and Mårten Stenius (1998). DIVE: A scaleable network architecture for distributed virtual environments. *Distributed Systems Engineering*, 5(3):91.

[Gamma et al., 1995]

Gamma, Erich, Richard Helm, Ralph Johnson, and John Vlissides (1995). *Design Patterns: Elements of Reusable Object-Oriented Software*. Addison-Wesley Longman Publishing Co., Inc.: Boston, MA.

[Khronos Group Inc., 2017]

Khronos Group Inc. (2017). OpenXR, Cross-platform, Portable, Virtual Reality. https://khronos.org/openxr. (accessed July 1, 2017).

[Kreylos, 2008]

Kreylos, O. (2008). Environment-independent VR development. In *Proceedings of Advances in Visual Computing: 4th International Symposium, ISVC 2008*, Las Vegas, NV: Springer Berlin Heidelberg, December 1–3. Proceedings, Part I, pages 901–912.

[OSVR, 2017]

OSVR (2017). Open Source Virtual Reality. http://osvr.com/software.html. (accessed July 1, 2017).

[Seffah, 2010]

Seffah, Ahmed (2010). The evolution of design patterns in HCI: From pattern languages to pattern-oriented design. In *Proceedings of the 1st International Workshop on Pattern-Driven Engineering of Interactive Computing Systems*, Berlin, Germany: ACM, pages 4–9.

[Steed, 2008]

Steed, Anthony (2008). Some useful abstractions for re-usable virtual environment platform. In *Proceedings of the IEEE VR SEARIS Workshop*, Reno, NV.

[Steed, 2015]

Steed, Anthony (2015). Yther: A proposal and initial prototype of a virtual reality content sharing system. In *Proceedings of the 25th International Conference on Artificial Reality and Telexistence and 20th Eurographics Symposium on Virtual Environments, ICAT–EGVE '15*, Aire-la-Ville, Switzerland: Eurographics Association, pages 151–158.

[The Stonefox, 2017]

The Stonefox (GitHub handle) (2017). VRTK—Virtual Reality Toolkit. https://vrtoolkit.readme.io/. (accessed July 1, 2017).

[Usoh et al., 1999]

Usoh, Martin, Kevin Arthur, Mary C. Whitton, Rui Bastos, Anthony Steed, Mel Slater, and Frederick P. Brooks (1999). Walking>walking-in-place>flying, in virtual environments. In *Proceedings of the 26th Annual Conference on Computer Graphics and Interactive Techniques*, Los Angeles, CA: ACM Press/Addison-Wesley Publishing Co., pages 359–364.

[VRML, 1997]

VRML (1997). ISO/IEC/DIS14772, The Virtual Reality Modeling Language. https://web3d.org/files/specifications/14772/V2.0/index.html

[X3D, 2013]

X3D (2013). ISO/IEC IS 19775-1, X3D Abstract: Node Definitions. http://web3d.org/documents/specifications/197751/V3.3/index.html

7

WebXR

Virtual Reality... in the Browser

Luis Diego González-Zúñiga and Peter O'Shaughnessy

7.1 Do Virtual Reality... in the Browser

Virtual Reality allows us to create and experience immersive spaces by putting the user in the center of the data and environment. While this is exciting, desirable, and (kind of) new, the ease of entry into the medium for developers and consumers is far from being accessible, comfortable, or affordable. Among the many challenges that pose barriers towards massive adoption of Cross Reality (XR, referring to the collection of VR, AR and MR) we can cite: (1) device and content availability, (2) scattered and scarce content, and (3) a lack of social interactions in the available experiences. Thankfully, each of these barriers are waning.

The standard way for distributing XR content nowadays is through the traditional app store model. While this is appropriate for some experiences, it has disadvantages and might not be the ideal distribution channel for all types of experiences. The current paradigm requires users go to a closed environment (app store) to wait several minutes to download onto their devices hundreds of megabytes, for an experience they will most likely use once. An interesting alternative might be to look to the web browser, since it allows frictionless XR experiences at the tap of a link, with no third-party policies or store-approval required.

The commoditization of the web browser has led us to underestimate its power. We associate it with email, social media, and other web pages we visit only when there is no default app for the task at hand. What we might not be aware of is that recent improvements in the web platform give modern browsers growing access to device sensors (like geolocation, accelerometer, biometric), external devices (gamepads, MIDI, Bluetooth, USB) and native-like features (push notifications, ability to work offline, access to file system). In this growing set of features for web browsers, WebXR (formerly WebVR) is poised to be an API that enables a form of Cross Reality (XR) by using web technologies.

For the consumer, WebXR can theoretically enable most devices with a modern web browser to experience immersive content, even without a headset, by means of the 'magic window' (refer to the section "*Progressive Enhancement of WebXR Applications*"). It also permits experiences to adapt to the device they are being accessed through. This makes consuming content an easy endeavor, and ensures that content is truly accessible.

From a developer's perspective, WebXR removes a lot of the complexity associated with hardware configurations and leverages existing standard web knowledge to create these immersive environments. Every developer with basic experience of HTML, CSS, and JavaScript can create XR applications with just a text editor and a web server. Exploiting this abstraction is key for a fast expansion of diverse XR content.

Additionally, this means that the cost of entry for a user to experience XR is gone, or greatly reduced, since they can use their own mobile devices and laptops to access the content. It is the same for developers, where no significant investment is required to start testing or developing content for limited experiences. (Full room-scale experiences require high end tracking sensors).

7.2 The "Immersive Web" Specification

We have mentioned WebXR in the previous section. It is important to explain specifically what this is. WebXR is an experimental JavaScript API that provides interfaces to XR hardware (VR/AR/MR), allowing developers to build compelling and comfortable experiences on the web. At the time of writing (February 2018), the WebXR specification is in active development and its stable release is version 1.1 [Vukicevic 2017].

The group formerly known as the "W3C WebVR Community Group" is behind it, and they announced in December 2017 that going forward they were expanding the scope (of WebVR) and renaming the group as the *Immersive Web Community Group*. Also, the term *WebXR* would now be used to refer to its expanded scope and the API [W3C 2017]. As such, the effort that was formerly known as the WebVR 2.0 specification will become the "WebXR Devices API" specification. It is important to say that this does not change the focus of developers and designers interested in WebVR, as 1.1 is still the stable version and the easiest way to build WebXR experiences today. You can contribute and see the ongoing work the WebXR GitHub repository found in [WebVR_CG 2017].

This specification is not an official W3C Standard, nor is it on the W3C Standards track—yet. Needless to say, the excitement and collaboration surrounding this technology is huge, with support from browser vendors like Mozilla, Samsung, Google and Microsoft.

In a nutshell, the WebXR API specification introduces interfaces to the DOM (Document Object Model) to support runtime access to VR (and eventually AR/MR) functionality. Presently, the "v1.1" is standard and supported in many browsers, and work continues towards the WebXR spec.

This specification covers a wide range of elements associated with VR, ranging from device ids, pose data (for headset and accessories), eye parameters and frame data, to extensions of other Web APIs like the Gamepad API. We will not cover these interfaces directly, since they are bound to change soon. Thankfully for developers, many of these changes will not be visible since we can create experiences through frameworks that wrap and abstract the underlying API. Please refer to the 1.1 spec document for information. And get in touch with the Community Group if you have interest in shaping the future of WebXR.

7.3 Distribution and Accessibility of Content Made Easy

The implementation of virtual reality in a web browser, like all other things that adhere to web standards, best practices, and an open technology stack, benefit from having a strong distribution and great accessibility. In its simplest form, a WebXR experience is a web page. As such, it is accessed through a URL, easily shared through a link, and compatible with other web technologies. This is extremely powerful, and allows anyone to build innovative experiences that can span across physical and digital locations and devices.

7.3.1 Transcend Virtual Barriers with Physical Web

A physical "*web beacon*" is a low-powered, battery efficient device that broadcasts content over Bluetooth. Right now we can set up a physical web beacon with a URL that's picked up by a service provided by a browser or app (like "CloseBy" in Samsung Internet or "Project Magnet" by Mozilla). This URL generally generates a notification that will redirect you to a web page on your mobile device. This page might be WebXR enabled, whereby you can "experience" it on a headset (Samsung Gear VR, Google Daydream or Cardboard). All of this in little more than half a minute. You could even save the app to your home screen (using the Service Worker API to create a Progressive Web App, which is a web site that can work offline and have access to push notifications) to use as a direct access to relaunch a VR experience whenever you want. Put simply, in only two taps you can be providing your users a VR experience (Figure 7.1).

This can provide a frictionless way to engage our users. Imagine a user who might be walking in front of a movie theater or museum and receives a notification about a VR experience related to an exhibition available. The user can opt in if they prefer to get this type of notification, and they can immediately go to the browser and pan around their smartphone to get a preview or interact with the experience (Figure 7.2).

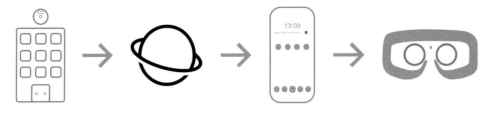

Figure 7.1

"From a physical object to the browser to your home screen to your headset."

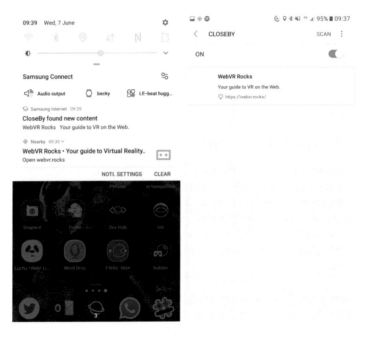

Figure 7.2

Samsung's "CloseBy" and Android's "nearby" notifications.

7.3.2 Engage through a Magic Window

Around 85% of users view WebVR content this way through a magic window [Bozorgzadeh 2017]. Much of the value derives from users being engaged early on and in a friction-less manner, thus "WebVR's magic window is the gateway for pushing VR to billions of people". To date there is no other way of consuming VR content that is as accessible (content and device-wise) or that has this type of massive reach.

The web can become the preferred way of distributing VR content; the same way it became the preferred way to distribute video content. It is compatible with many devices, platforms, and its core technologies support interactivity, communication, and boost sharing in unprecedented ways for VR (Figure 7.3).

Figure 7.3

Delivery platform for WebVR content.

7.4 Write Once, Run Anywhere

It is the promise that many frameworks have tried to deliver for a long time—the holy grail of development. It is no secret that standard web technologies are as close as it gets to writing once and running everywhere. WebVR 1.1 support has been implemented in several browsers. As WebVR is adopted by more browser platforms, a growing number of devices can support the same WebVR experience (Figure 7.4).

Overall, we see that *Samsung Internet, Firefox Nightly, Chromium, Chrome for Android, Oculus Browser* (formerly *Carmel*), *Microsoft Edge,* and *Mozilla Servo* all support the specification. These implementations are referred to as experimental and subject to change. This generally means WebXR implementation in browsers is disabled by default, except *Oculus Browser* and *Samsung Internet for Gear VR* 5.6. *Firefox 55* now supports WebVR 1.1 since August 2017 and *Chrome on Android* on Daydream-compatible devices will enable this with an origin trial (i.e. data developers can register to have it enabled for all users on their domain for a fixed period of time).

Noteworthy is the fact that all major VR consumer platforms (except for PSVR) are covered. In theory, we can run our WebVR 1.1 applications in all platforms, with support for peripherals varying through VR headsets. With one codebase, we can target

	Samsung Internet	Firefox	Chromium	Chrome	Oculus Browser	Edge	Servo
SAMSUNG **Gear VR**	✓				✓		✓
Google Cardboard			✓	✓			
Daydream			✓	✓			
oculus		✓	✓				
VIVE		✓	✓				✓
HoloLens						✓	

* ✓Compatible with WebVR

source: webvr.rocks

Figure 7.4

WebVR support as of October 2017.

six different HMDs, and with an elegant design we can make the experiences in these headsets perform optimally.

In the case of browsers not supporting the specification, there is an option to use a JavaScript implementation of the WebVR/WebXR specification. These implementations are the WebVR *Polyfill* [GoogleVR 2017] by the Google VR team and the the WebXR Polyfill from Mozilla, which supports building AR applications using WebXR. These decide which rendering mechanism to use depending on the configuration of the browser. Mobile devices provide device motion events, can render in stereo, include mesh-based lens distortion and handle the user interface (UI) and user experience (UX) to enter and exit VR mode. "Polyfilled" desktop browsers use mouse events and keyboard arrow keys to look around a scene. The WebVR Polyfill can be seen here https://github.com/immersive-web/webvr-polyfill, while the WebXR Polyfill can be seen here https://github.com/mozilla/webxr-polyfill.

7.5 Available Tools for Fast and Easy VR Creation

There are several options available to start building content for WebVR/WebXR. They adapt to different scenarios making it an easy to find an option that fits your needs. Beginning with the simplest and progressing to the most complex, the most popular alternatives are:

7.5.1 GuriVR

GuriVR is a free, open source project created to allow anyone to make Virtual Reality experiences with the lowest possible learning curve. It provides an online editor that creates Virtual Reality scenes from the users' natural language. This method of creating VR does not require any coding. An example from the GuriVR website (https://gurivr.com) (Figure 7.5):

> For example my first scene will last 500 seconds and display an image located at https://s3.amazonaws.com/gurivr/logo.png along with a text saying: "Guri is cool!" to my left and a panorama located at https://s3.amazonaws.com/gurivr/pano.jpg

Figure 7.5

GuriVR example output.

7.5.2 Vizor.io

Vizor.io allows the user to create spherical 360° tours, stories, sites, and WebVR experiences by dragging and dropping elements. The company also has a visual programming tool named **"Patches"** which lets you create scenes and add interactivity and motion. It also has a hosting option for publishing experiences (Figure 7.6).

7.5.3 A-Frame

A-Frame is a web framework for building virtual reality experiences. It allows the creation of WebVR content with HTML and the *"Entity-Component"* design pattern. It is one of the easiest and most powerful ways to develop WebXR content. Built on top of the popular 3D graphics library *Three.js* (more on this below), it allows developers to define a scene in a declarative, extensible and composable way. It is supported by Mozilla and maintained by the community. It also features a visual inspector in which you can modify and create scenes hierarchically.

7.5.4 React VR

React VR is a project from Facebook Open Source that lets you build VR apps using only JavaScript. It uses the same design as the popular React library, letting you compose a rich VR world and UI from declarative components.

7.5.5 BabylonJS

BabylonJS is a complete JavaScript framework for building 3D games with HTML5, WebGL and WebAudio.

Figure 7.6

Vizor.io Patches' visual programming tool.

7.5.6 PlayCanvas

PlayCanvas is a free and open source engine. It can be used to develop 3D HTML5 and WebGL games, along with WebVR content. PlayCanvas created the WebGL 2 demo *"After the Flood"* which showcases the updated shading language (OpenGL ES Shading Language 3.0), Multiple Render Targets and other new features [Gilbert & Albeza 2017].

7.5.7 ThreeJS

You can also create WebVR content directly in **Three.js**, with THREE.VRControls on the camera and THREE.VREffect on the renderer. It is worth noting that A-Frame wraps ThreeJS, giving A-Frame access to the underlying ThreeJS library and all the accompanying features including inputs, etc.

7.6 Web APIs: They Get Along Very Nicely with WebXR

There is also the ability to integrate other Web APIs into VR experiences, broadening the development options. Some of these are still experimental technologies.

7.6.1 Play with Positional Audio

The browser provides a powerful system for audio manipulation through the Web Audio API. This API allows developers to choose audio sources, add effects to these sources, analyze them to create visualizations and apply spatial effects, among other functionalities.

In a similar way that a 'context' exists for graphics in the browser, there is a context for audio. This context permits the creation of audio nodes that can be sources, effects or destinations and routes them through a graph to achieve the desired effect (Figure 7.7).

These nodes are linked into chains and simple graphs (webs) by their inputs and outputs. Among the available effect-nodes in the Web Audio context are: Biquad filters, convolution effects, delays, dynamic compression, and gain (volume). Of special interest for a VR experience is the Panner node, because it represents the position and behavior of an audio source (signal) in space. This type of node describes its position with right handed Cartesian coordinates, its movement using a velocity vector and its directionality using a directionality cone.

You can refer to a demo of using the Web Audio API to spatialize audio in https://developer.mozilla.org/en-US/docs/Web/API/Web_Audio_API/Web_audio_spatialization_basics. You can also achieve this effect with tools in selected frameworks, such as using A-Frame's sound component (Listing 7.1).

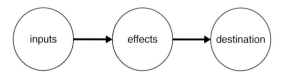

Figure 7.7

Types of nodes in the WebAudio context.

```
<a-sound src="src: url(click.mp3)" autoplay="true" position="0 2 5"></a-sound>
```

7.6.2 Add Gamepads to Your Experience

Virtual Reality applications that allow for user interaction are more engaging. In an immersive environment, you can have objects with different Degrees of Freedom (DOF). Degrees of Freedom refer to the movement of a rigid body inside space, which in VR relates to translation and rotation.

From a controller point of view, you can have 3-DOF orientation (pitch, yaw, and roll) or 6-DOF orientation and location (where you additionally access location in X, Y, and Z). There are several methods with which we can allow a user to select and manipulate objects ranging from no controller (sometimes referred to as 0-DOF) where the user stares at an element and actions it (aka "fuse button"), to 3-DOF where you can track a device's orientation and 6-DOF where additionally you can track their location in space.

Currently supported in *Samsung Internet, Edge, Chrome, Firefox,* and *Opera* browsers, the Gamepad API is a way to access and use gamepads and other game controllers from the browser (see Figure 7.8). Any controller that works as a standard Bluetooth controller can be used. Its buttons, triggers and analog sticks get mapped to buttons and axes on the Gamepad object. Two hardware examples that can be used with a browser are the Xbox One controller and Nintendo Switch Joy-Cons [González & Cannon 2017].

You can respond to the connection and disconnection events of a controller, as well as gain access to buttons and axes (Figure 7.9).

Additionally, the WebVR 1.1 specification enhances the Gamepad API by facilitating information on a controller's pose, if supported by the device. Another way of accessing gamepads is through wrappers over the Gamepad API developed for specific frameworks, like A-Frame 0.6.0 which brings controller support to Daydream and Gear VR.

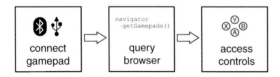

Figure 7.8

Access gamepads from the browser.

7.7 Making Your WebXR Content Accessible Offline

The web can now allow websites to work without an internet connection. It is important that VR experiences are not entirely dependent upon having internet access because even the best web app in the world would then provide a bad UX if it suffered a loss of connectivity. Browsers will display a generic offline UI and the experience is lost. More worrisome is the fact that this loss of connectivity is not infrequent, and that our dependence

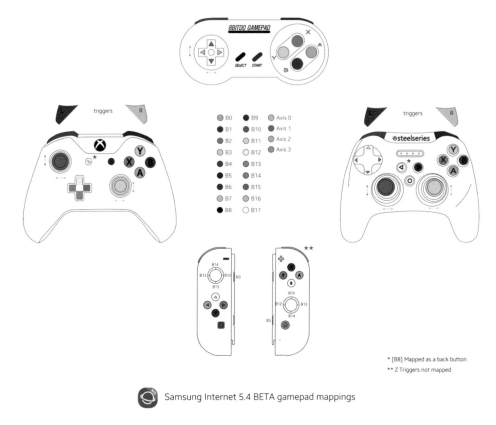

Samsung Internet 5.4 BETA gamepad mappings

* [B8] Mapped as a back button
** Z Triggers not mapped

Figure 7.9

Gamepad mappings. (Courtesy of Samsung Internet.)

of network coverage or Wi-Fi is quite high. A common myth about web experiences is that they require connectivity to work. The most recent attempt at fixing this problem are Service Workers [Russell, Song, Archibald, & Kruisselbrink 2016]. They allow the control of AppCache-implied behaviors with a fine degree of granularity. This means that it can be easily used to tell an app to use cached assets first, enabling a default experience when the XR app has no connectivity.

Service workers are key to enable "Progressive Web Apps" (referred from now on as PWAs), for which support exists in *Chrome, Firefox, Samsung Internet, Edge* and *Opera*. PWAs are experiences that are responsive, fast, secure, independent of connection and have the reach of the web. They can provide the best of the web capabilities and the best of native technologies, by allowing the use of push notifications, access to device sensors, and placement of the app on the home screen.

We can see in Figure 7.10 how a service worker will attempt to first match a resource request from a page with cached resources. This is key since it allows developers to download the resources the first time the user visits a page hosting a VR experience, allowing this experience to not only work offline but also load faster the next time it is accessed.

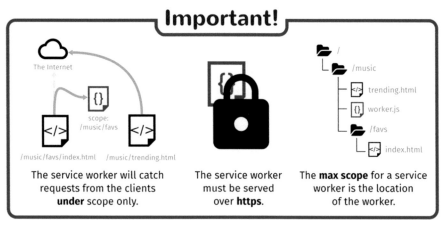

(a)

SERVICE WORKERS 101

Important!

The Internet

scope:
/music/favs

/music/favs/index.html   /music/trending.html

The service worker will catch requests from the clients **under** scope only.

The service worker must be served over **https**.

/
└ /music
    ├ trending.html
    ├ worker.js
    └ /favs
        └ index.html

The **max scope** for a service worker is the location of the worker.

✎ **Pro tip**: if you serve a service worker along with the `Service-Worker-Allowed` header, you can specify here a list of **max scopes** for this worker.

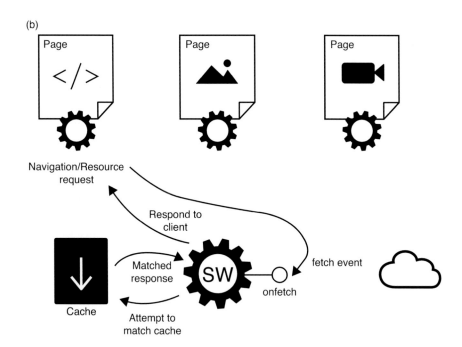

(b)

Page

Page

Page

Navigation/Resource request

Respond to client

Matched response

Cache

Attempt to match cache

SW

onfetch

fetch event

Figure 7.10

Service Workers 101. (Courtesy of Mozilla Hacks and Samsung Internet.)

Apart from providing a nice UX for the experience when offline, if the VR experience doesn't require assets from the network (say, a social media VR app that pulls down some data stream), then the entire app can reside as an independent, offline-first VR application. Any combination in between is possible, and enables VR apps like the 3D composition viewer *Progressive A-Painter* [Balouet 2017] to the offline 360° image viewer *Bubble* [Samsung Internet 2017].

To enable a WebXR application to become a PWA, you must comply with the same requirements needed for any other web page, from being served over an HTTPS connection to having the proper application file descriptors such as the manifest. For a detailed PWA check list, use developer tools like SonarWhal [SonarWhal 2018] and Google's Lighthouse [Google 2017]. Lighthouse can process a page to audit these requirements.

7.8 Progressive Enhancement of WebXR Applications

The reach of an application is only as good as how it adapts to different ways of experiencing it. If you limit your XR application's distribution to a store that only supports a small subset of hardware, you're restricting your reach. If you're developing your experience to be tailored to a specific hardware, then you're losing reach as well. Maximizing reach is about elegant design, a design that doesn't leave users behind and is flexible enough to work in a case where there is no headset involved, all the way up to the case where there is room tracking (Figure 7.11).

With a browser, you can poll for available functionality and adapt your experience to it. It's a good practice and web developers are accustomed to providing fallbacks when a specific API or feature is not implemented. This translates to XR experiences that can start engaging users with the "magic window effect" and tapping the screen to interact with objects.

This "magic window effect" refers to the ability to consume WebXR on a desktop or mobile device without a headset, where the content can be seen through the device as if this were a window into the XR world. In mobile devices, orientation sensors help position the visualization accordingly, while in desktops you can pan around with the mouse.

Users can also go into VR mode and put their phone into a Google Cardboard, to get a slightly more immersive experience, and from there the experience adapts to extra components of functionality. This includes controllers with 3 degrees of freedom (3-DOF) like the Daydream and Gear VR controllers and more complex 6 degrees of freedom (6-DOF) experiences with room position tracking. With a combination of WebAPIs and a robust feature check in place, you can make sure your experience is as accessible to as many devices as possible.

| 6DoF | 3DoF | 0DoF | mobile only |

Figure 7.11

Different type of experiences available with WebVR.

7.9 Recommendations When Creating WebXR Experiences

When you are creating WebXR experiences, there are some recommendations to take into consideration, which can enhance the experience.

Take advantage of the browser: Part of the benefit of doing immersive experiences in the browser is that you have at your disposal a wide array of APIs that can help you achieve innovative experiences. You can also take advantage of different APIs to achieve things like speech recognition and Bluetooth device integration with your applications.

Make your experience comply with Progressive Enhancement: With many devices supporting modern browsers, you want to expand the reach of your application to as many of them as possible. Making a progressively enhanced experience doesn't mean having the same experience in every device, but rather having *any* experience on every device.

Add Sound: Often overlooked, audio is an important part of any immersive experience. The easiest way to proceed with audio is to set a background sound that acts as ambient noise. Different frameworks provide different ways of playing sounds, but they generally provide straightforward ways of positioning and playing audio through JavaScript. Remember to test in different platforms, since mobile browsers handle audio differently from their desktop and VR counterparts.

7.10 Summary

Creating immersive experiences is now possible in a browser. There is a specification for an API in the works, and several frameworks and tools available to do so. In targeting web browsers, there is a broad set of devices that can engage with those experiences, but we have to take this into account to ensure the experience can be used to some degree in every device. Using web technologies to build immersive experiences also opens the door to combining different technologies built into the browser, like speech recognition, or geolocation, along with access to a plethora of devices that can be accessed through JavaScript APIs—indeed it is possible to add room tracking with a Kinect to a Cardboard-based experience for example, or even to control real Bluetooth devices from the virtual world.

The strength of the web lies in its ability to connect. These connections enrich experiences, allowing for more social, sharable, frictionless, open, and interactive applications.

Acknowledgements

We would like to thank Salvador de la Puente González (Mozilla) and Thomas Balouet (Virtuleap) for their review of the content in this chapter.

References

[Balouet 2017]

Balouet, Thomas (2017). "Progressive Web A-Painter: 3D VR in *Your Pocket.*" Retrieved from Medium.com: https://medium.com/@tombalou/progressive-web-a-painter-3d-vr-in-your-pocket-ef15a425559

[Bozorgzadeh 2017]

Bozorgzadeh, Amir-Esmaeil (2017). "WebVR's Magic Window is the Gateway for Pushing VR to Billions of People." Retrieved from UploadVR: https://uploadvr.com/webvrs-magic-window-gateway-pushing-vr-billions-people/

[Gilbert & Albeza 2017]

Gilbert, Jeff, and Belén Albeza (2017). "WebGL 2 Lands in Firefox." Retrieved from Mozilla Hacks: https://hacks.mozilla.org/2017/01/webgl-2-lands-in-firefox/

[González & Cannon 2017]

González, Diego, and Ada Cannon (2017). "The Gamepad Reloaded." Retrieved from Samsung Internet Medium: https://medium.com/samsung-internet-dev/the-gamepad-reloaded-5ba866770003

[Google 2017]

Google (2017). "Lighthouse." Retrieved from Tools for Web Developers: https://developers.google.com/web/tools/light

[GoogleVR 2017]

GoogleVR (2017). googlevr/webvr-polyfill. Retrieved from GitHub: https://github.com/immersive-web/webvr-polyfill

[Russell, Song, Archibald, & Kruisselbrink 2016]

Russell, Alex, Jungkee Song, Jake Archibald, and Marijn Kruisselbrink (2016). "Service Workers 1." Retrieved from W3C: https://w3.org/TR/service-workers-1/

[Samsung Internet 2017]

Samsung Internet (2017). "Bubble." Retrieved from bubble: https://bubble.pictures

[SonarWhal 2018]

SonarWhal (2018). Retrieved from SonarWhal.com: https://sonarwhal.com/

[Vukicevic 2017]

Vukicevic, Vladimir, Brandon Jones, Kearwood Gilbert, and Chris Van Wiemeersch (2017). "WebVR, Editor's Draft, 2" October 2017. Retrieved from GitHub: https://immersive-web.github.io/webvr/spec/1.1/

[W3C 2017]

W3C (2017). "W3C Community Groups." Retrieved from WebVR Community Group: https://w3.org/community/webvr/

[WebVR_CG 2017]

WebVR_CG (2017). "WebVR Spec." Retrieved from GitHub: https://immersive-web.github.io/webvr/

Greyhouse

Building the Neighborhood Coffee Shop in Unreal Engine for VR

Booker Smith and David Whittinghill
Purdue University

8.1 Introduction

Greyhouse is a locally famous coffee and pastry shop near our laboratory, well liked and often visited by the Purdue community. Progress being what it is, recent construction is shaking things up, and the beloved old shop will be getting a new look later this year. Out with the old, in with the new. For the sake of posterity, we have decided to virtually preserve the old place, using the Unreal game engine to create a VR representation of the shop optimized for the HTC Vive system (Figure 8.1).

8.2 Unreal in Virtual Reality

Fortunately for us, VR in Unreal is quite simple for the Vive. Developers can use the standard templates, which easily permit a Vive preview, or they can use the Unreal "Virtual Reality" template which allows deeper control of the controls and headset and includes handy functions for teleporting and other VR capabilities. For this chapter, we are going to stick with the standard templates. The Virtual Reality template requires a bit of Blueprint

Figure 8.1

The Greyhouse.

(Unreal's visual scripting language) coding, which is a bit beyond the scope of a purely introductory chapter.

The Vive depends upon Valve's Steam software platform for drivers and application loading. Vive developers must install Steam and enable SteamVR and make sure the SteamVR plugin is enabled in the editor. SteamVR is the mediator between the VR hardware and any games or applications that seek to communicate with it. In the case of Unreal Engine, when the editor first opens it checks for the presence of SteamVR and, if it finds it, it loads the "Virtual Reality" development template; when SteamVR is not present, this template option is not displayed. Since we are using standard templates, we will use the template called "First Person." This template delivers a VR experience controlled via a traditional WASD keyboard/mouse input scheme (Figure 8.2).

8.3 Casing the Greyhouse

We first photographed Greyhouse the way it presently is to capture its light, color geometry, and overall ambience. We have elected to use Unreal to block out a BSP representation of what is a fairly simple scene but one that is, to us, fairly familiar. Initially, we chose to use Unreal's VR editor and though the tools are promising and quite a lot of fun to use, at the time of this writing they are still experimental. Rather than risking the final release of Unreal VR Editor being dramatically different than the present experimental build, we chose to build using the traditional 2D mouse and keyboard interface.

We also chose to build our Greyhouse scene using only BSP's and starter content shipped with the engine. If one were trying to model a scene for a professional VR production they would use static meshes and custom-made 3d models. This chapter is

Figure 8.2

VR preset.

instead meant to be a fairly simple learning exercise through which new Unreal developers can gain some familiarity with the Unreal Editor and get familiar with the environment. Using Unreal's more advanced "Virtual Reality" development templates not only enables the use of motion controllers, avatar teleportation, and other fun VR features, but also requires coding and thus will be left to more advanced lessons elsewhere. Our hope is that we provide the reader a window into the process of using only in-platform assets to approximate an interesting real world scene. Our goal was not high-fidelity simulation, but rather to see just how far we could re-purpose the engine's off-the-shelf content to make a nonetheless interesting VR scene that captures some of the spirit of the source material.

8.4 Pre-Production

- Visit the location to recreate, and take pictures that capture enough detail and information such that you have a robust reference package from which you can derive the location's color, lighting, dimensions, and general ambience. Pay attention to the location's various architectural shapes and cues, materials, lighting, and other interesting details.

- It helps to have your reference images always visible during level construction. We like using a dual monitor configuration in which the reference materials are on the secondary screen while our level construction is completed on the primary screen.

8.5 Getting Started with Unreal

The Unreal Engine is a free download available from www.unrealengine.com and runs on Windows and Mac. Once you have created your unique user account, download the Launcher application, which will allow you to download the game engine and editor. For this particular project, we used version 4.16.2.

At the top of the screen (Figure 8.3), you will see multiple tabs, click on the one named "Unreal Engine." On the left is the Library button, click on it and the main window presents a button called "Add Versions." Click to select your version of choice (in this exercise, we are using 4.16.2). Click "Launch" to begin.

Creating a Project

- Choose the "New Project" tab, the "Blueprint" tab, then select the "Virtual Reality" icon;
- Select the "Desktop/Console," "Maximum Quality," and "With Starter Content" settings; and
- Select a location in your file system where you want to store your project.

Note, the Unreal Editor is often performing numerous file writes in the background during development. As such, having your files stored on an external or networked drive will cause the editor to feel sluggish and result in much slower loading. We highly recommend you save your work to a location on your local file system and then, if you want to maintain a backup, use a source control program or manually copy your project files to your backup location periodically.

Once the project is loaded you will be presented with a scene containing various VR Template items (Figure 8.2). We will not be using the elements in this scene (Figure 8.4),

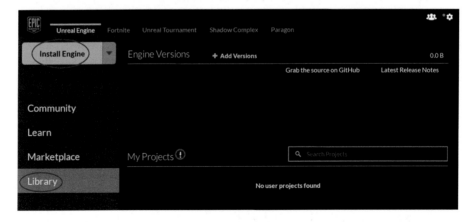

Figure 8.3

Choosing an engine version.

Figure 8.4

Opening scene with starter content.

except for "SkyLight" and "ExponentialHeightFog." You can see the items in World Outliner, click to highlight them, and delete all other items. The World Outliner is one of the panes in Unreal Engine that allows the developer to view the contents of their scene as a textual, hierarchical list rather than as a three-dimensional world (Figure 8.5). The World Outliner and the Viewport do in fact represent the exact same data.

Figure 8.5

The World Outliner (in red).

8.6 Recreating the Greyhouse

First, we construct the basic room. We did not measure the physical Greyhouse's dimensions so we instead used a best guess approximation. In the Modes window (Figure 8.6), select the Geometry tab where a number of pre-fab objects are available to drag into the Scene window. We constructed the walls, floors, and ceilings out of nine "Box" BSP's which were then scaled into flat planes and placed to form the room. We constructed the floor as four BSP's so that we could have different textures on them (to more closely match Greyhouse's floors).

8.6.1 The Floor

There will be no other characters walking through the scene when it is completed. Without some patrons walking about, it is more difficult to perceive the "feel" and flow of the space. To compensate, we provide some subtle visual hints by rotating the texture of the wood floor strategically, as the anisotropic effect of the wood grain serves as vision lines, drawing attention to interesting aspects of the scene. For instance, the diagonal wood in the entry and retail section point to the counter and display, alerting the user to the cash register.

Moving forward, one encounters wood whose direction is against the grain, acting as a visual cue of a barrier. Following its lines, the viewer sees the employee-only door. Customers only encounter this region after a purchase, so the spatial layout of the shop and the sight lines of its decor both urge your mind's eye to the next region, a region

Figure 8.6

In the Modes window, select the Place tab overhead tab, then the Geometry left tab.

whose wood grain pattern matches that of your current location. This layout encourages customers to sit down and enjoy their purchases in that area of the shop. It also is based on shopping psychology in real life: it causes one to pause and see the other wares, or in Greyhouse's case, items like sugar and creamer, which then moves the customer forward, reducing congestion in the main commerce space/entryway. In low traffic times, this is welcoming, because there is no line, and in high traffic times, it draws people from the eaves to the display counter and menu, because the flow of people creates a space that customers want to fill. Designing a virtual space, even a simple one like this, can be enhanced by simple visual cues like rotated textures, because in so doing, we model the same subtle human mechanics one finds in real life. This helps realism!

One extremely helpful feature in the Unreal Editor is snapping (Figure 8.7). Snapping causes objects that are dragged and dropped into the scene to "snap" to gridlines that run through the world. These gridlines can be set to any desired granularity. Each transformation tool: Translation, Rotation, and Scaling has its own snap values, which the user can customize. Using snapping helps maintain right angles between objects and helps prevent object overlap (which can cause "z-fighting" in the final render)—and it generally makes a level designer's work a whole lot easier.

8.6.1.1 Usability Note: ALT-drag

In the following data value tables frequent references are made to the ALT-drag sequence. This is a simple way to clone a piece of geometry in the scene while retaining the original geometry's orientation in the scene. It is an extremely handy feature for building walls as in most cases a left-hand wall and right-hand wall are oriented similarly. Cloning like this removes the need to reposition new geometry along all three axes. Naturally, this is also handy for any situation in which uniform orientation is necessary (ceilings/walls, etc.).

8.6.1.2 Usability Note: Surface Properties Submenu

The Surface Properties submmenu is not displayed by default for geometry. To enable this submenu, from within the Modes window select the Paint option (Figure 8.8). This will then make the Surface Properties submenu appear in the Details pane (Figure 8.9).

8.6.2 Floor Segments

There are **four** floor panels. Each row below in Table 8.1 lists attribute values used to create the floor pieces. Enter the values below in the Details window for each floor piece.

Figure 8.7

Transformation tools and their accompanying snap values.

Figure 8.8

The Paint Tab.

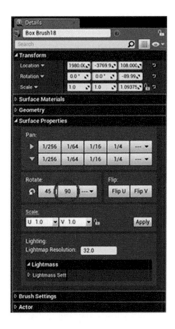

Figure 8.9

The Surface Properties submenu and the 90° rotation button.

Table 8.1 Floor Segments

	Location x, y, z	Rotation x, y, z	Scale x, y, z	Brush Type	Brush Shape	Brush x, y, z
1	0, 0, 0	0, 0, 0	6, 6, .08	Additive	Box	300, 600, 200
2	Use ALT-drag to clone Floor 1 along the Y green axis					
	Surface Properties—rotate: 90° menu button					
3	Use ALT-drag to clone Floor 2 and drag along the X (red) axis					
	1795, −1840, 0	0, 0, 0	6, 1, .08	Additive	Box	300, 600, 200
4	Use ALT-drag to clone Floor 3 and drag along the Y (green) axis					
	0, −4200, 0	0, 0, 0	6, 6, .08	Additive	Box	300, 600, 200
	Surface Properties—rotate: 90° menu button					

8.6.3 Walls—Base Architecture

Creating walls is very similar to how floors are created: Box BSP's are placed and rescaled to create each structure. Since walls are more (but not entirely) uniform, to save work we will be applying materials and cloning them with the materials applied using ALT-drag.

Drag a BSP into the scene and set its Location to (−945, 0, 108), its Scale to (1, 6, 1), and its Brush value to (300, 600, 200).

To create materials, open the Content Browser. In the Content Browser open Starter Materials/Materials. Find the material named M_Basic_Wall, right-click it, and click duplicate. Now right-click the duplicated material, and rename it whatever you like; we renamed ours "New_Wall." Drag the New_Wall material into the Scene pane and onto the new wall Box that was just created.

For the remaining walls, create duplicates of the first wall using ALT-drag. Each duplicate will have the attributes provided in Table 8.2.

8.6.4 Walls—Windows and Doorways

To create openings within walls for windows and doorways, we again used Box BSP's, except we now use the Subtractive Brush type (Figure 8.10). Subtractive geometry is used to "carve out" openings in another piece of geometry. As was the case for walls, Box BSP's are dragged and dropped onto the Scene pane, which we then follow up by manually editing the values in the Details pane.

The window and door attributes are as in Table 8.3.

Table 8.2 Walls: Base Architecture

	Location x, y, z	Rotation x, y, z	Scale x, y, z	Brush x, y, z
1	This piece was created in the instructions above			
2	−945, −3135, 108	0, 0, 90	1, 1, 1	1200, 200, 200
3	−710, 1610, 248	0, 0, 45	2.4, 1, 2.4	200, 50, 200
4	865, −1950, 657	0, 0, 0	1, 1, 1	200, 200, 200
5	45, 1700, 108	0, 0, 0	1, 1, 1	200, 200, 200
6	800, 120, 120	0, 0, 90	1, 1, 1	200, 200, 200
7	1670, −1590, 552	180, 0, 0	1.34, 1.09, 1.34	200, 200, 200
8	1700, −2200, 212	0, 0, 0	1.34, 1.09, 1.34	200, 200, 200
	Repeat the material creation and application process above, but use M_Brick_Clay_New			
9	Clone this from Wall 8 so that it inherits the M_Brick_Clay_New material			
	1980, −3770, 108	0, 0, −90	1, 1, 1.09	200, 200, 200
10	−100, −5100, 482	0, 0, 0	1.34, 1.09, 1.34	200, 200, 200
	Repeat the material creation and application process above, but use the M_Wall_New material			
11	−100, −5100, 112	0, 0, 0	1.34, 1.09, 1.34	200, 200, 200
	Repeat the material creation and application process above, but use the M_Wood_Floor_Clay_Walnut_Worn material			
12	2130, −2990, 110	0, 0, 0	1, 1.65, 1	200, 200, 200
	Repeat the material creation and application process above to create a dark gray material			

Figure 8.10

Setting Additive vs. Subtractive brush type.

Table 8.3 Walls: Windows and Doors

	Location x, y, z	Rotation x, y, z	Scale x, y, z	Brush Type	Brush Shape	Brush x, y, z
1	710, 1610, 270	0, 0, 45	2.4, 1, 2.4	Subtractive	Box	180, 60, 210
2	−875, −95, 415	0, 0, 0	.5, 12, 1.25	Subtractive	Box	200, 200, 200
3	−875, −3350, 415	0, 0, 0	.5, 12, 1.25	Subtractive	Box	200, 200, 200
4	−675, −4975, 180	0, 0, 0	.5, 12, 1.25	Subtractive	Box	200, 200, 200
5	−675, −4975, −180	0, 0, 0	.5, 12, 1.25	Subtractive	Box	200, 200, 200
6	−410, −4975, 180	0, 0, 0	.5, 12, 1.25	Subtractive	Box	200, 200, 200
7	−145, −4975, 180	0, 0, 0	.5, 12, 1.25	Subtractive	Box	200, 200, 200
8	120, −4975, 180	0, 0, 0	.5, 12, 1.25	Subtractive	Box	200, 200, 200
9	375, −4975, 180	0, 0, 0	.5, 12, 1.25	Subtractive	Box	200, 200, 200
10	640, −4975, 180	0, 0, 0	.5, 12, 1.25	Subtractive	Box	200, 200, 200
11	905, −4975, 180	0, 0, 0	.5, 12, 1.25	Subtractive	Box	200, 200, 200
12	1170, −4975, 180	0, 0, 0	.5, 12, 1.25	Subtractive	Box	200, 200, 200
13	1435, −4975, 180	0, 0, 0	.5, 12, 1.25	Subtractive	Box	200, 200, 200
14	1700, −4975, 180	0, 0, 0	.5, 12, 1.25	Subtractive	Box	200, 200, 200
15	1955, −4975, 180	0, 0, 0	.5, 12, 1.25	Subtractive	Box	200, 200, 200
16	1080, −3650, 145	0, 0, 0	2.12, .43, .46	Subtractive	Box	200, 200, 200
17	610, 1815, 355	0, 0, 0	1, 1, 1	Subtractive	Box	200, 200, 200

8.6.5 Ceiling

The ceiling is a clone of the floor. Hold CTRL and select the four floor pieces. Release CTRL, and ALT-drag the selected pieces upwards to clone. While the four pieces are still selected, right-click on any of the pieces and select Group. We recommend setting a value of 775 for the Location Z value.

8.6.6 Decor

Here we illustrate how we created the "furniture" and decor used to furnish our space. Remember, we are purposely avoiding creating proper 3D models and are instead trying to capture the feel of the original Greyhouse while using only BSP's, primitives, and "canned" assets found in the Unreal's Starter Content package. As such, from here forward the work we are illustrating is more "art" than science. We ask the reader to allow us some creative license as quite a bit of imagination will be required of the viewer's eye. This is the MacGuyver of virtual spaces.

The decor item properties are as shown in the following subsections (Tables 8.4–8.7).

8.6.6.1 Open-Air Shelving Unit

Table 8.4 Open-Air Shelving Unit

BSP Box					
Location x, y, z	Rotation x, y, z	Scale x, y, z	Brush Type	Brush Shape	Brush x, y, z
1070, −3650, 110	0, 0, 0	2.44, .44, 1	Additive	Box	200, 200, 200
All faces material: M_Wood_Pine (drag onto BSP from Starter Content/Materials)					

8.6.6.2 Cashier's Counter

Table 8.5 Cashier's Counter

BSP Box					
Location x, y, z	Rotation x, y, z	Scale x, y, z	Brush Type	Brush Shape	Brush x, y, z
145, 0, 108	0, 0, 0	1, 6, 1	Additive	Box	300, 600, 200
Countertop material: M_Rock_Marble_Polished					
Customer-facing material: M_Wood_Oak					

8.6.6.3 Pastry Display

Table 8.6 Pastry Display

BSP Cylinder				
Location x, y, z	Rotation x, y, z	Scale x, y, z	Brush Type	Brush Shape
150, 845, 205	90, 0, 180	.75, 1, 8.44	Subtractive	Cylinder
Z: 200; outer radius: 200; sides: 60				
150, 900, 205	90, 0, 180	.75, 1, 8.44	Additive	Cylinder
Z: 200; outer radius: 200; sides: 60				

8.6.6.4 "Piano" (Yeah, Yeah, This One's a Stretch...)

Table 8.7 "Piano"

		BSP Box			
Location *x, y, z*	Rotation *x, y, z*	Scale *x, y, z*	Brush Type	Brush Shape	Brush *x, y, z*
1775, −4700, 145	0, 0, 30	2.09, .69, 1	Additive	Box	200, 200, 200
All-faces material: M_Tech_Panel					

8.6.6.5 Tables

For the tables we will be using the static mesh tables that are included as part of the Starter Content. From within the Content Browser, navigate to Props/SM_TableRound (Figure 8.11).

Drag the table icon onto the Scene Pane and set the positional parameters as in Table 8.8.

Figure 8.11

Locating the table prop.

Table 8.8 Tables

	Location *x, y, z*	Rotation *x, y, z*	Scale *x, y, z*
1	530, −2630, 10	0, 0, 0	3, 3, 2
2	−74, −2960, 10	0, 0, −135	3, 3, 2
3	−180, −3583, 10	0, 0, −130	3, 3, 2
4	−550, −4690, 10	0, 0, −90	3, 3, 2
5	630, −4660, 10	0, 0, 0	3, 4, 2
6	435, −4110, 10	0, 0, 0	3, 4, 2
7	1765, −4140, 10	0, 0, 0	2, 2, 2
8	1765, −3455, 10	0, 0, 0	2, 2, 2

Table 8.9 Stools

	Location	Rotation	Scale
	x, y, z	x, y, z	x, y, z
1	−720, −3115, 10	0, 0, 0	1, 1, 2.25
2	−720, −2260, 10	0, 0, 0	1, 1, 2.25
3	−720, −1035, 10	0, 0, 0	1, 1, 2.25
4	−720, −180, 10	0, 0, 0	1, 1, 2.25
5	−720, 675, 10	0, 0, 0	1, 1, 2.25
6	−710, −1800, 10	0, 0, 0	1, 1, 2.25

8.6.6.6 Stools

The stools will use the same static mesh as our tables. They will just be stretched and narrowed to be more "stool like". From within the Content Browser, navigate to Props/SM_TableRound. Drag the table icon onto the Scene Pane and set the positional parameters as in Table 8.9.

8.6.6.7 Props

Last of all we place the various plants, sculptures, and miscellaneous objects about the scene. Below are the values we used to approximate the original Greyhouse but, frankly, placement is a matter of taste. Feel free to move around as you see fit. We do, however, include recipes for distorting and reshaping Starter Content assets such that they no longer resemble their original. For instance, we got a lot of mileage (yours may vary) with the SM_Table_Round: elongating it upward and scaling its X and Z makes it a nice barstool, uniform-scaling it way down and rotating it makes it a desk fan, and so on. We include these examples to hopefully inspire the reader to take their own creative license with the Starter Content materials and make their own interesting creations.

8.6.6.8 Plants

The plants will use the following static mesh from the Starter Content package: Content Browser/Starter Content/Props/SM_Bush. Place as in Table 8.10.

8.6.6.9 Ceiling Light Fixtures

The ceiling light fixtures used the following static mesh from the Starter Content package: Content Browser/Starter Content/Blueprints/Blueprint_CeilingLight. After placing the first light, use ALT-drag to duplicate the other lights. Place as in Table 8.11.

Table 8.10 Props

	Location	Rotation	Scale
	x, y, z	x, y, z	x, y, z
1	1705, −4745, 245	0, 0, 0	.6, .6, 1.875
2	200, 500, 210	0, 0, 0	.6, .6, 1.875
3	200, 800, 210	0, 0, 0	.6, .6, 1.875
4	200, 1060, 210	0, 0, 0	.6, .6, 1.875
5	200, 1310, 210	0, 0, 0	.6, .6, 1.875

Table 8.11 Ceiling Light Fixtures

	Location x, y, z	Rotation x, y, z	Scale x, y, z
1	1830, −3325, 765	0, 0, 0	.6, .6, 1.875
2	1830, −3600, 765	0, 0, 0	.6, .6, 1.875
3	1830, −3765, 765	0, 0, 0	.6, .6, 1.875
4	1830, −4040, 765	0, 0, 0	.6, .6, 1.875
5	1830, −4355, 765	0, 0, 0	.6, .6, 1.875
6	1830, −4630, 765	0, 0, 0	.6, .6, 1.875

8.6.6.10 Point Lighting

If this were a professional production, then designers would study the lighting in the Greyhouse in order to determine its particular layout of diffuse lighting sources. However, the spirit of this chapter is for beginner friendliness and rapid prototyping. As such, we used point lights to create some ambient illumination throughout the scene. It may not be accurate per se, but it does capture the ambiance of the original location.

Open the Modes window, Lights, Point Light (Figure 8.12), and drag lights onto the Scene Pane, setting their attributes as in Table 8.12.

8.6.6.11 The Doors

The doors used the following static mesh from the Starter Content package: Content Browser/Props/SM_Door. After placing the first door, use ALT-drag to clone the other doors. Place as in Table 8.13.

Figure 8.12

Selecting a point light.

Table 8.12 Point Lighting

	Location x, y, z	Intensity x, y, z
1	500, −1250, 395	1000
2	500, −750, 395	1000
3	500, −250, 395	1000
4	500, 250, 395	1000
5	500, 750, 395	1000
6	500, 1250, 395	1000
7	635, −4730, 395	1000
8	1750, −5250, 395	1000
9	1750, −3250, 395	1000

Table 8.13 The Doors

	Location x, y, z	Rotation x, y, z	Scale x, y, z
1	−592, 1738, 18	0, 0, −45	1, 1.94, 2.47
2	−839, 1491, 18	0, 0, 135	1, 1.94, 2.47
3	860, −1830, 10	0, 0, 0	2.59, 2.59, 2.59
4	2025, −3175, 10	0, 0, −180	1.88, 1.66, 1.88
5	2025, −2875, 10	0, 0, 0	1.88, 1.66, 1.88

Table 8.14 The Doors' Frames

	Location x, y, z	Rotation x, y, z	Scale x, y, z
1	712, 612, 13	0, 0, −45	2.56, 3.84, 2.5
2	870, −1945, 8	0, 0, 0	2.56, 2.56, 2.59

8.6.6.12 The Doors' Frames

The door frames used the following static mesh from the Starter Content package: Content Browser/Props/SM_DoorFrame. After placing the first door frame, use ALT-drag to clone the other frame. Place as in Table 8.14.

8.6.6.13 Miscellaneous

The remaining items constitute the various minutia around the shop and serve to give the space a personal touch (Figure 8.13). Place items as in Table 8.15.

8.7 The Finished Product

In the end we arrived at a decidedly *approximate* recreation of the original Greyhouse that we hope captures the essence of the original if not necessarily the specifics. This tutorial was designed to help an absolute beginner get started with Unreal for VR while

Figure 8.13

The simulated environment versus the original.

Table 8.15 Miscellaneous Decoration

	Location x, y, z	Rotation x, y, z	Scale x, y, z
Weird unreal orb thing	1745, −3450, 150	0, 0, −30	.125, .125, .125
Content Browser/Props/SM_MatPreviewMesh_02			
Statue	610, −4855, 150	0, 0, 0	1, 1, 1
Content Browser/Props/SM_Statue			
Decorative rock	1155, −3640, 100	0, 0, 0	.125, .125, .125
Content Browser/Props/SM_MatPreviewMesh_02			
Arch Thing	1155, −3640, 100	0, 0, 0	.125, .125, .125
Content Browser/Props/SM_MatPreviewMesh_02			
Old-timey camera	1225, −3640, 100	0, 0, 0	2, 2, 2
Content Browser/Props/SM_CornerFrame			
Shelf 1	−845, −85, 280	0, 0, 0	4, 12, 1
Content Browser/Props/SM_Shelf			
Shelf 2	−845, −3282, 280	0, 0, 0	4, 12, 1
Content Browser/Props/SM_Shelf			
Desk fan	1228, −3653, 208.57	0, 0, 0	.125, .125, .125
Modes/geometry/cone			
	1215, −3620, 255	−90, 0, 20	0.375, 0.375, 0.375
Content Browser/Props/SM_CornerFrame			

demonstrating how existing assets can be repurposed to let the reader get started right away on creating interesting original virtual environments.

Upon loading this map, you will be able to view the world using your HTC Vive headset and navigate it with the keyboard and mouse. To take the experience to the next level and enable motion controllers and avatar teleportation functionality, study Unreal's "Virtual Reality" template and Blueprint's visual scripting system.

9

Bridging Scientific Visualization and Unreal VR

Kees Van Kooten
NVIDIA

This chapter presents a practical solution integrating consumer virtual reality (VR) hardware into a scientific visualization pipeline. To this end, it shows the benefits of such hardware, but especially the challenges of using it with existing scientific visualization tools. The proposed solution then is to use the Unreal Engine for solving the rendering problem and the setup of a VR environment with interaction; then, a pair of plugins is described bridging the Unreal engine application to existing scientific visualization tools. After a technical explanation of the bridge, the workflow and interactions with it are shown. What follows is an explanation on how to integrate the bridge into your own scientific visualization application of choice. Lastly, some practical limitations and future directions will be discussed.

9.1 Benefits and Challenges of Consumer VR

The rise of consumer VR hardware in the gaming space has had a domino effect in other areas too. It is already a commodity in professional visualization, where it provides a means for architectural tours, previews of consumer products and design collaboration. It is also being employed in professional trainings, in education, and in psychological or occupational therapy. It even finds a use in object and environment reconstruction, for example, in the field of archeology.

It is therefore not surprising that there is considerable interest to use this technology in scientific visualization as well. The increased depth perception of current HMDs over standard monitors is useful for analyzing complex datasets. The ability to navigate and position oneself within a dataset is easier than with a traditional mouse and keyboard. Many types of interactions with the dataset feel more natural using consumer VR instead of the standard desktop UI. Additionally, the cost and space requirements as compared to a CAVE setup are much smaller; a basic setup at the desktop usually suffices.

There are of course drawbacks associated with the usage of consumer VR. For one, consumer VR is not yet easy to use for augmented-reality purposes, for example in combination with the physical environment, or in collaboration with other users in the same room. The headset is still too bulky for that, making it cumbersome to don and doff. While in-HMD exterior views are often supported via an outward-facing camera, they are not yet capable enough for precision tasks. However, these aspects are expected to improve considerably as technology matures.

Furthermore, it takes a considerable engineering effort to adapt an existing scientific visualization pipeline to the VR use-case. First off, a smooth experience in a VR HMD requires a high-frequency low-latency graphical update loop, which does not slow down under the various possible interactions with the scientific data. The whole scientific visualization pipeline should help maintain this requirement, from the generation of the geometry to the actual rendering.

Additionally, the interaction style in VR is different from keyboard and mouse at a standard monitor. Often it is not even clear which parts of the interaction are most comfortably done from within the VR environment, prompting a full redesign of the interaction with the scientific visualization software. This includes a lot of prototyping and testing. While such activities are usually not a problem for commercial use-cases, it does pose a problem for scientific visualization, where there is a comparatively small budget and time window for development and especially maintenance of software not directly related to a particular research project.

9.2 Leveraging Existing Technology

This chapter focuses on the aforementioned problem of integrating VR into a scientific visualization pipeline. It has been designed to affect existing scientific workflows as little as possible, while at the same time requiring very little investment in terms of money and engineering effort. It does this by leveraging technology from the gaming space, where lots of effort has already been put into the software platforms for design of virtual interactive environments, in the form of freely available game engines.

These engines have been developed using large budgets and lots of manpower over many years, where they have been put to the test in countless applications. Some of these engines employ the latest technological developments for VR rendering, so the developer does not have to take care of supporting new rendering algorithms or hardware features. The added benefit is that this technology is designed to be easy to use, for people who do not necessarily have software engineering or visualization skills themselves. Mostly, it will not require any programming in order to set up and prototype new interaction or exploration ideas.

Understandably, it is impractical to try and integrate existing scientific visualization tools directly into a game engine or vice versa. A considerable amount of work has been spent over the last decades across multiple disciplines to develop visualization technology and plugins, for all the data management and geometry generation that is necessary before the rendering can even begin. Copying this work would be too costly to undertake or to maintain. So instead, it is preferable to use the scientific software for its data management and generation strengths, and the game engine for its rendering and prototyping strengths. Using plugins, both can be coupled to show the 3D data of the scientific visualization that would traditionally be displayed on a standard monitor in the virtual VR environment created by the game engine.

The next sections describe an example bridge between one specific scientific visualization tool and one specific game engine: ParaView and the Unreal Engine. Both are widely used, familiar to many, and therefore enjoy a lot of community support. Furthermore, the Unreal Engine already has many applications in professional visualization, and is one of the foremost platforms for integration of the latest developments in VR rendering technology. The bridge allows the user to build their own application using the Unreal Engine, which then connects to ParaView while running in a standalone fashion.

While both VTK and ParaView already contain VR integrations (as described by [O'Leary et al. 2017; Martin et al. 2016] respectively) that perform rather well for selected situations, they neither offer the freedom of scene creation and prototyping of interaction, nor many of the advanced rendering effects available in the Unreal Engine. This solution therefore attempts to make a bridge in a similar fashion as in [Rajlich 1995], but with a larger focus on maintaining VR rendering performance under geometry modification.

At the time of writing, the plugin was tested to work with Unreal Engine 4.14 and ParaView 5.4, and supports both the Windows platform as well as Linux. It will be made available on the website that accompanies this book.

9.3 A Bridge of Plugins

The most straightforward way of bridging ParaView and Unreal is to use plugins for both technologies. Therefore, the bridge will consist of a plugin in ParaView that reacts to any change in the ParaView visualization pipeline, and identifies the changed geometry, texture, and transformation data. The ParaView plugin sends those changes over to a shared memory block, that can in turn be read by the Unreal plugin. The Unreal plugin takes the changes and uses them to update geometry, textures, and transformations for specific actors and meshes within the virtual reality environment. These two plugins are in combination referred to as the "External Visualization Plugin."

Note that the choice for sending data over shared memory forces the user to execute the instance of the ParaView client application on the same machine as the instance of the Unreal application—the rendered geometry should be fully present on one single workstation. The technology does not support use of the Unreal application to render images remotely on for example a High Performance Cluster, or use images as they are streamed from rendering processes on an HPC. Of course, it is entirely conceivable that an HPC processes geometry on its nodes before it is sent over to a ParaView client process, after which the client workstation could automatically display an up-to-date scene in the Unreal VR environment.

To increase the efficiency of the shared memory buffer for reading and writing, the buffer is split in two (double-buffered), so that ParaView can write to one part of the buffer while Unreal reads from the other part. Once either application is done reading or writing, it makes its part of the buffer available for the next write or read respectively. This way, Unreal does not have to wait for ParaView to finish writing before it can start reading. Conversely, ParaView does not have to wait for Unreal to finish updating its graphics resources before it can provide the next batch of geometry.

To illustrate the two plugins working together, Figure 9.1a shows a typical ParaView screen with imported geometry that is being rendered as a mesh in the ParaView OpenGL output window. This particular dataset is a timeseries dataset, so the geometry changes from one timestep to the next. For every new geometry that ParaView generates for the individual timesteps, the ParaView plugin sends the geometry via the shared memory block to the Unreal plugin. As the Unreal plugin runs in an Unreal application on the same machine, it automatically updates the timeseries data within a mesh belonging to a specific actor placed in the Unreal VR application. The output of the Unreal application is represented by Figure 9.1b.

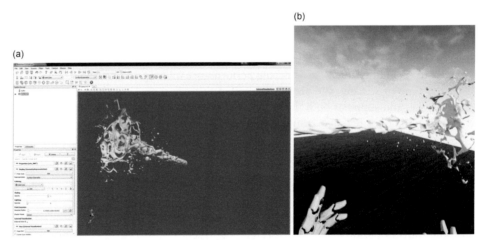

Figure 9.1

(a) A typical time-series data running in ParaView. (b) The time-series data is automatically transferred to an Unreal VR application, running simultaneously on the same machine. (Dataset courtesy of the Juelich Supercomputing Center, Institute of Combustion Technology.)

The choice of which Unreal actor should receive geometry from which separate geometry in ParaView is completely up to the user of the ParaView plugin. The plugin gives the user control over which geometries belong to an actor chosen from a list of actors available in the Unreal scene, so that any mapping of pieces of ParaView geometry to Unreal actors is reasonable. This is further explained in Section 9.6.

9.4 The Execution Model

As previously noted, it is imperative that the Unreal application is rendering frames at 90 Hz, or the VR experience will be unbearable. The rendering part of the Unreal VR application therefore cannot wait for large geometries to be updated before proceeding with rendering, especially if it happens as frequently as with timeseries datasets.

Unreal provides a multi-threaded environment whereby different CPU cores on the system to work on separate aspects of the application. Whenever a visualization transfer plugin is added to an Unreal application, an additional "External Visualization Thread" will be added to the existing set of threads. This new thread handles geometry updates, so that the render loop can run without stalling. It reads geometry from the shared "Geometry Transfer Buffer" and copies it into graphics resources. As long as the threads are properly synchronized, geometry updates should not influence the frequency at which rendering is performed. The standard Unreal Engine application employs this strategy to separate game logic execution from rendering; by default, any application based on it will contain both a game thread and a render thread. The former executes game logic while the latter fills the graphics command buffer and synchronizes with the graphics hardware executing that command buffer.

A summary of the different stages in the execution model is represented by Figure 9.2. From left to right, it shows the ParaView plugin filling the Geometry Transfer Buffer with geometry, while the External Visualization Thread of the Unreal plugin is reading previously submitted geometry from another part of the buffer. That thread is part of the Unreal Engine application, which additionally contains the game and render thread.

Note that the External Visualization Thread can run at a much lower frequency than the game thread or the render thread, as the lower frequency of geometry updates will not

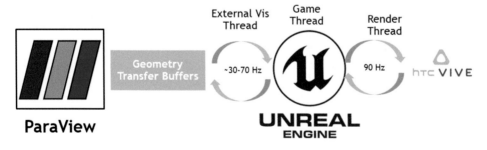

Figure 9.2

The ParaView-Unreal execution model, with ParaView on the left side and Unreal with its threads on the right side. The shared Geometry Transfer Buffer is used for streaming data from one side to the other.

be detrimental to the experience of the user within the VR environment. This allows for arbitrarily large geometries to be transferred, merely at the cost of animation smoothness.

9.5 Updating the Graphics Resources

The previous section described the External Visualization Thread of the Unreal plugin, which is responsible for reading geometry and texture data from the Geometry Transfer Buffer and copying it into graphics resources. However, the graphics API is generally assumed not to be multithreaded, so any kind of graphics resource creation or update API call in the External Visualization Thread must still be synchronized with the render thread API calls to execute properly. This can result in render thread stalls. For example, if a geometry update would require the creation of a large rendering resource, that act alone would stall the rendering pipeline, even though the eventual filling of that graphics resource can be performed asynchronously. Further complications exist for updating the graphics resource: while it is possible to get a pointer to a resource for asynchronous updates on another thread than the one where rendering takes place, the programmer still must ensure this update does not happen in a block of memory that is concurrently used for rendering operations. So how does the External Visualization Thread get around these problems?

The solution to updating graphics resources within an Unreal application while rendering, is again based on double-buffering, similar to the solution for transferring data between the two applications. At the start of the application, the External Visualization Thread pre-allocates a number of graphics resources, like vertexbuffers, indexbuffers, and texturebuffers of different sizes. These resources are exclusive to the External Visualization Thread, and are therefore initially not used for rendering. Whenever ParaView provides new geometry to the Unreal application, the best-fitting resource is selected and updated asynchronously from the render thread. This can trivially be done in a safe manner, as the resource is not used for rendering. Once the resource is updated, it can be handed off to the render thread for use in the display of a mesh or material. This resource is marked as used by the External Visualization thread and can therefore not be updated again.

Any subsequent geometry update will pick an as-of-yet unused resource from the pool for updating. Once the update is finished and the resource sent to a geometry that was already using an older resource, the reference to the resource is simply flipped to the new one, which doesn't delay the render thread at all. At the next rendered frame, the new resource will simply be used instead of the old one. The old resource is marked to be freed up again, but it cannot immediately be reused. It may still take several frames before the rendering thread and driver is truly finished with the resource. Therefore, the render thread increases a counter on all such marked-for-free resources at every rendered frame, and once that counter hits a certain value for a particular resource, that resource can be freely used by the External Visualization Thread again. As long as the amount of resources pre-allocated by the External Visualization Thread is sufficient to support the maximum scene complexity targeting a 90 Hz framerate, there will always be resources available for the next update.

There is one caveat to the system of updating graphics resources as described above. Within one frame, only a limited amount of graphics resources can be written to before it saturates the PCIe bus, which then again causes slowdown on the render thread. Therefore, the External Visualization Thread will update only a fixed amount of data per frame, waiting for subsequent frames to continue writing into graphics resources. Therefore, while it can take multiple frames for the External Visualization Thread to finish updating all graphics resources, the impact to the rendering frequency is minimized.

9.6 ParaView to Unreal Logical Mapping

In the Unreal software architecture, geometry is represented by one or more meshes belonging to actors in an Unreal scene. Actors are typically independent from the perspective of user-interaction, as they are at the top of a transformation hierarchy. ParaView on the other hand uses pipelines; one pipeline is generally a collection of stages, consisting of data inputs and outputs and filters in between. Those stages work in a serial fashion, transforming inputs from the previous stage in the pipeline, creating or modifying geometry, and passing their output to the input of the next stage. Any stage can provide its intermediate geometry as visual output. Because of that, the ParaView rendering backend allocates a separate vtkActor for each such output. Therefore, it is logical to be able to map any ParaView pipeline stage (vtkActor) to any Unreal actor. This is highlighted in Figure 9.3.

The External Visualization plugin allows the user to choose which ParaView stages should be grouped within the same actor in Unreal, and which ones will be part of a separate Unreal actor. The goal of such a grouping is to be able to independently interact with parts of the ParaView visualization, or to join separate parts of the ParaView visualization within one Unreal actor.

To support this, every Unreal actor's mesh is broken up into different sections, each one belonging to a unique ParaView stage. Whenever a ParaView stage is created, a new section is reserved within the Unreal mesh belonging to the Unreal actor to which the ParaView stage maps. From that point, the External Visualization Thread can add and remove graphics resources like vertex and index buffers to the reserved sections, and update or replace these when new geometry comes in, as explained in Section 9.5.

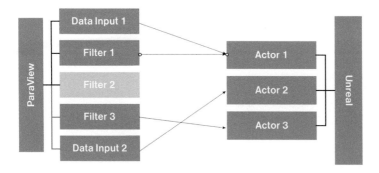

Figure 9.3

Each individual stage in a ParaView pipeline can show its intermediate output by being mapped to one or more Unreal actors (containing meshes) or one or more ParaView actors can map to a single Unreal actor. Filter 2 creates no geometry, and therefore is not mapped to any Unreal actor.

Note that one geometry buffer coming from the pool of buffers held by the External Visualization Thread may be assigned to one mesh section at one point in time, and a different one at another point in time. Each section has a reference to its own material, thereby supporting multiple materials over an actor's entire mesh. The assignment of geometry buffers from the External Visualization Thread's pool of resources to the different mesh sections is depicted in Figure 9.4.

Textures are updated in a similar fashion: a pool of textures is pre-allocated and assigned to the geometry sections' materials on-demand. To prevent that run-time changes of a texture's size will stall the rendering pipeline, all pre-allocated textures are chosen to be of a size at least as large as maximally required during operation of the plugin, and smaller textures simply update only a sub-region of a pre-allocated larger texture resource. This is possible due to the number of required surface textures in scientific visualization typically being small. The original geometry's texture coordinates are adjusted during the geometry update to fall within the larger texture's sub-region. Figure 9.5 shows a textured ParaView actor being represented in an Unreal Engine application.

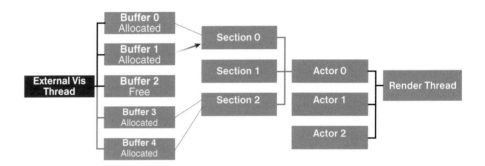

Figure 9.4

Mapping of the pre-allocated graphics resources from the External Visualization Thread to the reserved sections of an actor's geometry on the render thread. While Buffer 1 is assigned to Section 0, it has to wait until the render thread finishes with Buffer 0 to reuse it. Section 1 has no buffers attached, and therefore contains no geometry to render.

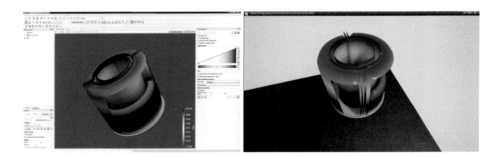

Figure 9.5

A ParaView actor with color mapping, as represented by the External Visualization plugin in an Unreal Engine application.

9.7 The Unreal-ParaView Workflow

Usage of the ParaView plugin is easy: once it is loaded into ParaView, it will automatically transport any visible geometry to a running Unreal Engine application. This only holds for mesh geometry; volume data or points and lines are not supported. The "Display" section of the "Properties" panel of a ParaView pipeline stage will automatically show the "Surface ExternalVis" representation for any geometry that can be sent over. Changing this representation will disable the item from being transferred to the Unreal VR scene. Also, the plugin adds the header "External Visualization" to the "Display" section of the "Properties" panel. Under this header, the user can set options for that control how the ParaView pipeline stage is sent to Unreal VR. One such option is the "External Actor Id." All pipeline stages with the same identifier are grouped into one actor in the Unreal VR scene, whereas stages with different identifiers are grouped into different actors. The options explained above are shown in Figure 9.6.

The Unreal plugin works a bit differently, as there is no such thing as a monolithic Unreal Engine application. Rather, one uses the Unreal Editor to construct a scene out of standard elements and possibly custom ones coming from plugins. Once the scene has been constructed, it can be converted into an application. The editor provides tools for rapid prototyping interactions and graphics even before the standalone application is generated, which allows the user to create any kind of virtual environment around the data that will come from ParaView and test it.

To start building your own environment using the Unreal Engine, I recommend following one of the many online tutorials, like the ones from [Epic Games 2017; Looman 2016]. Unreal comes with a standard VR template containing basic VR controls and an environment in which to play around. When creating a new project, just choose

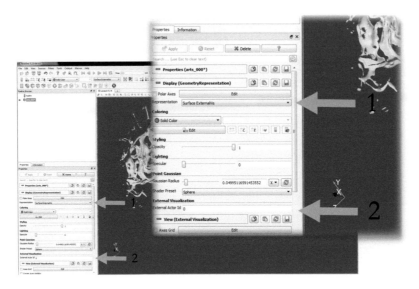

Figure 9.6

(1) shows the representation—changing it disables sending data over to Unreal.
(2) represents the actor identifier in the Unreal scene.

the "Virtual Reality" option in the "Blueprint" tab to get going. To include the External Visualization plugin, go to the project folder generated by the Unreal Editor, create a "Plugins" folder and unzip the External Visualization plugin into it.

The External Visualization plugin can be included within any application generated by the Unreal Editor, not just a VR application. It gives the user a new actor class called the "External Vis Actor," and by inserting instances of this class in the scene, the user chooses where it is possible to spawn ParaView geometry. These are the actors that the user can then choose under the "External Visualization" header in the ParaView pipeline stage property menu. This is shown in Figure 9.7.

Before the actor can be used, it has to be given a proper scale, and a material that allows for two-sided rendering and automatic texturing. Such a material is included in the plugin, under the name "M_BaseMatDoubleSided" in "StarterContent/Materials." Just drag the material called "M_BaseMatDoubleSided" onto the "Material" section of the External Vis Actor in the Unreal VR scene. This process is demonstrated in Figure 9.8.

The External Vis Actor can be made subject to interactions and visual transformations like any other normal actor, opening a host of possibilities for prototyping. For example, it is quite easy to set up interactions for grabbing the object, scaling it and clipping through its geometry. In fact, grabbing objects is already supported by the standard VR template: just create a blueprint around the External Vis Actor that implements the Pickup Actor Interface (see the "BP_PickupCube" blueprint as an example in the standard VR template), and add a physics collision box component to register overlap with the motion controller. Figure 9.9 shows two possible interactions in a VR scene.

Figure 9.7

After opening an Unreal VR template project with the plugin included, the External Vis Actor appears in the Unreal Editor and can be dragged into the scene.

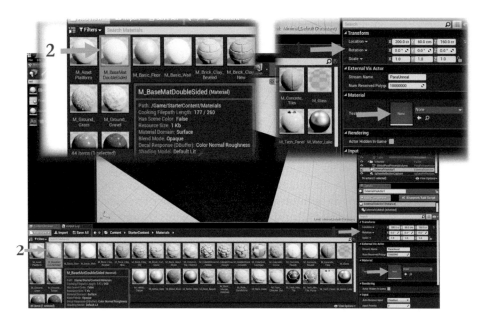

Figure 9.8

The External Vis Actor should be scaled appropriately at (1), the M_BaseMatDoubleSided material can be copied from the plugin content folder and selected using (2), and that material can then be dropped onto the actor in (3).

Figure 9.9

The first two images show the mechanism of grabbing an object and placing it at a new position. The third image shows geometry clipping in action, using a sphere shape to clip away an area around the hand.

9.8 Integration into Other SciVis Tools

The ParaView-Unreal bridge demonstrates an automatic process to send arbitrary geometry to an Unreal VR scene from within ParaView. In the future, it would be beneficial for the area of scientific visualization if any arbitrary scientific visualization tool or pipeline could send its geometry over to an Unreal VR scene. Therefore, the sourcecode of the ParaView plugin contains a header and implementation file that allows anyone to create a bridge between their favorite visualization tool and the Unreal Engine. These files define the class `ExternalVisBridge`, which provides a shared memory connection with the Unreal VR scene and the convenience functions to send geometry and other data.

The process that `ExternalVisBridge` follows for sending user data to Unreal VR is summarized by Listing 9.1. Upon creation of a class instance, the necessary shared resources are created with "`OpenStream`." Before the user can transfer data, the application has to request ownership over the shared memory block to communicate with Unreal VR, as only one instance of the same application may be connected to the Unreal VR scene at a time. This is done with the function "`GrabOwnership`". Once ownership over the communication channel has been obtained, the shared buffer has to be free for writing, which is tested by calling `StartProduce()`. At that point, writing to the shared buffer can start.

Listing 9.1. Pseudo Code demonstrating the use of `ExternalVisBridge`.

```
void main()
{
  //Create an instance of ExternalVisBridge
  externalVisBridge = new ExternalVisBridge;

  //This initializes the shared memory resources.
  externalVisBridge->OpenStream();

  //Make sure no two applications are communicating
  //with Unreal at the same time, and,
  //wait until there is space to fill the shared buffer.
  //(use "false" for non-blocking call)
  if externalVisBridge->GrabOwnership()
      && externalVisBridge->StartProduce(true) {
    for every geometry {
      if added or updated {
        //Request a geometry data for the specified actor/section,
        //which allocates sufficient memory for the requested number
        //of vertices (with requested attributes),
        //indices and texels
        ExternalVisGeomData* geomData =
            externalVisBridge->ProduceGeomData(actorId, sectionId,
            numVertices, AF_NORMALS | AF_TEXCOORDS,
            numIndices, texWidth, texHeight);

        //Copy actual vertex, index and texel data over to the
        //shared memory pointer to by geomData
        if geomData {
          geomData->TexFilter = TF_NEAREST;
          geomData->TexAddressX = TA_CLAMP;
          geomData->TexAddressY = TA_CLAMP;
          memcpy(geomData->FirstIndex(), userIndices,
              geomData->IndexSize() * numIndices);
          memcpy(geomData->FirstTexel(), userTexture,
              geomData->TexelSize() * texWidth * texHeight);
          memcpy(geomData->FirstVertex(AF_POSITION), userVerts,
              geomData->VertexSize(AF_POSITION) * numVertices);
          //Do a similar copy while replacing AF_POSITION with
          //AF_NORMALS and AF_TEXCOORDS
```

```
        }
    } else {
        //Send a request via shared memory to erase geometry
        //referenced by actorId and sectionId.
        ExternalVisGeomData* geomData =
            externalVisBridge->ProduceEmptyGeomData(actorId, sectionId);
    }
}

    //Explicitly tell ExternalVisBridge that the current batch of
    //geometries have been copied to shared memory. This makes the
    //buffer available for Unreal to be read.
    externalVisBridge->EndProduce()
}

//Destroy the ExternalVisBridge instance,
//which closes all handles to shared resources.
//The shared resources may or may not be destroyed,
//based on whether any other process is still using them.
delete externalVisBridge;
}
```

The process of copying data is fairly simple: for every geometry to be created or updated, request an "ExternalVisGeomData" structure using "ProduceGeomData", which reserves part of shared memory and returns a pointer towards it. The request is initiated by providing the number of vertices, indices, and texture size, along with the required vertex attributes, which together define the size of the reserved shared memory. The structure is initialized with an actor id and section id to identify what has to be updated on the Unreal side.

The actor id and section id passed along with the ExternalVisGeomData structure are chosen by the user application itself, and can be any arbitrary value. Usually every different chunk of geometry has a unique section id, and the actor id is chosen based on which geometries should be grouped within the same Unreal actor, as explained in Section 9.6. If a certain actor or section is sent over that does not exist in Unreal, a new one is automatically created by the Unreal plugin. For future updates to the geometry, the same actor and section id have to be used in order for the geometry to be replaced correctly in Unreal.

After creation of the ExternalVisGeomData structure, the vertex, index and texture data still have to be copied to shared memory manually. To this end, one can retrieve the "FirstVertex", "FirstIndex" and "FirstTexel" pointers, into which all vertices, indices, or texels can be copied contiguously. All vertex attributes, indices, and texels have to adhere to a strict format, which is outlined in the ExternalVisBridge header file. Along with the data, some vertex and texture properties can be passed along, such as the texture filter and addressing functions.

To remove a geometry call "ProduceEmptyGeomData" instead of "ProduceGeomData", with the actor and section id of the geometry to be removed. No further data has to be filled into the ExternalVisGeomData structure that the function returns.

Once the batch of geometries is copied to shared memory, calling "EndProduce" makes the shared memory section available for reading by the Unreal plugin.

Not all data that is communicated from a scientific visualization application to Unreal necessarily has to be transferred via shared memory. Examples of this are plenty: one could wish to change Unreal graphics settings from outside the Unreal application, trigger an animation sequence, or play certain sound effects. Many of those commands do not involve much data and the requirement for asynchronous resource updates on the Unreal side. Even more importantly, this also pertains to commands issued from Unreal to the scientific visualization application. Examples there include the specification of a position in 3D space to generate new streamlines, controlling replay of a timeseries dataset, or enabling certain pipeline filters.

The Unreal-ParaView bridge contains an example of a TCP/IP-based communication channel for the utilities mentioned above. Due to the application-specific nature of such communication, this feature has not yet been fleshed out, and will not be described in detail in this chapter. However, it would be quite simple to use the communication channel to achieve the goals listed above. The files "vtkPVExternalVisCommunicator.h" in ParaView and "ExternalVisCommunicator.h" in the Unreal plugin can be inspected to find out how the communication channel can be set up.

9.9 Limits on Performance and Data Sizes

Sections 9.4 and 9.5 showed how the Unreal VR plugin is able to maintain a 90 Hz rendering loop while transmitting geometry data from ParaView and updating graphics resources within Unreal. Even though it decreases rendering stalls, there is still a number of performance bottlenecks in the execution of the application.

For one, the number of static polygons that can be rendered at 90 Hz in an Unreal VR environment is bounded to around 15 million on a single GTX 1080. While it is possible to dynamically update a full 15 million polygon geometry, it requires multiple frames to send all data over the PCIe bus. Within scenes that are not expensive to render, 1–2 million polygons per frame can be transferred before it starts to impact the framerate. That means it takes roughly 10 frames of latency for the full geometry to become visible in the VR scene. The more complex a scene becomes to render, the longer the latency, as the PCIe transfers and the rendering still happen synchronously on the driver level.

Furthermore, there is a limit on how fast ParaView updates its geometry for every step in a time-series dataset. This limits the frequency at which ParaView can send updated geometry to the Unreal VR scene. Naively, ParaView loads the geometry anew from disk each timestep, but this can be mitigated by inserting a "Temporal Cache" filter below the geometry output. Once a timestep has been processed, this filter stores the result in memory for the next time the timestep is loaded. Even with such an optimization in place and some customizations to prevent ParaView from rendering its data when the Unreal VR application is active, ParaView is only able to update timeseries data for timesteps consisting of 1–2 million polygons at around 20 Hz, using a typical 3.5 GHz Intel Haswell desktop processor.

9.10 Conclusion and Future Work

The ParaView-Unreal bridge provides a low-cost opportunity for integration of the latest VR rendering techniques into scientific visualization pipelines. It also opens up an easy-to-use workflow for prototyping different visualization and interaction strategies in a VR environment. This is of much use to many branches of research that require the enhanced depth perception of VR and could benefit from the improved rendering quality offered by the game engine. However, due to the single-workstation constraint, the bridge is not yet usable for visualization in most large-data HPC use-cases.

One possible way to resolve this could be to develop a multi-node Unreal rendering backend for visualization of larger datasets. While this would certainly enable rasterization rendering of larger datasets, it is costly to develop, and it is not yet clear how the solution would handle the large latencies of rendered frames coming back from the HPC system. Given the interface of the bridge, it should not be a lot of effort to make it work across a range of other scientific visualization tools in the near future, such as VMD or VisIt. However, these packages often benefit from rendering techniques that are different from rasterization, like raytracing and volume rendering. Such techniques are less efficient for VR, as they often have a somewhat lower baseline performance and can therefore not meet the 90 Hz refresh rate requirement.

Even though other rendering techniques may be hard to achieve for a VR use-case, there should still be an effort to include them in order for VR to become more mainstream in scientific visualization. The reason other rendering techniques are so useful for scientific visualization is manifold: raytracing can provide more insight into data by a more natural support of global lighting techniques, which increases the user's perception of shape for complex geometries. Also, as datasets get larger, these complex geometries may even be more efficient to render with a raytracing method than using rasterization. Then, there will be a great need for rendering transparent geometry and especially volume data. While the latter requires a rendering method that quickly gets too expensive for higher levels of detail in VR, the former is challenging as well. Rasterization of transparent geometry requires considerable effort to sort rendering primitives (whether triangles or pixels) to correctly render the image. While it may be possible to break up geometry automatically in ways to support this, it will still have a negative impact on the performance of transferring dynamic geometry into a VR scene. Lastly, scientific visualization sometimes requires specialized shading routines and materials, which may not be easy to replicate in the model employed by the Unreal engine. The developer will have to perform a custom translation from one rendering pipeline into another, which requires a large investment of resources. It would be beneficial if all these techniques could just simply be combined with the rasterization that is provided by the Unreal Engine, instead of replicating the benefits of one method into another in a less-than-ideal form.

An important part of the bridge that has only briefly been touched on in Section 9.8, is communication from Unreal back into the ParaView. A fundamental goal of the bridge is for the user to be able to efficiently perform certain actions in the VR environment that they are familiar with in ParaView as well. Examples include control over how to play time-series datasets, inserting streamlines and changing isosurface contours. It is important that these operations are not performed natively in the Unreal application, but that communication with the ParaView application exposes such functionality, along with any other functionality that the SciVis software offers.

Another area in which future development of the bridge could take place is easy collaboration in VR, especially concerning manipulation of datasets. The ease of collaboration enabled by CAVE-style VR systems is still one of their major selling points, and hard to currently match with consumer VR.

References

[Epic Games 2017]

Epic Games (2017) Unreal Basic Scene and Lighting Tutorial: Lighting Quick Start Guide. Accessed October 4, 2017. https://docs.unrealengine.com/latest/INT/Engine/Rendering/LightingAndShadows/QuickStart/index.html

[Looman 2016]

Looman, Tom Blog: VR Template Guide for Unreal Engine 4, Sept. 9, 2016. http://tomlooman.com/vrtemplate/

[Martin et al. 2016]

Martin, Ken, David DeMarle, Sankhesh Jhaveri, and Utkarsh Ayachit (2016) Blog: Taking ParaView into Virtual Reality, Sept. 22, 2016. https://blog.kitware.com/taking-paraview-into-virtual-reality/

[O'Leary et al. 2017]

O'Leary, Patrick, Sankhesh Jhaveri, Aashish Chaudhary, William Sherman, Ken Martin, David Lonie, Eric Whiting, James Money, and Sandy McKenzie (2017) Enhancements to VTK enabling scientific visualization in immersive environments. In *Proceedings of IEEE Virtual Reality (VR)*, Los Angeles, CA: IEEE, pp. 186–194.

[Rajlich 1995]

Rajlich, Paul J. (1995) An object oriented approach to developing visualization tools portable across desktop and virtual environments, *MS Thesis*, Computer Science, University of Illinois at Urbana-Champaign. http://visbox.com/prajlich/T/bigT.html

SECTION III
Interaction

10

Brownboxing
The Secret to Rapid VR Prototyping

Shawn Patton
Principal Game Designer at Schell Games

10.1 Introduction

Creating a Virtual Reality (VR) game or experience can be a large undertaking. In the consumer marketplace, VR is a new medium and expectations can vary widely. As a developer, production costs can quickly balloon past original estimates as the depth of the interactions required to maintain presence quickly eat through resources. To an investor faced with increasing costs, confused and cautious consumers, and a small install base, VR is a risk.

So what is a fledgling industry to do?

Well, first, be confident in VR's innate ability to transport a person to other worlds. Virtual Reality may be new to the mainstream consumer, but it has been proving its power and allure in smaller venues for decades. Once people try "good" VR they are hooked; now we simply need to provide that content. You would not be reading this book if you did not believe that.

Second, know that you will be able to employ tools to bring the cost of development time down. That is what this chapter is all about. Fast iteration is the key to making great experiences and games in general—with VR content this is doubly so. In VR development, physical prototyping is the third dimension to paper prototyping's two. Just as paper prototyping speeds up creation of 2D games, physical prototyping is the closest analog to VR we have. What better way to create physical prototypes than with cardboard? So come with me as we dive into the world of brownboxing: creating physical prototypes with cardboard (Figure 10.1).

10.2 Benefits

We will start by discussing the benefits of this, perhaps unorthodox, approach. After all, if you are going to convince your manager or producer that setting up a "box fort" in the office is worthwhile, you had better have good reasons.

1. **Leverage a Low-tech Solution to a High-tech Problem**

    Having naïve people play your game, or playtesting, is key to making it the best it can be. You will learn so much. What are they thinking? Why are they thinking it? When and why are they frustrated? Learning these lessons as quickly as possible as early as possible is the goal of brownboxing. You can brownbox a 3D set or a key interaction with no specialized skills, no engineers, no artists—just some cardboard, tape, and relevant props you find lying around. This method keeps other team members free to work on the underlying systems. Or, if they are not so engaged, they can join in on the crafting fun. Creating a brownbox setup together

Figure 10.1

Henry inspects a brownbox after completing his playtest.

can be a great way for a new team to get to know each other, and when lessons are learned by the whole team at once, they are that much more powerful.

As an example of this phenomenon, while building a phone circuit board interaction for *I Expect You to Die*, I discovered that the location we had imagined for the interaction would be too far from the phone itself. Working with one of the artists, we started to move the interaction closer but got called away for a meeting or some other interruption. When I returned I found another artist and our tech lead had finished it off with some details I would not have contemplated but that tied it all together well. This cooperative building with physical materials is refreshing in an industry where most of our work is done on a screen and, well, doesn't involve duct tape.

2. **Quickly Define Spheres of Interaction and Attention Draws**

Early in the process of creating new VR content, be it an experience or a game, you need to clearly understand what your player can, and will, reach for. Certainly this problem changes based on whether you are room scale, have in-world movement, are in a cockpit, have full 6 DOF position tracking, 3-DOF orientation-only tracking, or are further limited by the tracking technology (e.g. is turning around a problem?), but the question remains. Players are going to want to grab some things (while surprising you by not grabbing others) and will generally explore their surroundings. Brownboxing is perfect for quickly testing and understanding player expectations in this sphere of interaction.

Having worked on the spatial puzzler *Water Bears VR*, the escape-the-room puzzler *I Expect You to Die*, the RTS *Frostbound VR*, and the creative builder and puzzler *Lego Brickheadz Builder VR*, my direct experience leans more toward stationary puzzlers, but one can anticipate that there are lessons to be learned for most VR experiences through this brownbox approach. Certainly it makes sense for room scale and games with cockpits, but even titles based around warping movement have key set pieces that can be mocked up in our world and thus explored quickly. Once mocked up, take particular note of where your players look first; what do they gravitate toward or away from? The player's attention is prized above all in a medium where you can look anywhere, so understanding early what draws the player will be advantageous.

3. **Rapidly Iterate**

As soon as you start putting naïve people in your brownbox world you will find aspects you want to change. And you can! Easily. Need to add an in-world sign describing a weird interaction? Grab a marker! Need to move that console a foot to the left? Pick it up and move it! That cabinet should open to the left instead of the right so it doesn't block that indicator light, right? Move that duct tape hinge and you're good! Every creative process chases the dream of rapid iteration, but few come as close as brownboxing. Yes, there are limitations, and we will discuss those in the next section, but for now revel in your freedom to iterate quickly! Tear that piece off, cut a hole there—you can always tape it back up.

Have a knick-knack on your desk that kind of looks like what you might model later? Bring it over. Need a sound effect for when that door opens? Your phone has a voice memo app and your voice has all the sound effects you could need, so get recording. Embrace your inner toddler: build with blocks, imagine and make real.

It is quite freeing once you get started. Worried what your manager or producer will say? Show them the quick progress you've made, the time shaved off the schedule of three other employees because of the issues you discovered and squashed, or, failing all that, show them this chapter; I'll talk to them for you (Figures 10.2–10.4).

10.3 Limitations of Brownboxing

Yes, there are some; it is not all spray adhesive and glitter. Only by understanding the limitations will you maximize the results of your brownbox building.

1. **Requires Physical Space**

    It should not be surprising that building an interactive space out of cardboard takes up room, but choosing that space is where it all starts, so let's think it

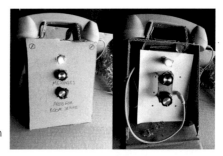

Figure 10.2

A phone created by a group effort and then iterated on.

Figure 10.3

Lucy inspects her immediate surroundings.

Figure 10.4

A newspaper went through many iterations to get the text just right.

through. Every office and workspace is different, but a single cardboard prototype of a device or interactable should be able to fit in some corner somewhere. Keep in mind lighting conditions, general employee traffic patterns, and noise levels when you are choosing a spot. You don't want an overly public location because you don't want to distract anyone while conducting playtests. A conference room would probably be the best space but those are often hard to find—especially for any significant duration.

Also, while room scale is doable, creating multiple rooms within a building (such as would be traversed by warping) would be problematic. Where brownboxing primarily shines over its cousin "whiteboxing" is in creating an interaction rich space around the participant. So find an out-of-the-way corner, grab some cardboard, and get to work! (Whiteboxing is a stage of desktop game development where basic in-engine levels are created from cubes and some simple models with flat single color textures—i.e. the world-scape is mostly white. It is usually the first time people can play a new game or experience.)

2. **Difficult to Simulate Magic and Projectiles**

In *I Expect You to Die*, you play as a late 1950s era secret agent, trying to complete missions while, well, not dying. You are aided by telekinetic implants that allow you to pick up and manipulate far away objects via telekinetic beams (TK beams). This conceit dates back to the original prototypes which were mouse-based (a control scheme the game still supports to this day). You have an aiming reticle you can move left/right and up/down with the mouse, and it auto-picks depth. When you click to pick objects up, you can use the mouse wheel to "reel" them in or out. This also allows for the game to have room-size areas easily supported on non-room-size VR platforms, as well as being darn convenient in general. (Trust me, I miss it while playing other games.) Even with hand input we support the TK beams, and brownboxing TK-related puzzles is difficult. You can try to describe and entice players to try out the ability, but it's just not the same. As a result, when testing I make mental concessions and encourage the player in certain ways that I would never do in a normal playtest. Then I need to account for that when assessing the strengths and weaknesses of the level and revisit the issue during the subsequent whitebox testing phase.

Similarly, when players need to shoot something, well, you kind of just need to wing it. Do you err on the side of them always being awesome shots? Probably, but your game may call for a different approach; either way, be aware of the shortcomings and you'll be fine.

3. **False Results Due to Level of Polish**

Probably the easiest trap to fall into when judging what draws players' attention with a brownbox is that interactable items tend to have more love put into them than non-interactable ones. For example, when an entire console is brown cardboard and there are two nifty red buttons inserted into it, those will both stand out and draw the eye. When the final game model is made, will both still stand out, or is one lost in that freshly baked shadow? The opposite is true as well; a handle that would be obvious in a real piece of furniture tends to blend in when everything is cardboard. You might find you have to "art up" a larger area to make a key piece of information blend in (Figures 10.5–10.7).

Figure 10.5

Sometimes a folding sound-dampening wall presents itself as useful. And yes, the ladder was part of it.

Figure 10.6

The author facilitating the use of telekinesis to bring a box over.

Figure 10.7

The inside of the engine had to have extra bits added in to make the functional parts not pop quite as much.

10.4 Practical Process

We have talked about the pros and cons (and how to mitigate them), but let us talk now a bit about the practical process of building and some tips and tricks that may be helpful along the way.

1. **Set Clear Goals**

    Whether you are creating a single room experience, a multi-dungeon plat-former, or something in between, I am confident brownboxing can speed up the early stages of your VR development, but you have got to go into it with some clear goals. How will a player explore Room A? What will a player try to do with Device B? When they hear Audio C, will they grab Doodad D or reach for Thing-a-ma-jig E? These are great questions for brownboxing.

That said, you will also get answers to questions you never even thought to ask, such as: Do we need to make the metal tray cover ricochet bullets back at the assassin? (Apparently the answer to that is a resounding yes, because the majority of players think that should work!) So set your goals and questions ahead of time, but also have a broad enough information gathering process to catch unexpected diamonds.

2. **Collect Materials Ahead of Time**

Since the first brownbox on the original *IEYTD*, Schell Games has kept a stockpile of cardboard and odds and ends lying around. Big box stores now crush, horde, and recycle their refrigerator boxes, so don't count on them being available. However, with the dominance of online shopping and meal kit delivery services (meal kit boxes are really nicely sized), a quick office email should net you more than enough raw material if everyone chips in.

Items such as PVC tubes of various thicknesses go a long way as well as tiny LED party favors and other knick knacks that can be scrounged or purchased from your local dollar store (and I'm talking a true dollar store, not one of those "around a dollar" stores).

3. **Location**

I touched on it before, but the best location for a brownbox has as many of the following qualities as possible:

A. Away from people trying to work/prying eyes
B. Lighting that can be controlled
C. Enough space for the finished product and, ideally, storage for leftovers/scraps
D. Power outlets (for lamps and things)
E. Relatively distraction-free but with the ability to make noise when necessary (see A)

4. **Construction tips**

• I know you want to use duct tape for everything, but know that if you hang the load wrong or your brownbox is in direct sunlight, you will find structural integrity failing after a day or so. Pens, PVC tubes, and random bolts often make much better hinges.

• Hot glue is your friend for anything you really want to stay where you put it. It also peels off of most painted drywall & plaster easily, though please do a spot test first. It also sticks to most masonry if you're working in one of those fancy new old-exposed-brick offices.

• Thick markers are always better than thin. Think about easy-to-read labels and signage. Save yourself some hassle and spring for a couple wide-tip markers. Red and black should be enough. If you need finer text, go with the next tip:
  – Printed labels—adhered with spray adhesive or rolled scotch tape is key. (I must have gone through six iterations on one printed prop to get the wording exactly right.)
  – Think outside the box. We used a folding sound dampening wall on wheels for a large part of one brownbox we made. Don't be afraid to put a folding table or lamp with a few modifications in. Let your imagination go wild.

5. **Some Details Matter, Some Don't**

When we talk about where to spend your time budget while brownboxing, it's in the details. While you want to avoid the false positives described above, you also need to make sure certain things read well and that you're providing as much feedback to the player as possible. That way, if it works for the player in brownbox and the feedback only gets better in the final game, you will know you're designing a good experience. For example, have a bell that goes off to get the player's attention, put a flashing LED on a console that you stop when they do the correct thing, and record sounds or scratch dialogue on your phone for those key moments. As a rule, if you are about to spend some art love on an aspect of your brownbox, ask if it is providing valuable feedback to the player. If the answer is yes, go for it (Figures 10.8 and 10.9).

Figure 10.8

A pile of cardboard and a bunch of random stuff is key.

Figure 10.9

An LED for attention, a car jack for heft, and a bell for arrival feedback are examples of details that will really sell your brownbox.

10.5 Playtesting

After a couple days (maximum) you should have something you can begin testing with. That rough layout will serve to discover so many things from the first run-through that you will be altering it soon enough anyway. Once you have spent a day or so preparing this awesome brownbox experience to test a naïve person with—how do you go about it? First, find a person not on your immediate team, ideally in your target demographic, and find a good time for them to play. Book the appointment and make sure you have the following figured out:

1. **The Script**

   After all the brainstorming has run its course, start by condensing all the ideas into a player experience document. That is to say, from the player's perspective, what they experience. From that create a brownbox script. Record any information needed to seed the player to give every player the same experience. Also, map out the most likely side branches and deviations from the "best path" through the game and how they should be handled. If you will need helpers to "trigger events" or play audio, consider making special versions of the script just for them or at least highlight their parts. This document will change very quickly the first few playtests as you hammer out the largest issues, so have your red pen handy.

2. **Your Role**

   The role you play as brownbox moderator is akin to a D&D game master or improv actor. You need to know when and how to present new information, what to describe in more detail, when to hold your tongue and let things play out, and you need to do it all in real time. The first couple run-throughs will be rough, but that's all part of the process of making interactive content. At first your brownbox world will be pretty broken, so don't hesitate to make big changes quickly or improvise on the spot. It is better to get at the heart of what your guest wanted to do and what they expected would happen than to shut them down because the script doesn't support it. Once you get the experience to a state where a player can run through it start to finish, then lock it in.

   Now, go make changes and print out a new script or record new audio prompts for those contingencies you just discovered. Make any "permanent" structural changes to boxes that need to be made. As things progress, when you test new players, try to stick more closely to the script and say and do the same actions the same way each time. Pretend you are the computer AI, taking in player input as actions and spitting out what your internal algorithm tells you to. Have no fear, you will change it again later, but try to get at least four solid playthroughs this way.

3. **Guest expectations**

   A few notes on guests for brownboxing. They probably cannot be people off the street, not yet at any rate. These should be developers not on your team who have good imaginations. As host, make it clear that they are helping you; if anything is confusing or frustrating it's your fault, not theirs. Let them know that the brownbox nature will necessitate you having to describe some things or usher them through some interactions. Ask them to speak their thoughts out loud as they play, asking for clarification when they need it and generally keeping you in

Figure 10.10

Tom contemplates his options as the game master waits patiently off to the side.

the loop of what they are thinking. Not just useful for note taking, this running commentary will make clear whether they are jumping to incorrect conclusions because of the rough cardboard setup or because of flawed or faulty game design.

4. **Data Collection Methodology**

If you can, it is nice to have someone taking notes while you host. You can still jot down notes privately yourself in the script, but it doesn't hurt to have two records. Video can be good to have, either to show the team later if they cannot be there for the playthroughs or as reference. Even if you don't end up using much of it, there will probably be a couple of times when you are glad you had it.

Then there are post-playtest questions. The goal is to get unadulterated feelings from the testers. You do not want to lead them in any way, but you want to find out what they were thinking. Obviously every experience is different, but I highly recommend the following four questions for games in general, but VR specifically:

1. What was the most frustrating moment or aspect of what you just played?
2. What was your favorite moment or aspect of what you just played?
3. Was there anything you wanted to do that you couldn't?
4. If you had a magic wand to wave, and you could change, add, or remove anything from the experience, what would it be?

I ask them in that order, every time, and write down what they say, in order. You might see some overlap in responses, but that's ok, that just means it was really important to them. Most of the time you will see different answers for number 3 ("Wanted") and number 4 ("Wand"), which is good intel. Also, you will be able to compare answers from different players who played the same version of the brownbox. Recognizing frustration trends and acting to fix them is obviously key. However, calling out favorite moments and capitalizing on them by putting in more content "like that" in a polish phase later can turn an ok experience into a great one (Figure 10.10).

10.6 Conclusion

Virtual Reality is here to stay. It is a flourishing medium that will take its place next to PC, console, and mobile. As developers it is our job to create compelling content for this growing medium in a cost-effective manner. Making fun interactions that have depth and preserve immersion takes iteration, and iteration takes time. Brownboxing can be an efficient first step to creating a fun VR space. The information learned helps inform the next steps, typically the in-engine, roughly outlined, whitebox stage of development. So grab some cardboard, tape, and markers and start making the future of interactive content!

11

Bi-Manual Interaction for Manipulation, Volume Selection, and Travel

Using the Leap Motion, Game Controllers and Mobile Devices

Elliot Hunt, Rajiv Khadka, and Amy C. Banić
University of Wyoming

In this Gem, you will learn how to set up a basic bi-manual (two-handed) interaction, specifically through object manipulation and selection/manipulation of a selection volume. These techniques will be demonstrated using a LEAP Motion Hand Tracker, standard game controllers, and Android-based mobile devices. The programming code in this chapter has been tested with Unity (v 5.6.1f1), using MonoDevelop (v 6.1.2.44) and Android Studio (v 2.3.1), though your solution is not limited to this compiler or Unity version.

11.1 Part I: Getting Started with Unity and Leap Motion Hand Tracking

To get started, in this part we will build a Unity scene that incorporates the finger skeletal information provided by the LEAP finger tracking device from Leap Motion. With the finger tracking, users will be able to manipulate objects in a virtual environment using their bare hands. The basics learned in this part will serve as a foundation to learn how to manipulate a selection volume to select multiple objects or data points. These examples provide details on manipulation through specific translation, rotation, and scaling tasks.

11.1.1 Step 1: Set Up a Basic Unity Scene

Set up a basic Unity scene (see Unity help files for basic setup) with a plane and a few 3D objects in the scene to manipulate. Simply right click within the hierarchy and find "Plane" under the "3D Object" sub-menu as shown in Figure 11.1. As part of a basic scene, we will add a plane to serve as the 'floor' of the environment (should you want to add gravity to the environment). When objects are picked up by a user and dropped, then the objects can be stopped by a *"Plane,"* instead of falling forever. The values of X: 0.0, Y: 0.2, and Z: −5.0 were used to position the camera at the edge of the plane. Add a few 3D objects in your environment, for this Gem we added a cube to interact with and manipulate. Navigate to **Assets → LeapMotion → Modules → InteractionEngine → Examples → InteractionObjects → Prefabs** and there is a list of several objects that can be put into the scene. Pick one and drag it to the hierarchy. In this Gem the cube was positioned at (X: 0.0, Y: 0.4, Z: −5.0). Let's name the scene; we call ours *"GemScene."*

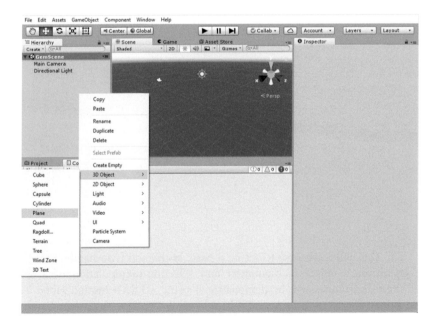

Figure 11.1

Create a plane object by right-clicking in the hierarchy. This plane will serve as our floor.

11.1.2 Step 2: Import LEAP Assets

Now that we have a basic scene to work with, we can import the LEAP's core assets. But before you unbox that LEAP, we have some downloading to do. On LEAP Motion's website, http://leapmotion.com, download the latest drivers (this GEM uses 3.2.0 Orion). Find your way to the developer section of LEAP's website and download Unity Assets for Leap Motion (4.2.0) as well as the "Leap Motion Interaction Engine" (1.0.1) Module. Install those drivers, restart if necessary, and re-open the Unity project. Drag and drop your downloaded Core Assets file and Interaction Engine into the Assets folder within the Project window and the files will be imported. Alternatively, you can right click within the Project window, go to Import Package, then to Import Custom Package, navigate to your downloads, and select the "*Leap Motion*" package.

11.1.3 Step 3: Adding Virtual Hands

Right click on our scene and, if you haven't already, save it! Then right click again, and click "**Unload Scene.**" As you navigate through the folders in the Project window, you'll find within **LeapMotion** → **Core** → **Scenes,** five example scenes provided by LEAP with basic implementations of the LEAP Motion Core Package. To try any of these out, double-click on each demo scene, one at a time, in the prefab assets folder. You can switch between scenes in this way to view LEAP's example scenes. There are examples for both Augmented Reality and for use with a Virtual Reality headset within the Scenes folder. We will be modeling ours after the "*Leap_Hands_Demo_Desktop*" scene. The Virtual Reality Headset implementation with a LEAP is simple, and will be explained at the end of this section. For now, however, let's return to our scene and implement the LEAP and Virtual Hands.

Several example implementations of LEAP's core asset package are provided within the core asset package itself. You can find those examples as "Scenes" located in the Assets/Scenes/directory (Figure 11.2).

To add LEAP support to your unity scene, first make sure to return to you "*GemScene*" scene, then select **LeapMotion** → **Core** → **Prefabs** within the Project window. Within the Prefabs folder, should be a Unity prefab asset named "*LeapHandController.*" Drag this into the Hierarchy and release it on top of our "*Main Camera*" object and it will become a child of "*Main Camera.*" If you are familiar with scene graphs, you will be aware that the child of an object within Unity inherits many features of its parent, including any real-time updates to position information. From now on, when and if we move Main Camera, "*LeapHandController*" will move with it. The opposite is not true, however, as we can still move "*LeapHandController*" independently of (relative to) its parent.

At this point, plug in the LEAP device. However, the physical hands in the real world will not yet be associated with any virtual objects. Let's fix this! In order for the LEAP to correctly access a set of virtual hand models (which we will add in our scene now), we must start by adding an empty object. Right click within the *Hierarchy*, select *Create Empty*, and a new object will appear within the Hierarchy. This object will not have a visible representation within the scene and is best thought of as merely a container to hold objects. Name it anything you'd like—this Gem uses the name "*HandFolder*". Now, it is time to add the virtual hand models that LEAP has included (though you can import other hand models from the Unity Asset store). Drag *CapsuleHand_L* and *CapsuleHand_R* to the top of "*HandFolder*" to place them as children of "HandFolder."

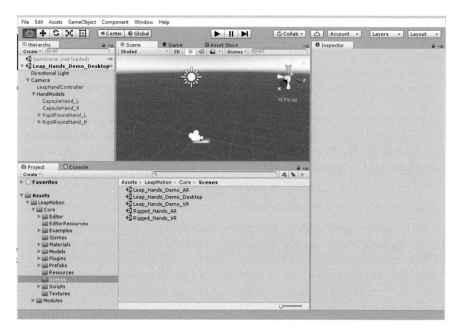

Figure 11.2

Five example scenes are available under the "Scenes" folder in the Leap Motion Unity package.

Now, select "*LeapHandController*" and in the Inspector panel, scroll to the bottom. You should find a section titled "*Hand Pool (Script).*" Under Models Parent, drag the Empty Object—"*HandFolder*"—to this box. Now the Hand Controller knows where to find the models! Change the *Model Pool's* Size value to 1 and drag "*CapsuleHand_L*" to the *Left Model* field, and "*CapsuleHand_R*" to the Right Model field from the hierarchy. Make sure '*Is Enabled*' is checked, as well as '*Can Duplicate,*' and rename the Group Name. In the interest of modelling our controller after the "*Leap_Hands_Demo_Desktop*" example, above "*Hand Pool (Script)*" in "*Leap Service Provider (Script),*" check the box next to "*Override Device Type*" and make sure "*Override Device Type With*" is set to "*Peripheral.*" By the time you're done, your screen should look like Figure 11.3.

You should now be able to plug in the LEAP motion, hit the play button, and control the Virtual Hands with your real ones!

11.1.4 Setting-up Physics for the Hands

Adding physics attributes to the hands allows us to pick up objects and interact with them within Unity. In reality, each of your hands is controlling two hands: A visual hand—i.e., the Capsule Hands—and another (invisible) hand that occupies the same space. This second hand—the Physics Hand—is what detects collisions and lets us pick up objects.

In LEAP's interaction engine (version 1.0.1), the physics hands are handled internally, so all you need to do is create an *Interaction Manager* object as well as *Interaction* objects. Navigate to **Assets → LeapMotion → InteractionEngine → Prefabs** and drag the

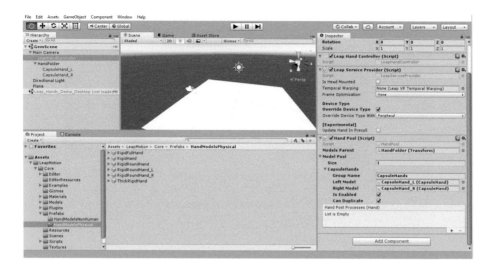

Figure 11.3

Using the Inspector panel to fill in the proper values in the "HandModelsVisible" object.

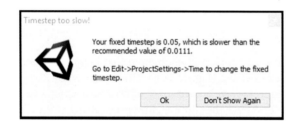

Figure 11.4

For HMD virtual reality experiences, 90 Hz (.0111 ms/frame) is the modern standard visual rendering rate.

"*Interaction Manager*" object into your hierarchy window. Press play—you may receive a warning about your Timestep at this point that looks like Figure 11.4.

Simply follow the instructions and change the associated value. This is due to modern VR headsets that operate at a much higher refresh rate rather than a standard monitor [Oculus VR 2018; Niehorster et al. 2017]. *Tip*: There is also the potential that a second error message relating to the gravity of the project being set too high will appear. This can safely be ignored and may be altered in future iterations of the *Interaction Engine*. Try pressing play again—everything should work this time!

11.1.5 Supporting Interaction with Objects

As you can see in Figure 11.5, there are three axes with arrows to shift the object's location—simply click and drag the Z-axis arrow to shift your cube to be roughly between the *Capsulehands* located on screen—i.e., to bring it within reach of the LEAP. Press the play button and experiment with using the LEAP to pick up the object you've created!

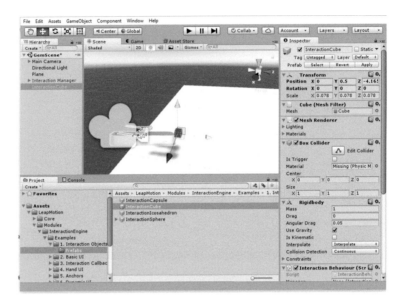

Figure 11.5

The arrows emanating from an object allow the developer to manipulate the object's location using the mouse. Here we bring an object to be within reach of the LEAP device.

There may be a strange clipping phenomenon that happens to both the virtual hands and the object as they intersect (Figure 11.6). This is caused by objects that are too near the camera. Unity cameras have a parameter of how near objects can be before they are "clipped" from view. To reduce the clipping, lower the setting of the Clipping Plane "*Near*" value, to perhaps 0.1 (default is 0.3 m). You can also turn off the forearm portion of your capsule hands. To remove them, find "*CapsuleHand_L*" and "*CapsuleHand_R*" in the Inspector and find the "*Show Arm*" checkbox, which you can toggle within the Inspector.

(a) (b)

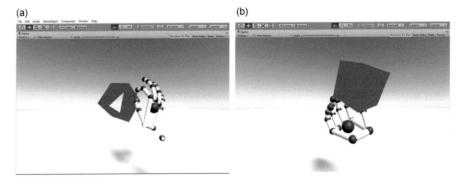

Figure 11.6

By default, objects are clipped (a) as they approach the camera (i.e. the user's eyes) within 30 cm. By decreasing the near clipping distance for the camera (b) the rendering can be improved.

11. Bi-Manual Interaction for Manipulation, Volume Selection, and Travel

11.2 Part II: Bi-Manual Object Manipulation

11.2.1 Step 1: Basics of Object Manipulation in Unity

We now explore the use of C# scripting to enable the manipulation of objects within the virtual world. Scripts are added to the objects in the scene. To add a script to the object you would like to modify (i.e., the cube in Figure 11.6), click on the object in the hierarchy panel and scroll to the bottom of its Inspector panel. At the bottom should be a button titled "*Add Component*"—click it. We're going to want to add a "*New Script,*" so scroll to the bottom of the new menu and click again. For this Gem, title the script "*Simple Grow Script.*" We'll be adding different versions of this script later. Double click on your script and it should open in a code editor. We prefer MonoDevelop—if MonoDevelop is not the default, you can change your default compiler by going to **Edit → Preferences → External Tools → External Script Editor** and select your compiler of choice.

Tip: It may also be worth considering updating your project to a more recent .Net Framework to reduce the number of build errors present. To do this in MonoDevelop, right click on your project(s), "*Assembly-CSharp*" and "*Assembly-CSharp-Editor*" in this case, select "*Options,*" then **Build → General.** Change "*Target framework*" to "*Mono/.NET 4.0*" as in Figure 11.7.

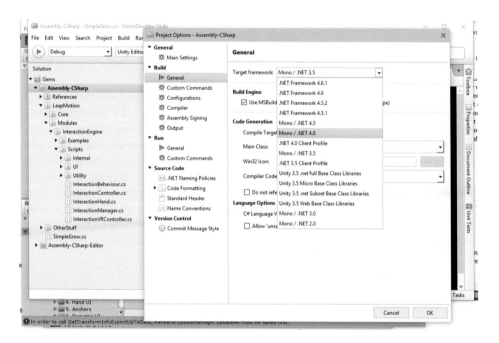

Figure 11.7

The target compiling system of your Unity project can be changed to "Mono/.NET 4.0", which enables you to compile your code using a MonoDevelop Project, a GNOME-based IDE primarily designed for C# and other .NET languages. (These examples have been tested on this framework, you may use another but we cannot guarantee these examples will compile without modification in that case.)

Creating a new script produces a default skeleton of the script's code (Listing 11.1):

Listing 11.1. The initial (skeletal) C# Unity script.

```csharp
using System.Collections;
using System.Collections.Generic;
using UnityEngine;

public class SimpleGrow : MonoBehaviour {

    // Use this for initialization
    void Start () {

    }

    // Update is called once per frame
    void Update () {

    }
}
```

Change `Update()` to the alternative `FixedUpdate()`, because `FixedUpdate()` is called more regularly than `Update()` and is beneficial for performing physics calculations. Next, we will implement the feature that uses the data from the LEAP controllers to manipulate objects in the scene. To do this we will use functions specific to the Unity API. (Of course, the specific syntax may change someday with future updates to Unity, much as updates to LEAP's interaction engine may alter the previous steps slightly, but the structure of the algorithm should remain.)

To manipulate the scale of an object we will use the *localScale* variable that is a part of the *Transform* class. This is connected to the *Scale* values as seen in the Inspector panel of Unity—with the script, we alter the values at runtime. (Note that one feature of Unity is that changes made during runtime are temporary, and revert back to the initial state when the execution ends.) The "*localScale*" is represented as a *Vector3* type with three float (real) values. To make an object that increases in size, we can continually increase these Vector3 values as exemplified in Listing 11.2. Unity C# scripts can implicitly use the "this" operator for components that are part of the object to which the script is attached. For example the "this." in Listing 11.2 is unnecessary—the "transform" component of the associated object implies it. However for clarity, it can be beneficial to include it nevertheless.

Listing 11.2. Change `Update()` to `FixedUpdate()` and increase the scale of the object.

```csharp
    // FixedUpdate is called regularly and roughly once per frame
    void FixedUpdate() {
        this.transform.localScale = transform.localScale + new Vector3(0.0005F, 0.0005F, 0.0005F);
    }
```

Note that the C# "+=" notation allows a value to be added-to a variable, so we can simplify our added line of code as this:

```csharp
        this.transform.localScale += new Vector3(0.0005F, 0.0005F, 0.0005F);
```

Press *control S* (^S)—or Command-S (⌘-S) on OS/X systems—to save your script and press the Play button in Unity—your interaction object should swell larger and larger! Larger numbers instead of 0.0005F, such as 0.001F, will make the cube grow faster, and each value can scale at an independent rate if you so choose.

You can also change the values of position (i.e. location) and orientation of the object in a similar way. Here are examples of code to do each of these actions, respectively:

```
this.transform.position += new Vector3(0.0005F, 0.0005F, 0.0005F);
```

Or change the position along each individual axis:

```
this.transform.position += new Vector3(0.0005F, 0.0F, 0.0F); // X axis
this.transform.position += new Vector3(0.0F, 0.0005F, 0.0F); // Y axis
this.transform.position += new Vector3(0.0F, 0.0F, 0.0005F); // Z axis
```

Example of how to change the orientation of the object:

```
// three values each represent a rotation angle for X,Y,Z axes respectively
this.transform.rotation += Quaternion.Euler(new Vector3(0.0005F,
    0.0005F, 0.0005F));
```

Example of how to change the orientation of the object local to its own axis:

```
// local object y axis
this.transform.Rotate(Vector3.up * rotationAngle, Space.self);
// local object x axis
this.transform.Rotate(Vector3.right * rotationAngle, Space.self);
// local object z axis
this.transform.Rotate(Vector3.forward * rotationAngle, Space.self);
```

To regulate rotation rate based on the framerate, be sure to add "* **Time**.deltaTime", for example:

```
this.transform.Rotate(Vector3.up*rotationAngle*Time.deltaTime,Space.self);
```

11.2.2 Step 2: Object Translation and Scaling Using Two Hands (Distance between the Two Hands)

In this step, you will learn to manipulate the size of the cube to correlate to the distance between the two hands. That is to say, no matter whether you are holding it or have it sitting on the ground, it will grow and shrink with every motion between your hands. A slight change in the code will enable change in position instead of scale. In step 3, you will learn a variation of this in which a user can use a pinch gesture to initiate the scaling. In step 4, you will add rotation.

Let's get started. To create a new script, right click on the old script within the inspector window and click Remove Component. Next, add a new script in the same way we did previously. We'll need to include LEAP's library for this script, thus in this script, under the other "using" statements, write "using Leap;". *Tip*: A list of classes that are within the LEAP API can be found on the Leap Motion webpage: https://developer.leapmotion.com/documentation/csharp/api/Leap_Classes.html

Remember to change Update() to FixedUpdate(). The Leap Motion sends information about every frame to its libraries for processing and to access this, we must create a controller object. The controller represents the physical leap controller and the data it sends every frame. Declare a controller within the fields section of our script so that update can access it and let's initialize it upon the object's initialization—within `Start();` (Listing 11.3).

Listing 11.3. An example implementation of a Leap Motion controller Unity C# script.

```
using Leap;      // Add this for access to LEAP Motion API
public class DirectGrow : MonoBehaviour {
    Controller controller; // Gives us data from the LEAP Controller.
    // Use this for initialization
    void Start() {
        controller = new Controller();
    }
    // Continues in Listing 11.4
```

For this to work in real time, we need to access each and every frame sent by the Leap controller—and we need each and every hand within that frame. Every update within our script should have hands present. We can do so with the following within `FixedUpdate();` It is best to make sure our controller is connected before we do anything with it. The following shows that we add both to `FixedUpdate()`:

Listing 11.4. In each frame, obtain the Leap Motion controller data via the LEAP API.

```
    void FixedUpdate() {
        if (controller.IsConnected) {
            // Gather a frame from LEAP controller with every update.
            Frame frame = controller.Frame();
        }
    }
}
```

Now, we need to access the information for each hand within a frame to calculate the distance between them. Thankfully, our controller's frames will each provide a list of hands that are detected—all we have to do is access them and create *Hand* objects.

```
        List<Hand> hands = frame.Hands;
        Hand firstHand = hands[0];
        Hand secondHand = hands[1];
```

Notice any problems? What if there is only one hand is on screen? Add a conditional ("if") statement to prevent unnecessary processing:

```
        if (frame.Hands.Count > 1) {
            List<Hand> hands = frame.Hands;
            Hand firstHand = hands[0];
            Hand secondHand = hands[1];
        }
```

The positioning of each part of the hand is stored as a vector—and for this particular script, we are going to tether everything to the positions of palms of the hands. We can use Unity's *DistanceTo()* function of a Vector to calculate it, as shown:

```
float distance;
distance = firstHand.PalmPosition.DistanceTo(secondHand.PalmPosition);
```

This distance is going to be a little much for our object—so we can use a factor value to change the ratio of object scaling verses the motion of the hands. At this point, the code will look like Listing 11.5.

Listing 11.5. The complete C# Script for changing the size of an object based on the distance between two LEAP-detected hands.

```
using System.Collections;
using System.Collections.Generic;
using UnityEngine;
using Leap;    // Add this for access to LEAP Motion API
public class DirectGrow : MonoBehaviour {
    Controller controller; //Gives us data from the LEAP Controller.

    // Perform initialization
    void Start() {
        controller = new Controller();
    }

    // FixedUpdate is called roughly once per frame
    void FixedUpdate() {
        if (controller.IsConnected) {
            // Gathers a frame from LEAP controller with every update.
            Frame frame = controller.Frame();
            if (frame.Hands.Count > 1) {
                //The two first hands in each frame.
                List<Hand> hands = frame.Hands;
                Hand firstHand = hands[0];
                Hand secondHand = hands[1];
                float distance;
                distance = firstHand.PalmPosition.DistanceTo(secondHand.PalmPosition);
                // distance between two hands' palms.
                distance = distance * 0.001F; //0.001F is a factor to adjust the
                                        //   distance to something more usable.
                // The scale of the object will always be related to the distance
                //   between a user's two palms.
                this.transform.localScale = new Vector3(distance, distance, distance);
            }
        }
    }
}
```

Remember to add the script to the cube object in the scene hierarchy, and then hit play in Unity and test out your new scaling script!

To use two hands to change the position of the object using the distance, simply replace the line of code that updates the scale with this line of code:

```
this.transform.position = new Vector3(distance, distance, distance);
```

11.2.3 Step 3: Object Scaling with Two Hands (Pinch to Scale)

In this version, we will create a script that enables a user to pick up the object, and while holding it, increase and decrease the scale with two hands. Scroll down to the *Interaction Behaviour* script component within the Inspector panel—make sure that the box under *Grasp Settings* titled "*Allow Multi Grasp*" is checked. *Tip*: In previous versions of the interaction engine, this box was located in the Interaction Manager, so it may exist elsewhere in alternative versions of Unity.

For this operation, we will title this script '*PinchToGrow.*' Include the code as we have it thus far, or you can start with a new script. In your class declaration line, put the title of your new script in instead of the old one. Follow this example:

```
public class DirectGrow : MonoBehaviour {
```

turns into this:

```
public class PinchToGrow : MonoBehaviour {
```

This section focuses on two main aspects: first, we are going to calculate distance from the pointer finger position rather than the palms; and second, we are going to detect when the hands have both grasped the object. Fingers are stored similarly to the way hands are stored in the Leap code and there are multiple methods to access them. In this Gem, we access them as a list. We will make two lists—one for each hand—and assign the active finger as the pointer finger—number 1 in the list. The following code demonstrates this:

```
List<Finger> firstFingers = firstHand.Fingers;
List<Finger> secondFingers = secondHand.Fingers;
Finger firstFinger = firstFingers[1];    // Index finger on hand #1
Finger secondFinger = secondFingers[1];  // Index finger on hand #2
```

Using the LEAP API to find the location of the tips of the user's fingers, we calculate the distance between them:

```
distance = firstFinger.StabilizedTipPosition.DistanceTo(secondFinger.
        StabilizedTipPosition);
```

Tip: In this calculation, TipPosition can be used instead of StabilizedTipPosition—however it is preferred to use the more Stabilized version for Virtual Reality to allow for more precise real-time interaction.

Next, we demonstrate how to detect object grasp. For this version of the Unity engine and LEAP API two handed grasping of the object is detected with the "*InteractionBehaviour*" script object. *Tip*: This is something that has frequently changed with Leap's *Interaction Engine* updates and it may again change in the future. First, add *Leap.Unity.Interaction* to the using list:

```
using Leap.Unity.Interaction;
```

Use Unity's GetComponent to initialize the *InteractionBehaviour* object itself. Use the following code in the fields section to declare it:

```
InteractionBehaviour iB;
```

Initialize it as follows:

```
iB = GetComponent<InteractionBehaviour>();
```

Now we will use it! With the following code, it can be determined how many hands are grasping the current object. If the number is two, then scale. If the number of hands is other than two, scale will not be permitted.

```
if (frame.Hands.Count > 1 && iB.graspingHands.Count == 2)
    { … }
```

The script should now resemble Listing 11.6.

Listing 11.6. The complete "PinchToGrow" C# script.

```csharp
using System.Collections;
using System.Collections.Generic;
using UnityEngine;
using Leap;                      // Add this for access to LEAP API
using Leap.Unity.Interaction;   // Add this for setting up interaction metaphors similar
                                //    to physically interacting with objects using your
                                //    hands, such as grasp, hover, or touch an object
public class PinchToGrow : MonoBehaviour {
    Controller controller;          // Gives us data from the LEAP Controller.
    InteractionBehaviour iB;        // Gives us information about the object's state in Unity.

    // Use this for initialization
    void Start() {
        // Get InteractionBehaviour from object.
        controller = new Controller();
        iB = GetComponent<InteractionBehaviour>();
    }

    // FixedUpdate is called roughly once per frame
    void FixedUpdate() {
        if (controller.IsConnected) {

            // Gathers a frame from LEAP controller with every update.
            Frame frame = controller.Frame();

            if (frame.Hands.Count > 1 && iB.graspingHands.Count == 2)  {
                // The two first hands in each frame.
                List<Hand> hands = frame.Hands;
                Hand firstHand = hands[0];
                Hand secondHand = hands[1];

                // Accesses the pointer finger of each hand.
                List<Finger> firstFingers = firstHand.Fingers;
                List<Finger> secondFingers = secondHand.Fingers;
                Finger firstFinger = firstFingers[1];
                Finger secondFinger = secondFingers[1];

                // distance between two hands' palms.
                float distance;
                distance = firstFinger.StabilizedTipPosition.DistanceTo(secondFinger.
                    StabilizedTipPosition);

                // Adjusts the distance to something more usable.
                distance = distance * 0.001F;
```

```
            // The scale of the object will always be related to the
            //   distance between a user's two palms.
            this.transform.localScale = new Vector3(distance, distance, distance);
        }
    }
}
```

Press play and test it out! Pick up the object and grab it with two hands and see how big and little you can make the object!

11.2.4 Step 4: Object Rotation Using Two Hands

There are many methods for changing the rotation based on the hands. The following rotation examples are based on the methods [Ulinski et al. 2007]: Hand-in-Middle, Hand-on-Corners, and Two-Corners. A simple method uses direct manipulation, where the rotation from a single hand is used to rotate an object, as to simulate that a hand grasped the object from the center. Notice in the example below the function "ToQuaternion()". This function servers to convert from Leap Quaternion to Unity Quaternion. The following example represents a direct change in rotation. To implement a relative change, use "+=" instead of "=".

```
this.transform.localRotation = firstHand.Rotation.ToQuaternion();
```

If you wish to offset the rotation by some amount based on the actual hand's position, i.e., if the hand was located on the outside of the object, instead of the center, then follow this example.

```
Vector targetDir = firstHand.PalmPosition - this.transform.position;
// order matters depending on which hand you want to initiate the
//   direction
float rotateBy = speed * Time.deltaTime; // Where speed is a float value
this.transform.rotation = Quaternion.RotateTowards(Transform.forward,
    targetDir.ToVector3(), rotateBy, 0.0f);
```

You may not wish to use the direct rotation or if your Leap controller is mounted in such a way that the orientations of the hands are different than the orientation of the objects in relation to a user's view, you may want to obtain the rotational values in a different way. The following provides such an example where direction is the directional vector from the palm towards the fingers.

```
float pitch = firstHand.direction().pitch();
float yaw = firstHand.direction().yaw();
float roll = firstHand.palmNormal().roll();
```

Another method of rotating an object or volume with your hands involves the use of the position of the two hands to define the rotation. The positions of the two hands relative to one another define a vector by which the object or volume will be rotated. This vector can be aligned along each of the x, y, and z axes of the object/volume or can be aligned along the diagonal. Notice that the "Vector" here is a Leap Vector, so we need to convert it to a Unity Vector3, using the ".ToVector3()" command.

```
// This code rotates the object or volume about its local z-axis based
//    on the directional vector defined by the positions of the two hands
// Substitute "transform.forward" for "transform.up" for the local y-axis
//    and "transform.right" for the local x-axis.
Vector targetDir = firstHand.PalmPosition - secondhand.PalmPosition;
// order matters depending on which hand you want to initiate the
//    direction
float rotateBy = speed * Time.deltaTime;    // Where speed is a float value
this.transform.rotation = Quaternion.RotateTowards(Transform.forward,
        targetDir.ToVector3(), rotateBy, 0.0f);
```

11.2.5 Alternative Software Implementations

The scripts in Sections 11.3.2 and 11.3.3 are designed using the Leap Motion Tracker—however, with the most recent iteration of Leap's interaction engine, support for HTC Vive, and Oculus Touch controllers are supported within the interaction engine itself. Whether you want to go about it this way through Leap's interaction engine is entirely up to you—but the general concept of scaling in this way is applicable so long as the distance between objects can be calculated. It is also worth considering that the Leap has been designed to be mounted on a Virtual Reality headset. When it comes to alternative Software Implementations of the above, it is important to realize that a direct one-to-one scaling like this is useful on its own, but can be altered in many ways. The maximum size can be limited, for example—restricting scale to not create objects that are too big for the screen. Indirect scaling can be used instead of a direct one-to-one mapping. Instead of scaling all three values of a vector, the position grasped on the object could determine which way the object is skewed. Or the height of the object can be fixed so only the width and depth can be skewed. Different pinches with different fingers could represent different ways of stretching and skewing an object.

Another implementation of the code in Section 11.3.4 can be implemented to select virtual objects or volumes of data. By using a collider to detect multiple impacts, one could trigger multiple objects to be selected—much in the same way you click and drag your cursor on a desktop to create a box, selecting multiple files. This would allow many objects to be simultaneously moved, stretched, skewed, and otherwise manipulated rather than each one at a time.

11.3 Part III: Manual Volumetric Selection and Manipulation

Volumetric selection and manipulation in virtual reality is really a special case of object manipulation. First, the volume is created (for example as a rectangular volume). Then, using the Bi-manual Interaction for Object Manipulation in a similar way, the volume for selection can be controlled and manipulated (Figure 11.8). *Components to Volumetric selection:* (1) Manipulation of the Selection Volume, (2) Visual Feedback, and (3) Selection Identification/Indication.

a. Manipulation of the Selection Volume can be done exactly as we have shown you how to manipulate an object.
b. Next, you will need to see the boundaries of the volume and what is in the volume, therefore the object or mesh you are using for the volume should be rendered using wireframe. You will need a wireframe object to serve as your volume. You

Figure 11.8

Example of physical (a) bimanual selection of objects (b) and volumetric data (c).

can easily do this by creating a mesh and only rendering the lines between the points. If you would like to use a simple cube as your volume, Unity has this capability and can be done easily as in Listing 11.7.

Listing 11.7. Draw a cube with wireframe rendering to use as a tool for volume selection in Unity.

```
using UnityEngine;
using System.Collections;
public class ExampleClass : MonoBehaviour {
    void OnDrawGizmosSelected() {
        Gizmos.color = Color.yellow;
        Gizmos.DrawWireCube(this.transform.position, new Vector3(1, 1, 1));
    }
}
```

c. Third, you will need to incorporate Selection Identification, which is to identify what objects or data are within the volumetric space. We can accomplish this in Unity using colliders. Your volume should have a collider and the objects or meshes that represent the data in the scene should also have colliders. In this Gem, we will demonstrate how to identify those objects and then to add/delete from a list of selected objects in the scene.

First, make sure that your cube has a collider and is set to serve as a trigger. In the Inspector tab, with the selection volume cube selected, you can click the 'isTrigger' checkbox, as shown in Figure 11.9.

To set add a 'Box Collider' using scripting, use the following code where you create the volume selection primitive.

Figure 11.9

After adding the 'Box Collider' component in the inspector tab, click on this checkbox next to 'Is Trigger' to set it to serve as a trigger.

11. Bi-Manual Interaction for Manipulation, Volume Selection, and Travel

```
BoxCollider boxC = gameObject.AddComponent<BoxCollider>();
```

To set the "isTrigger" mode using scripting, you would use the following code where you create the volume selection primitive.

```
boxC.isTrigger = true;
```

Set up each object to have the variable "*isSelected*".

```
using UnityEngine;
using System.Collections;
public class selectionClass : MonoBehaviour {
    bool isSelected;
    bool isIdentified;
    ...
}
```

Next you want to set up the volume selection primitive, such as the cube, to recognize what objects are within its bounds and identify them as 'selected.' *Handy Tip: Make sure that the objects you are trying to select all have rigidBodies in order for the Collider to work.*

Listing 11.8. Sample Unity C# code to demonstrate how to identify which objects are within the volume selection tool.

```
void OnTriggerStay(Collider object) {
    if (collision.gameObject.GetComponent<selectionClass>().isIdentified == false) {
        collision.gameObject.GetComponent<selectionClass>().isIdentified = true;
    }
}
```

Then provide the user a means of activation such as a button press (or other input) to communicate that the objects within the bounds are to be selected (or unselected). The example code in Listing 11.9 is for handling the input.

Listing 11.9. Sample code to demonstrate how to mark objects, that are within the swept volume (identified from listing 11.8), as selected with a button press.

```
GameObject objectsToAdd[];
if (Input.GetButtonDown(buttonNameOfSelection)) {
    objectsToAdd = FindObjectsOfType<GameObject>();
    for (int i = 0; i < objectsToAdd.Length(); i++) {
        // keep track of your own list
        if (objectsToAdd[i].GetComponent<selectionClass>().isIdentified == true) {
            objlist.add(objectsToAdd[i]); // add to the list of selected objects
                                          //    or add the element of selected
            objectsToAdd[i].GetComponent<selectionClass>().isSelected = true;
        }
    }
}
```

You can do a similar step to deselect objects using a different button.

Listing 11.10. Sample Unity C# code to demonstrate how to 'deselect' objects, that are in the volume tool (identified from Listing 11.8), with a button press.

```
GameObject objectsToAdd[];
if (Input.GetButtonDown(buttonNameOfDeselection)) {
    objectsToAdd = FindObjectsOfType<GameObject>();
    for (int i = 0; i < objectsToAdd.Length(); i++) {
        // keep track of your own list
        if (objectsToAdd[i].GetComponent<selectionClass>().isIdentified == true) {
            objlist.remove(objectsToAdd[i]);    // remove from the list of selected objects
                                                 //   or remove the element of selected
            objectsToAdd[i].GetComponent<selectionClass>().isSelected = false;
        }
    }
}
```

You can even change the properties of the objects, such as color, to provide feedback to the user that they have been selected.

Listing 11.11. Sample Unity C# code to change a property of the selection objects as a way to provide feedback to the user to know which objects are currently selected.

```
GameObject selectedObjects;
Color newColor = new Color(redValue, greenValue, blueValue, alphaValue);
selectedObjects.FindGameObjectsWithTag("SELECTED");
for (int i = 0; i < selectedObjects.Length(); i++) {
    selectedObjects[i].GetComponent<Renderer>().material.color = newColor;
}
```

11.4 Part IV: Bi-Manual Travel Using Typical Game Controllers

11.4.1 Step 1: Set-Up Controllers with Unity

Simple controllers can be added to any VR environment. They are especially useful when working with adaptable VR displays, such as Google Cardboard or another type of headset that can be used with a mobile device. This portion of our gem demonstrates how to add micro controllers to a Unity project and script them to control objects for selection or manipulation or even the camera to perform travel.

11.4.1.1 Setting Up the Controllers for Input

In order to use the input from any input device or controller, we need to register the input device and buttons with Unity. To do this select "*Edit*" from the top menu in Unity, then **Project Settings → Input**. In the inspector tab and "*InputManager*" will appear. In this tab, we will map the input device settings. There will be a number of input devices that will appear (such as "*Mouse X*" and "*Mouse Y*") depending on what devices you have connected to your computer. For more details about the

11. Bi-Manual Interaction for Manipulation, Volume Selection, and Travel

"*InputManager*" please refer to the Unity documentation at https://docs.unity3d.com/Manual/class-InputManager.html.

For the joystick controller horizontal and vertical, for the purpose of following this Gem, the settings should be as follows (Figure 11.10). You may change the axis and names depending on how you would like to program your own input control.

It is recommended to delete existing elements in the *InputManager* that you are not using for your Unity project. You can create new elements by modifying exiting ones or duplicating existing elements and then modifying them. We will need to add an element for each of the buttons we are using on the controller. Begin by either modifying an existing element you will not use or duplicate and modify. Change the name to "*ButtonA.*" For the purpose of following this Gem, we will assign "*ButtonA*" to "joystick button 3." If you wish you can assign an alternative button, such as "mouse 0" in order to test your script is working if the controller device may not be. Figure 11.11 shows the resulting parameters.

Next, we create "*ButtonB,*" "*ButtonX,*" and "*ButtonY.*" Then we assign "joystick button 2," "joystick button1," and "joystick button 0," respectively. Use the input device manager to determine which physical buttons from your input device map to the corresponding output.

11.4.1.2 Adding the Controller Model for Demonstration

We use a model of one of the controllers to demonstrate the controller input and manipulation on objects (Figure 11.12). First, we add the model to our Unity environment.

Figure 11.10

InputManager settings for joystick controller.

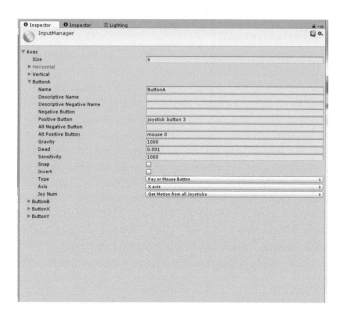

Figure 11.11

Parameters for ButtonA in the *InputManager*.

Figure 11.12

The model of the controller is shown in the scene view with separate object components for each of the buttons that will be manipulated using the input from the controller. (Thank you to Daniel Wilches for creation of the model.)

Select "*Assets*" from the top menu in Unity, and then select "*Import New Asset,*" navigate to where you have stored the BlackController.skp and select. Once in the assets directory, you can drag and drop the controller into the hierarchy window tab to add to your Unity scene.

11. Bi-Manual Interaction for Manipulation, Volume Selection, and Travel

11.4.1.3 Using Controller Input to Manipulate Objects

Once you have the model set up or any other objects for manipulation, we want to associate the controller input with object manipulation. We can start with one button control. Within the *"Assets/Scripts"* directory, right-click and select "Create" then "C# Script." Rename the script to *"InputController"* for the purpose of following this Gem. Of course the name of the script can be changed. There will be two default functions within the new script of "Start()" and "Update()".

Once you have created your script, the script will still need to be associated with a game object. This can be done in a number of ways. For simplicity, we create an "Empty Game Object" by right-clicking in the Unity game hierarchy, select "Create Empty". Rename this to *"GameController"* for the purpose of following this Gem. Once created, click on the "Inspector" tab for the object and click on *"Add Component,"* then select "Scripts," and then you will find and select your script *"InputController."* The Inspector tab will look like the following image in Figure 11.13.

You may use the "Start()" function to initialize any variables used. To control one button, we will add a variable *"buttonA"* of type Transform class to keep track of the current and new position of the A button game object. The Transform class is further documented by Unity at https://docs.unity3d.com/ScriptReference/Transform.html.

```
public Transform buttonA;
Vector3 buttonA_position;
```

Once you add these variables in your script, the inspector tab will update to include the transform object for button A as seen in Figure 11.14.

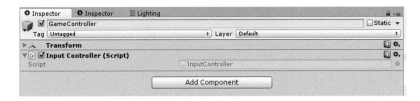

Figure 11.13

View of Inspector Tab after adding a script to an object. The *InputController* script was added in this case.

Figure 11.14

View of Inspector Tab after adding a variable, a button in this case, to the class of that object.

Once this appears, we want to associate the *Transform* class variables with an object we wish to manipulate. Click on the small circle to the right of "*Button A,*" None (*Transform*), circled in Figure 11.14. The following list of game objects (Note: your list may be slightly different) will appear and select the object you wish to manipulate. To follow this Gem, we will select button A game object shown in the list of game objects that appears (Figure 11.15) when clicking on the small circle in Figure 11.14.

Once button A game object is selected, the Inspector tab should result as shown in Figure 11.16.

Let's revisit our script. Within the "Update()" function, first to retrieve and store the current position of the game object button A, add the following code:

```
buttonA_position = buttonA.localPosition;
```

Figure 11.15

List of game objects that can be manipulated.

Figure 11.16

"Button A" Transform object is now associated with the transform of the "A" game object.

Then add the following lines of code to continuously check at each frame if an input event occurred and whether that event was the button press of button A.

```
if (Input.GetButtonDown("ButtonA")) {
    ...
}
```

This code checks whether the button was pressed down once. We can also check whether the button was released with the following code.

```
if (Input.GetButtonUp("ButtonA")) {
    ...
}
```

Using these two if ("conditional") statements we can manipulate the button in the model up and down at the moment the user is pressing the button in and out on the controller. The following code will update the position of the button: either inside the controller (when button is pressed down) or return outside the controller (when button is released). The position of the button game object is modified along the y axis since this axis is perpendicular to the model of the controller. The position is modified and then the "*local position*" of the button A game object is updated. In our Unity project we also use the following scale 1 mm = 0.001 units in our VR environment.

```
if (Input.GetButtonDown("ButtonA")) {
    buttonA_position.y -= 0.001F;
    buttonA.localPosition = buttonA_position;
}
if (Input.GetButtonUp("ButtonA")) {
    buttonA_position.y += 0.001F;
    buttonA.localPosition = buttonA_position;
}
```

Depending on where you may align the game object controller model in your Unity environment, you may manipulate the objects along different axes.

Run the Unity project to test that your button A is responding to your input.

Now that you have one button working, we can duplicate this process to manipulate the other buttons on the controller. We can simplify the code by creating a function that will check each of the buttons using the button name and appropriate Transform object. Create a Transform object for each button, or you can create a list of buttons.

```
public Transform buttonA, buttonB, buttonX, buttonY;
```

Once we add these Transform objects, we will associate them each with the appropriate game objects we wish to manipulate as we did with button A earlier. In Figure 11.17, in the Inspector tab for *InputController* game object, we see each Transform object associated with the appropriate game objects.

Create the new function "CheckButtonPressed" as follows:

```
void CheckButtonPressed(string buttonName, Transform buttonTransform) {
    ...
}
```

Figure 11.17

Transform objects are now associated with the appropriate game objects for manipulation.

Then add the code from above modified to use the functions arguments as in Listing 11.12.

Listing 11.12. Sample code to translate the object "button" to make it appear to be pressed in the scene as a result of the user pressing the that corresponding button from the mapping in Figure 11.16.

```
void CheckButtonPressed(string buttonName, Transform buttonTransform) {
    Vector3 tmpPosition;
    tmpPosition = buttonTransform.localPosition;
    if (Input.GetButtonDown(buttonName)) {
        tmpPosition.y -= 0.001F;
        buttonTransform.localPosition = tmpPosition;
    }
    if (Input.GetButtonUp(buttonName)) {
        tmpPosition.y += 0.001F;
        buttonTransform.localPosition = tmpPosition;
    }
} // end CheckButtonPressed
```

Within the "Update()" function, we can now add the function calls to check for each of the button events.

```
CheckButtonPressed("ButtonA", buttonA);
CheckButtonPressed("ButtonB", buttonB);
CheckButtonPressed("ButtonX", buttonX);
CheckButtonPressed("ButtonY", buttonY);
```

Run the Unity project to test that all of your buttons are responsive and moving the corresponding objects.

Next, we can add a function that will check and retrieve input from the joystick of the controller. First be sure to add the following variables to our script:

```
public Transform joystick;
private Vector3 initialJoystickPosition;
```

Be sure to associate the joystick Transform object with the appropriate game object for manipulation as seen in Figure 11.18.

Figure 11.18

Joystick Transform object is now associated with the appropriate joystick game object for manipulation.

Then, create a new function called "UpdateJoystick()" that will be called in the "Update()" function:

```
void UpdateJoystick() {
    ...
}
```

The joystick has two axes we can retrieve variable input from with the following lines of code which each return a float value.

```
float x = Input.GetAxis("Horizontal");
float y = Input.GetAxis("Vertical");
```

This float value represents the displacement of the amount the joystick has moved from the stationary position. We can obtain the original position of the joystick game object in the "Start()" function so that we may update the position with this displacement when the joystick is moved by the user.

```
void Start() {
    initialJoystickPosition = joystick.localPosition;
}
```

You can then use these values as a scaling factor to manipulate an object's position or other properties. The following code demonstrates the change in position of the joystick game object as the actual joystick is updated.

Listing 11.13. Sample Unity C# code using the valuators for translating an object.

```
void UpdateJoystick() {
    float x = Input.GetAxis("Horizontal");
    float y = Input.GetAxis("Vertical");
    Vector3 tmpPosition = initialJoystickPosition;
```

```
    tmpPosition.x -= 0.002F * x;
    tmpPosition.y -= 0.002F * y;
    joystick.localPosition = tmpPosition;
} // end UpdateJoystick
```

To use the joystick controller for object manipulation outside of the object's script which has been 'selected,' first you will need a method to identify the object for selection and store it as the selected Object. This can be completed through a selection method described in an alternative VR Gem chapter. Once selected, you can perform translation, rotation, and scale on that object. Here are a few code snippets of translation, rotation, and scale respectfully.

Listing 11.14. Sample Unity C# code that demonstrates how to use joystick valuators to translate, rotate, and scale, in that order in the code.

```
// This code fragment grabs the values from the joystick provided by it's
//    up/down left/right input.
GameObject selectedObject;
Vector3 tmpPosition;
float x= Input.GetAxis("Horizontal");
float y= Input.GetAxis("Vertical");
// performs translation on an object
tmpPosition = selectedObject.localPosition;
tmpPosition.x += x * scaleFactor;
tmpPosition.y += y * scaleFactor;
selectedObject.localPosition = tmpPosition;
// performs rotation on an object
Vector3 tmpRotation;
tmpRotation = selectedObject.transform.rotation;
Quaternion rotateBy = Quaternion.Euler((new Vector(x,y,0) * Time.deltaTime);
selectedObject.MoveRotation(tmpRotation * rotateBy);
// performs scale on an object
Vector3 tmpScale;
tmpScale = selectedObject.transform.localScale;
tmpPosition.x += x * scaleFactor;
tmpPosition.y += y * scaleFactor;
selectedObject.localScale = tmpScale;
```

Listing 11.14 is for 2D manipulation, or explicitly setting the axis of control. In the next two steps 2 and 3, this example will be extended to divide the axial control between the two hands, or rather two controllers.

11.4.2 Step 2: Configure Controller Input for Travel Control

One method for setting up bi-manual control for travel is to use one hand controller to control steering (rotation around the camera's vertical axis) and another hand controller for control of forward/back and left/right (assuming you are navigating by foot or in a vehicle in the virtual environment. An example for 6-DOF travel will be provided later in this example). To begin, we will reuse our code from the controller input but instead of manipulating an object, we will manipulate the camera game object to simulate travel. We will demonstrate this through two types of travel: (1) gaze-based travel (assuming you

11. Bi-Manual Interaction for Manipulation, Volume Selection, and Travel

have additional controls or sensors to update the camera view) and (2) pointing-based travel. Similarly, you could set up pointing-based travel with additional sensors.

11.4.2.1 Accessing the Camera to Manipulate It for Travel

Using input from the controller, instead of changing the position of the buttons in our 3D Model of the controller, we can add this control to our camera to control travel through a VR environment. In the Unity project file, for virtual reality you will need to have set up your stereoscopic camera rig (either explicitly or through a loaded plugin from the provider of your head-mounted display). First, add your main camera (for a VR environment add a left/right camera rig for stereoscopic viewing, or appropriate rig for your VR viewer or Head-Mounted Display) as shown in Figure 11.19.

Once you have this set up and configured (out of the scope of this chapter), then we will use the main camera to control travel. (Note: if there is no main camera, then use either the left or right eye camera but choose the one which serves as the 'parent' camera so that moving one camera will also appropriate move the other cameras). First, select the main or other 'parent' camera in the scene, shown in Figure 11.20.

Then, add a new script to handle the updates for the camera manipulation (Figure 11.21).

Figure 11.19

Image of the scene hierarchy (scene graph) with the camera rig for stereoscopic viewing.

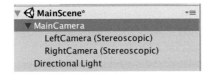

Figure 11.20

Image showing the main parent camera selected from the stereoscopic camera rig.

Figure 11.21

Image showing in the inspector tab for the main parent camera, the script that was added as a component.

In this script is where you will set up travel control based on updates from the controller:

a. gaze-based travel example:

Once your camera is in your environment, then select the main camera in the hierarchy tab, and add a new script in the inspector tab. You can name your script *travelController*. In here is where the camera will be updated based on the joystick input. Translating the camera along its forward and back vectors will use "*transform.forward*." If you use the *Vector3.forward* then it will use the world coordinate system forward vector and not the local coordinate system of the camera.

```
float x = Input.GetAxis("Horizontal");
float y = Input.GetAxis("Vertical");
float scaleFactor = 0.002f * Time.deltaTime;
// use a value according to the scale of your VR environment
//   and the speed at which you want the camera to travel
this.transform.Translate(transform.forward * x * scaleFactor);
this.transform.Translate(transform.forward*-1 * y * scaleFactor);
```

Handy Tip: The example provided should be in a script in the camera object. However, you could have the camera update from the `JoystickUpdate()` function. In this case, you would need to fetch the game object for the camera and then perform the translate command.

```
GameObject camera;
Camera = GameObject.Find("MainCamera");
camera.transform.Translate(camera.transform.forward * x *
    scaleFactor);
camera.transform.Translate(camera.transform.forward * -1 * y *
    scaleFactor);
```

b. Pointing-based travel, i.e., Input Controller axis-based travel example:

Once your camera is in your environment, then you will need to identify the vector to move the camera in the direction. This can be accomplished through various tracking equipment. Attach your tracker on your joystick controller and using the appropriate method from your tracking system, retrieve the axis from the trackable used on the joystick. Once you have this vector, we will refer to as "*Vector3 Direction*;" then you can update the camera in the `JoystickUpdate()` function:

```
GameObject camera;
Camera = GameObject.Find("MainCamera");
camera.transform.Translate(Direction * x * scaleFactor);
camera.transform.Translate(Direction * -1 * y * scaleFactor);
```

If you do not have a tracker, this is a great opportunity to use two controllers and divide the travel control between the two controllers for bi-manual travel control. Please continue to step 3 to learn how to implement two controllers for bi-manual travel control.

11.4.3 Step 3: Finalizing Bi-Manual Controller Travel

In both travel examples above, a rotation of the camera view (tracked head-mounted display) or the controller (tracked) will handle travel rotation. If no tracker is present or simply wish to use two controllers, then the following examples will provide details of how to divide the travel control. If the directional vector is not rotated, then you will need to add rotation (or otherwise steering) for travel. In the next two sections, examples are provided to set up separate directional and steering control between the two controllers/hands. Two full examples will be shown: (1) reduced degrees-of-freedom (DOF) travel (for human walking/running or vehicle travel) and (2) full 6-DOF travel will be shown. There are other various combinations for how to divide the travel control between the two controllers.

11.4.3.1 Add the Second Controller to Your Unity Environment

To set up the second controller, both controllers will need to be recognized and connected through the Bluetooth. Once connected, you will perform a similar step to adding the second controller as when the first controller was added in "Part IV: Bi-manual Travel using Controllers, Step 1" of this chapter. When doing so, there is an added step to differentiate the input for each controller. In Unity, select the menu **Edit → Project Settings → Input** to open the *Input Manager* in the Inspector tab. Then the single controller will have "horizontal" and "vertical" input as shown on the left in the following image. For the second controller, right click over the horizontal input tab, and select "*Duplicate Array Element*," as shown in the right in Figure 11.22.

Then a new horizontal tab will appear, as shown in the left of the following image. Rename this to differentiate from the first controller, such as "*Horizontal2*," and specify that input comes from joystick 2 as shown on the left in Figure 11.23. Next, do the same

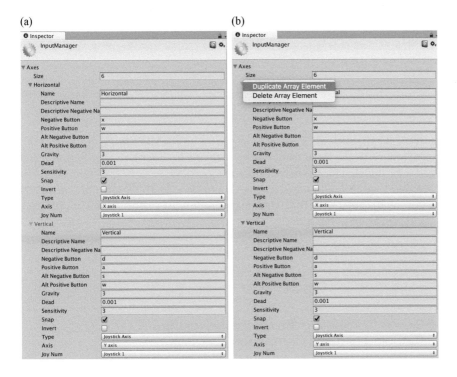

Figure 11.22

Image showing the elements and values for the *InputManager* (a). Further showing the selection of 'duplicate array element' when right-clicking the 'horizontal' element (b).

(a)

(b)

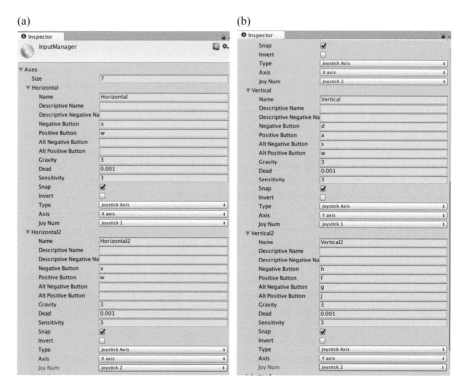

Figure 11.23

Image showing the duplicated elements producing 'Horizontal2' (a) and 'Vertical2' (b) and the added values.

for the vertical axis, such as "*Vertical2*," as shown on the right in Figure 11.23. For both horizontal and vertical axes, if using the joystick as a keyboard, the key button mappings will need to be updated for the output from the joysticks.

Remember to grab the input from your controllers. In the *BimanualControllerTravel* script in the main camera, the following lines of code will be added to the "void Update () { ... }" function in the script.

```
x = Input.GetAxis("Horizontal");   // x and y are type float
y = Input.GetAxis("Vertical");
x2 = Input.GetAxis("Horizontal2"); // x2 and y2 are type float
y2 = Input.GetAxis("Vertical2");
```

11.4.4 Step 4: Configuring the Controllers for the Mapping of Travel Components

11.4.4.1 Mapping for Hand Controller 1 (Speed and Steering)

Using one controller (after configuring the controller in Unity in step 1), this example shows how to set up the vertical axis of the controller to increase/decrease speed and the horizontal axis of the controller to control steering (rotation around the camera's vertical

11. Bi-Manual Interaction for Manipulation, Volume Selection, and Travel

axis, or yaw rotation). In this example, full 6-DOF is not implemented so Pitch and Roll rotations are not implemented here—but provided later in this example).

First, set up a variable for the speed of travel. You may need to set up a variable to represent the change in speed.

```
float travelSpeed;
float deltaTravelSpeed;
```

Then, set a base value in the "void Start () { ... }" function of the BimanualControllerTravel script in the main Camera. The value can be based on your environment scale and the amount of speed corresponding to the travel (i.e. walking vs. running vs. vehicle travel).

```
travelSpeed = 1.0F * Time.deltaTime; // 1.0F is the travel scale factor
deltaTravelSpeed = 0.5F;
```

Next, the other code will be added to the "void Update() { ... }" function of the BimanualControllerTravel script in the main Camera. In this example, y will be used for increasing/decreasing speed and x will be used for steering control. The change in input from the vertical axis of the controller will automatically change whether increasing or decreasing (in other words, so there is no need to add a 'negative' assignment for travelSpeed).

```
travelSpeed += y * deltaTravelSpeed;
```

Next, set up steering. First, set up a variable for the angle of steering.

```
float steeringSpeed;
```

Then, set a base value in the "void Start() { ... }" function of the BimanualControllerTravel script in the main Camera. The value can be based on your environment scale and the amount of angle corresponding to the travel (i.e. walking vs. running vs. vehicle travel).

```
steeringSpeed = 15.0F * Time.deltaTime;
```

Next, the other code will be added to the "void Update() { ... }" function of the BimanualControllerTravel script in the main Camera.

```
this.transform.Rotate(this.transform.up,y * steeringSpeed);
```

11.4.4.2 Mapping for Hand Controller 2 (Directional Control—Forward/Back, Left/Right)

To set up one controller for directional control, extend the code from the example above, only instead of using the vector direction defined from the tracking, use the directional vector from the camera and then use the values from the controller to update. The following example demonstrates how to do this in the "void Update () { ... }" function of the *BimanualControllerTravel* script in the *Main Camera*.

```
this.transform.Translate(this.transform.forward * x2 * travelSpeed);
this.transform.Translate(this.transform.forward * y2 * travelSpeed);
```

Handy Tip: since we are adding this to a script in the camera object, there is not a need to access the camera object. If you decide to instead add the travel control code to a controller object or another object, then remember that you will need to access the camera first:

```
GameObject camera;
camera = GameObject.Find("MainCamera");
```

And then replace any "`transform.XXX`" with "`camera.transform.XXX`".

11.4.4.3 For 6-Degrees-of-Freedom Control, Divide the Axial Control between the Two Controllers

To set up two controllers for 6-degrees of freedom control, you will need to decide how to set up the mappings between them. If you have two axes per controller, then you may need to use the A and B buttons to change manipulation mode.

One example mapping is to use separate buttons to activate a particular mode. For example, button A on the non-dominate hand controller activates translation and button B on the non-dominate hand controller activates rotation. When in translation mode, the vertical axis on the dominate hand controller can be used to control forward/back movement (local z-axis translation) while the horizontal axis on the dominate hand controller can be used to control left/right movement (local x-axis translation) (relative to the camera/user's view). Then the vertical axis on the non-dominate hand controller can be used to control the up/down movement (local y-axis translation).

When the mode is switched to rotational control, the vertical axis on the dominate hand controller can control rotation around the local x-axis (pitch) while the horizontal axis on the dominate hand controller controls rotation around the local y-axis (yaw) (relative to the camera/user's view). At the same time, the horizontal axis on the non-dominate hand controller controls the rotation around the local x-axis (roll).

This is only one example mapping and may not reflect the most optimal performance. Hinckley and his collaborators provide other possibilities [Hinckley et al. 1997]. More recent research literature reflects advice on task division for performance [Balakrishnan and Hinckley 1999].

Listing 11.15 provides a code example for the description of a 6-DOF mapping using the dominant and non-dominate hands for bi-manual interaction.

Listing 11.15. Sample Unity C# code that access the input from two devices and updates the rotation and translation of the camera or could be applied to any object.

```
float xDom, yDom;   // The X and Y location of the dominante hand
float xNonD, yNonD; // The X and Y location of the non-dominante hand
xDom = Input.GetAxis("Horizontal");    // x and y are type float
yDom = Input.GetAxis("Vertical");
xNonD = Input.GetAxis("Horizontal2");  // x2 and y2 are type float
yNonD = Input.GetAxis("Vertical2");

[…]

if (Input.GetButtonDown("ButtonA_NonD")) {
    mode = 1; // for translation
}
```

```
if (Input.GetButtonDown("ButtonB_NonD")) {
    mode = 2; // for rotation
}
if (mode == 1) {
    this.transform.Translate(this.transform.forward * yDom * travelSpeed);
    this.transform.Translate(this.transform.right * xDom * travelSpeed);
    this.transform.Translate(this.transform.up * yNonD * travelSpeed);
} else if (mode == 2) {
    this.transform.Rotate(this.transform.right, yDom * steeringSpeed); // pitch
    this.transform.Rotate(this.transform.up, xDom * steeringSpeed);  // yaw
    this.transform.Rotate(this.transform.forward, xNonD * steeringSpeed); // roll
}
```

11.5 Part V: Bi-Manual Manipulation and Travel Using Mobile Devices

In this portion of this chapter, we will take what we have learned about bi-manual control and apply it in another context, through the use of mobile devices (tablets, phones, etc.). Our examples focus on implementation with Android mobile devices. In this section, you will learn (1) how to establish a connection with the mobile device and your VR environment, (2) how to collect the two-dimensional touch gesture data from the devices and translate that into input into a virtual environment, (3) how to divide the input from two mobile devices as bi-manual control for 3D object manipulation, and (4) how to further extend step 3 for travel in a virtual environment.

11.5.1 Step 1: Set-Up Two Mobile Devices or Players (Instructions Based on Android)

There are several ways to set this up, but we will demonstrate two methods: (1) Via Bluetooth and (2) Via Wi-Fi (local wireless network). First, you will need to create a .java project that will run on each of your mobile devices. An easy way to do this is to use Android Studio, the official IDE for Android project development [Android Studio 2018]. If you do not have Android Studio, download Android Studio from their official website, https://developer.android.com/studio/. After downloading the Android Studio, create a new project by selecting "Start a new Android Studio project" as shown in Figure 11.24.

When creating your new project, provide an application name, such as a name that describes your project, and company domain, such as your institution or where you want your application to have credit for, as shown in Figure 11.25.

Since you will need to have your .java file run on the mobile devices, you will need to select which platform you are targeting to build the project. In this example, we will use **Phone and Tablet → Minimum SDK (API 19: Android 4.4 Kitkat).** The menu selection is shown in Figure 11.26. This will enable our project to run on devices which have at least Android version 4.4 "Kitkat". This version came out on October 13, 2013, so all modern Android devices will be able to use our program.

We will then create a new activity to describe the user interface for the interaction with the phone as shown in Figure 11.27.

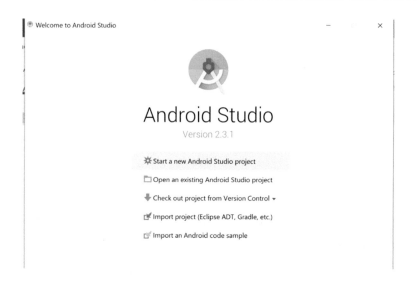

Figure 11.24

Image showing option to create a new Android project.

Figure 11.25

Image showing application name and company domain for the new project created.

After the "Activity" name is defined, click the finish button which will create the project, after which will proceed in setting up Bluetooth or Wi-Fi connection depending upon our requirement for transferring of data between server and client described in the following two steps.

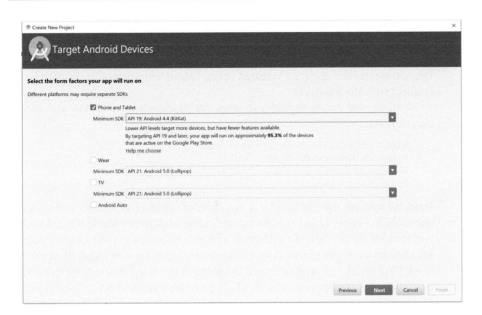

Figure 11.26

Image showing platform and minimum SDK selection for the target project.

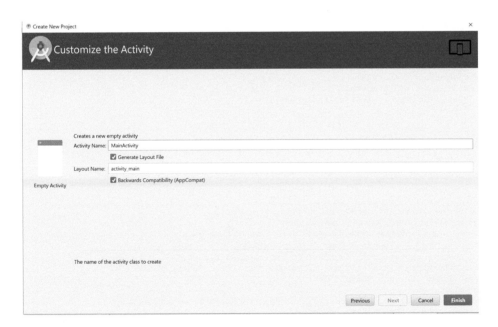

Figure 11.27

Image showing where to input "Activity" name for creating a user interface for interaction with the phone.

1. You have the option to use either Bluetooth or wireless network for connection. In this section, we will describe connecting mobile using Bluetooth for transfer of the information between server and client. After we have created an Android Project, we use the "Activity" created called "MainActivity.java" to initialize and connect with the Bluetooth.

Next, we will create variables to store the Bluetooth information and socket connection.

```
BluetoothAdapter bluetooth1 = null;
BluetoothDevice device1 = null;
BluetoothSocket socket1 = null;
PrintStream ps1;
```

Next, we will use the onCreate() function to initialize Bluetooth and a socket connection. Listing 11.16 provides example code to establish Bluetooth and socket connections. Note: the code will create a Bluetooth socket to start a secure outgoing connection to the mobile device that you are using for user input. The number is a UUID which is a service record to lookup RFCOMM channel. RFCOMM is a simple set of transport protocols which provides emulated RS-232 serial ports. The number is a universally unique identifier (UUID) which is different for each Android Phone. A user can get their UUID of the Android phone by navigating **to Menu → Settings → About Phone → Status.**

Listing 11.16. This Android Java source listing provides a code example to set up the Bluetooth connection using a socket to send/receive the data from the touch-based device to your virtual environment run from your Unity 3D project.

```java
public void onCreate(Bundle savedInstanceState) {
    super.onCreate(savedInstanceState);
    setContentView(R.layout.startscreen);
    bluetooth1 = BluetoothAdapter.getDefaultAdapter();

    try {
        // bluetooth mac address(iq's)
        device1 = bluetooth1.getRemoteDevice("XX:XX:XX:XX:XX:XX");
    } catch(Exception e) {
        Toast.makeText(this, "No Device", Toast.LENGTH_SHORT).show();
    }

    try {
        socket1 = device1.createRfcommSocketToServiceRecord(UUID.
          fromString("######-##-####-####-##########"));
        // The number ######-##-####-####-########## is a UUID which is a
        //   service record to lookup RFCOMM channel. RFCOMM is a simple set
        //   of transport protocols which provides emulated RS-232 serial
        //   ports. The number is a universally unique identifier (UUID) which
        //   is different for each Android device.
    } catch (Exception e1) {
        Toast.makeText(getApplicationContext(), "no socket"+e1.getLocalizedMessage(),
                    Toast.LENGTH_LONG).show();
    }
    try {
        socket1.connect();
        ps1 = new PrintStream(socket1.getOutputStream()); // adds the info to the message stream
```

11. Bi-Manual Interaction for Manipulation, Volume Selection, and Travel

```
    } catch (Exception e1) {
        Toast.makeText(getApplicationContext(), "no connection"+e1.getLocalizedMessage(),
                    Toast.LENGTH_LONG).show();
    }
}
```

2. In this example we will be using a local Wi-Fi network for the data transfer in our project. First, we need to allow our "Activity" created (described in the previous step on Bluetooth connections) to use the sensor of the Android phone. We have created the "Activity" called MainActivity.java so this will implement **SensorEventListener.**

```
public class MainActivity extends Activity implements
    SensorEventListener{ … }
```

We will then set up a variable for our Wi-Fi connection.

```
    private WifiManager wifiManager;
    private WifiManager.WifiLock wifiLock;
```

We will now use the OnCreate() function to initialize and start the *activity*. Listing 11.17 provides a code example for initializing and starting *activity* for Wi-Fi connection management.

Listing 11.17. This Andoird Java listing provides a code example for initializing the Wi-Fi connection on the mobile device that you are using for input.

```
@Override //overriding the parent class
    protected void onCreate(Bundle savedInstanceState)
    {
        super.onCreate(savedInstanceState);
        setContentView(R.layout.activity_main);
        // Register sensors
        sensorManager = (SensorManager)getSystemService(Context.SENSOR_SERVICE);

        wifiManager = (WifiManager)this.getSystemService(Context.WIFI_SERVICE);
        wifiLock = wifiManager.createWifiLock("TrackTableWifiLock");
    }
```

Now that we have initialized the "Activity" for the Wi-Fi Connection, we need to obtain the IP address of the mobile phone connected using the Wi-Fi Connection. We will use the getIpAddress() function to initialize and get the IP address. Listing 11.18 provides a code example for obtaining the IP address of the phone connected to the Wi-Fi network.

Listing 11.18. This Android Java listing provides a code example for obtaining the IP address of the mobile device or phone which is connected to the Wi-Fi network.

```
    private String getIpAddress()
    {
        try {
            String ips = "";
```

```
        Enumeration<NetworkInterface> enumNetworkInterfaces = NetworkInterface.
            getNetworkInterfaces();

    while (enumNetworkInterfaces.hasMoreElements()) {
        NetworkInterface networkInterface = enumNetworkInterfaces.nextElement();
        Enumeration<InetAddress> enumInetAddress = networkInterface.getInetAddresses();

        while (enumInetAddress.hasMoreElements()) {
            InetAddress inetAddress = enumInetAddress.nextElement();

            if (inetAddress.isSiteLocalAddress())
                ips += inetAddress.getHostAddress();
        }
    }
    return ips;
}
catch (SocketException e) {
    Log.e(TAG, "Main:" + e.getMessage());
    throw new RuntimeException(e);
}
}
```

Now that we have made a Wi-Fi connection with the phone, we need to create a socket connection which will send the information from the server to the client (i.e., mobile device) connected to it. We will create a new class **ServerSocketTransfer** which will handle our data transfer through a socket using threads.

```
public class ServerSocketThread extends Thread {...}
```

Next set up variables to store socket and port information in the **ServerSocketTransfer** class created.

```
private String TAG = "ServerSocketTransfer";
public const int PORT = 8080;
private ConcurrentLinkedQueue<String> currentClientQueue = null;
private ServerSocket serverSocket = null;
```

Next will create a run function run to initiate a thread to transfer the data through the socket to a port defined above. Listing 11.19 provides a code example to create and set up socket connection to transfer data through a port defined above.

Listing 11.19. This Android Java listing provides a code example to set up and manage the socket connection to send/receive data from your mobile device you are using for Input to the virtual environment run by your unity 3D project.

```
@Override //overriding the parent class
    public void run()
    {
        try {
            serverSocket = new ServerSocket(PORT);
            while (true) {
                Log.e(TAG, "Waiting for a connection ...");
                Socket socket = serverSocket.accept();
```

```
                Log.e(TAG, "Received a connection !");
                handler.sendEmptyMessage(1);
                if (currentClientQueue != null)
                    currentClientQueue.add(ClientSocketThread.STOP_WORKER);
                // Avoid two clients using the same queue, create one new and forget old one
                currentClientQueue = new ConcurrentLinkedQueue<>();
                // Start the client attendant
                new ClientSocketThread(socket, currentClientQueue, handler).start();
            }
        }
        catch (IOException e) {
            if (!e.getMessage().equals("Socket closed")) {
                Log.e(TAG, "Server:" + e.getMessage());
                throw new RuntimeException(e);
            }
        }
        finally {
            freeServerSocket();
        }
    }
```

After the Wi-Fi connection and socket have been set up, we will create a function to use the sensor to obtain and then send the information of the position (x & y) of a touch on the screen and send the values that represent the physical orientation of the mobile. We will use **onSensorChanged()** function in the MainActivity class created above to get the sensor information of position from the touch event and orientation from the IMU sensor. This function will be called automatically when the mobile sensor detects any changed information. Listing 11.20 provides a code sample to get mobile sensor information on change detect.

Listing 11. 20. This Android Java listing provides an example of how to send the position (x,y) values from the touch event and the quaternion (quat[0..3]) representing the orientation values from the IMU.

```
@Override //overriding the parent class
    public void onSensorChanged(SensorEvent event)
    {
        if (event.sensor.getType() == Sensor.TYPE_ROTATION_VECTOR) {
            SensorManager.getQuaternionFromVector(quat, event.values);

            serverThread.sendData(
                    // Orientation:
                    quat[1],
                    quat[2],
                    quat[3],
                    quat[0],
                    // Location:
                    deltaX, deltaY);
                    // NOTE: deltaX and deltaY are declared globally within
                    //    the scope of the script class
            deltaX = deltaY = 0;
        } else {
            Log.e(TAG, "Main: Unknown sensor type" + event.sensor.getType());
        }
    }
```

In summary, in this step you have learned how to initialize either a Bluetooth or Wi-Fi connection between a mobile device and server, created socket and ports for data transfer and then set up the sensor to detect and send information to/from a mobile device using the socket created. In the following section, we will set up Unity (running on the computer that will run the virtual environment) to receive the sensor data obtained from the socket.

11.5.2 Step 2: How to Set Up Unity to Receive Input from the Mobile Device

In step 1, we established a Bluetooth or Wi-Fi connection with a mobile device and can run the code on the device to set up a server and socket communication link. Now we will create a new Unity Project as described in previous sections (see the section: **Set Up a Basic Unity Scene**). Within our Unity Project, we will create a new GameObject (which we will call "GameController") in the hierarchy (shown in Figure 11.28) which will include our scripts for connecting with the socket and port.

Next, we attach the script to the "GameController" Object (Figure 11.29). Our script is called SocketConnection.cs which has the code to connect to the server socket and port.

Next, in your "ServerConnection" script, we will create a variable to store the socket and data from the socket port in the script. This variable will be used initialize the socket and port and then read the data from it. The following are example code to include in your script to declare the socket, later used in Listing 11.21.

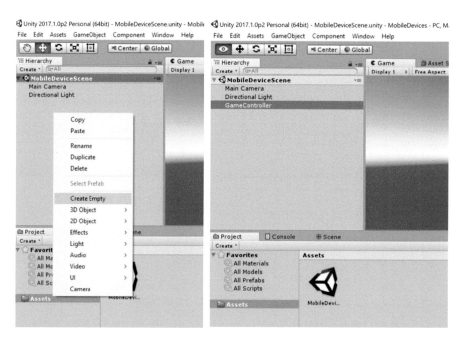

Figure 11.28

Create a GameObject (renamed to "GameController") for attaching the script for the socket connection.

Figure 11.29

Add the script to the GameObject named "GameController".

```
private string host;
private int port;
private Socket socket;
private StreamReader reader;
```

Next, we will add a function to our script that will initialize the socket and read data from this socket in the Unity project. Listing 11.21 provides a code sample to create a new socket for connection and read the data from it.

Listing 11.21. This listing provides example code to read the data from the socket.

```
protected override void InitializeDevice()
{
    socket = new Socket(AddressFamily.InterNetwork, SocketType.Stream, ProtocolType.Tcp);
    socket.ReceiveTimeout = readTimeout;
    socket.Connect(host, port);
    reader = new StreamReader(new NetworkStream(socket), System.Text.Encoding.UTF8);
    cmd_queue.Enqueue("_Client Connected");
}
```

Next, we use this data from the socket to move an object in the unity environment. We will create a 3D Object (Cube) and move that cube in the environment using the sensor data from the mobile device (Figure 11.30).

Next, we will attach our script to this new cube Gameobject. This script has the code to get the data information from the socket and apply it to the translation and rotation of the cube in the Unity environment.

We will add variables to store the translation and orientation data obtained from the socket and use them to move the cube accordingly when we interact through the mobile interface.

```
public Transform translationLocalAxes;
private Quaternion objectOriginalRotation;
```

Figure 11.30

Add a 3D Gameobject (here a cube) into the Unity environment.

Now, we can use the Unity `Update()` function on the manipulation object (or grab the reference to the game object as in Listing 11.14) to update the translation and orientation of the object in each frame. Listing 11.22 provides a code example to take the data from the socket connection and use it to interact with the object created in the unity environment.

Listing 11.22. This Unity C# script provides an example of how to use the data from the socket to update the rotation and translation of an object.

```
// Update is called once per frame
void Update()
{
    string data = implObject.GetNextReading();
    if (data == null)
        return;
    // Rotation
    Quaternion rotation = AdjustRotation(new Quaternion(data.quat_x, data.quat_y,
                                         data.quat_z, data.quat_w));
    this.transform.rotation = rotation;
    // Translation
    this.transform.Translate(this.transform.right * data.pos_x,
                           this.transform.up * data.pos_y, 0, Space.Self);
    // Note: You can also modify the localPosition, here is another way:
    //    this.transform.localPosition = translationLocalAxes.right *
    //    data.pos_x - translationLocalAxes.up * data.pos_y;
}
```

Listing 11.23 shows another great example of controlling an object is that you can use the orientation of one device to determine the directional translation, but not rotate the object.

Listing 11.23. This Unity C# listing provides an example of using the orientation of the IMU to determine direction of the translation that will result from the touch events.

```
// Update is called once per frame
void Update()
{
    string data = implObject.GetNextReading();
```

```
    if (data == null)
        return;
    // Rotation
    Quaternion rotation = AdjustRotation(new Quaternion(data.quat_x, data.quat_y,
                                              data.quat_z, data.quat_w));
    Vector3 dirX = this.transform.TransformDirection(this.transform.right * rotation);
    Vector3 dirY = this.transform.TransformDirection(this.transform.forward * rotation);
    // Translation
    this.transform.translate(rotation * this.transform.right * data.pos_x,
                      rotation * this.transform.up * data.pos_y, 0, Space.Self);

}
```

Thus far, we have a specific example that gathers the orientation of the IMU sensor data from the mobile device to update the rotation of a cube in a virtual environment. While this example is basic, it can be extended to more complex interactions with multiple objects and menus in the virtual environment. Interaction options include modifying what sensor data is used (see step 1) and/or how that data is translated into modifications of the virtual environment within Unity (step 2). In the next step, we will demonstrate how to set up a second mobile device for bi-manual use and control.

11.5.3 Step 3: Adding the Second Mobile Devices

With one mobile device connected, sending data, passing the data to the Unity project, and updating the virtual environment (steps 1 and 2), we can now add a second mobile device for bi-manual control. Once the dual-connection is established, we will explore further interface examples in steps 4 and 5 using two mobile devices. The procedure to add a second mobile device is similar to steps 1 and 2 for one mobile device; the only difference is that you will need to create an additional socket and port in the server through which to make either the Bluetooth or the Wi-Fi connection for the second mobile phone. The following example configures the second socket and port for an already established Wi-Fi connection.

```
public static final int PORT = 8080;
public static final int PORT2 = 8082;
private ConcurrentLinkedQueue<String> currentClientQueue = null;
private ConcurrentLinkedQueue<String> currentClientQueue2 = null;
private ServerSocket serverSocket = null;
private ServerSocket serverSocket2 = null;
```

Follow the example in Listing 11.18 by copying the entire section, and for all the variable names add a "2", for example:

```
serverSocket2 = new ServerSocket(PORT2);
Socket socket2 = serverSocket2.accept();
currentClientQueue2 = new ConcurrentLinkedQueue<>();
```

For the Unity project, we will also create additional variables as described in the previous step to store the socket and data read from the socket of the second mobile device. Of course, you will also need to add a second socket listener in your Unity project. The following is an example of the variables you will need to add to your Unity **SocketConnection.**

cs file (alternatively you can create a second **SocketConnection2.cs** file to add to your GameObject).

```
private string host;
private int portOne;
private int portTwo;
private Socket socketOne;
private Socket socketTwo;
private StreamReader readerOne;
private StreamReader readerTwo;
```

Next, we will read and update the stream data from the socket connection and use it for the translation and rotation actions in each frame. Be sure to copy the lines of code in Listing 11.21, but modify the variable names for your second mobile device. The following are a few lines of excerpted code to provide an example of this.

```
socketTwo = new Socket(AddressFamily.InterNetwork,
                     SocketType.Stream, ProtocolType.Tcp);
socketTwo.ReceiveTimeout = readTimeout;
socketTwo.Connect(host, port);
readerTwo = new StreamReader(new NetworkStream(socketTwo),
                     System.Text.Encoding.UTF8);
```

Using these values, you can access the data from your second socket to update objects in the virtual environment, similar to Listing 11.22. Now that you have two mobile devices connected and updating data in a virtual environment, you are ready for steps 4 and 5 to set up bi-manual interaction control.

11.5.4 Step 4: Configure Bi-Manual Interaction for Manipulation Control

Using two mobile devices provides us with one method to interact with a virtual environment using both hands (i.e. Figure 11.31). With access to input from both hands, we can divide the tasks between them to control and manipulate the world in an efficient manner. There are a number of ways to conduct this division. Here, we will provide three basic examples.

Figure 11.31

Examples of bi-manual control using mobile devices.

11. Bi-Manual Interaction for Manipulation, Volume Selection, and Travel

Example 1: We can divide our bi-manual interaction between our two hands by having one hand control translation of an object and another hand control the orientation. Listing 11.24 provides a code sample for this form of interaction.

Listing 11.24. This listing Unity C# script provides an example of reading data from two different mobile devices then using one to update the translation of an object and the other to update the rotation.

```
// Update is called once per frame
void Update()
{
    string dataOne = implObject.GetNextReading();
    string dataTwo = implObject.GetNextReading();
    if (dataOne == null || dataTwo == null)
        return;
    // Rotation
    Quaternion rotation = AdjustRotation(new Quaternion(dataOne.quat_x, dataOne.quat_y,
                                            dataOne.quat_z, dataOne.quat_w));

    this.transform.rotation = rotation;
    // Translation in the x/y plane.
    this.transform.translate(this.transform.right * dataTwo.pos_x,
                        this.transform.up * dataTwo.pos_y, 0, Space.Self);
}
```

This code updates the data obtained from the stream each frame. The first mobile phone connection controls the rotation and the second mobile phone controls the translation of the object—a bi-manual interaction. As in this example interaction, we can divide the translation and orientation control, however, with translation updated only from one touch plane, a mode will need to be added for full translational control in all three dimensions. While we can use a button to mode switch between movement in the x-y, x-z, and y-z planes, mode switches are cognitively demanding. Thus, in example two, we extend this interface to full 6-degrees of freedom control by dividing the axial translation among the two hands.

Example 2: One hand controls orientation, but the 3-degrees of freedom for translation are divided between the two mobile devices (i.e. the two hands). One hand (preferably the non-dominate hand) controls translation in the x-y plane and the other hand (preferably the dominate hand) controls translation in the x-z plane. Of course, these divisions of axial control can be customized to the preference of the user.

Listing 11.25. This Unity C# listing provides an example of how to use the 2D plane from each touch device to update translation in the x/y plane and the x/z plane separately.

```
// Update is called once per frame
void Update()
{
    string dataOne = implObject.GetNextReading();
    string dataTwo = implObject.GetNextReading();
    if (dataOne == null || dataTwo == null)
        return;
    // Rotation from device one.
```

```
Quaternion rotation = AdjustRotation(new Quaternion(dataOne.quat_x, dataOne.quat_y,
                                                    dataOne.quat_z, dataOne.quat_w));
this.transform.rotation = rotation;
// Translation in the x/y plane on device one.
transform.translate(this.transform.right * dataOne.pos_x,
                    this.transform.up * dataOne.pos_y, 0, Space.Self);
// Translation in the x/z plane on device two.
this.transform.translate(this.transform.right * dataTwo.pos_x, 0,
                         this.transform.forward * dataTwo.pos_y, Space.Self);
// or you can have the device only control z, for example:
// this.transform.translate(0, 0, this.transform.forward * dataTwo.pos_y, Space.Self);
}
```

A unique benefit of using bimanual interaction is that you can provide coordinated interaction. In *Example 3:* both hands work together to update rotation and translation of an object. Specifically, hands can be rotated 'in-phase,' meaning the rotation of an object can be manipulated through directional motion actions. Similarly, touch gestures can be executed 'in-phase' or singularly for translation. Listing 11.26 demonstrates an example for scale operations, where touch gestures can be moved in 'anti-phase,' meaning in opposite directions at the same time.

Listing 11.26. This Unity C# script provides an example of how to scale using combined touch input from both devices.

```
// Update is called once per frame
void Update()
{
    string dataOne = implObject.GetNextReading();
    string dataTwo = implObject.GetNextReading();
    float minDistance =  1.0;
    float maxDistance = 10.0;
    float minDistScale = 0.1;
    float maxDistScale = 1.0;
    if (dataOne == null || dataTwo == null)
        return;
    positionFirstMobile = new Vector3(dataOne.pos_x, dataOne.pos_y, 0);
    positionSecondMobile = new Vector3(dataTwo.pos_x, dataTwo.pos_y, 0);
    float distanceBetweenSwipe = (positionFirstMobile - positionSecondMobile).magnitude;
    // Normalizing
    float normValue = (distanceBetweenSwipe - minDistance)/(maxDistance - minDistance);
    // Changing the value to Vector3(1,1,1) * some_value_of_scale
    float minScale = Vector3.one * minDistScale;
    float maxScale = Vector3.one * minDistScale;
    // Interpolate between between the maxScale and minScale
    this.transform.localScale = Vector3.Lerp(maxScale, minScale, norm);
}
```

To this point, we have explored basic examples to divide the input between the two mobile devices to set up bi-manual control. Starting from these basic examples and reading about the most recent bi-manual interaction techniques in research you have the tools to implement new and more advanced methods of bi-manual control interfaces.

11. Bi-Manual Interaction for Manipulation, Volume Selection, and Travel

11.5.5 Step 5: Configure Bi-Manual Interaction for Travel Control

Here, we provide basic examples of bi-manual interaction for travel control. These examples are similar to step 4, but we now use the data to travel by controlling the stereoscopic camera rig, instead of an object.

Example 1: First, we set up one device to control roll, pitch, and yaw of the camera while both devices can control travel along the local axes of the camera. Listing 11.27 demonstrates example code for the Update() function of the camera rig (from "**Step 2: Configure Controller Input for Travel Control**" earlier in this chapter).

Listing 11.27. This Unity C# listing provides an example of using the data from two touch-based devices to update rotation and translation of the camera.

```
void Update()
{
    string dataOne = implObject.GetNextReading();
    string dataTwo = implObject.GetNextReading();
    float scaleFactor = 0.002f * Time.deltaTime;
    if (dataOne == null || dataTwo == null)
        return;
    // One device controls roll,pitch, yaw
    Quaternion rotation = AdjustRotation(new Quaternion(dataOne.quat_x, dataOne.quat_y,
                                         dataOne.quat_z, dataOne.quat_w));
    this.transform.rotation = rotation;
    // One device controls forward/back translation
    this.transform.Translate(this.transform.forward * dataOne.pos_y * scaleFactor);
    // Another device controls left/right and up/down translation
    this.transform.Translate(this.transform.right * dataTwo.pos_x * scaleFactor);
    this.transform.Translate(this.transform.up * dataTwo.pos_y * scaleFactor);
    // Remember, if this code is not added to a script within the parent camera of the
    //camera rig, be sure to reference the camera GameObject (ie. Camera.transform.Translate)
}
```

We can use additional data to adjust for the speed of the travel. We will add the **onFling()** function to the Mainactivity class created previously in **Step 1.** This onFling() function detects fling events when they occur and provides the speed of fling in x and y position. A 'fling' event is a 'swipe' event based on an ending velocity. Listing 11.28 provides a code sample to detect fling gestures which will return the velocity of a fling in position x and y.

Listing 11.28. This listing provides an example Android Java function to return the velocity of a fling gesture in position x and y.

```
@Override //overriding the parent class
    public boolean onFling(MotionEvent e1, MotionEvent e2, float velocityX, float velocityY)
    {
        return super.onFling(e1, e2, velocityX, velocityY);
    }
```

This function provides the speed of the fling in the x and y directions which we send through the server socket as before. *Example 2*: Thus now we can use the fling data to affect the translation speed of the movement, with orientation controlled by data from another mobile phone. For Listing 11.29, we can alter Listing 11.27 to instead use these values for the speed of travel.

Listing 11.29. Unity C# sample Unity C# script code that uses the fling event to control the speed of travel.

```
void Update()
{
    string dataOne = implObject.GetNextReading();
    string dataTwo = implObject.GetNextReading();
    float scaleFactor = 0.002f * Time.deltaTime;

    if (dataOne == null || dataTwo == null)
        return;

    //One device controls roll,pitch, yaw
    Quaternion rotation = AdjustRotation(new Quaternion(dataOne.quat_x, dataOne.quat_y,
                                                        dataOne.quat_z, dataOne.quat_w));
    this.transform.rotation = rotation;
    //One device controls forward/back translation
    this.transform.Translate(this.transform.forward * dataOne.pos_y * velocityY);
    //Another device controls left/right and up/down translation
    this.transform.Translate(this.ransform.right * dataTwo.pos_x * velocityX);
    this.transform.Translate(this.ransform.up * dataTwo.pos_y * velocityY);
    //Remember, if this code is not added to a script within the parent camera of the
    //camera rig, be sure to reference the camera GameObject (ie. Camera.transform.Translate)
}
```

You now have the wherewithal to set up your two devices for travel control. You can modify the division of tasks to your preferences for travel or combine with other devices or methods.

11.6 Conclusion

In summary, this chapter provides instructions for bare-handed bi-manual object manipulation and volume selection tool control, as well as bi-manual manipulation and travel using two input controllers. While the instructions and examples provided in this chapter provide assistance to create basic interactions in a virtual reality environment, they also serve as a foundation and can be easily extended to provide more complex interaction.

Specifically, this chapter provided details for how to set up Unity with Leap hand tracking and then incorporate that input to translate, rotate, and scale objects with one and two hands. You can use these examples to employ your bare hands to control objects in a real application, such as picking up or throwing objects, modeling or changing properties of objects, and even using your hands to navigate in the VE. More sophisticated bare-handed selection and manipulation techniques published in recent research can be implemented from the basis of the knowledge gained in this chapter.

Second, this chapter expands on the basic hand interaction examples to set up a basic volumetric selection tool. Examples demonstrate how to identify objects for selection, change properties, and control the volume selection tool using two hands. With these examples, you can use your hands to manipulate a multi-object selection tool. While these examples use solid objects, objects can also be defined as sprites or data points to be used in a real-time volumetric data renderer in Unity or another application. Furthermore, other selection techniques published in recent research could be implemented using the hand tracking and manipulating the basic volume in a different way as defined by those techniques.

Third, this chapter instructs how to set up Unity to utilize input from two input controllers for object translation, rotation, and scale as well as travel (by moving the camera). Examples demonstrates reduced degrees-of-freedom travel and full 6-degrees-of-freedom travel. These examples are great to use for mobile VR applications with VR viewers (e.g. Google Cardboards) due to the small form factor of the controllers and the wireless communication over Bluetooth. They could be further extended for more advanced interaction techniques now that you know how to set them up, access the input values, and use those values to control objects in Unity.

Lastly, this chapter provides details of how to set up two mobile devices for bi-manual input control of a Unity virtual environment. In the last section (Part V), you were able to connect two mobile devices over Bluetooth or Wi-Fi to manipulate objects in a Unity virtual environment. Further you learned to use the data to set up bi-manual control of orientation, translation, and scale of those objects as well as travel. While these are basic examples, they can be extended further to perform more advanced interaction control using the mobile devices. Further you can use these examples as a foundation to assess other buttons or sensor data to increase the amount of interaction functionality or more appropriately balance interaction tasks across devices for advanced interaction in virtual environments.

In conclusion, we hope that you are able to use these examples to get started or as a foundation for more advanced bi-manual control. Feel free to contact the authors regarding the details in this chapter or for more advice on bi-manual interaction techniques.

References

[Android Studio 2018]

Android (2018, October 23). *Detect Common Gestures*. Retrieved from https://developer.android.com/training/gestures/detector#java

[Balakrishnan and Hinckley 1999]

Balakrishnan, Ravin, and Ken Hinckley (1999). The role of kinesthetic reference frames in two-handed input performance. In *Proceedings of the 12th Annual ACM Symposium on User Interface Software and Technology* (pp. 171–178). ACM, Asheville, North Carolina.

[Hinckley et al. 1997]

Hinckley, Ken, and Randy F. Pausch, and Dennis Proffitt (1997). Attention and visual feedback: The bimanual frame of reference. In *Proceedings of the 1997 Symposium on Interactive 3D Graphics* (pp. 121–ff). ACM, Providence, Rhode Island.

[Niehorster et al. 2017]

Niehorster, Diederick C., Li, and Markus Lappe (2017). The accuracy and precision of position and orientation tracking in the HTC Vive virtual reality system for scientific research. *i-Perception*, 8(3). doi:10.117/2041669517708205.

[Oculus VR 2018]

Oculus VR LLC. (2018). *Oculus Developer Guide. URL: https://developer.oculus.com/rift/.*

[Ulinski et al. 2007]

Ulinski, Amy, Catherine Zanbaka, Zachary Wartell, Paula Goolkasian, and Larry F. Hodges (2007). Two handed selection techniques for volumetric data. In *2007 IEEE Symposium on 3D User Interfaces*. IEEE, Charlotte, North Carolina.

12

Effortless 3D Selection through Progressive Refinement

Doug A. Bowman
Center for Human-Computer Interaction, Virginia Tech

Regis Kopper
Duke University

Felipe Bacim
Apple, Inc.

Most virtual reality (VR) applications need a 3D selection technique—a way to pick or target objects in the virtual scene. While basic techniques like ray-casting can work in many situations, a more advanced form of 3D selection can give your users a better experience if your scene has many small, distant, cluttered, or moving objects. This chapter describes several such techniques based on the concept of progressive refinement, and it will help you choose which techniques to use for your application.

12.1 Introduction

3D selection, in which a user picks one or more objects in a VR environment, has been called one of the "universal" 3D interaction tasks [LaViola et al. 2017]. Selection takes place in almost every VR application, except for those that are purely passive experiences (such as watching a VR film).

Examples of 3D selection include:

- Targeting or "shooting" an object to be destroyed in a game
- Activating an interactive virtual object, such as a virtual switch that turns on a machine
- Picking an item in a menu
- Choosing an object for a follow-up action, such as manipulation, scaling, copying, or deleting

Like most 3D interaction tasks, selection has some real-world analogs that are often used as the basic metaphors for VR selection techniques. The most obvious is the *touching* metaphor, which selects objects when they are contacted or grasped by a virtual hand or virtual tool, which is typically controlled via tracked movements of the user's own hand or a handheld controller.

Touching is clearly easy to understand, because it maps directly to users' experiences in the real world, but it is not easy to use for selection of objects at a distance, or when selection is used for shooting. Such selection tasks often make use of a *pointing* technique, in which the user's finger or a tool is used to indicate the direction to the desired object. Laser pointers or guns provide real-world metaphors for selection by pointing.

Basic versions of these techniques are simple to implement and work well in many 3D selection scenarios. For example, in the game *Fantastic Contraption*, selection of parts to be used in building a contraption is performed simply by touching them with the handheld controller. Pointing is used in the Oculus Home menu, which employs a simple laser pointer approach to select apps and controls.

Not all selection tasks in VR, however, are so simple. Straightforward touching and pointing techniques can be difficult or impossible to use when objects are far away, small, densely packed, and/or moving. To address these issues, a wide variety of more advanced 3D selection techniques has been proposed (see LaViola et al. [2017] for an overview).

In this chapter, we'll take a look at a class of 3D selection techniques based on *progressive refinement*, which is the idea of gradually reducing the set of selectable objects until only one remains. When implemented well, progressive refinement techniques allow users to perform very difficult selection tasks with very little physical or mental effort, without increasing the time needed for selection.

We begin by looking more closely at four characteristics of 3D selection tasks that cause problems and increased difficulty. Next, we'll define progressive refinement more precisely and explain how and why the approach works. In the remainder of the chapter, we'll describe the design and implementation of three 3D selection techniques based on progressive refinement, and how developers can use these techniques to make demanding selection tasks seem effortless to users.

12.2 Common Problems in 3D Selection

As we discussed in the introduction, many selection tasks can be easily handled with basic touching or pointing techniques, but other tasks are significantly more difficult. If appropriate interaction techniques are not used in these scenarios, then users can spend significant time and effort on object selection, and may make many selection errors. This can lead to frustration, fatigue, and an all-around poor user experience. The primary factors that cause difficulty in 3D selection are distance, size, density, and movement.

12.2.1 Distance

The most obvious issue is that selection targets may be far away from the user. Objects beyond arm's reach cannot be selected at all by basic touching techniques—unless the user can travel (move within the virtual environment) to bring the object within arm's reach.

One obvious solution to the distance problem is to use a pointing-based selection technique, like ray-casting [Mine 1995]. In some cases, this is all that's needed. However, the ability of users to point accurately depends on the visual size of objects, and faraway objects will have a smaller visual size. Accurate pointing is hindered by both tracking jitter and natural tremor of the user's hand. Small movements of the hand and slight noise in the tracker signal can result in large movements at the end of the ray. Thus, an object that would be easy to select within a few meters can become very hard to select when it is much farther away [Wingrave and Bowman 2005].

Touching metaphors can still be used to select distant objects through the concept of arm extension [Bowman and Hodges 1997]. For example, the Go-Go technique [Poupyrev et al. 1996] allows the user to reach much farther into the environment with the virtual arm than is possible in the real world, by applying a non-linear mapping from the physical reach distance to the virtual reach distance. Like ray-casting, however, this scaling of reach comes at the cost of accuracy. Small physical hand movements will make the virtual hand move larger distances, making it sometimes difficult to touch distant objects with the virtual hand.

12.2.2 Size

Closely related to the problem of distance is the issue of target size. Touching and pointing techniques work well when objects are nearby and large enough. However, when targets are too far away or too small, tracker jitter and hand tremor make it hard to position or orient the hand accurately enough for selection.

There are several different aspects of size that deserve consideration. First, there's the distinction between absolute size and visual size. A sphere with a 1-m diameter has a 1-m diameter regardless of its location relative to the user—that's absolute size. But as we hinted in the previous subsection, that same sphere appears smaller and smaller (in visual size) to the user as it moves farther away. The accuracy of touching-based techniques depends on the absolute object size, while the accuracy of pointing-based techniques depends on visual size.

We should also note that objects don't have a single size; they may be sized differently in different dimensions. Imagine a square brick wall—it is relatively large in width and height, but relatively small in thickness. If a pointing technique is being used to select the wall, then it will be much easier to select when looking at the front or back of the wall, but more difficult to select when looking at the wall edgewise. On the other hand, with a distant touching technique like Go-Go, it is likely to be *more* difficult to select the wall when looking at the front or back, because the wall object is small in the depth dimension, and the technique provides less precision in the depth dimension.

Many 3D selection techniques have been designed to address the dual problems of distance and size. For example, the 3D Bubble Cursor [Vanacken et al. 2007] uses a volume cursor instead of a point cursor, and this volume (called the "bubble") changes size dynamically so that it always contains a single object. In this way, the user can always select the nearest object to the cursor without having to position the cursor precisely. Similarly, the Bent Pick-Ray technique [Riege et al. 2006] is a pointing-based technique that reduces precision requirements. It automatically bends the pointing ray so that it intersects the object closest to the unbent ray. Finally, PRISM [Frees et al. 2007] is an example of a technique that dynamically changes the level of precision (known as the control-display ratio) to allow both long-distance movements of the hand and precise placement. When the user's hand is moving quickly, the virtual hand moves very quickly; however, when the user slows down, the virtual hand moves even slower.

12.2.3 Density

A third confounding factor for 3D selection is object density (i.e., how close selectable objects are to one another). With high density of objects, there will be more occlusion, and therefore targets will have smaller visual size. Imagine a pizza box sitting on the table. Selecting it from the side would be difficult with a pointing technique due to small visual size, but it would be easy enough to raise your hand so you were pointing at the top of the box. But if instead we have a whole stack of pizza boxes, and we want to select a box in the middle of the stack, we have no choice but to select it from the side, because only the side is visible.

In addition, when objects are very near to one another, small movements of the user's hand (caused by tremor or tracker jitter) can cause the selection target to jump from one object to another and back again quickly and unpredictably. This is the downside of techniques like 3D Bubble Cursor and Bent Pick-Ray—they only work well when there is empty space (no selectable objects) around the target. Otherwise, the user will have to touch or point to the objects precisely.

Figure 12.1 shows a virtual supermarket, developed as the test environment for the first IEEE 3DUI Contest [Figueroa et al. 2010]. Users had to find three marked objects in the supermarket and select them to put them in their shopping carts. Note how this environment has a very large number of objects, many of which are far away, small, and densely packed. Even state-of-the-art 3D selection techniques can be frustrating and error prone in an environment like this.

12.2.4 Movement

Object movement is a fourth issue that can negatively impact the effectiveness of 3D selection. When objects are moving, users not only have to provide precise position, distance, or direction information, but also precise *timing*. Most 3D selection techniques do not explicitly consider moving objects, and therefore are difficult to use for moving object selection.

Many 3D environments consist primarily or exclusively of static objects, but moving objects are common in certain types of 3D applications. Targeting moving enemies in a game is probably the most prominent example. But selection of moving objects may also occur in 3D simulations and animations. Of course, it is always possible to include a "pause" function to stop the movement before selection, but this approach may not always be desirable.

12. Effortless 3D Selection through Progressive Refinement

Figure 12.1

Virtual supermarket illustrating the issues of distance, size, and density in 3D selection.

A few researchers have considered the moving object selection problem and developed techniques specifically to address this issue. For example, the Hook technique [Ortega 2013] is based on the observation that users must track and pursue moving objects in order to select them. Therefore, it looks at the distances from the hand/cursor to each object in the scene over time and maintains a score for each object, indicating the probability that the user is trying to select the object. When the user indicates a selection (e.g., by pressing a button), the object with the highest score is selected.

12.2.5 The Need for a New Approach

All of the techniques described above can help users overcome the problems of distance, size, density, and movement during 3D selection tasks. However, they often require extra effort from the user when the circumstances of selection are difficult. For example, Go-Go allows selection at a distance, but requires even more hand precision for distant objects, and Hook allows selection of moving objects, but requires users to follow the desired object for a while before it becomes selectable. These "immediate selection" techniques require the user to perform selection in a single precise step and result in users spending more time to select targets in order to be more accurate (an effect known as the speed-accuracy trade-off). The progressive refinement techniques we describe in the rest of the chapter take a different approach.

12.3 Progressive Refinement

While traditional selection techniques use immediate selection and require great care and precision from the user, progressive refinement techniques gradually refine the set of selectable objects to reduce the required precision of the task. For most progressive refinement techniques, this means that a series of rough or imprecise actions can be used to accomplish a precise result, reducing the overall interaction effort.

There is an inherent tradeoff between immediate techniques and progressive refinement techniques. Progressive refinement requires a process of selection, often using multiple steps, although each step can be very fast and accurate. Immediate techniques, on the other hand, involve a single high-precision spatial selection at the expense of having a higher error probability for difficult selection tasks.

The goal of progressive refinement technique design, therefore, is to make the multiple selection steps as simple and fast as baseline immediate selection techniques are, while being much more accurate when the target is small. This can be thought of as "beating" the speed-accuracy tradeoff. By using the concept of progressive refinement, we have shown it is possible to provide highly accurate selection techniques that require significantly less precision from the user when compared to immediate techniques.

For more information on the theory of progressive refinement, including a design space that can be used to generate ideas for new progressive refinement techniques, see our publications [Kopper et al. 2011; Bacim et al. 2013; Bacim 2015].

There are several selection techniques in the literature that can be classified as progressive refinement. For example, the Flower Ray [Grossman and Balakrishnan 2006] uses ray-casting to intersect a number of objects, and then displays those objects in a flower-like menu surrounding the ray to allow the user to specify the desired target. Other 3D selection techniques based on progressive refinement include Expand [Cashion et al. 2012], StarGazer [Hansen et al. 2008], and Shadow Cone-Casting [Steed and Parker 2004]. We focus on three progressive refinement techniques developed in our lab.

12.4 Techniques

In the 3D Interaction Group at Virginia Tech, we have designed, developed, and evaluated dozens of novel 3D selection techniques, including several based on the progressive refinement concept. Three of the best techniques are described below: SQUAD, FRIZ, and Double Bubble.

12.4.1 SQUAD

Sphere-casting refined by quad-menu selection (SQUAD) was the first progressive refinement selection technique developed in our lab. We designed it specifically for situations like the supermarket shown in Figure 12.1, with distant, small, and densely packed objects. SQUAD achieves rapid yet precise selection by dividing selection into two discrete steps, the first being spatial and in-context and the second being out-of-context.

12.4.1.1 Description

The first step of SQUAD uses a modified version of ray-casting that casts a sphere onto the nearest intersecting surface in the VE to determine the set of selectable objects. This subtask is called sphere-casting. The user simply has to ensure that the desired object is inside or touching the sphere, so that it can be picked from among the other objects in the next phase. Figure 12.2 illustrates this selection phase. Sphere-casting avoids the precision issues of ray-casting and allows selection of occluded objects.

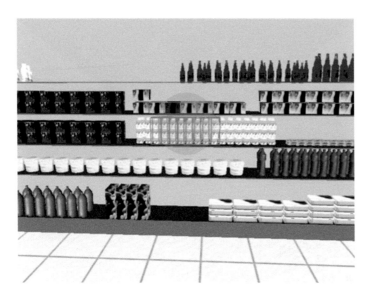

Figure 12.2

Sphere-casting.

Upon completion of the first phase, all objects that are inside or touching the sphere are evenly distributed among four quadrants on the screen. This phase is called quad-menu refinement. Users refine the selection by ray-casting anywhere in the quadrant that contains the target item, each time reducing the number of objects per quadrant until the desired object is the only one left. The selection is completed after a refinement action is performed on a quadrant containing a single object. This process is illustrated in Figure 12.3. The maximum number of selections necessary in the quad menu is the ceiling of $(\log_4 n)$, where n is the initial number of items coming from the sphere-casting phase. For example, if the sphere has between 17 and 64 objects inside it, SQUAD would require at most four clicks to select the target (one click for sphere-casting and three clicks for the quad-menu). Up to 256 objects requires at most 5 clicks and up to 1,024 objects requires at most 6 clicks.

12.4.1.2 Implementation

Sphere-casting could be implemented by casting an invisible ray into the scene in the natural pointing direction defined by a tracked handheld controller. Naïvely, the first intersection of this ray with a geometric object in the scene could determine the center of the sphere. In practice, however, this can cause the sphere to jump between objects at different depths because of tracker or hand jitter. Therefore, we implement sphere-casting by first casting a cone into the 3D environment and centering the sphere at the depth of the nearest object that falls inside the cone.

In order to improve confidence that the desired object will be available, the sphere's radius increases the farther the user is from the nearest intersecting surface, keeping the visual size of the sphere constant while increasing its volume. In our implementation the sphere's radius was set to appear to have a 26° visual size.

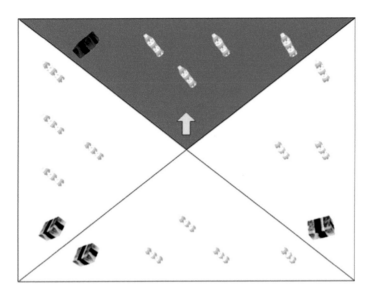

Figure 12.3

Quad-menu refinement.

Objects inside or touching the sphere should be highlighted to let the user know whether the desired target will be selectable after sphere-casting. Testing all objects in the scene could be very compute-intensive, so it is helpful to use a data structure like an octree to limit calculations to those objects in cells that the sphere touches or contains. Once the candidate objects have been determined, it is usually sufficient to test for collisions or containment with the objects' bounding boxes, since the worst thing that will happen is that a few objects outside the sphere but near it will be made selectable.

The quad-menu step is implemented as a full-screen overlay. In a projection-based VR system, this may mean simply taking over one of the physical screens and displaying the quad-menu instead of the virtual environment. In a head-worn display, the quad-menu can be displayed on a polygon that is attached to the user's head so that it will be in view no matter which way the user is looking. However, this polygon should be far enough away from the user's eyes that it does not cause eye fatigue, and large enough so that it fills most or all of the field of view.

The highlighted objects from the sphere-casting step are distributed evenly (perhaps randomly) into the four quadrants, with each quadrant storing its own list of objects. Our implementation creates copies of the objects rather than moving the objects from the 3D scene. Objects will also need to be scaled so that they appear to be approximately the same visual size as all the others. We found it helpful to animate the objects in the quad-menu to rotate slowly in place, so that users could clearly see the 3D shape of the objects. Note that object distribution doesn't have to be random; it could be based on spatial location within the sphere, size, color, shape, or any other relevant criterion.

Selecting a quadrant from the quad-menu uses a simple ray-casting approach. The quadrants should be considered to extend beyond the edges of the screen, so that users only have to point roughly up, down, left, or right to hit the desired quadrant. We highlight the

12. Effortless 3D Selection through Progressive Refinement

entire quadrant background so that it is clear which quadrant will be selected. After the first selection, the items in that quadrant are redistributed to all four quadrants, and this continues until the selected quadrant had only one object, which is selected.

An alternative implementation for the quad-menu display is to decouple the view of the quad menu from the gesture used to refine. For example, the quad-menu can be displayed in a portion of the field of view, and the quadrants can be chosen based on the direction the user is pointing. This alternate design benefits applications where keeping the spatial context is important. One example is in a VR game where the user selects an item from an inventory while keeping track of possible foes in the scene.

12.4.1.3 When to Use It

Because the quad-menu refinements are done out of context, it is important that the target be visually distinct from any other objects. Alternatively, if the goal is to select any one object from multiple instances regardless of spatial location, SQUAD is also effective. For example, in Figure 12.2, if the goal was to select a water bottle, any bottle would suffice.

SQUAD should be used when the targets are small (in our study, it was faster than ray-casting when objects were less than 0.5° across) and/or the object density is not too high (up to 16 objects inside the sphere). The biggest strength of SQUAD, however, is its precision. Our study found that even when ray-casting is faster, it greatly increases the chance of error [Kopper et al. 2011]. However, SQUAD leads to virtually 100% success, regardless of target size or density.

For this reason, SQUAD is well suited for situations where the cost of an erroneous selection is higher than the cost of a slower selection. SQUAD is also appropriate for situations where there are many objects arranged along a surface or clustered in space. Finally, SQUAD can address the selection of moving objects, since as long as the target object is inside the sphere in the first phase of selection, it will be available (and not moving) in the quad-menu.

SQUAD is not well suited for situations where the spatial context is important to determine the selection target. In those scenarios, other progressive refinement techniques are preferred.

12.4.2 FRIZ

The primary limitation of SQUAD is that it requires target objects to be visually distinct. This happens because users have to perform the refinement phase of selection outside of the objects' spatial context. One way to increase accuracy in selection without taking objects out of their spatial context is to increase the target size. In order to do this, users can zoom into the region of the screen containing the target. This is the idea behind a family of Zoom selection techniques. In this section, we describe Flexible Rapid Incremental Zoom (FRIZ), the most effective Zoom-based technique we implemented in our work.

12.4.2.1 Description

We tried two basic approaches to Zoom-based selection. The first was Discrete Zoom, in which users point to discrete regions of the screen (e.g., quadrants), and that region zooms in to fill the entire screen until the target object is large enough to select directly via ray-casting (Figure 12.4).

The second approach we tried was Continuous Zoom, in which the user can zoom in continuously in the direction of a 2D cursor controlled by a tracked handheld device.

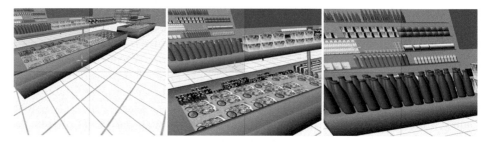

Figure 12.4

Three refinement steps of the Discrete Zoom technique.

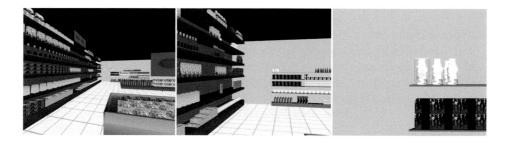

Figure 12.5

Three snapshots of different zoom levels achieved with the Continuous Zoom technique.

This way, users can simply point roughly toward the object and zoom in until the target is large enough for selection (Figure 12.5).

The best feature of the Discrete Zoom technique was the low precision it required in selecting the quadrants for zoom. Its main issue, however, was that every refinement phase required users to perform a new visual search for the target. On the other hand, while Continuous Zoom only required users to perform visual search once, it required more precision than Discrete Zoom. FRIZ is a hybrid of the two approaches that combines the strengths of both techniques into one improved design.

To maintain low precision requirements, we use discrete zoom steps: every time the user presses the zoom in/out button, a pre-determined amount of zoom is used and a short animation is shown, like in the Discrete Zoom technique. A zoom preview window indicates what part of the screen the next level of zoom will show. A 2D cursor is displayed at the location on the screen where the ray is pointing, and the user can choose to select the object under the cursor at any time. Moreover, the cursor stays in the same location in the zoomed image as it was before the zoom operation. Figure 12.6 shows two refinement steps in which the cursor stays in place and the image simply grows around it, as indicated by the blue preview window.

12.4.2.2 Implementation

Zooming in 3D computer graphics is usually done either by applying a scale to the model-view matrix or by scaling the width and height of the view volume [Shreiner 2009]. However, these techniques zoom in to the center of the current view, whereas our technique needs

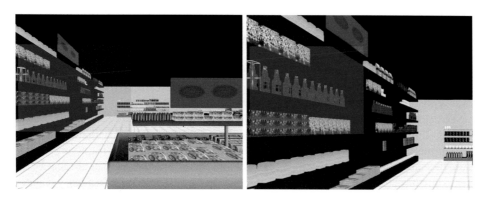

Figure 12.6

Two refinement steps of the FRIZ technique.

to be able to zoom into specific areas of the screen. We considered rendering the scene to a texture and then magnifying it, but this would reduce visual detail. We also considered simply moving the camera rather than zooming, but this can cause occlusion issues.

Instead, we implement zooming by adjusting the frustum to do off-axis projection while also reducing the field of view (Figure 12.7). Most 3D computer graphics make use of *on-axis* perspective projection, in which the viewing direction is perpendicular to the view plane and goes through its center (as in the left image in Figure 12.7). However, in order to get an undistorted and zoomed-in view of a certain region of the original view frustum, we need to use an *off-axis* projection, where the viewing direction is not perpendicular to the

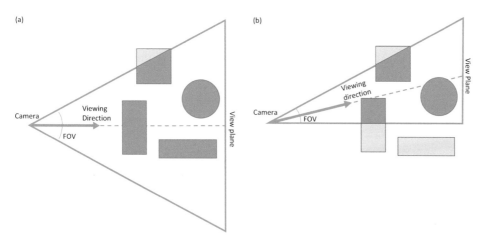

Figure 12.7

Zooming implementation in FRIZ. The large triangle represents the view frustum (shown in 2D for clarity); dark blue shapes are rendered, while light blue shapes are clipped. (a) Original viewing situation. (b) After the user selects the upper portion of the view for zooming, we render an off-axis projection with a reduced field of view, resulting in an exact replica of the image seen within the zoom window in step 1.

view plane (right image of Figure 12.7). In most graphics engines, this requires the creation of a custom projection matrix. At the same time, we must also modify the viewing frustum to give it a narrower field of view. This generates the exact same image as the one shown in the selected region of the screen initially (see Figure 12.6 for an example), and zoom is correctly applied in the image plane without distortions or spatial aliasing. For more detail on off-axis projections, see [Cruz-Neira et al. 1993; Kooima 2019].

Several alternatives for zoom window positioning were considered for the final design of FRIZ. The zoom window could always have the cursor at the center, which would allow users to zoom into regions of the screen not visible in the original view. The zoom window could be snapped to the edges of the screen to avoid this effect, but in either alternative the user would have to re-adjust the cursor position every time zoom is performed.

The solution was to snap the zoom window to the edges of the screen, but zoom in the direction of the cursor position and guarantee that the cursor will point at the same object in the 3D environment after zooming in or out. We do this by matching the position of the cursor in the current zoom level and the next level (illustrated by the zoom preview window), creating an off-axis projection frustum that has the cursor at the same position. This feature also eliminates visual search once a refinement is made.

12.4.2.3 When to Use It

Our studies [Bacim 2015], run on a large projection screen VR system, show that FRIZ, like other progressive refinement techniques, results in almost perfect selection accuracy. It has the desirable property that easy-to-select objects can be selected directly by ray-casting; zoom is always optional and can be used only when needed. FRIZ is sometimes a bit slower than other state-of-the-art progressive refinement and immediate techniques, possibly because users zoom in farther than necessary to be able to select the target accurately. Overall, FRIZ is a solid technique choice in 3D environments with high levels of density, small targets, and/or distant targets.

However, it should be noted that FRIZ would not be ideal for selecting moving objects, since objects might move out of the zoomed-in region before they could be selected. We also have not tried FRIZ in a head-worn display. Zooming may feel strange to users when there is no fixed screen, and it is unclear how head tracking should affect the view when it is zoomed in.

12.4.3 Double Bubble

Similar to SQUAD and FRIZ, Double Bubble implements selection in two phases. As its name implies, Double Bubble uses two selections based on the Bubble Cursor approach [Grossman and Balakrishnan 2005], in which the cursor is a sphere that dynamically changes size so at least one object is selectable at all times. The first selection is done in the 3D environment, and, if there is more than one object inside the bubble, a second selection is done in an on-screen overlay menu with original relative locations and distances preserved (Figure 12.8). A Bubble Cursor is used in this second phase as well to allow fast direct selection of the target object.

12.4.3.1 Description

We saw earlier that SQUAD reduces the precision required to select small objects by casting a large sphere into the environment and making all objects inside the sphere selectable.

     12. Effortless 3D Selection through Progressive Refinement

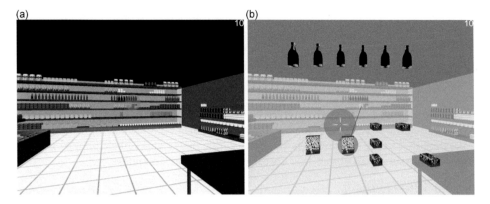

Figure 12.8

Two selection phases of Double Bubble: Bubble Cursor for initial in-context selection (a), and Bubble Cursor used to enhance selection of object in the menu (b).

However, this approach is not very practical in cluttered environments, as the user may end up with a very large number of objects inside the sphere, which will result in more time spent in the quad-menu phase to disambiguate selection. The use of a Bubble Cursor in the first phase of Double Bubble reduces the size of the sphere without necessarily increasing the precision needed for pointing.

The second refinement phase in Double Bubble lays out the objects selected in the first phase in a screen-space grid, similar to Expand [Cashion et al. 2012]. A standard 2D Bubble Cursor, in which the bubble always contains exactly one object, is used for direct selection of the target object in this grid.

Double Bubble also addresses the main limitation of SQUAD: objects needing to be visually distinct to recognize them in the second phase. Double Bubble uses a transparent menu background and a quick animation that shows the objects moving from their original positions in the scene to their new positions in the menu. This allows users to keep track of the target object as it moves. We also show a line that connects the currently highlighted object in the menu to its original counterpart in the scene. The right side of Figure 12.8 shows these improvements.

To further improve users' ability to understand the relationship between the objects in the menu and their counterparts in the scene, Double Bubble distributes the objects based on their original spatial layout. For example, if object A is to the left of object B when they are selected, object A will be to the left of object B in the menu as well. This means relative locations of objects are preserved in the menu. Similarly, Double Bubble also preserves relative distances between objects. For instance, if object C is close to object A, but far from object B, this will be reflected in the menu.

12.4.3.2 Implementation

The first refinement phase in Double Bubble uses a slightly modified version of the original 2D Bubble Cursor. All visible objects are projected onto the screen as 2D objects, and only those objects are initially selectable. Selection is always done in 2D screen space, and the bubble changes its radius based on the closest selectable pixel, which is associated with an object. We use 2D screen-space selection to ensure that all objects "underneath" the bubble are selectable, no matter their depth in the 3D environment. The main difference from the original Bubble Cursor [Grossman and Balakrishnan 2005] is that we introduce a minimum bubble size, and if the bubble contains more than one selectable object inside it when the user performs selection, they are sent to the second selection phase.

Positioning the proxy objects in the menu in the second phase of Double Bubble is done by calculating the relative position of all the objects inside the sphere in screen space, and remapping that to the entire screen. In practice, this menu works like a popped-out and zoomed-in version of all objects that are selectable from the first phase.

12.4.3.3 When to Use It

Double Bubble has been shown to be highly accurate in a wide variety of selection task scenarios, and speed of selection is comparable to other progressive refinement and immediate selection techniques. It was also considered to be very easy to use by participants in our studies [Bacim 2015]. Like FRIZ, it can be used in 3D scenes that have very small and distant objects, and high object density. Easy-to-select objects can be selected directly with the first Bubble Cursor, avoiding the second stage. Unlike FRIZ, it is also appropriate for moving objects, since objects "caught" in the first bubble will show up in the second phase menu.

Overall, Double Bubble is a great general-purpose technique if any 3D selection tasks are expected to be difficult for users. It has a number of nice properties:

- It provides proper spatial cues and preserves spatial relationships between objects in the menu
- It reduces visual search time in the menu due to the spatial cues
- It balances the amount of effort and precision required in both phases of selection
- It decreases the amount of pointing precision needed by providing Bubble Cursor snapping in both phases and larger targets in the second phase

As with FRIZ, we have not experimented with Double Bubble in head-worn displays. Some tweaks to the design would be required, since the camera might be moving due to head-tracking during the second selection phase, but we expect that Double Bubble would remain highly effective with head-worn displays.

12.5 Conclusion

Many VR applications require users to select 3D objects, and the complexity of 3D environments will only continue to increase. To ensure that users are not frustrated by the difficulty of selection tasks, developers should consider state-of-the-art techniques for increasing speed and accuracy as compared to the standard touching and pointing techniques.

In this chapter, we introduced the concept of progressive refinement techniques for 3D selection. These multi-stage techniques are more complex, both from the developer's and the user's perspective. However, they offer speed that is comparable to baseline techniques while greatly increasing accuracy. By using multiple selection steps, where each step is quick and effortless, progressive refinement techniques can beat the speed-accuracy trade-off. They allow users to be confident in their selections without expending too much physical or mental effort, so they can focus on what's most important in the VR application: the experience.

References

[Bacim 2015]

Bacim, Felipe (2015). Increasing selection accuracy and speed through progressive refinement. *Ph.D. dissertation*, Virginia Tech.

[Bacim et al. 2013]

Bacim, Felipe, Regis Kopper, and Doug A. Bowman (2013). Design and evaluation of 3D selection techniques based on progressive refinement. International Journal of Human-Computer Studies, 71(7), 785–802.

[Bowman and Hodges 1997]

Bowman, Doug A., and Larry F. Hodges (1997). An evaluation of techniques for grabbing and manipulating remote objects in immersive virtual environments. In *Proceedings of the Symposium on Interactive 3D graphics*, Providence, RI: ACM (pp. 35–ff).

[Cashion et al. 2012]

Cashion, Jeffrey, Chadwick Wingrave, and Joseph J. LaViola Jr. (2012). Dense and dynamic 3D selection for game-based virtual environments. IEEE Transactions on Visualization and Computer Graphics, 18(4), 634–642.

[Cruz-Neira et al. 1993]

Cruz-Neira, Carolina, Daniel J. Sandin, and Thomas A. DeFanti (1993). Surround-screen projection-based virtual reality: The design and implementation of the CAVE. In *Proceedings of the 20th Annual Conference on Computer Graphics and Interactive Techniques*, Anaheim, CA: ACM (pp. 135–142).

[Figueroa et al. 2010]

Figueroa, Pablo, Yoshifumi Kitamura, Sébastien Kuntz, Lode Vanacken, Steven Maesen, Tom De Weyer, Sofie Notelaers, Johanna Renny Octavia, Anastasia Beznosyk, Karin Coninx, Felipe Bacim, Regis Kopper, Anamary Leal, Tao Ni, Doug A. Bowman (2010). 3DUI 2010 contest grand prize winners. IEEE Computer Graphics and Applications, 30(6), 86–96.

[Frees et al. 2007]

Frees, Scott, G. Drew Kessler, and Edwin Kay (2007). PRISM interaction for enhancing control in immersive virtual environments. ACM Transactions on Computer-Human Interaction, 14(1), 2.

[Grossman and Balakrishnan 2005]

Grossman, Tovi, and Ravin Balakrishnan (2005). The bubble cursor: Enhancing target acquisition by dynamic resizing of the cursor's activation area. In *Proceedings of the SIGCHI Conference on Human Factors in Computing Systems*, Portland, OR: ACM (pp. 281–290).

[Grossman & Balakrishnan 2006]

Grossman, Tovi, and Ravin Balakrishnan (2006). The design and evaluation of selection techniques for 3D volumetric displays. In *Proceedings of the 19th Annual ACM Symposium on User Interface Software and Technology*, Montreux, Switzerland: ACM (pp. 3–12).

[Hansen et al. 2008]

Hansen, Dan Witzner, Henrik H. T. Skovsgaard, John Paulin Hansen, and Emilie Møllenbach (2008). Noise tolerant selection by gaze-controlled pan and zoom in 3D. In *Proceedings of the 2008 Symposium on Eye Tracking Research & Applications*, Savannah, GA: ACM (pp. 205–212).

[Kooima 2019]

Kooima, Robert (2019). Perspective projection for VR. In Sherman, W. R., editor, *VR Developer Gems*, Chapter 33. A K Peters/CRC Press: Boca Raton, FL.

[Kopper et al. 2011]

Kopper, Regis, Felipe Bacim, and Doug A. Bowman (2011). Rapid and accurate 3D selection by progressive refinement. In *Proceedings of IEEE Symposium on 3D User Interfaces*, Singapore: IEEE (pp. 67–74).

[LaViola et al. 2017]

LaViola Jr., Joseph J., Ernst Kruijff, Ryan P. McMahan, Doug Bowman, and Ivan P. Poupyrev (2017). *3D User Interfaces: Theory and Practice*. Addison-Wesley Professional: Boston, MA.

[Mine 1995]

Mine, Mark R. (1995). Virtual environment interaction techniques. *UNC Chapel Hill CS Dept. Technical Report*.

[Ortega 2013]

Ortega, Michael (2013). Hook: Heuristics for selecting 3D moving objects in dense target environments. In *Proceedings of IEEE Symposium on 3D User Interfaces*, Orlando, FL: IEEE (pp. 119–122).

[Poupyrev et al. 1996]

Poupyrev, Ivan, Mark Billinghurst, Suzanne Weghorst, and Tadao Ichikawa (1996). The Go-Go interaction technique: Non-linear mapping for direct manipulation in VR. In *Proceedings of the 9th Annual ACM Symposium on User Interface Software and Technology*, Seattle, WA: ACM (pp. 79–80).

[Riege et al. 2006]

Riege, Kai, Thorsten Holtkämper, Gerold Wesche, and Bernd Fröhlich (2006). The bent pick ray: An extended pointing technique for multi-user interaction. In *Proceedings of IEEE Symposium on 3D User Interfaces*, Alexandria, VA: IEEE (pp. 62–65).

[Schreiner 2009]

Shreiner, Dave (2009). *OpenGL Programming Guide: The Official Guide to Learning OpenGL, Versions 3.0 and 3.1*. Pearson Education: London.

[Steed and Parker 2004]

Steed, Anthony, and Chris Parker (2004). 3D selection strategies for head tracked and non-head tracked operation of spatially immersive displays. In *Proceedings of 8th International Immersive Projection Technology Workshop* (pp. 13–14).

[Vanacken et al. 2007]

Vanacken, Lode, Tovi Grossman, and Karin Coninx (2007). Exploring the effects of environment density and target visibility on object selection in 3D virtual environments. In *Proceedings of IEEE Symposium on 3D User Interfaces*, Charlotte, NC: IEEE.

[Wingrave and Bowman 2005]

Wingrave, Chadwick A., and Doug A. Bowman (2005). Baseline factors for raycasting selection. In *Proceedings of HCI International*, Las Vegas, NV.

13

Travel in Virtual Reality

Jason Leigh
University of Hawai'i at Mānoa

13.1 Introduction

Travelling in virtual reality (VR) is needed to provide a user the freedom to move in a virtual space beyond the limits of the physical space in which the VR hardware is situated. For example, while in the real world I may only be able to move a few feet while tethered to my VR hardware, in the virtual world I might like to travel greater distances. This may occur with the push of a button, a flick of a joystick, the tilt of a VR controller, or by walking atop an omnidirectional treadmill.

In this chapter however we focus on the most common use cases—where a user may be holding one or more VR controllers each capable of detecting 6-degree of freedom (6-DOF) motion (location in X, Y, Z, and rotation around X, Y, Z), and typically equipped with at least a joystick and/or directional pad, and multiple buttons.

Before we begin we'll consider criteria that make up a good travel scheme. Then we will examine a number of VR travel schemes in the context of these criteria. You can use this to help you decide which scheme is most appropriate for your application and audience. Most of these schemes can be found online, especially in the Unity Asset Store. One gem of a travel scheme which is not in the Asset Store is the Omni-navigator—a minimalistic but elegant full 6-DOF travel scheme that is most useful when first prototyping a new VR application where you want the flexibility of being able to look at your VR world from any perspective without constraint. We will describe how to implement this travel scheme in detail in this chapter.

13.2 What Makes a Good Travel Scheme?

An effective travel scheme should attempt to meet as best as possible, the following criteria:

1. It should minimize the number of interface controls used (e.g., buttons).
2. It should maximize the degrees of freedom of movement possible.
3. It should be as easy to learn as possible.
4. It should minimally fatigue the user.
5. It should minimize the potential for nausea and eye strain.
6. It should maximally maintain presence.
7. It should be applicable to a wide range of VR hardware such as Head Mounted Displays (HMDs), Room-based environments such as CAVEs [Cruz-Neira et al. 1992], CAVE2s [Febretti et al. 2013, 2014], CyberCANOEs [Kawano et al. 2017] and SunCAVEs.

Against these criteria we will describe and evaluate the following travel schemes: (1) first-person-shooter-style travel, (2) tele-hop, (3) waypoint navigation, (4) grappling hook navigation, and (5) the omni-directional navigator. Then we will go into detail in the implementation of the Omni-directional navigator.

13.3 The Contestants

The Table below (Table 13.1) summarizes all the travel schemes compared against our seven criteria for evaluating them.

13.3.1 First-Person-Shooter-Style

This scheme first appeared in projection-based virtual environments such as the CAVE in the early 1990s. The CAVE is a ten-foot-shaped room whose walls are rear-projected with stereoscopic 3D images (see Figure 13.1 for some examples). Most CAVEs tended to leave the rear open for entry and exit. And on rare occasion there were a few with screens on all six sides.

The popular travel scheme, which is still applicable today and pre-dates all first-person-shooter video games, uses the joystick on the VR controller/wand to move forward and backward along the direction of the wand, and turn left/right along the vertical axis. Strafing (moving sideways) is achieved by pointing the wand in the direction of strafe and pushing the joystick forwards or backwards. This scheme is most commonly used for traveling along a horizontal plane although movement upward and downward is possible by pointing the wand upward or downward and pushing the joystick forwards or backwards. The main advantage of this scheme is that it allows the traveler to always face the front of the CAVE while traveling. For HMDs this can help mitigate the user getting tangled up by the display cord.

With the advent of the popular video game DOOM in 1993, the use of WASD keys for moving forwards, backwards, strafing left and right became a de-facto standard for

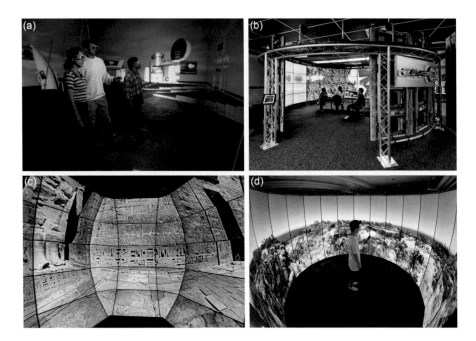

Figure 13.1

The CAVE™: CAVE Automatic Virtual Environment (a) and the CAVE2™ (b) at the Electronic Visualization Laboratory at the University of Illinois at Chicago; the SunCAVE Environment (c) at the Qualcomm Institute at the University of California San Diego; and the CyberCANOE: Cyber-enabled Collaboration Analysis Navigation & Observation Environment at the Laboratory for Advanced Visualization & Applications at the University of Hawai`i at Mānoa (d).

first-person-shooter video games. Turning under this scheme was performed by moving the mouse left and right, while looking up and down was performed by moving the mouse up and down. Pictured in Figure 13.2b the VR equivalent of this scheme is to use the joystick or direction pad to mimic WASD and to use the physical turn of one's head to mimic the movement of the mouse. The direction of strafe is applied perpendicularly to the forward vector of the user's head. As with the previous travel scheme, this scheme is ideal for moving along a horizontal plane as found in most first-person-shooter games. This scheme takes better advantage of the fact that HMDs allow the user to face any direction at the risk of getting tangled up in the display cord (until cords are eventually eliminated in future HMDs). It is however not well suited for supporting pitching and rolling in a fully three-dimensional environment, unless additional input controls are incorporated. This scheme is also not well suited for CAVEs, CAVE2s, etc., where rotation de-coupled from the view is often desired.

13.3.2 The Tele-Hop

Tele-Hop works by having a user point a virtual target at the destination and pressing a button (Figure 13.3). In most VR applications the target extends at the end of the VR controller/wand in an arc that intersects with the horizontal surface intended as the

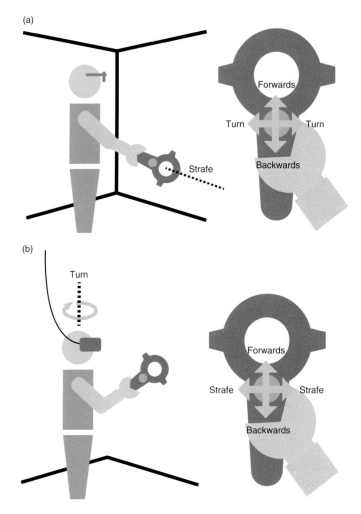

Figure 13.2

First-person-shooter-style travel in CAVE (a) and in Head Mounted Display (b).

destination of the tele-hop. The chief advantage of this scheme is that the potential for motion sickness is very low. It is also very easy for novice users to learn to use. The disadvantage however is that tele-hop can disrupt the users' sense of mental immersion (presence) in the VR environment. This scheme was frequently used in the earliest Oculus and HTC Vive applications as their software developers feared that the VR experiences might cause their novice audience to become motion sick, thereby potentially "killing" the VR market before it had left the starting block.

13.3.3 The Grappling Hook

The grappling hook is similar to the tele-hop scheme in that the user points at a destination to travel toward. It differs from the tele-hop scheme in that, once a target

Figure 13.3

The tele-hop control scheme.

is selected, the VR camera will then interpolate a path toward the target. This scheme's main advantage is that it is easy to learn how to use while maintaining a sense of presence in the environment. Anecdotal evidence suggests that if the movement is highly accelerated such that the experience becomes akin to "warping," then motion sickness can be mitigated as the images are presented as a brief series of strobes (which at 4–8 Hz has been shown to reduce motion sickness) [Reschke et al. 2006]. Motion sickness in head mounted displays can be further mitigated by reducing the field of view during warping [Ruddle 2004].

13.3.4 Waypoints

Waypoints are perhaps the easiest means of traveling in VR for the user. It is essentially auto-pilot for VR. In general, a user is given four buttons—two of the buttons are for moving to the next and previous waypoints (Figure 13.4). The third button is to move to the home waypoint (to reset the VR experience). The last button is to play and pause the entire set of waypoints in a sequence. Movement between waypoints generally involves a smooth interpolation of location and orientation of the VR camera. This scheme is good at maintaining presence at the risk of introducing motion sickness. This scheme is also very useful for creating pre-scripted tours of a virtual environment hence alleviating the user from having to learn any kind of travel scheme.

Figure 13.4

The waypoint control scheme.

13.3.5 The Omni-Navigator

All the previous travel schemes imposed constraints on movements in one form or another. Tele-hop and grappling hook travel schemes typically do not allow for any change in orientation. Waypoints impose pre-set travel points from which the user cannot deviate. The first-person-shooter-style travel schemes are not ideal if pitching and rolling is needed.

In the Omni-navigator scheme the user imagines that they are holding an airplane or bird in their hand and how they position and orient the bird determines how the user will navigate through the space. To use this navigation scheme, the user begins by holding the wand at an initial origin/starting position and orientation. Then by pressing a button and moving the wand from that origin, the distance, direction and orientation from the initial origin determines the direction, rate of translation (movement in location) and rotation about all three axes (Figure 13.5). For example, to move forward, the user presses the trigger button and moves the wand forward. The distance from the starting position of the wand determines the speed of movement. To move upward, the user presses the button and moves upward. The distance from the starting position again determines the speed of movement. To pitch, yaw, or roll, the user presses the trigger button and tilts the wand in one or more of the three axes. The greater the angle of tilt the more rapid the rotation.

This travel scheme has the advantage that with only the use of one button and the position of the wand, the user can achieve full 6-degree of freedom movement in addition

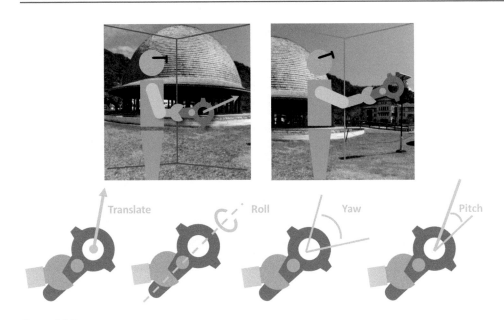

Figure 13.5

The Omni-navigator control scheme.

to rate of movement. Of course, if desired, some degrees of movement can also be constrained. For example, if a VR developer wanted to adapt this scheme to a first-person-shoot-style of movement along a horizontal plane, one simply has to exclude vertical movement, pitching and rolling.

One potential disadvantage of this scheme, of those we have covered, is that it is perhaps the least intuitive for novices. However, the difficulty can be mitigated by reducing the speed of movement as well as drawing a paper airplane or bird in the navigation hand so the user has a frame of reference for understanding the travel scheme. Another potential disadvantage of this scheme is that it can cause motion sickness for users (and in a CAVE, their riders) with poor travel skills. However, once mastered, users typically find the degree of control unparalleled by any other travel scheme.

The next section explains in greater detail the algorithm and its implementation in SteamVR and Unity.

13.4 The Omni-Navigator in Detail

In most VR environments there is the notion of a "container" in which the user's head and wand controllers are held. So when travel is performed it is this container that is moved through the larger virtual space, and then from within the container the user may walk around the limited physical space constrained by the VR hardware—it's like riding on a rectangular, invisible platform or vessel. In SteamVR the container is called the "Camera Rig" ([CameraRig]) and is encapsulated in a Unity Game Object (Figure 13.6).

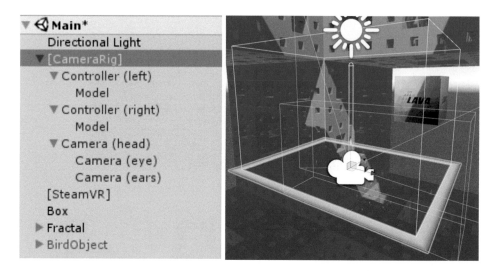

Figure 13.6

During navigation the Unity *[CameraRig]* acts like a "container" that carries with it the head, and wand. In SteamVR, the bright blue box is referred to as the SteamVR_Play Area, which essentially marks the boundaries of the "container".

The algorithm below describes how to use the aforementioned interaction scheme to move the "container" through space.

1. First obtain the starting position and orientation (transform) of the wand controller before travel is enacted.
2. Measure the distance between the new position of the wand and the starting position. Incrementally move the container in the direction and speed determined.
3. Measure the angular difference between the new orientation of the wand and the starting orientation of the wand. Incrementally rotate the container by the angular difference determined. The rate of rotation is determined by the magnitude of the angular difference.

Now let's look at the algorithm in greater detail by examining its corresponding C# source code fragments for SteamVR using the Unity game engine. Additional information on how to use the script is provided after the description of the algorithm and code.

1. if travel button is pressed the first time (changes state from being unpressed) store the wand's position and orientation in local coordinate space (startPosition, startRotation)

```
startPosition = wand.transform.localPosition;
startRotation = wand.transform.localRotation;
```

Else steps 2 & 3:

2. Perform translation:
   a. Find the difference between startPosition and current position of wand in local coordinates, call this movement. In essence this is the vector describing the direction and speed we want to move in.

      ```
      Vector3 movement = wand.transform.localPosition - startPosition;
      ```

   b. As mentioned earlier, since we want to be able to move independently of the direction we are looking there is the notion of a "container" in VR, and it is this container that is moving through space and the head and wands are inside this container. In SteamVR this container is the [CameraRig] object. The Unity Editor is used to attach the navigation script to the [CameraRig] object (see Figure 13.9).

   c. The movement vector is applied to the [CameraRig] to create the appropriate translation (movement) through space.

      ```
      this.transform.Translate(movement * Time.deltaTime * moveSpeed);
      ```

3. Next we address the rotation:
   a. We obtain the current orientation of the wand in local coordinates—call this newRotation

      ```
      Quaternion newRotation = wand.transform.localRotation;
      ```

   b. Calculate "diffAng"—the angle between the startRotation and newRotation angle.

      ```
      diffAng = Quaternion.Inverse(startRotation *
                      Quaternion.Inverse(newRotation));
      ```

   c. We apply a spherical interpolation (slerp) between the angle diffAng and the identity to determine the fractional angle to turn at each time step.

      ```
      frac_rotate = Quaternion.Slerp(Quaternion.identity, diffAng,
                               Time.deltaTime * rotateSpeed);
      ```

   d. We apply this fractional angle to the current rotation angle of the [Camera Rig].

      ```
      // NOTE: in the following line we use the implicit "this." operator
      for the transforms.
      transform.localRotation = transform.localRotation * frac_rotate;
      ```

13.4.1 Adding Constraints

If we wish to constrain movement so that no movement in the upward direction (y) occurs (such as for applications where we would like navigation to only involve walking rather than flying) we can set the y component of the movement vector to zero after step 2. We can likewise do the same for the x and z components if our application calls for such constraints.

If we wish to lock rotation so that it only occurs around one of the three axes we zero out the other two axis components in both startRotation and newRotation after step 3. Lastly, it is often useful to be able to reset navigation to an initial starting location and orientation. To achieve this one can simply interpolate from the current position and orientation of the [CameraRig] to the initial position and orientation.

For more details on how the aforementioned constraints are implemented in C#, the reader should examine the source code for the Omni-navigator provided for this book.

13.5 Setting Up the Omni-Navigator Script in Unity

Figure 13.7 shows the demonstrational Unity environment for the Omni-navigator included with the book. In the environment you will be surrounded by a large blue fractal. Within the fractal is an orange cube with the LAVA logo on it. When you press the trigger of the right wand controller, a bird will appear indicating that you are in travel mode. With the trigger pressed you can motion with the wand to perform travel as described earlier. To stop travel at any time, release the trigger. When you hold the side button on the wand, the Omni-navigator brings you back toward its designated home position (which is set to 0, 0, 0 in the demonstration).

Figure 13.8 shows the development screen for the application. The Omni-navigator script is a component of the [CameraRig] object.

A Capsule Collider and a Rigid Body component are used to prevent the [CameraRig] from falling through the ground or passing through walls. As mentioned earlier, the head and wand are children of the [CameraRig], which acts as the "container" that travels through the virtual space. The function `AdjustPlayerCollider()` in the full script is used to adjust the position of the collider based on the position of the user's head. This ensures that collisions are detected against the user (who may move independent of the container) rather than the container itself. So for example if you are standing close to the orange cube and attempt to walk into it, the collider will move with you and in the process prevent you from passing through the orange cube. Furthermore `AdjustPlayerCollider()` also adjusts the collider's height, so if a user crouches the collider reduces in height. This allows a user to then crawl through low spaces if necessary.

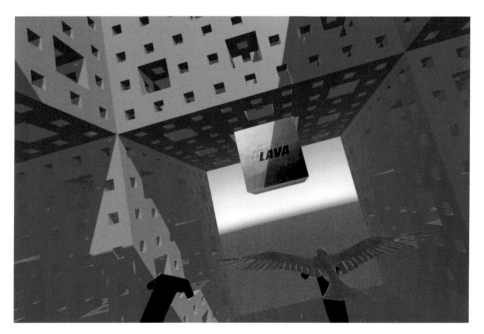

Figure 13.7

The demonstration environment for the Omni-navigator.

13. Travel in Virtual Reality

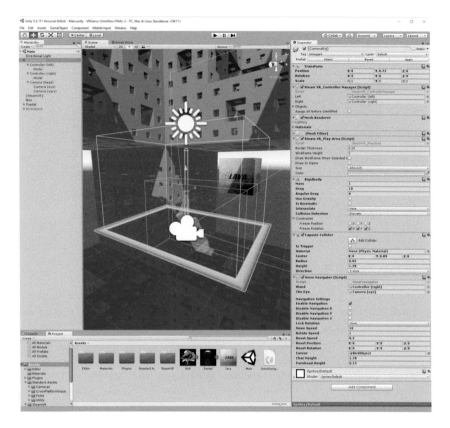

Figure 13.8

The Unity development environment showing the *[CameraRig]* settings in the Inspector view (on the right).

If instead, in your application, you prefer to collide between the virtual world and the container then you can omit calling `AdjustPlayerCollider()` and leave the default collider component locked to the center of the container.

13.6 The Knobs (Script Settings)

Once you have installed the Omni-navigator script into the [CameraRig] you can adjust its options within the field box for each public setting (see Figure 13.9 for the Unity Editor view). The meaning of the fields are:

- **Wand** (GameObject): The Unity game object representing the wand to use for travel.
- **The Eye** (GameObject): The Unity game object representing the user's eye in SteamVR (useful for determining the height of the capsule collider).
- **Disable Navigation** (in X, Y, Z): Disable movement along the selected axes.

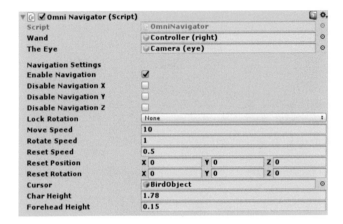

Figure 13.9

A close-up view of the Omni-navigator script component.

- **Lock Rotation**: Lock rotation around an axis (either X, Y, or Z). Lock rotation so that it only occurs along one of the axes.
- **Move Speed**: Movement speed in (grid-units/s).
- **Rotate Speed**: Rotation speed in (degrees/s).
- **Reset Position** (Vector3): Position considered the home position for the environment.
- **Reset Rotation** (Vector3): Specify the home rotation angle about X, Y, and Z
- **Cursor** (GameObject): Specify a 3D model asset to make visible when in navigation mode (in this example the bird is assigned as the cursor).
- **Char Height**: Anticipated height of the user (set to 1.78 m by default).
- **Forehead Height**: Height of the user's forehead (set to 0.15 m by default).

13.7 Conclusion

Table 13.1 summarizes the relative advantages and disadvantages of the various travel schemes and is a good place to look to help you decide on an appropriate scheme to use in your VR application. The Omni-navigator is excellent if you don't want to rush into committing to a travel scheme yet, but want the ability to explore your environment before making the final choice. As such, even if you were to choose one of the other travel schemes as the primary scheme for your users, the Omni-navigator still makes an excellent "god-mode" travel scheme that lets you to move through the virtual space completely unconstrained.

Acknowledgments

This work was co-sponsored by the Academy for Creative Media System and the National Science Foundation awards ACI 1550126 and CNS 1530873.

Table 13.1 Comparison of Common Virtual Reality Travel Schemes

	First-Person-Shooter 1990s	First-Person-Shooter Post-DOOM	Tele-Hop	Grappling Hook	Waypoint Nav	OmniNav
Number of controls used	Joystick/DPAD & 6-DOF wand	Joystick/DPAD & 6-DOF head & wand	Button & 6-DOF wand	Button & 6-DOF wand	3 buttons	Button & 6-DOF wand
Deg of freedom enabled	4	4	3	3	1	6
Fatigue	Low	Low	Low	Low	Very Low	Low
Difficulty	Easy	Easy	Easy	Easy	Very Easy	Medium
Motion sickness	Medium	Medium	Low	Medium	Medium	Medium
Presence	High	High	Low	Medium	Medium	High
HMD	OK	OK	OK	OK	OK	OK
6-wall CAVE	OK	OK	OK	OK	OK	OK
WAVE, walls, 4- or 5-wall CAVE, CAVE2, CyberCANOE	OK	Cannot see rear to navigate	Cannot turn	Cannot turn	Cannot see rear waypoint	OK
Advantages	Easy to learn 2D travel scheme that also works in wall-based VR environments	Easy to learn 2D travel scheme	Good for traveling long distances and minimizing nausea at the cost at immersion	Good for traveling long distances	Good for novices and traveling long distances at the cost of immersion	Most flexible generic navigation scheme. Good for "god mode"

References

[Cruz-Neira et al. 1992]

Cruz-Neira, Carolina, Daniel J. Sandin, Thomas A. DeFanti, Robert V. Kenyon, and John C. Hart (June 1992). The CAVE: Audio visual experience automatic virtual environment. *Communications of the ACM.*

[Febretti et al. 2013]

Febretti, Alessandro, Arthur Nishimoto, Terrance Thigpen, Jonas Talandis, Lance Long, J. D. Pirtle, Tom Peterka, Alan Verlo, Maxine Brown, Dana Plepys, Dan Sandin, Luc Renambot, Andrew Johnson, and Jason Leigh (2013). CAVE2: A hybrid reality environment for immersive simulation and information analysis. In *Proceedings of the Engineering Reality of Virtual Reality 2013*, San Francisco, CA: IS&T/SPIE Electronic Imaging, February 4, 2013.

[Febretti et al. 2014]

Febretti, Alessandro, Arthur Nishimoto, Victor Mateevitsi, Luc Renambot, Andrew Johnson, and Jason Leigh (2014). Omegalib: A multi-view application framework for hybrid reality display environments. In *Proceedings of 2014 IEEE Virtual Reality (VR)*, Minneapolis, MN: IEEE, pp. 9–14. doi:10.1109/VR.2014.6802043.

[Kawano et al. 2017]

Kawano, Noel, Ryan Theriot, Jack Lam, Eric Wu, Andrew Guagliardo, Dylan Kobayashi, Alberto Gonzalez, Ken Uchida, and Jason Leigh (2017). The destiny-class CyberCANOE—A surround screen, stereoscopic, cyber-enabled collaboration analysis navigation and observation environment. In *Proceedings of IS&T International Symposium on Electronic Imaging Science and Technology*, Burlingame, CA, pp. 25–30.

[Reschke et al. 2006]

Reschke, Millard F., Jeffrey T. Somers, and George Ford (Jan 2006). Stroboscopic vision as a treatment for motion sickness: Strobe lighting vs shutter glasses. *Aviation Space Environment Medicine*, 77(1), pp. 2–7.

[Ruddle 2004]

Ruddle, Roy A. (2004) The effect of environment characteristics and user interaction on levels of virtual environment sickness. In *Proceedings of IEEE Virtual Reality*, Chicago, IL: IEEE. 11, pp. 141–148. doi:10.1109/VR.2004.1310067.

14

From Painting to Widgets, 6-DOF and Bimanual Input Beyond Pointing

Bret Jackson
Macalester College

Daniel F. Keefe
University of Minnesota

In this chapter, we present an approach to designing expressive 3D user interfaces that make use of handheld input devices tracked in 3D space to go beyond a simple pointing metaphor. We show how employing the State Design Pattern can be useful for implementing interfaces in this style, and we provide examples from recent work highlighting particular design considerations. We hope that the reader will come away with the knowledge and inspiration to design more complex and expressive 3D user interfaces.

14.1 Introduction

What would you do if you could hold a magic wand in your hand? Better yet, one in each hand! From the early days of virtual reality (VR), hardware and software designers have continued to return again and again to the concept of VR wands—handheld, tracked 6-degree-of-freedom input devices—as a primary means of input. Note, by 6-degree-of-freedom, abbreviated 6-DOF, we mean 3 degrees for positioning (location) plus 3 degrees for rotating (orientation). The names of these devices (e.g., wand, stylus, 3D mouse, game controller) and number of buttons, joysticks, trackpads and other options have changed over the years, but there seems to be something fundamentally appealing and exciting about the opportunity to interact with the computer by moving one (or more) 6-DOF tracked devices through the air.

Despite this fundamental appeal and the consistent evolution of hand input VR hardware over the years, we find that the majority of VR applications simply do not take advantage of the amazing opportunity provided by holding a magic wand in one's hand. The most obvious thing to do with one of these devices is to point. Thus, there are countless examples of VR laser pointers and flying metaphors (i.e., point the wand in the direction you wish to fly). These metaphors are a fine and useful starting point, but what else is possible? How do we go beyond pointing and/or integrate it within larger, more complex interfaces? Surely, there must be more we can do with a magic wand in our hands!

Conceptually, 6-DOF stylus input can support many interactions that go beyond or build upon pointing. We encourage readers to consider designing interfaces that support more expressive, complex poses and gestures, often made in a body-centric way, and we provide several examples later in the chapter. Many of these "beyond-pointing" interfaces will take advantage of user interaction within arm's reach, perhaps involving direct manipulation with virtual content. Beyond-pointing interfaces built upon 6-DOF input devices can also be used to define spatial relationships (3D poses, orientations, distances) relative to one's body; grab objects and rotate, translate, scale, and twist them; and make sweeping movements and gestures over time. All these types of interactions may be made directly in 3D space or relative to some form of virtual widget. What's more, with two 6-DOF tracked devices, one in each hand, a bimanual user interface can be created whereby each of these beyond-pointing interactions can be combined to create simultaneous and composite interactions. Just as we might hold a piece of pottery in one hand while painting on it with the other, in a composite 6-DOF interaction, one hand can set the context for the other. This potential to harness natural, body-scale, and coordinated (e.g., bimanual) input is where we believe VR will shine.

Given this broad design space and great potential, why don't we see more beyond-pointing interfaces in current VR applications? We believe there are several reasons. First, it requires a different approach to programming. In desktop-based programming, our most common computing paradigm, the assumption is that the user controls just a single cursor. Thus, most programs rely upon this single cursor to set focus for input events and so on. In recent years, as multi-touch user interfaces have become more widely utilized, it has been exciting to see this assumption challenged more and more often, and new multi-cursor infrastructure for desktop, tablet, and phone platforms is emerging. This is useful for VR, as many new VR programmers may at least be familiar with the concept of multi-cursor input now. Yet, there are still important differences. For example, in VR, each cursor has more degrees of freedom; users often stand up without access to a keyboard or other complementary devices; and often it is dark or the view of our hands is blocked, so we work with input devices we cannot see. Whereas pointing and clicking is the dominant interaction mode in desktop computing, the VR situation is different, and user interface concepts such as gesture and spatial proximity become much more important. Thus, a different approach is needed when designing and implementing these VR interfaces.

How then does one design and program useful VR beyond-pointing interfaces? Answering this question is the key message of this chapter. Our approach is to first introduce a general framework and terminology that can apply to any VR bimanual user interface. Then, we walk through a series of three examples that build upon each other to demonstrate how sophisticated 6-DOF, beyond-pointing, bimanual VR user interfaces can be built upon this framework.

14.2 VR Bimanual UI Framework and Terminology

The framework we promote is event-based. Inputs, such as button presses, generate events; the VR program listens for these events and then responds appropriately. We also treat movements of the 6-DOF trackers as events, similar to the way modern windowing systems report mouse move events. Since this movement is often nearly continuous, this means that an application can expect to respond to tracker move events almost every frame.

Although event-based user interfaces are common in desktop computing, there are several important nuances in VR. For example, the need to work with multiple 3D coordinate systems and the need to interpret input relative to the current digital and physical context. It is possible today to purchase a VR input device with more buttons than we have fingers. Many developers will thus be tempted to simply assign one system action to each button. This is fine for expert users who are willing to put time into training and who will eventually develop a mental map of the input devices, but we advocate a different approach. We demonstrate several examples where the context in which input events occur can be used to disambiguate users' intent. Thus, context (from both the physical and virtual worlds) is important. The state machine design pattern that we suggest for programming VR interfaces helps programmers to track and respond appropriately to changes in context.

14.2.1 Definitions

Before demonstrating with examples how this framework can be applied to create exciting VR interfaces, let's begin with just a few definitions:

14.2.1.1 Coordinate Systems

Tracker Space: The raw data from the tracking system is reported in a Tracker Space coordinate system (origin and axes), as shown in Figure 14.1a. This coordinate system may align with the Room Space coordinate system, but does not always. In a calibrated system, the raw data is converted into Room Space before being reported in the tracker matrix.

Room Space: A coordinate system defined relative to the physical space the VR display hardware occupies. The Room Space coordinate system provides a way to relate tracking

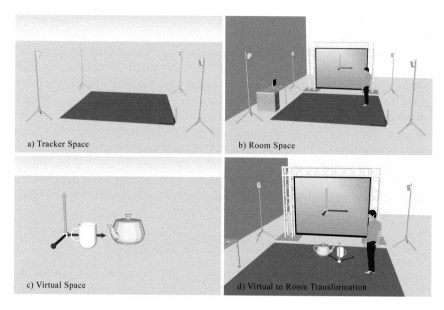

Figure 14.1

(a) Tracker Space is defined relative to the specific 3D tracking hardware. (b) Room Space is defined relative to the physical VR display. Sometimes this is the same as Tracker Space, but often it differs slightly, for example, in a projection-based VR display, the origin of Room Space may be defined conveniently to be located at the center of the display or the center of the walkable area. The virtual cameras set up in the VR graphics engine will be defined in Room Space; so, Room Space provides the essential link between tracking hardware and graphics rendering. Some virtual content (e.g., cursors, menus) may be defined in Room Space coordinates when the intent is for their virtual positions to stay consistent within the physical room. (c) The main content of the virtual scene is typically defined in a separate coordinate system called Virtual Space. (d) This Virtual Space content may be scaled, translated, or rotated relative to Room Space in order to make large viewpoint adjustments (travel through the virtual world).

data to graphics, since the virtual cameras used to render VR graphics are also defined in Room Space coordinates.

Virtual Space: A coordinate system used to define virtual content that may move relative to the physical room. Virtual Space content may be rotated, scaled, or translated relative to the Room Space coordinate system, but Room Space content will stay fixed within the room. A virtualToRoom 4×4 transformation matrix is used to encode the transformation between Virtual Space and Room Space.

14.2.1.2 Devices, Events, and Widgets

6-DOF: 6-Degree-of-Freedom. Three Position (Location) + three Rotation (Orientation).

Tracked Device: A VR input device, such as a wand or stylus, that can be tracked in 3D space, often with 6 degrees of freedom. Often the device will have buttons or other inputs. When the device is moved, a Tracker_Move event is generated, and when a button is depressed and later released, Button_Down and then Button_Up events are generated.

Event: A discrete programmatic signal generated in response to user input, for example a press or release of a button or movement of a tracked device to a new location or orientation relative to its last move event.

Tracker and **Tracker Matrix:** Each tracked device has (or can be modeled as having) a 6-DOF tracker attached to it. The Tracker Matrix is the raw data, typically a 4×4 transformation matrix, reported by this tracking hardware. These are the data reported by Tracker_Move events. The Tracker Matrix is reported in Room Space coordinates.

Cursor and **Proxy Matrix:** An icon or other visual representation of the tracked device displayed in VR for the user to see. In some applications the cursor may be drawn at the exact location defined by the Tracker Matrix, but we will discuss several examples where it is useful to offset this location slightly. For example, imagine a snap-to-grid mode, where small positional movements of a physical tracker are ignored in order to keep the virtual tracker locked onto a grid point. Thus, we add the concept of a Proxy Matrix, which stores the current position (location) and orientation of a virtual proxy for the tracker. The cursor is drawn at the position and orientation specified in the Proxy Matrix, which is defined in Room Space and is often close to, but not necessarily the same, as the Tracker Matrix.

Widget: A virtual user interface object, such as a menu, that responds to and provides a visual target for user input. Widgets may be defined in Room Space so that they appear to occupy the same space as the user (often useful for menus), or they may be defined in Virtual Space so that they move together with a virtual scene.

14.2.1.3 Context-Based User Interface

Interface Context: A discrete set of circumstances defined by both the virtual environment and the physical environment that requires input events to be interpreted differently. The circumstances are often significant enough that each interface context would include a change in visual feedback for the user.

State: We suggest an implementation based upon the state design pattern, where each state is a programmatic representation of the interface context.

14.2.2 State Design Pattern

There are many ways to implement beyond-pointing VR interfaces. We make two recommendations. First, and most importantly, recognize the importance of the interface context (defined above) in VR and choose a style of implementation that is designed to handle this context elegantly—in contrast, the approach we have too often seen is to handle state changes via one long conditional (**if**) statement, which does not scale well. Second, we recommend a specific approach that makes use of the state design pattern used extensively in object-oriented software design. Since this is the approach used in the remainder of the chapter, we begin with a brief description of the State Pattern.

"The State Pattern allows an object to alter its behavior when its internal state changes. The object will appear to change its class" [Freeman et al., 2004]. Figure 14.2 shows an example diagrammed in Unified Markup Language (UML).

In our approach, a client (e.g., your program's main loop), will notify UITechnique that some input event has occurred by calling onEvent1(), onEvent2(), etc. But, the way in which the user interface responds could be quite different depending upon which ConcreteState is currently active. Thus, your job as a software designer and programmer

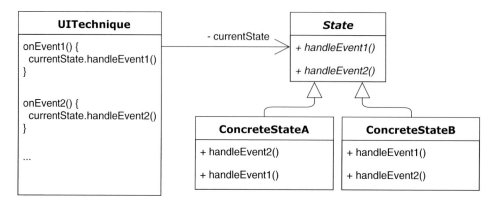

Figure 14.2

A generic illustration of the state design pattern applied to handling user input events. UITechnique always maintains one current state. When your program calls UITechnique::onEvent1() or UITechnique::onEvent2(), these calls are passed on to whichever ConcreteState class is pointed to by currentState.

is to determine how to properly divide your desired functionality into states and to implement these in separate ConcreteState* classes. The remainder of this chapter provides a series of increasingly complex examples to demonstrate how this may be accomplished.

14.3 Example 1: Implementing a 3D Painting User Interface

Our first example demonstrates how to implement a basic 3D painting user interface. There is a long history of VR applications based on 3D painting metaphors. Early work in this style can be found in Clark's surface designing system [Clark, 1976], 3-Draw [Sachs et al., 1991], 3DM [Butterworth et al., 1992], and Holosketch [Deering, 1995]. A second generation of 3D painting user interfaces can be found in applications, such as BLUI [Brody and Hartman, 1999], CavePainting [Keefe et al., 2001, 2005], Surface Drawing [Schkolne et al., 2001], FreeDrawer [Wesche and Seidel, 2001], and Digital Tape Drawing [Grossman et al., 2002]. More recently, Drawing on Air [Keefe et al., 2007, 2008a, 2008b], Shape Modeling with Sketched Feature Lines [Perkunder et al., 2010], Mockup Builder [De Araùjo et al., 2012, 2013] and Lift-Off [Jackson and Keefe, 2016] are representative of an ongoing emphasis within the VR research community on improving control in free-hand 3D painting and drawing user interfaces. In parallel, 3D painting applications built in industry, including Tilt Brush [Google, 2017], have leveraged commodity hardware and modern graphics rendering to make the techniques widely accessible and even more compelling. The examples pictured in Figure 14.3 are from CavePainting and Drawing on Air.

3D painting interfaces are excellent examples for our discussion of how to build beyond-pointing VR interfaces. The common interaction in all of them—creating new virtual forms via sweeping, gestural movements of a tracked wand in space—requires interpreting 6-DOF input in a way that goes well beyond pointing. Artists report making dance-like, gestural movements that incorporate not just the 3D path of the brush but also

Figure 14.3

3D Paintings created in VR using the CavePainting and Drawing on Air interfaces.

the orientation along the path [Zen, 2004; Mäkelä et al., 2004; Keefe, 2011]. There are many possible extensions in these tools that also go beyond pointing, ranging from interaction with physical props and virtual widgets to bimanual precision 3D drawing interfaces.

Let's begin the technical discussion by describing the core hardware and input events we expect in a bimanual interface for 3D painting. Our description assumes that the user is holding two tracked devices, each with a single button. When the button on the device held in the dominant hand is pressed, the event named DH_Down is generated, and when it is released, DH_Up is generated. Likewise, the button on the device held in the non-dominant hand generates NDH_Down and NDH_Up events. Finally, DH_Move and NDH_Move events are generated whenever the tracking system reports a change in the position or orientation for the corresponding tracked device.

The basic 3D painting interface described in this example (Example 1) supports two key user interactions. First, the dominant hand is used to paint—when users press and hold a button on this tracked device, a stream of virtual "paint" begins to emerge from the brush, and as they move and twist the brush through the air, additional paint, which could take almost any form in VR, is deposited along the path. Second, the non-dominant hand is used to "grab onto" the virtual painting and move it around. We call this reframing the painting. While reframing, changes in the full position (location and orientation) of the non-dominant hand are applied to the virtualToRoom matrix, so it is possible to both translate and rotate the painting in order to get a good look at it from different angles and place it in a comfortable position for making the next brushstroke. While reframing, it is also possible to enter a scaling mode. Simultaneously holding down the dominant hand button (so now, the button on each hand is depressed) activates a scaling mode where the scale of the virtualToRoom matrix is adjusted to scale the painting up or down in proportion to the distance between the two hands.

Figure 14.4 is a diagram of a state machine that can be used to implement this basic functionality. The interaction technique begins in the IDLE state. Notice that when a DH_Down event is generated, the state transitions to the PAINT state. This is the most important interaction in the whole user interface. When PAINT is entered, a new brush stroke is created. While in the PAINT state, each DH_Move event adds a new segment of geometry to this stroke. Finally, a DH_Up event triggers a transition back to the IDLE state.

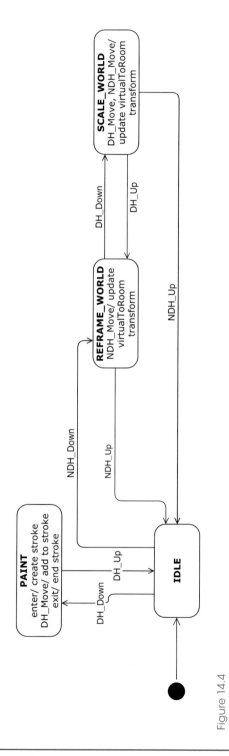

Figure 14.4

The finite state machine for a basic 3D painting user interface.

14. From Painting to Widgets, 6-DOF and Bimanual Input Beyond Pointing

Reframing is engaged from the IDLE state. A NDH_Down event triggers a transition to the REFRAME_WORLD state. From here, a DH_Down event triggers a further transition to the SCALE_WORLD state.

This last transition, from REFRAME_WORLD to SCALE_WORLD, is the first example in this chapter of a common pattern that we argue is a critical component of beyond-pointing user interfaces. Here, the DH_Down event triggers a different response depending upon the current state. In the REFRAME_WORLD state, DH_Down transitions to a scaling mode, whereas in the START state, DH_Down starts painting. Thus, the meaning of DH_Down is overloaded; it takes on a different meaning depending upon the context.

In this case, this overloaded behavior makes perfect sense. In general, the dominant hand is for painting and the non-dominant hand is for reframing, but once we have engaged a reframing operation, it is natural to extend this operation just a bit to adjust the scale in response to the motion of the two hands. There is no need to add a separate button to the input devices to support this, instead, we can reuse the same dominant hand button used for painting. This has an intuitive meaning for the user. Reframing and scaling can be described as, "grab on to the painting with one hand to translate and rotate, and grab on with two to scale it", and the user only needs to be able to locate a single button on each tracked device in order to perform all of the operations.

Now that we have designed an appropriate state machine, we can begin to translate the idea into actual code. Figure 14.5 is a class diagram that illustrates how this

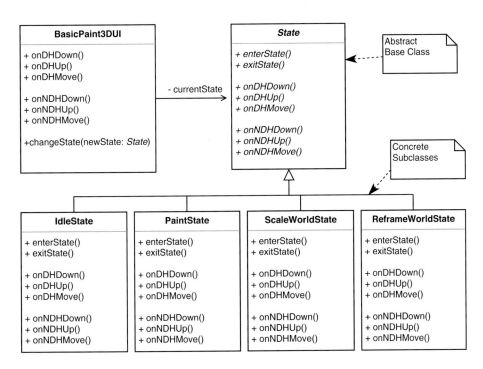

Figure 14.5

UML class diagram for the classes needed to implement the state machine diagrammed in Figure 14.4.

basic 3D painting state machine can be implemented using the State Design Pattern. BasicPaint3DUI serves as the main class that should be connected to the rest of your program. It includes a currentState member variable that points to an object of type State, which is an abstract class. There are four concrete implementations of State, one for each of the states defined in Figure 14.4. When BasicPaint3DUI is created, it will create one instance of each of the four concrete implementations and save a reference to each. Then, the job of BasicPaint3DUI is simply to act as a pass-through object. When your program tells it that a DH_Down event has occurred by calling onDHDown(), it simply passes this event through to the current state, which will handle the event appropriately. In C++, the code to implement this pass-through feature can be very simple, as shown in Listing 14.1.

Listing 14.1. Pass through an input event to the current state handler.

```
void BasicPaint3DUI::onDHDown() {
    currentState->onDHDown();
}
```

The implementation for passing other events through to the current state would follow the same pattern.

It is also important for BasicPaint3DUI to implement a method for changing the state, as shown in Listing 14.2.

Listing 14.2. Handle a state transition.

```
void BasicPaint3DUI::changeState(State *newState) {
    if (newState != currentState) {
        currentState->exitState() ;
        currentState = newState;
        newState->enterState();
    }
}
```

The concrete implementations of State may then call BasicPaint3DUI::changeState(..) whenever they receive an event that should trigger a state change or otherwise determine that a state change is required.

With these key code snippets in mind, consider the following example implementation of PaintState in Listing 14.3, one of the concrete states in the basic painting interface.

Listing 14.3. Example implementation of the PaintState.

```
class PaintState {
public:
    PaintState(BasicPaint3DUI *in_uiTechnique, State *in_startState) {
        uiTechnique = in_uiTechnique;
        startState = in_startState;
    }
```

14. From Painting to Widgets, 6-DOF and Bimanual Input Beyond Pointing

```
    void enterState() {
        // create a new brush stroke object here.
    }

    void onDHMove() {
        // add geometry to the brush stroke object here.
    }

    void onDHUp() {
        uiTechnique->changeState(startState);
    }

private:
    BasicPaint3DUI *uiTechnique;
    State *startState;
};
```

Of course, in a real implementation the code needed to create a new brushstroke and add geometry to it is likely to be quite complex, so this PaintState class would need to interface with graphics libraries and be much more detailed in practice. Keeping this complexity isolated to a single class is another reason why treating the user interface code for the painting context as its own class is useful.

14.4 Example 2: Adding Proximity Events and Widgets

This second example builds upon the first, adding the features needed to turn the basic 3D painting interface of Example 1 into a complete application. The first addition is an interface to resize the virtual brush; it introduces the notion of proximity events, which are used several times throughout the remainder of the chapter. The second addition makes it possible to interact with 3D widgets (e.g., menus, color pickers, other virtual objects). As in Example 1, context will be important in both of these new features. If the artist user is in the middle of a grand, sweeping brushstroke and happens to move the brush into a widget, we wish to just ignore that contact with the widget and continue on with the painting operation. On the other hand, if the user is not actively painting at the moment, then moving the virtual brush within close proximity of a widget is a good indication that the user intends to work with that widget.

Figure 14.6 adds two new features to the same finite state machine pictured in Figure 14.4. The first feature, brush resizing, makes it possible for artists to adjust the thickness of the paintbrush, essentially adjusting the line weight of the virtual 3D marks it will create. Since this operation is similar to scaling, a similar interface is used. The brush size is set to be proportional to the distance between the hands. The brush cursor is also adjusted during this operation—immediate visual feedback is important.

The most interesting aspect of this brush resizing interaction for our discussion is the way it is activated. Notice in Figure 14.6 that the RESIZE_BRUSH state is entered only after first entering a HANDS_TOGETHER state. This is a new state that we enter only when we determine that the two hands are within close proximity to each other, and serves to disambiguate the meaning of the DH_Down event. Since paint brushes are relatively small compared to the size of our bodies, users naturally put their hands close together in order to adjust the brush size. In contrast, the hands are rarely held close to each other

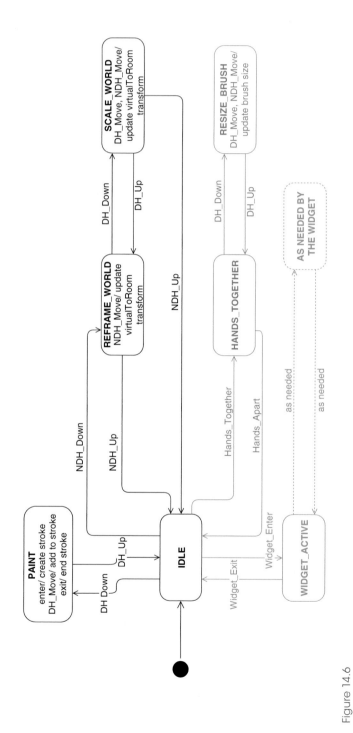

14. From Painting to Widgets, 6-DOF and Bimanual Input Beyond Pointing

Figure 14.6

The basic 3D painting state machine is extended here to support brush resizing (blue) and interaction with a widget (green).

while painting, since that is performed with the dominant hand while the non-dominant hand is at one's side. Thus, we use the proximity of the hands as a cue to disambiguate the user's intent. If the distance between the two hands is within a threshold (e.g., 15 cm), then we wish to transition from the IDLE state to the HANDS_TOGETHER state. From within the HANDS_TOGETHER state, a DH_Down event will trigger a transition to the RESIZE_BRUSH state. In contrast, if the hands are not within the proximity threshold, then a DH_Down event within the IDLE state will trigger a transition to the PAINT state as before. Visual feedback helps users understand how this proximity-based interface works, so it is recommended to include a change in the brush cursor to indicate that a button press will engage the resizing operation when within the HANDS_TOGETHER state.

There are several possible ways to implement this proximity-based functionality. Sticking with the event-based framework described thus far, we recommend detecting the instant the distance between the two hands falls under a threshold and treating this as a discrete Hands_Together event. Similarly, when the distance between the hands is greater than the threshold, this can also be treated as a significant event, which we call Hands_ Apart. The advantage of this approach (generating new events) as opposed to including distance calculations and logic directly within the state machines is that the transitions remain simple—the state machine simply transitions whenever it receives the appropriate event. Of course, the distance calculations do need to happen somewhere, and for this we introduce the idea of Proximity Events—events, just like those generated from a regular input device, but generated dynamically in response to tracker input.

The Proximity Events needed for the features described in this chapter can be generated by the state machine diagrammed in Figure 14.7. We call this our "Proximity Checker." The state machine contains two orthogonal regions running in parallel to output different types of Proximity Events.

For each new event received by the application, the event is passed first to the Proximity Checker, which acts as a virtual input device, and then on to the larger, application-oriented finite state machines, such as the one diagrammed in Figure 14.6. If the Proximity Checker generates new events, these are simply added to the current event queue. For example, notice in the left half of Figure 14.7 that the Hands_Together and Hands_Apart events mentioned earlier are generated in response to specific distance calculations. The same strategy is used to generate Widget_Enter and Widget_Exit events.

The second key feature introduced in the updated finite state machine diagrammed in Figure 14.6 is the ability to interact with widgets. For a 3D painting application, common widgets include a color picker, texture picker, menu of 3D style types (i.e., different styles of geometry for the paint), and menu of system control operations (e.g., load, save, print, undo, redo). All of these can be implemented with the same pattern illustrated in green within Figure 14.6. Here, the Widget_Enter event generated by the Proximity Checker is used to control the state transition. Because the system only responds to Widget_Enter when in the IDLE state, a widget (e.g., menu) can be activated as intended from this state but if we happen to hover over the menu while in the process of painting (i.e., while in the PAINT state), the Widget_Enter event is ignored, elegantly avoiding an unintended activation of the menu.

The Proximity Checker can be extended to test proximity to multiple widgets, each with its own _Enter and _Exit events. It is flexible for widgets needing to respond differently depending on how many hands are inside the widget. The right half of Figure 14.7

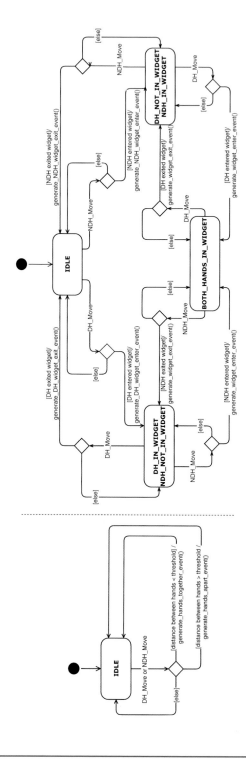

Figure 14.7

This Proximity Checker state machine, shown with two orthogonal regions running in parallel, acts as a virtual input device, interpreting Tracker_Move events from regular input devices and generating new events, for example, a Hands_Together event to signify the instant the tracked devices held in the hands come within a short distance of each other.

14. From Painting to Widgets, 6-DOF and Bimanual Input Beyond Pointing

shows how a DH_Enter_Widget event is generated when the dominant hand enters a widget and a NDH_Enter_Widget event when the non-dominant hand enters.

The Proximity Checker can also be extended to test for more elaborate gestures. For example, _Enter events might be redefined to mean that a tracked device is approaching the location of the widget but does not yet fall within its bounds or to mean that a tracked device is pointing toward the widget or has performed some other more elaborate gesture. In some versions of the CavePainting system a menu palette is activated at the location of the non-dominant hand when the user turns over their hand to look at their palm, a gesture that naturally defines a surface plane and evokes the idea of holding a palette in one's hand. Regardless of the method of activation, once the widget is activated, the system transitions to a WIDGET_ACTIVE state and further movements and button presses are handled as determined by the widget's state(s). Multiple widgets can be included in the design simply by duplicating the same pattern within the finite state machine (and renaming WIDGET_ACTIVE to be specific to each widget). Some widgets may be simple to implement, having just one state, and others may define additional states and transitions that hang off of their widget active state.

Figure 14.8 shows several example widgets from various versions of the CavePainting application developed at Brown University between 2000 and 2007. These widgets (various styles of menus, a 3D color picker) are relatively simple in that they can be implemented by adding just one or two "widget" states to the diagram in Figure 14.6. The next section builds upon these simple widgets, describing an example of a more complex, dynamic widget that includes multiple interaction modes and responds in real-time to the positions and orientations of both hands.

14.5 Example 3: Adding Constraints, Control, and Dynamic Widgets

This example presents additional possibilities for adding smart constraints, improving control, and integrating dynamic computation into VR widgets that are inspired by the

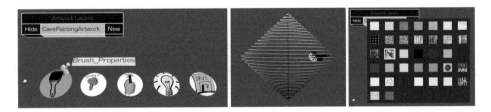

Figure 14.8

Example widgets used in CavePainting. Left: The blue "Artwork Layers" widget is an example of a 3D menu with a standard box-like layout. The palette of circular menus at the bottom activate in the location of the non-dominant hand when users flip their hand over, as if to look at their palm. The brush, controlled by the dominant hand, is currently hovering over the "Brush_Properties" sub-menu. Clicking and holding at this point would activate a range of choices displayed radially outward. Middle: A 3D color picker widget maps the Hue-Saturation-Value color space to a true 3D space, users work with this widget simply by moving the hand within the bounds of the double-sided cone. Right: A texture selection widget is used to change the visual appearance of the virtual paint strokes.

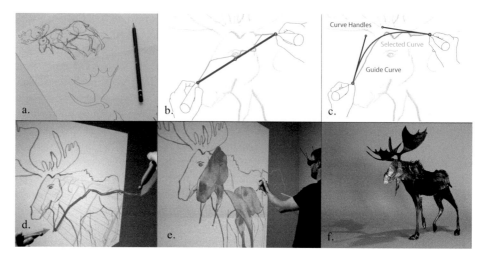

Figure 14.9

The Lift-Off 3D modeling interface. (a) 2D sketches are placed as 3D slides in the VR environment. (b) When both hands are within the activation distance of a slide, a guide curve (shown in red) is projected on the slide. (c) Rotating the tracked devices moves the curve handles changing the shape of the curve guide. The selected curve (shown in green) is influenced by the guide but is constrained to follow curve features identified automatically in the image. (d) The selected curve is lifted off the slide and placed in space as a rail. Rotation of the tracked devices changes the shape of the rail by bending to adjust depth. (e) Multiple rails create a wireframe. Surfaces are swept between rails to create the model. (f) The resulting 3D model rendered with Blender.

Lift-Off 3D modeling interface [Jackson and Keefe, 2016] shown in Figure 14.9. The Lift-Off modeling interface makes use of several bimanual interactions and 3D widgets that go beyond pointing and are more complex than the previous examples. We will start by briefly summarizing the user interface followed by more in-depth discussions of specific implementation details.

14.5.1 Overview of the Lift-Off Interface

The Lift-Off workflow starts by creating 2D pencil-and-paper sketches (Figure 14.9a). These sketches are integrated into the VR environment as 3D slides placed in space. Slides are chosen and placed using the slide selection and placer widget shown in Figure 14.10.

After the slide is placed in space, the artist can select a curve from the 2D imagery. This is accomplished by placing both tracked devices inside the activation area of the slide. The curve selection widget shows a cubic Bézier guide curve (shown in red in Figure 14.9b and c) that is projected on the surface of the slide. Each tracked device controls two of the Bézier control points (shown as the blue curve handles) to adjust the position and curvature. The guide curve gives visual feedback and functions like a magnetic rope. It pulls along the selected curve (shown in green) which settles onto the closest curve identified in the underlying pixel data of the slide texture. Clicking the button on the dominant hand's tracked device confirms the curve selection, and the curve now becomes a dynamic 3D widget called a rail that can be adjusted and bent in 3D space by rotating the tracked devices (Figure 14.9d).

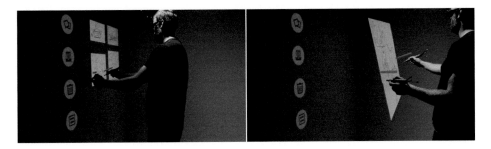

Figure 14.10

Left: A slide selection widget. Placing both tracked devices near a slide and creating a DH_Down event selects the slide, like lifting a picture off of a wall. Right: The selected slide sticks to the tracked devices until a second DH_Down event confirms the position. Rotating the tracked devices changes slide orientation and moving them further apart adjusts the scale. Note the red cursor representations of the tracked devices. The cursors are offset using a proxy matrix to avoid occlusions of the stereo images by the hands.

After a series of these rail creation actions, the artist builds up a wireframe of connecting rails defining the outlines of the 3D model that they are creating (Figure 14.9e). Connections are facilitated by snapping the virtual cursors to the endpoints of existing rails, either in 3D space or projected onto the surface of the slide, when the tracked device is close to an existing endpoint.

Two final modeling operations are needed: first, the ability to divide a rail into two pieces to add new endpoints for future connections, and second, a way of creating surfaces between the rails to form the geometry of the 3D model. Approaching a rail with the tracked device will highlight it. Clicking and releasing a button will divide the rail. However, if the tracked device is swept away from the highlighted rail before releasing the button, then a surface will be created filling in the spaces between the particular rails indicated by the direction of the sweep gesture.

14.5.2 Implementing Gesture-Based State Changes

There are several interesting design and implementation details that make this interface more complex than the previous two examples. The complete Lift-Off finite state machine is diagrammed in Figure 14.13. Here, we explore the implementation details of a subset of the state machine used to split rails in two pieces or to create surfaces between them, as described in the previous section. The subset of the state machine is shown in Figure 14.11. This interaction illustrates an important difference from previous examples because changes from one state to another depend on gestural 3D movements, in addition to proximity or button presses.

Gestural state changes can be challenging to implement because they depend on device input over a sequence of time. The possible output states can also be divergent. For example, in Figure 14.11 from the RAIL_ACTIVE state, a DH_Down event can signal the start of two possible transitions. If the DH_Up event is received before the tracked device is moved significantly, then the rail is split, and the state transitions to the back to IDLE. However, if the stylus is moved more than a specified distance from the rail, the system

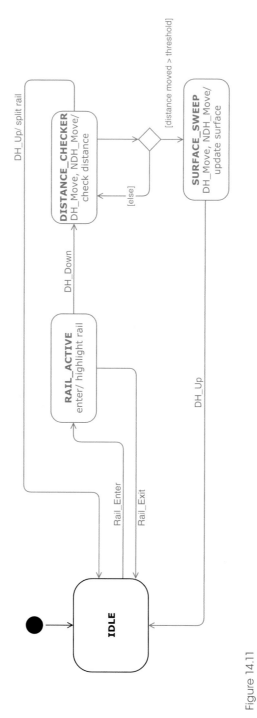

Figure 14.11

A subset of the Lift-Off modeling state machine used for dividing rails or sweeping surfaces between them.

enters the SURFACE_SWEEP state and a surface is created. A DH_Up at this point will finalize the surface creation and return the state back to IDLE.

To implement this type of gestural state change, we introduce a new state called DISTANCE_CHECKER. In this state, the DH_Move event is used to update the cursor position, but the state also calculates the distance the cursor has moved from the rail. If this distance increases above a threshold, then it will automatically transition to the SURFACE_SWEEP state.

14.5.3 Implementing Dynamic Widgets

Compared to the basic Proximity Checker used to activate widget states in Example 2, Lift-Off presents an added challenge. What makes this interaction different than the previous examples is that the slide and rail widgets are dynamic. They do not exist at the start of the program and their number depends on how many the user has created at runtime. Figure 14.12 extends the subset of the Lift-Off state machine shown in Figure 14.11. In this example the transition from IDLE to the RAIL_ACTIVE or SLIDE_ACTIVE states depends on the Proximity Checker calculating the distance to the *closest* slide or rail to determine whether it is within a threshold. This requires additional computation, a common occurrence for dynamic widgets.

To implement this efficiently, the Proximity Checker, acting as a virtual input device, must contain a reference to a shared data structure holding a list of dynamic widgets, updated as they are created. The 3D_RAIL_PLACEMENT state also needs to contain a reference to this data structure since it will add new rail widgets to the list.

At runtime, the list of dynamic widgets can be sorted to find the closest one using a custom comparison function. For each widget in the list, the function calculates the distance to the tracked object. Storing the widget data in a KD-Tree [Bentley, 1975] or other space-partitioning data structure will accelerate this process. The comparison function can also take into account the relative priority for different types of widgets. For example, the Lift-Off interface gives preference to slides when determining the closest object so that users can start to select new curves even when a 3D rail lies near a slide.

Implementing dynamic widgets also calls for interpreting the DH_Move events differently. For static widgets, which are typically defined in Room Space coordinates, data provided by Tracker_Move events can be interpreted directly since they are also provided in Room Space coordinates. However, for dynamic widgets the tracker events might need to be interpreted in Virtual Space. Here, the relative position of the slides and rail widgets directly depends on the virtual model being created, and the events must be interpreted in the same coordinate system, Virtual Space.

The slide widgets are dynamic in another way as well. Each slide contains a different 2D texture that is determined at runtime. As a result, the user interface to select curves must be flexible and controlled enough that users are able to indicate their desired selection regardless of the particular texture. In the next section, we describe how to implement contextual constraints (e.g. real-time image processing) to improve control of 3DUIs.

14.5.4 Contextual Constraints to Improve Control

A major challenge for beyond-pointing interfaces is that they can be difficult for users to control effectively. For example, CavePainting [Keefe et al., 2001] allows a user to create

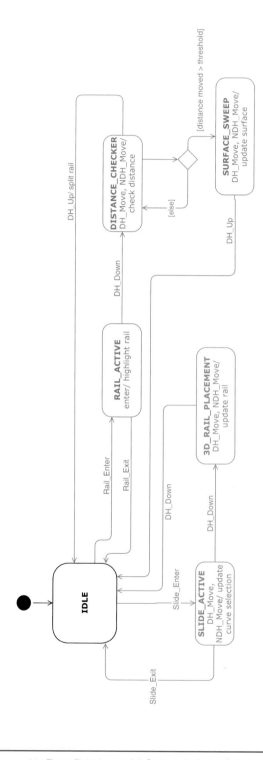

Figure 14.12

The Lift-Off modeling state machine is extended here to support rail creation (green).

14. From Painting to Widgets, 6-DOF and Bimanual Input Beyond Pointing

exciting gestural lines swept through the air, but it falls short of allowing an artist to draw a precise curve or even a perfectly straight line.

Using Lift-Off as an example, we advocate for using smart contextual constraints to improve control while limiting the impact on freedom of expression. The use of this state-based framework for beyond-pointing interfaces makes them easier to implement because the interpretation of events (i.e. the interface context) is encapsulated inside a class representing a particular state.

Lift-Off makes use of contextual constraints in several ways. In the SLIDE_ACTIVE state, each hand only has 3-DOF (two for the xy-position of the guide curve endpoint on the slide texture and one for rotation to indicate the position of the curve handle). This level of constraint is possible because the actual selection is based on image-based computations to set the selected curve.

Control is further improved by adding the ability to snap the cursor to an endpoint of a previously selected curve when the cursor is nearby, constraining the movement to ignore small hand jitters. Snapping is accomplished by adjusting the cursor position. In this situation the cursor position differs from the tracked object position by means of a Proxy Matrix. Actions that are based on the tracker's position (like selecting curve endpoints) in either room or virtual space should take this Proxy Matrix into account.

Contextual constraints are also used in the 3D_RAIL_PLACEMENT state. In this state, the user input is interpreted within the context of the guide surface (the transparent grid extending from the slide in the extruded shape of the selected curve, Figure 14.9d). Cursors are constrained to follow the closest point on the guide surface to each of the tracked objects' positions. The 3D rail is constrained to lie on the surface, although its shape can now be bent along this surface in 3D. These constraints make it possible to create precise curves and straight lines to model complex shapes with precision.

Lift-Off's finite state machine has a series of state transitions that linearly follow a series of steps. As seen in Figure 14.12, this still fits within the state framework described above. In fact, it would be challenging to implement it without the state design pattern. This raises the question of when to add a new state to a program. We recommend creating a new state (i.e. a new program class) when the context of an interaction changes and input events must be interpreted differently. This is usually correlated with changes in visual feedback and the ways that the input should be constrained to add control. In this example, the SLIDE_ACTIVE and 3D_RAIL_PLACEMENT states are distinct because the way they constrain the cursors and interpret the DH_Move and NDH_Move events is different.

When you want to enhance control in VR, turn to constraints. In developing user interfaces, you should find the things that you can do well with 6-DOF input and do them. Then, find the things that do not work very well and add constraints.

14.5.5 Putting It All Together

In this example we have described how the Lift-Off interface can serve as inspiration for gesture-based state changes with dynamic widgets involving computation that can improve users' control through constraints. In addition to the rail creation process described in Section 14.1, Lift-Off also supports rail creation by directly painting rails in the air in the style of the 3D paint application in Example 1. It has additional states for reframing and scaling, as well as saving and loading models, and deleting the artwork. The full finite state machine for Lift-Off is diagrammed in Figure 14.13. In contrast to

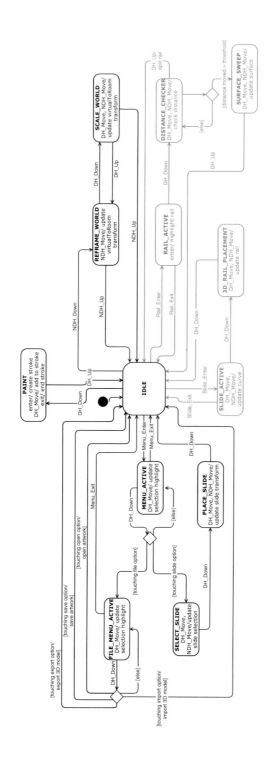

Figure 14.13

The Lift-Off modeling state machine builds on the basic 3D painting application. It has more complex transitions, including many states that are chained together. This transitional logic would be challenging to elegantly implement without the State Pattern.

14.   From Painting to Widgets, 6-DOF and Bimanual Input Beyond Pointing

the previous two examples, this example shows how a more complex user interface can be implemented using states, and hopefully it provides motivation for adoption of this approach. Creating a complete system of this scale and complexity would be extremely challenging without the organizational structure of the state framework.

14.6 Conclusions

Many VR user interfaces can be implemented using this state-based UI framework. The examples presented here show only a few possibilities, but we hope that they have inspired the reader to create user interfaces that go beyond pointing to accomplish more complex tasks. In designing new user interfaces, you should take full advantage of the amazing opportunity VR affords by holding magic wands in our hands, and you should use *both* hands. When you get two hands involved in the interaction, you should use state and the interaction context intelligently to provided significant functionality with a small number of buttons. Resist the urge to add one more button to the device for every new feature that comes along—your users will thank you when one button magically does what they want depending on the context.

References

[Bentley, 1975]

Bentley, Jon Louis (1975). Multidimensional binary search trees used for associative searching. *Communications of the ACM*, 18(9):509–517.

[Brody and Hartman, 1999]

Brody, Arthur William, and Chris Hartman (1999). BLUI: A body language user interface for 3D gestural drawing. *In: Proceedings of SPIE: Human Vision and Electronic Imaging*, 3644(3):356–363.

[Butterworth et al., 1992]

Butterworth, Jeff, Andrew Davidson, Stephen, Hench, and T. Marc Olano (1992). 3DM: A three dimensional modeler using a head-mounted display. In *Proceedings of the 1992 Symposium on Interactive 3D Graphics*, New York: ACM, pages 135–138.

[Clark, 1976]

Clark, James H (1976). Designing surfaces in 3-D. *Communications of the ACM*, 19(8):454–460.

[De Araùjo et al., 2012]

De Araùjo, Bruno R., Géry Casiez, and Joaquim A. Jorge (2012). Mockup builder: Direct 3D modeling on and above the surface in a continuous interaction space. In *Proceedings of Graphics Interface 2012*, GI '12, Toronto, ON: Canadian Information Processing Society, pages 173–180.

[De Araújo et al., 2013]

De Araújo, Bruno R., Géry Casiez, Joaquim A. Jorge, and Martin Hachet (2013). Mockup builder: 3D modeling on and above the surface. *Computers & Graphics*, 37(3):165–178.

[Deering, 1995]

Deering, Michael F (1995). HoloSketch: A virtual reality sketching/animation tool. *ACM Transactions on Computer Human Interaction*, 2(3):220–238.

[Freeman et al., 2004]

Freeman, Eric, Elisabeth Robson, Bert Bates, and Kathy Sierra (2004). *Head First Design Patterns: A Brain-Friendly Guide*. California: O'Reilly Media, Inc.

[Google, 2017]

Google Inc. (2017). Tilt brush. https://tiltbrush.com/.

[Grossman et al., 2002]

Grossman, Tovi, Ravin Balakrishnan, Gordon Kurtenbach, George Fitzmaurice, Azam Khan, and Bill Buxton (2002). Creating principal 3D curves with digital tape drawing. In *Proceedings of the Conference on Human Factors in Computing Systems*, New York: ACM, pages 121–128.

[Jackson and Keefe, 2016]

Jackson, Bret and Daniel F. Keefe (2016). Lift-off: Using reference imagery and freehand sketching to create 3D models in VR. *IEEE Transactions on Visualization and Computer Graphics*, 22(4):1442–1451.

[Keefe, 2011]

Keefe, Daniel F. (2011). From gesture to form: The evolution of expressive freehand spatial interfaces. *Leonardo*, 44(5):460–461.

[Keefe et al., 2001]

Keefe, Daniel F., Daniel Acevedo Feliz, Tomer Moscovich, David H. Laidlaw, and Joseph J. LaViola Jr. (2001). CavePainting: A fully immersive 3D artistic medium and interactive experience. In *Proceedings of I3D*, North Carolina: ACM, pages 85–93.

[Keefe et al., 2005]

Keefe, Daniel F., David B. Karelitz, Eileen L. Vote, and David H. Laidlaw (2005). Artistic collaboration in designing VR visualizations. *IEEE Computer Graphics and Applications (CG&A)*, 25(2):18–23.

[Keefe et al., 2007]

Keefe, Daniel F., Robert C. Zeleznik, and David H. Laidlaw (2007). Drawing on air: Input techniques for controlled 3D line illustration. *IEEE Transactions on Visualization and Computer Graphics*, 13(5):1067–1081.

[Keefe et al., 2008a]

Keefe, Daniel F., Daniel Acevedo, Jadrian Miles, Fritz Drury, Sharon M. Swartz, and David H. Laidlaw (2008). Scientific sketching for collaborative VR visualization design. *IEEE Transactions on Visualization and Computer Graphics*, 14(4):835–847.

[Keefe et al., 2008b]

Keefe, Daniel F., Robert C. Zeleznik, and David H. Laidlaw (2008). Tech-note: Dynamic dragging for input of 3D trajectories. In *Proceedings of IEEE Symposium on 3D User Interfaces*, Nevada, pages 51–54.

[Mäkelä et al., 2004]

Mäkelä, Wille, Markku Reunanen, and Tapio Takala (2004). Possibilities and limitations of immersive free-hand expression: A case study with professional artists. In *Proceedings of the 12th Annual ACM International Conference on Multimedia*, New York: ACM, pages 504–507.

[Perkunder et al., 2010]

Perkunder, Helen, Johann Habakuk Israel, and Marc Alexa (2010). Shape modeling with sketched feature lines in immersive 3d environments. In *Proceedings of the 7th Sketch-Based Interfaces and Modeling Symposium*, SBIM '10, Aire-la-Ville, Switzerland: Eurographics Association, pages 127–134.

[Sachs et al., 1991]

Sachs, Emanuel, Andrew Roberts, and David Stoops (1991). 3-Draw: A tool for designing 3D shapes. *IEEE Computer Graphics and Applications (CG&A)*, 11(6):18–26.

[Schkolne et al., 2001]

Schkolne, Steven, Michael Pruett, and Peter Schröder (2001). Surface drawing: Creating organic 3D shapes with the hand and tangible tools. In *Proceedings of the SIGCHI Conference on Human Factors in Computing Systems*, CHI '01, New York: ACM, pages 261–268.

[Wesche and Seidel, 2001]

Wesche, Gerold, and Hans-Peter Seidel (2001). FreeDrawer: A free-form sketching system on the responsive workbench. In *Proceedings of the ACM Symposium on Virtual Reality Software and Technology*, VRST '01, New York: ACM, pages 167–174.

[Zen, 2004]

Zen, Jen (2004). Painting in air. In *Proceedings of ACM SIGGRAPH 2004*, 38(3):7–9.

Section IV
Agents & Avatars

15

Making Virtual Reality Social
Getting Virtual Humans into Your Virtual Environment

Andrew Cordar, Yao Heng, Fatemeh Tavassoli, Jeffrey Wood, and Benjamin Lok
University of Florida

15.1 Overview of Virtual Humans

Virtual humans are the embodiment of realistic computer-modeled characters for virtual worlds. Incorporating virtual humans into your virtual environment can provide a sense of life to the experience. Incorporating social interactions with the virtual humans can expand the applicability to scenarios including training, therapy, and education. In this article, we briefly explore the applications of virtual humans, components of a virtual human, and work through a concrete example of how to incorporate a virtual human into a virtual environment. Finally, we discuss upcoming trends in virtual humans.

Virtual humans are composed of a 3D shape model, animations, sounds, and models for behavior, emotion, and cognition. As an example, Figure 15.1 shows a virtual human playing the role of a patient for which medical students can practice patient observation and communication skills. The virtual human patient is part of the Neurological Exam Rehearsal Virtual Environment project [Rivera-Guiterrez et al. 2014]. The virtual human's appearance was made to resemble a patient who had been injured in a bike accident and has come into the clinic complaining of double vision. To create the virtual human with the injury, 3D modeling tools were used with reference images of similar patients. The behaviors

Figure 15.1

An example of virtual human patient complaining of double vision after a bike accident [nervesim 2014].

and emotions of the virtual human were elicited through interviews with domain experts (neurologists) and realized by graphical artists. The flexibility to control attributes of the virtual human's form (e.g., showing abnormalities in eye movement as in the medical training scenario) is one of the strengths of using virtual humans in virtual reality. The virtual human's physical and behavioral traits can be explicitly specified and controlled. Physical traits such as gender, race, ethnicity, and body shapes can be explicitly defined. Behavioral traits, such as facial expression, body language, and personality features, are also defined and controlled by the virtual environment authors. This level of control of virtual social actors with which the user can interact is a powerful attribute of virtual humans. The concept of "virtual humans" is also referred to as "virtual agents," "embodied conversational agents," or occasionally "avatars"—though the term "avatar" is more properly limited to the embodiment of *actual* human users in the virtual environment.

Virtual humans are used in many fields, including extensively in medicine, psychology, and the military. In medicine, virtual humans are used in training, such as patients and teammates. Virtual humans provide additional opportunities to train team and patient communication skills. In psychology, virtual humans are used to reduce phobias, stress, and post-traumatic stress disorder in patients. Patients use virtual reality and interact with virtual humans through therapist-controlled exposure therapy sessions. For example, people who have a fear of public speaking can practice in front of a virtual crowd. In the military, virtual humans are used as teammates and combatants to train soldiers on strategic decision making, reaction time, and teamwork. Virtual reality simulations and virtual humans provide inexpensive and repetitive training opportunities to hone skills.

15.2 Components of a Virtual Human

Creating a virtual reality experience that incorporates virtual humans includes considering (1) the inputs, cognitive model, and outputs for the virtual human and (2) the virtual environment. The virtual environment that the interaction occurs within is critical in developing and setting the context and is critical to achieving social training goals. As a concrete example in the next two sections, we will consider a virtual human conversation partner for users learning English. The user will practice basic social conventions and communication with the virtual human. Such a scenario would be beneficial to those traveling to an English-speaking country, allowing practice and cultural exploration before one's trip.

The virtual environment sets the context for the experience and is important for domain learners to properly situate the interaction. The virtual environment should focus on establishing a narrative for the social interaction. Social interactions are affected by the environment they occur in, so the virtual environment chosen will impact how the user will interact with the virtual human. In our example of creating a virtual human to help people to practice their English oral skills, the environment should reflect the verbal lesson we are trying to impart. For example, presenting an airport ticket counter virtual environment would be appropriate to practice speaking about ticket booking or travel issues. By practicing the conversations with virtual humans in the appropriate virtual environment, we anticipate improved training capabilities of the virtual experience. High quality virtual environment models can be found through online resources (both free and paid) such as TurboSquid, SketchUp, 3D Warehouse, and Unity's Asset store. These third-party acquired models often require processing for importing and model complexity reduction to work within a real-time rendering system.

A virtual human has three components: *inputs, cognitive processing, and outputs.* The *inputs* are how the user communicates (e.g., body posture, speech, and gestures) to the virtual human. The *cognitive processing* is how the system processes the inputs and generates the virtual human's response. The *outputs* are the form of the virtual human and how the virtual human responds to the user's input. In our example, if the user speaks "Hello, my name is John" while waving their hand, the virtual human system would process the input, identify the intent behind the user's speech (in this case a greeting), and either generate or retrieve an appropriate response, e.g., "Hello, my name is Susan how can I help you today" while playing an animation of hand waving.

Inputs: The inputs to the virtual human are analogous to the inputs (verbal and non-verbal) humans perceive when interacting with other humans. Verbal cues are usually captured with a microphone recording the audio of a user speaking to the virtual human. The audio is then processed by a speech-to-text engine—we have found the Google Cloud Speech API and IBM Watson Speech-To-Text to perform well for one-on-one conversations with virtual humans. Other common input formats include typing to the virtual human or a selecting from a predefined set of dialogue options [Google Cloud Speech API 2017; Watson 2017].

The non-verbal inputs of the user to the virtual human includes capturing the body and facial gestures. Some commercial tracking systems are image-based and can capture multiple peoples' form. Inexpensive, commodity body tracking system includes the Kinect One Motion Sensor for the body form and the Leap Motion Controller for hand gestures.

Cognitive Processing: Given the verbal and nonverbal inputs to the virtual human, a cognitive system generates the best response from the virtual human. The multitude of ways to approach modeling the cognition of the virtual human is an extensive topic beyond the scope of this article. However, generally the cognitive system is generative-based (i.e., the system generates in real-time a response to the user's inputs), retrieval-based (i.e., the system has a set of predefined responses and tries to identify which response to present given the inputs), or uses a Wizard of Oz approach (i.e., an observing human controls the responses of the virtual human) [Wilson and Rosenberg 1988]. As retrieval-based systems are the most common approach used in virtual human applications, we outline a retrieval-based system for our English-language practicing conversation partner.

For a given interaction scenario, a virtual human's script is constructed to enable the virtual human to respond to user's questions. A question-answering virtual human script includes a set of similar questions for each response the virtual human will generate (Figure 15.2). To construct the script, the script author (typically a person with domain expertise) uses a system to input the set of questions the virtual human will respond to and the corresponding response. For example, if the user says "Hello," or "Hi, my name is John," "Hi there," or any of dozens of similar greetings, the virtual human ticket agent would say "Hi, my name is Susan, how can I help you today?"

The challenge is anticipating the large set of dialogue that the user would speak to a virtual human. To quickly create a virtual human capable of answering basic questions, there are systems such as USC's Virtual Human Toolkit and the University of Florida's Virtual People Factory that provide prebuilt templates of common questions and responses for virtual humans. These systems also leverage natural language understanding libraries to assist the author in rapidly creating a robust virtual conversation partner [USC's Virtual Human Toolkit 2017; Virtual People Factory 2017].

When the user asks the virtual human a question, the system would search the set of anticipated questions to find the question most similar to the one asked. If a similar question in the virtual human script is identified, the virtual human will use the corresponding

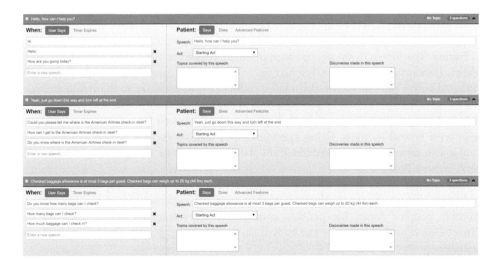

Figure 15.2

Virtual human script example.

answer as a response. The response would include the text to be displayed, the audio file of a voice talent speaking the text, and associated gestures and animations.

Other approaches to virtual humans include connecting with machine learning-based intent recognizers (e.g., Google's Dialogflow—nee Api.ai, Facebook's Wit, and Microsoft's LUIS). If the number of intents is relatively small and the conversation is structured (which would be the case for a conversation partner encompassing small topics such as purchasing airline tickets), then intent recognizers can provide an accurate and rapid way to generate virtual human responses [API.ai 2017; Wit.ai 2017; Microsoft 2017].

In addition to the language model for the virtual human, the virtual human behavior script refers to the output audio of the virtual human's responses and the virtual human's animations. Combined with proper outputs (audio, gestures, and animations) accurate responses help a virtual human appear to behave like a real person.

Outputs: The outputs of a virtual human system include the virtual human's visual appearance, audio, and animations and gestures. To create the virtual human's visual appearance, a virtual human modeling system is commonly used. Virtual human modeling systems include Adobe Fuse [2017], Autodesk Character Generator [2017], Reallusion Character Creator [2017]. A virtual human modeling system typically provides base virtual human models (Figure 15.3). The base virtual human models have varying races, ethnicities, and genders. The base models are customizable including changing facial characteristics, body size and proportions, and colors or textures of clothes. When building a virtual human, the developer should consider how a user will likely respond to the particularities of that virtual human model. In our example of a virtual human for practicing English language conversations, the character should appear welcoming, from the region being visited (including dress, mannerisms, style), and use an appropriate voice talent.

After creating the 3D model, the next step is to rig and animate the virtual human. Rigging and animating the virtual human involves integrating a virtual set of control points (called a skeleton) for the virtual human and enabling textures to properly be applied (skinning). The rigged virtual human allows for motion-captured animations to be applied. By using a rig, the same animation (e.g. hand-waving) can be applied to

(a)   (b)

Figure 15.3

(a) Interface to quickly create characters using a library of high-quality 3D content, from faces and bodies to clothing and textures. (b) Simple character size and proportion settings automatically adjust the clothing and other attributes [Adobe Fuse 2017].

(a)   (b)

Figure 15.4

(a) Auto rigging a 3D model in Mixamo. (b) Browsing animations from a library of animations in Mixamo.

multiple virtual humans. Animation and rigging can be applied by using systems that have pre-built or easily modifiable animations. For example, Mixamo's Online 3D Animation Service [2017] can rig a 3D model with a full skeleton and skinning weights and make it ready for animation. Mixamo also has a library of animations to apply to your virtual human (Figure 15.4).

The process of lip-synching synchronizes the virtual human's facial animations to the virtual human's auditory response. For lip-synching, tools such as LipSync pro for Unity [2017], FaceFX [2017], and SALSA [2017] convert audio to facial animations. Some of these tools allow controlling eye and eyebrow movements as well as facial expressions to make talking animations more plausible and engaging.

15.3 Building a Virtual Human: A Step by Step Tutorial

In this tutorial, an example conversational virtual human will be created for a virtual environment. Continuing with the example of practicing English with a virtual human ticket agent, first an environment of the airline ticket counter will be integrated into a Unity 3D project (Figure 15.5). Unity 3D is a popular game engine easily deployed to multiple platforms including mobile, web, desktop, and VR platforms. The Unity version shown in this tutorial is 5.6.2f1.

To create the virtual human, there are several tools that we can use to generate a 3D model. In this example, Autodesk Character Generator (charactergenerator.autodesk. com) will be used. Autodesk Character Generator is an online tool that will allow you to create your own custom 3D characters after you register for an account. Though you can create a free Autodesk account, it may be worth considering opting for a paid account to access the Premium features. Registering for an education account will also give you access to the Premium features. The Premium features allow you to generate high resolution models that will be compatible with lip-synching tools. When creating a new character, select a base model. After character selection, the next step will allow for altering aspects of the character such as hair style, skin tone, or clothes.

After creating the virtual human ticket agent, export the model for import into the Unity environment. The virtual human ticket agent should be in the "Character Designs"

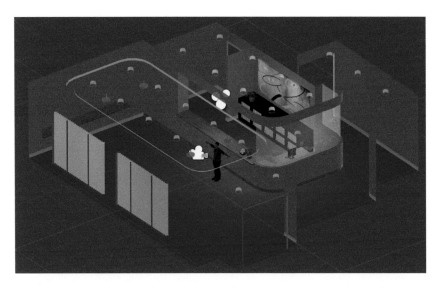

Figure 15.5

A ticket counter environment is imported into the Unity project.

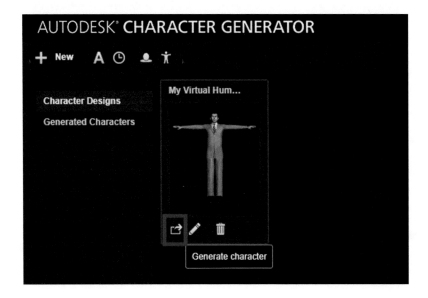

Figure 15.6

Your virtual human in the Character Designs window.

window (Figure 15.6). Select the "Generate character" icon which will prompt you with choosing the export options for your character. If you have a premium account, then you will want to choose most of the options in Figure 15.7. When it comes to Facial Expressions, the selection you make in the export settings will depend on the software

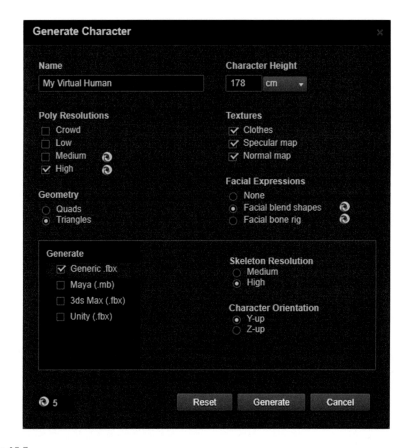

Figure 15.7

Settings to export your model from Autodesk Character Generator into Unity.

you choose to use for lip-syncing. For example, the Unity extension LipSync Pro supports both Facial blend shapes and Facial bone rig but the extension SALSA with RandomEyes only supports Facial blend shapes. Once the appropriate settings have been chosen, select "Generate." The result will be an FBX file containing your virtual human.

Generating your character will take several minutes and you'll be left with a 3D model that you can import into a virtual environment.

Open up the Unity scene with your virtual environment. Import the FBX file to the project. If successful, a prefab for the virtual human ticket agent can be dragged and dropped into the scene.

The next step is to add animations. For this step, Mixamo (www.mixamo.com) will be used, so temporarily set aside the Unity interface. Mixamo is an online tool that allows you to animate your own 3D characters with a free account. Upload the virtual human ticket agent 3D model into Mixamo and set it as the current character (which enables animation preview). To begin, choose an idle animation (Figure 15.8). The idle animation will play when the virtual human ticket agent is waiting for user inputs. Typical idle animations include shifting one's weight, looking around, and making subtle gestures.

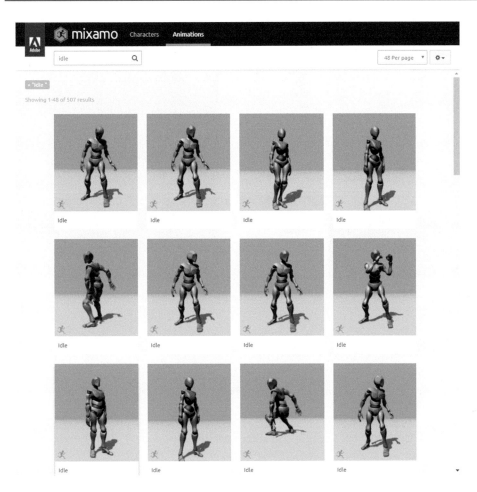

Figure 15.8

A few examples of idle animations provided by Mixamo.

Next, select the animations to be associated with the virtual human's responses (e.g. greeting the user, asking for the destination of the ticket, stating the price, and closing). After selecting the animations to apply to your virtual human, download the animations into your assets. Load the animations into Unity using *"Import New Asset"* and select "Fix now" for any errors that may pop up during the import process.

To attach the animations to the virtual human in Unity, create a new Animator Controller (Listing 15.1) and add it to the virtual human's Animator component (Figures 15.9 and 15.10).

Open the Animator Controller, which should be empty except for an "Any state" bubble and an "Entry" bubble (Figure 15.11). Drag and drop your idle animation into this view and name it Idle in the Inspector window (Figure 15.12).

To verify that it works correctly, click the Play button to view the virtual human ticket agent performing the idle animation.

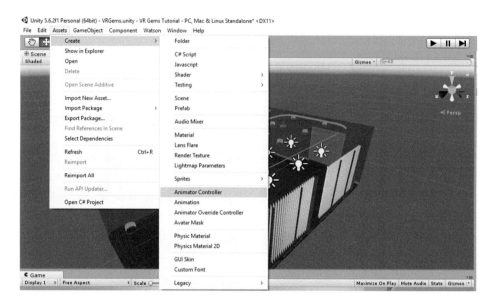

Figure 15.9

Create a new Animator Controller.

Listing 15.1. Create an Animator and several AudioClip variables. Use the GetComponent method to finish creating the Animator variable.

```
// Declare an Animator Controller variable and three AudioClip variables
private Animator anim;
public AudioClip helloResponse, goodbyeResponse, howAreYouResponse;

// Bind variable anim to the Animator Controller we have created in Unity
void Start() {
        LogSystem.InstallDefaultReactors();
        Debug.Log("ExampleStreaming", "Start();");

        anim = this.GetComponent<Animator>();

        this.StartRecording();
}
```

The next step is to record audio and generating lip-syncing animations. In this example, four phrases will be recorded for the virtual human ticket agent (e.g., "Hi, my name is Susan, how can I help you today?") A good microphone is recommended, and common sound editing software such as Audacity can enable the voice talent to rapidly record phrases. Export the audio files in a format supported by Unity (e.g. .aif, .wav, .mp3, and .ogg). Import the audio file assets into the Unity project under a new folder named "Audio." Different lip-syncing tools use varying methods to link the animation to the audio. As mentioned before, some of these lip-syncing tools may require the facial expressions of the virtual human's 3D model to be generated with a facial bone rig, and others may use

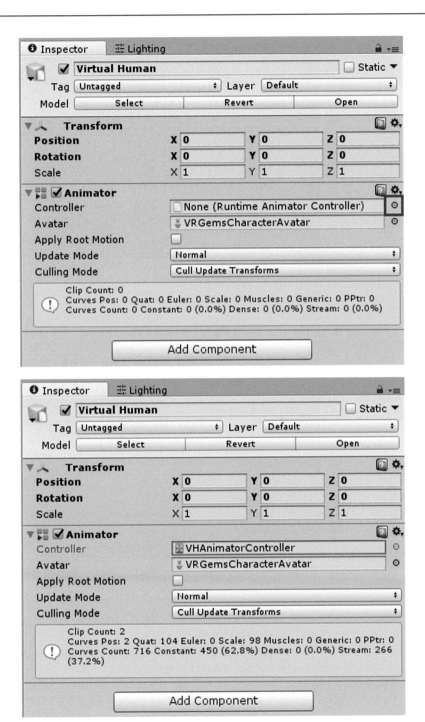

Figure 15.10

Add the Animation Controller you created to your virtual human.

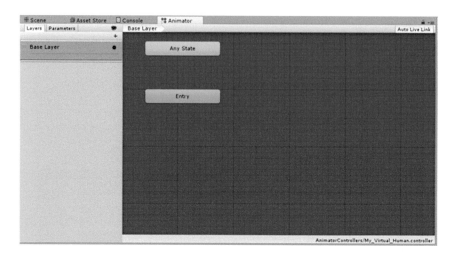

Figure 15.11

Your empty Animator Controller.

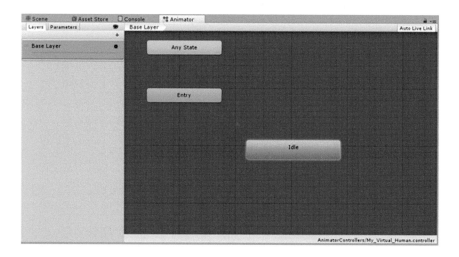

Figure 15.12

The idle animation is added to the virtual human.

facial blend shapes (which will require regeneration of the virtual human model with the appropriate changes made to the settings shown in Figure 15.7).

In the airline ticket conversation example, the user will speak common English phrases with the virtual human. In this tutorial, we'll use IBM Watson Speech-to-Text to process the user's spoken voice in real-time. You will need to register for an IBM Bluemix account to take advantage of this service. Though the Speech-to-Text is a paid service, a 1-month free trial can be used for this tutorial. IBM Watson Speech-to-Text has a downloadable SDK for Unity (This tutorial uses SDK version 0.13.0.), which includes a variety of sample scenes that demonstrate how to interface with the Speech-to-Text API. Specifically, the sample scene called "ExampleStreaming" uses a simple script to demonstrate how to use the Speech-to-Text API. The script can be altered, or another controller script can be written to determine when to play animations and audio based upon the text result from the Speech-to-Text service. Listing 15.2 shows an example alteration.

Listing 15.2. Alterations to the ExampleStreaming scene to enable an animation and audio to play given the results of the Speech-to-Text processing.

```
// This function shows how to use the Speech-to-Text API to enable the
//    virtual human to respond user's spoken voice in real-time
private void OnRecognize(SpeechRecognitionEvent result) {
    if (result != null && result.results.Length > 0) {
        foreach (var res in result.results) {
            foreach (var alt in res.alternatives) {
                string text = alt.transcript;
                Debug.Log("ExampleStreaming", string.Format("{0} ({1}, {2:0.00})\n",
                            text, res.final ? "Final" : "Interim", alt.confidence));

                // if the service has reached a final decision on what the user said
                //    we want to trigger an audio clip and an animation
                if (res.final) {
                    // first we must get the AudioSource that our clip will be
                    //      played from
                    AudioSource audio = this.GetComponent<AudioSource>();

                    // now we need to check for what the user said using
                    //    an if statement
                    if (text.Trim().Equals("hello")) {
                        // to have our virtual human response, we cause an animation
                        //    to play and play the appropriate audio clip as a response
                        anim.SetTrigger("IsSpeaking");
                        audio.clip = helloResponse;
                        audio.Play();
                    } else if (text.Trim().Equals("goodbye")) {
                        anim.SetTrigger("IsSpeaking");
                        audio.clip = goodbyeResponse;
                        audio.Play();
                    } else if (text.Trim().Equals("how are you")) {
                        anim.SetTrigger("IsSpeaking");
                        audio.clip = howAreYouResponse;
                        audio.Play();
                    }
                }
            }
        }
    }
}
```

Of note is the Trigger called "IsSpeaking." IsSpeaking notifies the Animation Controller to play a particular animation once and then revert back to the previous animation. Going back to the Animation Controller, add the remaining gestures to the controller. Make the appropriate transitions in both directions between the Idle animation and the new animation and add a new Trigger Paramater named "IsSpeaking" to the controller so that it looks like Figure 15.13.

For the transition from the Idle animation to the new animation, add *"IsSpeaking"* to the list of Conditions and make sure *"Has Exit Time"* is unchecked as in Figure 15.14.

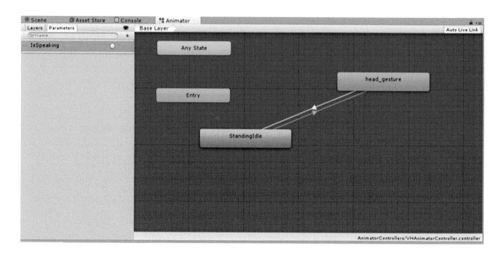

Figure 15.13

Adding the head_gesture animation with transitions using the IsSpeaking Trigger.

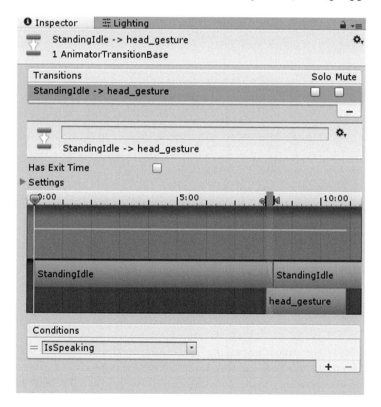

Figure 15.14

Settings for incorporating additional animations to transition between the idle animation and the new animation.

15. Making Virtual Reality Social

Congratulations, you now have a conversational virtual human with whom a user can practice English communication (Figure 15.15). Press Play and try speaking to the virtual human ticket agent using one of the phrases tagged in the script. Now that you understand the basics of what makes a virtual human, try incorporating an intent recognition services such as Microsoft's LUIS [2017] and API.ai [2017] to make a more conversational character.

15.4 Future of Virtual Humans

15.4.1 Overview

With expected improvements in graphical realism, animation, artificial intelligence, virtual humans will continue to develop in their ability to present increasingly realistic and complex social interactions. These enhancements will enable virtual humans to be applied to a growing list of scenarios. More interestingly is that the conversational virtual humans will be applicable in a spectrum of systems from augmented to mixed to virtual reality.

With the ticket agent virtual human, a user can interact with a conversational 3D virtual human through a face-to-face interaction (Figure 15.15) inside a VR head-mounted display. In the future, as augmented reality devices reach consumers, they can take the conversation with their virtual human companion with them. New world-scanning technologies will enable the virtual human to be aware of and capable of discussing items in the real world. Thus in the future, there will be a continuum of devices (see Figure 15.16)

Figure 15.15

A virtual human ticket agent that would respond to being spoken to by the user.

Figure 15.16

Continuum of devices a virtual human can embody.

through which users can interact with virtual humans: from cell phones to head-mounted displays.

The availability of tools facilitating important input, behavioral, and output components has made the creation of "fleshed out" virtual humans much easier. With conversational agents becoming more and more ubiquitous, it is very likely that people will interact with virtual humans daily to automate or assist many aspects of their life.

References

[Adobe Fuse 2017]

Adobe Fuse (2017). http://adobe.com/products/fuse.html, accessed 6/25/17

[API.ai 2017]

API.ai (2017). https://api.ai/, accessed 6/24/17

[Autodesk Character Generator 2017]

Autodesk Character Generator (2017). https://charactergenerator.autodesk.com/, accessed 9/18/17

[FaceFX 2017]

FaceFX (2017). https://facefx.com/, accessed 9/18/17

[Google Cloud Speech API 2017]

Google Cloud Speech API (2017). https://cloud.google.com/speech/, accessed 9/26/17

[LipSync pro for Unity 2017]

LipSync pro for Unity (2017). https://lipsync.rogodigital.com/, accessed 9/18/17

[Massive 2017]

Massive (2017). http://massivesoftware.com/, accessed 6/24/17

[Microsoft 2017]

Microsoft (2017). https://luis.ai/, accessed 6/24/17

[Mixamo 2017]

Mixamo (2017). http://mixamo.com, accessed 9/18/17

[nervesim 2014]

nervesim (2014). http://nervesim.com/, accessed 6/25/17

[Reallusion Character Creator 2017]

Reallusion Character Creator (2017). https://reallusion.com/character-creator/, accessed 9/18/17

[Rivera-Guiterrez 2014]

Rivera-Gutierrez, Diego, Andrea Kleinsmith, Teresa Johnson, Rebecca Lyons, Juan Cendan, and Benjamin Lok (2014). Towards a reflective practicum of embodied conversational agent experiences. In *IEEE International Conference on Advanced Learning Technologies (ICALT)*, Athens, Greece: IEEE.

[SALSA 2017]

SALSA (2017). http://crazyminnowstudio.com/unity-3d/lip-sync-salsa/, accessed 9/18/17

[USC's Virtual Human Toolkit 2017]

USC's Virtual Human Toolkit (2017). https://vhtoolkit.ict.usc.edu/, accessed 9/26/17

[Virtual People Factory 2017]

Virtual People Factory (2017). http://vpf2.cise.ufl.edu/, accessed 9/26/17

[Watson 2017]

Watson (2017). https://ibm.com/watson/developercloud/conversation.html, accessed 6/24/17

[Wilson and Rosenberg 1988]

Wilson, James, and Daniel Rosenberg (1988). Rapid prototyping for user interface design. In *Handbook of Human-Computer Interaction*, M. Helander (Ed.). Amsterdam: North-Holland, pp. 859–875. Doi:10.1016/B978-0-444-70536-5.50044-0.

[Wit.ai 2017]

Wit.ai (2017). https://wit.ai/, accessed 6/24/17

16

Building a Social VR App

Bernie Roehl
Virtual Escapes Inc.

Please note that specific details of the various interfaces may have changed considerably since this chapter was originally written. These instructions use Unity version 2017.3.1f1, SteamVR version 1.2.3, and VRTK version 3.1.0. Of course, the gist of this chapter is on the networking aspects, so the design of the virtual world itself is secondary. You can build any world you like. Please refer to the online documentation of the various libraries for more up-to-date information.

This chapter provides a step by step tutorial on how to create a shared social virtual reality space. We will create an interactive world in the Unity game engine using the VRTK toolkit for VR interactions, and then add the ability to connect with other people using the Photon networking toolkit. The "Altspace" experience provides a commercial example from which we can draw inspiration (Figure 16.1 shows a typical Altspace social world).

Figure 16.1

Two users share a private space in the Altspace social VR application. They can speak to each other, display emoticons that float upward from their head, and here they are watching a video together.

16.1 Introduction

The VR industry has a crisis of content. Everyone knows that VR games are great and provide a far better experience than a desktop PC or a console, but the problem is that the selection of games is still quite limited. Even more limited is the selection of genres... you can only kill so many zombies or react to so many jump scares before the novelty starts to wear off.

The challenge, of course, is that building games is a massive, time-consuming and expensive process that companies aren't willing to invest in until there's an established market. And yet, where will that market come from if the content selection is limited?

The answer is to look beyond games, and to start thinking of virtual reality not as a "game" but as an actual place—one where you can interact with other people in much the same way you do in the real world. The result is an endless supply of content, because the "content" is other people.

16.2 Games vs Worlds

Back in the day, I was one of the beta testers for Second Life. When I showed it to friends, everyone said the same thing—"cool game." I explained (over and over) that it wasn't actually a game, but they didn't seem to get it. It certainly *looked* like I was playing a game, and if it wasn't a game... what was it?

The way I finally got them to understand the difference was to say "Okay, it's a game." Their next question was "great, how do I play?", at which point I would say "well, there aren't any rules." Then they would ask "so how do I win?" I explained that you can't win, and you can't lose. Finally, they would say "well, it's not really a game then." And, of course, they'd be right.

A Social VR environment is a place, not a game. You can certainly *play* games within a virtual world—I've played catch, paintball, charades, Dungeons & Dragons and Cards Against Humanity in various virtual worlds—but the world is a place where you play those games, not a game in itself.

16.3 What's Out There

As I write this in the summer of 2017, there are a number of "social VR" systems out there. Altspace [Altspace], VR Chat [VRChat], High Fidelity [High Fidelity], vTime [vTime], Rec Room [Against Gravity], Big Screen [Big Screen], Oculus Rooms [Oculus 2016], Facebook Spaces [Facebook], Janus VR [JanusVR], Sansar [Linden Research], Anyland [Lowe & Lenssen] and many others. They all have a variety of features and many different kinds of user interface, but over time they're all learning from each other and starting to converge on a common set of features.

What they all have in common are the following:

- Users are represented by avatars
- Users can move around the virtual world
- Users can talk to each other
- There's some indication of who's speaking, so you can associate the voice with an avatar

In addition, most of them allow you to interact with virtual objects (tossing a ball around, building forts out of blocks, that sort of thing).

In this chapter, we're going to build a simple social VR application from scratch that implements all of those basic features. And we're going to do it all in an afternoon, using less than 200 lines of code.

Let's get started.

16.4 Choices

Before we begin, we have some choices to make. It is still early days for VR, so it is not yet possible to build an application once and have it run everywhere. That day will come, but until it does we need to decide on the following:

- What platforms are we targeting?
- What engine should we use?
- What networking technology should we use, or should we "roll our own"?
- What toolkits should we use for building the app?

Let's examine each of those more closely.

16.5 Platform

Broadly speaking, there are two types of platform for VR—desktop and mobile. Desktop-based systems (such as the HTC Vive and the Oculus Rift) are much more powerful, and generally include some sort of hand-held controllers. Mobile systems lack the graphics and computing power that desktop-based systems have, and they have much more limited input devices (if any at all). If we're going to target desktop, then it will be difficult or impossible to port our app back to a mobile platform. If we design for a mobile platform, moving to a desktop-based system is a lot easier. For this reason alone, it is tempting to go mobile-first (especially since it has a much lower price and consequently a much larger install base).

However, we really want to give our users a sense of presence that can only be achieved by actually touching and interacting with virtual objects. We therefore will be targeting desktop VR systems such as the Vive and the Rift. Those two devices are similar enough that we can support both, and possibly even the new Microsoft-designed "Mixed-reality" headsets that are coming out from Dell, Acer and others in the near future. Theoretically, we could also support Sony's PlayStation VR.

16.6 Engine

Our choice of engine is important. The available engines are different enough that changing from one to another mid-project is equivalent to starting over from scratch, which is why nobody does that. While there are a half-dozen engines that support VR, there are really only two which, at the time of this writing, have a significant install base—Unity and Unreal.

While Unreal certainly has its virtues, the overwhelming majority of VR development has taken place in Unity. Unity has always been multi-platform, so it is easier to port to new systems if there's a need for it. It also has the best support from VR hardware developers—when a new input device comes out, it has Unity support from Day 1 and support for other engines comes later (or doesn't). So, for this project at least, we'll be using Unity.

16.7 Networking

At one time, there were four of five different networking solutions for Unity. However, the choice has now narrowed to just two major options—Photon [Exit Games] or UNET [Unity UNET]. Both systems work well, and are well-supported. They have different approaches, but very similar APIs. UNET comes directly from Unity Technologies, so it has tight integration with the engine. Photon is cross-platform, and supports everything from 2D shooters on mobile phones all the way through massive multi-player games.

The deciding factor, at least for us, is that Photon has built-in support for voice chat. While voice chat can certainly be added to UNET (e.g. using the DFVoice package from the Unity Asset Store), the simplicity of having it already integrated into the networking system makes Photon the winning choice.

It is worth noting at this point that the choices we've made are the same as the ones made by the majority of existing Social VR systems—Altspace, VR Chat, Rec Room, Anyland and many others all use Unity and Photon. So we're in good company.

16.8 Toolkits

While it is certainly possible to build a VR application directly in Unity, especially with the additions that came out starting with Unity 5.6 (and have continued to be enhanced through new Unity editions), there is a lot of basic functionality that is common to a range of VR apps. Things like moving around, teleporting, interacting with objects, and so on are becoming standard, and there are several toolkits out there that implement those features.

As of this writing, the most popular and most comprehensive toolkit is VRTK [Extend Reality]. Originally designed for the Vive (through SteamVR [Valve SteamVR]), the toolkit now also supports the Oculus SDK [Oculus SDK] and has some preliminary support for Google Daydream [Google VR].

As with all toolkits, this one has its strengths and weaknesses. Its greatest strengths are that it covers all the basic functionality we'll require, has good documentation and a comprehensive set of examples and tutorial videos. It is also completely free.

The biggest challenge to using VRTK is that it is in a constant state of flux. Whenever you upgrade to the latest version, some things will break and force you to spend time tracking down and fixing the issues rather than working on your own code. The constant changes also mean that some of the documentation and online tutorials are outdated, and are no longer applicable to the version you're using. For our project, we're using the very latest version of VRTK (3.1.0). However, by the time you read this, some things may have changed.

Despite these problems, VRTK is by far the best toolkit out there and we'll be making extensive use of it in our project. Note that VRTK is open source, and that means that it won't necessarily be fully supported by the original author. However there is a community of users, and since it's open source, that community can always work on any issues that arise.

16.9 Setup

Now that we've chosen our platform and tools, it is time to get them set up. Open up Unity, go to the Unity Asset Store and download and install SteamVR, VRTK, Photon Unity Networking (PUN) and Photon Voice (Figure 16.2). Follow the installation instructions for Photon, including going to their web portal (https://photonengine.com) and choosing a Photon plan (perhaps the free option for now), and requesting a pair of app ids (one for PUN and one for Voice). Make sure these are set in the Photon configuration (Figure 16.3).

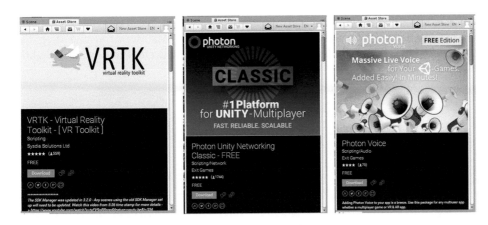

Figure 16.2

For this Gem, we will make use of three packages from the Unity Asset Store: VRTK, Photon Networking and Photon Voice.

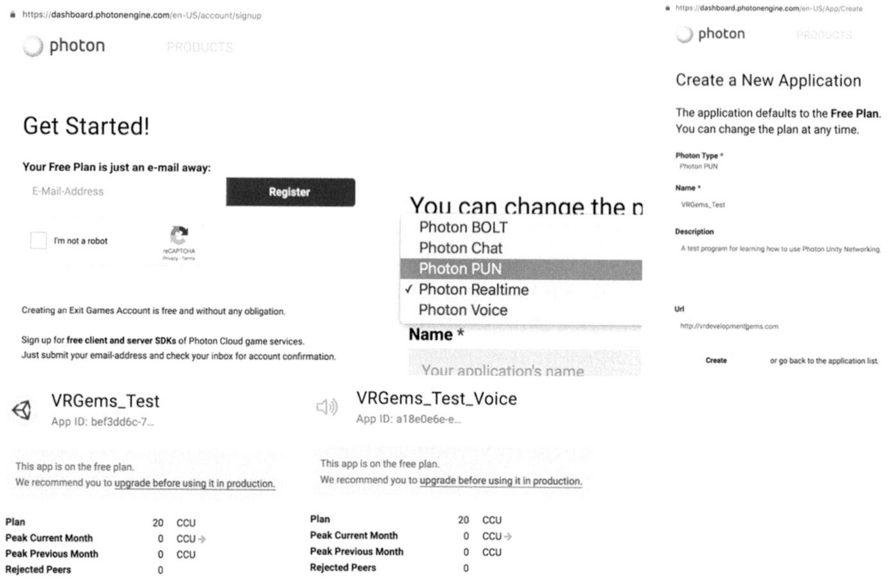

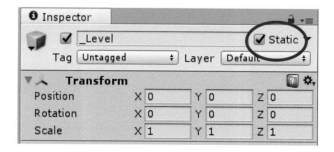

Figure 16.3

Go to the Photon Cloud signup page, get an account, and create two new applications, one for Photon for Unity Networking (Photon PUN) and the other for Photon Voice. You will be provided an "App ID" for each (partially shown in this example).

Also download a sample world. I used the free "3D Modular Kit" from Barking Dog and just started from their demo scene (renaming it to "VRGemsMultiUser"), but you can use whatever you like. Once downloaded, drag the world into your hierarchy or scene view. Mark it as static (see Figure 16.4), and add a mesh collider if it doesn't already have one—the 3D Modular Kit demo scene does. Advanced features such as marking lights as Mixed, baking the lighting, and adding occlusion culling are beyond the scope of this chapter.

Next, we'll set up SteamVR. Remove or disable the MainCamera, and drag the *[CameraRig]* prefab from the SteamVR prefabs folder into the scene. Position it just slightly

Figure 16.4

Set our "_Level" object (or whatever your terrain is called) to be Static—click on the empty box in the upper right corner (indicated by the red circle) making the checkmark appear.

Figure 16.5

The Unity hierarchy window showing a simple world with the SteamVR "[CameraRig]", and "[VRTK]". Add three empty gameObjects under [VRTK] naming them PlayArea, LeftController, and RightController.

above where you want the user to start out in the scene. In a full Social VR application, you would have multiple spawn points and a script to randomly assign users to one of those locations when they arrive, but for now we'll keep it simple.

Our next step is to set up VRTK. This has become much more straightforward in recent versions of VRTK which are designed to make it easier to change platforms. In the past, you would have to operate on the children of *[CameraRig]* and duplicate your work for each platform. Now you operate on a kind of "shadow" copy of those, and the *[CameraRig]* (or other rig) gets set up for you automatically at runtime. (These instructions pertain to VRTK version 3.1.0. The ease of setup has continued to evolve with more recent versions.)

Create an empty GameObject called *[VRTK]*, and put three empty GameObjects under it—naming them *PlayArea*, *LeftController* and *RightController* as shown in Figure 16.5.

The *PlayArea* object represents the tracking volume, and corresponds to the *[CameraRig]*. As shown in Figure 16.6, you should add the VRTK_BodyPhysics component to it, to prevent the user from walking through walls, and you should also add the VRTK_HeightAdjustTeleporter component on it to enable teleporting.

16.10 Travel

Our travel scheme is based on the one used in High Fidelity. The left-hand controller will be used for walking and comfort mode turning (rotating in instantaneous steps), and the right controller will be used for teleporting. Altspace has recently adopted a similar approach, and hopefully others will follow soon.

To implement walking and turning, we add a VRTK_TouchpadControl to our *LeftController* object. We also add a VRTK_SlideObjectControlAction component to handle forward/backward movement, and a VRTK_SnapRotate ObjectControlAction component to handle comfort-mode turning (See Figure 16.7).

Note that in VRTK_TouchpadControl we've set the Primary Activation Button to Touchpad_Press. The default is Touchpad_Touch, which is unpleasant

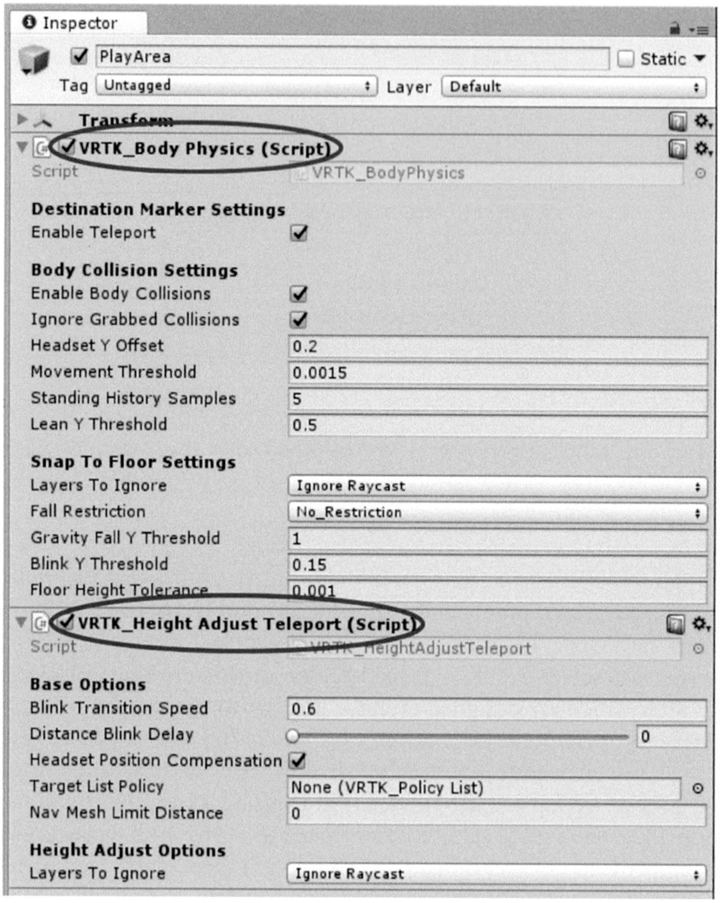

Figure 16.6

Add the VRTK_BodyPhysics and the VRTK_HeightAdjustTeleport scripts as components to the PlayArea GameObject.

since whenever the user casually comes in contact with the touchpad they'll unexpectedly go spinning and sliding away. We also set Action Modifier Button to Undefined.

On the VRTK_SlideObjectControlAction component we've changed the Listen On Axis setting to be the Y axis (i.e., pushing up and down on the touchpad—the touchpad's Y axis—will slide the user forward and back). We'll also set the Maximum Speed to be 1.4 m/s, which is normal human walking speed. And we point the Object Control Script to point to the VRTK_TouchpadControl on this very object.

On the VRTK_SnapRotateObjectControlAction component, we've used the default X axis (i.e. pushing left and right on the touchpad) for the step-turn (comfort) style of turning the user left and right. We've also set the blink transition speed to zero to prevent a fade-out/fade-in whenever we turn. And again we point the Object Control Script to the VRTK_TouchpadControl on this LeftController.

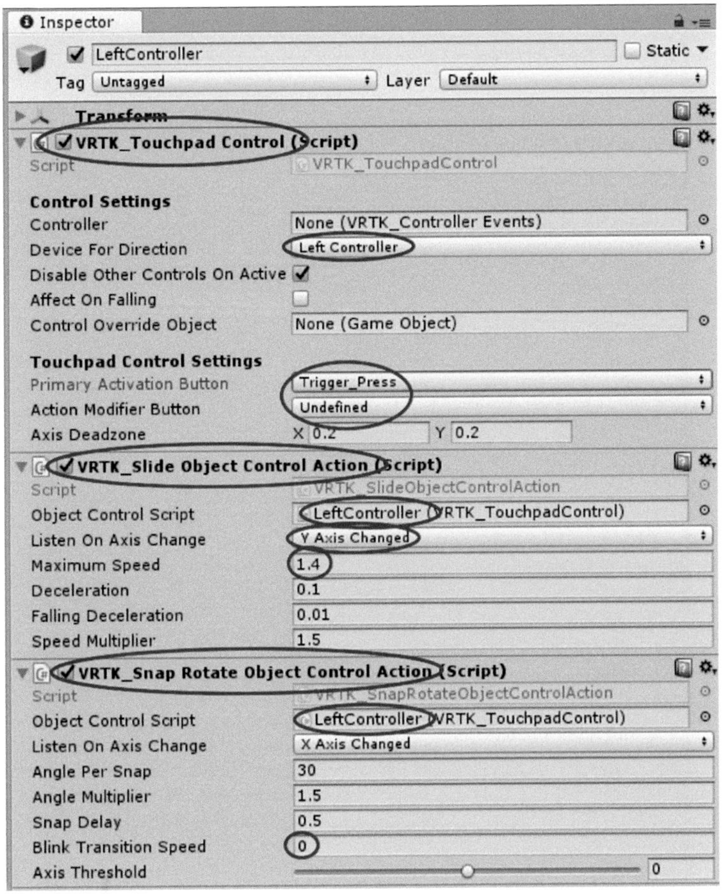

Figure 16.7

Add script components VRTK_TouchpadControl, VRTK_SlideObjectControlAction and VRTK_SnapRotateObjectControlAction to the LeftController GameObject. Change the parameters as shown (and discussed in the text).

To implement teleportation, we add a VRTK_Pointer component to the *RightController*. See Figure 16.8 for a sample configuration. We also add a VRTK_BezierPointerRenderer to display the teleport beam. Make sure the Pointer Renderer field of VRTK_Pointer references the VRTK_BezierPointerRenderer component (circled in the figure). We can optionally set the pointer color, and add custom objects for the tracer, the cursor and the valid/invalid location objects. You may also want to increase the tracer density a bit.

16.11 Interaction

We want both controllers to let you pick up objects by using the trigger (which is the convention that most Social VR apps have adopted). To implement this, we add

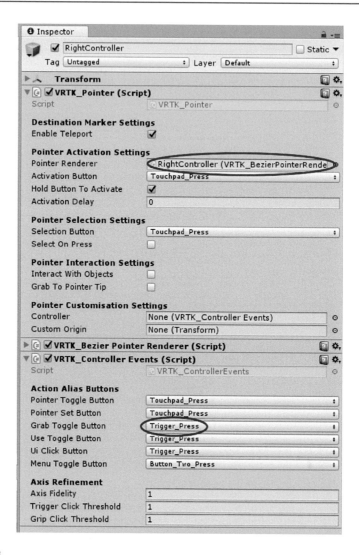

Figure 16.8

On the RightController add the VRTK_Pointer and VRTK_BezierPointerRenderer scripts to travel by short teleports ("tele-hopping").

a VRTK_InteractGrab component to both controllers, along with a VRTK_ControllerEvents component that maps the inputs to abstract events. Set the Grab Toggle Button to be Trigger Press (circled in Figure 16.9).

16.12 Adding an Object

Now we need something to interact with. Let's create a ball that we can toss around.

Add a sphere to the scene, resize it to be a bit smaller, position it someplace above the ground in your scene, and optionally give it a material to make it stand out a bit. You can

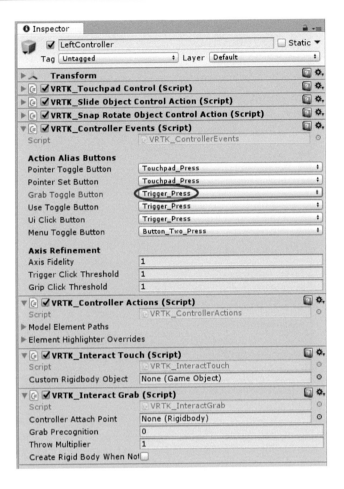

Figure 16.9

In addition to the scripts we've already added, for each controller add the VRTK_ControllerEvents, the VRTK_ControllerActions, the VRTK_InteractTouch and the VRTK_InteractGrab scripts. For the Controller Events script, set the "Grab Toggle Button" field to the "Trigger_Press" option (circled).

use the VRTK Interactable Object Wizard (found in the Unity editor menus as Window/VRTK/Set Up Interactable Object) to make the sphere interactable. As a floating window, a bug prevents all the controls from appearing, so drag it into a tab. (I moved it to share the panel with the Inspector tab.)

Set Hold Button to Grab and change the Grab Attach Mechanic to Fixed Joint (See Figure 16.10). You can also optionally set a highlight color (I happen to like green).

With your "ball" selected in the hierarchy, when you hit the big "Setup Interactable Object" button at the bottom all the necessary components will be added to our ball, then close the wizard. In the Inspector tab you can see all the components added to the ball object (See Figure 16.11). If you don't want to use the wizard, then you can add the

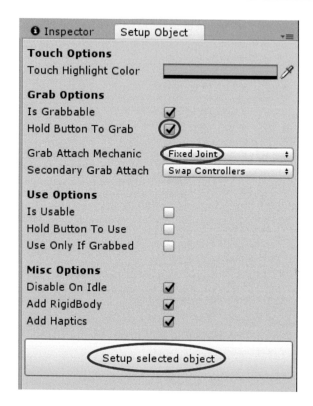

Figure 16.10

Bring up the "Setup [Interactable] Object" wizard using the Unity Editor menu under Window → VRTK → Set Up Interactable Object (you can leave it as a floating panel, or drag it to be a tab of one of the editor panels). With this wizard, you can make adjustments to how interactions operate. Here we enable the "Hold Button To Grab" entry and set "Grab Attach Mechanic" to be "Fixed Joint" (circled). Then to apply these settings to the selected object(s), press the large "Setup selected object" button at the bottom of the panel (circled). When this button is pressed, all the components needed for interaction will be added to the selected objects in the hierarchy.

necessary components by hand. It gets tedious, especially if you have a large number of objects to set up, so I recommend using the wizard.

16.13 SDK Configuration and Testing

Finally, we add a VRTK_SDKManager to the [VRTK] object and do a Quick Select of the SteamVR runtime (See Figure 16.12). Then click the auto-populate button. If you've set everything up correctly, all the fields should be filled in. You may have to click the auto-populate button four or five times to get it to "take". If that doesn't work, then you will need to manually drag your *LeftController* and *RightController* objects (the children of *[VRTK]*) into the Script Alias Left Controller and Script Alias Right Controller fields respectively.

(a)

(b)

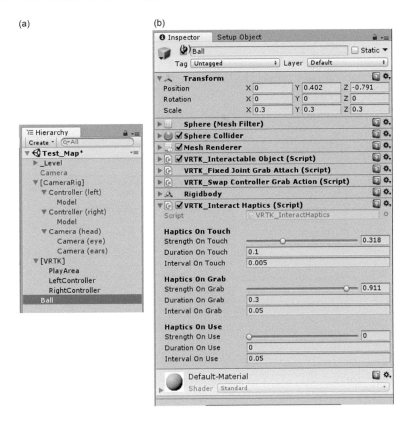

Figure 16.11

With the "ball" object selected in the hierarchy (a), the setup object wizard will add all the additional components needed to interact with that object using the hand controllers (b). Note that the haptic settings are zero by default, so if you want to feel vibrations when touching or grabbing the ball, experiment with the settings like we have done here.

At this point you should be able to walk forward and backward and comfort-turn using the left controller, teleport using the right controller, and pick up and throw objects with either hand. Not bad, considering we haven't written a single line of code! That's the advantage of using a toolkit like VRTK.

16.14 Creating Avatars

There are two basic types of avatars. There are fully articulated avatars that consist of a single mesh with a skeletal structure and vertex weights, like the ones seen in VR Chat or High Fidelity. Then there are much simpler avatars, made up of a collection of one or more separate body parts (like the ones in Altspace or Rec Room). Since the first type requires complex operations like inverse kinematics, we're going to keep it simple and just treat our body segments as separate objects.

As this is a zero-budget project, we can't hire an artist to create these avatars. Instead, we'll have to fall back on "programmer art". See Figure 16.13 for an example.

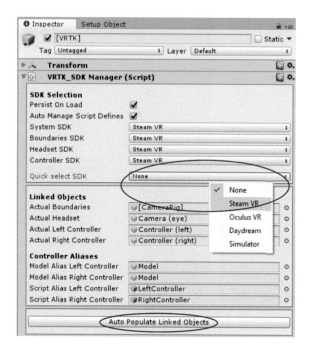

Figure 16.12

Add the VRTK_SDKManager script to the [VRTK] GameObject and populate the fields—Ideally, the "Auto Populate Linked Objects" button will do this for you.

Figure 16.13

A humanoid-like avatar created using the basic shapes provided in Unity.

I'm sure you're very impressed.

The avatar consists of a head, a torso and a pair of hands. The hands are made up of boxes, and are actually taken from one of the VRTK examples. The torso is just a capsule, with a flattened blue cylinder for a chest plate so we know which way the body is facing. The chest plate could be used to display the user's picture, the way it is done in Oculus Rooms for example.

The head is a sphere, with two smaller spheres for eyes and a stretched cube for a mouth. The eyes and mouth are children of the head, so the head is effectively one piece. The chest plate is a child of the torso. The left hand is exactly the same as the right, but scaled by −1 in the X axis. They should all be given contrasting materials so you can see the features.

Note that the head and torso models are children of corresponding empty GameObjects. This allows us to make adjustments to the scale and rotation of the models that remain unaffected by the transforms of their parent objects (which will be synchronized over the network, as we'll see later).

Figure 16.14 shows what the head and torso look like in the Hierarchy pane of the Unity editor:

We also need to set all the body parts (head, hands and torso and all their descendants) to be on the layer called "IgnoreRaycast" (See Figure 16.15). Otherwise VRTK's body physics will cause us to collide with our own body, which would lead to confusing results (most commonly, flying off into the air).

Alternatively, you could define a new layer for this purpose and add it to the list of layers that the body physics component ignores. Or simply remove all the colliders from those objects and their descendants.

16.15 All about Networking

We'll soon be writing some code, but before we do it is important to understand how the networking system works. Much of this is common to both Photon and UNET, so even though we'll be using Photon for this project, the concepts and API are very similar in

Figure 16.14

Unity hierarchy showing the [VRTK], Head, Torso and dependent child nodes.

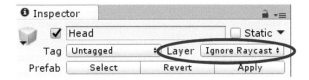

Figure 16.15

To avoid avatar objects from colliding with each other, set the layer to be "Ignore Raycast".

UNET. (Note that there are other approaches to sharing state information in multi-user networks. The approach taken by Photon and UNET is just one way of doing things.)

16.16 Shared State

The key idea is that objects in the world will be sharing state information. If you think about it, there are basically three kinds of objects in the world—(1) static objects that never change and are essentially part of the background (and are generally marked as static in Unity), (2) objects whose state is entirely a function of some common set of values (like the hands of a clock, which move constantly but whose value can be determined entirely from the time of day and a knowledge of your shared world's timezone), and (3) dynamic objects whose state is controlled by something unpredictable. That "something" can be a user, an NPC (non-player character), or a physics engine. It is these dynamic objects we must be concerned with.

Any dynamic object needs to have a single, authoritative source of state information at any given time. In the case of an avatar, the user's actions (as captured by their VR headset and controllers) are the source of the 6-DOF position information of their body parts. In the case of an NPC, there's some code running somewhere that controls the NPC's avatar. In the case of objects controlled by physics, there's a physics simulation running somewhere that provides definitive position information for that particular object.

State information can consist of anything at all, not just locations and orientations ("rotations"). The color of a material, the intensity of a light source, the volume of a sound and so on are all examples of state information. Sharing state information from the authoritative source to the other instances of an object running on other users' client machines is called *synchronization*. In Photon, this is carried out using a `PhotonView` component on the object.

A `PhotonView` observes one or more components of some set of GameObjects in your scene and serializes them onto the network. It also deserializes updates from the network and applies them to the GameObjects in your scene. Any observed component will have its `OnSerializePhotonView()` method called periodically to handle serialization and deserialization.

The most common case is sharing location and rotation. There's a special component called a `PhotonTransformView`, which handles smoothing and interpolation of those values. If you add that component to an object, it will automatically add a `PhotonView`, but you still need to add the `PhotonTransformView` to the list of observed components on the `PhotonView`. We'll do exactly that for our head, torso, left hand and right hand GameObjects. We'll also make sure that the "position" and "orientation" of `PhotonTransformView` are enabled, so they get synchronized over the network.

We'll do the same for the ball we created earlier, but we'll include the scale information since we resized the ball from 1 meter down to something more reasonable. An alternative approach is to make the ball a child of an empty GameObject, and move all the components from the Sphere to the new object. The reason you would do this is that you can then scale the sphere independently of the parent GameObject, which means the scale of the parent is 1, 1, 1 and never needs to be sent over the network. That reduces your bandwidth use substantially.

Because the ball is controlled by physics, you'll also need to add a `PhotonRigidbodyView` component and make sure it is added to the list of components that the PhotonView observes. This component will send the velocity and angular velocity to the other clients so that they can update their physics engines to simulate the ball's motion. Also change the Interpolate Option on the PhotonTransformView to LERP and set the speed to 5 (See Figure 16.16).

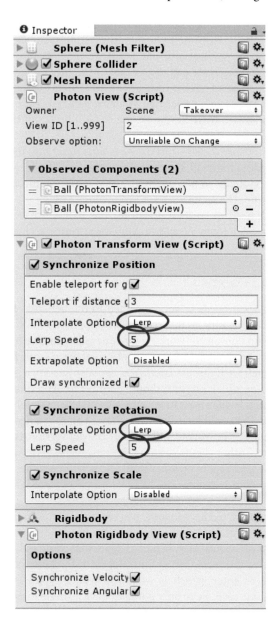

Figure 16.16

For the PhotonView object, set the two synchronize features (position and rotation) to interpolate using LERP, with a speed of 5.

There are some subtleties to all this that we'll cover later in the section on Object Ownership.

16.17 Instantiating Objects

You may be familiar with the `Object.Instantiate()` method in Unity, which can create new GameObjects at runtime by using an existing GameObject as a prototype. That's fine for single-user applications, but when we instantiate an object in a multi-user application we need to create copies of it on all the other clients. We do this using `PhotonNetwork.Instantiate()`. Instead of a local prefab asset, it takes the name of a prefab that must be stored in a folder that you create called "Resources." That way the other clients can also look in their Resources folder for a prefab of the appropriate name to be instantiated.

Creating a prefab in Unity is easy—just drag a GameObject into the Project window. In our case, we'll be dragging the head, hands and torso into the Resources folder. You'll need to drag each one individually. When you've dragged them all into the Resources folder, you can delete them from the scene.

Note that we don't need to create a prefab for our ball, since it's already part of the scene. However, if you plan to create additional balls at runtime then you would create a prefab for them.

16.18 Servers and Rooms

When our app starts up, it needs to get connected to the network. Photon's approach is very different from that of Unity, so this section only applies to Photon.

When you first set up Photon Networking for your app, you gave it a unique AppId that you obtained from the web portal. In fact, you got two of them—one for your app, and one for the voice chat (which we'll discuss later). You can also specify a geographic region for your game, to determine which server it should connect to. And finally, when you do the actual connection, you provide an arbitrary string (typically a version number) to identify which version of your app you'll be using. This allows you to change the specifics of how you share state or make RPC calls and still support the old version as well as the new one. Everyone will only "see" other clients running the same version of your app as they are.

The combination of geographic region, AppId and version number define a "game," i.e., a connection point for your virtual world. In order for two users to share the same virtual space, all three of those values must match.

When you first connect to the network, you're actually communicating with something called a Master Server. We're not going to talk about that in detail, but the Master Server maintains a list of "rooms" (i.e., instances of virtual worlds) that the user can enter. You can obtain that list from the server and present it to the user so they can choose a particular instance to enter, which is what you would typically see in Altspace or VRChat or vTime. In our case, we're only going to have a single instance which we'll call "Main room."

And now, at last, we're going to start writing some code.

We'll create a script called "NetMan.cs" that will manage our network connection. We can place it on any GameObject, and in our case we'll just put it on our existing

[VRTK] object. When `Start()` is called on our `NetMan` component, we connect to the MasterServer passing it a version number.

Listing 16.1. When the game is initialized, connect to the Photon Network.

```
// NetMan.cs - manage our Photon network connection
void Start()
{
    PhotonNetwork.ConnectUsingSettings("1.0");
}
```

When the connection is established, Photon calls our `OnConnectedToMaster()` method. It is here that we might present the user with a UI that lets them choose an instance of a world. Instead, we'll simply join our "Main room," creating it if it doesn't already exist.

Listing 16.2. When connected to the server, join the "Main room".

```
// OnConnectedToMaster() - put user in the Main room when joining a game
void OnConnectedToMaster()
{
    PhotonNetwork.JoinOrCreateRoom("Main room", new RoomOptions { MaxPlayers = 10 }, null);
}
```

Once we've successfully entered the room, we create instances of our avatar's various body parts. This causes them to also be instantiated on all the other connected clients. If a client joins later, they will automatically be informed of these objects without our having to do anything.

Listing 16.3. When joining the "Main room", initialize moving objects—in this case the user's avatar.

```
// OnJoinedRoom() - initialize objects that will move.  In this case, the avatar.
void OnJoinedRoom()
{
    head = PhotonNetwork.Instantiate("Head",
        headTracker.position, headTracker.rotation, 0);
    leftHand = PhotonNetwork.Instantiate("LeftHand",
        leftHandTracker.position, leftHandTracker.rotation, 0);
    rightHand = PhotonNetwork.Instantiate("RightHand",
        rightHandTracker.position, rightHandTracker.rotation, 0);
    torso = PhotonNetwork.Instantiate("Torso",
        headTracker.position, headTracker.rotation, 0);
}
```

You'll notice that we keep references to these objects around, as global variables. That is because we'll use `NetMan.cs` to perform one more important function—reading the input devices and updating the transforms of our head and hands (top of Listing 16.4).

In order to do that, we'll need to have references to those input devices. Fortunately, VRTK provides a way of doing that using its VRTK_DeviceFinder. We'll get those references in our Start() method and keep them around in global variables. Here are the declarations for all our globals, along with our updated Start() method:

Listing 16.4. Adding global variables, and storing in them references to the tracked user body parts.

```
// Top of the expanded NetMan.cs script
using UnityEngine;
using VRTK;

public class NetMan : MonoBehaviour
{

// these variables refer to the transforms that are tracked by the Vive hardware
private Transform headTracker; // position of the head as reported by the VR system
private Transform leftHandTracker, rightHandTracker;        // positions of the hands
// these GameObjects correspond to the various body parts
private GameObject head, leftHand, rightHand, torso;

void Start()
{
    headTracker = VRTK.VRTK_DeviceFinder.DeviceTransform(VRTK.VRTK_DeviceFinder.Devices.Headset);
    leftHandTracker = VRTK.VRTK_DeviceFinder.DeviceTransform(VRTK.VRTK_DeviceFinder.Devices.
        Left_Controller);
    rightHandTracker = VRTK.VRTK_DeviceFinder.DeviceTransform(VRTK.VRTK_DeviceFinder.Devices.
        Right_Controller);
    PhotonNetwork.ConnectUsingSettings("1.0");
}
```

And finally, we need an Update() method that will handle reading the input devices and updating the transforms of the body parts we instantiated:

Listing 16.5. Copy the User Input Transformations into the Avatar Objects.

```
// Update() - Copy the input transformation data from the user's body parts to their avatar.
void Update()
{
    // update network objects from trackers
    if (head != null) {
        head.transform.position = headTracker.position;
        head.transform.rotation = headTracker.rotation;
    }
    if (leftHand != null) {
        leftHand.transform.position = leftHandTracker.position;
        leftHand.transform.rotation = leftHandTracker.rotation;
    }
    if (rightHand != null) {
        rightHand.transform.position = rightHandTracker.position;
        rightHand.transform.rotation = rightHandTracker.rotation;
    }
}
```

The reason we check whether the head, leftHand, and rightHand are not null is so we don't get a null-reference error before the scene is loaded or after it's unloaded. Note that when the scene is unloaded (i.e., we leave the room) the game objects for our body parts, which were instantiated when we joined the room, are destroyed. Unity will cleverly cause destroyed objects to successfully compare to null.

Note that this updating does not need to be part of our network manager. You could have a completely separate script component just for copying the information from the input devices to the transforms. The main reason we put it here is that we have easy access to the GameObjects we instantiated for the head and hands.

You'll notice that there's no input device associated with the torso. If we had a Vive puck tracker, we could certainly attach it to our chest to track the torso. However, without a tracker, we can still make some assumptions—for example, the torso is under the head, and it generally tries to face the same way as the user's head. We'll add some code to the end of our Update() method:

Listing 16.6. Adding a simple IK (Inverse Kinematics) routine to cause the torso to move somewhat realistically.

```
// Simple IK algorithm to determine the direction of the torso
if (torso != null) {
    torso.transform.position = head.transform.position - 0.5f * Vector3.up;
    Vector3 headFacing = Vector3.ProjectOnPlane(head.transform.forward, Vector3.up);
    if (torsoTurning) {
        torso.transform.forward = Vector3.Lerp(torso.transform.forward,
            headFacing, 5 * Time.deltaTime);
        if (Vector3.Angle(headFacing, torso.transform.forward) < 10)
            torsoTurning = false;
    } else if (Vector3.Angle(headFacing, torso.transform.forward) > 30)
        torsoTurning = true;
}
```

We position the torso half a meter below the head. To find out whether we need to rotate the torso to follow the head, we first take the forward vector of the user's head (i.e., the direction the head is facing) and project it onto the ground plane. Since the torso is always upright, its forward vector is always parallel to the ground plane as well. That makes it easy to check the angle between them. If the user's head is facing more than 30° away from the direction the body is facing, we set a private boolean variable called torsoTurning to true which causes the body to re-align itself with the head. If the torso is turning, we lerp its forward vector towards the head facing direction and stop when the vectors are within 5° of each other.

Since the torso has a PhotonTransformView component on it, the updates we make to the torso's transform get synchronized over the network, just as if we were actually tracking the torso.

We're going to add one more feature. When the user enters a room, we're going to reduce the opacity of the models corresponding to their controllers in order to make the hands more prominent. We could even set the opacity to zero to hide the controllers altogether. When the user leaves the room (and their virtual hands go away) we restore the controllers to full opacity. This again is similar to what VRChat and Altspace do.

```
// OnJoinedRoom() - after initializing the objects, also reduce the opacity of the controller
//    models
void OnJoinedRoom()
{
    … // previous code

    // Reduce the opacity of the left and right tracker models (so the avatar can be seen better)
    leftHandTracker.GetComponent<VRTK_ControllerActions>().SetControllerOpacity(0.15f);
    rightHandTracker.GetComponent<VRTK_ControllerActions>().SetControllerOpacity(0.15f);
}

// OnLeftRoom() - when leaving a room restore the controller models to full visibility
void OnLeftRoom()
{
    // Set the visibily of the left and right controller objects to 100%
    leftHandTracker.GetComponent<VRTK_ControllerActions>().SetControllerOpacity(1);
    rightHandTracker.GetComponent<VRTK_ControllerActions>().SetControllerOpacity(1);
}
```

Note that we don't completely disable the controllers, since they need to be there for VRTK's grabbing to work.

We have to hide our own head as well. Because the camera is positioned inside the head, it will see the eyes and mouth. This is easy to fix—just turn off the renderers on our own head just after creating the head object:

Listing 16.8. Loop through all the game objects under the "head" object and disable their rendering (because we don't see our own face). [Add this to the OnJoinedRoom() method.]

```
// Disable the rendering For all the avatar objects that are part of the head
foreach (Renderer renderer in head.GetComponentsInChildren<Renderer>()) {
    renderer.enabled = false;
}
```

You can do the same with your torso, if you find it distracting.

For systems that use a single articulated mesh, this approach won't work. Instead, you can use an old trick—just set the scale of the bone associated with the head to zero:

Listing 16.9. In cases where an avatar mesh is used rather than component avatar parts (which is not the case described in this chapter), to eliminate the rendering of the head, set the size of it's "bone" (i.e. node in the skeleton) to zero.

```
// Set the "bone" (node) of the head to (0,0,0) so it doesn't obstruct the view
animator.GetBoneTransform(HumanBodyBones.Head).localScale = Vector3.zero;
```

This causes all the geometry that is rigidly attached to the head to shrink to invisibility. If you look closely at VRChat, you'll notice they use this trick too.

16.19 Object Ownership

As we mentioned earlier, it is important that each object have exactly one definitive source of state information at any given time. Photon has the concept of an object being "owned" by a particular networked client.

Whenever we instantiate an object through Photon, we are considered the owner of that object. So in the case of head, hands, and torso, our headset and controllers are always the source of state information. When we leave a room, the objects we created are automatically destroyed. This is what we want for our avatar, since it wouldn't make sense for it to hang around once we've left the world.

But what about the ball? It was never instantiated, since it's already part of the scene. Who owns it?

It turns out that Photon has the notion of a Master Client (not to be confused with the Master Server which we mentioned earlier, despite the similar names). The Master Client is an ordinary client machine in the simulation, but it's responsible for looking after the state of networked objects not owned by anyone else. The first client to enter the world becomes the Master Client, and when they leave a new Master Client is automatically assigned by the server. When the last client disconnects, the state of the world is lost (which means that when someone re-enters the world it will be in its default state). There are ways of persisting the state of objects in empty worlds, but we won't be covering that in this chapter.

Now that we understand Master Clients, we can begin to work out what happens with the ball. When the first client joins the world, it becomes the Master Client and takes ownership of the ball. It begins to run its physics simulation. The ball falls, and perhaps hits some object and bounces around, eventually coming to rest in the scene. As part of this simulation, the ball's position, rotation, velocity and angular velocity are all changing constantly.

When another client joins the world, it will also be running a physics simulation for the ball. However, it's not the owner of the ball—the Master Client is. The Master Client's values for the position, rotation, velocity, and angular velocity are definitive, and are sent out to the other clients which override their own values with the ones received from the network. In between updates, the velocity and angular velocity are used to do a kind of "dead reckoning" so the ball keeps moving as you would expect, but on the next update it will be moved to the correct location. That is why we specified LERP (**L**inear int**ERP**olation) when we first created the ball, and set the interpolation speed to 5, so the ball would quickly and smoothly move to the location received over the network.

All this works great until we pick up the ball. At that point, things get (even) more complex.

Whenever we pick up the ball, we want it to respond instantly when we move our hand. We do this with a script on the ball that registers two of its methods with the VRTK_InteractableObject component—one that gets called when the ball is grabbed, and the other that gets called when the ball is released.

When our method gets called that says the user has grabbed the ball, we tell Photon that we want to take ownership of the object. When the user moves their hand, VRTK updates the position of the ball. Since we own the ball, that information is definitive and gets sent out to all the other clients.

When our method gets called that says the user has released the ball, we return ownership to the Master Client.

However, if that's all we do, we'll have a problem. The physics engine on each client will be constantly trying to update the position of the ball, but the updates we send out will also be trying to update the ball's position according to the position of our hand. In between network updates, the ball will move according to physics instead of following our hand. When an update comes in, the ball will jump back to our hand only to be pulled away again by physics. In effect, the physics engine and the network are fighting for custody of the ball.

To solve this, we use another networking feature called a "remote procedure call" or RPC. A method can be declared as a remote procedure by prefixing it with [PunRPC], which means that it can be called from other clients. To call it, we just use the RPC method on our PhotonView. When making such a call, we can specify whether to call all the clients (including ourselves) or everyone but ourselves.

In Unity, rigidbodies designated as isKinematic are not controlled by the physics engine (though they can still interact with objects that are). Thus, when we grab the ball, we make an RPC call informing all the other clients to mark the rigidbody component of their copy of the ball as isKinematic while we ourselves mark it as not isKinematic. That way, physics for the ball will be run on our client but not on any of the others. Our client needs the ball to use simulated physics because VRTK uses physics for holding onto objects.

When we release the ball, we make another RPC call to mark it as non-kinematic for everyone and let all the clients again run their own physics simulations.

Here's the TakeOwnershipOnGrab.cs script component that we add to the ball:

Listing 16.10. The TakeOwnershipOnGrab.cs script initializes the object on startup (Awake), registers tasks to perform when the object is grabbed and released, and in those tasks, disables/enables the physics simulation's control over the object such that when the object is grabbed, it is controlled by the user rather than the simulation.

```
// Take network ownership of this gameobject when the user grabs it
// Written by Bernie Roehl, May 2017

using UnityEngine;
using VRTK;

public class TakeOwnershipOnGrab : Photon.MonoBehaviour
{

    private Rigidbody rigidBody;
    private VRTK_InteractableObject iObj;

    void Awake()
    {
        rigidBody = GetComponent<Rigidbody>();
        iObj = GetComponent<VRTK_InteractableObject>();
    }
```

```
void OnEnable()
{
    iObj.InteractableObjectGrabbed += ObjectGrabbed;
    iObj.InteractableObjectUngrabbed += ObjectUngrabbed;
}

void OnDisable()
{
    iObj.InteractableObjectGrabbed -= ObjectGrabbed;
    iObj.InteractableObjectUngrabbed -= ObjectUngrabbed;
}

private void ObjectGrabbed(object sender, InteractableObjectEventArgs e)
{
    photonView.TransferOwnership(PhotonNetwork.player);
    rigidBody.isKinematic = false;
    photonView.RPC("SetKinematic", PhotonTargets.Others, true);
}

private void ObjectUngrabbed(object sender, InteractableObjectEventArgs e)
{
    photonView.RPC("SetKinematic", PhotonTargets.All, false);
}

[PunRPC] // This prefix indicates that this method can be called from other clients.
public void SetKinematic(bool kinematic)
{
    rigidBody.isKinematic = kinematic;
}

}
```

Notice that we obtain and store references to the Rigidbody and the VRTK_ InteractableObject components in our Awake() method, in order to avoid the overhead of looking up those components all the time.

Note that you also need to change the field Fixed in the PhotonView to Takeover, and of course add the TakeOwnershipOnGrab component to the list of observables in the PhotonView (See Figure 16.17).

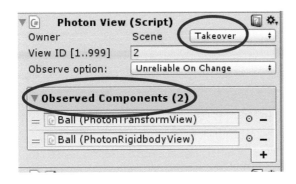

Figure 16.17

For our grabbable objects, the PhotonView should be set to "Takeover" scene mode, and have those objects added as "Observable Components."

This approach to sharing ownership works for 90% of the things you're likely to do. However, it is not perfect. There are cases where more sophisticated physics simulations will be needed, but that is a topic beyond the scope of this chapter.

16.20 Adding Voice Chat

As you recall from earlier, the main reason we chose Photon over UNET is that it provides built-in support for voice chat. Implementing voice chat is very easy—just add a `PhotonVoiceRecorder` component to the mouth of our avatar along with a `PhotonView`. You'll need to drag your Head prefab into the scene to access the mouth. Add the `PhotonVoiceRecorder` and `PhotonView` components to the mouth, select the Head, and click `Apply` at the top of the inspector to apply those changes to the prefab (See Figure 16.18). Once the prefab is created, you can delete it (the head) from the scene.

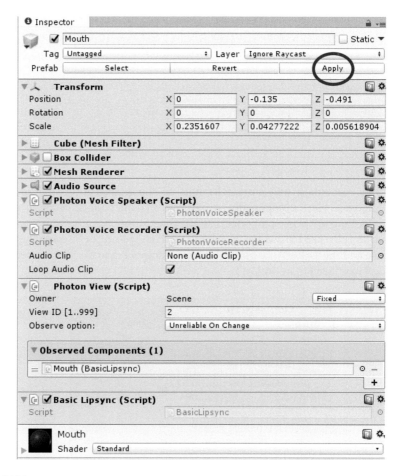

Figure 16.18

Add the PhotonVoiceSpeaker, PhotonVoiceRecorder and PhotonView scripts to the mount object in the hierarchy, and click "Apply" to update the prefab.

That is literally all there is to it. The `PhotonVoiceRecorder` component will automatically add an `AudioSource` component to the mouth object, along with a `PhotonVoiceSpeaker`. Together they will handle the entire process of capturing your voice input from a microphone device, sending it over the network, and playing it back. It will be spatialized by Unity, so you'll actually hear the person's voice coming from their mouth.

16.21 Lipsync

There are several approaches to doing realtime lipsync. Among these approaches are formant analysis, neural networks and other complex algorithmic approaches which extract phonemes from audio and map them into visemes (mouth poses).

In our case, we're going to keep it simple. We'll just use the amplitude of the audio signal to open and close the mouth of our avatar. This works well enough for puppets in the real world, and given how simple our avatar head is, we don't really want to do anything more complex.

At this point, we need to decide where to do the lipsync. We can either do it on the originating client where the audio is captured, or on the other clients where the audio is played back. Either way, there are trade-offs to consider.

If we do the lipsync on the source client, then we have to share that state information over the network. Since the voice and state information are handled independently by Photon, it is hard to ensure that the two will be synchronized. If they aren't, it will look like we're watching a badly-dubbed movie where the actors' mouths don't match with what they're saying. We could piggy-back the lipsync data on the audio so they travel together, but because Photon presents the voice chat interface as a "black box" there's no easy way to do that.

The alternative is to do lipsync on each client. That gives us perfect synchronization, and (slightly) reduces the amount of data we have to send over the network, but it does mean we have the computational overhead of doing lipsync for each character, on each client. Every client that enters the world puts an additional burden on the processors in all the other clients.

However, there are ways of managing the computational load. We could impose a limit to the number of clients that can join our world—for example, vTime (which runs on mobile devices with limited CPU power) imposes a hard limit of four users per world. Another approach is to monitor how far away an avatar is from the user, and not bother doing lipsync beyond a certain distance.

For our simple app, we'll be doing lipsync on each instance of our avatar rather than on the originator. The following code is based on a blog post by Chris Entropy [2016].

Listing 16.11. For lip-syncing, initialize the source and data storage in Awake(), and then calculate the volume (loudness) in the Update() routine, using that data to scale the avatar mouth.

```
// SimpleLipsync.cs - use the amplitude of the sound data to adjust the size
//   of the avatar's mount, doing the computation on the viewing-client side.
public class SimpleLipsync : MonoBehaviour
{
    public float mouthScale = 4;          // Adjust for how big to make the mouth
    public float updateStep = 0.1f;       // How much time should pass before recalculating
```

```
public int sampleDataLength = 1024;      // Size of the array for sampling the loudness

private AudioSource audioSource;
private float currentUpdateTime = 0f;
private float[] clipSampleData;
private Vector3 initialScale;

void Awake()
{
    audioSource = this.GetComponent<AudioSource>();
    clipSampleData = new float[sampleDataLength];
    initialScale = this.transform.localScale;
}

// Update() - For each sample window, calculate the amplitude of
//    the waveform by adding up and averaging all the wave offsets. Use
//    the calculated amplitude ("loudness") to scale the size of
//    the mouth object (in its own coordinate systems).
void Update()
{
    currentUpdateTime += Time.deltaTime;
    if (currentUpdateTime >= updateStep) {
        currentUpdateTime = 0f;
        float clipLoudness = 0f;
        if (audioSource.clip != null) {
            audioSource.clip.GetData(clipSampleData, audioSource.timeSamples);
            for (int i = 0; i < clipSampleData.Length; ++i)
                clipLoudness += Mathf.Abs(clipSampleData[i]);
            clipLoudness /= sampleDataLength;
        }
        this.transform.localScale = (1 + mouthScale * clipLoudness) * initialScale;
    }
}
}
```

The idea here is simple. We periodically (once every updateStep seconds) take a sample of the audio data. We average all the samples to compute the current amplitude. Note that none of this is related to networking at all—it would work fine to create a level meter in a single-player game, for example, and it will work with any audio source.

Drag your Head prefab into the scene, find the Mouth object, and drag the script onto it. Select the Head, hit Apply to update the prefab, then delete the head.

For this simple example, we use the amplitude to adjust the scale of the box representing our mouth. If we had an avatar with a jaw that they can open and close, then we could easily adapt the code to do that instead. Or we could go the route that Altspace has chosen for their "robot" avatars, and just change the emissive color value on one of the avatar's materials. Lots of options.

16.22 Opening and Closing the Hands

We're going to add one more feature. It may seem like a trivial one, but it introduces some important ideas. We're going to let the user open and close their hands using the triggers on their controllers.

You'll recall that the triggers have been configured in VRTK to do the grabbing of objects. Quite independent of that, we can read the value of the trigger and store it in a variable. We can then share that state information over the network, and apply it to the hands.

This example requires implementing our own network serialization and deserialization. Serialization is the process of taking values and sending them out over the network in a determined order, and deserialization is the reverse.

Listing 16.12. A script to put on a hand that uses the controller's trigger to reflect how far open the hand should be rendered. This data is then serialized and transmitted to the other clients sharing the world.

```
// Hand.cs - Determine the open-ness of each hand (using the controller triggers),
//   and transmit that (serialized) data to the other clients.
public class Hand : Photon.MonoBehaviour        // Note that we inherit from "Photon"
{
    public enum SIDE { LEFT, RIGHT };           // Create an enumeration to help decode the
                                                // network data
    public SIDE whichHand;

    private Transform gripFingers, pointerFinger;
    private VRTK_ControllerEvents controllerEvents;
    private float closeAmount = 0;              // How far closed?  0 (none), 1 (fully)

    void Start()
    {
        gripFingers = this.transform.Find("Container/GripFingerContainer");
        pointerFinger = this.transform.Find("Container/PointerFingerContainer");
        controllerEvents = (whichHand == SIDE.LEFT ?
                VRTK_DeviceFinder.GetControllerLeftHand() :
                VRTK_DeviceFinder.GetControllerRightHand()).
                GetComponent<VRTK_ControllerEvents>();
    }

    public void OnPhotonSerializeView(PhotonStream stream, PhotonMessageInfo info)
    {
        if (stream.isWriting)
            stream.SendNext(closeAmount);
        else
            closeAmount = (float)stream.ReceiveNext();
    }

    void Update()
    {
        if (photonView.isMine)
            closeAmount = controllerEvents.GetTriggerAxis();
        gripFingers.localEulerAngles = new Vector3(closeAmount * 90f, 0f, 0f);
        pointerFinger.localEulerAngles = new Vector3(closeAmount * 90f, 0f, 0f);
    }
}
```

The class derives from `Photon.MonoBehaviour` rather than `MonoBehaviour`, so it can override callback methods such as `OnSerializePhotonView()`.

Notice that we find and store references to the finger objects in our `Start()` method, as looking them up is a time-consuming operation that we don't want to repeat each frame. We also get a "which-hand" reference to the controller for each hand (as determined by a public variable on this component that we can set to `Left` or `Right` in the Unity inspector).

We use a variable called `closeAmount` to indicate how far the hand is closed, with 1 being fully closed and 0 being fully open.

In `OnSerializePhotonView()`, we write `closeAmount` to the network stream (if we're on the data sending side) or else read it from the network stream.

In `Update()`, we check to see whether we own the network view (i.e., is this our hand). If so, we set the variable `closeAmount` from the trigger value. This will later get sent out over the network in `OnSerializePhotonView()`. In any case, we use the `closeAmount` to rotate the fingers. The value of `closeAmount` will either have just been read from our trigger, or will have been set in `OnSerializePhotonView()`. We scale the value to the range 0°–90°.

Once you've got this script, you need to add it to each hand's prefab. You can just drag it onto the LeftHand and RightHand prefabs in the Resources folder. Be sure the set the "Which Hand" field to "Right" for the right hand (it defaults to "Left").

The reason this particular segment of code is important is that it forms the basis for sharing all kinds of other information from input devices. If you have eye trackers on your headset, this is how you would read and send the 2D or 3D vectors representing the user's gaze. If you have facial expression capture, this is how you would send the data (either as facial action units, or simple expression values). As VR input devices become more advanced, you'll use components like this one to share the data over the network.

16.23 Summary and Ideas for Further Work

So there you have it—a basic Social VR system with avatars, voice chat, lipsync, articulated fingers, and objects you can pick up and throw around. Not bad for a few hours of work and a couple hundred lines of code.

Of course, there are many things you can add. As mentioned, you can have multiple instances of your virtual world for the user to choose from; you can have a variety of different scenes, from western towns to moon bases; you can add multiple different avatar designs, and even support custom avatars the way VR Chat does (you may want to look into Unity asset bundles if you're going to do something like that).

You can add a UI system to allow the user to choose between worlds, change avatars, login and so on. You can use a backend database to maintain friends lists. You can allow people to mute and block others. You can add personal-space bubbles.

What you have now is a good foundation. Where you go from here is up to you. I'd love to hear what you come up with! Just drop me a line at broehl@bernieroehl.com. Also be sure to check out http://virtualescapes.ca/vrgems/ for any updates to the code in this chapter.

Many thanks to Erick Passos of Exit Games for checking the accuracy of the Photon portions of this chapter, and to Keith Makse of Red Meat Games for his help in beta testing.

References

[Against Gravity]

Against Gravity. URL: https://againstgrav.com/rec-room/

[Altspace]

Altspace. URL: https://altvr.com/

[Big Screen]

Big Screen. URL: http://bigscreenvr.com/

[Entropy 2016]

Entropy, Chris. Unity Forum Answer to "How do I get the current volume level (amplitude) of playing audio". URL: https://answers.unity.com/questions/1167177/index.html

[Exit Games]

Exit Games, Photon SDK. URL: https://photonengine.com

[Extend Reality]

Extend Reality, Extend Reality Ltd. VTTK documentation. URL: http://vrtk.io

[Facebook]

Facebook. URL: https://facebook.com/spaces

[Google VR]

Google VR, Google VR Daydream. URL: https://vr.google.com/daydream/developers/

[High Fidelity]

High Fidelity. URL: https://highfidelity.com/

[JanusVR]

JanusVR. URL: https://janusvr.com/

[Linden Research]

Linden Research. URL: https://sansar.com/

[Lowe & Lenssen]

Lowe, Scott and Philipp Lenssen. "Anyland." URL: http://anyland.com/

[Oculus 2016]

Oculus (2016), The Oculus Team, blog entry "Join Friends in VR with Oculus Rooms and Parties". URL: https://oculus.com/blog/join-friends-in-vr-with-oculus-rooms-and-parties/

[Oculus SDK]

Oculus SDK, Oculus Developers URL: https://developer.oculus.com/

[Unity UNET]

Unity UNET, Unity User Manual: Multiplayer and Networking page. URL: https://docs.unity3d.com/Manual/UNet.html

[Valve SteamVR]

Valve SteamVR, Valve Corporation, SteamVR Documentation. URL: https://steamcommunity.com/steamvr

[VRChat]

VRChat. URL: https://vrchat.com/

[vTime]

vTime. URL: https://vtime.net/

Avatar Embodiment, Behavior Replication, and Kinematics in Virtual Reality

Daniel Roth, Jan-Philipp Stauffert, and Marc Erich Latoschik
University of Würzburg

17.1 Introduction

Virtual reality (VR) strongly depends on a convincing place illusion typically achieved by accurate head-tracked stereoscopic view generation of a plausible artificial 3D environment [Slater et al., 2009]. However, the accorded sense of presence (or "being there") can be positively affected by avatars, virtual alter-egos which are located in the virtual space and which mimic one's body and its movements. Avatars can be defined as virtual characters driven by human movements. In contrast to avatars, virtual characters that are driven by computer algorithms are termed (embodied) virtual agents [Bailenson and Blascovich, 2004]. In a sense, avatars transfer the perception of the physical body to the perception of owning a virtual body [Slater et al., 2009; Lugrin et al., 2015; Latoschik et al., 2016; Roth et al., 2017a].

This fascinating illusion can evoke perceptual effects strong enough to perceive excitement or fear [Roth et al., 2016b; Argelaguet et al., 2016], taking the perspective of a virtual body.

The perception of the virtual body ownership is moderated by top-down (e.g., appearance realism and appearance personalization) as well as bottom-up effects (e.g., latency and replication coherence) [Maselli and Slater, 2013; Waltemate et al., 2018]. The effect of this illusion can be so strong that we change our behavior based on the visual characteristics of the virtual body in form of "afterglow" effects. Multiple previous works show that we adopt behaviors that we associate with avatar characteristics, such as behaving more confidently when being assigned a tall avatar or a reduction of negative stereotyping when being embodied as elderly avatar, which is known as the Proteus effect [Yee and Bailenson, 2006, 2007].

Additionally, avatar embodiment provides a direct way to include nonverbal behavior in virtual social interactions, and hence may affect aspects presence (e.g., social presence or "a medium's ability to connect people" [Nowak and Biocca, 2003]), as well as social judgments such as sympathy, empathy, or trust toward communication partners in virtual encounters [Roth et al., 2016c; Bente et al., 2008]. Previous research shows that nonverbal behavior is a substantial factor in social interactions, and estimates suggest up to 65% of the meaning in a social situation is communicated through nonverbal behavior—see Burgoon et al. [2011] for an overview. Therefore, one pragmatic goal for future VR simulations is to increase the extent to which human behaviors such as body motion, facial expression, and eye gaze are conveyed through avatars [Roth et al., 2017b].

17.2 Avatars as Animation Targets

A central aspect of a convincing avatar simulation is their dynamism, ideally mimicking exactly the motions of their owners. Virtual characters are typically visualized based on the rendering of a textured mesh (also called skin) and additional surface data, see Figure 17.1. Instead of transforming each mesh vertex individually to create an animation, a skeletal model (sometimes referred to as character rig or articulated model) is employed. In character animation, creating a character's skeleton is known as rigging. The skeleton of a virtual character consists of a number of bone objects, interconnected through joints, which can be bound to skin vertices by weighting the respective mesh parts. Bone transformations of the skeleton then manipulate the bound mesh vertices according to the predefined binding weights. These weights can be defined by automated, semi-automated or manual processes, often called skinning.

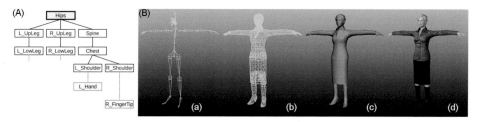

Figure 17.1

(A) Exemplary skeleton hierarchy. In this case, the hips describe the root node and the left hand, or in characters with more detail, the finger tips could be end-effectors. For more information on character hierarchies see Parent [2012]. (B) The illustration shows typical components of a virtual character: (a) the skeleton; (b) joints bound (weighted) to the mesh; (c) the mesh shaded using a material component, and (d) an applied texture.

The skeleton of humanoid characters is typically a topological structure of bones that approximate the structure of the human skeleton. The free end of each chain is often called end-effector. The range of motion of each joint connecting the bones is defined by the degrees-of-freedom (DOF) in movement and can be restricted to approximate human joint behavior using kinematic solvers. Modern game and simulation engines (such as Unity, Unreal Engine, and alike) often provide the infrastructure for humanoid kinematic or muscular models that, once defined and mapped, allow the developer to modify, restrict, or extend the movement space of the avatar on the basis of human limitations.

Skeletons are typically represented in hierarchical structure—see the ISO/IEC 19774:2005 H-Anim Standard [Human Animation Working Group et al., 2006] for one standard to use for joint labeling and structure. When representing hierarchical structures, a root node (root object, e.g., the hips) is defined, which is the parent node of one or more child nodes and constitutes the coordinate system of the hierarchy structure predefined by a known position in the global coordinate system. Child node positions are typically described in relation to the root node [Parent, 2012].

Creating rigged characters can be done with a variety of free and commercial products, such as MakeHuman [MakeHuman, 2016], Adobe Fuse [Adobe, 2017], Autodesk Character Generator [Autodesk, Inc., 2014], and many others. To achieve higher levels of realism and personalization, models can be reproduced from photogrammetry, a method for the extraction of surface points and surface properties from images, which can be used to create avatar meshes. Using personalized avatars can further improve embodiment in VR and support accepting the virtual body [Waltemate et al., 2018; Latoschik et al., 2017; Achenbach et al., 2017]. As a third option, characters made by 3D digital artists can be acquired from online shops, see also Chapter 15 of this book [Cordar et al., 2019]. To breathe life into a virtual character's lifeless state, a tracking system to sense motion behaviors such as body motion, facial expression or gaze is required. The required motion capture to drive avatar behavior is extensively used in the cinematic industry as well as in interactive simulations and games, see also [Roth et al., 2018c]. Several approaches for motion tracking exist, of which many are capable of replicating human movements within VR in real-time. Thus, we refine the definition of avatars in this context: an avatar requires a real-time connection between physical and virtual behavior.

17.3 Body Motion

The tracking of body movement is usually achieved by systems that are based on (1) active optical markers, (2) passive optical markers, (3) marker-less computer vision techniques (e.g., structured light coding/depth mapping/time-of-flight), (4) inertial sensor combinations, (5) artificial magnetic fields [Sherman and Craig, 2002, 2018; Roth, 2016], or a combination of those (see LaViola et al. [2017], Part 3 for general information on hardware systems for 3D user interfaces). For large-scale tracking systems, radio frequency-based techniques [Roth et al., 2018a] may be utilized and combined with trackers for feet and hands. With regard to body motion, we may often find ourselves utilizing systems built for digital animation for the cinematic industry or kinesiology research—i.e., motion capture (MoCap) systems. While MoCap systems are often capable of providing real-time tracking data, the real-time requirements for each field differ, as does the typical workflow as depicted in Figure 17.2.

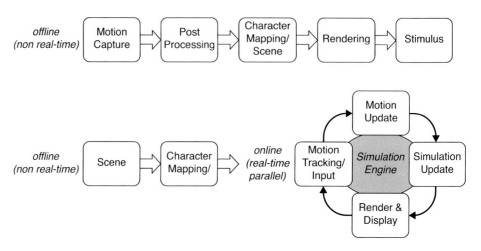

Figure 17.2

An illustration of how the workflows of cinematic digital animation (offline) and virtual reality simulations (firm/hard real-time) differ. Timeliness is of no concern in digital animation, and digital artists usually strive for image perfection (rendering) using post processed motion capture data. VR simulations on the other hand require real-time responsiveness and thus the simulation engine is confronted with real-time transformation updates for the character animation.

The choice of the system relies on numerous criteria, such as the required quality, the available budget, the scalability needs of the system (e.g., single-user vs. multi-user, prototype vs. consumer application), the allowable invasiveness of the system, and the pipeline into which it needs to be integrated. In the worst case, a very invasive system can end in what is described as the "cyborg's dilemma" [Biocca, 1997], which is the change of one's own body schema and identity due to potential technological burdens such as intrusive technologies or multiple heavy sensors. However, learning from our experiments, we find a general rule of thumb to be: for a higher degree of perceived avatar embodiment (virtual body ownership), minimal latency, quality and robustness of the tracking should be preferred over other requirements. This is because sensorimotor coherence is a key bottom-up factor in fostering this illusion [Maselli and Slater, 2013]. Spanlang et al. [2014] provide an introduction on how to build an embodiment lab for research purposes based on a passive-marker system. Today, state-of-the-art machine learning techniques boost the quality and speed of non-invasive, marker-less computer vision-based systems for full body tracking, making them competitive to marker-based solutions [Stoll et al., 2011]. Full-body markerless motion tracking is also available from sensors such as the Microsoft Kinect, which combine algorithms to reconstruct pose from RGB-depth or time-of-flight sensor data. However, the robustness of these systems is often insufficient for a first person perspective form of virtual embodiment. Yet by combining HMD tracking with markerless hand-tracking sensors (e.g., Leap Motion) some user embodiment (though reduced) can be evoked [Argelaguet et al., 2016].

Most motion tracking systems are able to output 6-DOF rigid body (defined by a combination of three or more non-collinear markers or features) or joint data to use as feature points for the animation. Although not truly rigid, the human body can be described as a combination of approximately rigid segments. Thus, some systems are capable of full body pose estimation and calculate a kinematic model through marker clusters or feature clusters, that can be used to drive a virtual character's behavior. In turn, as one would expect, the calculation of the kinematic model requires computational processes that may or may not be effective/precise and therefore may or may not deliver a satisfying result—depending on the objective and requirements for the simulation. A high-quality pose estimation and the reconstruction of realistic human movements requires sophisticated computation. This computation can increase the computational cost of the overall process and, in turn, the expected end-to-end latency from motion to visual feedback (also known as motion-to-photon latency [Lincoln et al., 2016]; see Friston and Steed [2014] for ways to measure latency that can also be adapted for simulations using body motion tracking).

17.3.1 Interfacing with Simulation Engines

Various frameworks provide substantial support for the integration of motion tracking into VR simulations: (1) the manufacturers of tracking systems often deliver SDKs for data streaming or plugins for the integration; (2) middleware such as middleVR [Kuntz, 2015] or OpenNI [Occipital, Inc., 2017] provide most required features; and (3) open and standardized protocols such as VRPN [Taylor et al., 2001] can be utilized.

Given their abundance, many developers will find themselves using a game or simulation engine (e.g., Unity, Unreal Engine, WorldViz or equivalent) which is why we consider this use case in providing the steps for the integration of full body skeleton data. State of the art tracking systems usually support this option. If one plans to use consumer hardware, for example, an RGB-depth (RGBD) based sensor such as the Microsoft Kinect, one might want to use the available SDKs or a toolkit such as FAAST [Suma et al., 2011a, 2011b] or Brekel Pro Body [Brekel, 2008], to interface with the engine.

17.3.2 Receiving the Data

For our realistically behaving avatar, our first task is to receive data from the tracking (client) application. As the tracking server will often continually send data (UDP is most common), it is useful to have two open communication channels/ports: the data connection as well as a command connection for invoking events and communicating the status from the simulation application back to the tracking application (tracking server).

In some cases, a conversion of the coordinates needs to be applied to the data received from the tracking server to match the coordinate system of the client application (e.g., left-handed to right-handed conversions).

Note that the following examples are based on a Unity application. To our hope, they are sufficiently abstract to show the concept and be implemented in any engine of choice. Many available integrations (from third parties or system suppliers, such as [NaturalPoint, Inc., 2018]) use similar concepts and inspired the following examples. For a conversion of Unreal/Unity terms see Joessu et al. [2017].

The interfacing consists of two parts: (1) adapting the rate that tracking data is provided to the rate it can be consumed at; and (2) translating the tracking data to data usable by the application. The issue of unequal data rates can be handled with a loop that conducts the simulation and rendering where the tracking data is queried once or multiple times per iteration at specific points in time. For tracking input (as opposed to button presses), only the most recent data is relevant.

One approach is to accept tracking data in a separate thread at the pace of the sending instance. This data is then provided to the application that queries at its own pace. Upon starting the application, we create a connection that runs in parallel. It calls a callback function when data arrives as shown in the code in Listing 17.1.

Listing 17.1. Upon establishing a connection, the message structure is negotiated before receiving tracking data.

```
// establish connection to the tracking server
client = new TrackingReceiver(serverAddress);

// get information from the server about the data layout
UpdateDefinitions();

// register callback that is called whenever new tracking data arrives
client.registerCallbackForData(OnDataReceive);
```

Before tracking data is received, the client requests information about how this data will be structured and what parts of the tracked body it represents. This request allows the required memory for the data exchange to be reserved. This memory will be updated every time new tracking information is received. On the other side, this memory is the reference that is used by the application to update its avatar representations. For our example, we refer to the variable pointing to this memory location as `skeletons` as it holds the bone transformation information of all tracked users.

When a data packet arrives, its content is dissected and translated to a representation consumable by the application. Here, for the sake of simplicity, we assume that one data frame contains updated positions and orientations for every joint of every tracked person (Listing 17.2).

Note that data might be in different formats, taking advantage of the hierarchical skeleton structure and forward kinematics. The position and orientation values could be sent only for the root node/the hips, followed by rotation values for each joint. While in many cases the extraction of the information from the data frame might be more extensive, the following code shows the general concept irrespective of the underlying pose solver.

Listing 17.2. For each received update, save the updated bone positions and orientations.

```
using System.Threading;
...

private SkeletonStream skeletons;
private Skeleton skeleton;
private mutex skeletonAccess;

// callback that is called when new data arrives
```

```
void OnDataReceive(data) {
    // use mutex lock to prevent other parts of the application
    //  from accessing the skeleton data while it gets updated
    lock(skeletonAccess);

    // update each bone in each skeleton with the received data
    foreach (var skeleton in skeletons) {
        foreach (var skeletonBone in skeleton.bones) {
            skeletonBone.position = data[skeleton.id][skeletonBone.id].position;
            skeletonBone.orientation = data[skeleton.id][skeletonBone.id].orientation;
        }
    }

    // release mutex lock to allow other parts of the application
    //  to access the newly updated skeleton data
    unlock(skeletonAccess);
}
```

As receiving data and updating the skeleton happens in a thread decoupled from the main application's thread, the update is protected by a mutex. A *mutex* is used to *mut*ually *ex*clude simultaneous access to a block of code, usually to prevent one stream from reading data that may be incomplete because another thread hasn't yet completed its task. In the main thread, the mapping of the source data to the target avatar takes place.

17.3.3 Mapping the Source Motion Data to the Target Character

To use the motion data in the application, the skeleton model has to be translated to the target skeletal representation of the avatar. Therefore, the real-time skeleton data stream needs to be linked to a virtual character which is thus animated by the user's behavior. Both Unity and Unreal come with animation systems (Animation Module/Mecanim [Unity Technologies, 2014]/Persona [Epic Games, Inc., 2017]) that allow virtual characters to be animated by prerecorded movements (movement cycles) in a state machine principle. However, for live user data we need to access the target avatars in real-time and map the received joint data accordingly. Note that with ongoing engine updates, the animation system interfaces are subject to change. In Unity, the target virtual character needs to be preconfigured and appropriately rigged/skinned to fulfill the criteria of a humanoid character (a minimum of 15 bones, rooted at the hip, and including all extremities). When these requirements are met, the character can be defined as "humanoid;" in special cases a "generic" definition can work. A humanoid avatar can then represent a humanoid pose that is abstracted from the skeleton rig[*].

In order to drive the humanoid target avatar we can construct a humanoid source avatar with the corresponding (Game) objects as an object tree to relate to the skeleton representations of the tracking system, see Figure 17.3. This process is often referred to as retargeting. References to the objects are handled through a bone id/game object map, see Listing 17.3.

---

[*] Note: The notion in Unity is that an "Avatar" object is a template object for an avatar not necessarily in need for a visual representation. Although this contradicts the definition stated above, we will stick with the Unity namespace for the examples for the sake of coherence.

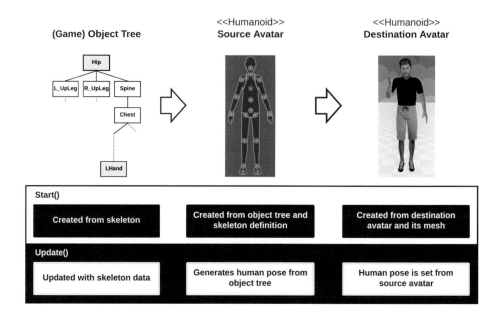

Figure 17.3

Retargeting pipeline. At the initialization (start) of the application, an object tree is created of each tracked skeleton. This object tree is the root of the humanoid source avatar. Similarly, a destination avatar is created. In the main application loop, the object tree is updated with the skeleton data. This implicitly updates the source avatar as it is built on the object tree's references. Finally, the updated pose of the source avatar is transferred to the target avatar.

Listing 17.3. A game object tree is created, relating to the structure of a skeleton and its bones.

```
private Dictionary<int, GameObject> boneObjectMap;
private GameObject rootObject;
...

void CreateBoneObjects(){
    boneObjectMap = new Dictionary<int, GameObject>(skeleton.bones.Count);
    rootObject = new GameObject(rootObjectName);

    foreach (var skeletonBone in skeleton.bones) {
        // create a new game object for each skeleton bone.
        GameObject boneObject = new GameObject(skeletonBone.Name);
        // set the bone in the right position of the object tree,
        // depending on the skeleton hierarchy.
        if (skeletonBone.parent == null) boneObject.parent = rootObject;
        else boneObject.parent = boneObjectMap[skeletonBone.parent.id];
        ...
        // store the reference to the boneObject in a bone id / game object map
        boneObjectMap[skeletonBone.id] = boneObject;
    }
}
```

The next step is to map the skeleton representation of the tracking system and the just created bone objects to the human anatomy of the engine's animation system, see Listing 17.4.

Listing 17.4. Map the skeleton representation to the human anatomy of the engine's animator.

```
void MecanimSetup() {
    ...
    // set up the HumanDescription for the source avatar.
    HumanDescription humanDescription = new HumanDescription();
    humanDescription.human = makeHumanBonesFromSkeletonBones(skeleton.bones);
    humanDescription.skeleton = retargetSkeleton(skeleton);

    // take the HumanDescription and the object tree root to build the source avatar.
    sourceAvatar = AvatarBuilder.BuildHumanAvatar(rootObject, humanDescription);

    // create pose handlers for the source and the target avatar.
    sourcePoseHandler = new HumanPoseHandler(sourceAvatar, rootObject);
    targetPoseHandler = new HumanPoseHandler(targetAvatar, targetRootObject);
}
```

Since the sourcePoseHandler was created with the references to the previously created bone object tree, any changes to the bone objects directly affect the human pose of the sourcePoseHandler. During the application loop, the bone objects are directly assigned the skeleton's values, using the BoneObjectMap. After allocating the skeleton values (see Listing 17.5), the sourcePoseHandler is used to extract the current pose of the source avatar. The pose is then assigned to the target avatar using the targetPoseHandler.

Listing 17.5. Skeleton values are assigned to the object tree during the application loop. The generated human pose is used to retarget the data to the corresponding target avatar.

```
void Update()
{
    // update the bone game objects with the current skeleton state.
    SkeletonState skeletonState = StreamingClient.GetLatestSkeletonState(skeleton);
    if (skeletonState != null){
        foreach (var skeletonBone in skeleton.bones) {
            TrackingPose currentBonePose;
            GameObject boneObject;
            skeletonState.BonePoses.TryGetValue(skeletonBone.id, out currentBonePose);
            boneObjectMap.TryGetValue(skeletonBone.id, out boneObject);

            if (currentBonePose != null && boneObject != null){
                boneObject.localPosition = currentBonePose.Position;
                boneObject.localRotation = currentBonePose.Orientation;
            }
        }
    }

    // interpret the streamed pose into Mecanim muscle space representation
    // and retarget the muscle space pose to the destination avatar.
    if (sourcePoseHandler != null && targetPoseHandler != null){
        sourcePoseHandler.GetHumanPose(ref humanPose);
        targetPoseHandler.SetHumanPose(ref humanPose);
    }
}
```

Once the input data is retargeted to the target avatar, the avatar's body motion should closely reflect the real user motion.

The approach presented here is one option to drive an avatar's body motion based on an OptiTrack passive marker system and the respective interface. The procedure is strongly dependent on the engine's animation system which is subject to change due to engine updates. On the upside, this procedure allows us to easily integrate almost any virtual character that respects the basic rules to be configured as humanoid by the engine and, thus, inherit a lot of flexibility in character usage. On the downside, the procedure strongly depends on the kinematic solving of the engine, which leaves us (at the time of writing) little control over how kinematic solving is applied and may result in unwanted artifacts such as "foot skating" due to a strong use of forward kinematic solving, i.e., solving the pose as function of a root position and consecutive child joint angles.

One alternative approach is to directly retarget raw skeleton input to a character rig. This approach can be very precise, but only works for certain combinations of tracking input and character skeletons, and is difficult to generalize. Another method is to gain more control over kinematic solving by using third party plugins such as FinalIK [RootMotion, 2018] that provides more control over the kinematic solving; this is discussed further in Section 17.5.

17.3.4 Character Scaling

One should keep in mind that the avatar has certain measurements that may not exactly match the (physical) human user. Thus, especially in the case of a first-person perspective rendering using a head-mounted display (HMD), appropriate scaling is necessary. Exact scaling is preferred, but without a photogrammetric copy, universal scaling of the character according to the user's height is a useful approximation, see Listing 17.6. In this case, the character measurements should be close to the user measurements to avoid contortions of the limb proportions. With pre-skinned characters, scaling individual bones will lead to unwanted artifacts in the mesh deformation. Thus, current approaches try to compensate for these artifacts while allowing avatar scaling based on the user's measurements [Takala and Heiskanen, 2018].

Listing 17.6. A rough but accessible approach to universal scaling.

```
// get character height during initialization
var smr = GetComponentInChildren<SkinnedMeshRenderer>();
var characterHeight = smr.sharedMesh.bounds.size.y;

// get user height, e.g., from menu
userHeight = Parameters.userHeight;

// adjust scale
multiplier = (userHeight / characterHeight);
character.transform.localScale = new Vector3(multiplier, multiplier, multiplier);
```

Integrations for tracking systems that support full skeletal data can often be retrieved from the system supplier as SDKs or plugins for leading game engines. In some cases, however, it may be necessary or beneficial to use a reduced set of features to reconstruct the full body motion.

17.3.5 Inverse Kinematic and Combined Approaches

In contrast to processing full body skeleton data for the simulation, it may be necessary or beneficial to approximate full human body movement from limited, but key features. Sparseness of tracking points can have different causes, for example: (1) the tracking system might not be capable of delivering the desired amount of tracking points; (2) the experience design requires minimal invasiveness (i.e., a demo application or a clinical research project); or (3) the application has crucial latency or latency jitter requirements [Stauffert et al., 2018], attainable only by gaining control over timeliness and performing the kinematic computation on the client [Roth et al., 2016b].

One way to approximate full human movement is with a set of rigid bodies, each defined by three or more markers. In this case, the concept of inverse kinematics (IK) comes in handy, as it allows us to approximate full body movement from fewer (e.g., five or six) key terminal end-effector positions. In contrast to forward (or direct) kinematics (FK) which describe the positions of the body parts as a function of joint angles, IK determines the character's pose and joint rotations from the positions of the end-effectors through the kinematic chain, i.e., the constraint locations for bones are specified and solved for joint angles with respect to the DOF of each joint. In our research, we show that using reduced (simpler) tracking (see Figure 17.4) can lead to lower end-to-end latency due to reduced tracking overhead as compared with a full marker set and predefined skeletal calculations—which usually utilize hybrid solving models based on FK/IK combinations. Users did not report any significant decrease in the quality of the experience [Roth et al., 2016b]. Yet, the situation was controlled, and the movement was limited to regular walking.

For real-time avatar animation, the usual practice is to track the hands/wrists, the head, and the feet as they represent the skeletal end-effectors. However, from experience, we find that it helps to introduce an additional feature point at the hips, which otherwise has to be approximated from the limbs, head and arm positions and may not result in satisfying realism for complex movements such as crawling or sitting. This approach can then be seen as a hybrid approach, but it still reduces potential tracking overhead and therefore calculation costs on the tracking system side. Alan Zucconi [2017] provides an introduction on how to use IK and its basic underpinnings. Tolani et al. [2000] summarize traditional mathematical solutions and present a combined solution. Further readings on numerical and analytical methods can be found in the fields of game programming and robotics [Buss, 2004].

Sensing solutions from VR devices such as Oculus Touch or the HTC Vive Trackers can be used to track IK feature points. More often than not, we can use the interfaces provided with a particular game or simulation engine. Most state-of-the art engines offer sophisticated IK solvers and custom middleware can be included (e.g., IKinema [IKinema Limited, 2017] or FinalIK [roo, 2018]). However, as these functions are mathematical approximations, different approaches can differ in their reconstruction quality. The code in Listing 17.7 gives a simple example of how to interface a tracking feature's position and rotation (transformation goal/target) with Unity's Mecanim animator for IK-driven animations. By doing so, hands and feet can be positioned via tracking data and the kinematic model of Unity's Mecanim then solves the character's pose. For further information and other extended examples see also [NaturalPoint, Inc., 2017; Unity Technologies, 2017a, 2017b].

```
private Animator animator;
...

// set up the inverse kinematics for one joint
if (TransformationGoal != null) {
    animator.SetIKPositionWeight(AvatarIKGoal.Joint, 1);
    animator.SetIKRotationWeight(AvatarIKGoal.Joint, 1);
    animator.SetIKPosition(AvatarIKGoal.Joint,TransformationGoal.position);
    animator.SetIKRotation(AvatarIKGoal.Joint,TransformationGoal.rotation);
}
```

17.4 Camera Properties, Placement and Calibration

Correct placement and properties of the virtual camera are important for applications supporting avatar embodiment. The virtual camera transformation should replicate the physical transformation of the user's eye positions as accurately as possible. The misplacement and wrong interconnection of the virtual camera can lead to strange camera movements, an increase of potential sickness effects, awkward perspectives, and clipping artifacts. In usual applications one might set a near frustum plane to an arbitrary level that fits the simulation requirements. However, in embodied applications, the near frustum needs to be set to a minimum level in order to not be able to see "through" your body. This typically prevents collisions of frustum and mesh and thus the user from seeing the "inside" of an arm or hand that is close to the virtual camera which could lead to a break in the perception of presence.

The HMD tracking (i.e., a tracking target that closely approximates the user's eye positions) or a rigid body tracking (see, e.g., NaturalPoint, Inc. [2017]) typically serve as physical reference for the virtual camera movement. In some cases, such as full body tracking or the reduced IK setup used in the example scene in Figure 17.4, the reference tracking target for the IK model might be the neck bone or the center of the head rather than the eye positions. In all cases, the virtual camera can be attached as child object of (or transformed with) the respective joint (e.g., the neck) data including a horizontal and vertical offset accounting for the translational difference between tracking target/joint and the eye positions to assure the proper rendering of the visual scene according to the physical movement. This is sometimes referred to as neck model or head-neck model.

In some cases, it can be useful to fuse data of two tracking systems, for example, absolute full body tracking with relative inertial measurement unit (IMU) tracking. IMU tracking data is usually available with lower latency and at higher frequency in comparison to absolute optical tracking systems, but can suffer from rotational drift. Therefore, combining (i.e., fusing) low latency rotational IMU tracking data with absolute positioning of a second system (e.g., marker-based full body tracking) can reduce simulator sickness effects. Logically, both systems have to be calibrated to the same coordinate space. Listing 17.8 shows such a rotational calibration in a camera update. To calibrate both systems, we provide a method for recalibrating the HMD orientation to match the more accurate absolute rotational data through the `cam.calibration` flag. In this simplified example,

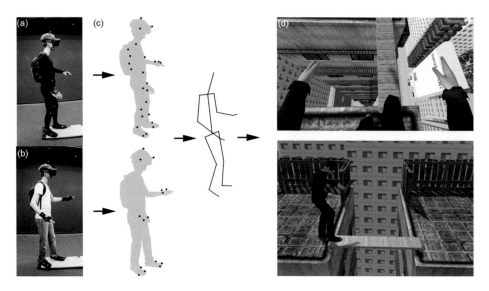

Figure 17.4

A prototypical scenario similar to the "Pit" [Meehan, 2001; Roth et al., 2016b] (using passive haptics on the feet). The user is either equipped with a full body suit and marker set (a), or a reduced IK rigid body marker set (b). Data from either tracking set is approximated to skeleton movements (c) via a kinematic model. The screenshots (d) display the respective first and third person view in the simulation that can be achieved by both approaches but with different quality and latency properties.

we modify the virtual camera's parent object coordinate system (camContainer) to represent the transformation required to compensate the accumulated drift in the y (up) axis. Such calibrations should be performed before a VR session and/or continuously (i.e., drift correction) when the influence of the drift makes a longer experience unpleasant. Using interpolation to transition through the correction prevents abrupt changes of the camera's orientation. In cases with a large lag between the input of both tracking systems, the HMD should be immobile during the initial calibration and more sophisticated prediction methods can be applied. Thus far, we found that calibrating the world-up axis results in the least perceptual artifacts.

Listing 17.8. When flagged, calculate and store a gyroscopic drift compensation offset for the camera view. The calibration modifies the orientation of an (empty) parent (Game)object camContainer, as some VR integrations may not allow modifying the camera directly or may overwrite the rotational compensation if applied directly to the camera (cam).

```
// recalibrate the camera (cam) y-rotation to compensate for
// drift if requested
void Calibration() {
    // check whether a calibration was requested
    if (cam.calibrationRequested) {
        // rotate container parented to camera to compensate current drift
```

```
camContainer.rotation =
    Quaternion.AngleAxis(headBone.eulerAngles.y, world.up)
  * Quaternion.Inverse(Quaternion.AngleAxis(cam.localRotation.eulerAngles.y, world.up));

  // reset calibration request
  cam.calibrationRequested = false;
  }
}
```

17.5 Facial Expression

Facial expressions have tremendous impact on our social interactions and the way we perceive others. Especially important in the detection of affective states, facial expressions as a nonverbal communication channel contribute to understanding others' intentions and their emotions [Roth et al., 2016a]. For embodied VR applications the replication of facial expressions to virtual characters makes sense when there is visual feedback of the self-representation (i.e., in the form of a virtual mirror) or in the case of multi-user environments.

In general, two major approaches to track and animate facial expressions can be distinguished ([Parke and Waters, 2008] is a good overview on the topic). First, a facial skeleton can be defined and transformed according to physical markers attached to the user (e.g., passive optical markers) or virtual markers that are positioned using tracking software (e.g., computer vision-based approaches). Second, and more widely used for real-time purposes, facial blendshapes (predefined morph targets) can be defined as morph properties of the avatar's face and deformed according to tracking software inputs [Orvalho et al., 2012]. Both animation methods have benefits and limitations.

Using facial skeletons, the limits in accurate weighting and skinning sometimes result in unnatural behaviors. Facial blendshapes seem, at first, to be limited in degrees of freedom, but weighted combinations of blendshapes can have numerous dimensions. However, the algorithmic models can break when too many blendshapes are evoked in combination. Recent state of the art computer vision and machine learning algorithms allow for non-intrusive RGB or RGBD based real-time tracking of facial expressions [Weise et al., 2011]. Although these performance captures are quite robust in their replication accuracy, latencies often go beyond 150 ms. Current sensor prototypes compatible with HMDs track lower facial expressions [Yu and Park, 2016; BinaryVR, 2017], including EMG sensors integrated into the HMD casing [Mavridou et al., 2017]. Research also found that a combination of sensory input (e.g., EMG or strain sensors plus RGBD cameras) mounted within an HMD can lead to good results while covering the full facial behavior [Li et al., 2015]. Treating the avatar as a display medium, replicating blendshapes for facial animation necessarily requires the target avatar to either directly support the set of blendshapes delivered as data from the tracking system, or a related set that can be retargeted (mapping similar source and target blendshapes) by appropriate weighting. Listing 17.9 shows an exemplary blendshape based implementation using influence weights. To retarget a larger set of facial blendshapes, lookup tables can be used [Roth et al., 2017b].

```
MeshRenderer avatarMesh;
BlendshapeStream float[] facialExpressionWeights;

...

// updates the avatar's facial blendshapes
void facialExpressionUpdate(float[] blendshapeWeights) {

    // retarget blendshape 1:1 match
    // e.g., source is 'smile' and target is 'smile'
    avatarMesh.SetBlendshapeValue(1, blendshapeSourceData[1] * blendshapeWeights[1]);

    // retarget blendshape 1:many match
    // e.g., source is 'smile' and targets are 'smileLeft' + 'smileRight'
    avatarMesh.SetBlendshapeValue(2, blendshapeSourceData[2] * blendshapeWeights[2]);
    avatarMesh.SetBlendshapeValue(3, blendshapeSourceData[3] * blendshapeWeights[3]);
}
```

17.6 Gaze

Human gaze is especially important in social interactions [Kleinke, 1986] (e.g., for signaling attention and for eye contact) and can increase behavioral realism to an even higher degree. Eye trackers (or gaze trackers), which were previously expensive investments have become available in low cost versions, first as desktop sensors and finally as HMD integrations (e.g., [Tobii AB, 2017; Pupil Labs, 2018; or FOVE, Inc., 2017]). Most eye trackers emit infrared light (or an infrared light pattern) which in turn delivers lighting for images captured by one or two cameras. Using image processing techniques an (auto-) calibrated system usually delivers virtual gaze targets (2D pixel values of the focus point on the screen) and/or eyeball position and rotation, and/or eye/head position and rotation. Using head or eye positions and gaze targets we can derive the direction the user is looking at in the scene, by constructing a ray into the scene originating from the center of the eyes.

With the position of the center between both eyes ($\vec{e}$) and a direction ($\vec{d}$) we can form the ray $\vec{r} = \vec{e} + t \cdot \vec{d}$. The tracker may already deliver these values. If not, they have to be derived. If the position of the center of the eyes is unknown, it can be approximated by using the head position with an offset. If the tracker delivers a gaze target, this has to be brought into 3D space by applying knowledge about the depth of the image plane relative to the user. With a 3D gaze target ($\vec{g}$) the direction can be derived as $\|\vec{g} - \vec{e}\|$. In turn, one can infer the avatar's eye rotations by utilizing the gaze target screen values (or respectively viewport values) and the user's head rotation by constructing a rotation according to these values with respect to the virtual camera's field of view and camera's aspect ratio. Multiplying this rotation with the inverse head rotation will then result in a local replication of the physical gaze behavior to the avatar's eye movements.

To increase smoothness, filters can be applied. Eye trackers with low quality might deliver some arbitrary null value if the user is not detected by the tracker. One way of coping with these null values is to simply use an upper or lower threshold for filtering

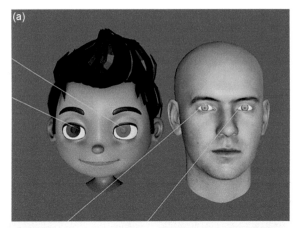

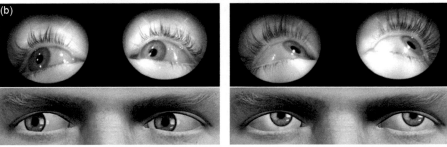

Figure 17.5

(a) Avatars following gaze targets accurately rotating their eyeballs (avatars by faceshift AG/infinite 3D head scan by Lee Perry-Smith). (b) HMD-based eye-tracking using a FOVE device. To prevent artefacts, the maximal rotation can be restricted (right example). Other refinements include the approximation of coupled behavior of eyeball and eyelids.

(else, take the old value), or to identify the null value and implement the necessary logic. In social scenarios, social gaze models could be one option to cope for disruptions in the transmission (Figure 17.5) [Roth et al., 2018b].

17.7 Conclusion

In this chapter, we covered the principles of avatar embodiment and behavior reproduction for VR simulations. Tracking techniques and implementations for replicating behaviors from body motion, facial expression, and gaze to avatars have been discussed. Using this knowledge, developers can include embodiment in their simulations to evoke illusions of virtual body ownership or increase the level of social behaviors transmitted. Tracking devices for real-time behavior replication have gained interest and many sensors as well as integrations for real-time behavioral replication are becoming accessible. Thus, one can expect further improvements in speed and accuracy, and behavioral realism (e.g., ongoing approaches to include finger movements), especially with the prominence of machine learning in current developments (Figure 17.6).

When working with motion tracking or on applications that evoke embodiment, we sometimes find ourselves confronted with bottlenecks that result from blackboxed integrations. Developers should be aware of system specifications and plan their pipelines and component combinations. Being constrained to the engine backend can have benefits, but restricts control over the pipeline.

The next generations of HMDs will most likely be equipped with integrated sensors for facial expressions and eye-tracking. Computer vision-based machine learning approaches to motion capturing and reconstruction will become more applicable for embodiment simulations. In the long run, we might expect brain-computer interfaces as sensors of intended behaviors [Slater, 2014]—short-cutting the loop between intention and motor activation. Our virtual bodies might be modified by additional limbs, e.g., to increase efficiency [Won et al., 2015]. Finally, artificially modified [Roth et al., 2015, 2018d] or visually transformed [Roth et al., 2018a] behaviors could drastically change communication paradigms in VR. Ethical discussions on transmission, data security, and modification need to be part of future developments. All together, these examples indicate the enormous potential of *Avatar Embodiment, Behavior Replication, and Kinematics in Virtual Realities*.

Acknowledgements

We thank Gary Bente, Julia Büser, David Fernes, Dmitri Galakhov, Peter Kullmann, David Mal, Christian Felix Purps, Felix Stetter, Sebastian von Mammen, Kristoffer Waldow, as well as Case Bowman & François Asseman (NaturalPoint/OptiTrack), Thibaut Weise (faceshift/Apple), and Kenneth Ryu (binaryVR) for their help, support and feedback during projects, developments and studies that led to the conclusions and knowledge described in this summary.

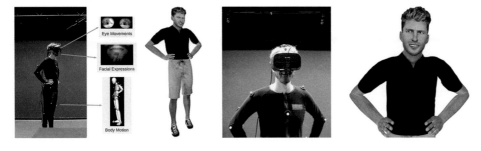

Figure 17.6

Full replication of body movement, lower facial expressions, and gaze behavior to a virtual avatar.

References

[Achenbach et al., 2017]

Achenbach, Jascha, Thomas Waltemate, Marc Erich Latoschik, and Mario Botsch (2017). Fast generation of realistic virtual humans. In *Proceedings of the 23rd ACM Symposium on Virtual Reality Software and Technology*, page 12. ACM, Gothenburg, Sweden.

[Adobe, 2017]

Adobe (2017). Adobe Fuse, Adobe Systems Software Ireland Ltd. http://adobe.com/products/fuse.html. Accessed: 2017-09-25.

[Argelaguet et al., 2016]

Argelaguet, Ferran, Ludovic Hoyet, Michael Trico, and Anatole Lécuyer (2016). The role of interaction in virtual embodiment: Effects of the virtual hand representation. In *Proceedings of Virtual Reality (VR)*, pages 3–10. IEEE, Greenville, South Carolina.

[Autodesk, Inc., 2014]

Autodesk, Inc. (2014). Autodesk Character Generator. https://charactergenerator.autodesk.com/. Accessed: 2017-09-25.

[Bailenson and Blascovich, 2004]

Bailenson, Jeremy N., and Jim Blascovich (2004). Avatars. In *Encyclopedia of Human-Computer Interaction*. Berkshire Publishing Group: Barrington, MA.

[Bente et al., 2008]

Bente, Gary, Sabine Rüggenberg, Nicole C. Krämer, and Felix Eschenburg (2008). Avatar-mediated networking: Increasing social presence and interpersonal trust in net-based collaborations. *Human Communication Research*, 34(2): 287–318.

[BinaryVR, 2017]

BinaryVR (2017). BinaryVR—BinaryVR Dev Kit V1. https://medium.com/@hyprsense/releasing-vr-sdk-1-1-2-today-6bf99f57ccb7.

[Biocca, 1997]

Biocca, Frank (1997). The cyborg's dilemma: Progressive embodiment in virtual environments. *Journal of Computer-Mediated Communication*, 3(2).

[Brekel, 2008]

Brekel (2008). http://brekel.com/brekel-kinect-pro-body/. Accessed: 2017-09-25.

[Burgoon et al., 2011]

Burgoon, Judee K., Laura K. Guerrero, and Valerie Manusov (2011). Nonverbal signals. *The SAGE Handbook of Interpersonal Communication*. In Knapp, M. L., Daly, J. A., editors, *SAGE*: London.

[Buss, 2004]

Buss, Samuel R. (2004). Introduction to inverse kinematics with Jacobian transpose, pseudoinverse and damped least squares methods. *IEEE Journal of Robotics and Automation*, 17(1–19): 16.

[Cordar et al., 2019]

Cordar, Andrew, Yao Heng, Fatemeh Tavassoli, Jeffrey Wood, and Benjamin Lok (2019). Making virtual reality social: Getting virtual humans into your virtual environment. In Sherman, W. R., editor, *VR Developer Gems*, Chapter 15. A K Peters/CRC Press, Boca Raton, Florida.

[Epic Games, Inc., 2017]

Epic Games, Inc. (2017). Animation editors. https://docs.unrealengine.com/latest/INT/Engine/Animation/Persona/. Accessed: 2017-09-26.

[FOVE, Inc., 2017]

FOVE, Inc. (2017). FOVE eye tracking virtual reality headset. https://getfove.com/. Accessed: 2017-09-26.

[Friston and Steed, 2014]

Friston, Sebastian, and Anthony Steed (2014). Measuring latency in virtual environments. *IEEE Transactions on Visualization and Computer Graphics*, 20(4): 616–625.

[Human Animation Working Group et al., 2006]

Human Animation Working Group et al. (2006). Information Technology Computer Graphics and Image Processing Humanoid Animation (h-anim). *ISO/IEC FCD 19774: 200x*. http://www.web3d.org/documents/specifications/197741/V2.0/HAnim/HAnimArchitecture.html.

[IKinema Limited, 2017]

IKinema Limited (2017). IKinema website. https://ikinema.com/. Accessed: 2017-10-20.

[Joessu et al., 2017]

Joessu, KitatusStudios, and SNDRKeene (2017). Transitioning from Unity to UE4—Epic Wiki. https://wiki.unrealengine.com/Transitioning_from_Unity_to_UE4

[Kleinke, 1986]

Kleinke, Chris L. (1986). Gaze and eye contact: A research review. *Psychological Bulletin*, 100(1): 78–100.

[Kuntz, 2015]

Kuntz, Sébastien (2015). MiddleVR a generic VR toolbox. In *Proceedings of Virtual Reality (VR)*, pages 391–392. IEEE, Arles, France. Unityplugin at http://middlevr.com/middlevr-for-unity/.

[Latoschik et al., 2016]

Latoschik, Mark Erich, Jean-Luc Lugrin, and Daniel Roth (2016). FakeMi: A fake mirror system for avatar embodiment studies. In *Proceedings of the 22nd ACM Conference on Virtual Reality Software and Technology*, pages 73–76. ACM, Munich, Germany.

[Latoschik et al., 2017]

Latoschik, Marc Erich, Daniel Roth, Dominik Gall, Jascha Achenbach, Thomas Waltemate, and Mario Botsch (2017). The effect of avatar realism in immersive social virtual realities. In *Proceedings of the 23rd ACM Symposium on Virtual Reality Software and Technology*, page 39. ACM, Gothenburg, Sweden.

[LaViola et al., 2017]

LaViola Jr., Joseph J., Ernst Kruijff, Ryan P. McMahan, Doug Bowman, and Ivan P. Poupyrev (2017). *3D User Interfaces: Theory and Practice*. Addison-Wesley Professional: Boston, MA.

[Li et al., 2015]

Li, Hao, Laura Trutoiu, Kyle Olszewski, Lingyu Wei, Tristan Trutna, Pei-Lun Hsieh, Aaron Nicholls, and Chongyang Ma (2015). Facial performance sensing head-mounted display. *ACM Transactions on Graphics (TOG)*, 34(4): 47.

[Lincoln et al., 2016]

Lincoln, Peter, Alex Blate, Montek Singh, Turner Whitted, Andrei State, Anselmo Lastra, and Henry Fuchs (2016). From motion to photons in 80 microseconds: Towards minimal latency for virtual and augmented reality. *IEEE Transactions on Visualization and Computer Graphics*, 22(4): 1367–1376.

[Lugrin et al., 2015]

Lugrin, Jean-Luc, Johanna Latt, and Marc Erich Latoschik (2015). Avatar anthropomorphism and illusion of body ownership in VR. In *Proceedings of Virtual Reality (VR)*, pages 229–230. IEEE, Arles, France.

[MakeHuman, 2016]

MakeHuman (2016). MakeHuman. http://makehuman.org/. Accessed: 2017-09-25.

[Maselli and Slater, 2013]

Maselli, Antonella, and Mel Slater (2013). The building blocks of the full body ownership illusion. *Frontiers in Human Neuroscience*, 7: 83.

[Mavridou et al., 2017]

Mavridou, Ifigeneia, James T. McGhee, Mahyar Hamedi, Moshen Fatoorechi, Andrew Cleal, Emili Balaguer-Ballester, Ellen Seiss, G. Cox, and Charles Nduka (2017). FACETEQ: A novel platform for measuring emotion in VR. In *Proceedings of the Virtual Reality International Conference-Laval Virtual*, page 9. ACM, Laval, France.

[Meehan, 2001]

Meehan, Michael (2001). Physiological reaction as an objective measure of presence in virtual environments. *PhD thesis*, University of North Carolina at Chapel Hill.

[NaturalPoint, Inc., 2017]

NaturalPoint, Inc. (2017). OptiTrack manual—Unity plugin. http://v20.wiki.optitrack.com/index.php?title=OptiTrack_Unity_Plugin. Accessed: 2017-10-20.

[NaturalPoint, Inc., 2018]

NaturalPoint, Inc. (2018). OptiTrack Unity Integration. http://optitrack.com/unity-integration/index.html. Accessed: 2017-10-20.

[Nowak and Biocca, 2003]

Nowak, Kristine L., and Frank Biocca (2003). The effect of the agency and anthropomorphism users' sense of telepresence, copresence, and social presence in virtual environments. *Presence*, 12(5): 481–494.

[Occipital, Inc., 2017]

Occipital, Inc. (2017). OpenNI. https://structure.io/openni. Accessed: 2017-09-25.

[Orvalho et al., 2012]

Orvalho, Verónica, Pedro Bastos, Frederic I. Parke, Bruno Oliveira, and Xenxo Alvarez (2012). A facial rigging survey. In Cani, M., Ganovelli, F., editors, *Eurographics (STARs)*: 183–204.

[Parent, 2012]

Parent, Rick (2012). *Computer Animation: Algorithms and Techniques.* Elsevier/Morgan Kaufmann Publishers, Waltham, MA.

[Parke and Waters, 2008]

Parke, Frederic I., and Keith Waters (2008). *Computer Facial Animation.* CRC Press, Boca Raton, Florida.

[Pupil Labs, 2018]

Pupil Labs (2018). Pupil Labs. https://pupil-labs.com/.

[RootMotion, 2018]

RootMotion (2018). Final IK—RootMotion. http://www.root-motion.com/final-ik.html

[Roth et al., 2015]

Roth, Daniel, Marc Erich Latoschik, Kai Vogeley, and Gary Bente (2015). Hybrid avatar-agent technology—A conceptual step towards mediated "social" virtual reality and its respective challenges. *i-com*, 14(2): 107–114.

[Roth, 2016]

Roth, Daniel (2016). The study of interpersonal communication using virtual environments and digital animation: Approaches and methodologies. In *Presentation on the 66th Annual Conference of the International Communication Association (ICA)*, June 9–13, Fukuoka, Japan.

[Roth et al., 2016a]

Roth, Daniel, Carola Bloch, Anne-Kathrin Wilbers, Marc Erich Latoschik, Kai Kaspar, and Gary Bente (2016). What you see is what you get: Channel dominance in the decoding of affective nonverbal behavior displayed by avatars. In *Presentation on the 66th Annual Conference of the International Communication Association (ICA)*, June 9–13, Fukuoka, Japan.

[Roth et al., 2016b]

Roth, Daniel, Jean-Luc Lugrin, Julia Büser, Gary Bente, Arnulph Fuhrmann, and Marc Erich Latoschik (2016). A simplified inverse kinematic approach for embodied vr applications. In *Proceedings of Virtual Reality (VR)*, pages 275–276. IEEE, Greenville, South Carolina.

[Roth et al., 2016c]

Roth, Daniel, Jean-Luc Lugrin, Dmitri Galakhov, Arvid Hofmann, Gary Bente, Marc Erich Latoschik, and Arnulph Fuhrmann (2016). Avatar realism and social interaction quality in virtual reality. In *Proceedings of Virtual Reality (VR)*, pages 277–278. IEEE, Greenville, South Carolina.

[Roth et al., 2017a]

Roth, Daniel, Jean-Luc Lugrin, Marc Erich Latoschik, and Stephan Huber (2017). Alpha IVBO-construction of a scale to measure the illusion of virtual body ownership. In *Proceedings of the 2017 CHI Conference Extended Abstracts on Human Factors in Computing Systems*, pages 2875–2883. ACM, Denver, Colorado.

[Roth et al., 2017b]

Roth, Daniel, Kristoffer Waldow, Marc Erich Latoschik, Arnulph Fuhrmann, and Gary Bente (2017). Socially immersive avatar-based communication. In *Proceedings of Virtual Reality (VR)*, pages 259–260. IEEE, Los Angeles, California.

[Roth et al., 2018a]

Roth, Daniel, Constantin Kleinbeck, Tobias Feigl, Christopher Mutschler, and Marc Erich Latoschik (2018). Beyond replication: Augmenting social behaviors in multi-user virtual realities. In *Proceedings of the 25th IEEE Virtual Reality (VR) Conference*, Reutlingen, Germany.

[Roth et al., 2018b]

Roth, Daniel, Peter Kullmann, Gary Bente, Dominik Gall, and Marc Erich Latoschik (2018). Effects of hybrid and synthetic social gaze in avatar-mediated interactions. In *Proceedings of the 17th IEEE International Symposium on Mixed and Augmented Reality (ISMAR) Adjunct*. IEEE, ACM, Munich, Germany.

[Roth et al., 2018c]

Roth, Daniel, Jean-Luc Lugrin, Sebastian von Mammen, and Marc Erich Latoschik (2018). Controllers & inputs: Masters of puppets. In Banks, J., editor, *Avatar, Assembled—The Social and Technical Anatomy of Digital Bodies*, 106, Digital Formations, 281–290. Peter Lang Publishing, Inc.: New York.

[Roth et al., 2018d]

Roth, Daniel, David Mal, Christian Felix Purps, Peter Kullmann, and Marc Erich Latoschik (2018). Injecting nonverbal mimicry with hybrid avatar-agent technologies: A naïve approach. In *Proceedings of the* 6th *ACM Symposium on Spatial User Interaction (SUI)*. ACM, Berlin, Germany.

[Sherman and Craig, 2002]

Sherman, William R. and Alan B. Craig (2002). *Understanding Virtual Reality: Interface, Application, and Design*. Elsevier/Morgan Kaufmann: Burlington, MA.

[Sherman and Craig, 2018]

Sherman, William R. and Craig (2018). *Understanding Virtual Reality: Interface, Application, and Design*, 2nd edition. Elsevier/Morgan Kaufmann: Amsterdam, the Netherlands.

[Slater, 2014]

Slater, Mel (2014). Grand challenges in virtual environments. *Frontiers in Robotics and AI*, 1(3).

[Slater et al., 2009]

Slater, Mel, Daniel Pérez-Marcos, H. Henrik Ehrsson, and Maria V. Sanchez-Vives (2009). Inducing illusory ownership of a virtual body. *Frontiers in Neuroscience*, 3(2): 214.

[Spanlang et al., 2014]

Spanlang, Bernhard, Jean-Marie Normand, David Borland, Konstantina Kilteni, Elias Giannopoulos, Ausiàs Pomés, Mar González-Franco, Daniel Perez-Marcos, Jorge Arroyo-Palacios, Xavi Navarro Muncunill, and Mel Slater (2014). How to build an embodiment lab: Achieving body representation illusions in virtual reality. *Frontiers in Robotics and AI*, 1: 9.

[Stauffert et al., 2018]

Stauffert, Jan-Philipp, Florian Niebling, and Marc Erich Latoschik (2018). Effects of latency jitter on simulator sickness in a search task. In *Proceedings of the* 25th *IEEE Virtual Reality (VR) Conference*, Reutlingen, Germany.

[Stoll et al., 2011]

Stoll, Carsten, Nils Hasler, Juergen Gall, Hans-Peter Seidel, and Christian Theobalt (2011). Fast articulated motion tracking using a sums of Gaussians body model. In *Proceedings of Computer Vision (ICCV), 2011 IEEE International Conference*, pages 951–958. IEEE, Barcelona, Spain.

17. Avatar Embodiment, Behavior Replication, and Kinematics in Virtual Reality

[Suma et al., 2011a]

Suma, Evan A., Belinda Lange, Albert Skip Rizzo, David M. Krum, and Mark Bolas (2011). FAAST: The Flexible Action and Articulated Skeleton Toolkit. In *Proceedings of Virtual Reality Conference (VR)*, pages 247–248. IEEE, Singapore.

[Suma et al., 2011b]

Suma, Evan A., Belinda Lange, Skip Rizzo, David Krum, and Mark Bolas (2011). Flexible Action and Articulated Skeleton Toolkit (FAAST). https://projects.ict.usc.edu/mxr/faast. Accessed: 2017-07-18.

[Takala and Heiskanen, 2018]

Takala, Tuukka M., and Heikki Heiskanen (2018). Auto-scaled full body avatars for virtual reality: Facilitating interactive virtual body modification. In *Proceedings of the 25th IEEE Virtual Reality (VR) Conference*, Reutlingen, Germany.

[Taylor et al., 2001]

Taylor II, Russell M., Thomas C. Hudson, Adam Seeger, Hans Weber, Jeffrey Juliano, and Aron T. Helser (2001). VRPN: A device-independent, network-transparent VR peripheral system. In *Proceedings of the ACM Smposium on Virtual Reality Software and Technology*, pages 55–61. ACM, Banff, Canada. Available at https://github.com/vrpn/vrpn.

[Tobii AB, 2017]

Tobii AB (2017). Tobii eye tracking in virtual reality. https://tobii.com/tech/products/vr/. Accessed: 2017-09-26.

[Tolani et al., 2000]

Tolani, Deepak, Ambarish Goswami, and Norman I. Badler (2000). Real-time inverse kinematics techniques for anthropomorphic limbs. *Graphical Models*, 62(5): 353–388.

[Unity Technologies, 2014]

Unity Technologies (2014). Mecanim animation system. https://docs.unity3d.com/462/Documentation/Manual/MecanimAnimationSystem.html. Accessed: 2017-09-26.

[Unity Technologies, 2017a]

Unity Technologies (2017). Unity user manual—Animation system overview. https://docs.unity3d.com/Manual/AnimationOverview.html. Accessed: 2017-10-20.

[Unity Technologies, 2017b]

Unity Technologies (2017). Unity user manual—Inverse kinematics. https://docs.unity3d.com/Manual/InverseKinematics.html. Accessed: 2017-10-20.

[Waltemate et al., 2018]

Waltemate, Thomas, Dominik Gall, Daniel Roth, Mario Botsch, and Marc Erich Latoschik (2018). The impact of avatar personalization and immersion on virtual body ownership, presence, and emotional response. *IEEE Transactions on Visualization and Computer Graphics*, 24(4): 1643–1652.

[Weise et al., 2011]

Weise, Thibaut, Sofien Bouaziz, Hao Li, and Mark Pauly (2011). Realtime performance-based facial animation. In *Proceedings of ACM SIGGRAPH* 2011, pages 77: 1–77:10, New York. ACM.

[Won et al., 2015]

Won, Andrea Stevenson, Jeremy N. Bailenson, and Jaron Lanier (2015). Homuncular flexibility: The human ability to inhabit nonhuman avatars. In Scott, R. A., Buchmann, M. C., editors, *Emerging Trends in the Social and Behavioral Sciences: An Interdisciplinary, Searchable, and Linkable Resource*.

[Yee and Bailenson, 2006]

Yee, Nick, and Jeremy N. Bailenson (2006). Walk a mile in digital shoes: The impact of embodied perspective-taking on the reduction of negative stereotyping in immersive virtual environments. *Proceedings of PRESENCE: The 9th Annual International Workshop on Presence,* August 24–26, Cleveland, OH.

[Yee and Bailenson, 2007]

Yee, Nick, and Jeremy Bailenson (2007). The Proteus effect: The effect of transformed self-representation on behavior. *Human Communication Research*, 33(3): 271–290.

[Yu and Park, 2016]

Yu, Jihun, and Jungwoon Park (2016). Real-time facial tracking in virtual reality. In *Proceedings of SIGGRAPH ASIA* 2016 *VR Showcase, SA '16*, pages 4: 1–4, New York. ACM.

[Zucconi, 2017]

Zucconi, Alan. (2017). FOVE Eye Tracking Virtual Reality Headset. http://alanzucconi.com/2017/04/10/robotic-arms/. Accessed: 2017-09-26.

SECTION V
Third Person POV Cameras

Recording and Replaying Virtual Environments for Development and Diagnosis

Anthony Steed, Mingqian Wang, and Jason Drummond
University College London

18.1 Overview

The user of a virtual reality experience has a lot of freedom to move and interact. As a developer, or experimenter, understanding user experience can be very hard. From a video of the session it can be difficult to determine what happened. Sometimes you want to put yourself in the shoes of the user and ask why something specific happened, or why the user chose to make a particular action.

In attempting to develop and debug our own virtual reality applications, we have found that recording and replaying elements of the virtual environment can be very useful. In our experimental work, we have often used recordings for later analysis. For example, checking whether users witnessed a particular event occur, or to count collisions between the user and obstacles in an environment. Recording and replaying also has uses in creating demonstrations or tutorials for software, or simply for creating new content to be used in animations.

We have implemented or used many variants of record and replay over the years; from systems that could completely record the application state and replay it, through to custom mechanisms that would record only key information. The former is attractive for low-level debugging, but it is hard to engineer and can generate extremely large log files.

Not all software is amenable to this unless you have the complete source code. The latter can fail to capture all the details of the application, but it is very quick to implement. This latter variant can also easily use file formats that can be imported into other software for inspection and analysis.

In this chapter we outline some simple tools for recording and replaying on the Unity platform. We support basic recording to comma-separated value (CSV) files which can be easily loaded in Excel or Matlab. We illustrate the use of the tools with two examples. The first is recording of the user's behavior in a simple scene with a puzzle. The operator can record the movement of a user and then play this back. During the playback they see a simple avatar representation of the previous user and can experience this from a first person point of view. This allows them to see what the user was doing from an immersive perspective and potentially generate hypotheses about how the user was tackling the puzzle. The second example is recording of a skeletal animation. In this example the operator gets some simple tools to edit recordings of the motion. Although not a fully featured motion editor, this example illustrates the main principles of recording an animation for content production.

18.2 Design

18.2.1 Overview

In this chapter we focus on recording movement of objects in the scene. The goal is to provide simple scripts that are easy to extend to support more complex use cases. Many use cases will need other variables or properties to be recorded and replayed, but these can be added in a straight-forward manner, see Section 18.4.1.

A secondary goal is to output the recording files into a format re-usable by other software. Thus, we use a very simple file format using comma-separated values, which is very easy to parse by other tools. For example, one common use is simply to load them into Excel to plot user trajectories around the space.

18.2.2 Recording Types and Rate

A key question is what to record and how often. Frequently we want to reconstruct what users did, and what they saw, because we want to reconstruct the users' experiences. However, we also might want to recreate the complete state of the environment. For example, we might want to make a world persistent, so that it is available for users to re-experience later, see Section 18.4.2. Logging systems often rely on *serialisation* procedures; that is, all objects that make up the scene are asked to record their state to disk. This technique is common across many types of systems and is a common functionality in many programming languages. However, it generates large files that have state that is usually difficult to re-use in other applications. Given the high update rates of modern virtual reality systems, this type of approach needs careful implementation so that the system doesn't become slower simply because of the repeated serialisation.

Therefore, a key decision is to focus on extracting only data that we want to record and replay from the scene. The code we demonstrate focuses on recording and replaying the positions of objects. In some ways, it is similar to the motion capture format *Biovision Hierarchy* (BVH), which is commonly used to store movement animations. In fact, one use we will demonstrate is the simple recording and replaying of files that would be easy to edit into a BVH-compatible format. A key difference is that BVH focuses on animation of skeletal rigs, whereas we need a format that can cope with arbitrary sets of moving objects including skeletal rigs (i.e., mostly animated by rotations of joints) and entities moving in six degrees of freedom.

In this chapter our demonstrations focus on user or character motion. A simple extension could record other values that are necessary to recreate the state of the application, such as floating point values that are needed by shaders or flags that indicate the state of objects. If scene behavior is non-deterministic or dependent on the full history of user behavior (e.g., imagine a game level with multiple moving agents that are stalking the user), then we would need to be mindful of what to record in order to reconstruct the appearance of the scene.

Having settled on what information to record, a second issue is how often to record information. Given that current consumer hardware has a display rate of around 90Hz, we record at the display rate. Replaying at faster or slower speeds is relatively simple for motion behaviors, but leads to problems with other values where the results of an interpolated value might not make sense. For example, a binary flag can't be interpolated, but the game state might not make sense if an interpolated frame is added for a motion, but doesn't exist for the flag (e.g. consider a flag that occurs when a moving object hits another object). Issues like this are why completely general record and replay systems are hard to build.

18.2.3 Recorder Script

The key to our implementation is the *Recorder* script which saves motion state to a log file. Initially, we will not worry about the user interface for recording. See Section 18.3 for examples that use different interface types.

In Listing 18.1 we show the overall form of the script. The script has an array of reference to `Transform` components. The first `logPositionRotationObjects` is an array of single objects for which the script will record the full position and rotation each frame. The second `logRotationTreeObjects` is an array of the roots of sub-graphs for which the script will record the rotation of each child. Rotation-only sub-graphs are very commonly used in skeletal animation. If the animation includes translations and rotations, then each member of the sub-tree would need to be added to the `logPositionRotationObjects` independently.

The script is quite naive in the way that it records to the file with the given name (`file-Name`). Everything happens inside the standard Unity `Update()` function. Each time recording mode is activated by setting the public flag `recording` it calls `initializeFile` which creates a header line on the file (Listing 18.1), and then it writes the current state of the specified objects to the file.

Listing 18.1. The declaration of the Recorder class, the main public variables and the per-frame update function.

```
// Recorder.cs
// Recorder class: starts and stops the recording process
//      Add script to an empty gameObject
```

```
using System.IO;
using System.Text;

public class Recorder : MonoBehaviour {

    public Transform[] logPositionRotationObjects; // objects to record full transforms
    public Transform[] logRotationTreeObjects; // sub-graph nodes recording rotations
    public string fileName; // file to store recorded log data
    public bool recording = false; // set this to true to begin recording

    private bool isInitalised = false;
    private int frameCount = 0;
    private float startRecordingTime = 0.0f;

    void Update() {
        // Change recording state
        if (recording && !isInitalised) {
            Debug.Log("Start_recording");
            startRecordingTime = Time.unscaledTime;
            initializeFile(fileName);
            isInitalised = true;
        }

        if (!recording && isInitalised) {
            Debug.Log("recording_finished");
            isInitalised = false;
            frameCount = 0;
        }

        if (isInitalised) {
            frameCount++;
            writeDataToFile(fileName);
        }
    }
}
```

The `initializeFile` and `writeDataToFile` functions are defined in Listing 18.2. The function `initializeFile` starts to build a header line for the log file with the current time and a frame count, then calls helper functions to append the relevant details from the lists of objects that are slated for storage.

Similarly, `writeDataToFile` writes the time and frame count, and calls helper functions for the lists of objects.

Listing 18.2. Writer methods for the data logging.

```
// Write a line to the file that indicates the values for each "column" of data.
private void initializeFile(string fileName) {
    StringBuilder headerBuilder = new StringBuilder();
    headerBuilder.Append("Time" + "," + "FrameCount" + ",");
    foreach (Transform t in logPositionRotationObjects) {
        appendPositionRotationHeader(t, headerBuilder);
    }
    foreach (Transform t in logRotationTreeObjects) {
        appendRotationTreeHeader(t, headerBuilder);
    }
    File.AppendAllText(fileName, headerBuilder.ToString(0, headerBuilder.Length - 1));
}
```

```
     // Write time & frame count followed by transform data in arrays
     private void writeDataToFile(string fileName) {
         StringBuilder dataBuilder = new StringBuilder();
         dataBuilder.Append("\n" + (Time.unscaledTime - startRecordingTime) + "," + frameCount +
","); 
         foreach (Transform t in logPositionRotationObjects) {
             appendPositionRotationData(t, dataBuilder);
         }
         foreach (Transform t in logRotationTreeObjects) {
             appendRotationTreeData(t, dataBuilder);
         }
         File.AppendAllText(fileName, dataBuilder.ToString(0, dataBuilder.Length - 1));
     }
```

Listing 18.3 shows the helper functions. The function `appendPositionRota-`
`tionHeader` appends a header showing the six values that will be logged. The associated function `appendPositionRotationData` outputs those values. The function
`appendRotationTreeHeader` does a recursive output of the names and three rotation values for the tree. The associated function `appendRotationTreeData` outputs
the rotation values in the same order.

Listing 18.3. Helper methods for creating the data log strings.

```
     // Appends the name of a single position and rotation variable to a string.
     private void appendPositionRotationHeader(Transform rootnode, StringBuilder stringbuild) {
         stringbuild.Append(rootnode.name + "PosX" + "," + rootnode.name + "PosY" + "," +
                 rootnode.name + "PosZ" + "," + rootnode.name + "RotX" + "," +
                 rootnode.name + "RotY" + "," + rootnode.name + "RotZ" + ",");
     }

     // Appends the position and rotation values to a string.
     private void appendPositionRotationData(Transform rootnode, StringBuilder stringbuild) {
         stringbuild.Append(rootnode.localPosition.x + "," + rootnode.localPosition.y + "," +
                 rootnode.localPosition.z + "," + rootnode.localEulerAngles.x + "," +
                 rootnode.localEulerAngles.y + "," + rootnode.localEulerAngles.z + ",");
     }

     // Appends the variable names in a tree of rotations to a string
     private void appendRotationTreeHeader(Transform rootnode, StringBuilder stringbuild) {
         stringbuild.Append(rootnode.name + "RotX" + "," + rootnode.name + "RotY" + "," +
                 rootnode.name + "RotZ" + ",");
         for (int i = 0; i < rootnode.childCount; i++) {
             Transform child = rootnode.GetChild(i);
             appendRotationTreeHeader(child, stringbuild);
         }
     }

     // Appends the values in tree of rotations to a string
     private void appendRotationTreeData(Transform rootnode, StringBuilder stringbuild) {
         stringbuild.Append(rootnode.localEulerAngles.x + "," +
                 rootnode.localEulerAngles.y + "," +
                 rootnode.localEulerAngles.z + ",");
         for (int i = 0; i < childCount rootnode.childCount; i++) {
```

```
        Transform child = rootnode.GetChild(i);
        appendRotationTreeData(child, stringbuild);
    }
  }
}
```

18.2.4 Replayer Script

The *Replayer* script (Listing 18.4) mirrors the *Recorder* script. The code similarly references arrays of `Transform` objects that will be modified. The code assumes that the structures of the transforms are the same. There is no enforcement for the transforms to have the same names as those recorded, as it is common in our own recordings to use a different set of objects to play back recordings than those used for the recordings. However, it would be simple to add name checking, and to check whether the structures of the `Transform` objects and their sub-trees match.

To read the file, a helper function `loadDataToArray` reads one line into an array `currDataArr` which is of size `columnCount`. The count of columns is done in an initialization phase wherein the header is parsed. The function `updateAll` iterates through all the objects to be replayed. It uses the two functions `updatePositionRotationObjects` and `updateRotationTreeObjects` to update the `Transform` objects appropriately. The former function skips through the array of stored data six indices at a time (three locations, three orientations). The latter recurses through the tree taking three float values at a time (orientation only). Both `loadDataToArray`, and `updateAll` are called from the Update callback in the *Replayer* script, see the online materials for full details.

Listing 18.4. Replayer methods for loading data from a log file and setting the appropriate position and rotation values for objects in the scene graph.

```
// Reads one line from the log file into an array of values
private void loadDataToArray() {
    string[] values = sr.ReadLine().Split(',');
    for (int i = 0; i < columnCount; i++) {
        currDataArr[i] = float.Parse(values[i]);
    }
}

// Call once to update all the objects that are replayed. Must have previously
// loaded a line from the log file into the array currDataArray (see loadDataToArray())
private void updateAll() {
    int idx = 2; // Skip time and frame count
    foreach (Transform t in replayPositionRotationObjects) {
        idx = updatePositionRotationObjects(t, idx);
    }
    foreach (Transform t in replayRotationTreeObjects) {
        idx = updateRotationTreeObjects(t, idx);
    }
}

// Reads the position and rotation for a single object
private int updatePositionRotationObjects(Transform rootnode, int idx) {
    rootnode.localPosition = new Vector3(currDataArr[idx], currDataArr[idx + 1],
            currDataArr[idx + 2]);
```

```
            rootnode.localEulerAngles = new Vector3(currDataArr[idx + 3], currDataArr[idx + 4],
                    currDataArr[idx + 5]);
        return idx + 6;
    }

    // Recursively reads the rotation for an object in a rotation tree
    private int updateRotationTreeObjects(Transform rootnode, int idx) {
        rootnode.localEulerAngles = new Vector3(currDataArr[idx], currDataArr[idx + 1],
                currDataArr[idx + 2]);
        idx = idx + 3;

        for (int k = 0; k < rootnode.childCount; k++) {
            Transform child = rootnode.GetChild(k);
            idx = updateRotationTreeObjects(child, idx);
        }
        return idx;
    }
```

Another useful function of the *Replayer* script is the ability to skip to any frame in the log file. We could store the whole log file in memory, but this is rather onerous; some of our log files are over an hour in duration. Thus, we use file access mechanisms to re-scan the file. See the online materials for the full class for replaying.

18.3 Examples

18.3.1 User Motion

Our first example is of recording a user doing a tangram puzzle inside a head-mounted display. We are interested in where the user looks while doing the puzzle. The demonstration below is configured for the HTC Vive system. It was developed for Unity 5.6.2f.

The scene set up is very simple (Figure 18.1). The main scene graph follows the *Vehicle Pattern* as described in Chapter 6 of this volume. The Vehicle contains simple functionality to support the HTC Vive using the SteamVR package. The responsibility of this scene sub-graph is to provide the functionality to move around the scene, manipulate objects and create any first-person representation of the user's own avatar. The Zone object contains the scene itself (Tangram for the puzzle, and HMDLab for the room and furniture) and the Record and Replay object which has the record and replay scripts, and an avatar which is a simple collection of objects to represent the user during the replay. The replay avatar consists of models of a head-mounted display and two hand controllers.

In Figure 18.2 we see the Unity property inspector for the Record object. The *Recorder* script's field Position Rotation Objects (which matches the class variable log-PositionRotationObjects, see Section 18.2.2) is set up to track four objects from the Vehicle: the head, left hand, right hand, and overall position of the user in the scene which is controlled by the Vehicle object's transform.

The Record and Replay object has a script (RecordReplayControl—Listing 18.5) to start and stop the recording and replaying. An excerpt from its script is below. On the key "Q," the recording starts with a log file name composed of the exact time of day. The key "W" stops the recording. The key "O" starts the replay of the latest recording, and "P" stops the replay. The function newestLogFile finds the latest log file.

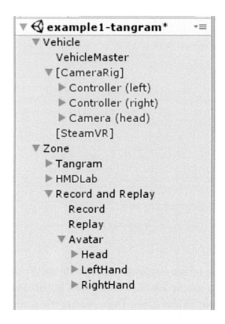

Figure 18.1

The Unity scene-graph for the first example—the tangram puzzle world.

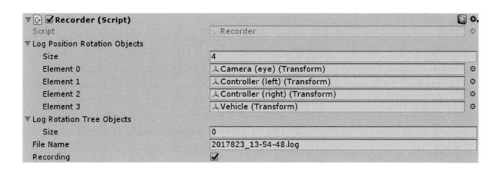

Figure 18.2

Part of the Unity inspector for the Recorder object. We can see the list of four recorded objects that are required to record the user's main behaviour. The recording is currently active.

Listing 18.5. Part of the RecordReplayControl showing keyboard controls for recording and playback.

```
// Update() function reads key presses to control the recording and replaying
void Update() {
    if (Input.GetKeyDown(KeyCode.Q)) {
        DateTime now = System.DateTime.Now;
        recorder.fileName = now.Year.ToString() + now.Month.ToString() +
```

```
            now.Day.ToString() + "_" + now.Hour.ToString() + "-" +
            now.Minute.ToString() + "-" + now.Second.ToString() + ".log";
        recorder.recording = true;
        replayer.playing = false;
        avatar.SetActive(false);
    }
    if (Input.GetKeyDown(KeyCode.W)) {
        recorder.recording = false;
    }
    if (Input.GetKeyDown(KeyCode.O)) {
        replayer.fileName = newestLogFile();
        Debug.Log("Newest_log_file_is_" + replayer.fileName);
        replayer.playing= true;
        recorder.recording = false;
        avatar.SetActive(true);
    }
    if (Input.GetKeyDown(KeyCode.P)) {
        replayer.playing = false;
        avatar.SetActive(false);
    }
}
```

Figure 18.3 shows a view of the replay in progress. We used simple objects to represent the user. The rays coming from the head and hands help visualise the gaze and pointing targets of the user.

18.3.2 Character Animation

Our second demonstration is more complex. It is a system for creating recordings during content development. The scene shown in Figure 18.4 has two human characters controlled by skeletal rigs. In this demonstration, the first character in purple and yellow is controlled by an external source. Our normal use of this tool is to have this character

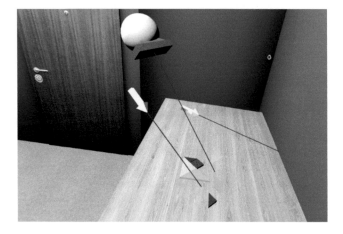

Figure 18.3

A fragment of a screen capture of the Unity Editor showing an example scene replaying the puzzle solving task.

Figure 18.4

The second example scene. The character in purple and yellow is playing a motion capture animation. The character in green and orange is a replay of a recording. The slider and buttons at the top of the screen allow the user to scroll through the animation. The small control at the bottom right allows the user to edit the recorded animation.

controlled by a motion capture rig such as a Perception Neuron. However, in the example provided it is actually replaying a motion capture animation. The second character in green and orange is replaying a recording.

The demonstration provides a user interface for scrolling through the animation (top of Figure 18.4) and functionality to mark sections of an animation for replacement (bottom right of Figure 18.4). This interface exploits the same simple functionalities of the record and replay scripts as the first example. Under the hood, editing an existing file is done by composing fragments of previous files.

18.4 Discussion

18.4.1 Extensions

The code presented in this chapter is a framework that is easy to extend for other purposes. For example, it would be easy to add logging information for input devices such as joystick and button values. When we run experiments, we often record secondary values that can be more easily calculated by the game engine than external tools. For example, determining whether a particular object was touched by the user or whether the user looked at a particular object.

Another type of extension is linking the recording of the virtual environment behavior to external recordings. It can be useful to log timestamps from video cameras, external sensors (e.g. heart-rate sensors), voice recordings of the user, etc. While some of these devices may involve separate recording systems, we recommend that some time signal or flags be brought into the Unity scene so that synchronization can be maintained. Unity has a variety of useful plugins to connect to other sensors, so in many cases it may be possible to control an external device, and its logging, directly from within Unity.

A final type of extension is additional visualization tools on top of the raw replay of the events, or visualization of multiple replays simultaneously. Although the operator can be immersed within the replay, it can be difficult to understand the user's actions or intentions. It can be useful to visualize aggregate behavior such as lines showing the route users took through the environment or heatmaps of gaze directions.

18.4.2 Related Work

There is a considerable amount of previous work in this area. A large proportion of games include a game replay mechanism. If the game is deterministic, then a replay mechanism can be constructed simply by recording the determinants of the initial state (e.g. random numbers) and then the sequence of inputs. Otherwise the state of the scene elements can be stored and replayed with a similar mechanism to that we have described.

The concept of recording and replaying as a resource for re-use in virtual environment also has a long history. Perhaps the first demonstration was the virtual mail system, where users could record segments of the virtual environment and send them to other users [Imai et al., 1999]. Today, as an example, the Altspace system allows events to be recorded and replayed to new audiences [Altspace, 2016]. Many useful reasons for recording experiences are described by Dolinsky et al. [2012].

There is a strong relationship between the requirement to network systems together, and the ability to record events. The networking protocols that underpin a collaborative virtual environment need to record short-term behavior and copy it to other sites [Steed and Oliveira, 2009]. However, the requirements are slightly different; for example, network sharing only needs to reconstruct an approximation of state, so it is typical to simplify the information that is sent. The record and replay of the Massive system is a good demonstration of some advanced uses of recording multiple users' activities and replaying them within a scene [Greenhalgh et al., 2002].

A common mechanism for recording application state is the use of *serialization* mechanisms. Serialization allows a program to save the state of a group of objects, by having each object have its own functionality to save and load its state to a file or database. These mechanisms have internal or core library support in many languages. The Javascript Object Notation (JSON) is one example that now has broad support [JSON, 2017]. It provides for data-only write and read of Javascript objects, though there are readers and writers available in many languages. Alternatively, the implementer of a virtual environment could also add their own serialization. It is easy to implement such a mechanism in Unity [Daily, 2014].

18.5 Conclusions

In this chapter we have given an overview of the utility of record and replay mechanisms for developers of virtual reality experiences. Because it can be hard to understand what users do inside the virtual environment, we have found that creating recordings allows us to visualize behavior to uncover problems with the system, or discover how users tackle interaction tasks. We have also found recording and replaying useful during creation of new content for our environments. Finally, we have previously advocated for broader sharing of experiment log files within the virtual reality research community [Friedman et al., 2006; Steptoe and Steed, 2012] to facilitate new types of analysis and allow validation of experimental results.

The implementation and examples we provide are very simple, but they are a good basis for exploration. Recording and replaying more complicated systems is potentially a difficult task because of the complex interaction between data and functionality that is common in scene-graph and scripting-based systems. However, even as they are, the tools are already useful for recording diagnostic information about user performance that can aid in developing new applications.

The examples included are on the accompanying website. The avatars we use are simple open source models we created ourselves. The second example uses a basketball motion capture from the Carnegie Mellon University Graphics Lab Motion Capture Database. These motion captures are available as a Unity package on the asset store [cMonkeys, 2017].

References

[Altspace, 2016]

Altspace (2016). AltspaceVR Blog, VR Capture. https://altvr.com/vrcapture/. Accessed: 2017-07-25.

[cMonkeys, 2017]

cMonkeys (2017). Huge FBX Mocap Library part 1. https:/assetstore.unity3d.com/en/#!/content/19991/. Accessed: 2017-07-25.

[Daily, 2014]

Daily, Eric (2014). How to Save and Load Your Players' Progress in Unity. https://gamedevelopment.tutsplus.com/tutorials/how-to-save-and-load-your-players-progress-in-unity--cms-20934/. Accessed: 2017-07-25.

[Dolinsky et al., 2012]

Dolinsky, Margaret, William Sherman, Eric Wernert, and Yichen Catherine Chi (2012). Reordering virtual reality: Recording and recreating real-time experiences.

[Friedman et al., 2006]

Friedman, Doron, Andrea Brogni, Christoph Guger, Angus Antley, Anthony Steed, and Mel Slater (2006). Sharing and analyzing data from presence experiments. *Presence: Teleoperators and Virtual Environments*, 15(5): 599–610.

[Greenhalgh et al., 2002]

Greenhalgh, Chris, Martin Flintham, Jim Purbrick, and Steve Benford (2002). Applications of temporal links: Recording and replaying virtual environments. In *Proceedings IEEE Virtual Reality 2002*, Orlando, FL, pp. 101–108.

[Imai et al., 1999]

Imai, Tomoko, Andrew E. Johnson, Jason Leigh, David E. Pape, and Thomas A. DeFanti (1999). The virtual mail system. In *Proceedings IEEE Virtual Reality (Cat. No. 99CB36316)*, Houston, TX, p. 78.

[JSON, 2017]

JSON (2017). Introducing JSON. http://json.org/. Accessed: 2017-07-25.

[Steed and Oliveira, 2009]

Steed, Anthony, and Manuel Fradinho Oliveira (2009). *Networked Graphics: Building Networked Games and Virtual Environments*. Elsevier, Amsterdam.

[Steptoe and Steed, 2012]

Steptoe, William, and Anthony Steed (2012). Multimodal data capture and analysis of interaction in immersive collaborative virtual environments. *Presence: Teleoperators and Virtual Environments*, 21(4): 388–405.

19

Capturing Cinematic Shots of Virtual Reality Scenes in Unity

Andrew Cunningham
University of South Australia

Maxime Cordeil
Monash University

19.1 Introduction

Producing compelling videos of VR content is valuable to many domains, whether as a marketing resource to sell a product or game, or a tool to educate users on a particular VR application, or to capture and document a research project. Compelling videos should make use of well-established cinematic techniques such as multiple camera shots and points of view, as these techniques are well known to help strengthen the narrative conveyed in a video [Arijon, 1991].

Shooting high-quality video of interactive VR scenes can be both a difficult task and take a considerable amount of time to produce; time that is at a premium due to the novel development involved in VR applications. Furthermore, videos captured directly from a VR user's view can be of a poor quality because of the small erratic head movements that occur as a natural part of the human sensorimotor interaction process. While these movements are a completely natural, unconscious process, to an outside viewer they can be distracting and, in the worst case, confusing.

This chapter introduces a set of behaviors for Unity designed to address the need for producing high-quality video of VR applications. These behaviors are implemented through a camera director and a toolbox of cameras each providing different cinematic shots suited towards capturing specific aspects of a VR application. These cameras are: (1) a smoothed camera to eliminate erratic user head movements, (2) an orbit camera to capture the broad scope of the VR world, and (3) a shoulder-style camera to capture the user's hand controller interactions. These cameras are presented with general guidelines on where they are best used.

19.2 Camera Director

The purpose of the camera director is to provide a means to select between any of the cinematic views of a VR scene—all of which can be captured independently of the user's actual point of view. To achieve this, the director facilitates switching between various cameras placed by the user in the scene to provide more cinematic variety in the shots captured.

The camera director behavior (Listing 19.1) contains a list of camera references that can be switched between by pressing the numeric keyboard keys. By default, the first camera in the director's list will be the active camera when starting up. The camera director may be attached to any game object within the scene, though to facilitate easy access and referencing, a good convention is to place the behavior on an empty game object within the root of the scene hierarchy and to name the object "[CameraDirector]".

Listing 19.1. A camera director behaviour, responsible for user-controlled switching between a list of cameras.

```
// CameraDirector.cs
// This script is responsible for the user-controlled
//     switching between a list of cameras
// Attach this script to any game object in the scene
//     (e.g. empty "[CameraDirector]")
using System.Collections.Generic;
using UnityEngine;

public class CameraDirector : MonoBehaviour
{
    [SerializeField]
    List<Camera> videocameras = new List<Camera>();

    void Start() {
        SetCamera(0);
    }

    void Update() {
        // map number keys to camera in the list of cameras
        for (int i = 0; i < videocameras.Count; i++) {
            if (Input.GetKeyDown(KeyCode.Alpha1 + i)) {
                SetCamera(i);
            }
        }
    }

    // enable a camera by number
    void SetCamera(int idx) {
        for (int i = 0; i < videocameras.Count; ++i) {
            videocameras[i].gameObject.SetActive(i == idx);
        }
    }
}
```

19.3 Cameras

Along with a camera director, it is useful to have a "toolbox" of cameras to provide a variety of potentially interesting shots that can be used to emphasize various aspects of the scene or narrative. Depending on what you are trying to emphasize with a particular shot, you would use a different type of camera. This section presents three types of cameras that can be used to capture VR content, and discusses where each type of camera is best suited.

19.3.1 Smooth Follow Camera

The first camera we consider aims to smooth the natural but erratic head movements that a user in VR may not be conscious of. This camera will closely follow a target camera, specifically the active VR camera, using a smoother linear interpolation function. The result of this is a smooth tracking camera producing a view that is much easier for outside viewers to watch and understand. The resulting footage appears to a viewer as though the user is controlling their viewpoint with a specific purpose.

The smoothed camera is enabled through a `SmoothFollow` behavior attached to a camera within the scene, as presented in Listing 19.2. This camera contains a reference to the transform to follow (generally being the main VR headset camera) as well as a `speed` parameter and an `isSmoothed` boolean parameter. The `speed` parameter will control how quickly the smoothed camera will follow the target camera. The `isSmoothed` boolean will disable the smoothing effect on or off and is useful for contrasting the effect of the smoothing with the default camera.

Listing 19.2. A smooth follow-camera behaviour that will linearly interpolate to follow a referenced transform.

```
// SmoothFollow.cs
// Linearly interpolate a camera to follow a given transform (game object)
// Attach this script to the moving camera in the scene
using UnityEngine;

public class SmoothFollow : MonoBehaviour
{
    public Transform target; // the object to follow (typically HMD view)

    public float speed = 2.0f;
    public bool isSmoothed = true;

    private void Update()
    {
        // toggle the smoothing when 'S' key is pressed
        if (Input.GetKeyDown(KeyCode.S)) {
            isSmoothed = !isSmoothed;
        }
    }

    // smooth follow is applied in LateUpdate() to ensure the target transform
    //    has already updated its movement for the current frame
    void LateUpdate()
    {
        if (isSmoothed) {
```

```
        // use LERP (Linear intERPolation) to transition to the target
        this.transform.position = Vector3.Lerp(this.transform.position, target.position,
            Time.deltaTime * speed);
        this.transform.rotation = Quaternion.Lerp(this.transform.rotation, target.rotation,
            Time.deltaTime * speed);
    } else {
        this.transform.position = target.position;
        this.transform.rotation = target.rotation;
    }
  }
}
```

This style of camera is useful for shots that need to show what a user is seeing in VR in an understandable and clear manner. It is also useful for situations where hand controller interaction occurs in front of the user's face, although it is worth noting that many VR interactions occur just below the user's chest where the user can leverage proprioception over visual cognition. In those cases, other cameras such as the shoulder camera presented below are better suited. Finally, when trying to capture a shot that conveys frantic action, a "shakey cam" camera with no smoothing may be preferable, in which case you can disable the isSmoothed boolean in the SmoothFollow behaviour.

19.3.2 Orbit Camera

An orbit camera will orbit around any game object at a set speed, determined by a speed property, and distance, determined by the initial relative distance to the target game object. This type of camera is useful for conveying a sense of space or to provide an overview of a scene. The orbit camera behavior presented here will orbit around a specific transform, whether it is a stationary object in the scene or the transform of the user's head itself.

This behavior presented in Listing 19.3 has a target transform referencing the object that is being orbited. You may add an empty game object into the scene to orbit around an arbitrary point in the scene, or attach it to the user's camera to orbit around the user as they move. The speed parameter determines the orbit speed in units per second.

Listing 19.3: The orbit camera behaviour will orbit around a referenced transform within the scene.

```
// OrbitCamera.cs
// Orbit a camera around a given transform (game object)
// Attach this script to the moving camera in the scene
using UnityEngine;

public class OrbitCamera : MonoBehaviour
{
    public bool orbit;                  // toggle to enable/disable orbiting
    public float speed = 1.0f;          // orbiting speed
    public Transform target;            // game object around which to orbit

    // incrementally move the camera to the next position
    void LateUpdate()
    {
```

```
        if (target != null && orbit) {
            this.transform.Translate(Vector3.right * speed * Time.deltaTime);
            this.transform.LookAt(target);
        }
    }
}
```

Consider using an orbit camera in shots where you want to provide an overview of the scene without showing too much detail, or to provide an overview of the user's hand controller interaction from multiple different angles.

19.3.3 Shoulder Camera

As the name suggests, a shoulder camera will follow the user's point of view from slightly above and behind his shoulder. This section presents a more generalized version of a shoulder camera that may be positioned anywhere relative to the user's viewpoint. The code for the shoulder camera behavior is presented in Listing 19.4. This behavior contains an offset vector that determines the offset from the target transform. The tracking of the target transform occurs using a SmoothDamp function that provides more dynamic movement than a typical linear interpolation, giving the impression that the camera is handheld.

Listing 19.4: A generalized shoulder camera.

```
// ShoulderCamera.cs
// Move camera to follow the user over their shoulder
// Attach this script to the moving camera in the scene
using UnityEngine;

public class ShoulderCamera : MonoBehaviour
{
    public Transform target;            // object to follow
    public Vector3 offset;              // distance from action
    public float smoothTime = 1.0f;     // how fast to smooth the movements

    Vector3 velocity = new Vector3();

    void LateUpdate()
    {
        if (target != null) {
            var targetPosition = target.position + target.TransformVector(offset);
            this.transform.position = Vector3.SmoothDamp(this.transform.position, targetPosition,
                ref velocity, smoothTime);
            this.transform.LookAt(target);
        }
    }
}
```

A shoulder style camera is useful for capturing hand controller interactions, especially where the interactions take place at or below the user's torso—an area that is generally not captured by a headset camera.

19.4 Putting It All Together

With the camera director and camera toolbox scripts in your Unity project, the next step is to instance and link the various elements together. Begin by adding the camera director script to a new (empty) game object within the VR scene. Add camera objects to the scene for each of the cameras types presented in the toolbox and add their respective behaviors to the game object. From Unity 5.6 onwards, Unity favors displaying non-stereo cameras to the main display, so ensure that the *Target Eye* property of each camera is set to "None (Main Display)." Setup any transform references to point to the transform (game object) you wish to track, and add any additional stationary cameras you may need. Finally, drag references for each of these cameras into camera list of the camera director.

To test the cameras, run the scene through Unity. By default, the first camera in the camera director will become active. Switch between the camera using the numeric keyboard keys as required. Once you have tested the camera setup, use screen capture software to record the footage of your project, either from within Unity itself or from a built executable. Follow the general guidelines for each camera presented in this chapter and, if time permits, capture multiple shots of the same scene and activity with different cameras to provide you with more variety when editing the final video together. On single-display setups, multiple shots can be captured sequentially by re-enacting interactions and activating different cameras using the camera director. On multi-display setups, different cameras can be assigned to each display and captured simultaneously, either within the editor by using multiple "Game" windows, or from a built executable using the Display class from UnityEngine. It should be noted that rendering to multiple displays and, at the same time, recording those displays can introduce performance issues such as lowered frame rates.

While there are a multitude more potential types of cameras that may be implemented, the cameras presented in this chapter were selected specifically for the value they bring to capturing VR applications, as summarised in Table 19.1. Notably, the smooth follow camera will provide immediate benefits when replacing the default camera, as illustrated in Figure 19.1 and with some experimentation you will be able to determine the best use-cases for the other cameras presented. Once you have mastered these cameras, you may want to investigate more traditional cinematic camera techniques such as the dolly zoom or the dutch angle.

Table 19.1 A Summary of the Cameras Presented in this Chapter

Camera Type	Value in VR
Smooth follow	Filter out the erratic unconscious head movements from the VR user, resulting in a view that is much easier for outside viewers to watch.
Orbit	Orbit around a point in the scene, providing an immersive overview of the VR scene.
Shoulder	Follow from a relative distance from the user, providing a method for clearly capturing hand controller interactions.

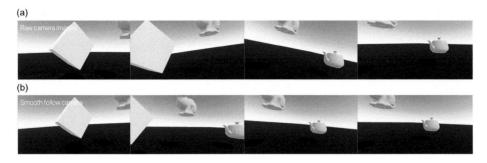

(a)

Raw camera images

(b)

Smooth follow camera

Figure 19.1

A series of images illustrating the effect of capturing a smooth follow camera compared to a standard camera. (a) A series of images showing the raw capture of a user's head camera, where the user is tilting their head unconsciously as they look from left to right. (b) A smooth follow camera following the head camera. The horizon is much more stable and the motion is easier for a viewer to track.

Acknowledgements

This work has been supported by the Data to Decisions Cooperative Research Centre whose activities are funded by the Australian Commonwealth Government's Cooperative Research Centres Programme.

Reference

[Arijon, 1991]

Arijon, Daniel (1991). *Grammar of the Film Language*. Los Angeles, CA: Silman-James Press.

20

A Stereoscopic 3D View for Virtual Reality Spectators

Andrew Guagliardo
University of Hawai'i at Mānoa

Jason Leigh
University of Hawai'i at Mānoa

Ming-Der Yang
National Chung Hsing University

A major part of Virtual Reality's appeal over other forms of media, is the sense of immersion a virtual environment provides, and therefore there is much desire to be able to share that experience. Whereas room-based VR environments such as CAVEs allow several people to share a VR experience simultaneously, head-mounted displays (HMDs), such as the Vive or Oculus, are primarily solitary experiences. In order for audience members to see what the HMD-wearer is seeing, the default approach is to present a monoscopic preview window on a monitor. However, given the low cost of 3D televisions today it is possible to also give audience members a more immersive experience by providing a simultaneous stereoscopic view.

The gem presented in this chapter, called the Stereoscopic Spectator View (SSV), is a script for the Unity engine to enable VR applications to be enhanced with a simultaneous stereoscopic 3D view for audience members. This chapter will first explain briefly the fundamentals of stereoscopic computer graphics, and then provide an overview of the approach to make the stereoscopic view work in Unity. At first glance one might think that it is sufficient to simply mirror the left- and right-eye images of the HMD-wearer. This is only a partial solution. From our experience, a simple mirroring can cause the audience to experience eye strain, especially as the viewpoint of the HMD wearer's head changes so rapidly from moment to moment. To implement the SSV experience well, it is important to smooth out the HMD-wearer's viewpoint changes before presenting them to the audience. This will be elaborated on further in this chapter as well.

20.1 Stereoscopic 3D in a Nutshell

Human vision allows for perceiving the world with depth—in three dimensions. This is possible because our eyes are offset on our heads and so each eye simultaneously sees a slightly different image from the other. The brain fuses these two images, and as a result we perceive depth. To achieve this in virtual reality, two cameras, offset like our eyeballs, must simultaneously take two pictures and present them to each eye of the viewer. Using polarizing filters or alternating the left and right eye images, it is possible to feed these two different pictures to a person's left and right eye achieving the perceived stereoscopic effect. A passive stereo display creates an interlaced image, whereby the left and right eye views are interleaved in alternating rows from the top to the bottom of the display. Wearing polarized glasses, with an opposing pair of linear or circularly polarized lenses, allows the user to receive the distinct images in their left and right eyes, enabling stereoscopic depth perception. Two ways of conveying stereoscopic pairs to the display are either to stack the left and right images on top of each other or place them side by side. A passive 3D television will take those images and perform the necessary interleaving to match the interleaved lines of polarization on the display, whereas an active 3D television image will take the two images and alternate between showing the left and right images rapidly while simultaneously triggering the viewer's glasses to allow only the correct image to be received by each of the viewer's eyes.

20.1.1 The Nuts and Bolts of a Stereo Spectator View in Unity

The Unity script that we will describe can present 3D images in both side-by-side and interleaved modes making it useable on both passive stereo and active stereo 3D televisions. Performing the image interleaving is slightly more complex than presenting the images side-by-side, and so this chapter will focus on the former.

Three things are required to produce the interleaved images:

1. Two cameras that will serve as the "eyes." These cameras will provide the different views needed for the effect.
2. A shader that will take the two images from the "eyes" and interleave them, so that they display properly for a passive stereo effect.
3. A script to control the creation of the cameras and their movement. The script also ensures that the camera's views are correctly connected to the shader and properly creates the interleaved effect for the display.

All three of these items will be attached to a Unity *GameObject* either as a *prefab*, or an object in your Scene.

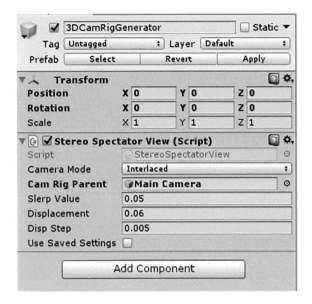

Figure 20.1

Inspector panel view of the game object containing the SSV script.

20.1.2 The Final Game Object

Pictured in Figure 20.1 is the final *GameObject* we will be creating, as seen in the inspector panel of Unity.

We will require both a script named *StereoSpectatorView* as well as a shader to do the actual interlacing of our images. We'll start with our *StereoSpectatorView* script (Listing 20.1).

20.2 Stereo Spectator View Script

Listing 20.1. The settings and internal variables for the SSV script.

```
// StereoSpectatorView.cs script
using UnityEngine;
using System;
using System.Collections;
using System.Collections.Generic;

public class StereoSpectatorView : MonoBehaviour {
    public GameObject CamRigParent;                      // the viewpoint to track
    public float slerpValue = .05f;                      // the rate at which we follow the viewpoint
    public float displacement = 0.2f;                    // the displacement between the "eyes"
    Camera rightCamera, leftCamera, interlacedCam;       // camera references for SSV effect
    Texture2D interlaceMask;                              // opacity mask for interleaving lines
    Material mat;                                         // the material with our interlacing shader
```

```
// We will create & enhance Start() and Update() as we go along
void Start() { }

void Update() { }

}
```

After setting up the basic script we need a function to create our cameras (Listing 20.2).

Listing 20.2. The MakeCameras() method creates and initializes the SSV camera objects.

```
void MakeCameras()
{
    rightCamera = new GameObject().AddComponent<Camera>();
    rightCamera.name = "rightCamera";

    leftCamera = new GameObject().AddComponent<Camera>();
    leftCamera.name = "leftCamera";

    interlacedCam = this.gameObject.AddComponent<Camera>();
    interlacedCam.name = "interlacedCam";

}
```

Now that we have our two "eyes" (*rightCamera* & *leftCamera*) and our *interlaceCam* we need to put everything in place (Listing 20.3).

Listing 20.3. Link and position all the viewer cameras.

```
void SetCameraProperty()
{
    // position the right eye camera
    rightCamera.transform.parent = this.transform;
    rightCamera.transform.localPosition = new Vector3(displacement, 0, 0);
    rightCamera.transform.localRotation = Quaternion.Euler(0, 0, 0);

    // repeat for the left
    leftCamera.transform.parent = this.transform;
    leftCamera.transform.localPosition = new Vector3(-displacement, 0, 0);
    leftCamera.transform.localRotation = Quaternion.Euler(0, 0, 0);

    // make sure they will render to the display, not the user in the headset
    rightCamera.depth = 1;
    rightCamera.stereoTargetEye = StereoTargetEyeMask.None;

    leftCamera.depth = 1;
    leftCamera.stereoTargetEye = StereoTargetEyeMask.None;

    // now the camera we will use for interlacing
    this.transform.localPosition = new Vector3(0, 0, 0);
    interlacedCam.stereoTargetEye = StereoTargetEyeMask.None;
    interlacedCam.depth = 1;
}
```

We should change our Start function to call the two functions we just made. It should now look as in Listing 20.4.

Listing 20.4. Initialize the cameras upon scene initialization.

```
void Start() {
    MakeCameras();
    SetCameraProperty();
}
```

Now that we have all of our necessary cameras we can create the three textures used to create the interlace effect. We will first need a texture to use as a mask, which will mask out every other row of a given image (Listing 20.5).

Listing 20.5. A function to procedurally generate a texture for masking every other line.

```
void MakeInterlaceTexture()
{
    interlaceMask = new Texture2D(Screen.width, Screen.height, TextureFormat.RGB24, false);

    for (int y = 0; y < Screen.height; y++) {
        if (y % 2 > 0) {
            for (int x = 0; x < Screen.width; x++) {
                interlaceMask.SetPixel(x, y, Color.green);
            }
        } else {
            for (int x = 0; x < Screen.width; x++) {
                interlaceMask.SetPixel(x, y, Color.red);
            }
        }
    }
    interlaceMask.Apply();
}
```

Next we need to direct the eye-cameras to send their rendered image to a render texture, rather than rendering to the display. This will provide the two textures on which the mask will be applied in order to create the interlaced image (Listing 20.6).

Listing 20.6. Set left & right eye camera views to render as textures such that they can be further processed into a single interlaced stereoscopic view.

```
void CreateRenderTextures()
{
    mat = new Material(Shader.Find("Custom/Interlace"));

    // assign interlaceMask
    mat.mainTexture = interlaceMask;

    // make our other textures to grab from the cameras
    RenderTexture leftCamTex = new RenderTexture(Screen.width, Screen.height, 24);
```

```
RenderTexture rightCamTex = new RenderTexture(Screen.width, Screen.height, 24);

// plug in right/left camera rendertexture to the right slot
leftCamera.targetTexture = leftCamTex;
rightCamera.targetTexture = rightCamTex;


// assign all these textures to our material
mat.mainTexture = interlaceMask;
mat.SetTexture("_Texture1", leftCamTex);
mat.SetTexture("_Texture2", rightCamTex);
}
```

Let's add these new functions to our *Start()* method as well (Listing 20.7).

Listing 20.7. Add the masking texture and render-texture placeholder creation to `Start()`.

```
void Start()
{
    ...
    MakeInterlaceTexture();
    CreateRenderTextures();
}
```

The "Interlace" custom shader referenced in Listing 20.6 must also be written. Create a new shader in the resources folder of your project hierarchy. If you do not have a resources folder yet, create one and place your new shader there. Listing 20.8 shows the code for the new shader.

20.3 The Interlace Shader

Listing 20.8. The CG GPU shader that will interleave two camera views into a single interleaved view suitable for passive stereoscopic monitors.

```
Shader "Custom/Interlace" {

    Properties
    {
        _MainTex ("Interlace Texture", 2D) = "" {}
        _Texture1 ("Left Eye", 2D) = "" {}
        _Texture2 ("Right Eye", 2D) = "" {}
        _Texture3 ("Interlaced Mask", 2D) = "" {}

    }

    SubShader
    {

        Pass{
            CGPROGRAM
```

```
#pragma vertex MyVertexProgram
#pragma fragment MyFragmentProgram

#include "UnityCG.cginc"

sampler2D _Texture3;
float4 _Texture3_ST;
int _Flip = 1;

sampler2D _Texture1, _Texture2;

struct VertexData
{
        float4 position : POSITION;
        float2 uv : TEXCOORD0;
};

struct Interpolators
{
        float4 position : SV_POSITION;
        float2 uv : TEXCOORD0;
        float2 uvSplat : TEXCOORD1;
};

Interpolators MyVertexProgram (VertexData v)
{
        Interpolators i;
        i.position = UnityObjectToClipPos(v.position);
        i.uv = TRANSFORM_TEX(v.uv, _Texture3);
        i.uvSplat = v.uv;
        return i;
}

float4 MyFragmentProgram (Interpolators i) : SV_TARGET
{
        float4 splat = tex2D(_Texture3, i.uvSplat);
        if ( _Flip < 1) {
                return
                        tex2D(_Texture1, i.uv) * splat.g +
                        tex2D(_Texture2, i.uv) * splat.r;
        }
        return
                tex2D(_Texture1, i.uv) * splat.r +
                tex2D(_Texture2, i.uv) * splat.g;
}

ENDCG
        }
    }
}
```

In a nutshell, this shader works by using a mask to pull out every other row of a texture map. One texture has the odd rows masked out, the other has the even rows masked out. By combining the results, we end up with a complete image, each row alternating as a piece of the image from the left and right "eyes." If you want to learn more, then you can look up splat map shaders, from which this shader is based.

20.4 The Final Pieces of the StereoSpectatorView Script

Add the code in Listing 20.9 to your *StereoSpectatorView* script.

Listing 20.9. Add the special OnRenderImage() method that finally "paints" the image on the display.

```
private void OnRenderImage(RenderTexture source, RenderTexture destination) {
    // use null for source to blit directly to main display
    Graphics.Blit(null as RenderTexture, mat);
}
```

And finally, add the code in Listing 20.10 to your update function. This code will allow the Stereo Spectator View to follow the *CamRigParent* object when it moves around. Note, we implement this with Unity's *Slerp()* function to enable the spectator to follow behind the VR camera while attenuating the jarring head-tracked view. The *slerpValue* can be reduced to near zero to provide smoother motion or set to 1 to produce the exact same view as the VR camera's view—though generally not recommended for the sake of the audience's comfort.

Listing 20.10. Set the SSV camera to generally follow the HMD camera.

```
void Update() {
    this.transform.position = Vector3.Slerp(this.transform.position,
        CamRigParent.transform.position, slerpValue);

    this.transform.rotation = Quaternion.Slerp(this.transform.rotation,
        CamRigParent.transform.rotation, slerpValue);

}
```

You will need to assign the *CamRigParent* in the inspector. This will be whatever *GameObject* you want the Stereo Spectator View to follow. Usually you will want to use the camera that the VR user sees through. For SteamVR this is labelled as the Camera (eye). You can also us other GameObjects in order to allow for third person views, or views other than that of the VR user. Now put an object in your scene, in front of the item you have set as the *CamRigParent*, and hit play to test it.

The game window should now show an interlaced image suitable for use on passive stereo displays (Figure 20.2). If you have a passive stereo display, test your project there. You should see that when wearing the properly filtered glasses each eye sees a slightly different perspective of the scene. However, it likely is not perfect and will need some calibration, which can be done by adjusting the displacement between the left and right cameras.

There are a few additional utility items that should be added to this script. These additional functions include a way to perform runtime calibration of the effect and a method for saving the calibration. Both of these features are already implemented in the StereoSpectatorView script that is included in the "3D View for Spectators" sample scenes with this book. Feel free to use them as provided, or implement your own methods for runtime calibration and saving and loading settings.

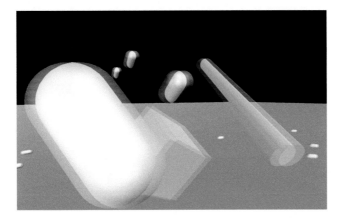

Figure 20.2

An interlaced stereoscopic rendering of a simple scene. The "ghosting" that appears in the image is really just how the results appear when not viewed through proper filtering glasses on an interlaced stereoscopic display.

SECTION VI
Virtual Worlds

21

The Utility of Virtual Reality for Science and Engineering

Kenny Gruchalla
National Renewable Energy Laboratory
University of Colorado at Boulder

Nicholas Brunhart-Lupo
National Renewable Energy Laboratory

In our daily usage of the large-scale immersive virtual environment at the National Renewable Energy Laboratory (NREL), we have observed how this VR system can be a useful tool to enhance scientific and engineering workflows. On multiple occasions, we have observed scientists and engineers discover features in their data using immersive environments that they had not seen in prior investigations of their data on traditional desktop displays. We have embedded more information into our analytics tools, allowing engineers to explore complex multivariate spaces. We have observed natural interactions with 3D objects and how those interactions seem to catalyze understanding. And we have seen improved collaboration with groups of stakeholders. In this chapter, we discuss these practical advantages of immersive visualization in the context of several real-world examples.

21.1 Introduction

Scientific visualization is the transformation of complex scientific data into visual images through computer graphics and data processing algorithms. The fundamental premise of scientific visualization is that the human mind excels at pattern matching and visual interpretation; we are readily able to identify patterns and anomalies in visual data, and we can contextualize those patterns with all our domain knowledge. A visual representation of data can engage more human cognitive machinery than looking at a list of numbers, and by doing so, we can gain a deeper understanding of the data in a shorter amount of time.

As an example, consider Anscombe's quartet (Table 21.1), which consists of four datasets synthesized by British statistician Francis Anscombe [1973]. Each set is very simple, consisting of 11 two-dimensional points. If we apply standard statistical metrics on these sets, the results are almost identical. The mean of x and y for each of the four datasets is 9.00 and 7.50 respectively, the correlation between x and y are also the same with 0.816, and the linear regression line for the datasets is the same. A researcher using these metrics might then be led to assume that the datasets were similar. However, when we plot these four datasets (Figure 21.1), at a glance, we can immediately see that each is very different. There is a general linear relationship in the first set, a clear non-linear relationship in the second, a strong linear relationship with an outlier in the third, and the fourth has very different distribution being heavily skewed by an outlier. By plotting these data, we can instantly see the differences in their character and distributions. Of course, there are other statistical methods that can tease out these differences in a more quantitative manner, but these require a level of sophistication far exceeding the simple action of plotting these data. Anscombe's point is that without a visual understanding of your data, you may not know which statistical techniques to apply.

While Anscombe's quartet demonstrates the value of visualizing our data, to truly make the most of our very sophisticated pattern matching and visual interpretation capabilities, we should consider that these visual and cognitive abilities have evolved from our sense of place and embodiment. We understand our world by moving through it, interacting

Table 21.1 Anscombe's Quartet: Data

1		2		3		4	
x	y	x	y	x	y	x	y
10.0	8.04	10.0	9.14	10.0	7.46	8.0	6.58
8.0	6.95	8.0	8.14	8.0	6.77	8.0	5.76
13.0	7.58	13.0	8.74	13.0	12.74	8.0	7.71
9.0	8.81	9.0	8.77	9.0	7.11	8.0	8.84
11.0	8.33	11.0	9.26	11.0	7.81	8.0	8.47
14.0	9.96	14.0	8.10	14.0	8.84	8.0	7.04
6.0	7.24	6.0	6.13	6.0	6.08	8.0	5.25
4.0	4.26	4.0	3.10	4.0	5.39	19.0	12.50
12.0	10.84	12.0	9.13	12.0	8.15	8.0	5.56
7.0	4.82	7.0	7.26	7.0	6.42	8.0	7.91
5.0	5.68	5.0	4.74	5.0	5.73	8.0	6.89

Mean $\bar{x} = 9$	$\bar{y} \approx 7.5$
Variance $\sigma_x^2 = 11$	$\sigma_y^2 \approx 4.12$
Correlation (x,y)	0.816
Regression	$y = 3.00 + 0.500x$

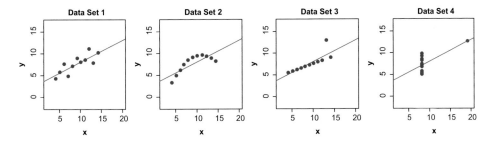

Figure 21.1

Anscombe's Quartet. The four datasets have nearly identical simple descriptive statistics (see Table 21.1), but are visually distinctive when plotted. The quartet provides a simple demonstration of the importance of visualizing data before analyzing it.

with it, and examining it from different perspectives. When we want to go somewhere, we walk. When we want something, we reach out and grab it. When we wish to see under something, we crouch.

VR promises to bring that embodiment to the visualization and understanding of data. Here, a combination of hardware and software provides a psychophysical experience of being surrounded by a computer-generated scene, physically immersing users in a virtual world wherein they can explore complex spatial structures by looking around them, walking through them, and viewing them from different points of view. The medium of VR is built on rapidly evolving technology, moving in the past few years from large laboratory installations to commodity head-mounted displays (HMDs) and now mobile platforms. VR systems provide a head-tracked, typically stereoscopic, view into a virtual scene. Different VR systems provide different *levels of immersion*. Bowman and McMahan [2007] define the *level of immersion* as an objective and measurable feature of a visualization system, measuring how close the system's visual output is to real-world visual stimuli. A system's level of immersion is dependent on a variety of factors including:

- head-tracking—the scene is rendered based on the physical location and orientation of the user's head
- stereoscopy—providing a depth cue by providing each eye a different perspective
- field of view (FOV)—the size of the visual field that can be viewed instantaneously
- field of regard (FOR)—the total size of the visual field surrounding the user
- resolution—the number of distinct pixels in each dimension
- frame rate—the frequency of generating images of the scene
- refresh rate—the frequency of the display hardware's redraw
- kinesthesia support—the awareness of the position and movement of one's own body.

CAVE-like [Cruz-Neira et al., 1993] environments are currently the state of the art and provide the highest level of immersion with head-tracked, stereoscopic images projected onto multiple surfaces in a room-sized installation that users can physically walk into (see Figure 21.2). Commodity VR HMDs (e.g., the HTC Vive) currently provide a lower

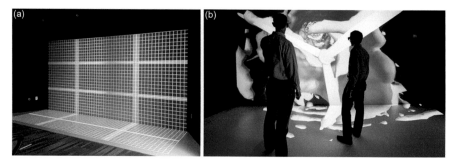

Figure 21.2

The immersive virtual environment at NREL Insight Center. (a) The system is an optically tracked space with a rear-projected wall and a front-projected floor. (b) Wind engineers standing inside the environment are evaluating the wake forming behind a wind turbine.

level of immersion with stereo and head-tracking, but relatively low FOVs and resolutions, and with no view of one's body, kinesthesia is limited to proprioception. Augmented reality (AR) HMDs (e.g., the HoloLens), which augment the user's view of physical space by layering in a rendered scene, fully support kinesthesia but currently suffer from low resolutions, and FOVs. The gaming industry revolutionized the field of visualization when they commoditized graphics processing units (GPUs). A similar transformation is approaching for immersive visualization with the commoditization of AR and VR headsets. The current state of the HMD technology is still inferior to state-of-the-art CAVE-style immersive environments. However, the level of immersion of the next generations of these HMD technologies could surpass these expensive high-end installations.

High-levels of immersion appear to provide cognitive benefits to the visualization of complex data by supporting natural body movements and well-practiced automatic brain function that facilitates reasoning in the virtual world. Additionally, the extra degrees of freedom afforded by VR can provide additional visibility into the relationships of complex multivariate data common to scientific and engineering analysis.

In this chapter, we explore some of the potential benefits of using immersive visualization for science and engineering supported by several real-world examples.

21.2 Background

We are not alone in believing that immersive visualization has benefits in the visual analysis of complex data. Scientific visualization has been a focal point for VR for many years [Bryson, 1996; van Dam et al., 2000, 2002; Kuhlen and Hentschel, 2014]. And there is growing evidence that higher levels of stereoscopy, head tracking, FOV, and FOR working together can be beneficial. For example, empirical studies show improved perception and understanding of spatially complex data [Ware and Franck, 1996; Richardson et al., 1999; Schuchardt and Bowman, 2007; Ragan et al., 2013; Laha et al., 2014] inside immersive environments. Likewise, studies with complex 3D interaction tasks have shown improved task performance [Narayan et al., 2005; McMahan et al., 2006] in immersive environments. The extra degrees of freedom afforded by VR have been shown to improve understanding of high-dimensional data representations [Arns et al., 1999; Raja et al., 2004; Ni et al., 2006] when searching for or comparing complex abstract data. Furthermore, installations that support multiple users have been shown to improve collaboration [Narayan et al., 2005; D'Angelo et al., 2008; Marai et al., 2016]. These studies, and others like them, substantiate the benefits of immersive interfaces. However, these studies are limited to isolated tasks and how they might relate to scientific and engineering workflows is not always obvious.

The benefits of immersion in real-world settings is less examined in the literature, as conducting empirical experiments in these settings is difficult with many confounding variables. However, there are a few controlled studies on *real-world applications* that also show similar benefits from VR. The oil and gas industry was one of the earliest adopters, and a controlled study [Gruchalla, 2004] found significant benefits for immersion when comparing oil-well path planning activities in a CAVE-style immersive environment compared to a stereoscopic desktop environment. Immersion was shown to have significant benefits for biological data analysis in laser confocal microscopy data that emphasized understanding of spatial relationships [Prabhat et al., 2008].

While there are few controlled studies on real-world applications, there is a breadth of anecdotal evidence of real discoveries made with the aid of immersive technologies. For example, there have been discoveries made in biology [Brady et al., 1995], molecular biology [Gruchalla et al., 2008], geoscience [Kreylos et al., 2006], remote sensing [Gardner et al., 2003], forestry [Bohrer et al., 2008], and archaeology [Acevedo et al., 2001]. While the benefits of immersive virtual reality may be difficult to verify scientifically for science and engineering applications, the anecdotal discoveries made while using immersive virtual reality are suggestive of the utility.

21.3 NREL VR Use Cases

The National Renewable Energy Laboratory (NREL) is the U.S. Department of Energy's (DOE's) primary national laboratory for renewable energy and energy efficiency research. The NREL Insight Center combines state-of-the-art visualization and collaboration tools to promote knowledge discovery in experimental data, high-resolution microscopy, and large-scale simulation data. One of the primary tools used in the NREL Insight Center is a large-scale (CAVE-like) immersive virtual environment. In our day-to-day usage of this environment for scientific and engineering workflows, we have observed multiple discoveries and witnessed the practical benefits of immersive technology, which we describe here.

21.3.1 System

The immersive virtual environment at the Insight Center is a custom design, composed of six active stereoscopic projectors that illuminate two surfaces: a wall and a floor (Figure 21.2). The projected space is 5 m wide, 2.5 m high, and 1.75 m deep with 3,540 × 1,728 pixels on the wall, and 3,540 × 1,080 pixels on the floor. A six-camera Vicon™ system optically tracks the whole volume. The system is driven by a single Linux server with dual 8-core Sandy Bridge processors, half a terabyte of RAM, and three NVIDIA Quadro M6000 GPUs. The primary input device is a commodity *Logitech*™ joystick augmented with optical markers to track its 3D position. In addition, we employ a variety of custom built input devices specialized to particular workflows. We handle all tracking and input control through VRPN [Taylor et al., 2001].

We support a variety of software applications in the space. Immersive ParaView [Shetty et al., 2011], FreeVR-enabled VMD [Sherman et al., 2013], and the commercial application Avizo provide scientists and engineers a pathway to move visualizations directly from their desktops to our immersive environment. We also support Unity-based applications, which provide a relatively easy programming model for scientists and engineers who wish to develop their own applications for the system. However, these tools are generally only used for preliminary investigations. The vast majority of the applications run in the system (and the applications detailed in this chapter) were custom built on our immersive software framework, *Isopach*, written in C++, and powered by Qt and OpenGL. *Isopach* is a high-performance scene-graph library and full stack application toolkit optimized for our multi-projector, multi-screen environment, and includes image handling, an object-component scene model, geometry operations, threading, and other utilities. By employing the most recent graphics API features (shaders) tuned to our hardware, we have a performance advantage over more general immersive software frameworks. It is also designed to facilitate coupling with other software, such as simulation codes written in C, R-based statistics scripts, and web data sources. The library provides a lower-level API compared to other frameworks, requiring more expertise to build a given visualization application, but allows the developer to uniquely tailor the user interface and experience for each investigation.

21.3.2 Improved Spatial Judgments

From our observations, one of the primary benefits of our immersive system is the improved ability for our users to make spatial judgments. Being able to physically move inside spatially complex datasets has allowed our scientists to identify structures—and the spaces between structures—that were not noticed or were impossible to notice using traditional desktop visualization.

One such discovery came when visualizing the morphology of organic photovoltaic (OPV) materials. These materials consist of interpenetrating networks of a polymer and fullerene materials, as can be seen in Figure 21.3. The polymer absorbs light, and the resulting excitation migrates, injecting a negative charge into the fullerene and leaving a positive charge behind in the polymer. These charges travel through the two material networks, ideally reaching electrodes to produce current. By examining the pathways for different morphologies, we can develop intuition about how modifying the materials will affect OPV device properties. Figure 21.3 is a typical representation of traditional analysis on these materials. While 2D renderings can be useful, the inner structure is largely occluded. Even when transparency is added, or matter is culled, the complex material network makes it difficult for the researcher to follow strands of material.

We built a visualization tool for our immersive system and invited the scientist leading these investigations to explore the 3D immersive version of these 2D renderings. When he stepped inside one of the morphologies, he uttered the three most exciting words in science, "Huh? That's funny." The visualization allowed him to physically explore the morphology. He could stand in the middle of his dataset, move to interesting places by walking and look behind the occlusions just by moving his head. In VR, depth is *depth*, and he could follow pathways with his finger from point to point. What he discovered was the heterogeneity of these morphologies that he could not easily appreciate in the

Figure 21.3

A simulated representation of a bulk heterojunction used in the active layer of organic photovoltaic devices (OPV), consisting of interpenetrating networks of polymer and fullerene material. Here a skeletonization of the polymer is shown in blue and a skeletonization of the fullerene in red. Understanding this structure and how electrons might transport through it, is a challenging problem. Using VR, scientists discovered structures in these materials that they had not seen using desktop displays.

desktop visualizations, features that the 2D perspective obscured. This new appreciation of his data was immediate and fostered changes to the statistical measures that were being applied to these materials. This observation was a real-world encounter of Anscombe's thesis; a qualitative understanding of the data helped the scientist develop his quantitative measurements.

We have seen similar discoveries in the visualization of molecular dynamics (MD) simulations of solar materials. MD simulations were being used to investigate how different polymer chains would stack inside the active layer of an OPV device. Based on x-ray diffraction imaging and traditional visualization of the MD results, researchers believed the stacking properties of two polymers to be qualitatively similar. However, when they examined these polymers using our immersive system (see Figure 21.4), they determined that only one exhibited a structure known as π-stacking while the other did not.

We have also seen users make spatial discoveries that were clearly relative to their bodies. We supported a project team that virtually constructed a large concentrating solar collector, a structure tens of meters in length, with curved mirrors that focus the light, using the resulting heat to generate electricity. These collectors are constructed in the field, requiring scaffold and supporting jig. The team wished to understand if there were flaws in the jig design which would complicate this assembly or challenge construction of the collector with the jig. The virtual assembly supplemented their traditional design and analysis using 3D CAD modeling tools and small-scale physical 3D models.

Figure 21.4

Investigating polymer stacking in the active layers of OPV devices. Using VR, scientist were able to qualitatively distinguish stacking characteristics between materials that were not obvious with more traditional visualization techniques.

We presented the collector, its assembly jig, and assembly platforms to the project team at a 1:1 scale inside the immersive environment. We provided props to the user, consisting of a foam tube and a foam beam with trackers; the visualization tool attaches geometry to these tracked objects, so the users could move collector struts in the virtual space (see Figure 21.5). The application highlighted the collision of parts with the base structure as the user moved those parts into position.

In a single working session, the project team discovered nearly a dozen issues with the jig design. They were able to identify numerous places where connecting components would require dangerous extensions to reach, where beams and struts would likely collide with the scaffolding, and positions where construction workers would likely have difficulty manipulating a rivet gun.

At this point, the design team had already gone through more traditional steps of design and analysis. They had thoroughly modeled the structure to the threads on the bolts, they had 3D printed models on their desks, but only by bringing the model to human scale, and allowing them to explore the collector as they would a real prototype, were they able to uncover these issues.

This example demonstrates a unique capability provided by immersive visualization that cannot be duplicated, or emulated, in traditional visualization. Users were able to ask and answer simple questions like "can I reach this?" Allowing users to test their creations without incurring significant fabrication costs and time investments is a powerful addition to the engineer's toolkit.

21.3.3 3D Interaction

The virtual assembly of the concentrating solar collector also demonstrates the utility of being able to manipulate 3D objects directly in 3D space. The engineers were able to

Figure 21.5

An engineer places a strut during the virtual assembly of a concentrating solar collector. The red strut in the figure is mapped to the prop held by the engineer. Using VR, engineers were able to identify design issues that they had not identified with their CAD/CAM tools and physical scale models.

precisely move and place components of the structure to better understand the workflow and the complexities of assembling the collector.

We have also seen the utility of 3D interaction for analyzing computational fluid dynamics (CFD) data of simulated flow inside the cabins of electric vehicles. The efficiency of heating and cooling electric vehicles is an area of research at NREL, as these loads can have a significant impact on the driving range of an electric vehicle [Kiss et al., 2015]. The airflow inside vehicle cabins can be quite complex (see Figure 21.6), and developing a visualization that provides a clear view of that flow is a challenging problem.

VR provides a medium to interactively investigate the flow by directly seeding particles into that flow. We transfer the velocity vector fields from CFD simulations into the working volume of our immersive environment, and we render a partial mesh of the vehicle's body as context. The user can release massless particles into this flow with a touch of a button on the tracked joystick, injecting up to 20,000 particles into the velocity vector field by 'painting' with the controller (see Figure 21.7). These particles are then advected by the flow and change color to reflect the temperature at their current location in the volume. The particles diminish in size over a fixed amount of time, so as to not clutter the visualization. Further, we stretch the particles along the velocity vector; this helps the eye catch fast moving particles. The particles are rendered using instance rendering, a feature found in most modern graphics APIs, which renders all 20,000 particles in a single draw call, keeping the visualization interactive.

Before being introduced to the immersive virtual environment, the vehicle engineers would evaluate the flows through 2D cross-sections. This VR application provides the

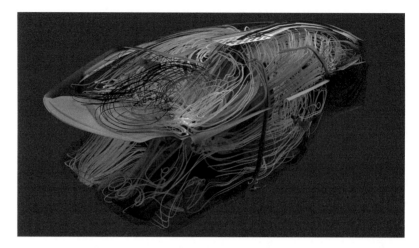

Figure 21.6

Streamline rendering of an electric vehicle simulation, displaying airflow inside the cabin. Note the mannequin's feet at the lower left of the image. Color represents relative temperature. The airflow inside the cabin is complex and difficult to understand.

Figure 21.7

Inside the same vehicle as Figure 21.6, a user interactively explores the airflow inside an electric vehicle cabin, by directly seeding particles into the flow. Using this VR system, engineers were able to identify flow characteristics they had not discovered using desktop visualization tools.

engineers a method to explore the air flows in a manner that is simply not possible in a 2D context. They can easily pick points to seed particles and move their bodies to follow the flow of particles. Engineers were able to probe areas of interest directly and quickly isolate the features in this complex flow. The engineers reported discovering vortices and regions of high flow in the immersive context that they had not found in their previous non-immersive visualizations of the data.

21.3.4 High-Dimensional Data

As an immersive environment provides extra degrees-of-freedom, we have seen benefits toward the exploration of high-dimensional and highly multivariate datasets. In the very simplest case, consider the two-dimensional scatter plot, which is the mainstay of data analysis; in VR the direct analog is a three-dimensional scatter plot. We have mapped additional dimensions to point size and color, providing five-dimensional data directly in the immersive environment. Users can probe individual points and use interactive planes for additive half-space selection to isolate regions of interest (see Figure 21.8).

Going further, many data visualization techniques for even higher-dimensional data have analogs in a 3D environment. For example, we have generalized the two-dimensional parallel-coordinates visualization technique as parallel-planes in VR. In traditional parallel coordinates, data dimensions are mapped onto coordinate axes as a series of parallel lines [Inselberg, 1985]. We map pairs of the multivariate dimensions onto a series of parallel 2D scatter plots and connect individual observations in the dataset with a polyline, as shown in Figure 21.9. This construct allows users to explore datasets with 12 or more variable dimensions in a convenient fashion. Regions of the rectangles can be "brushed" to highlight and select observations of interest. This brushing and selection action is used to explore existing data, but is also used to visually provide input parameter spaces to launch simulations or processes that provide additional data; it is in this manner that users can easily "paint" questions and have an attached model provide answers in near-real-time. We have observed that these immersive analytics tools can accelerate users' realization of insights about the simulation and its output [Brunhart-Lupo et al., 2016].

VR's extra degrees-of-freedom have also allowed us to re-imagine and bring new context to other highly multivariate datasets. For example, electric power distribution systems represent a significant visualization and analysis challenge, as they have a large number of temporally and spatially varying quantities (i.e., voltage, real power, and reactive power across three phases, solar irradiance, varieties of control equipment with different operational parameters and scenarios, and dynamically changing load). Even highly trained

Figure 21.8

A user interactively exploring and selecting clusters in a five-dimensional dataset on a three-dimensional scatter plot. Half-spaces, created by the planes, define the user's selection.

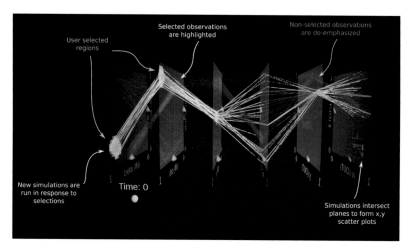

VR can support higher-dimensional visualization constructs, such as parallel planes that link observations on parallel 2D scatter plots in a high-dimensional parameter space.

engineers have difficulty fully comprehending these interactions, especially between variables using traditional two-dimensional geographic representations.

To help address this challenge, we developed an immersive three-dimensional visualization technique for distribution networks by elevating the power lines as a function of their voltage and sizing them as a function of their power flow (see Figure 21.10). There

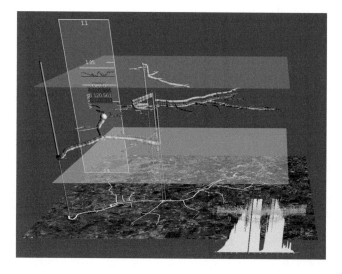

Figure 21.10

Three-dimensional visualization of a power distribution system, representing the highly multivariate space of a power flow simulation. Power system engineers used VR to augment their traditional analysis workflows.

are three phases of power in A/C distribution systems. Each line is "hung" in the vertical dimension by its per-unit voltage and shaped by the real and reactive power present on the line. By adding a degree of freedom, we have taken what is typically a four-dimensional visualization (i.e., network topology and two line variables mapped to width and color) and extended it to an eleven-dimensional space: three phases of voltage, three phases of real power, and three phases of reactive power embedded with the 2D network topology.

In addition to line information, we represent the state of other elements on the system. Voltage regulators are visualized as vertical cylinders, spanning their input and output voltages. Generation sources are spheres geographically positioned in the horizontal plane and positioned vertically by output voltage.

Users can manipulate floating 2D plots that provide details on demand; these are virtual billboards in the immersive space that the user can grab and re-position in three-space using the optically tracked joystick. A companion time-series view provides an overview of the study feeder's line loads and generation during a single day. This view provides the primary temporal interface for the three-dimensional views, allowing the user to set the current time or animate through time. Users can probe details of individual components by intersecting a component with the joystick and creating a three-dimensional tooltip with a button press. The tooltip provides both metadata (i.e., characteristics about the data itself) and time-series plots (e.g., time-varying variables applicable to the component).

This VR application has been used by power system engineers to evaluate complex control strategies on a distribution feeder [Palmintier et al., 2016] and provided novel visibility into the multivariate relationships in these data. The immersive visualization was used to support the traditional analysis of these power flow simulations, augmenting the power systems research engineers' typical workflow. Engineers would schedule time in our immersive environment to troubleshoot the simulation, posing questions about complex multivariate relationships that were not readily accessible using traditional two-dimensional displays and plots. Specifically, the immersive application was utilized to troubleshoot voltage imbalance between phases, as the immersive visualization provided topological context for the voltage profiles in all three phases. The engineers were readily able to identify gradual phase separations along the topology. The engineers also utilized the multivariate spatial information of the VR application to understand the location and cause of "over-voltages" on the system.

21.3.5 Collaboration

One of the benefits of our large-scale system that we repeatedly observe is how the space seems to facilitate collaborative reasoning about data. The large scale allows multiple researchers to gather inside the environment simultaneously, which many teams have indicated they find more collaborative than crowding around a small computer screen or sitting around a conference table.

One example is financial and investment modeling. A number of researchers at NREL are exploring how market forces can impact investments in renewable energy. These problems are highly interdisciplinary, bringing financial analysts, market specialists, and industry experts together with modeling and simulation groups. Through multiple meetings, attended by these professionals and held in our immersive environment and supported by the on-demand simulation request framework discussed in the previous section (and displayed in the parallel-planes projection), we have observed a highly proficient, frictionless environment. A cluster would form around an individual chosen as the ad-hoc primary visualization user; the group would ask questions of the model, and new results displayed for discussion. Frequently, groups would spin off to talk in depth about a certain notable data point before rejoining the main cluster for more questions-and-answers, replacing what would have been month-long conversations over email, and long-latency requests for new data. Though initially skeptical, the users reported enjoyment of the environment and noted the amount of research they could accomplish in a short amount of time.

In another example, we have been using the system for collaborative design and planning studies of the NREL campus (see Figure 21.11), where multiple stakeholders can gather and evaluate planning scenarios combining technical, economic, and policy perspectives. As before, we have facilitated these types of design and planning meetings by loosely coupling multiple simulation tools with our immersive, VR environment. For the NREL campus planning studies, this means an economic optimization model combined with an electrical power flow model of the campus to allow users to interactively manipulate the on-site power generation and electrical loads. Though in its early stages, we have already been able to discover opportunities for energy systems integration on our campus by bringing our site planners and leadership together in this environment, and have received requests to create similar models of other sites.

Our experiences in these kinds of studies are preliminary, but we are discovering that analysis can proceed at a rapid pace not only when immersive spaces allow collaboration between multiple users, but also when the visualization provides a substrate, either through simulation, machine learning, or statistical analysis, to let these users ask questions about their data, or request new simulations on the fly to test hypotheses. This machine-powered question and response format appears to be key in our future visualizations.

Figure 21.11

NREL campus planning study that allows groups of stakeholders to interactively evaluate the techno-economic impacts of design decisions.

21. The Utility of Virtual Reality for Science and Engineering

21.4 Conclusion

In our daily usage of the large-scale immersive virtual environment at NREL, we have observed multiple practical benefits of immersive technology. We have witnessed discoveries made in VR that had gone overlooked using traditional data analysis methods. We have seen how researchers can expedite analysis through intuitive 3D interaction with their data. We have been able to embed more information into our analytics tools, allowing engineers to agilely explore complex multivariate spaces. We have seen groups of stakeholders bring their perspectives together on planning decisions.

VR cannot and should not replace the entire visualization and analysis stack, but immersive visualization has its place as a valued tool in NREL's analysis stockpile and has augmented how some researchers do their science. For some NREL researchers, an immersive examination is now the first step in the data analysis workflow: a physical walk-through of the data, to get a qualitative understanding of the features, before developing the statistical or quantitative measures of those data. For others, it becomes part of an iterative debugging process to refine simulation models. Still, others use it to communicate and collaborate with a variety of audiences.

A transformation is approaching for immersive visualization. AR and VR are being commoditized by the entertainment industry with relatively low-cost HMDs, just as GPUs were commoditized more than a decade ago. While the level of immersion of these commodity systems cannot currently compete with the large-scale state-of-the-art immersive environments, like the one installed at NREL, their capabilities are rapidly advancing and will soon surpass these expensive high-end installations. As their capabilities improve, AR and VR will revolutionize analysis for many classes of complex scientific and engineering data.

Acknowledgments

This work was supported by the U.S. Department of Energy under Contract No. DE-AC36–08GO28308 with Alliance for Sustainable Energy, LLC, the Manager and Operator of the National Renewable Energy Laboratory. Funding provided by U.S. Department of Energy Office of Energy Efficiency and Renewable Energy. NREL is a national laboratory of the U.S. Department of Energy, Office of Energy Efficiency and Renewable Energy, operated by the Alliance for Sustainable Energy, LLC.

References

[Acevedo et al., 2001]

Acevedo, Daniel, Eileen Vote, David H. Laidlaw, and Martha S. Joukowsky (2001). Archaeological data visualization in VR: Analysis of lamp finds at the Great Temple of Petra, a case study. In *Proceedings of the Conference on Visualization '01*, VIS '01, Washington, DC: IEEE Computer Society, pp. 493–496.

[Anscombe, 1973]

Anscombe, Francis J. (1973). Graphs in statistical analysis. *The American Statistician*, 27(1): 17–21.

[Arns et al., 1999]

Arns, Laura, Dianne Cook, and Carolina Cruz-Neira (1999). The benefits of statistical visualization in an immersive environment. In *Proceedings IEEE Virtual Reality (Cat. No. 99CB36316)*, Houston, TX, pp. 88–95.

[Bohrer et al., 2008]

Bohrer, Gil, Marcos Longo, David J. Zielinski, and Rachael Brady (2008). VR visualisation as an interdisciplinary collaborative data exploration tool for large eddy simulations of biosphere-atmosphere interactions. In *International Symposium on Visual Computing (ISVC 2008)*, Las Vegas, NV. Berlin: Springer, pp. 856–866.

[Bowman and McMahan, 2007]

Bowman, Doug A., and Ryan P. McMahan (2007). Virtual reality: How much immersion is enough? *Computer*, 40(7): 36–43.

[Brady et al., 1995]

Brady, Rachael, John Pixton, George Baxter, Patrick Moran, Clinton S. Potter, Bridget Carragher, and Andrew Belmont (1995). Crumbs: a virtual environment tracking tool for biological imaging. In *Proceedings 1995 Biomedical Visualization*, Atlanta, GA, pp. 18–25, 82.

[Brunhart-Lupo et al., 2016]

Brunhart-Lupo, Nicholas, Brian W. Bush, Kenny Gruchalla, and Steve Smith (2016). Simulation exploration through immersive parallel planes. In *2016 Workshop on Immersive Analytics (IA)*, Greenville, SC, pp. 19–24.

[Bryson, 1996]

Bryson, Steve (1996). Virtual reality in scientific visualization. *Communications of the ACM*, 39(5): 62–71.

[Cruz-Neira et al., 1993]

Cruz-Neira, Carolina, Daniel J. Sandin, and Thomas A. DeFanti (1993). Surround-screen projection-based virtual reality: The design and implementation of the CAVE. In *Proceedings of the 20th Annual Conference on Computer Graphics and Interactive Techniques*, SIGGRAPH '93, New York: ACM, pp. 135–142.

[D'Angelo et al., 2008]

D'Angelo, David, Gerold Wesche, Maxim Foursa, and Manfred Bogen (2008). The benefits of co-located collaboration and immersion on assembly modeling in virtual environments. In *Proceedings of the 4th International Symposium on Advances in Visual Computing*, ISVC '08, Berlin: Springer, pp. 478–487.

[Gardner et al., 2003]

Gardner, Joseph V., Timothy Warner, M. Duane Nellis, and Tomas Brandtberg (2003). Virtual reality technology for lidar data analysis. In *Proc. SPIE*, vol. 5097, pp. 48–57.

[Gruchalla, 2004]

Gruchalla, Kenny (2004). Immersive well-path editing: Investigating the added value of immersion. In *Proceedings of the IEEE Virtual Reality 2004*, Washington, DC: IEEE Computer Society, pp. 157–164.

[Gruchalla et al., 2008]

Gruchalla, Kenny, Mark Dubin, Jonathan Marbach, and Elizabeth Bradley (2008). Immersive examination of the qualitative structure of biomolecules. In *International Workshop on Qualitative Reasoning about Physical Systems*, Boulder, CO, pp. 36–41.

[Inselberg, 1985]

Inselberg, Alfred (1985). The plane with parallel coordinates. *The Visual Computer*, 1(2): 69–91.

[Kiss et al., 2015]

Kiss, Tibor, Jason Lustbader, and Daniel Leighton (2015). Modeling of an electric vehicle thermal management system in matlab/simulink. In *SAE Technical Paper*. SAE International.

[Kreylos et al., 2006]

Kreylos, Oliver, Gerald Bawden, Tony Bernardin, Magali I. Billen, Eric S. Cowgill, Ryan D. Gold, Bernd Hamann, Margarete Jadamec, Louise H. Kellogg, Oliver G. Staadt, and Dawn Y. Sumner (2006). Enabling scientific workflows in virtual reality. In *Proceedings of the 2006 ACM International Conference on Virtual Reality Continuum and Its Applications*, VRCIA '06, New York: ACM, pp. 155–162.

[Kuhlen and Hentschel, 2014]

Kuhlen, Torsten Wolfgang, and Bernd Hentschel (2014). Quo vadis CAVE: Does immersive visualization still matter? *IEEE Computer Graphics and Applications*, 34(5): 14–21.

[Laha et al., 2014]

Laha, Bireswar, Doug A. Bowman, and John J. Socha (2014). Effects of VR system fidelity on analyzing isosurface visualization of volume datasets. *IEEE Transactions on Visualization and Computer Graphics*, 20(4): 513–522.

[Marai et al., 2016]

Marai, G. Elisabeta, Angus G. Forbes, and Andrew Johnson (2016). Interdisciplinary immersive analytics at the Electronic Visualization Laboratory: Lessons learned and upcoming challenges. In *2016 Workshop on Immersive Analytics (IA)*, Greenville, SC, pp. 54–59.

[McMahan et al., 2006]

McMahan, Ryan P., Doug Gorton, Joe Gresock, Will McConnell, and Doug A. Bowman (2006). Separating the effects of level of immersion and 3D interaction techniques. In *Proceedings of the ACM Symposium on Virtual Reality Software and Technology*, VRST'06, New York: ACM, pp. 108–111.

[Narayan et al., 2005]

Narayan, Michael, Leo Waugh, Xiaoyu Zhang, Pradyut Bafna, and Doug Bowman (2005). Quantifying the benefits of immersion for collaboration in virtual environments. In *Proceedings of the ACM Symposium on Virtual Reality Software and Technology*, VRST'05, New York: ACM, pp. 78–81.

[Ni et al., 2006]

Ni, Tao, Doug A. Bowman, and Jian Chen (2006). Increased display size and resolution improve task performance in information-rich virtual environments. In *Proceedings of Graphics Interface 2006*, GI'06, Toronto, ON: Canadian Information Processing Society, pp. 139–146.

[Palmintier et al., 2016]

Palmintier, Bryan, Julieta Giraldez, Kenny Gruchalla, Peter Gotseff, Adarsh Nagarajan, Tom Harris, Bruce Bugbee, Murali Baggu, Jesse Gantz, and Ethan Boardman (2016). Feeder voltage regulation with high-penetration PV using advanced inverters and a distribution management system: A Duke Energy case study. Technical Report NREL/TP-5D00–65551, National Renewable Energy Laboratory.

[Prabhat et al., 2008]

Prabhat, Andrew Forsberg, Michael Katzourin, Kristi Wharton, and Mel Slater (2008). A comparative study of desktop, fishtank, and CAVE systems for the exploration of volume rendered confocal data sets. *IEEE Transactions on Visualization and Computer Graphics*, 14(3): 551–563.

[Ragan et al., 2013]

Ragan, Eric D., Regis Kopper, Philip Schuchardt, and Doug A. Bowman (2013). Studying the effects of stereo, head tracking, and field of regard on a small-scale spatial judgment task. *IEEE Transactions on Visualization and Computer Graphics*, 19(5): 886–896.

[Raja et al., 2004]

Raja, Dheva, Doug A. Bowman, John Lucas, and Chris North (2004). Exploring the benefits of immersion in abstract information visualization. In *In Proceedings of 8th International Immersive Projection Technology Workshop*, pp. 61–69.

[Richardson et al., 1999]

Richardson, Anthony E., Daniel R. Montello, and Mary Hegarty (1999). Spatial knowledge acquisition from maps and from navigation in real and virtual environments. *Memory & Cognition*, 27(4): 741–750.

[Schuchardt and Bowman, 2007]

Schuchardt, Philip, and Doug A. Bowman (2007). The benefits of immersion for spatial understanding of complex underground cave systems. In *Proceedings of the 2007 ACM Symposium on Virtual Reality Software and Technology*, VRST '07, New York: ACM, pp. 121–124.

[Sherman et al., 2013]

Sherman, William R., Daniel Coming, and Simon Su (2013). FreeVR: Honoring the past, looking to the future. In *Proceedings of the SPIE*, vol. 8649, Burlingame, CA, pp. 864906-1–864906-15.

[Shetty et al., 2011]

Shetty, Nikhil, Aashish Chaudhary, Daniel Coming, William R. Sherman, Patrick O'Leary, Eric T. Whiting, and Simon Su (2011). Immersive ParaView: A community-based, immersive, universal scientific visualization application. In *Proceedings of the 2011 IEEE Virtual Reality Conference*, VR'11, Washington, DC: IEEE Computer Society, pp. 239–240.

[Taylor et al., 2001]

Taylor II, Russell M., Thomas C. Hudson, Adam Seeger, Hans Weber, Jeffrey Juliano, and Aron T. Helser (2001). VRPN: A device-independent, network-transparent VR peripheral system. In *Proceedings of the ACM Symposium on Virtual Reality Software and Technology*, VRST'01, New York: ACM, pp. 55–61.

[van Dam et al., 2000]

van Dam, Andries, Andrew S. Forsberg, David H. Laidlaw, Joseph J. LaViola, and Rosemary M. Simpson (2000). Immersive VR for scientific visualization: a progress report. *IEEE Computer Graphics and Applications*, 20(6): 26–52.

[van Dam et al., 2002]

van Dam, Andries, David H. Laidlaw, and Rosemary Michelle Simpson (2002). Experiments in immersive virtual reality for scientific visualization. *Computers & Graphics*, 26(4): 535–555.

[Ware and Franck, 1996]

Ware, Colin, and Glenn Franck (1996). Evaluating stereo and motion cues for visualizing information nets in three dimensions. *ACM Transactions on Graphics*, 15(2): 121–140.

22

Immersion and Visualizing Artistic Spaces in Virtual Reality

Margaret Dolinsky
Indiana University at Lafayette

This chapter explores how the experience of creating artwork for virtual reality systems relies on shifting sensory perceptions through "*emotables,*" or affective entities that establish aesthetics. Virtual reality (VR) art and design, framed in terms of a fine arts aesthetics encourages artists to build a visual rhetoric for VR that is distinct from that of video games or cinema. One such rhetorical approach emphasizes using art fundamentals such as line, shape, form, scale, and color to build visual metaphors I term "emotables." The results—construction of "emotables"—animates objects as symbolic building blocks to shape the environment and assist with the visitor's navigation through its visual environment. These emotables then are used to construct environments and establish "cyberity", the temperance for being that occurs while in cyberspace. Rather than see still images or videos that represent VR, a visitor has to be in the VR art in order to experience it and moreover, navigate it to understand it.

22.1 Introduction: The Rise of VR

The recent popular interest in virtual reality is the direct result of the wide availability of graphics hardware driven to serve the needs of the gaming community. Virtual reality, in some form or another, has been around much longer than graphical based games, and this chapter offers a point of view separate from the industry of competitive gaming and concentrates on shaping visual choices through art exploration and creative expression. Now that computer graphics technology is more accessible, VR has become a shifting quantity with a variety of displays available which influences the engagement with the environment.

The fine arts tradition emphasizes aesthetics as the approach towards VR experience pursuits (See Figure 22.1). Rather than a coded goal of "does it work?" the success here relies on the shape of a line—how lines are created as a source of flow through the environment, how shapes envelope, engulf and engage the visitor. It is critical that the emotables define a semblance of order to allow the visitor to find a unique path to uncover and experience choices. These choices are emphasized through the aesthetic moments to be experienced. I create plastic artworks (drawings, paintings, collages, and sculptures) that inform my virtual worlds. The shape of a line in a drawing suggests multiple interpretations for becoming multi-dimensional worlds that translate into a dynamic VR art experience. In the evolution of one's own creative voice, that voice expands through the shaping of movement in VR and real time interactive experience. Virtual reality can serve the artist in their quest towards discovering a visual voice through their cultivation of a visceral truth by combining the visual aesthetics of line, color, shape, proportion, volume and stature of the objects with the situation of consciousness and active exploration. Virtual reality situates the visitor's consciousness in an alternate world and asks them to act decisively, in the moment. This encourages the visitor to become actively involved in identifying and navigating an unfamiliar space. As a result, the visitor explores the environment by making it their own experience. They can decide the moment to move left or right, or to

Figure 22.1

Figuratively Speaking, in the Indiana University Virtual Reality Theater. Using large screen projection displays artists are dialoguing with art and walking in the worlds of their aesthetic visions.

22. Immersion and Visualizing Artistic Spaces in Virtual Reality

move their head up or down or to turn around or to look under objects. The experience is revealed through their conscious choices. Through artistic expression, the medium of VR forms a rhetoric distinct from traditional computer graphics.

Games are consumer driven, mass market products that challenge users with goal-oriented activities that are often linear, hierarchical, and designed with an assurance that a predictable comfort level will be maintained. This is accomplished by introducing mythological themes that are easily assimilated into the gaming culture such as searching for items, combatting foes, and accumulating wealth. It is possible to describe virtual reality as an extension of the gaming market, but that would be misleading. Virtual reality actually is an experience, much like the conceptual art of Agnes Denes [Denes 1993], Nancy Holt [Lee and Schaber 2015], Alice Aycock [Risatti 1985], James Turrell (Adcock and Turrell 1990], and Robert Smithson [Smithson and Smithson 1996], who present aesthetic experience by creating art as events, situations, or happenings. These moments of posturing visitors within time and light within a landscape enriches the viewing by shifting perceptions of truth and promoting special moments of being.

22.2 VR: An Evolving Medium

Since the 1960s, the investigation of VR has developed rich research communities at university campuses, corporations, and military complexes—earlier if one considers flight simulation as a type of VR. Today these places include the University of North Carolina at Chapel Hill, the University of Illinois at Chicago, the Virtual Reality Medical Center in San Diego, Ford Motor Company, Facebook, Intel Labs among so many more companies and emerging start-ups. Virtual reality has a legacy in visualization for scientific, mathematical and information visualization, medical training, architectural rendering and communication in the arts and humanities. Many fields develop strategies for interacting with data and complex information in three-dimensional space. No field has a particular protocol for creating virtual reality and no virtual reality environment follows a standard protocol. At the outset, software and hardware tended to be custom made and designed in-house or shared among a group of collaborative institutions. All of the environments offered unique opportunities for immersion and provided a strategy for navigation. Understanding navigation and interacting with visual and auditory information becomes the virtual reality challenge for the creator, and more likely, the creative team. Consumer market products for VR bring the research and development challenge for building environments right into the home. What does that offer us?

Virtual reality provides alternative strategies for creating immersive experiences. VR is typically understood or discussed in terms of video games, films, interactive videos and the like but it is actually redefining those genres in a distinctive way—it has the ability to extend these media. However, we can begin with VR as a strategy in and of itself because it presents experience—and currently that reality of experience is ill-defined. That is one of the reasons why VR has been so problematic as a "Wild West" frontier. Artists, developers, and visitors to virtual environments find themselves in dialogues about VR without a manual or lexicon.

The biggest reason why VR appears to be a wild frontier is that it is not easily contextualized. The term itself has been used to refer to large displays, small displays, and web displays with a plethora of supporting devices depending on who is claiming it at the time. And that is only the technology, never mind the environments themselves.

Approaching VR with an artistic strategy offers an opportunity for creating expression and affecting perception of a visitor within a multi-dimensional physicality of complex characterization of space and sound. Programming art in VR establishes a link between the computer and the imagination. The pleasure of pushing brightly colored paints around with a long handle paintbrush is extended to generating pixels that fly through the air. The immediacy, the smell, the sensuality, and the feeling of pure intoxication occurs when virtual environments appear from darkness. Now logical phrases calculate floating point number values to create three dimensional objects. Tools are available through 3D modeling packages and improved image manipulation software that allow artists to expand their ideas about static objects to how they should appear when they are experienced in relation to a navigational sequence. This becomes a narrative that exists in a 360° arena. VR becomes a fascinating challenge for the artist and designer to unfold experience from multiple vantage points. As creative director, one has to think about the artistic value, the design methodology, and the software solutions being offered to the visitor.

Tools will allow us to create environments and artwork directly inside virtual reality. It is imperative to understand VR as art and continue to expand the aesthetic role in interactive experience.

22.3 Immersion: A Key to Virtual Reality

Key to VR's interactive experience is *immersion*. Immersion offers a perceptual shift; it is mental awareness of a reality that enhances the normal or real world. Virtual reality offers a method to recognize an added component to everyday awareness. VR interaction can be subtle such as approaching an object or an emotable and having the entity react by changing its appearance through color, shape or size, or creating sounds, or by generating movement or placement changes. By making interactions possible for the visitor, choices engage the visitor and promote understanding and immersion within the environment.

Consider the mentally immersive medium of the book. An absorbing read enriches life. As if the author is sending us messages, whether fiction, non-fiction, imagined, or historical, these messages each in their own way form an immersion into a perceptual shift. Avid readers will consider a good book to be an escape or a type of friend. One can hold a book as if it is a companion that provides comradery late at night or in the adventure of a plane flight. The virtual environment is essentially the book; the emotables shape the story of the virtual environment by communicating ways to navigate its messages.

As an object, the emotable can be very apparent or rather subtle. However, aesthetics position the emotable as a tool of VR immersion. Through the act of reading the emotable, one is led or sometimes dragged or other times found tripping over the expression in order to realize the narrative. Our immersion is part of the drive to discover how the narrative unfolds and to become consumed by it so much so that we suspend our disbelief over to the reality of virtual circumstances. The most effective experiences add a layer to our conscious awareness. And that layer enhances the normal or real world, it is superimposed on our reality and we experience an awareness that is a simultaneous and parallel flow state. It is through this absorption into the language of the emotable that we sense an engagement with a virtual reality that can entertain, inform, and enrich us.

22.4 Making Special with Immersion and Perceptual Awareness

For me, VR serves a biological drive to create or "make special." According to Dissanayake's research in *"Art as Human Behavior: Toward an Ethological View of Art,"* humans are driven to create objects that are beyond a utilitarian design [Dissanayake 1980]. We make objects special in an effort to satisfy a desire towards creating something. We want to be surrounded by objects of greater value. This need to appreciate the significance of objects is an indicator of cognitive awareness. Making special is a drive for a perceptual shift and an appreciation of aesthetics. This drive enhances immersion. Creating emotables in virtual reality makes it is possible to achieve the feeling of "making special" for the artist creating the environment and for the visitor exploring the environment.

Emotables set the stage for mental immersion in virtual reality and indicates a direction for further pursuits.

VR combines two trajectories, technical (hardware, software) and experiential (perceptual, artistic, purposeful, scientific, training, etc.). One definition states that virtual reality is a "very powerful and compelling computer application by which humans can interface and interact with computer-generated environments in a way that mimics real life and engages all the senses" [Burdea and Coiffet 2003]. Sherman and Craig defined it as having four key elements: Virtual World, Physical and Mental Immersion, and Interactivity [Sherman and Craig 2002]; and then recognized two more key elements: the Participant, and the Creators [Sherman and Craig 2018]. Steuer writes that many people describe VR as a medium like television or the radio, but he considers it "a particular kind of experience" (unique) rather than a technological assemblage [Steuer 1992].

As a result, hardware people talk about the hardware, software people talk about the software, and art people talk about the aesthetics. Together, VR is experience. In fact, all of these components make up VR and go hand in hand. For example, the efficiency of the technological components and the efficacy of their execution provide for smooth navigation which allows the perceptual field to accept the environment more readily. This doesn't mean that the environment needs to approach realism for an effective experience. It means that the graphics must respond effortlessly to the rotation of your head or the pointing of your finger, etc. The interaction and visual motion should be smooth in order to provide a conscious psychological sense of immersion that is a result of aesthetics: making special with hardware, software, and displays.

Immersion in VR will improve as real time rendering improves. As VR operation becomes a smooth occurrence, VR begins to stabilize, the expectations of hardware and software become more predictable and so does the playback during engagement. As these smooth conditions become normative, we will be able to speak about ourselves in the state of VR with more certainty. I am proposing a name for this state. The status of existing in the virtual world—cyberity (as opposed to sobriety)—is the state of being cyber. Cyberity is the temperance or moderation of being cyber. Cyberity occurs in such spaces as virtual reality, artificial reality, augmented reality, cyberspace, cyber-presence, second life, etc.

Cyberity is determined by the experiential moment which is shaped by its artistry. The artistry can be to focus on the phenomena of art-making and perception-shifting using a variety of strategies from digital drawing, digital painting, and digital sculpting as well as scanning and photographic techniques to create virtual worlds. The experience is also defined by the VR displays which include CAVEs, ImmersaDesks, John-e-boxes,

Oculus Rift HMD, VIVE HMD, Wide-Angle Virtual Environment (WAVEs), Flat panels, IQ-walls, phones, HoloLenses, and other augmented reality displays. This wide berth of devices range from small single visitor displays to large group projection displays. CAVE-like rooms or wall displays for multiple persons allows groups of people to look directly at one another creating a level of co-existence between the people, VR, and shared time and place.

There are those who believe that VR is truly realized in a single visitor display such as a head mounted display (HMD) and that the HMD is the true source of immersion [Laurel 2016]. This attitude suggests that one must be alone in the environment isolated from the real world, and cut off from seeing one's body or others or the world we live in. The HMD separates the visitor from the self and the actual surroundings, which can be problematic if one's movements are not safely negotiated or monitored. Adherence to a single visitor display will prove to be a privileged vision with the proliferation of surround screens, touch walls, augmented reality, and the like which expands our relationships to include the natural environment and our graphics capabilities.

The configuration of displays and their supporting technologies provide very different types of physical immersion and as a result, very different experiences. The visual display delivers the virtual environment or destination in which to discover the artwork itself. The technology drives the real world environmental conditions for viewing. The technology can help to shape the experience but the visual phenomena combined with audio immersion is core to the experience. The artist should maintain a conscientious dialogue with their creative process when inviting visitors into an unknown world exemplifying a space we are wholly within, visually immersed and interactively and thoughtfully connected to.

22.5 Aesthetic Experience: VR Art Evokes Visitor Action and Reaction

The VR artist challenges the visitor to withhold their sense of disbelief in order to navigate a world that they may have never imagined facing before. In the initial encounter the visitor realizes that the newfound world fills their field of view. The sense of presence gained through the experience depends on how tracking devices and related peripheral devices are used to facilitate interaction.

Taking the opportunity to create artworks using state-of-the-art technologies and high performance networks for gallery and museum installations, dramatic theater events and operas widens the expression possibilities. This includes projection displays that incorporate 3D computer graphics, real-time animation, real-time video processing, facial detection, stereo audio, stereo video and real -time interaction. The real-time interaction includes some form of position tracking system integrated into the graphics output. Such systems could include an electromagnetic tracker, an infrared camera tracker or a facial detection tracking system. The artwork requires the ability to display the visual graphics in real time and may use many processor-intensive programs running simultaneously. The artwork does not require a sequential playback device; it requires the artwork to be generated during the time of the visitor's interaction. The work is realized as the visitor moves, manipulates, navigates or in some way alters the reality of the art experience.

Through various forms of VR which include CAVE, HMDs, surround screen 360° video, smartphone, second life, stereo cinema, 3D video, planetariums, domes, IMAX theaters, etc., different kinds of reality can be offered. The physical immersion experience is fundamental to VR but the available hardware requires specific software to display artwork in these various venues. A virtual reality artwork is not interchangeable as it is typically optimized for a specific display such as a handheld device, or a surround display like a planetarium.

Virtual reality requires having viewer-centered perspective, however domes and iMAX theaters do not have viewer centered perspective. They may display in stereo-vision but they are not VR because they have camera perspective. 360° video is physically immersive when seen on an HMD but it is not viewer-centered perspective. Viewers of 360° video are in the camera point of view which is a fixed POV. The visitor is not moving in virtual space; rather their head is rotating around to understand the view. A CAVE promotes viewer-centered perspective to the navigator. VR experiences can be considered as a venue much like a baseball stadium, symphony hall, or nightclub. As you arrive, you can feel that others are collectively creating the immersive space that everyone is sharing.

So how do we share VR through art? What makes VR an excellent arts space? Translating ideas into a three-dimensional space with 360° viewing is challenging. It is problematic in terms of understanding which direction to face. Visitors may be watching for some time before realizing the action is occurring behind them. The key is to establish a variety of viewpoints, to orient the visitor at the start and be able to reset that orientation for each visit. Each direction in VR art is a possibility for experience where every viewpoint offers the prospect of discovering an element of the environment. VR is distinguished from a 3D film because VR offers interaction beyond the photographic imagination, with non-linearity and non-hierarchical navigation and with the ability to experience environments without a predefined beginning, middle, and end.

In VR, the visitor is no longer bound to the fixed frame of a still image or the fixed point of view of a camera or the fixed length of a cinematic film. Rather than sitting in front of a flat display the visitor is immersed in in a three-dimensional sound environment. In VR, the visitor discovers and defines the walk through the imagery by interacting with its elements or emotables.

As an artist, I am interested in artistic expression of ideas that provoke perceptual pleasure and provide emotional possibilities. I have created the term '*emotable*' to define a digital character that represents ability, emotion, motive, and voice. The emotable helps to establish an aesthetic and place the visitor in an environment. An emotable represents an affective entity. An emotable may have a facial expression and a unique voice. An emotable represents an aspect of the environment that uses aesthetics as a method for establishing the terrain and wayfinding in order to immerse the visitor. It acts as its own entity to define the environment and establish the visitor's cyberity, or consciousness in VR.

The emotables depend on metaphors that provide objects with certain characteristics that define the environment and its expressive qualities. For example, an emotable on a wall can appear fixed until it is approached, whereupon it grows more dimensional, alters in size and reveals itself as a doorway. This is the metaphorical equivalent of walking down a hallway to discover doorways and windows and contemplate options in order to choose a particular path. By being attracted to an emotable and a direction, recognition and approach become levels of interaction with the emotable. By integrating the emotable into our consciousness we develop an understanding with the emotable. Visitors are having a reciprocal dialogue with the VR world. The emotable is an affective entity or element that establishes the interaction.

Much of my artwork is involved in communicating an emotion or a type of social communication. Art processes (painting, drawing, and sculpture) open up the possibilities to discover shapes and lines and colors that evoke the imagery to represent these various conscious and subconscious phenomena and establish them into VR circumstances. For me, creating pen, pencil, and brush markings allows me to immediately express the intrinsic associations I make with the world. I interpret these drawings by exploring the metaphors that they reveal in VR. VR allows me to expand on the associations I make with the real world. Artworks are metaphorically expressive as they portray realism or pure abstraction or data [Cox 2006] and metaphor is the approach for investigating how artistic virtual environments can be ascribed.

Much like swapping the letters in a JUMBLE puzzle to form a word, VR offers the ability to swap boundaries from reality to "virtuality." Many of my VR artwork experiences rely on portraiture or characters to situate the visitor within the environment. The human is the visitor in the virtual world of emotables. For example, in *Figuratively Speaking*," one encounters a VR artwork where abstract characters share a world where hearts fly in the sky and boats rock in the ocean and "guards" flail their arms in haphazard consternation. Some of the emotables in the environment are beckoning and others attempt blocking which allows for a responsive and intuitive navigation. The emotables fill the environment as characters (figures) and their parts configure the landscape. The emotables form the land and the figures by being interchangeable parts. For example, a nose can be singular entity on a face or can be multiples to establish a forest. By presenting the emotables with various configurations, the visitor is provided with multiple pathways of interpretation and direction.

The essential methodology for designing a virtual environment is to start with a familiar object in the real world and shape it characteristics—be they realistic, exaggerated or abstract. For example, I enjoy the homonym 'nose' and 'knows.' When I look at someone, I see their nose. I tend to draw the nose first when I create a portrait. The nose becomes a confrontation point and a discernment point. By combining these ideas, I created a forest of tall green noses that provide a shelter for two characters in an intimate conversation. They are having a dialogue in the *Forest of Knowses* (See Figure 22.2). The noses are not obvious noses unless you look at the characters in the forest, the trees are actually their noses grown tall and turned green. The audio sounds an imaginative dialogue that gives them a voice that whispers to the visitor as they approach.

22.6 Engaging Forward with "Emotables"

A critical aesthetic element of the VR art environment is what I term 'emotables.' An emotable's construction and placement situates consciousness by establishing the aesthetics of the environment to guide visitors through virtual reality. The emotable represents an affective entity and provides ability, emotion, motive, and voice to a VR scene. The emotables' abilities are signals for the visitor to explore their own abilities in the VR. The emotables' emotion situates consciousness through the mise-en-scène. The emotables'

Figure 22.2

"Forest of Knowses" in *Figuratively Speaking*. As an aesthetic strategy, the nose as an emotable is used in figurative elements and landscape elements to unify the environment. The forest of noses leads us to the figures that are whispering nose to nose. In effect, the emotables are speaking in the environment and parts of the faces are establishing the environment as a forest.

motives provide motivation for further exploration. The emotables' voices provide sound locators and substantiates the tone of the scene. An emotable is any element in the scene. The emotable can have facial expressions and a unique voice but it does not represent any person. It acts as its own entity and may mirror a receptive visitor. The emotable is opposite of an avatar that represents a particular person.

Aesthetics helps define a visual rhetoric for virtual reality and facilitate visitors with navigational strategies.

VR artwork communicates to the visitor through the emotable, an affective entity that defines the environment and the possibilities within it. The VR visitor's experience is established by their cyberity, their moderation of cyberspace and their ability to make special while in it. Artists will continue to define VR as they creatively define their voice and establish visual VR rhetoric and aspects of cyberity through aesthetic moments.

References

[Adcock & Turrell 1990]

Adcock, Craig E. and James Turrell. *James Turrell: the Art of Light and Space*. Oakland, CA: University of California Press, 1990.

[Burdea & Coiffet 2003]

Burdea, Grigore C. and Philippe Coiffet. *Virtual Reality Technology*, Vol. 1. Hoboken, NJ: John Wiley & Sons, 2003.

[Cox 2006]

Cox, Donna. Metaphoric mappings: The art of visualization. In: Fishwick, P. ed. *Aesthetic Computing*. Cambridge, MA: MIT Press, pp. 89–114, 2006.

[Denes 1993]

Denes, Agnes. Notes on eco-logic: Environmental artwork, visual philosophy and global perspective, *Leonardo* 26(5), 387–395, 1993.

[Dissanayake 1980]

Dissanayake, Ellen. Art as a human behavior: Toward an ethological view of art, *Journal of Aesthetics and Art Criticism* 38(4), 397–406, 1980.

[Dolinsky 2018]

Dolinsky, Margaret. Facing experience: A painter's canvas in virtual reality, Manuscript submitted for publication, 2018.

[Laurel 2016]

Laurel, Brenda. What is virtual reality? 2016. doi:10.13140/RG.2.1.4415.0643. https://researchgate.net/publication/301891235_What_Is_Virtual_Reality

[Lee & Schaber 2015]

Lee, Pamela M. and Ines Schaber. *Nancy Holt: Sightlines*. Oakland, CA: University of California Press, 2015.

[Risatti 1985]

Risatti, Howard. The sculpture of Alice Aycock and some observations on her work, *Woman's Art Journal* 6(1), 28–38, 1985.

[Sherman & Craig 2002]

Sherman, William R. and Alan B. Craig. *Understanding Virtual Reality*. San Francisco, CA: Morgan Kaufman Publishers, 2002.

[Sherman & Craig 2018]

Sherman, William R. and Alan B. Craig. *Understanding Virtual Reality,* second edition, San Francisco, CA: Morgan Kaufman Publishers, 2018.

[Smithson & Smithson 1996]

Smithson, Peter and Robert Smithson. *Robert Smithson: The Collected Writings*. Oakland, CA: University of California Press, 1996.

[Steuer 1992]

Steuer, Jonathan. Defining virtual reality: Dimensions determining telepresence. *Journal of Communication* 42(4), 73–93, 1992.

23

Embodied Montage
Constructing Meaning in Virtual Reality

Deniz Tortum and Ainsley Sutherland
MIT Comparative Media Studies

Virtual reality (VR) storytelling allows unprecedented levels of interactivity, sometimes at the cost of traditional methods for telling a story—a tradeoff described as the "narrative paradox" in gaming literature [Harrell 2013]. VR is positioned between gameplay and film. It demands new techniques that take advantage of the unique qualities of the medium. This chapter discusses *embodied montage,* a technique that draws from film montage, adapted to the physical, sensory world of VR storytelling. The "magic" of changing your body's abilities in the world is an ancient concept, and this section will describe how the technical affordances of VR open up new possibilities in this realm. We will discuss specific techniques by looking at examples of existing VR artwork. As you create your own VR projects, you will be able to consider carefully how to design interactive stories and mechanics that use perception in new and effective ways.

23.1 Don't Look Back

To begin thinking about this, consider the myth of Orpheus. In the famous myth of Orpheus and Eurydice, perception itself has dire consequences. Deeply in love with his wife, Orpheus seeks to bring her back from death. He travels to the underworld to save her. Hades offers him her return on one condition: Orpheus must not look back at her until they have left the underworld. If he looks back, she will stay there forever. Though they travel together towards the entrance to hell, Orpheus trusting that Eurydice is close behind, he grows increasingly doubtful. At the last moment, unable to bear the possibility that she might not be with him, Orpheus looks back. Eurydice, who had indeed been just behind him, is trapped in the underworld forever. This ancient myth has been ripe with meaning for philosophers and writers concerned with the consequences of our gaze. It also speaks to something quintessential in VR.

The act of looking has consequences for Orpheus. It creates "action at a distance;" though he doesn't touch Eurydice, his gaze both causes change in himself (he has knowledge, verifies her presence) and changes in the world (Eurydice must stay in the underworld). Generally, we are accustomed to the first consequence of looking, as sight is one of the primary ways in which people learn about and understand their environment. Sight changes our knowledge of the world. In this myth, however, sight changes the world itself.

23.2 Virtual Reality Systems and Perception

Uniquely, virtual reality enables the opportunity to bring these types of interactions to the fore more easily than in other media. Artists can create these types of moments in virtual reality because it is a dynamic computational medium, tracking all of a user's bodily input, from movement around a room to the direction of a look. **Tying action to consequence is a unique affordance of virtual reality, and creates the foundation of embodied montage.**

To understand why this is possible with VR, let's take a look at the affordances of real-time engines and head-mounted displays (HMDs). Real-time graphics engines are not new, they have been used in games since the 1990s. Crucially, they render a display based on user input: where the user is looking, what location the user has moved to, etc. This is in contrast to a linear display as you would see in a non-interactive animated film or movie. In VR, this adaptable display is even more closely aligned with our body and our natural movements. VR peripherals, like controls, microphones, and the head-mounted display work in tandem to provide information about our physical movements, such as gaze, voice, height, and so on to the computational system. Think about it like this: a traditional video game reacts to inputs in the form of button presses—intentional, discrete inputs. A VR system is graphically adjusting to much more complex and overlapping inputs: turning your head as you walk forward, holding an object as you sit down.

While we can design interactions in the same way—e.g., jumping causes you to move up and then down again—mimicking what we encounter in the physical world, it is important to register that as a *design choice*. The realism of virtual "reality" is constructed. By acknowledging this, creators can push the medium to more experimental and novel ends [Arnheim 1969].

Currently, a variety of unique VR experiences have experimented with what happens when we *don't* reproduce the physical world in our VR design choices. The framework of *Embodied Montage*, a concept borrowed from the montage of cinema, helps us to analyze and understand this type of design.

23.3 Embodied Montage

We expect certain outcomes from our body's movement and perception—like looking completely around to see what is behind us. That action isn't necessarily a given in a virtual reality environment and can be altered expressively. By breaking the illusion of naturalistic realism, particularly within the body, we are able to create new and additional meanings from adjacent sensations. Embodied montage originates in a study of film history, specifically the history of montage.

In the 1920s, Soviet filmmakers developed an approach to film editing called "montage." [Eisenstein and Leyda 1949] Rather than creating sequences in which shots follow each other seamlessly, these filmmakers placed contradicting shots directly after one another. These two shots when combined create a third meaning that does not exist in either of the shots alone, and the whole ends up being greater than the sum of each shot. The heart of montage lies in creative juxtaposition.

In VR the "third meaning" of montage can appear from new connections between the body and the environment, and between action and perception. For example, VR systems can create new perceptual experiences that we don't have access to in everyday life: such as projecting different images to each eye, or changing the field of vision, or the effect of mass and gravity on a body. Such separations between what we expect, and what we actually perceive allow the artists to make novel combinations between actions and their consequences and to reconfigure the body and its relation to the environment. Embodied montage offers a response to narrative paradox in interactive experiences and serves as a narrative tool for virtual reality.

23.4 Case Studies

In a nutshell, using virtual reality we break the existing, expected relationship between a user's actions and their consequences. For example, we expect walking to produce movement, we expect contact with an object to produce an effect on the body. But in virtual reality, we must design these interactions intentionally. Embodied montage can be additive or subtractive: it can either create a new pairing between action and consequence or it can break an already existing pairing. The case studies demonstrate how artists have broken and reconnected our expectations about how our actions produce effects in the virtual world (Figure 23.1).

Figure 23.1

Users move to where they look in Oscar Raby's *Assent*.

23.4.1 Assent—Oscar Raby

Created by Oscar Raby in 2013, *Assent* is a critically acclaimed virtual reality documentary. In this experience, users take on the perspective of the artist's father, a former soldier who served in the Chilean army during the Pinochet military regime. The piece centers on the experience of witnessing a mass execution during this time. The mechanic for moving in this experience is tied to the viewer's gaze. The user looks at a particular place (a technique known as "dwelling") for several seconds, and then moves towards it. This interaction mechanism combines the action of looking with the consequence of moving, linking these two acts. This gives new meaning to the act of looking. What emerges in this juxtaposition is that looking is active, has consequences in space, and is involved. This mechanic gains resonance when seen in the context of witnessing, where even observation can be a form of participation or suffering. In the physical world, our gaze doesn't move us. But by tying perception and consequence together in a new way in the virtual world, Raby has employed embodied montage to create meaning.

Action	Consequence	Analysis
Looking	Movement	Looking (and witnessing) is an active, rather than passive interaction with the world

23.4.2 *"Maquette"* section of *"The Sky is a Gap"*—Rachel Rossin

In this piece, the user finds themself in a 3D rendering of a house; the everyday objects in the house are presented as imperfectly rendered 3D objects. Rossin utilizes the optical trackers in the HTC Vive HMD system to track a user's movement in space. The user's movement in space also controls passage of time, making the room explode as the user moves. This causes the body to become an interface for changing temporality. If the user does not move, then time does not pass. For example, unlike a video, where time is fixed and linear, time itself could be controlled by a user's movement within a space. In games such as *A Slower Speed of Light* and *Braid*, "time control" is a kind of "game mechanic." In VR it can be more tightly linked to embodiment and perception—where the system responds in a nuanced way to subconscious or unintentional actions (Figure 23.2).

In this experience, time becomes a capability of the body. Cognitive scientist and linguist Mark Johnson writes that humans think about time through the analogy of moving in space: "We (adults) conceptualize time via deep, systematic spatial movement metaphors in which the passage of time is understood as relative motion in space" [Johnson 2007]. The embodied montage in "Maquette" allows this abstract concept to be enacted and observed.

Action	Consequence	Analysis
Walking	Control of the Timeline	Our perception of time is subjective, connected to our activity and location.

Figure 23.2

Users control the timeline with their movement in Rachel Rossin's *Maquette*.

23.4.3 Notes on Blindness—Arnaud Colinart et al.

Created by Arnaud Colinart, Amaury La Burthe, Peter Middleton, and James Spinney in 2016 as a companion piece to the film with the same name, Notes on Blindness has been a festival favorite, winning the Storyscapes Awards at Tribeca Film Festival 2016. This project attempts to represent the experience of a blind person. In the piece, as the user stares at dark and empty places in the environment where positional audio can be heard, the shapes of objects begin to take form. In this way, the act of staring is combined with the appearance of previously unseen shapes. This pairing is a representation of how important sound is to blind persons, and how they use sound to interpret the world. The user in Notes on Blindness also perceives objects (visually) through attending to the sounds they create.

Action	Consequence	Analysis
Listening	Seeing	Reversing the primacy of sight over sound mimics the sensory schema of a blind person.

23.4.4 Project Syria—Nonny de la Peña

Project Syria was created by Nonny de la Peña in 2014. This immersive journalism piece was commissioned by The World Economic Forum to raise awareness about the children displaced because of the Syrian civil war. This project recreates the experience of a bombing in Aleppo, Syria. A room-scale installation, Project Syria uses the virtual reality headset and optical tracking to positionally track the user. The user begins in a 3D modelled Aleppo streetscape. After a brief chance to walk and explore the street, there is an explosion, and a cloud of smoke covers the street.

This is a crucial moment of disembodiment within the piece. The explosion is created through sound and image only; no other bodily sense is stimulated. Simulations do not replicate reality point for point, but rather only selected elements of it. In Project Syria when the rocket strikes the street, the body of the user is unaffected; the action of explosion is detached from the perception of feeling pain. Even though debris strikes the virtual body of the user, her physical body is not affected. This is a ripe creative moment that virtual reality pieces should acknowledge and make creative use of. In Project Syria, such disembodiment could signify the impossibility of fully understanding such a situation.

Action	Consequence	Analysis
Collision with objects	No effect on body	A spectator in this virtual experience will always be a ghost, unable to completely understand or experience the violence of the situation.

23.5 Conclusion

As you design and develop your virtual reality experiences, consider how the embodied nature of the VR systems interact with the affordances of the real-time 3D engines. We have the opportunity to tell stories not just with images and words but by juxtaposing actions and perception. Embodied montage techniques don't assume that virtual reality must also be realistic: they make use of the medium formally to produce critical effects.

Though these VR works are early examples in a young field, they point towards the creative potential immersive media has to produce poetic meaning and deepen a narrative in new ways.

References

[Arnheim 1969]

Arnheim, Rudolf. *Film as Art*. Berkeley, CA: University of California, 1969.

[Eisenstein and Leyda 1949]

Eisenstein, Sergei, and Jay Leyda (ed. and trans.) *Film form: Essays in Film Theory*. New York: Harcourt, 1949.

[Harrell 2013]

Harrell, D. Fox. *Phantasmal Media: An Approach to Imagination, Computation, and Expression*. Cambridge, MA: MIT Press, 2013.

[Johnson 2007]

Johnson, Mark. *The meaning of the Body: Aesthetics of Human Understanding*. Chicago, IL: University of Chicago Press, 2007.

SECTION VII
Advanced Rendering for VR

24

Omnidirectional Stereoscopic Projections for VR

John E. Stone
University of Illinois at Urbana-Champaign

This chapter describes omnidirectional stereoscopic projections that are used by both immersive camera systems and by rendering software to produce images and movies suitable for viewing in a wide range of immersive displays such as low-cost commodity virtual reality (VR) HMDs. Omnidirectional stereoscopic projections provide the user with an opportunity to experience an immersive view of pre-generated imagery that supports intuitive exploration with at least two degrees of freedom of head orientation. This chapter describes common approaches for omnidirectional projections, their strengths and weaknesses, and methods for their implementation in rendering software.[*]

24.1 Introduction and Context

Omnidirectional stereoscopic projections (OSPs) are widely used to support capture or rendering, encoding, transmission, and playback of immersive image and movie content on a broad range of virtual reality HMDs, including power-constrained devices such as smartphone-based VR HMDs such as Samsung's GearVR, Google Cardboard and Daydream, and others [Stone et al., 2016a,b; Sener et al., 2014]. Ray tracing engines can

---

[*] Portions of this chapter ©2016 IEEE. Reprinted by permission (Stone et al., 2016b).

directly render a variety of omni-stereo projections including equirectangular (sometimes called latitude-longitude) — mapping from a rectangular image to spherical latitude-longitude angles), cube map (spherical projection mapped onto the six faces of a cube), and other special projections such as planetarium dome master (hemispherical projection mapped to a circular region inscribed within a square image). The images and movies produced by OSPs can often be imported directly into conventional image and video editing software, where with a few noteworthy differences, they can be edited and post-processed using the same tools used for standard planar images. Indeed, omnidirectional VR movies are supported in YouTube and Vimeo, allowing them to be streamed to a wide variety of playback hardware. By incorporating support for OSPs, rendering software and post-processing tools can then support production workflows for immersive content, directly producing images and movies for viewing with immersive displays such as HMDs.

Images captured by omnidirectional live-camera arrays require significant post-processing to align and feather images, filling the view in all directions, and warping or resampling images to obtain a complete OSP from the array of cameras. Non-stereoscopic omnidirectional projections can often be implemented with existing graphics programming APIs and libraries through multi-stage rendering and warping, but the need for stereoscopic output in OSPs presents an additional challenge that is often not explicitly supported by existing APIs. Widely used rasterization APIs such as OpenGL and Direct X lack support for non-planar projections, requiring special techniques to generate commonly used OSP encodings. In contrast, it is often easy to directly implement a wide variety of OSP encodings in renderers based on so-called ray casting or ray tracing methods. Custom-written CG-camera functions that control primary ray generation is an area of significant flexibility in most ray tracing engines, making OSPs easy to implement in practice (Figures 24.1 and 24.2).

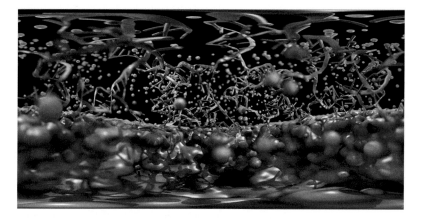

Figure 24.1

Left eye equirectangular subimage from an omnidirectional stereoscopic projection of a Satellite Tobacco Mosaic Virus (STMV) scene containing over 626,000 objects, shown with ambient occlusion lighting, depth of field focal blur, two directional lights, and shadows.

Figure 24.2

Left eye equirectangular subimage from an omnidirectional stereoscopic projection of an HIV-1 capsid scene containing 9.7-million objects, shown with ambient occlusion lighting using a maximum occlusion distance cutoff, a point-light "headlight" at the camera location, and shadows.

24.2 Methods

OSPs and related panoramic projections attempt to generate images that encompass most or all of the plenoptic function (all rays of light passing through a point in space) for a given eye location [Adelson and Bergen, 1991; McMillan and Bishop, 1995]. The images resulting from OSPs can be reprojected for arbitrary viewing orientations and fields of view by texture mapping OSP images onto a focal surface's proxy geometry surrounding the camera in a conventional rendering pipeline. Since any number of reprojections can be performed independently, using the OSP image as input, multiple independent views and therefore multiple users can be can be supported using the same shared head or camera location. OSP view-orientation-independence can be exploited to allow the use of advanced rendering techniques such progressive refinement ray tracing, where ongoing rendering continually refines the image presented to the user(s). Changes to a user's viewing direction does not change the omnidirectional projection. Progressive refinement rendering can continue until the camera location is moved to a new location, requiring that the progressive refinement rendering process be restarted.

24.2.1 Equirectangular and Cubic Omnidirectional Projections

Previously, one of the most widely used applications of omnidirectional projections was for environment texture mapping. Environment mapping provides a convincing graphical illusion of mirror-like reflections on shiny objects without the need to render mathematically correct reflections of the entire surrounding environment. Environment texture maps are typically stored either as a equirectangular projection of a sphere [Paeth, 1990; Musgrave, 1992] or as a cubic projection (i.e., unfolded cube) [Greene, 1986]. These two OSP encodings are fairly simple to render, but have some shortcomings. One shortcoming in particular is the uneven distribution of OSP image pixels per unit of solid angle (steradians of field of view). For example, in equirectangular projections, far more OSP image pixels are spent near the poles, performing unnecessarily dense rendering work there, even though ironically for areas less likely to be viewed (straight-up and straight-down), whereas pixel density (and rendering work/samples) is least-dense at the horizon. Other omnidirectional projections could be created on arbitrary focal plane surfaces other than spheres or cubes, to maximize uniformity of the solid angle sampled by each pixel (and rendering work), but these two projections are simple and benefit from high performance hardware support in modern GPUs and rendering APIs.

Because their support is entrenched in rendering hardware and software and within VR image and video formats, we focus on variants of the equirectangular or cubic projections to render, store, transmit, and reproject omnidirectional scenes for HMDs. All omnidirectional projection approaches involve compromises between the most efficient (most uniform) mapping of omnidirectional image pixels to the field of view (steradians of solid angle or area on a sphere), complexities in indexing and storage, and potential for image or video compression artifacts. Equirectangular projections oversample the regions surrounding the polar axis, so they are not as pixel-efficient as they could be. Cubic projections oversample regions near the cube corners, but to a lesser degree than the polar regions in equirectangular projections.

24.2.2 Stereoscopic Adaptation of Omnidirectional Projections

The popular equirectangular and cubic projections both work well for photographic applications and for monoscopic rendering (see Figure 24.3a), but as is they do not support stereoscopy — owing to the *backward-stereo* images produced when viewing to the rear, and *no stereo* effect when looking to the sides when displaying a pair of such projections rendered with laterally displaced eye locations. One solution described by Peleg and Ben-Ezra is a so-called "circular stereoscopic projection" (see Figure 24.3b) for photographic capture applications that provides a correct stereoscopic view over the full 360°circle. They describe image capture by sweeping a slit camera over circular path, laterally offset from the center of projection, with the camera view direction roughly tangent to the circle [Peleg and Ben-Ezra, 1999]. In related work Simon et al. [2004] and Bourke [2006] describe the use of circular projections with image warping, for stereoscopic viewing. Simon et al. note that stereo views reconstructed from the circular projection approach are perfect for the viewing direction, but moving off-axis, they gradually distort the view direction in the periphery of a user's field of view, emphasizing that the view is *"always correct where you are looking."* When rendering for VR HMDs, which often already suffer from a variety of other off-axis optical aberrations, this tends to be a satisfactory compromise.

Having decided upon equirectangular or cubic OSPs, we resolve a remaining obstacle for effective use with HMDs by combining these approaches with the circular projection technique. Stereoscopic circular projection is correct when the viewer constrains their viewing direction near the horizon, but not when the zenith or nadir points on the OSP polar axis are visible, since the viewer will see *backward-stereo* images in the hemisphere behind the pole (from the viewer's perspective). One can adapt the circular projection, as shown in Figure 24.3c, by modulating the stereoscopic eye separation such that it begins at normal eye separation near the horizon, and is smoothly decreased, reaching zero when either the zenith or nadir points on the polar axis are visible, producing a monoscopic image. The modulation of eye separation can be computed as a function of the

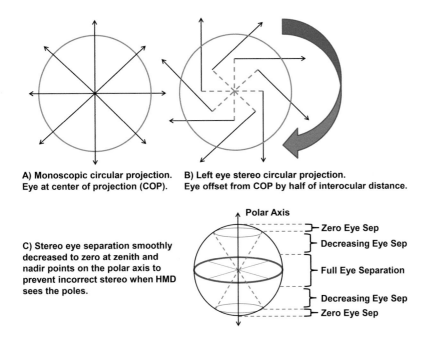

A) Monoscopic circular projection.
Eye at center of projection (COP).

B) Left eye stereo circular projection.
Eye offset from COP by half of interocular distance.

C) Stereo eye separation smoothly decreased to zero at zenith and nadir points on the polar axis to prevent incorrect stereo when HMD sees the poles.

Polar Axis

Zero Eye Sep
Decreasing Eye Sep

Full Eye Separation

Decreasing Eye Sep
Zero Eye Sep

Figure 24.3

Omnidirectional stereoscopic projection approach. (a) A conventional non-stereo omni-directional projection (at the horizon). (b) Circular stereoscopic projection adapted from (a), as described by Peleg and Ben-Ezra [1999] (c) Our omnidirectional stereoscopic projection (OSP) adapts (b) with modulation of the stereo eye separation distance, to prevent *backward-stereo* when either the zenith or nadir points of the polar axis are in view.

cross product of the viewing direction and the polar axis, and the display half-field-of-view angle. Furthermore, the OSP approach allows the system to handle the completely arbitrary HMD head poses necessary for independent multi-user viewing of the same OSP stereo image.

24.2.3 Image and Video Compression Considerations

State-of-the-art image and video compression algorithms take advantage of extensive knowledge about details of the human visual system and human perception. So-called "lossy" compression approaches purposefully discard image information that is considered redundant, low importance, or otherwise imperceptible to most viewers. As an example, software tools that implement popular image and video compression standards such as JPEG and MPEG typically begin the first stage of compression by converting images from an RGB color space to a luminance-chrominance colorspace (e.g., YUV or YCbCr) that allows better compression ratios by exploiting knowledge of biology of color vision related to the density of retinal rods and cones in the human eye. After colorspace conversion, the next steps in compression typically involve downsampling of chrominance information, on the basis that the retina in the human eye contains a much larger number of rods (brightness or luminance detection) than cones (chrominance detection).

Compression algorithms therefore preserve a full-resolution luminance channel, but typically downsample the two chrominance channels to half resolution (halved horizontal resolution) or quarter resolution (both horizontal and vertical resolution are halved).

In video compression terminology, the original full-resolution luminance-chrominance image would be referred to as a 4:4:4 chrominance sampling mode, half-horizontal resolution chrominance subsampling would be referred to as 4:2:2 sampling, and quarter-resolution chrominance subsampling would referred to as 4:2:0 sampling. The information loss due to chrominance subsampling is an early step where some "lossy" compression occurs, even before the much more sophisticated steps of image or video compression begin.

The video chrominance subsampling format notation is particularly useful to be aware of when considering the impact of compression on omnidirectional images. We can see that any subimage tile "edges" in an omnidirectional projection could potentially be blurred in the two chrominance channels if they occur on a pixel boundary with an odd-numbered index. It is therefore best to choose an image size and layout for omnidirectional projections that avoids putting any edges on odd pixel indices.

In addition to colorspace conversion and chrominance downsampling, many image and video compression approaches use a block-based scheme to decompose and compress an image or video sequence, attempting to exploit spatial or temporal redundancy to achieve higher compression ratios. Some commonly used compression block sizes are 8×8 and 16×16. To avoid block related compression artifacts, it is therefore advisable to ensure that any subimage edges in an omnidirectional image are placed only at compression block boundaries, and that the image is an even multiple of the block size used by the underlying compression scheme.

The equirectangular image layout provides unbroken continuity within the image, which is beneficial for minimizing compression artifacts, and is immediately compatible with any other image or movie post-processing workflow. The primary consideration when using image or video compression tools with the equirectangular omnidirectional image layout is to ensure that the overall image size is an even multiple of the compression block size, e.g., 16 in most cases.

Cubic projections present an extra challenge for artifact-free compression and post-processing when they are organized into a conventional rectangular image layout, since they are composed of six subimages that cannot be tiled to completely eliminate discontinuities at their edges. The edge discontinuities are therefore a source of potential problems for tools or post-processing workflows that do not take this into account. To make cubic projections compatible with conventional rectangular image storage and compression formats, the subimage tiles must either be arranged in a rectangular layout, or the unfolded cubic image would need to be padded with empty space to create a rectangular image from the six unfolded cube subimages. To ensure that block artifacts do not harm the edge boundaries for the individual cubic projection subimages (cube facets), they again should be sized to an even multiple of the compression block size, e.g., a multiple of 16.

24.3 Omnidirectional Rendering and Display

OSPs are ideally suited for display using HMDs connected to a conventional laptop or workstation, or by mobile phone-based or self-contained HMDs, but they can also be shown in stereoscopic full-dome theaters, CAVE-like displays, or on conventional 3-D

TVs and monitors. However, they are most aptly suited for viewing with HMDs, since HMDs have a particularly challenging requirement for smooth, low-latency, high-frame-rate display updates — not just for improved immersion, but most importantly, to prevent users from experiencing so-called simulator sickness.

24.3.1 Omnidirectional Stereo Rendering

It is a straightforward task to devise ray tracer camera implementations for the OSPs we have described, but it is worth noting a few details that may be beneficial for ray tracing software efficiency.

The left- and right-eye stereoscopic images resulting from an OSP can be rendered completely independently of each other. However, due to the highly parallel nature of ray tracing software on modern CPUs and massively parallel GPU hardware, it is usually advantageous for the renderer to aggregate as much work as possible into a single pass. By rendering both the left- and right-eye subimages at once, there are more independent items of work available for processing by tens (CPUs) or thousands (GPUs) of arithmetic units, often resulting in higher overall performance and reduced API overhead. Furthermore, within an individual left- or right-eye subimage, there may be several OSP sub-viewports and associated subimages, e.g., such as the individual cube facets in the cubic projection for one eye, as shown in Figure 24.4. By choosing an appropriate stereoscopic and per-eye image packing and encoding format, all of the views can be rendered in a single rendering pass, again maximizing available parallelism and reducing API overheads.

The only additional computational costs associated with the image and subimage packing described above is the requirement for a small amount of additional indexing logic to convert an incoming X or Y coordinate in the final packed image, into the appropriate internal coordinates and associated camera projection parameters required by its associated subimage and the kind of OSP being used. This generally amounts to a division of the incoming OSP image coordinate by subimage size, where the integral part of the quotient indicates which subimage the pixel/sample are associated with, and the fractional part of the quotient is used to compute the internal subimage coordinate need for rendering, e.g., for an individual cube face in a cubic projection. The cost of the subimage indexing operations can be minimized by precomputing arithmetic subexpressions common to all pixels, and by replacing costly operations such as divides by multiplies with their reciprocal values, for example.

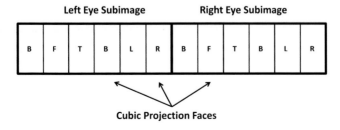

Figure 24.4

Example omnidirectional cube map side-by-side stereoscopic image layout associated with a GearVR sample application for viewing images and movies. Each cube subimage is labeled with the first letter of the cube face, as Back, Front, Top, Bottom, Left, or Right.

24.3.2 Omnidirectional Stereo Image Display

For convenience and efficiency in rendering, post-processing, and final display, it is beneficial to pack the resulting stereoscopic OSP subimages together in the same memory buffer. Each packed OSP image then contains a stereo pair in an over-under or side-by-side arrangement. The over-under stereo pair arrangement provides greatest software interoperability since subimages are stored contiguously in memory, but each subimage can also be directly accessed independently, e.g., by functions not explicitly designed for stereoscopic image pairs.

Renderers based on ray casting or ray tracing methods can produce such final-form packed OSP images in a single rendering pass, by determining the correct left/right eye projection assignment from the stereoscopic subimage that each pixel is associated with as each primary ray is generated. This works well for both equirectangular and cube map OSPs.

Once the OSP image has been rendered, the resulting OSP subimages are reprojected and rasterized, e.g., by OpenGL, for the display. Reprojection is achieved by texturing the

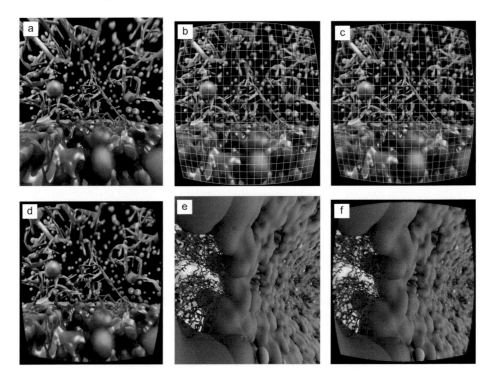

Figure 24.5

Left eye HMD images for Satellite Tobacco Mosaic Virus capsid and RNA (a-d), and the HIV-1 capsid (e,f), with roughly 100° FoV. The images show the HMD reprojection of the OSP images in Figures 24.1 and 24.2, with HMD lens distortion correction steps. The STMV images show the left eye OSP reprojection with: (a) no lens distortion corrections; (b) geometric lens distortion correction only (mesh shown); (c) geometric and chromatic aberration corrections (mesh shown); (d) final left eye HMD image. The HIV images show (e): no lens distortion correction; (f) final left eye HMD image.

OSP image onto an origin-centered spherical or cubic projection surface (as appropriate), with the camera also located at the origin (centered inside the projection surface), using a view frustum that matches the HMD or other display hardware. For stereoscopic display, the left and right eye subimages are reprojected and rasterized independently.

It is sometimes desirable to provide the user with graphical information in the form of heads-up display (HUD) overlays or other interfaces, or to draw special avatar geometry that represents the user's wand, hand, or arm pose along with sighting lines for various picking or manipulation operations. User interfaces and 3-D augmentation geometry can be drawn and composited on top of the OSP rendering prior to display using conventional texturing and depth buffering operations. The presentation of the OSP renderings on a particular display is finalized by applying any display-specific warping or distortion correction operations, which is particularly important for commodity HMDs. Figure 24.5 shows HMD eye images in various stages of applying distortion corrections.

24.4 Equirectangular Projection Sample Code

The C source code shown in Listings 24.1 and 24.2 implements a simple equirectangular camera with optional support for antialiasing. The sample code shown here is adapted from an implementation in the Tachyon parallel ray tracing engine [Stone, 1998]. The two functions below can be used to generate a stereoscopic equirectangular OSP image in a single rendering pass, based on the caller-provided camera location, stereoscopic interocular distance (IOD), and the X and Y coordinates of the pixel in the final OSP image plane.

Listing 24.1. The cam_stereo_equirectangular_ray() function uses the caller-provided X-Y OSP image coordinate to calculate the ray direction and origin, it traces the new ray and returns the resulting color.

```
/*
 * cam_stereo_equirectangular_ray()
 * Generate an omnidirectional equirectangular camera ray, with or without
 *  modulation of stereo eye separation by latitude angle, no antialiasing
 * This camera splits the image into over/under stereoscopic viewports
 *  that contain the left eye view in the top subimage,
 *  and the right eye view in the bottom subimage.
 */
color cam_stereo_equirectangular_ray(rayType *ray, float x, float y) {
  float sin_ax, cos_ax, sin_ay, cos_ay;   /* lat-long angle sin/cos values */
  float rdx, rdy, rdz;                     /* ray direction vector components */
  float invlen;                            /* unit vector normalization factor */
  float vpx, vpy, eyeshift;                /* viewport width/height and half-IOD */
  vector eye_axial;                        /* rightward stereo eye shift direction */
  scenedef *scene = ray->scene;            /* global scene data and attributes */
  /* compute stereo subimage viewport coordinates from image coordinates, */
  /*  with two vertically stacked viewports in Y (each with height vpszy) */
  float vpszy = scene->vres * 0.5;         /* viewport is half height of full image */
  vpx = x;                                 /* X coordinate is also viewport X coord */
  if (y >= vpszy) {
    vpy = y - vpszy;                       /* left eye viewport subimage on top */
    eyeshift = -scene->camera.eyeshift;    /* shift left, by half of IOD */
  } else {
    vpy = y;                               /* right eye viewport subimage on bottom */
    eyeshift = scene->camera.eyeshift;     /* shift right, by half of IOD */
  }
```

```
/* compute mx and my, the midpoint coords of the viewport subimage */
float mx = scene->hres * 0.5f;          /* viewport spans width of full image */
float my = vpszy * 0.5f;                /* two vertically stacked viewports in Y */
/* compute lat-long radians per pixel in the resulting viewport subimage */
float radperpix_x = (3.1415926f / scene->hres) * 2.0f;
float radperpix_y = (3.1415926f / vpszy);
/* compute the lat-long angles the pixel/sample's viewport (VP) cords */
float ax = (vpx - mx) * radperpix_x;    /* X angle from mid VP, longitude */
float ay = (vpy - my) * radperpix_y;    /* Y angle from mid VP, latitude */
sincosf(ax, &sin_ax, &cos_ax);
sincosf(ay, &sin_ay, &cos_ay);
/* compute the ray direction vector components (rd[xyz]) from the */
/*   lat-long angles and orthogonal camera basis vectors */
rdx = cos_ay * (cos_ax * scene->camera.viewvec.x +
               sin_ax * scene->camera.rightvec.x) +
               sin_ay * scene->camera.upvec.x;
rdy = cos_ay * (cos_ax * scene->camera.viewvec.y +
               sin_ax * scene->camera.rightvec.y) +
               sin_ay * scene->camera.upvec.y;
rdz = cos_ay * (cos_ax * scene->camera.viewvec.z +
               sin_ax * scene->camera.rightvec.z) +
               sin_ay * scene->camera.upvec.z;
/* normalize the ray direction vector to unit length, */
/*   and set the new ray direction */
invlen = 1.0 / SQRT(rdx*rdx + rdy*rdy + rdz*rdz);
ray->dir.x = rdx * invlen;
ray->dir.y = rdy * invlen;
ray->dir.z = rdz * invlen;
/* eye_axial: cross-product of up and ray direction, a unit "right" */
/*   vector used to shift the stereoscopic eye position (ray origin) */
VCross(&scene->camera.upvec, &ray->dir, &eye_axial);
/* optionally modulate eyeshift by latitude angle to  */
/*   prevent backward-stereo when looking at the poles */
if (scene->camera.modulate_eyeshift) {
   /* modulate eyeshift by latitude angle and cosine-power scale factor */
   eyeshift *= powf(fabsf(cos_ay), scene->camera.modulate_eyeshift_pow);
}
/* shift the eye (ray origin) by the eyeshift distance */
/*   (half of the IOD) */
ray->origin.x = scene->camera.center.x + eyeshift * eye_axial.x;
ray->origin.y = scene->camera.center.y + eyeshift * eye_axial.y;
ray->origin.z = scene->camera.center.z + eyeshift * eye_axial.z;
return trace_primary_ray(ray);     /* trace ray and return shaded color */
}
```

Listing 24.2. The cam_stereo_aa_equirectangular_ray() function calls cam_stereo_equirectangular_ray() to compute an antialiased color by jittering the requested image plane locations of multiple samples, averaging them together, and returning the final color to the caller.

```
/*
 * cam_stereo_aa_equirectangular_ray()
 * Generate omnidirectional equirectangular camera ray(s),
 *  potentially incorporating antialiasing.
 * This camera splits the image into over/under stereoscopic viewports
 *  that contain the left eye view in the top subimage,
 *  and the right eye view in the bottom subimage.
 */
```

```
color cam_stereo_aa_equirectangular_ray(rayType *ray, float x, float y) {
    color col, avcol;                                /* temp color, and color accumulator */
    int alias;                                       /* antialiasing sample counter */
    scenedef *scene = ray->scene;                    /* scene handle */
    float scale;                                     /* color averaging/normalization factor */
    col=cam_stereo_equirectangular_ray(ray, x, y);   /* trace un-jittered ray */
    /* perform antialiasing if enabled. */
    /* samples are run through a very simple box filter averaging */
    /*  each of the sample pixel colors to produce a final result */
    for (alias = 1; alias <= scene->antialiasing; alias++) {
        float jxy[2];
        jitter_offset2f(&ray->randval, jxy);
        avcol=cam_stereo_equirectangular_ray(ray, x + jxy[0], y + jxy[1]);
        col.r += avcol.r;                            /* accumulate antialiasing samples */
        col.g += avcol.g;
        col.b += avcol.b;
    }
    /* average sample colors, back to range 0.0 - 1.0 */
    scale = 1.0f / (scene->antialiasing + 1.0f);
    col.r *= scale;
    col.g *= scale;
    col.b *= scale;

    return col;
}
```

The primary ray generation function in Listing 24.1 is intended to be driven by a calling routine that iterates over all of the pixels in the final image. The function makes only read-only accesses to shared scene and camera data structures during rendering, so it supports parallel ray tracing with an arbitrary number of independent worker threads.

The function in Listing 24.2 provides a simple antialiasing implementation that iteratively accumulates antialiasing samples by calling the primary ray generation routine in Listing 24.1, averaging them together with a simple box filter. This routine also operates without the need to write to shared scene or camera data structures and is also inherently parallel.

Stereoscopic rendering is provided in an over/under stereo encoded format with the left eye image into the top half of a double-high framebuffer, and the right eye into the lower half. The subsequent OpenGL drawing code can trivially unpack and draw the two images with simple pointer offset arithmetic.

The sample source code in both listings is a starting point that is intended to be easy to understand and adapt to other ray tracing frameworks. Many CPU/GPU hardware-dependent optimizations are possible but are beyond the scope of this article.

24.5 Closing Thoughts

This chapter has provided an introduction to omnidirectional stereoscopic projections and their use. While these projections do not replace conventional stereoscopic projections and rendering approaches that have no limitations on head orientation, they can be used to provide immersive experiences that can be easily displayed even on low-cost commodity hardware devices such as smartphone-based HMDs with constrained rendering power. The stereoscopic equirectangular OSP image format described here can be used to generate content for online VR video streaming with YouTube and Vimeo. Both streaming services provide tools and video content uploading procedures for equirectangular format source material. Similarly, OSPs enable offline pre-rendering of immersive content that would not be feasible to render in real time on even the world's fastest supercomputers.

Acknowledgments

This work was supported in part by the National Institutes of Health, under grant P41-GM104601.

References

[Adelson and Bergen, 1991]

Adelson, Edward H. and James R. Bergen (1991). The plenoptic function and the elements of early vision. In Landy, M. and Movshon, J. A. (eds.) *Computational Models of Visual Processing*, pp. 3–20. MIT Press, Cambridge, MA.

[Bourke, 2006]

Bourke, Paul (2006). Synthetic stereoscopic panoramic images. In Zha, H., Pan, Z., Thwaites, H., Addison, A., and Forte, M. (eds.) *Interactive Technologies and Sociotechnical Systems*. Lecture Notes in Computer Science, vol. 4270, pp. 147–155. Springer, Berlin.

[Greene, 1986]

Greene, Ned (1986). Environment mapping and other applications of world projections. *Computer Graphics and Applications, IEEE*, 6(11):21–29.

[McMillan and Bishop, 1995]

McMillan, Leonard and Gary Bishop (1995). Plenoptic modeling: An image-based rendering system. In *Proceedings of the 22nd Annual Conference on Computer Graphics and Interactive Techniques*, SIGGRAPH'95, Los Angeles, CA: ACM, pp. 39–46.

[Musgrave, 1992]

Musgrave, Kenton (1992). A panoramic virtual screen for ray tracing. In Kirk, D. (ed.) *Graphics Gems III*, Chapter VI.4, pp. 288–294. Academic Press, San Diego, CA.

[Paeth, 1990]

Paeth, Alan W. (1990). Digital cartography for computer graphics. In Glassner, A. S. (ed.) *Graphics Gems*, pp. 307–320. Academic Press, Boston, MA.

[Peleg and Ben-Ezra, 1999]

Peleg, Shmuel and Moshe Ben-Ezra (1999). Stereo panorama with a single camera. In *IEEE Computer Society Conference on Computer Vision and Pattern Recognition*, Fort Collins, CO, vol. 1, p. 401.

[Sener et al., 2014]

Sener, Melih, John E. Stone, Angela Barragan, Abhishek Singharoy, Ivan Teo, Kirby L. Vandivort, Barry Isralewitz, Bo Liu, Boon Chong Goh, James C. Phillips, Lena F. Kourkoutis, C. Neil Hunter, and Klaus Schulten (2014). Visualization of energy conversion processes in a light harvesting organelle at atomic detail. In *Proceedings of the International Conference on High Performance Computing, Networking, Storage and Analysis*, SC'14, New Orleans, LA: IEEE Press, 4 p.

[Simon et al., 2004]

Simon, Andreas, Randall C. Smith, and Richard R. Pawlicki (2004). Omnistereo for panoramic virtual environment display systems. In *IEEE Virtual Reality, 2004. Proceedings*, Chicago, IL, pp. 67–279.

[Stone, 1998]

Stone, John E. (1998). An efficient library for parallel ray tracing and animation. *Master's thesis*, Computer Science Department, University of Missouri-Rolla.

[Stone et al., 2016a]

Stone, John E., Melih Sener, Kirby L. Vandivort, Angela Barragan, Abhishek Singharoy, Ivan Teo, Joao V. Ribeiro, Barry Isralewitz, Bo Liu, Boon Chong Goh, James C. Phillips, Craig MacGregor-Chatwin, Matthew P. Johnson, Lena F. Kourkoutis, C. Neil Hunter, and Klaus Schulten (2016). Atomic detail visualization of photosynthetic membranes with GPU-accelerated ray tracing. *Parallel Computing*, 55:17–27.

[Stone et al., 2016b]

Stone, John E., William R. Sherman, and Klaus Schulten (2016). Immersive molecular visualization with omnidirectional stereoscopic ray tracing and remote rendering. In *2016 IEEE International Parallel and Distributed Processing Symposium Workshop (IPDPSW)*, Chicago, IL, pp. 1048–1057.

Volume Lenses for VR

Jason W. Woodworth and Christoph W. Borst
University of Louisiana at Lafayette

25.1 Introduction

This chapter shows how to create lens effects for 3D scenes within virtual reality (VR), with implementation examples using Unity. We start with 3D box lenses that change shading or visibility of objects inside the lens volume. We then show how the same basic rendering technique can create a window or portal-like lens. We also show how Unity's built-in VR features can be used for immersive stereoscopic lens viewing in consumer devices such as the Rift or Vive. Examples were created with Unity 5.6 (we have also successfully tested them with Unity 2018.3). The code will be comprehensible to most Unity or VR developers, and we recommend basic knowledge of shaders for Unity.

25.2 Volume and Flat Lenses in 3D

Volume lenses are 3D regions, such as boxes, that show content or use a rendering style different from the rest of a 3D scene. For example, in 1996, Viega presented an X-ray volume that revealed bones beneath skin and described both "volumetric" and "flat" lenses for 3D scenes [Viega et al. 1996]. Such effects can be considered a 3D version of earlier 2D effects like the Magic Lenses in Toolglass [Bier et al. 1993] or magnifying portals in Pad [Perlin and Fox 1993]. In our own work, we explored interactive 3D lenses in VR for scientific data exploration, for example, changing surface appearance to enhance features in a selected terrain region [Borst et al. 2010], viewing weather data from different times in subregions [Borst et al. 2011], and arranging multiple dataset views in a 3D window system [Borst et al. 2007].

The difference between flat and volume lenses in 3D is illustrated in Figure 25.1. Both types can be rendered using volume lens rendering, although additional rendering methods can be considered for flat lenses. The flat lens behaves more like what one may expect from real-world lenses, and it can be used to render effects like a portal, window, or mirror that include stereoscopic visuals. The affected region depends on the user's point of view, which is notable in VR, because the head may move or because multiple users in shared environments have different viewpoints. In contrast, volume lenses are used so that a particular region is affected regardless of viewpoint.

25.2.1 Main Rendering Concept

In this chapter, we focus on lens rendering using a conceptually simple in/out test in a shader [Borst et al. 2007]. During rendering, a fragment (pixel) can easily be tested against a box lens boundary using a coordinate range test in the box's local space, against general planes using the plane equation, against an implicit surface model such as $F(x, y, z) = x^2 + y^2 + z^2 + R^2$ for a sphere, or with Boolean and mathematical combinations of such shapes. We use this idea to implement a box volume lens and a rectangular flat lens (portal) in Unity. Some other rendering approaches are mentioned at the end of this chapter.

25.3 Unity Implementation Details

Our first implementation example is a simple box volume lens that inverts the color of fragments (pixels) inside. This lens may rotate and scale so that it can be connected to a VR wand controller, among other things. We then present an object-replacement version showing a different world inside the lens. Finally, we'll show how to use a volume lens to render a portal-like flat lens that affects all objects behind a lens from the eye's point of view. Examples here are implemented using a per-object shader approach, meaning the associated shader code will need to be placed in every shader used by affected objects. An alternative approach will be mentioned at the end of this chapter. The code will be comprehensible to Unity developers with moderate knowledge of shaders. It is recommended to read Unity's "Gentle Introduction to Shaders" before starting [Zucconi 2015].

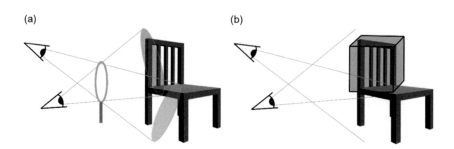

Figure 25.1

Flat lens (a) vs. Volume lens (b) in 3D.

25.3.1 Color Inversion Lens

To invert the color of fragments in a lens (demonstrated in Figure 25.2), we first test whether a fragment is inside or outside the lens. For a box lens, this is accomplished by bounds checks on each fragment in a shader. To support the checks, the fragment attributes include fragment position with respect to a lens object's local coordinate system. To provide a needed transform matrix, create a standard Unity cube and apply a script including the code in Listing 25.1 in the Update loop. This cube will be made partially transparent so viewers can see both the cube boundary and the effect inside.

Listing 25.1. Provide shaders access to the object's transformation matrix.

```
void Update() {
    // ...
    // Adding this line to Update() sets a matrix that is accessible to all shaders.
    //     The line should be added at the end of Update, if anything is done to affect
    //     the transform (movement, rotation, etc…)
    Shader.SetGlobalMatrix("_LensMat", this.transform.worldToLocalMatrix);
}
```

This code sets a global matrix accessible to any shader as a uniform variable. The matrix transforms world-referenced coordinates into the local, or "canonical," lens space, where in/out tests will be done. Doing in/out tests in this lens space supports a simple bounds check that is independent of lens position, orientation, or scale.

The in/out test will be included in any shader used by objects that you want to be considered by the lens. For this example, we will assume you are using a Unity surface shader. A later section will mention adaptation to a vertex and fragment shader.

Unity can provide the world position for each fragment. The code in Listing 25.2 applies the transform that converts to lens space. As exemplified in Listing 25.2, make sure that your surf() function input struct contains a definition for worldPos, and that the shader

Figure 25.2

An example scene in which a box volume lens inverts the color of all objects within it. The square on the floor and darker parts of the chairs indicate that they are within the lens.

declares a variable for the lens's matrix. In the surf function, multiply the world position by the lens matrix to get the desired position:

Listing 25.2. Convert current fragment's position into a lens-space position.

```
// Unity Shader
struct Input {
    // Various other parameters
    float3 worldPos; // Input world position used to calculate local position
                     //     (lens space position) in the surf() function.
}
uniform float4x4 _LensMat; // Set by setting global matrix in the lens cube object.
void surf(Input IN, inout SurfaceOutputStandard o) {
    float4 pos = float4(IN.worldPos.x, IN.worldPos.y, IN.worldPos.z, 1);
    pos = mul(_LensMat, pos);
    // Rest of shader code
        ...
}
```

The lens's bounds range from -0.5 to 0.5 in each dimension, in its local coordinate space. Thus, the in/out test only requires checking three position elements against those bounds and returning a value specifying the result (in or out), as in Listing 25.3.

Listing 25.3. Check whether a fragment is within the boundary of the lens.

```
// Unity shader (cont)
float inoutCube(float4 pos) { // pos is fragment position in lens space
    // Repeatedly check for the six bounds, return 1 if not inside
    if (pos.x < -.5 || pos.x > .5)
        return 1;
    if (pos.y < -.5 || pos.y > .5)
        return 1;
    if (pos.z < -.5 || pos.z > .5)
        return 1;
    // If all checks are passed, it is inside the lens.
    return -1;
}
```

The in/out test function returns a -1 if the fragment is found to be inside the lens. The main surf function will thus check for this and apply the desired effect (here, invert the color), as shown in Listing 25.4.

Listing 25.4. Apply an effect (in this example, invert the color) when the fragment is inside the lens.

```
// Unity shader color reverse surf() example
void surf(Input IN, inout SurfaceOutputStandard o) {
    // Adjust fragment albedo based on in/out position test
```

```
        float io = inoutCube(pos);
        if (io < 0)
            o.Albedo = float3(1,1,1) - o.Albedo;
}
```

25.3.2 Object Replacement (Visibility) Lens

Our next example makes the lens appear to replace the scene with another scene (shown in Figures 25.3 and 25.4), and is implemented by controlling visibility of objects based on in/out tests. The visibility shader will include a property that allows the developer to specify whether a material should be hidden or shown inside the lens (or outside of it). As seen in Listing 25.5, instead of inverting the albedo as before, the surf function will now clip (discard) fragments based on the in/out test.

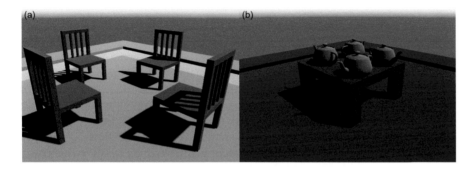

Figure 25.3

A view of the two separate worlds, the main world (a) and hidden world (b).

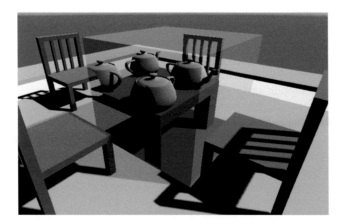

Figure 25.4

A cubic visibility lens reveals the hidden world and hides the main world. The lens boundary is shaded for emphasis.

Listing 25.5. A lens effect to reveal a hidden world. Object fragments are discarded based on their position in relation to the lens.

```
// Unity shader hidden world surf() example
// NOTE: Properties is a special Unity shader block that exposes shader values to Unity's
//   material inspector.
Properties {
    // Other properties such as color go here
    // Materials should specify if they exist in world 1 (main world), or 0 (hidden world)
    _World("World Number", int) = 1
}
void surf(Input IN, inout SurfaceOutputStandard o) {
    // Compute fragment position in lens space
    float io = inoutCube(pos);
    if (_World) // If the fragment is in the main world, discard if it's in the lens
        clip(io);  // standard clip() function: discard fragment when (io < 0)
    else // If the fragment is in the hidden world, discard if it's outside the lens
        clip(-io); // discard fragment when (io > 0)
}
```

One way to build your Unity scene in a manageable way is to create two scenes, one for each world (in/out), with each having materials using one "_World" value. The two scenes can then be loaded into the editor simultaneously to facilitate working on them together, while keeping each scene separable for working with it individually. An object in the main scene (the world that is shown outside the lens) can have a script on it to additively load the second scene on start, allowing it to work in Unity builds.

Use of a standard rendering engine such as Unity limits control of interaction between the two scenes in terms of light or shadows. So, we present a few different approaches for handling shadows. The objects in each scene can be on a per-world layer, with the culling mask of each light set up so the light only affects the desired world's layer. The initial #pragma tag in a shader can contain a parameter for specifying how Unity will handle shadows for the shaded object. Combining the standard shadow parameter, *fullforwardshadows*, with standard forward rendering will result in clipped fragments casting and receiving shadows, giving objects an undesirable "ghost" appearance. Changing to deferred rendering will cause clipped fragments to only cast shadows, which will only appear in the corresponding world when lighting is properly layered. However, Unity is known to not fully support certain features, such as partial transparency, in deferred rendering mode. If the scene must be rendered with forward rendering, the shadow parameter can be changed to *addshadow* to have clipped fragments neither receive nor cast shadows. However, depending on the application, this may be undesirable due to apparent gaps in the shadows (see Figure 25.5). A different approach to avoid light interactions, not detailed here, is to render two completely separate images for inner and outer lens content and compose the results, considering both color and depth buffers from the renders.

25.3.3 Flat Portal for 3D, or General Convex Polyhedral Lenses

To illustrate the relationship between volume lens rendering and flat lenses, and as an example of handling convex polyhedral lens shapes that can be more general, we show a portal-like flat lens implemented using general plane boundaries. As illustrated in early 3D lens work [Viega et al. 1996], a flat lens for 3D can be rendered as a 3D volume lens

Figure 25.5

Deferred rendering with fullforwardshadows (a) compared to forward rendering with add-shadow (b). Compare shadows in the two images to note the shadow gaps in the right image, e.g., under the table and the left chair.

shaped to contain exactly the part of the scene behind a 2D lens object, from the point of view of the eye (camera), and considering perspective projection. This 3D shape is analogous to a perspective view frustum, as the volume lens can be considered the frustum that would be used if we were projecting to the flat lens surface (see Figures 25.6 and 25.7). It can also be considered analogous to a shadow volume, to the extent that its sides are an extrusion of an object silhouette through the view frustum.

For a rectangular flat lens in any orientation, the corresponding 3D volume lens shape (frustum) can be represented by the five planes that bound it: one for the front face (the flat lens's plane) and one for each of its four sides. In Unity, we will represent the lens in-game with a quad that is used as the front face of the volume (frustum) shape. The other planes are calculated to pass through the quad's edges and through an eye point.

The plane equation below computes a signed distance between a point and the plane:

$$F(P) = P \cdot N + D,$$

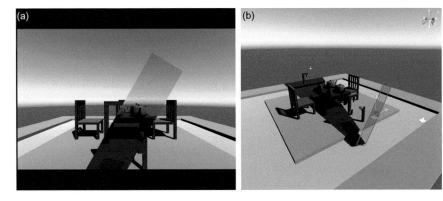

Figure 25.6

An example of our scene with the flat portal lens. To the viewing camera (a), it appears that the second world is viewable through the rectangular lens. In the scene view (b), we see that the affected volume is more of a pyramid in shape.

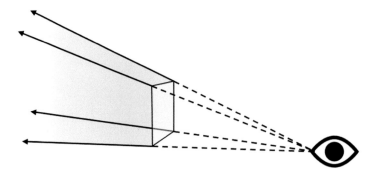

Figure 25.7

An example of a frustum defined by the viewing camera and a quad. All fragments within the bounds of the frustum behind the grey quad should be affected.

where: P is the 3D point coordinate being evaluated, N is the plane's normal (we choose the inward-facing normal), and D is precomputed as $(-P_0 \cdot N)$ where P_0 is a known point on the plane.

A lens in/out test can use this to determine on which side of the plane a fragment lies. The in/out test for a whole volume then consists of checking whether the fragment is to the inner side of every bounding plane. This approach extends to handle any convex polyhedral volume lens, although its cost can be high when there are many sides.

For simplicity of finding normals, we represent everything in the world coordinate system. We will calculate the plane normals facing the inside of the lens frustum. The front face plane uses the 2D lens quad's forward vector (negated, depending on which side of the quad the camera is on) and D is computed using the quad's world position as P_0 above. For each side plane of the frustum, the normal can be found by the cross product of two edge vectors: one between two lens corners and the other between the camera position and a corner. D can be computed using the camera position or one of these corners as P_0 above.

To ensure inward-facing normals regardless of which side the quad is viewed from, we first distinguish its back or front using the sign of the dot product between the quad's forward vector and the vector from the lens to the camera. Normals are negated depending on this sign.

All planes should be set up in a script on the portal lens (quad). In that script, a plane can be represented as a Vector4, with the first three values being the 3D normal and the fourth value being D, and all information can be passed to the shader at once. The Update loop would thus include the code from Listing 25.6.

Listing 25.6. Setup a flat-lens using 5 planes in a Unity C# script.

```
// Add to Update() function after any adjustments to transform are made.

// If we're facing the back side of the lens, we need to negate the normals.
Vector3 vectorToCamera = this.transform.position - Camera.main.transform.position;
float dot = Vector3.Dot(this.transform.forward, vectorToCamera);
```

```
int negateFactor;
if (dot < 0)
    negateFactor = -1;
else
    negateFactor = 1;

// Assign position values for the corners of the quad
Vector3 topRight = transform.TransformPoint(.5f, .5f, 0f);
Vector3 topLeft = transform.TransformPoint(-.5f, .5f, 0f);
Vector3 bottomLeft = transform.TransformPoint(-.5f, -.5f, 0f);
Vector3 bottomRight = transform.TransformPoint(.5f, -.5f, 0f);

// Compute forward normal
Vector3 forwardNormal = -transform.forward * negateFactor;
float forwardD = -Vector3.Dot(transform.position, forwardNormal);
Vector4 forwardNormalWithD = new Vector4(forwardNormal.x, forwardNormal.y,
        forwardNormal.z, forwardD);

// Compute the right plane normal
Vector3 v1 = topRight - Camera.main.transform.position;
Vector3 v2 = bottomRight - Camera.main.transform.position;
Vector3 rightNormal = Vector3.Cross(v1, v2).normalized * negateFactor;
float rightD = -Vector3.Dot(topRight, rightNormal);
Vector4 rightNormalWithD = new Vector4(rightNormal.x, rightNormal.y, rightNormal.z, rightD);

… // The setup code for other planes goes here. All other side planes can be computed
  //   similarly, just using different corners of the quad.

// Set uniform shader variables for all normals
// Note that the lens matrix is no longer needed now that we work in world space
Shader.SetGlobalVector("_ForwardNormal", forwardNormalWithD);
Shader.SetGlobalVector("_RightNormal", rightNormalWithD);
Shader.SetGlobalVector("_LeftNormal", leftNormalWithD);
Shader.SetGlobalVector("_TopNormal", topNormalWithD);
Shader.SetGlobalVector("_BottomNormal", bottomNormalWithD);
```

The surface shader can then perform a volume in/out test by checking on which side of each boundary plane the tested fragment lies, as shown in Listing 25.7.

Listing 25.7. The in/out test and fragment modifier for a flat-lens frustum.

```
// The following functions should be placed directly above the surf() function in the shader.

float distPlane(float3 fragmentWorldPos, float4 normal) {
    return dot(fragmentWorldPos, normal.xyz) + normal.w;
}
float inoutFrustum(float4 fragmentWorldPos) {
    // Repeatedly check if the fragment is behind the plane
    // Return 1 when outside and -1 when inside
    if (distPlane(pos.xyz, _RightNormal) > 0)
        return 1;
    if (distPlane(pos.xyz, _LeftNormal) > 0)
        return 1;
    if (distPlane(pos.xyz, _TopNormal) > 0)
        return 1;
```

```
    if (distPlane(pos.xyz, _BottomNormal) > 0)
        return 1;
    if (distPlane(pos.xyz, _ForwardNormal) > 0)
        return 1;
    return -1;
}
// Unity shader surf() example for hidden world revealed in frustum instead of cube
void surf(Input IN, inout SurfaceOutputStandard o) {
    float worldPos = float4(IN.worldPos, 1);
    float io = inoutFrustum(worldPos);
    if (_World)
        clip(io);
    else
        clip(-io);
}
```

When running a scene with a quad portal lens, you should see from the main camera perspective that the "hidden world" is revealed only through the quad, even when varying quad scale and rotation. This portal could be held in a tracked virtual hand to give your users an easy-to-use portal into a hidden world.

25.3.4 Stereoscopic Flat Lens Rendering

The technique above described portal rendering for a single eye. For stereoscopic rendering, which is standard in VR, there are two eyes in different positions. The region seen through flat lenses should be different for each eye (seen in Figure 25.8). So, we need to define different planes per eye.

Left and right images can be rendered using two separate rendering passes (in Unity, we use two separate cameras), changing lens planes between passes. A per-camera script can run the code to compute the normals for the camera's position. Alternatively, for emerging multi-projection features (sometimes called single-pass stereo), a shader would need to choose between two sets of planes based on which projection (eye) is being processed.

To set this up for a head-mounted VR display using Unity's built-in VR features, create two co-located cameras, parent them to a new empty GameObject representing the head, and change the "Target Eye" parameter in the Camera's inspector to Left or Right (one of

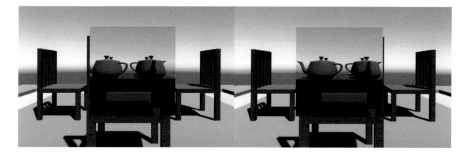

Figure 25.8

A side-by-side view for two eyes viewing the scene. Note that the lens covers slightly different parts of the scene in each eye.

each). Also check the "Virtual Reality Supported" checkbox and choose the appropriate VR SDK in Unity's Player Settings, so Unity will move and rotate these two cameras based on your tracked HMD and will render the images for their respective eyes. Also in Player Settings, set the stereo rendering method to multi-pass to allow the cameras to render separate images. Multi-pass rendering has each camera render the entire scene, then move to the next camera, while single-pass renders a single object to each camera, then moves on to the next object. Note that if you are using a premade VR rig from Oculus OVR or SteamVR, it must use two eye objects to work as above. SteamVR typically uses a single camera object.

To set up different lens planes per camera, the normals should be computed and set up for the shader in the OnPreRender function for each camera. This means the script should be placed on each camera and have a reference to the lens quad. The OnPreRender function can find the eye position and use it for normal calculation as shown in Listing 25.8.

Listing 25.8. Calculate the normals for each camera (of a stereoscopic view) for proper lens effects in VR.

```
// Place this C# script on each camera to properly calculate the normals required for
//     the lens operations in a stereoscopic view
void OnPreRender() {
    // Get the position of the appropriate eye
    if (GetComponent<Camera>().stereoTargetEye == StereoTargetEyeMask.Left)
        eyePos = XR.InputTracking.GetLocalPosition(XR.XRNode.LeftEye);
    else if (GetComponent<Camera>().stereoTargetEye == StereoTargetEyeMask.Right)
        eyePos = XR.InputTracking.GetLocalPosition(XR.XRNode.RightEye);
    // Assuming there is a parent "head" object, transform eyePos into world space
    eyePos = this.transform.parent.TransformPoint(eyePos);

    // Determine if negation is necessary, as shown in Listing 25.6
    … // (Here is where you place a dot product check as in Listing 25.6)

    // Calculate planes, making sure to use eyePos for camera position,
    //     and a reference to the lens quad for its position
    Vector3 forwardNormal = -lensQuad.forward * negateFactor;
    float forwardD = -Vector3.Dot(lensQuad.position, forwardNormal);
    Vector4 forwardNormalD = new Vector4(forwardNormal.x, forwardNormal.y,
                                         forwardNormal.z, forwardD);

    // Compute the right plane
    Vector3 v1 = topRight - eyePos;
    Vector3 v2 = bottomRight - eyePos;
    Vector3 rightNormal = Vector3.Cross(v1, v2).normalized * negateFactor;
    float rightD = -Vector3.Dot(topRight, rightNormal);
    Vector4 rightNormalD = new Vector4(rightNormal.x, rightNormal.y, rightNormal.z, rightD);

    // All other side planes should be computed similarly, and global vectors set
    //     for the shader as shown in Listing 25.6
    //     * use eyePos and lensQuad as above
    //     * the shader global vector is the same
    …
}
```

The visibility shader can remain the same, and will run with different values for each camera. The resulting script should work for standard Unity-compatible HMDs.

25.4 Other Notes

Though this chapter has given examples using Unity's surface shader, it is possible to use these techniques with standard vertex and fragment shaders. When converting the fragment position to canonical lens space, it is possible to perform the matrix multiplication in the vertex shader, with the results being interpolated by hardware into fragment values [Borst et al. 2007]. If using a polyhedral shape constructed from planes, the distance from a point to a plane can be interpolated from vertex to fragment values as well. The fragment shader should still test this in/out value to determine whether the fragment should be clipped.

Whereas this chapter primarily discusses a per-object approach (with a shader applied in each object that should be affected), a more global approach is possible. A Unity feature called Replacement Shaders [Unity 2017] allows a camera to replace the shader of every object seen with another specified shader. The replacement shader can read properties from the materials it sees, and so can still render using those values. However, they will have to be used in the same manner (e.g., same lighting applied, or some monolithic shader that handles all cases). This technique avoids per-object script requirements and allows for all checks to be done in a single shader, and the whole scene will be more easily affected. On the other hand, the per-object approach we described simplifies some per-object control, e.g., affecting objects in a room but not the walls surrounding them.

We elsewhere discuss some other rendering approaches and their tradeoffs [Borst et al. 2010]. Viega used six general clipping planes available in SGI's graphics hardware to divide the scene into seven subregions related to cube lens boundaries, each region being rendered by a separate pass [Viega et al. 1996]. Another technique uses three-pass depth peeling, essentially using two depth buffers to distinguish pixels behind the lens, inside the lens, or elsewhere [Ropinski and Hinrichs 2004]. Other approaches have considered stencil buffer techniques [Fuhrmann and Groeller 1998], ray-traced volume data rendering [Wang et al. 2005], and 3D texture-based volumetric data rendering [Plate et al. 2007]. Note that with volume lenses, unlike with flat lenses, exterior-world objects may be visible both in front of and behind ("through") a volume lens. Flat lenses have commonly been rendered with other techniques that do not apply to the more general volume lenses.

This chapter did not cover advanced 3D lens rendering concepts. For a starting pointing, interested readers can consider work such as multi-lens combinations [Borst et al. 2010, 2011, Mendez et al. 2006] or speedup techniques [Borst et al. 2010, 2011].

Acknowledgment

Part of this material is based upon work supported by the National Science Foundation under Grant No. 1451833.

References

[Bier et al. 1993]

Bier, Eric A., Maureen C. Stone, Ken Pier, William Buxton, and Tony D. DeRose, Toolglass and magic lenses: The see-through interface, *Proceedings of the SIGGRAPH,* Anaheim, CA, pp. 73–80, 1993.

[Borst et al. 2007]

Borst, Christoph W., Vijay B. Baiyya, Christopher M. Best, and Gary L. Kinsland, Volumetric windows: Application to interpretation of scientific data, shader-based rendering method, and performance evaluation, *Proceedings of CGVR*, Las Vegas, NV, pp. 72–78, CSREA, 2007.

[Borst et al. 2010]

Borst, Christoph W., Jan-Phillip Tiesel, and Christopher M. Best, Real-time rendering method and performance evaluation of composable 3D lenses for interactive VR, *IEEE Transactions on Visualization and Computer Graphics*, vol. 16, no. 3, pp. 394–410, 2010.

[Borst et al. 2011]

Borst, Christoph W., Jan-Phillip Tiesel, Emad Habib, and Kaushik Das, Single-pass composable 3D lens rendering and spatiotemporal 3D lens," *IEEE Transactions on Visualization and Computer Graphics*, vol. 17, no. 9, pp. 1259–1272, 2011.

[Fuhrmann and Groeller 1998]

Fuhrmann, Anton and Eduard Groeller, Real-time techniques for 3D flow visualization, *Proceedings of the IEEE Visualization*, NC, pp. 305–312, 1998.

[Mendez et al. 2006]

Mendez, Erick, Denis Kalkofen, and Dieter Schmalstieg, Interactive context-driven visualization tools for augmented reality, *Proceedings of ISMAR*, Santa Barbara, CA, pp. 209–218. IEEE and ACM, 2006.

[Perlin and Fox 1993]

Perlin, Ken and David Fox, Pad: An alternative approach to the computer interface, *Proceedings of the SIGGRAPH*, Anaheim, CA, pp. 57–64, 1993.

[Plate et al. 2007]

Plate, John, Thorsten Holtkaemper, and Bernd Froehlich, A flexible multi-volume shader framework for arbitrarily intersecting multi-resolution datasets, *IEEE Transactions on Visualization and Computer Graphics*, vol. 13, no. 6, pp. 1584–1591, 2007.

[Unity 2017]

Rendering with Replaced Shaders, 2017. Unity online manual, Retrieved from https://docs.unity3d.com/Manual/SL-ShaderReplacement.html

[Ropinski and Hinrichs 2004]

Ropinski, Timo and Klaus Hinrichs, Real-time rendering of 3D magic lenses having arbitrary convex shapes, *International Conference in Central Europe on Computer Graphics (WSCG)*, Bory, Czech Republic, pp. 379–386, 2004.

[Viega et al. 1996]

Viega, John, Matthew J. Conway, George Williams, and Randy Pausch, 3D magic lenses, *Proceedings of the ACM UIST*, Seattle, WA, pp. 51–58, 1996.

[Wang et al. 2005]

Wang, Lujin, Ye Zhao, Klaus Mueller, and Arie Kaufman, The magic volume lens: An interactive focus+context technique for volume rendering, *Proceedings of the IEEE Visualization*, Minneapolis, MN, pp. 367–374, 2005.

[Zucconi 2015]

Zucconi, Alan, A gentle introduction to shaders, *Unity online tutorials* Retrieved from 2015. https://unity3d.com/learn/tutorials/topics/graphics/gentle-introduction-shaders, 6/10/2015.

SECTION VIII
Perception for Immersion

26

Check Your Work

Evaluating VE Effectiveness Using Presence

Richard Skarbez
La Trobe University

Mary C. Whitton
University of North Carolina at Chapel Hill

A virtual reality (VR) application may target any of a variety of domains, from architectural walkthroughs to psychological therapy. Regardless of the specific application domain, however, there may be a need to evaluate the effectiveness of the virtual experience. In some cases, this evaluation may involve objective measurements, such as user performance on a standard test following training in virtual reality. In many cases, though, evaluating the general, overall effectiveness of a virtual reality application will involve measuring one or more subjective constructs. The most commonly encountered such construct is *presence*.

Presence, commonly defined as a user's sense of "being there" in a virtual environment, has been studied in conjunction with computer-mediated environments since at least 1983 when Akin and colleagues defined the term *telepresence*. Perhaps the main reason for the continuing interest in the presence construct is that it is applicable to a wide range of virtual experiences. This is desirable for several reasons: first, to the extent of its generalizability, it is not necessary to develop a new measure specifically to evaluate each individual VE, and second, it enables comparisons between different VEs.

That said, presence is not the only dimension of user experience in virtual reality, and it may not be the best measure for all applications. As discussed later in this chapter, we believe that presence can be decomposed into Place Illusion, Plausibility Illusion, and Social Presence Illusion, and that, depending on your application, these subcomponents may be more relevant than an overall sense of presence. Other constructs that may be useful for evaluating a virtual experience include immersion and coherence (discussed later in this chapter), involvement/engagement [McQuarrie and Munson, 1992], and flow [Csikszentmihalyi, 1990].

26.1 Presence and Related Constructs

Presence is most commonly defined as the sense of "being there" in a virtual space. Presence is inherently subjective and internal (philosophers call such feelings *qualia*); this subjective and internal nature makes the measurement of presence very difficult. The following sections will talk more about the measurement of presence, setting out several broad categories of presence measures as well as pointing out several specific ones, along with best practices for their use. The remainder of this section, however, focuses on the definition of presence and some related terms, as well some thoughts regarding what the structure of presence might be. A more extensive treatment of the various ways presence is defined and measured can be found in [Skarbez et al., 2017a]. (If you're not interested in presence theory, feel free to skip to the next section, but we'll try to keep it brief.)

First, we discuss the constructs of *Place Illusion* and *Plausibility Illusion*. As the introduction suggests, over the 30+ years that the term *presence* has been associated with mediated and virtual environments, many researchers and developers have proposed their own definitions of it. This has resulted in the term presence being both used widely and used with different meanings. To address the latter problem, Mel Slater proposed that we focus on two constructs, Place Illusion and Plausibility Illusion, rather than on presence. *Place Illusion* corresponds to the definition of presence as "being there"; specifically, Slater defines it as "the... illusion of being in a place in spite of the sure knowledge that you are not there." *Plausibility Illusion* is a new introduction to the literature, which Slater defines as, "the illusion that what is apparently happening is really happening (even though you know for sure that it is not)" [Slater, 2009].

Place Illusion and Plausibility Illusion, then, are also qualia—subjective and internal sensations. But it is sometimes helpful to think about the objective characteristics of the virtual experience that enable Place Illusion and Plausibility Illusion to occur. To that end, we define the terms *immersion* and *coherence*.

Immersion is another term that has multiple definitions in the literature. We follow Slater in considering immersion an objective characteristic of a VE system. Specifically, we define *immersion* as the set of valid actions supported by a VE, and we define a *valid action* as any physical action a user can take that changes the state of the environment or their perception of it. For example, a head-tracked VE system is more immersive than a non-head-tracked system because the action of turning or moving your head results in a change to your viewpoint in the VE. The immersion of a VE constrains a user's Place Illusion, but it does not determine it. Place Illusion also depends on how a user interacts with the VE—if you don't move your head at all, it doesn't matter whether your display is head-tracked—as well as on the user's traits (relatively permanent characteristics, such as their innate tendency to experience Place Illusion) and state (their temporary characteristics, such as whether or not they are distracted at the time). That is, Place Illusion is a function of immersion and individual characteristics.

We have defined the term *coherence* to be to Plausibility Illusion as immersion is to Place Illusion—an objective characteristic of the virtual experience that constrains a user's Plausibility Illusion. Specifically, we define *coherence* as the set of reasonable circumstances supported by a VE, and a *reasonable circumstance* as a state of affairs that is self-evident given prior knowledge. For example, if you've been led to believe that a VE represents the "real world," a version of that VE where people walk on the ground would be more coherent than one where they float through the air. Again, Plausibility Illusion is a function of coherence as well as individual differences.

Another important concept is *social presence*. Once again, there are varying and conflicting definitions in the literature, but we follow Biocca in defining *social presence* as the awareness of the copresence of another sentient being combined with a sense of engagement with that being, and *copresence* as the sense of being with an *other* in the same space. In other words, social presence is the sense of engaging with another intelligence who is in the space with you. We argue for the use of the term *Social Presence Illusion* instead of social presence, to avoid the ambiguity associated with the terms presence and social presence. Social Presence Illusion arises from the existence of another seemingly sentient being in the space (we call this *company*), the coherence of that being's behavior, and the traits and state of the user.

Given that there is now the term Place Illusion to refer to the sense of "being there," the general term presence can be redefined to match its meaning in common practice. Many practitioners already use the term presence loosely to mean the overall "goodness" of a virtual experience. We therefore propose a redefinition of the term presence to mean the perceived realness of a mediated or virtual experience.

The relationships between the concepts discussed in this section are shown in Figure 26.1.

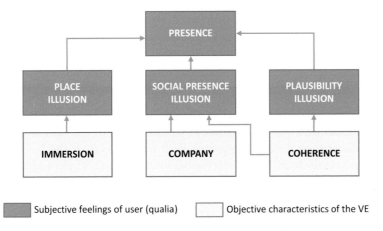

Figure 26.1

Proposed relationships between presence and related constructs.

26.2 Measuring Presence

The literature on virtual environments reports many methods for evaluating the quality of the user's experiences—that is, the level of presence the user experiences. Some measures are subjective responses from the users, some are objective readings from sensors (physiological or otherwise), and some are based on experimenters' observations. We present a short primer on measures and then discuss the most frequently used measures.

26.2.1 Characteristics of a good measure

The sub-discipline of psychology called *psychometrics* teaches that for results from any measure to be credible, the measure must be *valid*, *reliable*, *objective* and *sensitive* [Lipsey and Hurley, 2009; Singleton and Straits, 2009].

- *Validity* means that the measure in fact measures what it says it is measuring. Validity is often demonstrated by showing a strong correlation between results from a new measure and results from an existing measure that is known to be valid.
- *Reliability* means that the results of the measure are stable and consistent over time. Reliability is demonstrated by repeating the stimulus and measure after a period of time and showing strong correlation between the sets of results.
- *Objectivity* means that the measure is free from bias resulting from the participant's or the experimenter's thoughts and feelings while completing or scoring the measure.
- *Sensitivity* concerns whether the reported measure can distinguish between multiple levels of the factor being measured.

Another factor important for evaluating VEs is how *contemporaneous* measurement taking is with the VE experience, i.e., is the measurement made during the experience or sometime later. When we take measures after the VE experience, we are asking users to remember and accurately report how they felt during the experience. The possibility of faulty or uncertain memory after even a short time can confound results, so best practices suggest that measures be made during or as soon after the VE experience as possible. Another concern is that by taking only a single measurement after the fact, we are unable to measure any variations in presence that occurred over the course of the experience.

Unfortunately, the desire for a contemporaneous measure can conflict with the desire for a measurement technique that does not induce *breaks in presence* [Slater and Steed, 2000]. If, for example, a measure requires a user to wear additional hardware, or to adjust a dial to indicate their feeling of presence, such intrusions from the "real world" may confound your results by artificially decreasing the very construct you set out to measure.

Another desirable measurement characteristic is that collecting the measure does not require modifying the virtual experience. Post-experiment questionnaires, for example, can be administered after any virtual experience without changing the experience. On the other hand, physiological metrics have generally been validated only for VEs that are known to induce stress. If you want to evaluate a non-stress-causing VE, you either need to artificially add stress-inducing content, or find another measure.

Table 26.1 Pros and Cons of Measure Types

Type of Measure	Pros (+)	Cons (−)
Questionnaires	• There are several well accepted presence questionnaires • Easy to administer and score	• Subjective, self-report • Cannot measure concepts about which there are no questions • Administered post-experience
Behavioral	• Contemporaneous • Minimal interference with experience • Objective, within limits of rubric and human observers	• Requires scoring rubric • May require multiple trained observers (unless scored algorithmically) • May be difficult to judge subtle behaviors
Physiological	• Contemporaneous • Objective • Demonstrated correlation of change in heart rate with SUS questionnaire results [Meehan et al., 2002]	• Requires gathering base-line data • Few stimuli evoke useful levels of signal change • Equipment can encumber user • Lag time between stimulus and change in measure
Psychophysical	• Combines subjective and objective; results come directly from contemporaneously reported user preferences for varying levels of stimuli	• Requires the ability to modify the physical stimulus level during testing • Ranks multiple experiences or implementations, rather than yielding a single "score"
Interviews	• Users will tell you things about the system and experience you never thought to ask about	• Possible interviewer and scorer bias • Analysis may require multiple scorers • Cost of recording and transcription

26.2.2 Kinds of Measures

Measures used to judge how well a VE evokes the feeling of being present in the virtual scenario include presence questionnaires, observations of behavior, physiological data, psychophysical analyses, and interviews. Each type of measure has strengths and weaknesses (see Table 26.1).

Because there is no psychometrically perfect, completely objective, and generalizable measure of VE quality, we recommend you, if possible, use multiple measures of presence. If all of your results point toward the same interpretation, you can have increased confidence in the validity of your conclusions. This multiple measure technique, very common in qualitative research in the social sciences, is called *triangulation*.

26.3 Questionnaires

Questionnaires are the dominant type of measure in which users self-report their level of feelings of presence. They are typically administered immediately after the user experiences the VE and are scored on one scale or on several sub-scales as defined by the questionnaire developers. The questions most often require a rating, ranking, or a Likert-type response. Experimenters often supplement formal questionnaire data with user responses to experimenter-developed questions. These supplemental questions are often specific to the VE experience and can be open-ended to elicit longer and richer responses from users.

Table 26.2 Some Widely Used Questionnaires

Questionnaire	# items	Subscales	Intended Use
SUS	6	No separate subscales	Virtual environments
WS PQ	19+	Control; Sensory; Distraction; Realism	Virtual environments
ITC-SOPI	44	Sense of Physical Space; Engagement; Naturalness; Negative Effects	Cross-media
SSQ	16	Nausea; Oculomotor; Disorientation	Simulators (also often used in virtual environments)

We next describe several of the most widely used questionnaires and summarize information about them in Table 26.2.

26.3.1 Slater-Usoh-Steed (SUS) Presence Questionnaire

The SUS questionnaire asks specific questions about "being there", so it directly measures the level of *Place Illusion* (see Section 26.1) experienced by the user. The SUS is short and easily administered orally, online, or with pencil and paper. It allows some tuning of the questions for a specific virtual environment, e.g., the generic question "How present did you feel in the virtual place?" can be customized to "How present did you feel in the elevator?" [Usoh et al., 2000].

Be careful with statistical analysis of Likert-type data. Responses to the SUS questions are chosen from Likert-type scales, where values typically range from 1 to 7. A problem that is inherent to analysis of Likert-type data is that they are ordinal, not interval. (In other words, we don't know whether the distance between 2 and 3 is the same distance as between 4 and 5; all the values represent is an ordering.) It is not good practice to use statistics such as the mean as it cannot be meaningfully computed for ordinal data. A more appropriate way to summarize such data is convert the response for each question to a binary value (say, responses of 6 or 7 are counted at HIGH, and all other scores are not), and then for each individual, the total count of HIGH scores is their SUS score. Note that this same method can be used for other questionnaires with Likert-type responses; it is not only for the SUS questionnaire.

26.3.2 Witmer-Singer Presence Questionnaire (WS PQ)

The WS PQ generates an overall score as well as four subscale scores reflecting a model of Presence having four factors: users' ability to *control* events in the environment; the extent and quality of *sensory* information; the degree to which the system enables the user to avoid *distraction*; and the consistency, meaningfulness, and *realism* of the virtual stimuli. Each of the 19 questions with demonstrated reliability in the questionnaire addresses an aspect of one of these four factors [Witmer et al., 2005].

Don't arbitrarily subset questionnaires. If you're going to use a questionnaire, use the whole thing (or at least entire subscales). While it may be tempting to use a subset of an entire questionnaire if you're interested in how well your VE performs in a specific area, e.g., realism, this is a mistake: There is no guarantee that the subset of questions has the same validity and reliability as the entire questionnaire, so you should give less credence to those results when developing your conclusions. Furthermore, your results can no longer be meaningfully compared with other evaluations that used the same questionnaire.

There's no free lunch. When you choose a questionnaire, pay attention to what is in it, as well as what isn't: you can only get out of a questionnaire information about concepts that are covered in the questions. The Witmer-Singer PQ has a subscale devoted to attention and distraction factors. As a result, subjecting questionnaire responses to additional analysis, such as a factor analysis, is likely to reveal that attention is an important and distinguishable component of presence. On the other hand, the WS PQ does not have any questions relating to Social Presence Illusion or factors contributing to it. So even if the social aspects of a VE are very important to the overall experience, that will not be apparent in your analysis if you've used the WS PQ as your only measure.

26.3.3 ITC Sense of Presence Inventory (ITC-SOPI)

The ITC-SOPI was developed by researchers supported by the UK's Independent Television Commission (ITC) with the intention of being applicable across a range of media—not only immersive virtual environments, but also television, computer games, and more. Therefore, there are no questions that ask specifically about properties of the system or of the content. The questionnaire was not designed with subscales in mind, but a subsequent factor analysis revealed four factors: sense of physical space, engagement, naturalness, and negative effects [Lessiter et al., 2001].

26.3.4 Simulator Sickness Questionnaire (SSQ)

Simulator sickness is the name given to undesirable side effects of a VE experience such as nausea, dizziness, and eye fatigue. The Simulator Sickness Questionnaire has long been the standard for quantifying the severity of these side effects [Kennedy et al., 1993]. The rule of thumb is that the higher the SSQ score, the lower the presence. A high SSQ score across a group of users typically implies one or more problems in the VE system. The SSQ subscale scores can help developers target their efforts to improve the system and reduce the incidence of simulator sickness.

26.4 Other Measures

26.4.1 Behavioral Measures

Theory says that if users are sufficiently present in the VE, they will "react as if real" [Slater, 2009]. Behaviors can be physical movements: Some are large enough to be seen and categorized by observers/raters, e.g., ducking to avoid a limb while riding a bicycle in a VE. Other movements are subtle, such as how users move their heads when trying to locate the source of a sound, and are best captured in signals from sensors.

Behaviors are also important when evaluating the quality of the *Social Presence Illusion*. Observers can score body language and the content and tone (e.g., friendly, condescending, angry) of verbal interactions between users and virtual humans/intelligent entities. Sensors, e.g., head and eye trackers, can capture data for coding and analysis of behaviors such as eye contact between real and virtual humans.

Use multiple observers. In order to avoid introducing bias, always use multiple observers/raters for behavioral observations, whether they score during live sessions or from video. The experimenters and observers should develop a scoring rubric and then the observers should train using it until their ratings match most of the time.

Define algorithmic measures. In some instances, it may be possible to derive behavioral measures from recorded sensor data. This can reduce or eliminate the reliance on human raters. For example, if users' positions in the virtual environment are logged and time-stamped, it is possible to determine the amount of time a user spent in a given virtual room via direct analysis of the logs.

Log, log, log. Today, disk space is plentiful and cheap, but gathering experimental data remains time-consuming, for both experimenters and participants. Especially in light of the previous paragraph, one should record as much data as can be readily gathered. It is generally difficult or impossible to gather additional data for a given participant after the fact. It is better to have it and not need it, than to need it and not have it.

26.4.2 Physiological Measures

Physiological measures were one of the first contemporaneous, objective correlates of presence that was developed [Meehan et al., 2002]. The physiological responses most often measured are heart rate, skin temperature, and galvanic skin response (GSR) (also known as skin conductance response or electrodermal activity). Users put in a stressful situation, e.g., crossing a ravine on a worn-out bridge, exhibit changes in each of these signals—heart rate and GSR increase (your heart beats faster and your palms sweat), while skin temperature decreases at the extremities.

In the general population, there is wide variation in the baseline values of these three factors, so the signals' *change from baseline* is the data preferred for analysis. Baseline measures should be taken over about 3 min while users are in the VE, but before exposing the user to the high-stress environment. Change in heart rate has proven the most useful in our work.

Choose measures and sensors carefully. Skin temperature changes slowly, and thus requires longer VE exposures both to gather baseline and to gather data in the target VE. Users should be encumbered as little as possible by physiological monitoring equipment and the sensors should mount firmly to the user to accommodate user motion when in the VE. For example, our older GSR sensors did not mount securely to fingers, so data collection was unreliable.

Ethical treatment of users. Be sensitive to issues of privacy and gender if, for instance, EEG sensors must be placed on a user's torso. This is one example of a broader topic of ethical treatment of users. Find out whether you need approval from your local ethics board (in the United States, the Institutional Review Board) to carry out VE experience evaluations. Apply for and get that approval if it is needed. The board review will insure that you follow required guidelines that protect your users, you, and your institution.

26.4.3 Psychophysical Measures

Often used to determine at what level a stimulus becomes noticeable, psychophysics is the study of the relationship between physical stimuli and individuals' perceptions of those stimuli. The physical stimuli are objectively described; the users' reports are subjective. For example, psychophysical techniques have been used to investigate how low VE system latency must be before the user does not notice it.

More recently, psychophysical techniques have been used to evaluate factors that contribute to Place Illusion and Plausibility Illusion in virtual experiences [Slater et al., 2010; Bergström et al., 2017; Skarbez et al., 2017b]. In such studies, users are exposed to a high-quality VE and instructed to remember, for example, "how real it feels." They are then placed in a lower-quality VE and given the option to improve various objective aspects of the VE (such as illumination quality or field of view) until it feels "as real" as the experience they were asked to remember. The order in which aspects are upgraded is recorded. This method results in an objective ranking of which VE factors are most important to users' subjective experiences.

Consider how you choose and present your physical stimuli. Make sure that within each category, you can at least argue a priori for an ordering of the "steps" from best to worst. This is easy for some factors (usually immersion), like field of view, but complicated for others (usually coherence), such as virtual body quality. Similarly, try to make sure that the steps are roughly equal in the amount of perceived improvement between categories.

26.4.4 Interviews

Post-experience interviews are almost always an illuminating addition to other measures of VE effectiveness. Users are often eager to tell you what they think about your VE—good and bad. What experimenters look for in their analysis of interview data are things that are complete surprises and things, expected or unexpected, that are mentioned by multiple users. Data from interviews is often used to support and explain results from other measures, helping triangulate overall conclusions.

Interviews can be *structured* or *semi-structured*. While structured interviews, interviews asking each user the same set of questions, can be administered online, unless they allow open-ended responses they do not encourage respondents to elaborate on and explain their responses. We believe a face-to-face *semi-structured* interview is superior. In such an interview, the interviewer has a set of questions to cover with each interviewee, but can also ask follow-up questions and follow threads and ideas introduced by the user to elicit as much information as possible.

Getting the most from your interviews. There are commercial content analysis tools that help identify themes that emerge in the interviews. Recording and transcribing interviews allows you to revisit all interviews once the themes emerge and to quote interesting remarks precisely.

26.5 Conclusion

In this chapter we have discussed methods and best practices for evaluating virtual environments, focusing on the presence construct and the various ways it is measured. While there are a variety of constructs that one can measure, and a variety of ways that one can choose to measure each construct, we believe that there are some general principles that apply regardless of what you seek to measure.

First, **put some thought into your choice of constructs.** We have focused primarily on presence in this chapter, but presence is not the only or necessarily the best construct for evaluating every virtual experience.

Second, **put some thought into your choice of measures.** Even within a category of measure, not all measures are created equal. Questionnaires may address different subscales, or physiological measures may have different physical characteristics. Choose measures that suit your application.

Finally, if possible, **use multiple measures for the construct that you care about.** No single measure is perfect, and we have discussed some of the pros and cons associated with different types of measures in Table 26.1. But if you collect multiple measures and they all indicate the same thing, you can report your results with much greater confidence.

This chapter has by no means provided an exhaustive discussion of how to evaluate users' experiences of virtual environments. But we hope that we have provided some illumination and some helpful suggestions on how you might do so in the event that you do, at some point, need to make sure that your VE is actually doing what you want it to do.

References

[Bergström et al., 2017]

Bergström, Ilias, Sérgio Azevedo, Panos Papiotis, Nuno Saldanha, and Mel Slater (2017). The plausibility of a string quartet performance in virtual reality. *IEEE Transactions on Visualization and Computer Graphics*, 23(4):1352–1359.

[Csikszentmihalyi, 1990]

Csikszentmihalyi, Mihaly (1990). *Flow: The psychology of optimal experience.* Harper and Row, New York.

[Kennedy et al., 1993]

Kennedy, Robert S., Norman E. Lane, Kevin S. Berbaum, and Michael G. Lilienthal (1993). Simulator sickness questionnaire: An enhanced method for quantifying simulator sickness. *The International Journal of Aviation Psychology*, 3(3):203–220.

[Lessiter et al., 2001]

Lessiter, Jane, Jonathan Freeman, Edmund Keogh, and Jules Davidoff (2001). A cross-media presence questionnaire: The ITC-sense of presence inventory. *Presence: Teleoperators and Virtual Environments*, 10:282–297.

[Lipsey and Hurley, 2009]

Lipsey, Mark W. and Sean M. Hurley (2009). Design sensitivity: Statistical power for applied experimental research. In Bickman, L. and Rog, D. J., eds., *The SAGE Handbook of Applied Social Research Methods*, 2nd edition, chapter 2, pp. 44–76. SAGE Publications, Inc., Thousand Oaks, CA.

[McQuarrie and Munson, 1992]

McQuarrie, Edward F. and J. Michael Munson (1992). A revised product involvement inventory: Improved usability and validity. *NA—Advances in Consumer Research*, 19:108–115.

[Meehan et al., 2002]

Meehan, Michael, Brent Insko, Mary Whitton, and Frederick P. Brooks Jr. (2002). Physiological measures of presence in stressful virtual environments. In *Proceedings of the 29th Annual Conference on Computer Graphics and Interactive Techniques*, SIGGRAPH '02, pp. 645–652. ACM, New York.

[Singleton and Straits, 2009]

Singleton Jr., Royce A. and Bruce C. Straits (2009). Measurement. In *Approaches to Social Research*, 5th edition, chapter 5. Oxford University Press, New York.

[Skarbez et al., 2017a]

Skarbez, Richard, Frederick P. Brooks Jr., and Mary C. Whitton (2017). A survey of presence and related concepts. *ACM Computing Surveys*, 50(6):1–39.

[Skarbez et al., 2017b]

Skarbez, Richard, Solene Neyret, Frederick P. Brooks Jr., Mel Slater, and Mary C. Whitton (2017). A psychophysical experiment regarding components of the plausibility illusion. *IEEE Transactions on Visualization and Computer Graphics*, 23(4):1369–1378.

[Slater, 2009]

Slater, Mel (2009). Place illusion and plausibility can lead to realistic behavior in immersive virtual environments. *Philosophical Transactions of the Royal Society of London. Series B, Biological sciences*, 364:3549–3557.

[Slater and Steed, 2000]

Slater, Mel and Anthony Steed (2000). A virtual presence counter. *Presence: Teleoperators and Virtual Environments*, 9:413–434.

[Slater et al., 2010]

Slater, Mel, Bernhard Spanlang and David Corominas (2010). Simulating virtual environments within virtual environments as the basis for a psychophysics of presence. *ACM Transactions on Graphics*, 29: 92: 1–92:9.

[Usoh et al., 2000]

Usoh, Martin, Ernest Catena, Sima Arman, and Mel Slater (2000). Using presence questionnaires in reality. *Presence: Teleoperators and Virtual Environments*, 9:497–503.

[Witmer et al., 2005]

Witmer, Bob G., Christian J. Jerome, and Michael J. Singer (2005). The factor structure of the presence questionnaire. *Presence: Teleoperators and Virtual Environments*, 14(3):298–312.

27

Misperception of Self-motion and Its Compensation in Virtual Reality

Frank Steinicke
University of Hamburg

One major benefit of wearable computers is that users can naturally move and explore computer-mediated realities. Walking through the real world is one of the most fundamental processes of humans, and its consideration in immersive virtual environments (IVEs—aka "virtual reality") is of major importance for many application domains, such as those requiring immersive walkthroughs. However, previous research shows that the user egocentric perception of space and motion severely differs in these environments compared with the real world—an effect often attributed to slight discrepancies in sensory cues, perhaps caused by tracking inaccuracy or system latency.

From a simple physics perspective, walking or more general self-motions can be defined by the three components (i) speed, (ii) distance, and (iii) time. Determining motions in the frame of reference of a human observer imposes a significant challenge to the perceptual processes in the human brain, and the resulting speed, distance, and time percepts are not always accurate (as illustrated in Figure 27.1). In previous VR research these components have been evaluated in different experiments, i. e., using largely different hardware, software and protocols. However, experiments show that in many situations these components are significantly misperceived. In particular, users largely underestimate virtual distances and slightly underestimate virtual speed while moving through the IVE. Using visual illusions and manipulations of certain rendering parameters can improve the perception of the motion components.

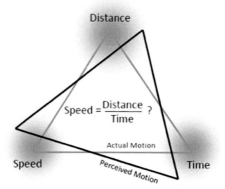

Figure 27.1

Illustration of the mathematically well-defined components of motion (the speed triangle) with the interrelations between actual and perceived motion speed, distances and time. The question remains whether this relation is also valid from a perceptual point of view.

In this chapter we explore the perception of the three components of self-motion during immersive walkthroughs, and how they can be altered using simple illusions.

27.1 Introduction

The motion of an observer or scene object in the real world or in a virtual world (VW) is of great interest to many research and application fields. This includes computer-generated imagery, e. g., in movies or games, in which a sequence of individual images evoke the illusion of a moving picture [Thompson et al., 2011]. In the real world, humans may move by walking or running, physical objects move and sometimes actuate each other, and, finally, the earth spins around itself as well as around the sun. From a simple physics perspective, such motions can be defined by three main components: (i) (linear or angular) speed and (ii) distances (or revolutions), as well as (iii) time. The interrelation between these components is given by the speed of motion, which is defined as the change in position (location) or orientation of an object with respect to time:

$$s = d/t \qquad (27.1)$$

with speed s, distance d, and time t. Motion can be observed by attaching a frame of reference to an object and measuring its change relative to another reference frame.

As there is no absolute frame of reference, absolute motion cannot be determined; everything in the universe can be considered to be moving [Bottema and Roth, 2012]. Determining motions in the frame of reference of a human observer imposes a significant challenge to the perceptual processes in the human brain, and the resulting percepts of motions are not always accurate [Berthoz, 2000]. Misperception of speed, distances, and time has been observed for different forms of self-motion in the real world [Efron, 1970,

Gibb et al., 2010; Mao et al., 2010]. This raises the question whether the mathematically well-defined components of motion (illustrated in Figure 27.1) and their interrelations are also valid from a perceptual point of view.

In the context of self-motion, walking is often regarded as the most basic and intuitive form of locomotion within an environment. Self-motion estimates from walking are often found to be more accurate than for other forms of motion [Ruddle and Lessels, 2009]. This may be explained by adaptation and training due to early childhood and evolutionary tuning of the human brain to the physical affordances for locomotion of the body [Choi and Bastian, 2007]. While walking in the real world, sensory information such as vestibular, proprioceptive, and efferent copy signals* as well as visual and auditory information creates consistent multi-sensory cues that indicate one's own motion [Wertheim, 1994]. However, a large body of research has shown that spatial perception in IVEs differs from the real world. Empirical data shows that static and walked distances are often systematically over- or underestimated in IVEs (cf. [Loomis and Knapp, 2003] and [Renner et al., 2013] for thorough reviews) even when the displayed world is modeled as an exact replica of the real laboratory in which the experiments are conducted [Interrante et al., 2006].

Less empirical data exists on speed misperception in IVEs, the available data suggests a tendency for underestimating visual speed during walking [Banton et al., 2005; Bruder et al., 2012a; Steinicke et al., 2010b; Durgin et al., 2005b]. There is evidence that time perception can deviate from accurate judgments due to visual or auditive stimulation related to motion misperception [Grondin, 2008; Roussel et al., 2009; Sarrazin et al., 2004]. Different causes of motion misperception in IVEs have been identified, including hardware characteristics [Jones et al., 2012; Willemsen et al., 2009], rendering issues [Thompson et al., 2011], and miscalibration [Kuhl et al., 2009; Willemsen et al., 2008].

As discussed, for distance and speed perception in IVEs, over- or underestimations have been well documented by researchers in different hardware, software and experimental protocols. In contrast, perception of time has not been extensively researched in IVEs thus far. The only empirical experiment in the area of time perception in IVEs has been conducted by Schatzschneider et al. [2016]. They found some environmental cues such as the movement of the sun can be artificially manipulated in VR, and thus have the potential to change the perception of time.

Remarkably, only Bruder et al. [2014] have compared self-motion estimation in the three components distance, speed, and time using the same setup and a similar action-based two-alternative forced-choice experimental design. Their experiments in an Oculus Rift HMD DK 2 showed that participants largely underestimated virtual distances, slightly underestimated virtual speed, and slightly overestimated elapsed time.

To summarize, several research efforts have shown that the user perception of self-motion severely differs in IVEs compared to the real world. A challenging question is whether and how such misperceptions can be compensated.

The main contributions of this chapter are:

- a summary of results in self-motion perception of speed, distances, and time in IVEs, and
- approaches to compensate the often-observed misperceptions of self-motion.

---

* An efference copy is an internal copy of a movement-producing signal generated by the motor

27.2 Self-motion Perception and Misperception

27.2.1 Distance Perception

During self-motion in IVEs, different cues provide information about the travel distance with respect to the motion speed or time [Mohler, 2007]. Humans can use these cues to keep track of distance traveled, the remaining distance to a goal, or discriminate travel distance intervals [Bremmer and Lappe, 1999]. Although humans are considerably good at making distance judgments in the real world, experiments in IVEs show that characteristic estimation errors occur such that distances are often severely overestimated for very short distances and underestimated for longer distances [Loomis et al., 1993]. However, current developments in the area of gaze-contingent and adaptive focus displays have slightly improved the situation, but misperception still occurs [Padmanaban et al., 2017].

Different misperception effects were found over a large range of IVEs and experimental methods to measure distance estimation. While verbal estimates of the distance to a target can be used to assess distance perception, methods based on visually directed actions have been found to generally provide more accurate results [Loomis and Knapp, 2003]. The most widely used action-based method is *blind walking*, in which subjects are asked to walk without vision to a previously seen target. Several experiments have shown that over medium range distances subjects can accurately indicate distances using the blind walking method [Rieser et al., 1990]. Other action-based methods include *triangulated walking* and *timed imagined walking* [Fukusima et al., 1997; Klein et al., 2009; Plumert et al., 2004]. Moreover, perceptual matching methods can be used, in which subjects match the distance or size of a target to the distance or size of a reference object, respectively [Loomis and Philbeck, 2008].

Although there is a large interest in solving the distance misperception problem, the reasons for this perceptual shift are still largely unknown, as are approaches to reduce such misperceptions. Kuhl et al. [2009] observed that miscalibration of HMD optics is a main reason for distance misperception, although subjects underestimated distances even for correctly calibrated HMDs [Kellner et al., 2012]. Willemsen et al. [2009] compared HMD properties with natural viewing in the real world and observed that mechanical restrictions of HMDs can cause slight differences in distance judgments. Jones et al. [2011, 2012] found that increasing the field of view of HMDs to approximate the visual angle of the human eyes helps alleviate distance misperception. Interrante et al. [2006] showed that the VE has an impact on distance judgments with underestimation being reduced if subjects are immersed in an accurate virtual replica of the real-world surroundings than in a hypothetical VE. Studies by Phillips et al. [2009] further showed that the visual rendering style affects distance judgments. They observed that distance underestimation was increased for a non-photorealistic rendering style than in a photorealistic (verisimilar) scene.

27.2.2 Speed Perception

Different sensory motion cues support the perception of the speed of walking in an IVE (cf. [Durgin et al., 2005a]). Visual motion information is often estimated as most reliable by the perceptual system, but can cause incorrect motion percepts. For example, in the illusion of linear vection [Berthoz, 2000] observers feel their body moving although they are physically stationary because they are presented with large-field visual motion that resembles the motion pattern normally experienced during self-motion. Humans use such optic flow patterns to determine their speed of movement, although the speed of retinal motion signals is not uniquely related to movement speed. Any translational motion from the visual velocity of any point in the scene depends on the distance of the point from the eye, i. e., points farther away move slower over the retina than points closer to the eye [Bremmer and Lappe, 1999; Warren, 1998]. Banton et al. [2005] observed for subjects walking on a treadmill with an HMD that optic flow fields at the speed of the treadmill were estimated as approximately 53% slower than their walking speed. Durgin et al. [2005a] reported on a series of experiments with subjects wearing HMDs while walking on a treadmill or over solid ground. Their results show that subjects often estimated subtracted speeds of displayed optic flow fields as matching their walking speed. Steinicke et al. [2010b] evaluated speed estimation of subjects in an HMD environment with a real walking user interface in which they manipulated subjects' self-motion speed in the VE compared to their walking speed in the real world. Their results show that on average subjects underestimated their walking speed by approximately 7%. Bruder et al. [2012b,2013] showed that visual illusions related to optic flow perception can change self-motion speed estimates in IVEs.

27.2.3 Time Perception

Although human temporal perception in IVEs is a relatively unexplored area, there has been some research exploring time perception in VEs. For instance, it has been shown that immersing chemotherapy patients in IVEs can reduce their perceived duration of certain treatments [Schneider et al., 2011]. Furthermore, experimental studies of time perception in the field of psychology have well established that estimates of stimulus duration do not always match its actual time interval, and are affected by a variety of factors [Efron, 1970]. Since the brain internally cannot directly measure time, it is theorized that it estimates time based on internal biological or psychological events, or external signals [Grondin, 2008]. The effect of exogenous cues (i. e., external cues used to reset a biological clock— *zeitgebers*) from the local environment on endogenous biological clocks (e. g., circadian rhythms) is studied in the field of chronobiology [Kramer and Merrow, 2013]. It is possible that differences in exogenous time cues between the real world and IVEs have an effect on internal human time perception. In particular, system latency is known to change the perception of sensory synchronicity [Shi et al., 2010] and can degrade the perceptual stability of the environment [Allison et al., 2001].

Space and time are interdependent phenomena not only in physics, but also in human perception [Grondin, 2008]. Helson coined the term *tau effect* for the phenomenon wherein the variation of the time between spatial events can affect judgments of their spatial layout (cf. [Helson and King, 1931; Jones and Huang, 1982; Sarrazin et al., 2004]). For instance, Helson and King [1931] conducted a tactile estimation experiment that stimulating three equidistant surface points p_1, p_2, and p_3 with $\|p_2-p_1\|=\|p_3-p_2\|$ at points in time t_1, t_2, and t_3 for different durations $\|t_2-t_1\|>\|t_3-t_2\|$ in which they observed that subjects judge the distance between p_1 and p_2 as longer than between p_2 and p_3. That is, even though the distances between successive points was the same, the lengthened temporal stimulation led to an increased distance perception.

Conversely, Cohen et al. [1953] coined the term *kappa effect* for the phenomenon wherein the variation of the spatial layout of events can affect judgments of their temporal layout (cf. [Grondin, 2008; Roussel et al., 2009]). They observed for a visual bisection task that three successive flashes at spatial points p_1, p_2, and p_3 for different distances $\|p_2 - p_1\| >$ $\|p_3 - p_2\|$ with points in time t_1, t_2, and t_3 with $\|t_2 - t_1\| = \|t_3 - t_2\|$ that subjects judge the duration between t_1 and t_2 as shorter than the duration between t_2 and t_3, which underlines the mutual effects of distances and time.

27.3 Visual Illusions and Manipulation to Compensate Self-Motion Misperception

As described above, several works have shown that the user perception of self-motion severely differs in IVEs compared with the real world. In this section, we explore how such misperceptions can be compensated for by using visual illusions and manipulations of the IVE.

27.3.1 Compensation of Distance and Size Misperception

Accurate perception of size and distance in IVEs is important for many applications. However, as described above, several experiments have revealed that spatial perception of VEs often deviates from the real world, even when the virtual scene is modeled as an accurate replica of a familiar physical environment. Previous research has elucidated various factors that can facilitate perceptual shifts. In this context, we consider the effects of modified geometric rendering parameters on spatial cues and spatial perception [Bruder et al., 2012a].

When presenting computer-generated images on a physical display, we distinguish between the virtual rendering parameters and the physical display setup. To provide a view of a virtual scene on a head-referenced display (such as an HMD) that matches what a user would see in a corresponding real-world scene, the computer graphics rendering system has to be calibrated to the physical display characteristics. In particular, the geometric field of view (GFOV) in the rendering environment has to be set to the visual angle covered by the display screens in front of the user's eyes. Furthermore, the geometric interpupillary distance (GIPD) of the user has to be applied to the binocular camera model as shown in Figure 27.2. Any discrepancy between these parameters will affect various size and distance cues and cause perceptual shifts [Bruder et al., 2012a].

In this section, we describe the effects of spatial transformations caused by variations of the GFOV and the GIPD in on-axis stereographic display environments. In a psychophysical experiment, we have evaluated the mutual impact of the two parameters on size and distance perception, and set the results in relation to the models for these cues. In this experiment, participants were asked to judge distance and size properties of virtual objects placed in a realistic virtual scene (see Figure 27.3). As visual stimulus, we used a virtual hallway scene of 3.8 m × 2.5 m × 35 m (in width, length, and height), which was rendered with Crytek's CryEngine 3. We used a split screen design of a virtual hallway (see Figure 27.3), with the left-hand side view being rendered with one pair of GFOV and GIPD, and the right-hand side view being rendered with another. We did not use the stereoscopic rendering facilities of the CryEngine 3, but added an interface to our own software which handled the generation of the split-screen stereo pair and provided accurate on-axis stereoscopic renderings. As illustrated in Figure 27.3, in both virtual scenes we placed a virtual avatar (Caucasian male, 1.85m height) as the focus object. We used the

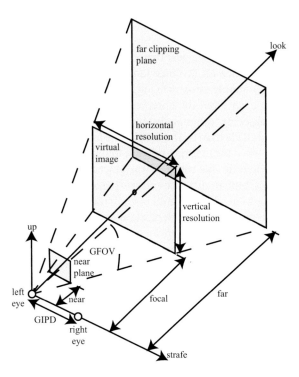

Figure 27.2

An idealized binocular camera model in three-dimensional computer graphics for HMDs. For better legibility, only the view frustum for the left eye camera object is shown. The right eye camera frustum results from a translation by GIPD along the strafe vector.

Figure 27.3

Illustration of the compensation approaches of distance and size misperception: View of the split-screen visual stimulus used in the experiment (here illustrated with red-cyan anaglyphs). Participants had to compare size and distance of the avatars displayed in the left and right view.

distance of the avatar from the observer as the between-subjects variable, and tested three distances: 4, 6 and 8 m.

The results of our experiment suggest that variations in the GFOV (within the tested range) have a strong influence on distance judgments, whereas variations in the GIPD (within the tested range) mainly affect size judgments. Larger GFOVs resulted in objects being judged as farther away from the observer. Larger GIPDs resulted in objects being judged as closer to the observer, although distance discrimination performance appears to be less influenced by the GIPD than by the GFOV. The tested GIPDs had only a slight effect on distance judgments when set in direct relation to the tested range of GFOVs.

Our results indicate that for cue conflicts introduced with increased GFOV and GIPD in realistic virtual scenes, human distance and size perception differs from the predictions of the models for reduced-cue visual stimuli (i. e., stereopsis and retinal size) described in [Bruder et al., 2012a]. In particular, for a typical range of miscalibrated GFOVs, the results indicate a strong effect on relative distance perception, with little effect on relative size perception. In contrast, for a typical range of miscalibrated GIPDs, the results indicate only a slight effect on relative distance perception, but a stronger effect on relative size perception. However, variations in both parameters can be used to alter the perception of size and distance.

27.3.2 Compensation of Speed Misperception

In this section we focus on the approaches to compensate misperception of speed.

27.3.2.1 Manipulating Visual Motions

Various researchers focused on manipulating landmarks in IVEs, which do not have to be as true as in the real world. For instance, Suma et al. [2010] exploited change blindness by shifting the position of landmarks, such as doors in an architectural model which often go unnoticed by observers when the altered landmark was not in the observer's view during the change. These changes can also be induced if the visual information is disrupted during saccadic eye motions or a short inter-stimulus interval [Steinicke et al., 2010a]. Less abrupt approaches are based on moving a virtual scene or individual landmarks relative to a user's motion [Razzaque, 2005]. For instance, Interrante et al. [2007] described approaches to upscale walked distances in immersive VEs to compensate perceived underestimation of travel distances in VR. Similarly, Steinicke et al. [2010b] proposed up- or downscaling rotation angles to compensate observed under- or overestimation of rotations. Although, such approaches can be applied to enhance self-motion judgments, and support unlimited walking through VEs even when restricted to a limited real world interaction space [Steinicke et al., 2010b], the amount of manipulation that goes unnoticed by users is limited. Furthermore, manipulation of virtual motions can produce some practical issues. Since the user's physical movements do not match their motion in the VE, an introduced discrepancy can affect typical distance cues exploited in some professions. For instance, counting steps as distance measure is a simple approximation in the fields of architecture or urban planning, which would be distorted if the mapping between the physical and virtual motion is manipulated. Another drawback of these manipulations results from findings of Kohli et al. [2005] and Bruder et al. [2009] in the area of passive haptics, in which physical props, which are aligned with virtual objects, are used to provide passive haptic feedback for their virtual counterparts. In the case of manipulated mappings between real movements and virtual motions, highly complex prediction and planning is required to keep virtual objects and physical props aligned.

27.3.2.2 Optic Flow Manipulations

Scaling user motion in VEs affects not only landmarks, but also changes the perceived speed of optic flow motion information. Manipulation of such optic flow cues has been considered as the contributing factor for affecting self-motion perception. However, the potential of such optic flow manipulations to induce *self-motion illusions* in VEs have rarely been studied in VR environments.

Apparent motion can be induced by directly stimulating the optic flow perception process, e. g., via transparent overlay of stationary scenes with three-dimensional particle flow fields or sinusoidal gradients [Giese, 1997], or by modulating local features in the visual scene, such as looped, time varying displacements of object contours [Freeman et al., 1991].

In this section we describe techniques for such optic flow self-motion illusions in IVEs [Bruder et al., 2012b]. In comparison with previous approaches these techniques neither manipulate landmarks in the VE [Suma et al., 2010] nor introduce discrepancies between real and virtual motions [Steinicke et al., 2010b]. In psychophysical experiments we analyzed whether and how much these approaches can affect self-motion perception in VEs when applied to different regions of the visual field. These manipulations can affect self-motion perception in VEs, but omit a quantitative discrepancy between real and virtual motions. In particular, we considered within which regions of the virtual view these apparent self-motion illusions can be applied, i. e., the ground plane or peripheral vision. Therefore, we experimentally introduced four illusions and demonstrated that optic flow manipulation can significantly affect users' self-motion judgments [Bruder et al., 2012b].

Through multiple trials, we either blended layered motion fields over the virtual scene using (1) particle flow fields, (2) sinusoidal gradients [Giese, 1997] or (3) motion of an infinite surface textured with a seamless tiled pattern approximating those in the virtual view (illustrated in Figure 27.4a–c). The illusion differs significantly from layered flow fields, because the edges in the rendered view move globally with virtual camera motions, but the illusion modulates the edges to stimulate local motion detectors of the visual system [Adelson and Bergen, 1985] (illustrated in Figure 27.4d).

Next, we studied illusory motion based on (4) change blindness by introducing a short-term gray screen as an inter-stimulus interval (ISI). We manipulated the one-to-one mapping to virtual camera motions directly with gains $gT_I \in \mathbb{R}$ and $gR_I \in \mathbb{R}^3$, similar to translation and rotation gains described in [Steinicke et al., 2010a], i. e., we introduced an offset to the actual camera location and orientation accumulated from the last ISI occurrence, and reverted to zero at each ISI onset. We apply an ISI of 100 ms duration for reverse motion (see Figure 27.4e). An example is shown in Figure 27.4f.

The experimental results show that the illusions can affect travel distance judgments in VEs. In particular, we established that the underestimation of travel distances observed in the case of a one-to-one mapping from real to virtual motions of a user can be compensated for by applying illusory motion with the points of subjective equality (PSEs) determined experimentally. We also evaluated potential of the presented illusions for enhancing applicability of scaled walking by countering the increased or decreased virtual traveling speed of a user through induced illusory motion. Our results show that

Figure 27.4

Screenshots illustrating layered motion with (a) particles, (b) sinusoidal gradients and (c) textures fitted to the scene, as well as (d) contour filtering, (e) change blindness and (f) contrast inversion. Please note that the illusory motion stimuli illustrated here are limited to peripheral regions.

participants judged real and virtual motions as equal, which under standard rendering they usually do not. This illustrates the potential of visual illusions to be applied when virtual motions must be manipulated with scaled walking gains that otherwise would be detected by users. Moreover, we found that illusory motion stimuli can be limited to peripheral regions or the ground plane only, which limits visual artifacts and distraction of users in immersive virtual worlds.

27.3.3 Manipulation of Time Perception

In this section, we describe the effects of manipulated zeitgebers (biological clock cues) on time estimation as yet unexplored factors of spatiotemporal perception in IVEs. We conducted an experiment to analyze human sensitivity to temporal durations while immersed in an HMD as well as a non-immersive display.

The experiment was performed in our laboratory, which was sealed from external cues during the experiment. Participants wore an Oculus Rift DK2 HMD for the stimulus presentation. The visual stimulus consisted of a virtual tropical island with sand, palm trees and ocean water. For rendering, system control, and logging we used an Intel computer with 4.0 GHz Core i7 processor, 16 GB of main memory and a Nvidia Quadro K5200 graphics card. The stimuli were rendered with the Unity 3D 5.0.3 engine. During the experiment, participants were seated in an MWE Lab Emperor chair, which provides a comfortable pose similar to the virtual sun lounger on the virtual beach in the VE. The virtual world shown to the participants during the experiment consisted of a virtual morning with a rising sun. We set the initial virtual local time of day to 7 am and approximated a sunny morning to ensure there would always be sufficient light available for the different tasks in the experiment. To simulate the virtual movement of the sun at different speeds, we implemented a realistic sun model in Unity 3D. In particular, a directional light was moved around the virtual hemisphere and the ambient lighting was manipulated using keyframe animations to simulate a natural change in color from red to blue after sunrise. A procedural skybox drew a white circle, dependent on the rotation of the directional light in the scene with sunshafts rendered as a post-effect (see Figure 27.5). The palm trees in the virtual scene were self-shadowing and cast soft shadows to provide additional cues about the position and movement of the sun.

We found that manipulations of external zeitgebers (cues) caused by a natural or unnatural movement of the virtual sun in the sky had a significant effect on time judgments. The key result is that whether the sun moved or was stationary was the major factor—there was

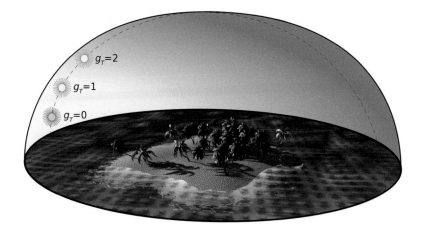

Figure 27.5

Illustration of the virtual island from a bird's eye perspective and movement of the sun in the virtual world scaled by the three time gains $g_t \in \{0, 1, 2\}$ corresponding to no, realistic and double speed sun movement.

little effect from altering the speed of the sun's movement across the sky. Thus, increasing the speed of the sun to twice its natural speed did not result in a significant change in time estimates. Hence, it appears that time estimation is improved in the presence of a dynamically moving sun while it is degraded in static virtual scenes. This is an important implication for implementing near-natural IVEs since it suggests that humans extract time information from the representation and movements of a virtual sun.

27.4 Conclusion and Future Directions

In this chapter we analyzed the triplet of self-motion speed, distance, and time perception in an IVE. As illustrated in Figure 27.1, differences in this self-motion triplet reveal perceptual biases, which may be effected by VR hardware and software or individual differences. We reviewed previous research work, which show that the user perception of self-motion severely differs in IVEs compared to the real world. Furthermore, we have summarized approaches to compensate these misperceptions of self-motion.

More research is necessary to understand the reasons, interrelations, and implications of such perceptual biases introduced by VR technologies in IVEs. This chapter can serve as a starting point to conduct research in the area of compensating misperception in IVE, which is important for the success of VR and associated technologies.

References

[Adelson and Bergen, 1985]

Adelson, Edward H. and James R. Bergen (1985). Spatiotemporal energy models for the perception of motion. *Journal of the Optical Society of America A*, 2(2): 284–299.

[Allison et al., 2001]

Allison, Robert S., Laurence R. Harris, Michael Jenkin, Urszula Jasiobedzka, and James E. Zacher (2001). Tolerance of temporal delay in virtual environments. In *IEEE Proceedings of the Virtual Reality (VR)*, Yokohama, Japan, pp. 247–253. IEEE.

[Banton et al., 2005]

Banton, Tom, Jeanine Stefanucci, Frank Durgin, Adam Fass, and Dennis Proffitt (2005). The perception of walking speed in a virtual environment. *Presence*, 14(4): 394–406.

[Berthoz, 2000]

Berthoz, Alain (2000). *The Brain's Sense of Movement*. Harvard University Press, Cambridge, MA.

[Bottema and Roth, 2012]

Bottema, Oene and Bernard Roth (2012). *Theoretical Kinematics*. Dover Publications, New York.

[Bremmer and Lappe, 1999]

Bremmer, Frank and Markus Lappe (1999). The use of optical velocities for distance discrimination and reproduction during visually simulated self-motion. *Experimental Brain Research*, 127(1): 33–42.

[Bruder and Steinicke, 2014]

Bruder, Gerd and Frank Steinicke (2014). Threefolded motion perception during immersive walkthroughs. In *Proceedings of the 20th ACM Symposium on Virtual Reality Software and Technology (VRST)*, Edinburgh, Scotland, pp. 177–185.

[Bruder et al., 2009]

Bruder, Gerd, Frank Steinicke, and Klaus H. Hinrichs (2009). Arch-explore: A natural user interface for immersive architectural walkthroughs. In *Proceedings of IEEE Symposium on 3D User Interfaces (3DUI)*, Lafayette, Louisiana, pp. 75–82.

[Bruder et al., 2012a]

Bruder, Gerd, Andreas Pusch, and Frank Steinicke (2012). Analyzing effects of geometric rendering parameters on size and distance estimation in on-axis stereographics. In *Proceedings of ACM Symposium on Applied Perception (SAP)*, Los Angeles, CA, pp. 111–118. ACM.

[Bruder et al., 2012b]

Bruder, Gerd, Frank Steinicke, Phil Wieland, and Markus Lappe (2012). Tuning self-motion perception in virtual reality with visual illusions. *IEEE Transactions on Visualization and Computer Graphics (TVCG)*, 18(7): 1068–1078.

[Bruder et al., 2013]

Bruder, Gerd, Phil Wieland, Benjamin Bolte, Markus Lappe, and Frank Steinicke (2013). Going with the flow: Modifying self-motion perception with computer-mediated optic flow. In *IEEE Proceedings of the International Symposium on Mixed and Augmenting Reality (ISMAR)*, Adelaide, Australia, pp. 67–74. IEEE.

[Choi and Bastian, 2007]

Choi, Julia T. and Amy J. Bastian (2007). Adaptation reveals independent control networks for human walking. *Nature Neuroscience*, 10(8): 1055–1062.

[Cohen et al., 1953]

Cohen, John, C. E. M. Hansel, and John D. Sylvester (1953). A new phenomenon in time judgment. *Nature*, 172: 901.

[Durgin et al., 2005a]

Durgin, Frank H., Krista Gigone, and Rebecca Scott (2005). Perception of Visual Speed While Moving. *Journal of Experimental Psychology: Human Perception and Performance*, 31(2): 339–353.

[Durgin et al., 2005b]

Durgin, Frank H., Adar Pelah, Laura F. Fox, Jed Lewis, Rachel Kane, and Katherine A. Walley (2005). Self-motion perception during locomotor recalibration: More than meets the eye. *Journal of Experimental Psychology: Human Perception and Performance*, 31(3): 398–419.

[Efron, 1970]

Efron, Robert (1970). Effect of stimulus duration on perceptual onset and offset latencies. *Perception & Psychophysics*, 8(4): 231–234.

[Freeman et al., 1991]

Freeman, William R., Edward H. Adelson, and David J. Heeger (1991). Motion without movement. *In SIGGRAPH '91 Proceedings of the 18th Annual Conference on Computer Graphics and Interactive Techniques*, Las Vegas, NV, vol. 25, pp. 27–30. ACM.

[Fukusima et al., 1997]

Fukusima, Sergio S., Jack M. Loomis, and José A. Da Silva (1997). Visual perception of egocentric distance as assessed by triangulation. *Journal of Experimental Psychology: Human Perception and Performance*, 23(1): 86–100.

[Gibb et al., 2010]

Gibb, Randy, Rob Gray, and Lauren Scharff (2010). *Aviation Visual Perception: Research, Misperception and Mishaps*. Ashgate, Farnham.

[Giese, 1997]

Giese, Martin Alexander (1997). A dynamical model for the perceptual organization of apparent motion. *PhD thesis*, Ruhr-University Bochum.

[Grondin, 2008]

Grondin, Simon, ed. (2008). *Psychology of Time*. Emerald Group Publishing Ltd., Bingley.

[Helson and King, 1931]

Helson, Harry and Samuel M. King (1931). The tau effect: An example of psychological relativity. *Journal of Experimental Psychology: General*, 14: 202–217.

[Interrante et al., 2006]

Interrante, Victoria, Brian Ries, and Lee Anderson (2006). Distance perception in immersive virtual environments, revisited. In *IEEE Proceedings of the Virtual Reality (VR)*, Alexandria, VA, pp. 3–10. IEEE.

[Interrante et al., 2007]

Interrante, Victoria, Brian Ries, and Lee Anderson (2007). Seven league boots: A new metaphor for augmented locomotion through moderately large scale immersive virtual environments. In *Proceedings of IEEE Symposium on 3D User Interfaces*, Charlotte, NC, pp. 167–170. IEEE.

[Jones and Huang, 1982]

Jones, Bill and Yih Lehr Huang (1982). Space-time dependencies in psychophysical judgment of extent and duration: Algebraic models of the tau and kappa effects. *Psychological Bulletin*, 91(1): 128–142.

[Jones et al., 2011]

Jones, J. Adam, J. Edward Swan II, Gurjot Singh, and Stephen Ellis (2011). Peripheral visual information and its effect on distance judgments in virtual and augmented environments. In *Proceedings of Symposium on Applied Perception in Graphics and Visualization (APGV)*, Toulouse, France, pp. 29–36. ACM.

[Jones et al., 2012]

Jones, J. Adam, Evan A. Suma, David M. Krum, and Mark Bolas (2012). Comparability of narrow and wide field-of-view head-mounted displays for medium-field distance judgments. In *Proceedings of Symposium on Applied Perception (SAP)*, Los Angeles, CA, p. 119. ACM.

[Kellner et al., 2012]

Kellner, Falko, Benjamin Bolte, Gerd Bruder, Ulrich Rautenberg, Frank Steinicke, Markus Lappe, and Reinhard Koch (2012). Geometric calibration of head-mounted displays and its effects on distance estimation. *IEEE Transactions on Visualization and Computer Graphics (TVCG)*, 18(4): 589–596.

[Klein et al., 2009]

Klein, Eric J., J. Edward Swan, Gregory S. Schmidt, Mark A. Livingston, and Oliver G. Staadt (2009). Measurement protocols for medium-field distance perception in large-screen immersive displays. In *IEEE Proceedings of the Virtual Reality (VR)*, Lafayette, Louisiana, pp. 107–113. IEEE.

[Kohli et al., 2005]

Kohli, Luv, Eric Burns, Dorian Miller, and Henry Fuchs (2005). Combining passive haptics with redirected walking. In *Proceedings of the 2005 International Conference on Augmented Tele-Existence (ICAT)*, vol. 157, Christchurch, New Zealand, pp. 253–254. ACM.

[Kramer and Merrow, 2013]

Kramer, Achim and Martha Merrow, eds. (2013). *Circadian Clocks. Handbook of Experimental Pharmacology*, vol. 217. Springer, Berlin.

[Kuhl et al., 2009]

Kuhl, Scott A., William B. Thompson, and Sarah H. Creem-Regehr (2009). HMD calibration and its effects on distance judgments. *ACM Transactions on Applied Perception (TAP)*, 5: 1–24.

[Loomis et al., 1993]

Loomis, Jack M., Roberta L. Klatzky, Reginald G. Golledge, Joseph G. Cicinelli, James W. Pellegrino, and Phyllis A. Fry (1993). Nonvisual navigation by blind and sighted: Assessment of path integration ability. *Journal of Experimental Psychology: General*, 122(1): 73–91.

[Loomis and Knapp, 2003]

Loomis, Jack M. and Joshua M. Knapp (2003). Visual perception of egocentric distance in real and virtual environments. In Hettinger, L. J. and Haas, M. W., (eds.) *Virtual and Adaptive Environments*. Lawrence Erlbaum Associates Publishers, Mahwah, NJ.

[Loomis and Philbeck, 2008]

Loomis, Jack M. and John W. Philbeck (2008). Measuring spatial perception with spatial updating and action. In Klatzky, R. L., Behrmann, M., MacWhinney, B. (eds.) *Embodiment, Ego-Space, and Action*, pp. 1–43. Psychology Press, New York.

[Mao et al., 2010]

Mao, Baohua, Zongzhong Tian, Haijun Huang, and Ziyou Gao, eds (2010). *Traffic and Transportation Studies 2010*. ASCE, Reston, VA.

[Mohler, 2007]

Mohler, Betty Jo (2007). *The effect of feedback within a virtual environment on human distance perception and adaptation. PhD thesis*, University of Utah, Salt Lake City, UT. ProQuest.

[Padmanaban et al., 2017]

Padmanaban, Nitish, Robert Konrad, Tal Stramer, Emily A. Cooper, and Gordon Wetzstein (2017). Optimizing virtual reality for all users through gaze-contingent and adaptive focus displays. *Proceedings of the National Academy of Sciences of the United States of America*, 114(9): 2183–2188.

[Phillips et al., 2009]

Phillips, Lane, Brian Ries, Victoria Interrante, Michael Kaeding, and Lee Anderson (2009). Distance perception in NPR immersive virtual environments, revisited. In *Proceedings of Symposium on Applied Perception in Graphics and Visualization (APGV)*, Chania, Crete, Greece, pp. 11–14. ACM.

[Plumert et al., 2004]

Plumert, Jodie M., Joseph K. Kearney, and James F. Cremer (2004). Distance perception in real and virtual environments. In *Proceedings of Symposium on Applied Perception in Graphics and Visualization (APGV)*, Los Angeles, CA, pp. 27–34.

[Razzaque, 2005]

Razzaque, Sharif (2005). *Redirected walking. PhD thesis*, University of North Carolina, Chapel Hill.

[Renner et al., 2013]

Renner, Rebekka S., Boris M. Velichkovsky, and Jens R. Helmert (2013). The Perception of egocentric distances in virtual environments—a review. *ACM Computing Surveys (CSUR)*, 46(2): 23.

[Rieser et al., 1990]

Rieser, John J., Daniel H. Ashmead, Charles R. Taylor, and Grant A. Youngquist (1990). Visual perception and the guidance of locomotion without vision to previously seen targets. *Perception*, 19(5): 675–689.

[Roussel et al., 2009]

Roussel, Marie-Ève, Simon Grondin, and Peter Killeen (2009). Spatial effects on temporal categorization. *Perception*, 38(5): 748–762.

[Ruddle and Lessels, 2009]

Ruddle, Roy A. and Simon Lessels (2009). The benefits of using a walking interface to navigate virtual environments. *ACM Transactions on Computer-Human Interaction (TOCHI)*, 16(1): 5: 1–5:18.

[Sarrazin et al., 2004]

Sarrazin, Jean-Christophe, Marie-Dominique Giraudo, Jean Pailhous, and Reinoud J. Bootsma (2004). Dynamics of balancing space and time in memory: Tau and kappa effects revisited. *Journal of Experimental Psychology: Human Perception and Performance*, 30(3): 411–430.

[Schatzschneider et al., 2016]

Schatzschneider, Christian, Gerd Bruder, and Frank Steinicke (2016). Who turned the clock? Effects of manipulated zeitgebers, cognitive load and immersion on time estimation. *IEEE Transaction Visualization Computer Graphics*, 22(4): 1387–1395.

[Schneider et al., 2011]

Schneider, Susan M., Cassandra K. Kisby, and Elizabeth P. Flint (2011). Effect of virtual reality on time perception in patients receiving chemotherapy. *Supportive Care in Cancer*, 19: 555–564.

[Shi et al., 2010]

Shi, Zhuanghua, Heng Zou, and Hermann J. Müller (2010). Temporal perception of visual-haptic events in multimodal telepresence system. In Zadeh, M. H. (eds.) *Advances in Haptics*, pp. 437–449. InTech.

[Steinicke et al., 2010a]

Steinicke, Frank, Gerd Bruder, Klaus Hinrichs, and Pete Willemsen (2010). Change blindness phenomena for stereoscopic projection systems. In *IEEE Proceedings of the Virtual Reality (VR)*, Waltham, MA, pp. 187–194. IEEE.

[Steinicke et al., 2010b]

Steinicke, Frank, Gerd Bruder, Jason Jerald, Harald Fenz, and Markus Lappe (2010). Estimation of detection thresholds for redirected walking techniques. *IEEE Transactions on Visualization and Computer Graphics (TVCG)*, 16(1): 17–27.

[Suma et al., 2010]

Suma, Evan A., Seth Clark, Samantha L. Finkelstein, and Zachary Wartell (2010). Exploiting change blindness to expand walkable space in a virtual environment. In *Proceedings of IEEE Virtual Reality (VR)*, Waltham, MA, pp. 305–306.

[Thompson et al., 2011]

Thompson, William, Roland Fleming, Sarah Creem-Regehr, and Jeanine Kelly Stefanucci (2011). *Visual Perception from a Computer Graphics Perspective*. A K Peters, Ltd, Wellesley, MA.

[Warren, 1998]

Warren Jr., William H. (1998). Visually controlled locomotion: 40 years later. *Ecological Psychology*, 10(3–4): 177–219.

[Wertheim, 1994]

Wertheim, Alexander H. (1994). Motion perception during self-motion, the direct versus inferential controversy revisited. *Behavioral and Brain Sciences*, 17(2): 293–355.

[Willemsen et al., 2008]

Willemsen, Peter, Amy A. Gooch, William B. Thompson, and Sarah H. Creem-Regehr (2008). Effects of stereo viewing conditions on distance perception in virtual environments. *Presence: Teleoperators & Virtual Environments*, 17(1): 91–101.

[Willemsen et al., 2009]

Willemsen, Peter, Mark B. Colton, Sarah H. Creem-Regehr, and William B. Thompson (2009). The effects of head-mounted display mechanical properties and field-of-view on distance judgments in virtual environments. *ACM Transactions on Applied Perception (TAP)*, 2(6): 1–14.

28

Exploring Large Environments with Redirected Walking

Mahdi Azmandian and Rhys Yahata
University of Southern California

Evan Suma Rosenberg
University of Minnesota

Enabling natural exploration of interactive virtual environments is highly desirable for many practical applications. Virtual reality applications that rely on controllers or mouse and keyboard movement do not fully replicate the physical and perceptual cues from the real world, and often fall short of providing a strong sense of immersion. On the other hand, research has shown that using a natural walking interface results in an enhanced sense of presence [Usoh et al., 1999] and efficient navigation [Ruddle and Lessels, 2009; Suma et al., 2010]. Furthermore, users who experience walking in an environment have improved spatial awareness and can develop better cognitive maps of virtual worlds [Ruddle et al., 2011]. However, supporting natural locomotion for exploring arbitrarily large virtual environments is not feasible because the dimensions of the physical tracked space will ultimately constrain the size of the virtual world that may be navigated.

Redirected walking is a perceptual illusion that aims to overcome this restriction by extending the range of environments that can be traversed on foot within a limited tracked space [Razzaque et al., 2001]. Leveraging the characteristics of human perception, redirection works by manipulating the mapping between physical and virtual motions. When employed properly, redirected walking offers a software-level solution to the seemingly intractable problem of limited physical space. This chapter provides tools to easily incorporate redirected walking into a virtual reality application. Though these techniques have been implemented in the open-source Redirected Walking Toolkit for the Unity game engine, they can also be extended for use in other platforms, as these concepts are universal [Azmandian et al., 2016].

28.1 The Theory of Redirected Walking

The general approach employed during redirected walking can be summarized as *manipulation of the mapping between physical body movement and the user's corresponding motions in the virtual environment*. Ideally, these manipulations will remain imperceptible and will keep the user contained within the tracked space.

28.1.1 Manipulating Perception

Redirection works by taking advantage of a key aspect of the human perceptual system: vision tends to dominate over vestibular sensation. According to previous work, visual and body-based spatial sensory systems are attuned to different ranges of motion frequency [Gibson, 1933], and when senses are in conflict, vision is dominant and is naturally used to correct accumulated error in the body-based senses [Burns et al., 2005; Posner et al., 1976; Souman et al., 2009]. Therefore, when injecting artificial motions during redirection, the discrepancy between sensory cues introduces a conflict that is resolved by relying on vision over other senses [Jürgens et al., 1999].

28.1.2 Decoupling Real and Virtual Motions

Conventionally, there is a static one-to-one mapping between the real and virtual coordinate systems. For instance, a forward motion of 1 m in the tracked space would result in a 1.0 m forward translation in the respective virtual environment. When applying redirected walking, however, the one-to-one relationship is disrupted. When motions are injected to the virtual user, the correspondence between coordinates is altered such that at any given moment, a single point in the tracking space can be mapped to a different point in the virtual environment. Thus, the shape of the user's real world and virtual world trajectories will be different. However, when wearing a virtual reality headset, the real world is not visible, and users will therefore rely primarily on the visual feedback from movement in the virtual environment. This divergence of trajectories is the key element that allows mapping a virtual path that would normally exceed the boundaries of the real world tracked space into one that can fit seemingly within it.

28.1.3 Redirection Gains

Redirected walking must adhere to a specific set of rules in order to remain imperceptible to the user. The manipulations must be restricted to a percentage multiplier of some component of the user's physical motion, which are generally referred to as *gains*. In the research literature, three different motion manipulation techniques have been identified: (a) translation gain, (b) rotation gain, and (c) curvature gain [Suma et al., 2012].

28.1.3.1 Translation Gain

Translation gain (g_t) involves scaling the user's velocity, usually in the forward direction, resulting in a displacement in the virtual world that is either faster or slower than the

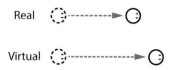

Figure 28.1

The user's virtual displacement is larger than the real displacement when $g_t > 1$.

actual physical movement. The term g_t is often expressed as the ratio between virtual and real translations. For instance, $g_t = 1.2$ would refer to a 20% upscaling and $g_t = 0.8$ equates to a 20% downscaling of virtual translation relative to real translation. Figure 28.1 illustrates the difference between real and virtual displacement when the translation gain is greater than 1.

It is worth mentioning that an alternative convention is to define g_t as the ratio of injected motion to real motion, making $g_t = 0$ the point of no gain applied, and positive and negative values refer to upscaling and downscaling respectively. The same definition can be used for rotation gain. We prefer the ratio convention for its mathematical elegance.

28.1.3.2 Rotation Gain

Rotation gain (g_r) refers to scaling the change in orientation as the user physically rotates, effectively increasing or decreasing perceived rotation. Similar to g_t, g_r is expressed as a scalar that measures the ratio of virtual to real rotation. Figure 28.2 illustrates the difference between real and virtual rotation when the rotation gain is greater than 1.

28.1.3.3 Curvature Gain

Curvature gain (g_c) involves applying a continuous rotation while the user is walking in the forward direction. In contrast with the other two gains, g_c does not directly scale a motion, but rather injects one type of motion (rotation) in response to another motion (translation). Therefore, the unit for curvature gain is "rotation applied per unit of translation." In practice, when curvature gain is applied, users will alter their physical trajectory to walk along a curved path in the real world even though the path in the virtual world appears straight (see Figure 28.3).

It should be noted since curvature and rotation gains both involve injecting rotations, it is common practice to only apply one of the two at a given point in time. This is to prevent gains from becoming noticeable. We will elaborate on this later in this chapter.

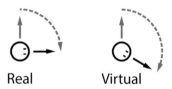

Real   Virtual

Figure 28.2

The user's virtual rotation is larger than the real rotation when $g_r > 1$.

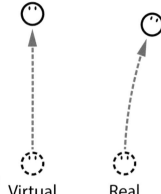

Figure 28.3

When curvature gain is applied, the real trajectory is curved while the perceived virtual trajectory is straight.

Virtual   **Real**

28.1.4 Gain Detection Thresholds

Redirected walking is a perceptual manipulation that should remain undetected by the user. In order to achieve this, each type of gain must be restricted to the user's *detection thresholds*. While these values are subjective and vary from one user to another, scientists have empirically measured these thresholds for the average person [Steinicke et al., 2010]. Reported results indicate that the range of unnoticeable values is [0.86, 1.26] for translation gain and [0.8, 1.49] for rotation gain. As for curvature gain, curving a straight virtual path into an arc with a radius of at least 22 m will remain imperceptible, which translates to a 2.6°/1 m traveled.

The efficacy of redirection is highly dependent on the detection thresholds. Therefore, in some use cases, it is desirable to prioritize redirection efficacy over perceptibility, applying stronger gains that can better redirect users at the compromise of potential detection. The most common example of this is using a curvature radius of 7.5 m (instead of 22), which has been often used by many researchers and is considered accepted practice [Hodgson and Bachmann, 2013].

28.1.5 Reorientation

Imposing limits on gains entails a restriction on the mapping capabilities of redirection. This in turn means applying redirection gains exclusively is not sufficient to ensure user containment within the tracked space. Thus, when the user inevitably reaches a physical boundary, a fail-safe mechanism must be triggered to prevent the user from leaving the tracked space. Such a safety measure is known as a *reorientation technique*. The purpose of a reorientation is not only to immediately prevent the user from leaving the tracked space, but also to manipulate the real to virtual mapping in a way that progression in the user's desired virtual direction becomes possible.

Note that reorientation techniques should be triggered before the user reaches hard boundary limits. This is typically implemented by placing triggers inside the tracked space within a fixed distance from each boundary limit, providing a buffer for the user to react to reorientation cues safely.

Also worth noting is that some advanced techniques in the literature involve performing a reorientation even when the user is not approaching a boundary. This is typically done as part of a planning strategy that strives to avoid multiple near-boundary reorientations by a priori activating an earlier reorientation.

28.1.5.1 Resets

The most widely used form of reorientation is a *reset*, which predates coining the term reorientation technique and is the first of its kind [Williams et al., 2007]. At a functional level, resets use gains (typically rotation) to reorient the user. Visually, resets are presented as a prompt, instructing the user to turn in place or walk in a specific direction. Once the task is complete, the prompt disappears and the user can continue walking in their original direction in the virtual world without leaving the tracked space.

The *2:1-Turn* reset is a popular reset option that instructs the user to perform a 360° rotation in place while scaling the virtual rotation by a factor of 2, resulting in a 180° rotation in the real world. Thus, by the time the reset task is complete, the user will be facing the center of the tracked space. This method can also be seen as rotation gain applied at the boundary, mapping a 180° real rotation to a 360 virtual rotation. As a result, the user can resume walking in the (pre-reset) intended direction, which now physically maps to the opposite direction in the tracked space.

28.1.6 Redirected Walking System

Redirection gains offer a non-intrusive unnoticeable mechanism for trying to keep users within the tracked space, while reorientations offer a guaranteed containment technique that temporarily interrupts users' navigation through the virtual world (Figure 28.4). These two methods combined form a redirected walking system for large-scale exploration that ensures users remain within the physical tracked space, regardless of the size of the virtual environment.

Bolstering redirected walking with reorientations forms a complete solution. However, it is important to note that reorientations alone are sufficient for exploring large environments. The user can freely roam the virtual environment and will simply ricochet off the real-world boundaries with a reorientation when needed. However, in practice, the goal

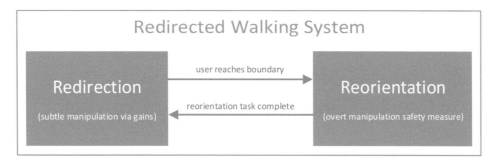

Figure 28.4

High level architecture of a redirected walking system.

(primary objective) is to minimize reorientations since they disrupt the flow of the experience. When redirected walking is employed effectively in conjunction with reorientation, the frequency of interruptions can be substantially reduced [Azmandian et al., 2015].

28.2 Implementation Options

Implementing redirected walking in a game engine requires providing a mechanism to dynamically adjust the mapping between the real and virtual worlds. This can be achieved by moving the GameObject node representing the entire real world relative to the virtual world GameObject node. If this movement were visualized, it would appear as two different planes of the real and virtual world shifting and sliding on top of each other, dynamically redefining the mapping between their coordinate systems. The next section will examine and compare two different approaches for accomplishing this mapping.

28.2.1 Static Real World

Perhaps the most intuitive approach is to keep the real -world static and inject virtual motions of redirection gains by manipulating the transform of the virtual world's GameObject node. To implement translation gain and upscale the perceived virtual movement by 20%, the entire virtual world will move in the opposite direction of the user's translation, at 20% of the user's instantaneous speed (Figure 28.5).

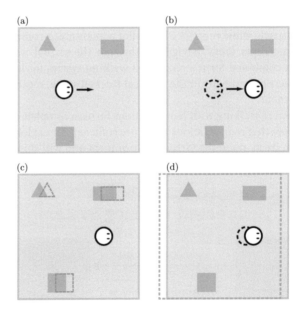

Figure 28.5

The effect of applying translation gain with a static virtual world vs a static real world. Dotted outlines correspond to the previous state of elements in the scene. Starting from state (a), after the user translates (b), either the real world (blue square) is kept static and the virtual elements move in the opposite direction (c) or the virtual world is kept static, and the real world including the real user are shifted along the direction of the user's translation. The blue square represents the physical tracked space.

28. Exploring Large Environments with Redirected Walking

Having a static real world can help with better understanding how redirection works and visualizing the movement, however translating and rotating the virtual world can cause artifacts derived by any physics engine simulations. In addition to repercussions with physics, moving a large virtual environment can also add substantial computational overhead in more complex environments.

28.2.2 Static Virtual World

To mitigate artifacts caused by moving the virtual world, gains can be implemented by moving the real world while leaving the virtual world static. Revisiting the static real world example, a translation gain of $g_t = 1.2$ is implemented by moving the real world along the opposite direction of the user's translation, at 20% of the user's instantaneous speed (Figure 28.5). Note that the tracked user is considered part of the real world, thus moving the real world will indirectly move the real user as well. Consequently, when gains are applied, the user's pose (location and orientation) relative to the real world (including the tracked space) will be preserved.

The remainder of this chapter will be expanding on the static virtual world implementation. The architecture and code presented will be in reference to the open-source Redirected Walking Toolkit for Unity [Azmandian et al., 2016]. The toolkit was designed to serve as a unified platform for developing, benchmarking, and deploying redirected walking algorithms. Encapsulated as a package for the Unity game engine, the toolkit seamlessly integrates with standard virtual reality configurations, requiring minimal configuration effort for content developers [Unity Technologies, 2017].

28.3 Setting Up the Scene Graph

Adding support for redirected walking involves setting up a representation of the dynamic real world as a `GameObject` that contains the tracked space along with the tracked user within that hierarchy (Figure 28.6). Everything outside of this structure is considered external and part of the virtual world which will remain unaffected by redirection. The primary objects in this structure are `Redirected User`, `Tracked Space`, and `Tracked User`.

Figure 28.6

Screenshot of the `GameObject` hierarchy in the Unity scene graph.

28.3.1 The Redirected User

The `Redirected User` node is the root object in the redirection hierarchy and is considered the representation of the real world. Assuming the origin of the virtual world is the origin of the scene's coordinate system, the transform of `Redirected User` is essentially the mapping from the virtual world origin to the real-world origin. With this design, applying redirection and affecting gains is simply enacted by manipulating the position and rotation of this object.

28.3.2 The Tracked Space

The `Tracked Space` node is assumed to be a rectangular plane with the dimensions matching the available physical tracked space. This element is key in determining when the user is approaching a boundary in order to react with reorientation tasks accordingly.

In addition to the dimensions of this object, the placement is also crucial. Depending on the configuration of the tracking system, the origin of the real world may or may not be at the center of the tracked space. Thus, a translational or rotational offset may need to be applied for this object to align with the physical tracked space. This offset must be applied during or prior to initialization and no further manipulation should be applied to this object's transform.

28.3.3 The Tracked User

`Tracked User` should contain the root object of the components used for determining the pose of the user in the tracked space. The arrangement of these components depends on the specific tracking hardware and software, but they must be placed under the `Redirected User` node. Furthermore, if the tracking system relies on any transforms (such as an origin reference object—aka "prop") they must also be placed under the `Redirected User` node to ensure the effects of redirection gains are also correctly propagated to those elements of the real world.

28.4 Execution Sequence in One Frame of Redirection

To minimize the chance of detection, redirection gains are applied gradually in a continuous fashion (at every frame) for a smooth, interwoven affecting of change. This process involves examining the changes that occurred since the last frame and using this information to determine the extent translations and rotations must be applied to the redirected user `GameObject`. Figure 28.7 illustrates the sequence of actions taken during each frame.

28.4.1 Keeping Track of Real Physical Movement

It is the user's change in pose that enables the application of undetectable gains. The amount of actual user translation determines how much translation and curvature gain can be applied and the amount of rotation determines how much rotation gain can be applied. Note that redirected walking can be formulated as a two-dimensional problem since the input and output of redirection lies in the horizontal plane (the ground). Consequently, only the user's translation in the horizontal plane is measured, and for rotation, only the angle change about the horizontal plane (heading) is calculated between frames.

28. Exploring Large Environments with Redirected Walking

Figure 28.7

Sequence of actions taken during one frame of redirection.

The two questions that need to be answered in this stage are: (1) how much did the user translate (expressed as a 3D vector represented solely on the horizontal plane) and (2) how much did the user rotate (expressed as an angle), both of which are relative to the last frame. These questions will be answered by following a sequence of three steps, two of which happen before applying gains and the third happens after the gains have been applied.

28.4.1.1 Step 1: Get Current Pose

The first step is to extract the pose of the user from the perspective of the horizontal plane. This pose can be expressed as a position vector `currPos` that lies in the horizontal plane and a direction unit vector `currDir` of the user's heading projected onto the horizontal plane.

Here the `Flat(Vector3)` helper function takes the given Vector3 input and projects it onto the horizontal plane by setting its y component to 0. Here the `Flat(Vector3)` helper function takes the given Vector3 input and projects it onto the horizontal plane by setting its y component to 0.

```
// Step 1: project the 3D position and direction vectors onto the 2D
//   horizontal plane
Vector3 currPos = Flat(headTransform.position);
Vector3 currDir = Flat(headTransform.forward).normalized;
```

28.4.1.2 Step 2: Measure the Changes

This step measures how `currPos` and `currDir` have changed for this new frame, relative to previously measured `prevPos` and `prevDir` variables from the previous frame.

```
// Step 2: calculate the movement delta
Vector3 deltaPos = currPos - prevPos;
float deltaDir = Utilities.SignedAngle(prevDir, currDir);
```

The helper function `SignedAngle` calculates the angle between two given vectors lying in the horizontal plane and assigns a sign to this angle based on its direction.

28.4.1.3 Step 3: Update Previous Pose

At the tail end of the redirection frame, the `prevPos` and `prevDir` variables need to be updated in order to be used by the next frame.

```
// Step 3: store current values for next frame
prevPos = Flat(headTransform.position);
prevDir = Flat(headTransform.forward);
```

Note that if step 3 happens immediately after step 2 (instead of after the gains are applied), the `deltaPos` and `deltaDir` calculations in the next frame will also include changes affected by the gains, which is incorrect. The objective is to ensure `deltaPos` and `deltaDir` explicitly measure only real physical movement, in other words how much of the translation and rotation since the last frame was caused strictly by user movement.

This situation also hints at a possible pitfall when using redirection with augmented travel capabilities such as teleportation. If the position and rotation measurements are taken at incorrect times, then a sudden teleportation can be measured as part of `deltaPos` and `deltaDir`, which can lead to a sudden injection of motion from gains. The key is to ensure all artificial motion injections (travel) happen between step 1 and 3, that is to say no injections take place after step 3 and before step 1 of the following frame. This ensures the measurements taken in step 2 reflect changes that were only caused by the user's locomotion.

28.4.2 Applying Gains

This section describes how to apply a translation gain of g_t, rotation gain of g_r and curvature gain of g_c in one frame of redirection. How the values for each of these variables is determined will be explained later in the chapter. It is important to reiterate that each gain value acts as a ratio or scaling factor, meaning the final degree of translation or rotation to apply also depends on the measured user movement since the last frame.

28.4.2.1 Translation Gain

To apply translation gain, calculate the amount of translation to apply using the scaling factor g_t and the vector of physical position change (in the horizontal plane). Then apply this translation to `Redirected User` (referenced as `redirectedUser`) relative to the virtual coordinate system.

```
// translate the user by the gain-modified movement
Vector3 translationToApply = (1 - g_t) * deltaPos;
redirectedUser.Translate(translationToApply, Space.World);
```

28.4.2.2 Rotation Gain

When applying rotation gain, the world must pivot around the user's head position (in the horizontal plane). Therefore, injecting rotation gain implicitly translates `Redirected User` in addition to rotating it.

```
```

```
// rotate the user by the gain-modified movement
float rotationToApply = (1 - g_r) * deltaDir;
redirectedUser.RotateAround(Flat(headPos), Vector3.up, rotationToApply);
```

28.4.2.3 Curvature Gain

Curvature gain is inherently similar to rotation gain in that they both apply a rotation around the user's head position. The difference is that their enabling element is different. Whereas rotation gain is activated in the presence of head rotations, on the other hand, curvature gain is instead reliant on the existence of body translation (as conveyed through head movement).

```
// add user rotation based on the distance moved
float curvatureToApply = g_c * deltaPos.magnitude;
redirectedUser.RotateAround(Flat(headPos), Vector3.up, curvatureToApply);
```

Since rotation and curvature gain have different causes yet similar effects, it is common to apply just one of the two in the same frame (time slice) in order to prevent two-fold rotations or alternatively the two partially fighting and canceling each other out. Furthermore, how a user's gain sensitivity thresholds can change when more than one gain is applied in a single frame remains an open question since previous research has only investigated these thresholds individually.

28.5 Redirection Strategies

At a high level, redirection can be summed up as the following actions in each frame:

1. measure user movement
2. determine gain values
3. apply gains

While in some cases gain values may be set manually, they are often determined by an algorithm known as a *redirection strategy*. A redirection strategy aims to adjust gains in a manner that would keep the user contained in the tracked space while keeping gains below detection thresholds.

Devising an optimal redirection strategy is a fundamental problem in redirected walking and a variety of approaches have been proposed. This chapter covers commonly used redirection strategies in virtual reality applications.

28.5.1 Steer-to-Center

The basic heuristic of "*steer-to-center*" is to apply rotations (via rotation and curvature gains) to steer the user towards the center of the tracked space (Figure 28.8a). This approach was originally proposed by Razzaque et al. [2001] and expanded on by Hodgson and Bachmann [2013]. In these implementations, the curvature radius was set to 7.5 m, and rotations gains were kept within [0.85, 1.3].

Hodgson et al.'s version of steer-to-center along with its pseudocode is covered in their 2013 study and its implementation can be found in our toolkit [Hodgson and Bachmann, 2013].

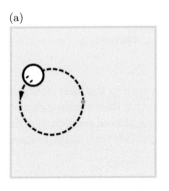 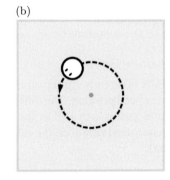

Figure 28.8

A demonstration of the user's path in the real world when the *steer-to-center* and *steer-to-orbit* strategies are used. With *steer-to-center*, when the user walks along a straight line in the virtual environment, the path will curve back to the center forming a circle passing through the center of the tracked space. On the other hand, for *steer-to-orbit*, the path is curved such that the user orbits around the center of the tracked space. The blue square represents the physical tracked space. (a) steer-to-center, (b) steer-to-orbit.

28.5.2 Steer-to-Orbit

The idea behind this strategy is to steer the user into orbit around the center of the tracked space using rotation and curvature gains (Figure 28.8b). *Steer-to-orbit* and *steer-to-center* are functionally very similar, but with different heuristics. Both were similarly presented and extended by Razzaque et al. [2001] and Hodgson and Bachmann [2013] respectively with similar gain restrictions.

Hodgson et al.'s version of of *steer-to-orbit* along with its pseudocode is also covered in their 2013 study and its implementation can be found in our toolkit [Hodgson and Bachmann, 2013].

28.5.3 Center-Based Translation

This algorithm was introduced by Azmandian et al. to improve the efficacy of redirection strategies that only inject rotations [Azmandian et al., 2015]. The "*center-based transla-tion*" method uses translation gains to slow down the user when moving away from the tracked space (Figure 28.9). Expressed in terms of gains, this implies using a constant maximum translation gain when the user's translation vector points away from the center of the tracked space (i.e., the dot product between the direction to the center and user's movement vector is negative). The upscaling of virtual movement boosts the user's prog-ress in the desired direction of movement before reaching a tracked space boundary.

The maximum translation gain value is set to 1.2 based on detection thresholds mea-sured by Steinicke et al. and its implementation can be found in the toolkit [Steinicke et al., 2010].

28.5.4 Zigzag Redirection

This technique was how redirected walking was originally introduced, demonstrating how it can be used effectively in a relatively small tracked space. Although the *zigzag*

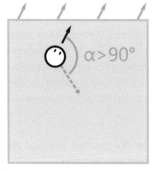 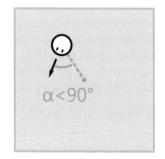

(a) User moving away from center   (b) User moving towards center

Figure 28.9

Center-based translation gain upscales virtual translations when the user is (a) moving away from the center of the tracked space, otherwise (b) no translation gains are applied. The dot product of the user's movement vector (solid black), with the vector toward the center (red dashed) is positive when moving toward the center, negative when moving away. The blue square represents the physical tracked space.

redirection technique is not a generalized approach, it serves as a useful method for any application aiming to expand the limits of room-scale tracking.

Zigzag redirection requires the user to walk along a zigzag-shaped path in the virtual environment. At each corner when the user turns, virtual rotations are downscaled such that in the real world the user rotates an entire 180°. As a result, the user walks back and forth along a single line in the tracked space, collapsing the zigzag path into stacked lines akin to folding an accordion (Figure 28.10).

Razzaque's original implementation used only rotation gain. However, our toolkit contains a more robust version, proposed by Azmandian et al., that uses all three gain types, and thus is more resilient to moderate deviations [Azmandian et al., 2014].

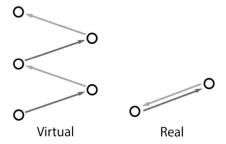

Figure 28.10

Using *Zigzag redirection*, a virtual trajectory shaped like a zigzag can map to a real trajectory of walking back and forth between two points, thus collapsing the path into a much tighter area.

28.6 Implementing Resets

Resets are a safety mechanism in the redirected walking system. They need to be enabled reliably, at the right time, and near the boundary, in order to safely stop the user from leaving the tracked space. The three main components of implementing resets are: (1) determining when to trigger the reset, (2) efficiently communicating the required task with appropriate cues, and (3) using rotation gain to execute the reorientation.

28.6.1 Reset Trigger and Reaction Time

Triggering a reset is based on where the user is in the tracked physical space, how they move, and how quickly they can be expected to react to reset cues.

The simplest way of setting rules for triggering resets is to use a buffer zone (Figure 28.11). This approach sets triggers at a fixed *safety distance* (d) away from each boundary such that when the user's distance to a boundary drops below d, a signal fires indicating the need for a reset (Figure 28.12).

The safety distance d is often determined based on some model of people's delay in reacting to cues and how rapidly they slow down (Figure 28.13). By modeling the user's slowdown in the worst case scenario (when they approach the boundary head-on (perpendicularly) as in Figure 28.14) the value of d is determined. In practice, $d = 1$ m is suitable for novice users and it can be lowered down to $d = 0.5$ m for more experienced users.

Strictly relying on boundary proximity for triggering resets can cause undesirable artifacts such as aggressive firing of resets. The most prevalent case is when the user slightly grazes the reset trigger without the intention of leaving the tracked space. More sophisticated implementations can be designed that account for: (a) the user's velocity (speed and direction) of movement when approaching the boundary and (b) the angle between the user's orientation and the tracked space center (as opposed to the angle with the nearest boundary). This information can help with dynamically adjusting the safety distance and also preventing back-to-back resets.

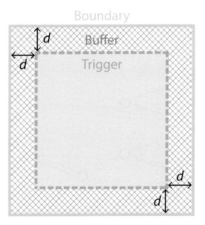

Figure 28.11

Resets are fired when a user collides with a reset trigger (dashed-square outline) placed at safety distance d from a hard boundary (outermost square outline). This grants the user the opportunity to safely react to the reset prompt within the buffer (cross-hatched area).

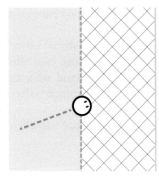

Figure 28.12

When the user reaches a reset trigger, a reset is fired and the reset prompt appears.

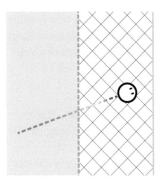

Figure 28.13

Once the user is prompted with the reset task, they eventually react to the prompt and slow down until coming to a full stop before reaching the tracked space boundary. The reset task is then performed typically within the buffer area.

 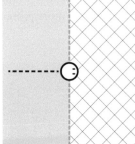

(a) best case for safe reset   (b) worst case for safe reset

Figure 28.14

The best and worst cases for determining reaction time. The best case (a) is when the user is walking almost parallel to the tracked space while the worst case is (b) where they approach the boundary head on.

28.6.2 Prompting Reset Task with Cues

The purpose of the reset task prompt is to communicate the necessary reset task and elicit the required response promptly. Although no formal studies have investigated the most effective manner of communicating the need for a reset, our intuition suggests that providing multimodal cues can reduce the expected response time. At the very minimum, visual cues should be displayed but when possible, audio cues along with haptic cues help quickly grab the user's attention.

Since a reset is a critical safety mechanism, it is recommended to have a tutorial introducing users to the reset instructions prior to the experience. This exposure can help familiarize users with the cues under safe conditions, help them understand what to expect, and ensure they are on alert when they encounter them later as a last-minute safety warning.

The following paragraphs introduce two categories of cues used to communicate when to do a reset and how close the user is to a boundary.

28.6.2.1 Reset Trigger Cues

This category of cues signals specifically when it is time to perform the reset task. An example of a common visual cue would be to simply show a heads-up-display text reading "Turn In Place" along with a stop sign icon (Figure 28.15). Additionally, an instant short beep audio cue and even a tactile vibration could help with notifying the user of a reset. More examples are discussed in Section 28.7.3.

28.6.2.2 Boundary Limit Cues

Ideally, reset trigger cues should be sufficient in grabbing the user's attention. However, if the user does not react quickly enough, as an extra safety measure a warning can be explicitly communicated indicating how close they are to a boundary.

One way of going about this is to tint the entire screen red, using increasingly stronger shades as the user approaches the edge of the tracking space. The audio counterpart to this would be to play a continuous sound clip (such as static noise) that increases in volume as a function of proximity to a boundary. Similarly, gradually increasing the intensity of haptic feedback can be included for a more pronounced warning.

Figure 28.15

Example of a basic reset prompt communicating the task of stopping and turning in place.

Another common metaphor is to gradually fade in some form of a wall (also referred to as a chaperone), explicitly informing the user where the approaching boundary is. This is an effective method that leverages people's natural instinct to speedily react to oncoming obstacles.

Note that boundary limit cues can intentionally be more intrusive by design since they serve as a last line of safety warning.

28.6.3 Reset Variations

A variety of reset types have been introduced in the literature within the broader corpus of reorientation techniques [Williams et al., 2007]. This chapter is specifically limited to the category of resets that requires the user to rotate in-place to complete the reorientation task. Within this scope, rotation gains are used to reorient the user to face toward the tracked space. The variations within this reset category are determined by what rotation gains are used and by the user's target orientation.

Note that in the techniques presented below, rotation gain is always greater than zero. However, a technique known as *freeze resetting* involves setting the gain to zero where the user's rotation in the horizontal plane (yaw) is immediately canceled out in each frame (by rotating the real world along with the user but in the opposite direction—such that the world seems to rotate along with the user). This can be technically categorized as a rotation-in-place reset, but in practice, freeze-resetting is more jarring than using normal—albeit possibly noticeable—rotation scaling ($g_r > 0$).

In all reset variations, below the user is instructed to stop and rotate in-place an entire 360°. What angle the user rotates in the real world depends on the specific reset type. Regardless of the real-world result, in the virtual world, the user always faces the original direction they were facing prior to the reset. This allows the user to continue progression along their intended virtual path without disrupting overall progression of the virtual trajectory. Naturally, once the 360° virtual rotation is complete, reset trigger cues are disabled allowing further advancement.

28.6.3.1 2:1-Turn Reset

The simple *2:1-Turn reset* uses a 2 to 1 ratio of virtual to real rotations, which is a constant rotation gain of $g_r = 2$. As a result, the 360° virtual rotation always maps to a 180° real rotation, causing the user to physically face opposite the direction they were facing when the reset was triggered (Figure 28.16). The intuition behind this approach is to have the user go back to where they came from, which is probably an unobstructed direction to walk along in the tracked space (but this heuristic is often suboptimal).

Turning to face the opposite direction of movement might not always be the most beneficial strategy, especially when approaching a boundary with a heading almost parallel to the boundary. An even worse of this is when the user is near a corner of the tracked space, causing back-to-back resets happening alternatively at adjacent boundaries (Figure 28.17).

28.6.3.2 Face-Center Reset

A better approach that overcomes the back-to-back problem is to scale rotations such that the user always faces the center of the tracked space by the end of the reset. Ensuring the user faces the center is a bit more involved than simply setting a constant rotation gain.

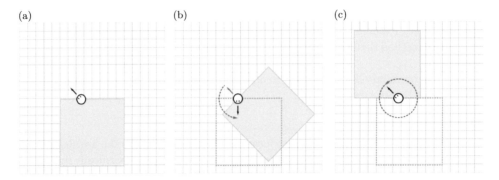

(a)   (b)   (c)

Figure 28.16

Progression and mechanics of the *2:1-Turn reset*. The user virtually rotates 360° while physically rotating only 180°. The user can then continue walking along the original virtual direction while now physically walking in the opposite direction within the tracked space. The blue square represents the physical tracked space. (a) initial state, (b) during reset, (c) terminal state.

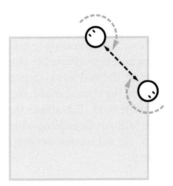

Figure 28.17

Undesirable scenario for *2:1-Turn reset* that leads to back-to-back resets. The blue square represents the physical tracked space.

The reason for this is that the user's turning direction during the reset affects the end result. For the *2:1-Turn reset*, +180° and −180° are essentially the same. However, if for instance a 150° rotation is required to face the center, a −150° rotation would not yield the same result.

To implement a *face-center reset*, first measure the target injection angle α by finding the angle between the user's initial heading and the target direction (the vector from the user's position to the center). Note that α is not an unsigned value. If the user rotates in the same direction as α, an upscaling would be required, setting rotation gain to $g_r^{+} = \dfrac{360 + |\alpha|}{360}$. However, if the user rotates in the opposite direction, the rotation must be downscaled by setting $g_r^{-} = \dfrac{360 + |\alpha|}{360}$ (Figure 28.18).

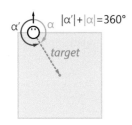 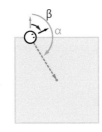 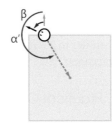

(a) determining target angles   (b) preferred rotation direction   (c) alternative rotation direction

Figure 28.18

(a) When a *face-center reset* is triggered, two different rotations α or α' can be applied to achieve the desired target orientation. (b) If α's direction matches the direction of the user's overall rotation (β), the real world will rotate α degrees during the reset. (c) Otherwise, if the user is rotating in the opposite direction, or not rotating, the face-center reset will inject a rotation of α' to achieve the target orientation. The blue square represents the physical tracked space.

The simplest way to accomplish this goal is to keep track of the user's overall real rotation since the beginning of the reset β. If at any point β changes directionality, then the rotation gain being applied also needs to switch from one value (g_r^+ or g_r^-) to the other (g_r^- or g_r^+). The rotation gain at the exact frame of directionality change however needs to be set such that all previous injections are undone, and the overall injection applied is $(1 - g_r^+) \cdot \beta$ or $(1 - g_r^-) \cdot \beta$ for the new target g_r^+ or g_r^- respectively. This extra calculation is to ensure erratic rotation residuals don't accumulate if the user keeps swiveling around their starting orientation.

These nuances in implementing face-center reset are addressed in the implementation available in the toolkit along with an alternative approach that makes better use of user rotation to prevent the need to undo previous injections if the user oscillates during the reset.

28.6.3.3 More Reset Tweaks

By default, resets take the user's initial head orientation as a reference for the user's initial direction and require a 360° virtual rotation that begins and ends with this vector. However, if for some reason at the moment a reset is triggered the user is facing a different direction than they are moving, then it might be preferable to instead take the user's recent average vector of velocity (using a short window leading up to the current moment), and consider that as the starting orientation—in lieu of determining the body direction by tracking the torso. This way when a face-center reset is enabled, once the reset task is complete, the user's direction of movement will face the center instead of the user's offset gaze.

Another modification that can be done is to redirect the user to physically face the farthest corner of in the tracked space (instead of the center as in face-center resets). The intuition for this is to maximize possible walking space along the direction of movement after the reset. However, no research evidence has shown this approach to be superior to face-center.

Lastly, another commonly used approach is to reorient the user perpendicular to the nearest boundary (known as the *away-from-wall* technique). However, this approach has flaws similar to *2:1-Turn*. Overall, using *face-center reset* is the recommended approach for general cases.

28.7 Practical Considerations

While the implementation details presented here in conjunction with the open-source toolkit are meant to facilitate an effortless plug-and-play system for redirected walking, applying redirection in a virtual reality application demands a bit of finesse, and is an art in its own right. Beyond the science and machinery of redirected walking, there is a degree of engineering and tailoring that is necessary to meet the needs of the target audience and specific deployment context. This section covers adjustments and alterations that can be made beyond a strict implementation in order to deliver the optimal redirected walking experience.

28.7.1 Setting Detection Thresholds

Though Steinicke's [Steinicke et al., 2010] empirically-measured detection thresholds are the de facto scientific standard for setting gain thresholds, plenty of researchers including Hodgson and Bachmann [2013] still recommend using more aggressive gain values. This section addresses the variety of reasons as to why in practice it is possible to use greater gain intensities without users noticing.

In order to understand why Steinicke's thresholds may be disregarded (loosened), it is important to understand how detection thresholds are measured. In a typical threshold estimation study, users are often instructed to first perform a task, and are then asked whether they noticed a visual discrepancy. What this means is that participants are fore-told about the presence of manipulations and are—as a result—unintentionally primed for noticing their existence. In fact, when inspecting user responses, it is not uncommon for users to claim they noticed something even when no gains were applied. This is argu-ably an inherent and perhaps inevitable flaw of gain estimation studies. However, it is not difficult to imagine unnoticeably applying stronger gains when users are unaware of the possibility of redirection gains. This is because a great deal of mismatch is required for an unsuspecting user to question the soundness of a presumed-to-be accurate one-to-one mapping tracking system.

The second potentially confounding factor is the generalization of detection thresh-olds. The variance of between-user thresholds is not negligible, and prescribing the aver-age detection threshold can be an overestimation for some while an underestimation for others. Not only is noticeability substantially subjective, but recent research has also hinted to the possibility of adaptation effects [Grechkin et al., 2016]. This means with exposure to gains, over time users can build up a tolerance, thus conditioning them to higher thresholds of detection. The degree of this adaptation effect can also vary from one individual to another.

Even if individuals have constant factors of detection sensitivity, a slew of other fac-tors affect the specific context in which redirection is applied. One such factor that varies from one experience to another is user engagement. Realizing that redirection is a form of illusion, as with any other of its kind, it can be all the more effective in remaining a mystery with the aid of misdirection. A user being preoccupied with a demanding task is conjectured to be less likely to detect redirection in comparison to a user wandering an environment with no pressing objectives.

Not all gain detection factors however are necessarily human-dependent. In practice, the density of the virtual environment can also be a determinant, which may be explained by optical flow and the stimulation of the periphery. Furthermore, the virtual reality hardware specifications can also affect the noticeability—including HMD intrinsics (such as field-of-view) and tracking fidelity. Of course, the matter is further complicated by the varying degree of impact each of these external factors has on different users.

The variety of influencing factors complicates how to estimate gain detection thresholds for an individual. As an improvement upon using reported detection thresholds, it is recommended to use a calibration process that gauges each user's detection sensitivity for a specific experience (virtual environment, objective, and hardware). This can be done rather efficiently by using *adaptive* methods for measuring gain sensitivity [Grechkin et al., 2016]. Additionally, a custom-tailored set of detection thresholds can also give higher priority to redirection efficacy by using more aggressive gains, aiming less for preventing detection and more for reducing resets. It is critical however to always prevent inducing simulator sickness and compromising the experience of redirected walking altogether.

28.7.2 Restricting Reset Gains

The intensity of rotation gains applied in rotate-in-place resets often violate the detection thresholds reported by Steinicke. Though this is a common compromise serving the goal of efficient recovery from an interrupted state, the strong manipulations can cause discomfort in addition to being noticeable by some users. The simplest remedy for users prone to simulator sickness is to instruct them to rotate 720° in the virtual world. The added rotation allows for using a lower rotation gain factor to alleviate user discomfort (although it may make them dizzy, and also the entanglement of a tether could start to be problematic).

28.7.3 Reset Prompt Choices and UI Options

Resets are arguably the least desirable component of a redirected walking system, and thus the main objective of a redirection strategy is to minimize their use. However, if employing a reset is absolutely necessary, it is essential to mitigate the level of disruption caused to the narrative and the flow of the experience. The ideal reset would present itself organically, integrate seamlessly within the narrative and be congruent with the theme of the virtual experience, all while efficiently reorienting the user and maintaining her sense of immersion.

A common approach for improving the reset interaction is to mask the reset prompt with a task that is germane to the experience without changing the underlying mechanics (known as *skinning* the reset). The first example of skinning resets was presented by Peck, who introduced the idea of reorientation with distractors [Peck et al., 2009]. Peck proposed using a virtual hummingbird to grab the user's attention, thus triggering the head rotations needed for reorientation. Suma et al. presented a context-sensitive reorientation as a photography-themed task in a tactical scouting experience [Suma et al., 2015]. Depending on the reset angle required, users were either asked to perform 360° visual rotation to capture a virtual panorama image (Figure 28.19) or turn and face a point of interest in the environment and snap a picture for reconnaissance (Figure 28.20). The environment was populated with points of interest that would be chosen as photography targets based on the user's location.

Grechkin also proposed the *rotate-and-walk* reorientation technique with a novel underlying mechanic [Grechkin et al., 2015]. This approach involved introducing *side objectives* as points of interest that would be newly spawned or highlighted. The user

Figure 28.19

The virtual panorama reset task requiring the user to rotate 360° to complete a panorama shot.

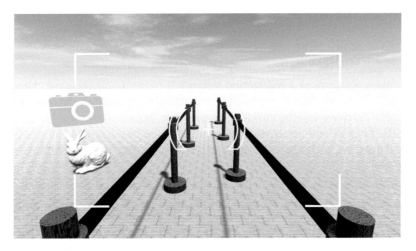

Figure 28.20

The virtual snapshot reset task requiring the user to turn to a point of interest and snap a picture before resuming progression.

would then be required to visit this point of interest before progressing further along the virtual path. The user's translations and rotations to and from the side objective provide opportunities for applying redirection gains for reorientation.

28.7.4 Tracked Space Requirements and Expected Performance

The most important practical question for redirected walking is "How much space is required to effectively deploy redirection?" Answering this question requires (a) a defined *performance metric*, (b) a method for measuring performance, and (c) knowledge of what influences performance.

Azmandian et al.'s simulation study is a seminal research endeavor that has attempted to formally address this matter [Azmandian et al., 2015]. Given that the frequency of resets is the main crux of any redirected walking experience, the performance measure they used was the average virtual distance traveled between resets (ratio of total virtual distance traveled to the number of total resets). Performance measurements were conducted using a simulation platform that eventually evolved into the Redirected Walking Toolkit [Azmandian et al., 2016]. The use of simulations made it possible to systematically control for a variety of interacting factors including: user behavior, tracked space dimensions, the structure of the virtual environment and type of the virtual path, as well as internal parameters of the redirection strategies such as detection thresholds and the reset type used.

The results indicated that the minimum viable size of physical tracked space for redirected walking in the most general case is approximately $6\,m \times 6\,m$ with performance continuously improving in larger tracked spaces. At the same time, no "optimal" tracked space size can guarantee the absence of contacts with the boundary. They also found that the best overall performance can be achieved using the steer-to-center strategy combined with center-based translation gain in conjunction with *face-center resets* deployed in square tracked spaces.

Using these results, the best guideline for determining what tracked-space size would meet one's requirements is to inspect the performance graph across varying (square-shaped) tracked spaces sizes (Figure 28.21). Note that the side length reported here is based on the effective walking area (inside the reset safety trigger) which can be calculated as (actual side length $-2 \times$ safety trigger length). If encountering a reset every 10 m of walking is satisfactory, then an effective tracked space of $8 \times 8\,m$ would be required. If that is not sufficient, to see resets every 20 m, then a space of at least $12 \times 12\,m$ would be necessary. Ultimately, the right choice of space dimensions comes down to what reset frequency is considered tolerable and the trade-off with the cost of the tracked space.

Though the results of this research shed light on some fundamental practical matters, what is important to point out is that these results are essentially a lower bound on expected performance for redirected walking. More advanced redirection strategies have been introduced in the literature that can drastically improve performance. These techniques leverage knowledge of the architectural layout of the virtual environment and the tasks the user will be required to perform. With foreknowledge of expected user movement actions, the VR experience designer can plan more effective redirection strategies. Although *Zigzag redirection* is a simple technique with limited applicability, it does exemplify and showcase how a planning algorithm can substantially reduce the need for resets and be more effective than a general redirection strategy.

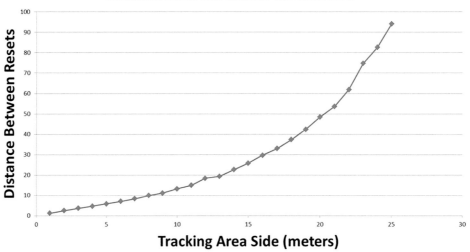

Figure 28.21

Expected performance for redirected walking in the general case for a given "effective walking area" (area within safety trigger).

In the current state of understanding in redirected walking research, in order to have a compelling room-scale redirection experience, advanced planning strategies should be used, which inherently limits the scope of viable virtual experiences. For instance, having an experience akin to first-person shooter games in VR where predicting user behavior is complex, planning algorithms may not be applicable, and therefore general strategies must be used, resulting in undesirable performance as seen in Figure 28.21. On the other hand, linear narratives, while restrictive, still offer immersive experiences conducive for redirection through optimal design strategies. More tools are expected to be made available for content creation and level design that are interwoven with planning strategies to deliver optimal redirected walking experiences.

References

[Azmandian et al., 2014]

Azmandian, Mahdi, Mark Bolas, and Evan Suma (2014). Countering user deviation during redirected walking. In *Proceedings of the ACM Symposium on Applied Perception*, Vancouver, BC, p. 4503.

[Azmandian et al., 2015]

Azmandian, Mahdi, Timofey Grechkin, Mark Bolas, and Evan Suma (2015). Physical space requirements for redirected walking: How size and shape affect performance. In *Eurographics Symposium on Virtual Environments 2015*, Kyoto, Japan: The Eurographics Association, pp. 93–100.

[Azmandian et al., 2016]

Azmandian, Mahdi, Timofey Grechkin, Mark Bolas, and Evan Suma (2016). The redirected walking toolkit: A unified development platform for exploring large virtual environments. In *2016 IEEE 2nd Workshop on Everyday Virtual Reality (WEVR)*, Kyoto, Japan, pp. 9–14.

[Burns et al., 2005]

Burns, Eric, Sharif Razzaque, Abigail T. Panter, Mary C. Whitton, Matthew R. McCallus, and Frederick P. Brooks Jr. (2005). The hand is slower than the eye: A quantitative exploration of visual dominance over proprioception. In *IEEE Virtual Reality, 2005. Proceedings. VR 2005*, Bonn, Germany: IEEE, pp. 3–10.

[Gibson, 1933]

Gibson, James J. (1933). Adaptation, after-effect and contrast in the perception of curved lines. *Journal of Experimental Psychology*, 16(1): 1–31.

[Grechkin et al., 2015]

Grechkin, Timofey, Mahdi Azmandian, Mark Bolas, and Evan Suma (2015). Towards context-sensitive reorientation for real walking in virtual reality. In *2015 IEEE Virtual Reality (VR)*, Arles, France: IEEE, pp. 185–186.

[Grechkin et al., 2016]

Grechkin, Timofey, Jerald Thomas, Mahdi Azmandian, Mark Bolas, and Evan Suma (2016). Revisiting detection thresholds for redirected walking: Combining translation and curvature gains. In *Proceedings of the ACM Symposium on Applied Perception*, Anaheim, CA: ACM, pp. 113–120.

[Hodgson and Bachmann, 2013]

Hodgson, Eric, and Eric Bachmann (2013). Comparing four approaches to generalized redirected walking: Simulation and live user data. *IEEE Transactions on Visualization and Computer Graphics*, 19(4): 634–643.

[Jürgens et al., 1999]

Jürgens, R., T. Boß, and W. Becker (1999). Podokinetic after-rotation does not depend on sensory conflict. *Experimental Brain Research*, 128(4): 563–567.

[Peck et al., 2009]

Peck, Tabitha C., Henry Fuchs, and Mary C. Whitton (2009). Evaluation of reorientation techniques and distractors for walking in large virtual environments. *IEEE Transactions on Visualization and Computer Graphics*, 15(3): 383–394.

[Posner et al., 1976]

Posner, Michael I., Mary J. Nissen, and Raymond M. Klein (1976). Visual dominance: An information-processing account of its origins and significance. *Psychological Review*, 83(2): 157.

[Razzaque et al., 2001]

Razzaque, Sharif, Zachariah Kohn, and Mary C. Whitton (2001). Redirected Walking. In *Proceedings of EUROGRAPHICS*, Manchester, UK, pp. 289–294.

[Ruddle and Lessels, 2009]

Ruddle, Roy A., and Simon Lessels (2009). The benefits of using a walking interface to navigate virtual environments. *ACM Transactions on Computer-Human Interaction (TOCHI)*, 16(1): 5.

[Ruddle et al., 2011]

Ruddle, Roy A., Ekaterina Volkova, and Heinrich H. Bülthoff (2011). Walking improves your cognitive map in environments that are large-scale and large in extent. *ACM Transactions on Computer-Human Interaction (TOCHI)*, 18(2): 10.

[Souman et al., 2009]

Souman, Jan L., Ilja Frissen, Manish N. Sreenivasa, and Marc O. Ernst (2009). Walking straight into circles. *Current Biology*, 19(18): 1538–1542.

[Steinicke et al., 2010]

Steinicke, Frank, Gerd Bruder, Jason Jerald, Harald Frenz, and Markus Lappe (2010). Estimation of detection thresholds for redirected walking techniques. *IEEE Transactions on Visualization and Computer Graphics*, 16(1): 17–27.

[Suma et al., 2010]

Suma, Evan, Samantha Finkelstein, Myra Reid, Sabarish Babu, Amy Ulinski and Larry F. Hodges (2010). Evaluation of the cognitive effects of travel technique in complex real and virtual environments. *IEEE Transactions on Visualization and Computer Graphics*, 16(4): 690–702.

[Suma et al., 2012]

Suma, Evan A., Grud Bruder, Frank Steinicke, David M. Krum, and Mark Bolas (2012). A taxonomy for deploying redirection techniques in immersive virtual environments. In *Proceedings—IEEE Virtual Reality*, Costa Mesa, CA, pp. 43–46.

[Suma et al., 2015]

Suma, Evan A., Mahdi Azmandian, Timofey Grechkin, Thai Phan, and Mark Bolas (2015). Making small spaces feel large: Infinite walking in virtual reality. In *ACM SIGGRAPH 2015 Emerging Technologies*, SIGGRAPH' 15, New York: ACM, pp. 16:1–16:1.

[Unity Technologies, 2017]

Unity Technologies (2017). Unity3D game engine. https://unity3d.com/. Accessed: 2017-02-02.

[Usoh et al., 1999]

Usoh, Martin, Kevin Arthur, Mary C. Whitton, Rui Bastos, Anthony Steed, Mel Slater, and Frederick P. Brooks Jr. (1999). Walking>walking-in-place>flying, in virtual environments. In *Proceedings of the 26th Annual Conference on Computer Graphics and Interactive Techniques*, SIGGRAPH' 99, New York: ACM Press/Addison-Wesley Publishing Co., pp. 359–364.

[Williams et al., 2007]

Williams, Betsy, Gayathri Narasimham, Bjoern Rump, Timothy P. McNamara, Thomas H. Carr, John Rieser, and Bobby Bodenheimer (2007). Exploring large virtual environments with an HMD when physical space is limited. In *Proceedings of the 4th Symposium on Applied Perception in Graphics and Visualization—APGV '07*, Tubingen, Germany, vol. 1(212), p. 41.

SECTION IX
DIY VR Hardware

29

Building and Interfacing Input and Output Devices

Kyle Johnsen
University of Georgia

In this chapter we will explore sensing and controls tasks that link the physical environment to a virtual environment. This chapter shows a complete pipeline for interfacing physical sensors and actuators to a Unity3D-based interactive simulator using a development microcontroller with basic analog to digital circuits. The example provided deals specifically with interfacing Arduino hardware to Unity3D; however, translating this code for other game engines or microcontroller platforms should be straightforward. Basic analog to digital circuits are included that cover the majority of direct current sensor and actuator types.

29.1 Introduction

This chapter provides a general method for electronic interfacing of custom input and output devices that allow the digital virtual reality world to interact with the analog physical world. Using this method allows VR devices to be tailored to an application, rather than the application being constrained to available off-the-shelf devices.

There are generally three levels to such interfacing.

- Highest-level: Using an embedded, but otherwise general purpose, computer. These devices are capable of similar interfacing as the VR computer, but are typically smaller, lower power, and can be wired directly to digital sensors and actuators. They are typically connected to the VR computer through a network.
- Intermediate-level: Using a data acquisition and control module. These devices can interface to a wide variety of analog sensors and actuators. They are most commonly wired to the VR computer through a bus (e.g. USB), and manufacturers provide the (typically proprietary) required device drivers and libraries.
- Low-level: Building a data acquisition and control module yourself. This offers the most flexibility in terms of sensing accuracy/precision/latency, control, size, power, and communication.

This chapter covers the low-level method.

29.2 Section I—Fundamental Electronics

Except for using an embedded computer to interface an off-the-shelf device, some knowledge of analog electronics is required, the most basic being an understanding of the terms **voltage** (SI unit "volt, V") and **current** (SI unit "ampere, A", often abbreviated "amps",)), which respectively describe the energy and flow of a **quantity of charge**, (SI unit "Coulomb", C), as well as **resistance** (SI unit "Ohm", Ω) to that flow and **power** (SI unit "Watt", W) generated/dissipated by it.

Electrical charge is a property of a substance. Most people remember that "like charges repel and opposite charges attract." This is true, *if the particles can move.* Most metals, such as copper, contain an enormous number of mobile negatively charged particles called electrons (1g of copper material contains approximately 9.4×10^{21} *mobile* electrons). Having many free charged particles allows metals to be used as electrical channels (conductors) through which charges move, which happens if an electric field (caused by separation of positively and negatively charged particles) is present. When charged particles move, they can generate light, heat and magnetic fields, which can be used to perform useful work, such as moving a motor.

Electrical current is a measurement of the *quantity* of charge (Coulombs) moving through a conductor *per unit time*. Its unit, the Ampere, is a measurement of (Coulombs/second), i.e., 1 A = 1 C/1 s. Given that 1 Coulomb represents the charge on -6.24×10^{18} electrons (a seemingly arbitrary negative value because Coulombs were defined before electrons were discovered), an enormous number of charged particles are moving through the conductor per second at 1 A. However, electrical current does not imply the *speed* of an individual charged particle, which is typically very slow, on the order of millimeters per second. Electrical current is analogous to a measurement of the amount of water moving through a pipe over time. The speed of an individual water molecule may be slow, but the overall quantity may be very large.

Electrical voltage is a measurement of the potential energy (SI unit "Joule", J) of a charged particle. Its unit, the Volt, is a measurement of (Joules/Coulomb), i.e., 1 V = 1 J/1 C.

Voltage can only be measured between two points, meaning it is the energy change to a quantity of charge that moves between those points.

Electrical resistance is a property of all **conductors**, and is the ratio of voltage to current, i.e., R = V/I, or more commonly stated V = IR. This relationship, called Ohm's Law, is the most fundamental equation in electronics.

Electrical power is the last term you should know, and is the most confusing because many people equate power and energy. Power is the *change in energy over time* (1 W = 1 J/1 s). In electronics, we mostly think about power generation and dissipation. Within a power source, this is the product of Voltage and Current between the positive and negative terminals. Within a conductor, it is the same, but can be related to resistance (by using Ohm's Law to substitute I or V for R) as $P = I^2R$ or $P = V^2/R$.

29.2.1 Analog Sensors

Analog sensors convert a physical state or event into a corresponding, *analog*ous measurable electrical one. Sensors come in many varieties, differing widely on the type of electrical output they produce. For the most part, a sensor exists for every physical property such as light, temperature, sound, or motion. Sensors are selected both by their measurement properties (accuracy, sensitivity, and range with respect to the physical property), and also by their electrical characteristics, and particularly how they are designed to interface with other electronics. Some produce a varying voltage, while others produce varying current or varying resistance. Still others *modulate* their output onto a carrier signal, such as by varying the frequency of a voltage sine wave or the time of a pulse.

For example, consider a normally-open push button. A normally open push button may be a mechanical sensor that converts the physical button state {unpushed, pushed} into the electrical resistance {∞, 0} by making a connection between two terminals when it is pressed down. By measuring the resistance, we can determine the state.

29.2.2 Analog Actuators

Actuating is the opposite of sensing. An analog actuator converts an electrical state or event into an analogous physical one, such as light, heat, sound, or motion. Many of the same qualities apply to actuators as sensors. The most significant difference is that actuation typically requires much more power than sensing.

29.2.3 Analog-Digital Conversion

To get data that a digital computer can process, the analog signal must be converted to a set of binary values. This process is managed by an analog to digital converter (ADC) unit. A typical ADC linearly maps a voltage range between 0 and a supplied reference voltage into an N-bit value. For example, a 10-bit ADC using a 5 V reference would typically map 0 V to 0000000000_2 and 5 V to 1111111111_2. A value of 2.5 V would be mapped to 0111111111_2. For a 10-bit ADC, there are 2^{10} possible binary values for the input voltage range, making the resolution 5/1023 V / bit.

Other properties to consider are the *sample time*, how much time it takes to reliably convert a stable voltage, and the *sampling period,* how much time passes between the start of each sample. Very fast (e.g. nanosecond-level sample period), high-resolution (e.g. 24-bit) ADCs can be found in cameras and sound cards. More typical ADCs are 10-bit or

12-bit resolution and sample in the high microseconds to low milliseconds (note, you'll often see the frequency, rather than the period). Higher sample times usually result in better accuracies. For current-based or resistance-based sensors, an intermediate current-voltage or resistance-voltage circuit is often needed if not included in the ADC.

When you convert a changing analog signal to digital samples, you may lose information if you do not sample fast enough. The Nyquist-Shannon Sampling Theorem provides some insight into this problem, showing that you can only recover information from signal frequencies that are less than half of your sampling frequency. In other words, if your signal is 10 Hz (10 oscillations per second), you should sample at more than 20 Hz. However, this is for pure sinusoidal signals. In practice, for VR input systems, sample as fast as your system can handle. The faster the sample time, the lower the input latency—a key quality measure for a VR input system.

Similarly, an N-bit digital value can be converted to a voltage within a reference range by a digital to analog converter (DAC). This voltage is typically meant as a control signal (rather than something used to power a device). If more power is needed (often the case), a transistor (electronic switch) or relay (electromechanical switch) can be employed as amplifiers. The maximum power of a DAC will be specified, and should not be exceeded by the power required from the device, or damage could occur to the converter and whatever is attached.

29.2.4 Digital Sensors and Actuators

Some sensors and actuators have control units that contain ADC, DAC, memory, and logic elements that are designed to communicate directly with another digital device using an established, typically standardized, protocol stack over one (Serial) or more (Parallel) communication links. The protocols used by the devices must match at both ends, making this a key consideration when choosing a digital sensor or actuator. Another important characteristic of digital devices is that they normally have a fixed latency between the physical event and digital signal that cannot be improved.

29.3 Section II—Interfacing

The remainder of this chapter covers practical cases of high, intermediate, and low-level interfacing. The Arduino, ecosystem is used for the embedded systems, while Unity3D is used for VR simulation and rendering.

29.3.1 Low-Level "Do-It-Yourself" Analog Interfacing

A low-level interfacing method is indicated when size, timing, and power are all critical to the application, all of which are critical to embedding sensors inside of a VR device. This flexibility comes at a cost of complexity and physical construction time relative to higher level methods.

A key component to this approach is the microcontroller, which usually contains all necessary ADC, DAC, and logic/timing components in a single package. These are also often embedded into a development board that provides power and standard external interfaces (ports, headers) for connecting to other devices as well as a crystal oscillator. The microcontroller this example uses is the ATMEGA328P, produced by Atmel Semiconductors. The development board is the Arduino Uno R3, which is widely available, and runs the microcontroller at 16 MHz and 5 V. It contains a USB-Serial adapter that simultaneously powers the device and emulates a corresponding serial device on the host PC (note that drivers for this are commonplace, and should work on most modern operating systems without additional installation requirements). On Windows, this will result in a virtual COM port, listed in device manager. On Mac and Linux, this will be a TTY device listed under "/dev".

The Arduino ecosystem, more broadly, is a complete development environment for embedded systems. It is an attempt at simplification of microcontroller programming process. Code is written in C++ within a text file, called a sketch, which at a minimum contains *setup()* and *loop()* functions. These are linked to a template file that contains the *main()* entrypoint, and subsequently calls a microcontroller-specific *init()* function, the sketch's *setup()* function once, and then the sketch's *loop()* function repeatedly. The default development environment further encapsulates the specifics of compiling and uploading the sketch to the microcontroller on the chosen development board.

Once a sketch is uploaded to the microcontroller (stored in flash memory, so the program is maintained when power is lost), it is independent from the computer (aside from power, which can also be supplied via a battery or AC/DC adapter). The USB connection can, however, still be used to interface with other programs on the computer.

Note that while the code below appears to be highly Arduino specific, all microcontrollers have similar features and the vast majority have C or C++ libraries and compilers. Also, the Arduino development board can be replaced by only the microcontroller, a suitable power supply, and a communications device. This can greatly reduce power usage and space.

29.4 Example 1: Build-Your-Own Motion-Controller Gamepad with Vibration

A gamepad is a composite set of buttons, joysticks, and motion sensors that are connected as a composite digital input/output device. An electronics design for a 3-button, 2-axis joystick gamepad with an accelerometer, vibration feedback, and light is presented here, alongside a generic Arduino-Unity interface that can be easily extended for custom designs. Note that with the accelerometer, we provide our gamepad with 3 Degree of Freedom (3-DOF) capabilities that most game controllers do not include (two exceptions being the Nintendo Wii remote and Google Daydream controllers).

The schematic is presented here, both as a circuit diagram (Figure 29.1), which describes the connectivity between components using standard circuit symbols, as well as a "breadboard" diagram, which shows a possible prototyping layout (Figure 29.2). Note that wire colors are irrelevant, and are used only for clarity.

The circuit shown in Figures 29.1 and 29.2 uses a 2-axis joystick module that outputs 0 to V_{cc} for each of the axes (centered at $V_{cc}/2$). It also has a built-in push-button that connects the SEL pin to GND while pushed in.

The three-axis accelerometer has three voltage outputs, that range from 0 to V_{cc} (centered at $V_{cc}/2$), and senses from -3 g to 3 g. This accelerometer, the ADXL335, has a maximum V_{cc} voltage of 3.6 V. In order to use the full range of the ADC, the V_{cc} voltage is attached to the A_{REF} pin to 3.3 V. This also means that the joystick must use 3.3 V for V_{cc} to have the same full range. Note, V_{cc} stands for common-collector, a term historically

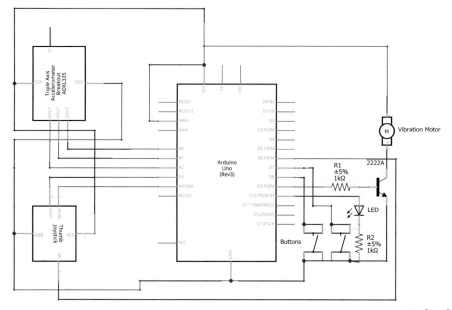

fritzing

Figure 29.1

The circuit schematic diagram for the game controller using the Arduino.

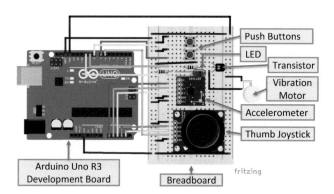

fritzing

Figure 29.2

The wiring diagram connecting the Arduino board to the game controller I/O on the breadboard. (Red wires are 3.3 V V$_{cc}$, black wires are GND, other colors are for wiring clarity, and do not signify anything in particular.)

associated with the device using bipolar junction transistors, but in modern use means where the positive power supply connection is made.

The two pushbuttons are connected to pins 7 and 8 respectively. Like the joystick button, while pushed in, the buttons connect the pin to ground. Each button is connected between an available input pin on the Arduino Uno Board (ADC or a "digital" input, which is a very fast 1-bit ADC, sometimes called a comparator) and ground (labelled GND). All ADC pins can be used as digital inputs, but only the ADC pins can be used for higher resolution (10-bit in the case of the ATMega328) analog conversions.

Pins 9 & 10 are output pins, for controlling a vibration motor and a light (LED) respectively. Most output circuits such as these require additional components to ensure that current limits (40 mA for each output pin on the Arduino Uno R3) are not exceeded. The LED pin current is limited with a 1K resistor connected between the pin and the anode of the LED. This allows for a bright light when pin 10 is set to HIGH voltage (5 V on the Arduino Uno), providing roughly 3 mA of current to the LED ($V_{forward}$ = 2 V), according to Ohm's Law: (5 V − 2 V_{LED})/1,000. The vibration motor is trickier to use, as it requires more current (usually over 100 mA) to operate. In these cases, a transistor can be used as an electronic switch. The circuit uses an NPN transistor, the PN2222A. When a small current moves from the base junction of the transistor to the emitter junction, a massive (approximately 300x) amount of current can move from the collector to the emitter. To limit the base current (which would otherwise be very high), another 1 K resistor is connected between pin 9 and the transistor base pin. This limits the base current to around 4 mA, and the collector current to about 1.2 A. The motor is then connected between 3.3 V and the collector, and the emitter is connected to ground.

Both pin 9 & 10 can be controlled in two ways, as binary outputs (HIGH or LOW), or as PWM outputs. PWM stands for pulse-width-modulation, and means that the pin can be set to turn its output HIGH for a certain period of time, then LOW for the remaining period of time. The ratio of the HIGH to the total period is called the "duty-cycle." The sample period is either 1/490s, or 1/980s depending on which PWM pin is used (the pins marked with a ~ on the Arduino Uno).

29.5 Section III—Software

Once the circuit is constructed, and all connections are verified, an Arduino program can be written to periodically sample and transmit each sensor reading through the Arduino serial port. It also reads commands from the serial port and controls outputs. The program is designed to be generic, and can be adapted for most controller types by changing only the upper block of code. It is further designed to minimize the amount of latency when writing and reading data from the serial port.

The program (Listing 29.1) starts with assigning variable names to pin numbers. Variable arrays are used to shorten the code, and allow for future expansion.

Listing 29.1. Arduino I/O communications program (C).

```
/*********** Gamepad Configuration *********/
const int NUM_DIGITAL_IN = 3;
int digitalInPins[NUM_DIGITAL_IN] = {6, 7, 8};          // Thumb, b1, b2
int digitalInPinTypes[NUM_DIGITAL_IN] = {1, 1, 1};      // 1 for pullup
const int NUM_ANALOG_IN = 5;
int analogInPins[NUM_ANALOG_IN] = {A2, A1, A0, A4, A3}; //  X,Y,Z,Horz,Vert
const int NUM_DIGITAL_OUT = 1;
```

```
int digitalOutPins[NUM_DIGITAL_OUT] = {10};              // LED
const int NUM_ANALOG_OUT = 1;
int analogOutPins[NUM_ANALOG_OUT] = {9};                 // Vibration Motor
int ADC_REFERENCE = EXTERNAL; // see Arduino documentation for analogReference()

/********** Serial Communication *********/
const unsigned long baudRate = 115200;
const int startByte = 0x72; //arbitrary (but avoid 0x00 & 0xFF)
int lastByte = 0; // book-keeping, do not change
int readIndex = 0;

/********** Microcontroller Initialization *********/
void setup() {
  Serial.begin(baudRate);
  for (int i = 0; i < NUM_DIGITAL_IN; i++) {
    pinMode(digitalInPins[i], digitalInPinTypes ? INPUT_PULLUP : INPUT);
  }
  for (int i = 0; i < NUM_DIGITAL_OUT; i++) {
    pinMode(digitalOutPins[i], OUTPUT);
  }
  for (int i = 0; i < NUM_ANALOG_OUT; i++) {
    pinMode(analogOutPins[i], OUTPUT);
  }
  analogReference(EXTERNAL);
}

/********** Called repeatedly by the Arduino base code ********/
void loop() {

  Serial.flush(); // wait for any prior serial output to complete
  Serial.write(startByte);

  // write inputs (bit packed)
  byte inputStates = 0;
  for (int i = 0; i < NUM_DIGITAL_IN; i++) {
    int shift = i % 8;
    int b = !digitalRead(digitalInPins[i]); // 1 (pressed) or 0 (unpressed)
    inputStates |= (b << shift); // put in bit field
    if (shift == 7 || i == (NUM_DIGITAL_IN - 1)) {
      writeByteWithEscapes(inputStates);
      inputStates = 0;
    }
  }

  // write analogs (packed into 2 little-endian bytes per analog)
  int analogStates[NUM_ANALOG_IN];
  for (int i = 0; i < NUM_ANALOG_IN; i++) {
    analogStates[i] = analogRead(analogInPins[i]);
    writeByteWithEscapes(analogStates[i] & 0x00FF);
    writeByteWithEscapes((analogStates[i] >> 8) & 0x00FF);
  }

  // read output commands
  while (Serial.available()) {
    byte b = (byte)Serial.read();
    // handle packet alignment with the possibility of escaped start bytes
    if (b == startByte && lastByte != startByte) {
      lastByte = b;
      continue; // must wait to see if it's escaped
    } else if (b != startByte && lastByte == startByte) {
      // start of a packet, reset the read index
      lastByte = b;
      readIndex = 0;
```

```
    } else if (b == startByte && lastByte == startByte) {
      lastByte = 0; // not the start byte
    } else {
      lastByte = b;
    }

    // read bit-packed digital outputs
    if (readIndex < (NUM_DIGITAL_OUT + 7)/8) {
      int offset = readIndex;
      for (int i = 0; i < 8; i++) {
        int pinIndex = offset * 8 + i;
        if (pinIndex >= NUM_DIGITAL_OUT) {
          break;
        }
        int pin = digitalOutPins[pinIndex];
        digitalWrite(digitalOutPins[i], (b & (1 << i) > 0) ? HIGH : LOW);
      }
      readIndex++;
    } else { // done with digital, next read the analog output commands
      analogWrite(analogOutPins[readIndex++], b);
    }
    if (readIndex >= (NUM_DIGITAL_OUT + 7)/8 + NUM_ANALOG_OUT) {
      readIndex = 0;
    }
  }
}

/********** Helper Function for handling start byte escaping *********/
void writeByteWithEscapes(byte b) {
  if (b == startByte) {
    Serial.write(startByte);
  }
  Serial.write(b);
}
```

Arduino digital pins are also known as general purpose input/output pins – this means that they can be used to detect digital signals (i.e. as inputs) or can be used to change digital signals (as outputs). The Arduino library function *pinMode()* is used (perhaps unsurprisingly) to select the pin mode for each connected pin. For input pins, there are two options: INPUT and INPUT_PULLUP. When set as INPUT, the pin's voltage is determined entirely by external circuitry. When set as INPUT_PULLUP, an internal resistor is switched on, connecting the pin to logic HIGH. However, the resistance value of the resistor is in the range of 25–50 kΩ. This means that it will not normally influence the pin voltage, except for when there is no connection to the pin, in which case the voltage will be read as HIGH. The button pins are set as INPUT_PULLUP, as they are connected to pushbuttons, such that when pushed they will connect the pin directly to LOW voltage. When unpushed, because of the pullup resistor, they will be read as HIGH. The output pins are set as an OUTPUT, indicating that their function is to power a device.

The *analogReference()* function is used to change the default ADC reference point from 5 V to the external voltage at A_{ref} (3.3 V in the example). This means 3.3 V will read as 1,023, and 0 V will read as 0. If this were not done, 3.3 V would read as 614, losing 2/5 of the possible resolution.

The configuration block also initializes some global bookkeeping variables necessary for our application's communication protocol. The "baud-rate" specifies the number of transmitted bits per second (for binary communications), and is a very important consideration. Choosing the highest reliable baud rate (normally 115, 200 bits/s) is normally acceptable and desirable. This will place an upper limit on the send rate. For example, if the packet size is 12 bytes (as it is in this example), the maximum number of transmissions/second is 115,200 / 8 / 12 or about 1,200 transmissions/s. This assumes that the Serial port is always in use. In practice, the update rate will be less, but it will be highly consistent.

The communication protocol is designed to ensure that each data packet sent through the serial port can be correctly aligned, i.e., the reader knows where it starts. Some protocols use ASCII encoding to do this, but this results in a significant overhead relative to using unencoded binary bytes. The protocol in use is typical of Serial communications. It uses a known "start byte" that has an arbitrary value. As the start byte could potentially occur within the data, any start bytes within the data are duplicated. Thus, a standalone start byte indicates the start of a message, while two in a row indicates one actual instance of the byte alone. This incurs overhead, but is minimal. Using a non-boundary (i.e. not 0x00 or 0xFF) value for the start-byte minimizes the probability of this byte occurring in the data.

29.6 VR Program

A corresponding program (Listing 29.2) on the VR system serves to read all inputs from the serial port, and send control outputs. This example is provided as a C# Unity3D script, and tested on the Microsoft Windows operating system. The script can be attached to any scene object. It is the complement to the Arduino program. The principle difference is the use of a C# thread. This difference is associated with Unity's Mono Development environment implementation of the .NET SerialPort class, which does not implement asynchronous access to the SerialPort. Thus, reading and writing must be done synchronously, and in a thread, so as not to slow down the VR rendering.

Listing 29.2. Unity I/O communications program (C#).

```
// Unity I/O Communications Program (ArduinoGamepad.cs)
using System.Collections;
using System.Collections.Generic;
using UnityEngine;
using System.IO.Ports;
using System;
using System.Threading;

public class ArduinoGamepad : MonoBehaviour
{
    // Configuration block
    public static int numDigitalIn = 3;
    public static int numAnalogIn = 5;
    public static int numDigitalOut = 1;
    public static int numAnalogOut = 1;
    const int startByte = 0x72;
    public string port = "\\\\.\\COM8";
    public int baudRate = 115200;
```

29. Building and Interfacing Input and Output Devices

```
// Private members
SerialPort p;
ThreadStart serialThreadStart;
Thread serialThread;
bool threadQuit = false;
bool[] digitalIns = new bool[numDigitalIn];
ushort[] analogIns = new ushort[numAnalogIn];
bool[] digitalOuts = new bool[numDigitalOut];
byte[] analogOuts = new byte[numAnalogOut];

// Start
// - Called once by Unity when the script is enabled, before Update
void Start() {
    p = new SerialPort(port, baudRate, Parity.None, 8, StopBits.One);
    p.ReadTimeout = 1;
    p.WriteTimeout = 1;
    p.Open();
    serialThreadStart = new ThreadStart(serialThreadFunc);
    serialThread = new Thread(serialThreadStart);
    serialThread.Start();
}

// getAnalogInput
// - retrieves the latest value for a particular analog input 0 - numAnalogIn
// - return values will be between 0 and 1023 for typical Arduino ADCs
public int getAnalogInput(int a) {
    lock(analogIns) {
        return analogIns[a];
    }
}
// setAnalogOutput
// - sets the strength of a particular analog output 0 - numAnalogOut     //
public void setAnalogOutput(int a, int v) {
    lock(analogOuts) {
        analogOuts[a] = (byte)v;
    }
}

// getDigitalInput
// - retrieves the latest state for a particular digital input 0 - numDigitalIn
// - returns true if the digital input is HIGH (1), false if the digital input is LOW (0)
public bool getDigitalInput(int d) {
    lock(digitalIns) {
        return digitalIns[d];
    }
}
// setDigitalOutput
// - sets the state of a particular digital output input 0 - numDigitalOut
// - set v to true if the digital output should be HIGH (1),
//      or false if the digital output should be  is LOW (0)
public void setDigitalOutput(int d, bool v) {
    lock(digitalOuts) {
        digitalOuts[d] = v;
    }
}

// writePacket
// - called by the serial thread to send digital and analog outputs to the Arduino
void writePacket() {
    p.BaseStream.WriteByte(startByte);
    lock(digitalOuts) {
        int bitField = 0;
```

```
        for (int i = 0; i < digitalOuts.Length; i++) {
            int shift = i % 8;
            if (digitalOuts[i]) {
                bitField = bitField | (1 << shift);
            }
            if (shift == 7 || i == (digitalOuts.Length - 1)) {
                if (bitField == startByte) {
                    p.BaseStream.WriteByte(startByte);
                }
                p.BaseStream.WriteByte((byte)bitField);
                bitField = 0;
            }
        }
    }
    lock(analogOuts) {
        for (int i = 0; i < analogOuts.Length; i++) {
            if (analogOuts[i] == startByte) {
                p.BaseStream.WriteByte(startByte);
            }
            p.BaseStream.WriteByte(analogOuts[i]);
        }
        p.BaseStream.Flush();
    }
}

// readPacket
// - called by the serial thread to handle incoming digital & analog inputs from the Arduino
void readPacket(byte[] buffer) {
    p.BaseStream.Flush();
    lock(digitalIns) {
        for (int i = 0; i < digitalIns.Length; i++) {
            digitalIns[i] = (buffer[i / 8] & (1 << i)) != 0;
        }
    }
    lock(analogIns) {
        for (int i = 0; i < analogIns.Length; i++) {
            int index = i * 2 + (numDigitalIn + 7) / 8;
            analogIns[i] = (ushort)((buffer[index + 1] << 8) | buffer[index]);
        }
    }
}


// serialThreadFunc
// - started by the monobehavior to handle serial communication with minimal delay
void serialThreadFunc() {
    byte[] buffer = new byte[numAnalogIn * 2 + (numDigitalIn + 7) / 8];
    int readIndex = 0;
    int lastByte = 0;

    while (!threadQuit) {
        int b = -1;
        try {
            b = p.ReadByte();
        } catch (TimeoutException) {
            writePacket ();
            continue;
        }

        if (b == startByte && lastByte != startByte) {
            lastByte = b;
            continue;
        } else if (b != startByte && lastByte == startByte) {
            lastByte = b;
```

```
                    readIndex = 0;
                } else if (b == startByte && lastByte == startByte) {
                    lastByte = 0;
                } else {
                    lastByte = b;
                }
                lock(buffer) {
                    buffer[readIndex++] = (byte)b;
                }

                if (readIndex == buffer.Length) {
                    readPacket(buffer);
                    writePacket();
                    readIndex = 0;
                }
            }
        }
        if (p.IsOpen) {
            p.Close();
        }
    }

    // OnApplicationQuit
    //  - called once by Unity when the application is stopped normally,
    //        or stop is pressed in the editor
    //  - this stops the thread
    void OnApplicationQuit() {
        threadQuit = true;
    }
}
```

29.7 Section IV—Conclusion

The approach taken here is one of many possibilities. Several adaptations may be desirable. For example, a simple change might be to only send values that change. However, this would require some overhead to specify which values changed, making the protocol more complex. Additionally, high frequency control is not possible with this scheme, as the serial bandwidth is too low. Smaller packets would help, as would a higher baud rate. Furthermore, wireless communication could be added. Several drop-in wired serial replacements are available, such as the Digi XBee (Series 1) devices. Other products use higher bandwidth protocols (e.g. SPI or I²C) such as the NRF24L01+, and would require more work, but provide lower latency. Finally, using WiFi or Bluetooth is also possible through Arduino, but these technologies add significant latency, and should be used with care for VR applications.

30

A Tinkerer's Perspective on VR Displays

J. Adam Jones
University of Mississippi

In this chapter, we look at virtual reality (VR) displays from a different perspective—that of the VR tinkerer. As a result, this chapter will be presented in a fairly informal manner. We will be focusing exclusively on components, hardware, and the effect they have on display design. Topics to be covered include display panels, optics, physical structure, head-mounting techniques, and the like. Regardless of your background or foreknowledge, I hope this chapter will be digestible and insightful.

30.1 Introduction

The motivation of a tinkerer may be different from your typical academic, scientist, or engineer, but these groups can, and often do, overlap. I want to take some time to give you an idea as to why this chapter is perhaps a little less technical and a little more practical than ones you may have seen elsewhere. Let's do this by talking about the motivations of the people who typically work with VR displays.

Academics and researchers are usually tool, or instrumentation, focused. They are often using VR as a means to study something else. This *something else* can be almost anything from brain function to automotive repair. Sometimes they are studying VR itself with the hopes of improving the technology, but in recent years advancements in VR technology seem to be coming more rapidly from industry. Since VR is a tool for their work, they are largely interested in having displays that are well-built, low-hassle, and high precision.

Engineers working in the development of VR displays, on the other hand, may be interested more in producing displays that will fill the needs of gamers, academics, scientists, or other clients. Some engineers may be more research centric, focusing on pushing the boundaries of what is possible, but still with the focus of eventually making a product.

Tinkerers, however, tend to be prototype oriented. Their focus is less on making a tool or a product. Instead, they may be more interested in how far they can get on creativity, wit, and limited resources. Their prototypes may not be cutting edge technology, but it will almost certainly be a feat of creative engineering. Best of all, anyone can be a tinkerer regardless of their day job, though tinkering tends to be an afterhours activity. This brings up another interesting characteristic of the tinkerer. They do not usually have a lab or a big budget for their prototypes. These are folks who are doing their work with pocket change and in their garage, dorm room, or wherever they can find work space. This is the target audience of this chapter.

We are going to cover the basic components and design considerations that you will need to build a workable VR display prototype similar to those shown in Figure 30.1. Often prototypes are not engineered with exacting precision, but with a little bit of foreknowledge you can greatly improve the quality of your prototypes. With time, practice, and some further investigation, you can produce prototypes that approach professional production standards. This chapter will not get you there by itself, but it will set you in the right direction and hopefully help you avoid some headache and frustration along the way.

30.1.1 Diving In

OK, let's do this—dive into the topic. First, we need to go over some up-front information. The VR display type that most people are familiar with is called the *head-mounted display*, or *HMD* for short. An HMD is a VR display that is meant to be worn on your head like goggles or a helmet. Some folks also call them head-worn displays since this sounds a

Figure 30.1

Students assembling a 3D printed display. You may notice the display's various components: display panel, optics, scaffoling, and other electronics.

30. A Tinkerer's Perspective on VR Displays

little less invasive. I can sympathize with this argument, but the acronym HMD is embedded deeply in VR culture. When you're wearing an HMD, the things that you are seeing and interacting with are usually called the *virtual environment*. You will sometimes hear people use the terms virtual environment and *virtual world* interchangeably.

What you see in the virtual environment is usually what theater goers call "3D." I put this in quotes because it is a little more complicated than that. In computer graphics terms, anything that shows a picture of a three-dimensional space is considered 3D graphics (including common on-screen computer games). The "3D" that you get when you watch a 3D movie is something very specific called *stereoscopic 3D*. This means that you are seeing two unique views simultaneously, one view with your right eye and another with your left (stereo = two, scopic = view). This is how most HMDs show 3D virtual environments — using stereoscopic views. Each eye sees a slightly different view of the world both in reality and virtual reality. This lets us get more 3D information about what we see than when just using one eye and results in the "pop-out" effect experienced in 3D movies. There are some HMDs that show 3D scenes from only one eye's point of view. These are called *monoscopic*. The HMDs that we're going to talk about in this chapter are all stereoscopic HMDs, but many of the things we will discuss could easily apply to monoscopic designs as well.

Every HMD has at least three components: an image source, a focusing mechanism, and a scaffolding to hold them all together. We are going to talk about some of the factors that you'll need to consider when dealing with these components and making a design that will work with them. We will begin by looking at image sources, or what actually shows your virtual environment. Next, we'll talk about the kind of optics you'll need to make the image of your virtual environment focusable. Finally, we'll end by going over the options you have to put these components together into a complete display. Hopefully, by the end of this chapter, you will be ready to build your own VR display prototype.

30.2 Display Panels

Virtual reality is largely about being visually immersed in a virtual world. This means that we will need some way to display images of this world to the user. Before we talk about displaying images in your HMD, let's take a moment to talk a little about how people see the world. One of the simplest ways of explaining human vision is to say that our eyes *detect* light from the world around us and turn it into a picture that our brains can actually *see*. This explanation has three distinct parts. First, the *world* provides us with light. Second, our *eyes* accept that light. Third, our *brain* interprets the light and tells us what we see (or at least what we *think* we see). In virtual reality, we are trying to replace the real world light with light that we control with a computer. People who study human vision call the light that enters the eye the *optical array*. This term makes a lot of sense if you think a bit about vision. Rays of *light* enter our eye and they show us the structure of the world around us. You can think of the optical array as just meaning structured light (optical = light, array = structure).

We can use a computer to generate a picture of a virtual world using pixels on a display. These pixels are seen as a 2D array or grid of colored dots of light. This means that our virtual world is visually composed of a *pixel array*. This pixel array becomes a synthetic optical array which we substitute for the real world. Herein lies a problem.... We can have a nearly infinite number of rays of light coming into our eyes from the real world, but an image rendered on a computer has a finite number of pixels. Essentially, we substitute pixels for rays of light in virtual reality. This is one of the most important tasks of a VR visual display, and it relies on the device that you choose to present images through your HMD.

Anything that you can use to display a picture can be used as an image generator for a virtual environment. We could use video projectors, LCDs, LEDs, lasers, or any number of devices, but for our purposes we're going to focus exclusively on LCD panels. Why are we looking at these? Because we are living in the age of the display panel! In the homes of most people I know, myself included, display panels outnumber people by at least 2:1. Take a minute and count the display panels in your home. They are in our TVs, desktop/laptop computers, tablet devices, smartphones, cameras, thermostats, and many other things (there is even an LCD panel in my vacuum cleaner). They are an essentially ubiquitous part of life in many places of the world. This has implications for the VR tinkerer. First, the prevalence of these display panels has driven down their price considerably. For instance, as of the writing of this chapter, you can easily find lightweight 7" LCD panels with moderately high resolution for under $50 from many online marketplaces. An example is shown in Figure 30.2. Second, it has also gotten easier to harvest LCD panels from broken or second hand goods. You may be surprised at the components you'd be able to harvest from your local second-hand stores. These low-cost, off-the-shelf display panels have become the workhorse of many VR tinkerers and hardware hackers.

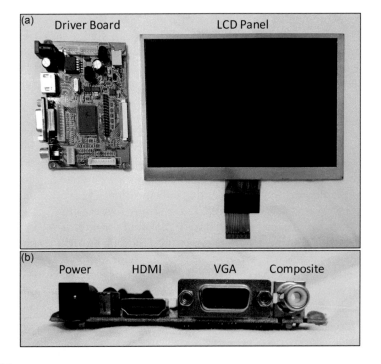

Figure 30.2

A common off-the-shelf LCD panel and its driver board (a). A thin ribbon cable is used to connect the panel and driver board. A close-up view of the ports available on the driver board is also shown (b).

30. A Tinkerer's Perspective on VR Displays

30.2.1 Resolution

One of the first numbers that people look at when getting a desktop monitor is screen resolution, or the total number of pixels in the screen. Usually this is given as the number of pixels along the width of the screen and the number of pixels along the height of the screen (e.g., 1920 × 1080). In some modern televisions, resolution is described in terms of only the vertical number of pixels and the ratio of horizontal to vertical pixels (e.g., 1080, 16:9). When picking a display panel for your project, you will probably be tempted to look for display panels with the highest resolution. This is a reasonable approach, but it isn't always the best approach. Working with VR displays is different than working with computer monitors or televisions. The difference is in how we use them. For instance, monitors and televisions usually sit in a room at some stationary position—on a desk, table, or mounted on the wall. They don't typically move around much, so if you want to get a look at the whole screen at once, you stand back, away from it. You could even stand far enough away that you can't make out individual pixels on the screen. On the other hand, if you want to get a close look at something on the screen, you move closer to it. You can get so close that you can see even individual pixels. How large the pixels appear depends on how close you are to the screen. This means that the *visual angle* (how much of your total vision is covered by something) occupied by a pixel changes based on your viewing position. If you think of it like that, when you're standing far from the screen, there are more pixels per degree of your vision and less when you're standing closer. This is called *angular resolution*, or how many pixels there are per degree of vision. In virtual reality, the display panel isn't sitting somewhere your room. It is attached to your head. You cannot get closer, you cannot get further away. This means that you are more interested in the angular resolution of your display than the traditional resolution. For this reason, you want to look for a display that has the smallest, most densely packed pixels that you can get. Why does this matter so much? When you display a virtual environment, you are creating a volumetric space that is composed of 3D pixels called voxels. These voxels are the overlap of two pixels (one seen by the right eye and one seen by the left eye). They define the smallest possible chunk of 3D space that you can draw (Figure 30.3). The smaller the pixels, the smaller the chunks of space you can represent, and the better your 3D resolution. For this reason, depending on what you want your display prototype to do, you may actually prefer to use a 1280 × 800, 5in display as opposed to a 1920 × 1080, 8in display.

30.2.2 Estimating Angular Resolution

How exactly can you figure out a VR display's angular resolution? That turns out to be a complicated question to answer because of the way most HMDs magnify the view of the display panel. The optical systems used in most off-the-shelf HMDs do not uniformly magnify the screen. This causes distortions in the image you see through the lenses making the angle subtended by the pixels change across your view! It is much easier to estimate the average angular resolution if you know the HMD's pixels resolution and *field of view (FOV)*. FOV is the total visual angle that one eye can see in the HMD. If you're trying to estimate the angular resolution of an off-the-shelf VR display, you'll want to consult the manufacturer's specifications to find the FOV. When manufacturer's quote field of view, they often use *diagonal field of view* or the field of view measured between opposite corners of the screen (upper left and lower right or upper right to lower left). Once you've gotten

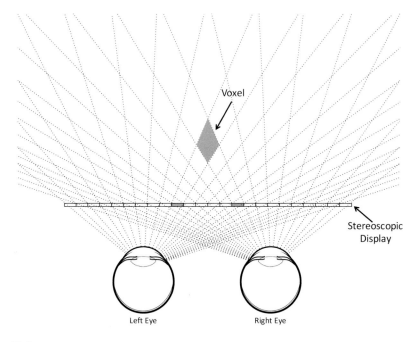

Figure 30.3

An illustration of voxels seen in a 3D display.

the diagonal FOV and the screen's resolution, you can estimate the average angular resolution as the ratio of degrees of FOV to the number of pixels across the screen's diagonal. We've got to do some math for this. Fortunately, the mathematics is pretty lightweight. If we are estimating angular resolution (A_{est}), we know the horizontal pixel resolution (p_x), the vertical pixel resolution (p_y), and the diagonal FOV (F_d), then the formula will be:

$$A_{est} = \frac{F_d}{\sqrt{p_x^2 + p_y^2}} \tag{30.1}$$

Sometimes, you may see manufacturers listing *total field of view*. This usually refers to the combined field of view of both eyes in the HMD. However, the views of each eye typically overlap to some degree. When calculating angular resolution, you want to know what *each eye can see*, not what both can see simultaneously. This is a common "gotcha" when estimating a VR display's angular resolution.

30.2.3 The Screen Door Effect

Having higher angular resolution also helps in avoiding the *screen door effect* (Figure 30.4). The screen door effect occurs when the virtual world appears pixelated almost as though it is being viewed through a window or door screen. This is largely an issue of the angular resolution of your HMD, but it is also exacerbated by empty gaps between pixels in your display panel. These gaps can give the appearance of a literal screen laying atop the pixels of the display, making low-resolution imagery more noticeable. Fortunately, prototypes

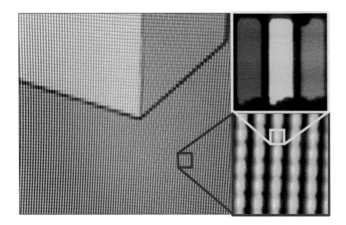

Figure 30.4

An example of the "screen door effect" at multiple scales. The red highlighted area provides a close-up view of large between-pixel gaps. The yellow highlighted area shows a microscopic view of a single pixel. Notice that tiny gaps are present even within the pixel itself. These can be discerned in very low resolution, high magnification HMDs.

usually have looser design requirements than production-grade designs. Depending on what you want to do with your prototype, you might be able to get by with a pretty modest display panel. Generally, I don't worry too much about the screen door effect in a prototype. This is because the effect is most noticeable when you're looking at a stationary image, but this isn't what you're usually doing in VR. You're almost always looking around, moving your eyes, head, or body. Our visual system is very good at filtering out visual noise, especially when moving. As such, the power of the screen door effect greatly diminishes when either the scene or user is in motion. After a few minutes, many people stop noticing it at all.

30.2.4 Design Considerations

From the tinkerer's perspective, your choice in display panel dictates a lot of your design constraints. This isn't very surprising since the display panel is a very functionally important component. It is what actually presents the virtual world to the user. It is also the single largest component that your design will have to accommodate. Another factor that must be considered is that the display panel almost always requires a separate driver board that serves as an interface with your computer (Figure 30.2). Of course, the panel's width and height will affect the minimum width and height of your HMD design as well. Essentially, your design will probably be centered around accommodating the display panel.

You also have to consider *how many* display panels you will need. There are generally two configurations that are seen in HMD designs: one panel or two panel designs. Older HMDs often had a separate display panel for each of the user's eyes. In this approach, a display panel and a focusing mechanism are physically attached to one another and present a single, monocular view to the user. By necessity, you would have two of these arrangements (one for each eye). These could then be adjusted independently to align with the user's eyes. This is a pretty big advantage because people's eyes are spaced differently from one person to the next (typical range is from 58 to 72 mm, average is 63 mm). Since each eye has its own independent, moveable display and optics, the two panel design could easily accommodate a wide range of users. The disadvantage of this approach was that you need additional circuitry to drive two display panels, not to mention mechanical parts to adjust for the eye separation. This often leads to either bulkier HMDs or completely separate display driver boxes to which the HMD must be tethered. However, as displays and driver boards are getting smaller and cheaper, the pendulum is swinging back toward the two panel design. Several consumer-level displays are now using this configuration.

Some modern consumer-level displays, however, opt for using a single display panel to present both the left and right eye views. As you would expect, the left eye's view is drawn on the left side of the screen and the right eye's view is drawn on the right side (Figure 30.5). This design has a couple advantages. Since you only have a single display panel, you only need one driver board which can often easily be packaged in the HMD itself without need for an external driver box. The second advantage is that it can be much cheaper! The display panel is likely to be the most expensive part of your proto-type, so keeping the number of panels low is financially desirable. However, there are some disadvantages as well. Since you have a single panel, the lenses are usually rigidly fixed to the panel and not easily adjustable. This makes accommodating a wide range of eye separations difficult. Additionally, the center of each eye's view will probably not be aligned with the center of the viewport on the screen. This can prove to be a more difficult rendering situation. However, this is more of a software issue that is beyond the scope of this hardware-oriented chapter. Just be aware that this may be an issue for single-panel configurations.

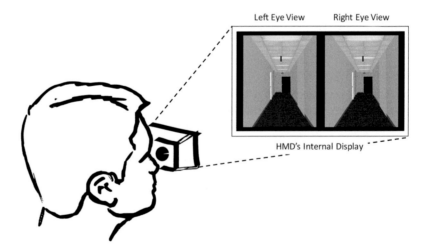

Figure 30.5

An example of a 3D scene as shown in a single panel VR display. This arrangement is called side-by-side stereo.

30. A Tinkerer's Perspective on VR Displays

30.3 Optics

Once you've gotten something that can display an image, you have to make it visible to the user. The naïve assumption would be that you can just put the display panel directly in front of the user as you would with a typical monitor, only a lot closer to the face. This should work, right? Let's do an experiment right now. Grab a piece of paper with some writing on it (or even a cellphone with some text on the screen). Now, hold it about 2 in. ($\approx$5 cm) from your eyes and try to read it. You probably can't. Why is this? The paper that you're trying to read is closer to you than your eyes can actually focus. In order for you to be able to read the text, you'll have to move the paper farther away from your eyes. Depending on your age and vision, this distance might be an arm's length or more away. For a head-worn VR display, having the screens this far away from your eyes would not be reasonable. Since we cannot physically move the display panel very far from your eye, can we *optically* move it farther away? The answer, of course, is yes! We can make our displays look farther away than they actually are by using lenses to bend light. This is the primary purpose of the *focusing mechanisms* in VR displays.

In many old-school VR displays (as well as many modern, professional displays), you'll find complicated focusing mechanisms consisting of multiple lenses, prisms, beam-splitters, or mirrors. However, most modern consumer-grade VR displays use a single lens per eye to focus and magnify the images that you see. Optical engineering is a pretty heavy subject and can be rather complicated. Fortunately, the astute tinkerer can get by with some basic knowledge and equipment.

Tinkering with optics can get expensive very quickly, especially if you are shopping for professional-grade equipment. Fortunately, if you know some basics about how optics work and where to look, you can do some pretty sophisticated stuff cheaply. Let's start off with lenses. The most common kind of lens you'll most likely be working with are convex lenses. Most off-the-shelf magnifying glasses are of this type. They are also usually made from lightweight plastic, very cheap, and widely available (from both online and brick-and-mortar retailers). This makes magnifying glasses a great source of inexpensive lenses for VR tinkering. It is no coincidence that some of the early consumer VR displays used single, plastic lenses like those found in magnifiers. One of the trade-offs for plastic lenses (especially those harvested from off-the-shelf magnifiers) is that they tend to produce more distortions in the image. They are often very clear when looking through the middle, but the periphery may appear less focused, blurry, or even wavy. This can sometimes be attributed to uneven cooling or other manufacturing problems that would not be evident when simply using them for their intended purpose. In my experience with off-the-shelf magnifiers, glass lenses usually produce better overall images and are only a few dollars more expensive than plastic lenses. However, glass lenses are usually much heavier than their plastic counterparts. In the end, your choice of glass or plastic will probably come down to a tradeoff of weight verses image quality. Take the lenses in Figure 30.6, for example. The left lens is glass and the lens on the right is plastic. Notice that the image seen through the glass lens is much clearer around the edges than with the plastic lens, but the plastic lens weighs almost half (7 g) as much as the glass lens (13 g)! If you are building a display where weight is important and image quality along the edge of your view isn't important, plastic lenses will probably be your best bet. On the other hand, if you're building a display

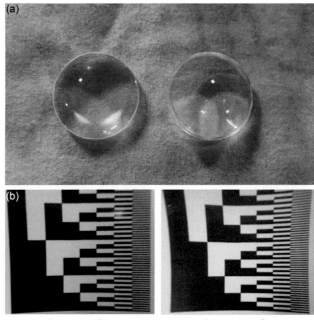

Glass Magnifier   Plastic Magnifier

Figure 30.6

Two off-the-shelf magnifiers, one glass (a), the other plastic (b). The images on the bottom illustrate the image clarity and distortions.

where image quality is more important, weight be damned, you'll almost certainly want to go with a glass lens.

30.3.1 Measuring Focal Length

When shopping around for lenses, you will need to know a couple things. First, what size lens are you going to need for your project? Lenses tend to come in a several standard diameters. Common lens diameters that are useful to the VR tinkerer are 50 and 38 mm. The 38 mm diameter lens is particularly common. The next thing you'll need to pick is a *focal length*. Every lens has a position at which light projected from a very far distance converges to a single point. Why is this number important? If you're using a single lens to focus your display, the focal length is going to dictate the maximum distance at which you can place your display panel and it still be focusable. When specifying lenses for your projects, you might also see focal length listed as *focal power*. Focal power has its own unit called diopters. Don't worry though; diopters are just the inverse of the focal length or, in other words, one divided by the focal length in meters (not millimeters). Since they are just straight inverses, you can also convert diopters to meters by dividing one by the focal power. A "gotcha" to keep in mind, however, is that we usually work in either centimeters or millimeters when building a display, so make sure you are converting your focal lengths to the correct units.

Since focal length is going to determine the spacing between your display panel and lens, it is a pretty important number. If you are buying professional-grade lenses from a well-established optics provider, the focal length provided in their specifications will probably be pretty close to the true focal length. However, such specifications are seldom provided with off-the-shelf magnifiers. In this case, you'll need to measure the focal length for yourself. It is also a good idea to confirm the focal length of lenses that may have been purchased from outlets that could be selling ultra-cheap lenses which might not have been manufactured to exacting standards. I have found some to be off by as much as 20 mm. In an optics lab, you might do this with an optical mounting rail, a special light source, and some complicated mounting hardware. Fortunately, we can approximate this setup using parts that you almost certainly have around your home or office. The trick to estimating a lens's focal length is understanding exactly what the focal length is in optical terms. The focal length is the distance at which parallel light rays entering one side of the lens converge to a single point on the other side of the lens. That sounds a bit abstract, so let's put that in more concrete terms. We can think of parallel rays as being light coming from a source that is very, very far away (effectively infinitely far) from your lens. The closer the light source is to your lens, the less parallel they are. The focal length can be thought of as the distance from the lens at which we get a clearly projected image of light sources that are very, very far away on the other side of the lens. Now that we know this, we can use a little trick to estimate the focal length of almost any lens.

I personally recommend working with 38 mm diameter lenses because this type of lens is common in magnifiers, lens sets, some HMDs, and in ophthalmology. This means that you can find them almost everywhere! These also work out well when improvising a mounting enclosure. The standard cardboard tube used with paper towels and other papers has a diameter of 43 mm (roughly 1.7 in.). As you can see in Figure 30.7, a small

Figure 30.7

An improvised 38 mm lens mount using a slice of a cardboard tube and a large binder clip.

piece cut from one of these tubes acts quite well as a lens enclosure and includes enough slack to act as a handle that can be held by a standard binder clip. (Tip: use the arms of the binder clip to brace the lens in its cardboard enclosure.) This gives us a fairly sturdy rig for holding our lens. You will also need an object to serve as a projection surface. A notecard in a binder clip will suffice. You will also need a ruler, preferably metric with millimeter divisions. Finally, you'll need to find a brightly lit window with about 6 m (roughly 20 ft) of space in front of it. Once you've gotten all of these things, place your lens (inside its holder) on your ruler at 6 m from your window with the ruler's length pointing toward the window. On the opposite side of the lens from the window, place your notecard. You will probably see some light blobs projected through the lens onto the notecard. This is the unfocused image of the window. Slowly slide the notecard along the ruler until the light blobs sharpen into a focused picture of the window (the image will be upside down, but this is okay). Figure 30.8 shows an example of what you should see when you've found the focal length. When you find the spot where the image of the window frame is most sharply focused, write down how far the notecard is from the lens on your ruler. You will want to repeat this measurement several times and take the average.

The measurement that you now have is going to be very close to your lens's focal length, but it is not quite right. Recall that the focal length is the distance at which light coming from an *infinitely far* light source converges to a single point after passing through your lens. Since your window is certainly not infinitely far away, this means that the measured distance is not the true focal length. However, we can apply a simple correction to this measurement to get us much closer to the actual value. You could derive this correction from optics equations, but I will spare you that task. If the average measurement is 93 mm or smaller, multiplying the measurement by 0.99 and rounding to the nearest millimeter will give you a very close approximation. For measurements greater than 93 mm, you will need to perform this correction and then subtract an additional 1 mm. For lenses with focal lengths of 125 mm or less, this approximation will give you an estimate within 99% of the lens's actual focal length. Of course, this is assuming that you've taken good, careful measurements.

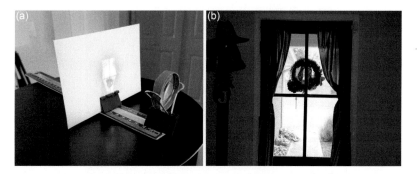

Figure 30.8

Here we see an example of the focal length measurement procedure (a) and the window being used as a focal reference (b). Notice that the projected image of the window on the notecard appears upside down.

30.3.2 Ballparking Focal Length

If you do not need very high accuracy, have enough room, or have the patience to do the above estimation procedure, you can "eyeball" a lens's focal length using the same setup as above. Lay your ruler on a flat surface, and place the lens at one end. This time, instead of a notecard, put a business card (or anything with writing on it) in a binder clip at the opposite end of the ruler. Now, you will need to look through the lens. Your view of the card will be very blurry. If it is not blurry you either have placed the card too close to the lens or you have a lens with a very long focal length. If it is the former, make sure you have the card and the lens as far apart on the ruler as possible. If it is the latter, then this method will not work well for this lens. Assuming that you see a blurry image of the card, begin to slowly move the card close to the lens until it becomes sharply focused. The distance at which your view of the card is sharply focused will be approximately the lens's focal length. Keep in mind, however, that this is a very, very rough estimation and will probably be off by multiple millimeters. This method also assumes that you have either normal (20/20) or corrected-to-normal (glasses, contact lenses, etc.) vision. Essentially, what you're measuring is the maximum distance from the lens where light is focused into your eye as opposed to onto a projection surface as in the previous method. Again, I must emphasize that this method is only a very rough, ballpark estimate.

30.3.3 Design Considerations

Though I recommend using the lens's focal length as the display separation, it can still be focusable at some distances shorter than the focal length, but only up to a point. The trick is that by using lenses to focus an image, what you're really doing is changing the angle that light *enters* one side of the lens and *leaves* the other. By changing the angle that light enters the eye, you can effectively make light appear to be coming from any distance you want. When your display panel is placed exactly at the focal length of the lens, the light entering the eye is composed of parallel rays and appears as though it's coming from a very, very far distance, so far in fact that is it effectively infinitely far away. Light that exits the lens in parallel rays is called *collimated* (the rays are parallel, forming columns, so they are collimated. Get it?). Many VR displays are collimated, especially research-grade displays. This can be an issue though. Not everyone has very good far vision. If you have normal or corrected-to-normal vision, viewing a collimated image in a VR display will be no problem. If you happen to be nearsighted, however, then you will still see a blurry image. For this reason, you may actually want the distance between the display panel and the lens to be slightly less than the focal length. Conversely, if you move the display panel beyond the focal length of the lens, the image is not naturally focusable by the human eye and will be seen as blurry to all users regardless of their visual acuity.

Choosing the separation between the display panel and lens is actually a really big decision. Why? Think back to what we said about how lenses focus light. They make the light at some distance appear to be coming from some other distance. Since your lens will be focusing light coming from your display panel, it will make all light coming from your display appear to be coming from one fixed distance. This means that your eye will be focused at that distance no matter at which distance you're actually looking in the virtual environment. This mismatch between where you are looking and where your eye is focusing can cause eye strain. To give an analogy, it is like putting on someone else's glasses and looking around. You might be able to see through them, but it makes your eyes feel weird or even hurt! You want to minimize this mismatch in your VR display. Generally speaking, collimated images (using the lens's actual focal length) are pretty comfortable for most viewing distances except those very close to the eye. However, if you are building a display where the user will only be viewing imagery that is within arm's length, such as a work bench or desktop, then you may want to separate the display and lenses by a distance slightly smaller than the focal length. Keep in mind, that if you move the display and lens too close to each other, you'll end up with a blurry, unfocusable image again. Regardless of your final decision, you'll need to know the separation that you will be using before moving on to designing the rest of your display.

30.4 Scaffolding

You have probably chosen a display panel and some lens for your prototype display. Now, you need to think about the part that most people seem to forget even exists—the *scaffolding*. This is the part of your display that holds all of your components in place, in particular the lenses relative to the display panel. Sometimes it is called the case or shell, but I prefer the term scaffolding. The reason behind this is that the scaffolding does not necessarily need to enclose the display. Its most important function is providing the structure for your display. Since you are likely to be tinkering with a prototype that you've hacked together, you will probably be making modifications and additions along the way. The scaffolding will act as the foundation upon which you make these modifications. Because of this, you will need to design your scaffolding with that in mind. In this section, we will discuss some helpful design recommendations that are geared toward 3D printed VR displays.

30.4.1 Open vs. Enclosed Scaffolding

Your next design choice is whether to have an open or enclosed scaffolding. An enclosed scaffolding is probably what you are used to seeing (e.g., Figure 30.9a). This kind of scaffolding acts both as a framework to hold your components and as a shell to cover and protect them. Open scaffolding acts simply as the framework to hold your components (e.g., Figure 30.9b). Both of these have their places. For instance, the enclosed scaffolding is almost certainly what you would want any production display to use. When you are shipping products out to thousands of users who will be using your display under a variety of unknown conditions, you want it to be as well protected as possible. However, the open scaffolding has certain advantages too. If you're building a prototype display, having an open scaffolding makes it much easier to access components, make structural modifications, or just fiddle with things. Since this chapter focuses primarily on building prototypes, we're going to talk mostly about open scaffolding.

30.4.2 Component-Based Design

If you've ever made a 3D printed prototype, then you likely know that muddled feeling of despair, anger, confusion, and utter frustration after having spent nine hours waiting for a print to finish only to find that you made the smallest error in your design. It might be just a mistake of a couple millimeters (or even less for things like threading), but the whole part is completely useless. You now have to modify your model and spend another nine hours waiting to find out what other mistakes you have made. To make matters worse,

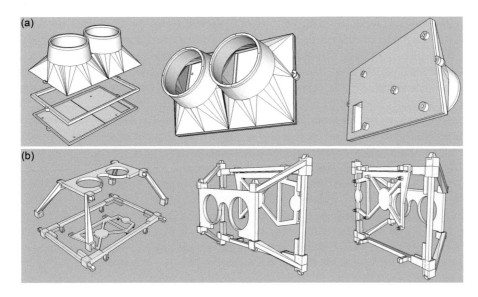

Figure 30.9

Examples of enclosed (a) and open (b) scaffoldings.

you're burning through filament! Will you have enough on this spool? No? How far into the print do you think you can make it on this spool? Four hours, maybe five? Who knows! It is the worst game of chance ever… I have seen many very good designers struggle with these issues, each having trash cans filled with failed prints.

I come from a computer science background where component-based design is a big deal. We are often taught to write programs in such a way as to have individual "components" that do specific functions that can easily be built and tested. I like to bring this design style to building physical prototypes, too. Whenever possible, I recommend opting to design a display prototype as a series of small interlocking parts instead of a single large part (e.g., Figure 30.9b). This will often require a little more up-front work when designing your prototype, but it will save you a lot of printing time and material in the long run. This idea works really well with open scaffolding style displays. For instance, the open scaffolding can consist of a series of individual parts that connect together to form a skeleton for your display. Conversely, component-based design doesn't really lend itself to enclosed scaffolding where it also serves as a shell for the display. If you are using an enclosed scaffolding, it usually has to accommodate the mounting of multiple internal parts while also covering the display's exterior. This often results in large, monolithic parts that cannot be easily decomposed. As such, an open scaffolding designed as a series of individual components is much more forgiving in terms of print time, filament use, error correction, and modification.

There are nearly infinite ways to design a display, but there are certain functional components that you will almost always see regardless of whether you use open or enclosed scaffolding. If you take a close look at most VR displays, they almost always have three basic components: lens mount, display panel frame, and circuit/electronics mount. The lens mount has the specific job of holding your optics relative to your display panel. Often this part will also serve as a faceplate, as can be seen in Figure 30.10. Above, you can see that the lens holder in the enclosed design is a single, large piece that forms the bulk of the display's case. In the open scaffolding display, you can see that the lens mount consists of five individual pieces. While there are five pieces, we only needed to design two models. We have one model of the faceplate and one model for the legs that attach the faceplate to the display panel frame. Why one model of the four legs? All of the legs are either rotated or mirrored copies of each other. If your lens mount is also acting as a faceplate, an important design feature that must be included is a significant amount of open space between the left and right lenses for the user's nose to sit comfortably.

The display panel frame has the modest, but important, purpose of holding the display panel stationary while attaching to the lens mount/faceplate. Even in enclosed display designs, this component is usually separate from the rest of the scaffolding and not part of the external casing. Regardless of scaffolding type, this can easily be a single part. If you are designing an open scaffolding, this will probably be your largest single component, so you might actually want to decompose it into several smaller pieces. For instance, in the example above (Figure 30.10b, c), the display scaffolding was intended to be part of a snap-together kit that would fit into a very small box. So that the display panel frame would fit, I opted to make it into four small parts. In the enclosed scaffolding example, on the other hand, you can see that this component is a single continuous, rectangular frame that would fit snuggly around the display panel.

The circuit/electronics mount is the part of your display that will serve primarily as the attachment point for your driver board. Regardless of display technology, you will almost always have a circuit board (usually packaged with the display panel) that takes some standard video input, such as VGA or HDMI, and translates it into the necessary signals to illuminate your display pixels. An example of this can be seen in Figure 30.2.

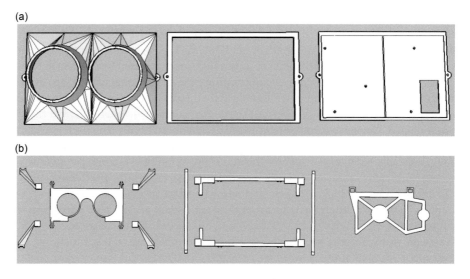

Figure 30.10

A deconstructed view of the enclosed (a) and open (b) scaffolding examples.

Usually, there is a single, very thin ribbon cable that attaches this circuit board to the display panel. Since this cable is pretty fragile, you do not want to leave the driver board hanging inside your HMD. You will need a way to rigidly attach it to the rest of the display. In the enclosed design above, the driver board is mounted on the backmost face of the enclosure. Also notice that there is a small window on the mounting to allow the ribbon cable to pass to the back of the display panel. It is not uncommon for the electronics of a display to be mounted in this part of the enclosure, but they are seldom outward facing as in the example above. In the open scaffolding example, however, notice that the driver board's mount is probably the most complicated part of the design. Don't be surprised if this is the case for you too. Though display panels and lenses tend to come in standard sizes, this is not the case for the display's driver board. They often have unique shapes, sizes, and attachment points from one manufacturer and model to the next.

30.4.3 Head Attachments

Once you have completed your display prototype and are satisfied with its function, you have the task of figuring out how to wear it. After all, these are *head-mounted* displays. There are actually several approaches you can take that can be both comfortable and easy to implement.

People often use ski goggles as an analogy for wearing a VR display (Figure 30.11a). This is a decent analogy, so it would seem reasonable to use a similar way to attach it to your head, right? Not always. Most ski goggles attach with a single elastic strap to hold itself against your face with pressure. This works well for ski goggles since they are pretty lightweight, but VR displays tend to be a lot heavier. Using a goggle strap results in the weight of the display being supported partially by the strap and partially by the user's nose. This quickly becomes uncomfortable and will likely leave the user's nose red and possibly bruised. As such, avoiding goggle-style straps is a good idea unless your display is exceedingly light.

There is a simple modification (Figure 30.11b), that you can make to the goggle strap approach that will make the display much more comfortable for the user. By adding a strap across the top of the user's head that attaches to the top of the HMD and to the back of the goggle strap, you lift the weight off the nose and distribute it over the head. This is

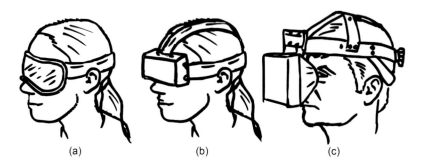

(a)　　　　　(b)　　　　　(c)

Figure 30.11

Examples of head mounting options including ski goggles (a), head straps (b), and rigid headgear (c).

generally a comfortable arrangement and can be implemented with as little as two long hook-and-loop fastener strips. Since this approach will likely have the user's face in direct contact with the display, you will need to add some padding to the faceplate. This can be done with felt or adhesive foam crafting sheets.

Another common method is to take the *headgear* approach, sometimes referred to as a *halo*. This method uses a rigid or semi-rigid harness to strap the HMD to the user's head. A common headgear implementation (Figure 30.11c) is to use the straps from an off-the-shelf welding mask. These straps can be easily found for under $20 from many online retailers. An advantage of this approach is that the headgear usually comes with a ratcheting adjustment knob that allows the user to easily adjust the size and tightness of the attachment.

30.4.4 Additional Attachments

When building a prototype display, you want to plan for modification. One way that I like to do this is by adding attachment points in the form of clips along the scaffolding. In the open scaffolding example above, you can see that the same style clip attachments that the circuit mount uses are also on the bottom of the frame. Why are they there? I don't know—at least not yet! Those attachment points can be used for the next idea you come up with to accessorize your display. I recommend coming up with an attachment scheme, like clips, that you can use as a standard on your prototypes. 3D printing also makes supporting this idea really easy. I have a model of just the clip attachment point (see Figure 30.12). I can take that clip model, stick it on any other model, and then print a piece that can have a new attachment point. This is very useful. Also, adding gaps between parts can be useful in case you need to run small wires, add head straps to your display, or accommodate some yet unknown accessory.

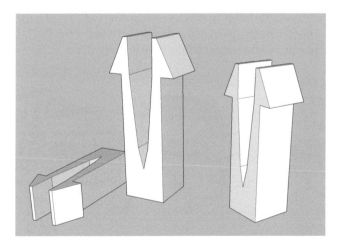

Figure 30.12

Attachment clip examples. These can be attached to various points on your design to accommodate accessories.

Unfortunately, you will never be able to plan for all possible modifications that you may want to make to your prototype. Similarly, you might not be sure what modifications you might want to undo in the future either. For this, you need to work out a sturdy but reversible attachment method. One of the best ways to accommodate unexpected modifications that may also need to be reversible is good ol' hot glue. This crafting staple can be your best friend in a pinch, but it is not perfect. Unfortunately, hot glue is hot... Big surprise, right? The problem is that many devices are made from plastic, and they can deform or discolor when heated. On some rough or porous surfaces, hot glue might not want to peel off when you try to remove it. For this reason, I'm actually not a fan of using hot glue by itself. I recommend using the combination of masking tape and hot glue. Apply the masking tape to the surface that you want to make your attachment and then hot glue your accessory to the tape. This serves several purposes. First, masking tape has an adhesive that is designed to be removed without damaging the surface to which it is attached (some even have pH neutral adhesives). Second, it acts as a thermal barrier between the hot glue and the underlying surface. In this sense, it works like a pot holder when taking a hot dish from your oven. Third, it prevents the hot glue from getting embedded into porous surfaces, making future removal of the attachment much easier.

30.5 3D Printing Tips

For prototyping VR displays, 3D printing is an awesome tool. You can go from having no manufacturing experience to making workable parts without tons of training or financial investment. I used to draw up designs and then bum shop time from family and friends. Turnaround time on a usable design could be days or weeks. Now, I can turn out several revisions of a part in a day! My modest little 3D printer is like having a tiny machine shop in my garage...just a really finicky machine shop that only works in plastic and runs on frustration. Don't get me wrong, I love 3D printing. It has completely changed the way (and how quickly) I build stuff. If you know its limits and how to work around them, you can do some really great prototyping. Keep in mind, I'm not a 3D printing guru. I'm just a computer science geek who likes to tinker. Having said this, I want to share some tips and tricks that I've come across while fiddling around in the garage.

After looking at the display design examples in the previous section, you might be tempted to go with an enclosed scaffolding for your prototype because it has far fewer parts. The enclosed design has three parts while the open design has ten! More parts, more things to go wrong and reprint, right? Also, more parts means more work, right? Maybe not. Take a closer look at the open scaffolding example. Even though there are ten total parts to the scaffolding, there are only five unique parts. The rest are either exact duplicates or mirrors of some other part. This can greatly reduce the amount of redesign work you will have to do in the future. For instance, if you make a mistake on the legs that attach to the display panel frame, you probably won't have to make a new lens holder. This design style also works well for accommodating changes to your designs. For example, if you decide to change to a different diameter lens, you'll only have to modify a single, quickly printable part of the display.

One of the catches to 3D printing is that you can't print in midair. This means that every layer that you print must have something printed below it for support. To allow you to print models that have overhanging parts, you usually have to print a removable support. These supports have to be removed once the print is complete. More often than not, the removal of these supports makes the surface of your print a little rougher, but this can be smoothed with a bit of sandpaper. However, this will usually leave the surface of your print looking scuffed. This is more of an aesthetic problem though. The bigger issue is that the support structure has to be disposed of once your print is completed. This can be a big waste of material. Many printers can print slants of around 40 degrees without the need for support structure. If you design your prototype with this in mind, you can make remarkably complex parts without the need for additional support structure. For instance, both of the scaffolding examples pictured earlier were printed without any support structure.

Another important "gotcha", especially for those of you who may be new to 3D printing, is sizing your parts. When printing parts that are intended to fit within each other, snap together, or screw together, you need to account for the sloppiness of 3D printers. Most additive 3D printers, specifically the kind that use plastic filaments, are essentially very precise hot glue guns (robotic hot glue guns, but hot glue guns nonetheless). They melt a tube of plastic and push it through a nozzle onto some surface where the plastic cools and sticks. Printers are very good at placing the nozzle almost exactly where it needs to go, but then it has to push out that gooey melted plastic. This is the sloppy part of 3D printing. Most printers are somewhat calibrated to account for this sloppiness, but it is affected by a lot of variables. Extrusion speed, nozzle size, tiny clogs, minute variations in filament thickness, air temperature, and tons of other factors can affect how the plastic is extruded. Because of this you usually need to account for sloppiness in your prints. For instance, let's pretend that you have a peg attached to some larger part that you want to fit into a hole in another part. You can reasonably assume that the centers of the peg and hole will be in the correct places, but you usually cannot assume that their diameters will be correct. In general, regardless of how you are manufacturing your parts, you will almost always need to very slightly undersize the peg to fit a hole of a given size. The extrusion slop in 3D printing usually requires you to further undersize your peg. I have had the opportunity to use several filament-based 3D printers from multiple manufacturers. With very few exceptions (exactly one), they all needed this adjustment. For very small peg/hole pairs, you may end up under-sizing the peg to the point that it is no longer a strong attachment point. For these circumstances, you will likely need to slightly oversize the hole in order to retain some strength at the attachment point.

30.6 A Final Note

I hope that this chapter has provided some insight into designing a VR display prototype. Getting started does involve a lot of tinkering and fiddling with your designs, but ultimately you will get the hang of it. I also believe the approach of tinkering with technologies, like VR, is a great way to learn. Through tinkering with something, you develop a more detailed understanding of how it works, what it is capable of, where its limits are, and what new things it *could potentially do*. This is something that I teach my lab students. I have noticed, however, that sometimes it can be hard for them to get started, especially when it comes to building a prototype. Once they get started, however, they almost can't stop! It can be fun, challenging, and informative. One important thing that I tell them is that no matter how well you plan your prototype, your first design will not be your final design. By default, this means that your first design won't work (at least not the way you planned). Regardless, just build something to get started. There are some things that you would never even think of without having first laid hands on your prototype. Don't be afraid of errors, failed builds, or design mistakes. Just build something, learn something, and then build something better.

31

Environmental Feedback for VR Systems

Chauncey E. Frend
Indiana University (IUPUI)

Contemporary virtual reality systems typically offer user feedback in the form of 3D spatialized visuals and sounds. Eye-sight and stereophonic hearing are the two most easily stimulated human senses in virtual reality (VR) thanks to readily available VR displays optimized for modern computer graphics and spatial audio. If you ponder the concept of immersive quality in terms of how realistic a VR experience feels you might find the immersive quality to be satisfactory in systems like the HTC Vive™ or Oculus Rift w/Touch™. However, there is always room for improvement. This chapter focuses on pragmatically engaging a user's senses beyond the default modes of sight and sound to strive for much higher physical and mental immersive qualities through multimodal feedback.

31.1 Background

Presenting environmental feedback for immersive experiences has always been an uphill struggle, typically relegated to pioneering VR practitioners. Providing a realistic sense of simple environmental conditions like hot and cold or humid and dry in VR is still relegated as novelty. VR systems using environmental effects are sparse throughout the world and usually found in expensive theme park installations or some university research labs.

Existing examples not only demonstrate the possibilities, but also reveal the inflexibility in how they can be incorporated into VR systems designed for the average VR user.

Among the pioneers of environmental feedback is Morton Heilig with his Sensorama system [Heilig 1962]. The Sensorama machine still exists and resembles an arcade kiosk where users watch stereoscopic films ranging from dune buggying, helicopter rides, motorcycling, and Belly dancing. Each experience was displayed with a wide field of view, wind effects, aromas, and vibrations. Sensorama users would sit and place their chin in a fixed position where the machine could display the 3D movie, wind, and aromas to them as they remain in a controlled pose. With the source footage being on film reel the multimodal effects were set to happen with known timings which could then be activated and controlled electromechanically. Each effect was contextually accurate to what was being shown on the screen. There are many more pioneers in this area not covered here including Laube Hans [1959], Yasuyuki Yanagida et al. [2003], and Disney Imagineer Mark Sumner [Moseley 2016] just to name a few.

Often creating a new environmental feedback system feels like one is reinventing the wheel. This is because multimodal feedback systems are few and far between, and thus difficult to experience first-hand. Developers often have to develop new hardware and software tools within their project cycle consuming considerable time and energy. Solutions often come to market and fade away. At trade and technical conferences, it is not uncommon to have opportunities to directly experience environmental feedback systems. Good conferences for these opportunities include IEEE Virtual Reality, Interservice/Industry Training Simulation & Education (IITSEC), and International Association of Amusement Parks & Attractions (IAAPA).

As a novel (or "novelty") area, there is still more research to be done, and many questions to be answered. For example, questions such as what are the typical fluid dynamics of wind on a person's body in common environments and how can this be simulated in VR? Or, how can the thermal resolution of a multimodal VR system be measured and optimized? Answering questions like these will lead the VR development community further down the road to a more purposeful and prevalent use of environmental feedback systems within—VR ultimately raising the bar for the state of the art.

31.2 A Traditional Approach

Two approaches to environmental feedback are to place the transducers on body-wearable "displays" versus mounting the effects as part of the room environment. Wearable displays might be used as a means to reduce cost and complexity. The focus of this chapter is on room mounted multimodal effects.

We will first explore adding a heat effect to a virtual world. Perhaps the virtual world has a pair of suns on an alien planet which provide warmth from two distinct directions matching the visuals. Or perhaps there is a dragon blowing fire at a user which should feel like a blast of hot air from a particular direction. In this example, we will work with the HTC Vive™ HMD VR system configured with a room tracked space of $3 \times 3\,m^2$.

A basic AC heat lamp inside a fixture is easily acquired for less than $15. (We will address safety issues later in the chapter, which you should read before setting out to implement this or other examples.) The first issue is that a heat lamp's effective radiation is only about 0.5 m so more than one will likely be needed for even coverage. (Space heaters have an effective range of about 1 m, but have a slow response.) A single heat source therefore is insufficient for a $3 \times 3\,m^2$ space. Envisioning the $3 \times 3\,m^2$ tracked space of our VR system as a cube with six sides where the user is allowed to move around freely reveals the difficulty. As heat in the real world has directionality it should in the virtual world as well. Thus, we could put four heat lamps and space heaters on each side to provide even coverage of the cube, but this would be 48 individual heat sources to mount and cable, as well as purchase.

Knowing the content of the VR experiences can mitigate the problem somewhat. For a virtual sun then there should be heating environmental feedback devices (EFDs) placed above the user to simulate the virtual warmth. If a dragon will be blowing fire towards the front of the tracked space, then you can focus on placing the heat EFDs on the front of the tracked space. There might be some confusion here regarding the tracked space orientation to a virtual dragon. Typically, an HTC Vive™ tracked space has a fixed orientation between the virtual and real worlds, which can be repositioned through the commonly used teleport feature, but you could assume the rotation will remain consistent. This might mean that the dragon is scripted to only blow fire towards portions of the tracked space that have heat EFDs present.

The next issue to consider is how the VR system will control all of the heat EFDs in synchronization with the other sensorial renderings of the virtual world?

Control solutions fall within the engineering versus software domain. Except for the "Maker" community, modern software engineers and programmers seldom delve into the programmatic control of electrical or mechanical systems. Before taking on this challenge one should know what has been used in the past within the VR community.

Hülsmann et al. [2013] published on the use of a lighting control system known as the MultiDim MKIII Dimmerpack system which controlled EFDs using serial digital multiplex (DMX) protocol [DMX 2017] which is common in live entertainment systems. Deligiannidis and Jacob [2006] published on a research system known as The VR Scooter where wind and vibrotactile EFDs were controlled using an AR-16 relay interface and the STA-16 status input interface from the Electronic Energy Control company. This control mechanism would be typically used by electricians on home or business automation systems. Programmable Logic Controllers (PLCs) are a type of control solution chosen for theme park attractions where many PLCs are networked together to control arrays of EFDs in synchronization with electromechanical ride vehicles and digital displays. Even prior to the use of VR content the conveyance of ride vehicles in theme parks has long been orchestrated by PLCs. Thus, the adaptation of PLC software for the control of EFDs is a natural fit for a theme park engineer. PLC code examples for integrating EFDs within a VR system remain few and far between. Some VR hobbyists have controlled EFDs using a USB connected series of mechanical relays called a Phidget™ interface kit. The four or eight relays available on a kit can each control an AC or DC EFD. Available application programmer interfaces (APIs) include C, C#, Java, Python, JavaScript, and Max/MSP.

One effort replicated by each of the listed control solutions is the development of a new driver software. Typically, this driver software is responsible for simultaneously controlling the EFDs as well as responding to communications that originate in the VR system's virtual world. Each EFD arranged around the VR system's tracked space needs to be recorded into a configuration file that might include location and orientation of the EFD in relation to the tracked space's 3D origin. This information may be utilized within the virtual world or the control system driver to appropriately control EFDs that relate to environmental stimulus simulated in the virtual world. For example, if wind in the virtual world is only occurring from the front of a user then only the fans located in front of the user should be activated.

The communications from the VR system are formed by code classes implemented to be consistent with what the driver code in the control device expects. Events within the virtual world prompt methods within these classes to assemble packets with commands and other information that are communicated to the control system. A packet is usually formatted with rules known as a protocol. For example, a DMX controller uses a protocol known as DMX512. Similarly, a PLC may be configured to utilize a protocol known as ModBus. These communications between a VR system and a control system generally occur over a serial or network connection. In summary, authoring the software layer for an EFD control solution typically requires code classes for events and communication within the virtual world, a configuration record of all attached EFDs, and a driver for the control hardware to receive and act on packets as well as electronically manipulate connected EFDs.

31.3 An Updated Approach

In the previous sections we discussed some of the decisions that have to be made in order to extend a VR system with environmental feedback support. Another way to think about the coverage of EFDs arranged around a user is the way most of us think about surround sound systems. Standard surround sound systems are marketed as 4.1, 5.1, and 7.1 where the first number represents the number of mid-hi toned speakers positioned around a viewing area and the second number indicates the presence of a sub-woofer for low tones. Each surround sound solution represents a step up in quality for the audio experience. These systems function based on a standardized design where audio streams are packaged into channels. The amount of channels used is standardized to match surround sound systems utilizing 4.1, 5.1, or 7.1 arrangements. For, example a 7.1 surround sound system will provide a rich audio experience for a user watching any film that supports 7.1 surround sound and eight audio channels are utilized. Seven channels are utilized for mid- to high-toned speakers and one channel for the subwoofer. Audio technicians also know the arrangement of each of these speakers around the viewing audience. This standard of speaker placement and channel design allows for audio mixing to accommodate sound emitting from different directions in relation to the movie. EFD arrangements may also be thought of in terms of surround configurations. A standard does not yet exist for environmental feedback systems, but as you work with these types of systems you will develop a sense for your own preferred arrangements. For example, a configuration of EFD coverage used for a seated VR experience is shown in Figure 31.1 [Frend 2016]. Four fans are mounted horizontally around the user from four angles, two heat lamps are mounted before and behind the user. Finally, a PVC manifold is mounted below the front heat lamp. This PVC device was custom made to emit scents. This EFD arrangement is generic and could sufficiently render environmental feedback for many different virtual worlds.

Popular VR systems today are generally not seated experiences and more experimentation might suggest a generic coverage for typical $3 \times 3\,m^2$ tracked spaces or larger. Envision once again the $3 \times 3\,m^2$ tracked space of our VR system as a cube with six sides where the user is allowed to move freely and consider how you might arrange fans and heat lamps to support many virtual worlds. This arrangement experimentation can be slow and discouraging without an effective EFD control solution.

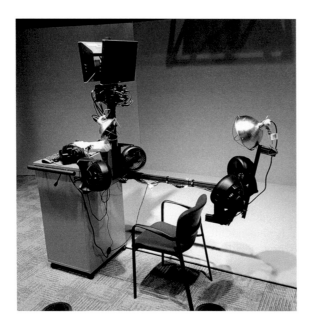

Figure 31.1

A seated multimodal VR system.

An updated approach to controlling EFDs can be found in a cy.PIPES™ device which was designed with VR developers in mind to enable rapid experimentation. For the rest of this chapter we will refer to the cy.PIPES™ EFD control solution as our example control system. This control system is pictured in Figure 31.2 [Cyutil 2017].

Figure 31.2

A cy.PIPES™ device used for controlling EFDs.

On the top face of the device there are six AC wall outlets as found in North America. Next to each socket is a light to indicate whether that EFD channel is on, along with a fuse access cap. On the front of the unit are four USB ports and an Ethernet socket. Inside are two circuits, the first is a computer system known as a Raspberry Pi 3, which is designed for embedded computing and has a distribution of Linux installed. The second circuit is a series of six solid-state relays. This control system is designed to communicate with a VR system using either a WiFi or a wired Ethernet connection. EFDs are connected to the outlets on the top of the device and extension cords may be used.

The software layer includes a "*Spatial Manager*" tool for coordinating a network configuration and an EFD configuration. A network configuration stores the unique IP address and ID number for each control device being used. Multiple control devices can be used and orchestrated as if they are all a single device. The advantage of using many control devices will be discussed later on. Within the EFD configuration each EFD is cataloged by which channel it is plugged into, the type of EFD, location, rotation, and scale of each device. The process for cataloging the EFD configuration will be discussed later.

The control device has a driver installed that is designed to interface with a Unity 3D integration plugin. The Unity 3D game engine is one of the most widely used development tools for VR applications.

31.4 cy.PIPES™ EFD Control System Integration

This section shows how to setup one particular EFD control solution—one geared specifically for virtual reality experiences. While this particular implementation is for commercial hardware, the interface software is available as open source [Frend 2017] and may be explored, and perhaps even extended to other hardware solutions.

Once you have a configured VR system you are now ready to incorporate EFDs using the cy.PIPES™ control solution. Each control device can support six EFDs from the six AC sockets on the top of the device. Sketch on a white board how you would prefer to arrange EFDs around your VR system's tracked space. Acquire your EFDs, mounting hardware, extension cords, network cables, and one control device for every six EFDs.

During installation of your EFDs connect each control device with a network cable prior to the power cable. (Making these connections first will help mitigate network connection issues.) As you plug in EFDs to each control device do not worry about sorting the order. You only need to make sure each EFD is actually plugged into a control device. The sorting process will be completed during the EFD configuration process described later.

Once all EFDs are placed and each control device is connected with network and power cables the next step is to create the network configuration. On your VR computer install and run the cy.PIPES™ Spatial Manager tool that comes with the system. Figure 31.3 shows what this interface looks like.

First the *Spatial Manager* needs to find all the control devices connected to your network. Click the "Run Network Scan" button to find all active control devices on the local network. This usually takes about 10–30 s (Figure 31.4).

The first control device found will be assigned as the master device and you will see its IP address and ID number displayed in the *Spatial Manager*. At this point the control devices are in a standby mode waiting for the network launch command. The network launch command orchestrates a series of processes on each control device to link them

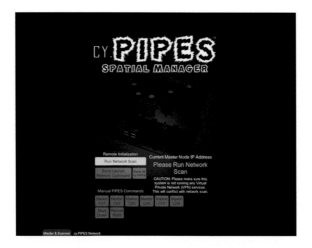

Figure 31.3

The cy.PIPES™ Spatial Manager interface.

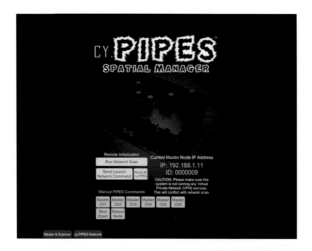

Figure 31.4

The cy.PIPES™ Spatial Manager interface displaying an IP address and ID number (in green).

to the master control device as children. Click the "Send Launch Command" button to activate the network configuration on all control devices. This activation prompts each control device to enter their active state and respond to command packets from the VR system. The buttons labeled "Master Ch1–6" allow you to sequentially test each channel on the master device.

Click on the tab below labeled "cy.PIPES Network" and all control devices attached to your network are listed on the right of the screen. You can manually test each channel (ch1–ch6) on each unit here by clicking the "ch" buttons. Figure 31.5 shows an image of this interface. This network configuration process has to be done every time you boot the

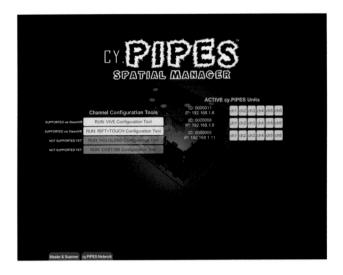

Figure 31.5

The cy.PIPES™ Spatial Manager interface displaying attached control devices.

system because each control device may be assigned a different IP address each reboot. At this point the network configuration is complete and the next step is to create the EFD configuration.

Ensure your VR system is configured and functioning before continuing on to the EFD configuration. On the left side "cy.PIPES Network" screen will be a series of buttons for various types of VR systems. With your VR system connected click the "RUN: VIVE Configuration Tool" or "RUN: RIFT+TOUCH Configuration Tool." This will launch a VR application that will allow you to configure each EFD's type, placement, orientation, and scale. Take a look around. You will see virtual control devices that represent the ones you have set up in the real world. An example screenshot is shown in Figure 31.6.

To start configuring, aim the ray coming from one of your hand controllers at one of the buttons labeled "CONFIGURE:" below any of the virtual control devices and pull the trigger. Now you will configure each channel of this device. Select the "Ch1" button and notice, when using the HTC Vive™, that the front facing camera turns on and a menu appears over one of your hand controllers. This experience is not optimized as an augmented reality tool, but the experience may resemble augmented reality to you. The purpose of the front facing camera is to help you collocate your hands with the EFD being configured. Also take notice that the EFD connected on channel 1 of the selected control device is activated. If you are using the Oculus RIFT™ you will have to peak under the headset through the nose piece or periodically lift the headset to see EFDs because it is not equipped with a camera. Figure 31.7 shows an example screenshot.

Your task now is to choose the type of EFD that is on this channel by pointing your other handset at the menu items shown over the first controller. For example, heat lamps or space heaters would be the item shaped like a yellow sun for a heat type EFD. Choose the left wind type for fans. For all other types of EFDs choose Other. The other types of effects include specialized EFDs like scent emitters, shake motors, or even air blast

31. Environmental Feedback for VR Systems

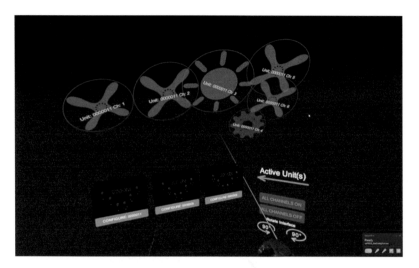

Figure 31.6

Screenshot of the cy.PIPES™ VR EFD Configuration Tool.

Figure 31.7

Screenshot of the cy.PIPES™ VR EFD Configuration Tool with the HTC Vive™ front facing camera activated.

emitters. After making the selection an icon matching the type you selected will appear near your second controller. You now need to superimpose it as close as you can to the real world EFD. Once it is placed use the scale slider to approximately match the scale of the device. Figure 31.8 shows a diagram of this concept.

Once you have completed this, save by selecting "DONE" below the virtual control device just configured and repeat the process for each channel. Once you have finished

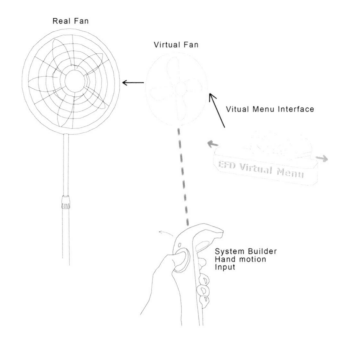

Real Fan

Virtual Fan

Vitual Menu Interface

EFD Virtual Menu

System Builder
Hand motion
Input

Figure 31.8

Diagram of placing a virtual fan EFD over a real fan EFD in three-dimensional space.

configuring all six channels on a control device select "FINISHED" and repeat for any other control device. If there is nothing attached to a channel it is ok to skip it. You only have to do this EFD configuration process once when you first setup your system. The EFD configuration data will persist on your machine as a configuration file for each cy.PIPES™ system associated by a unique "unit ID" number. Above it is mentioned that the IP address details for each cy.PIPES™ system may change, so the unique "unit ID" is utilized to reconnect to the correct EFDs. You will only need to repeat if you reconfigure your VR tracked space or rearrange the EFDs around your space. You may make adjustments to single channels as needed later without harming the entire EFD configuration. Once you have configured each channel on each unit you can simply close the VR configuration tool. The EFD configuration data is now saved on your system as a JSON (JavaScript Object Notation) file which will be used at runtime by any VR application utilizing the cy.PIPES™ Unity 3D plugin.

31.5 Safety Considerations

Before we move on to talk about building VR applications with EFD control systems here are a few important safety considerations. The cy.PIPES™ system itself uses high voltage sockets. Never plug anything into a cy.PIPES™ device that cannot handle 120 V AC current. Never take apart a cy.PIPES™ device as the internal components are energized with high voltage current while powered on. Electric shocks can cause injury or even death.

Basic EFDs that have been mentioned in this chapter include house fans, heat lamps, space heaters, and AC shake motors. More advanced EFDs mentioned include scent emitters and air blasts. These are not off-the-shelf and need to be custom made. This will be discussed below, but DO NOT attempt to make these yourself unless you are a trained electronics professional. You are responsible for the results of an EFD you choose. Verify that an EFD you choose is rated for 120 V AC and 5 A or less. A maximum of 600 W can be drawn from each channel before the fuse will blow and protect the internal relays. Use caution when installing heat lamps as they can shatter easily if finger oils are left on the glass bulb. Also be sure to cover the front of a heat lamp fixture or fan with a metal mesh or guard to protect users from the hot surface or fan blades. Let your users know before they enter your VR system of potential hazards like burns and collisions with EFDs. The cy.PIPES™ system offers the capability to modulate, turn on and off, the power outlets using intensity settings converted to pulse width modulation (PWM). For example, PWM can control fans to express various wind intensities. It is dangerous to purposely configure an outlet as a fan type EFD and plug a different type of EFD into this outlet. Applying PWM to EFDs that are not fans can cause damage to these EFDs or even ignite a fire. Please read and obey all safety procedures and warnings provided with EFDs and control devices.

31.6 VR Software Integration

As a new EFD control solution not many VR applications support the cy.PIPES™ device. This section explains how to integrate cy.PIPES™ support into your own VR application using the Unity 3D game engine. This section assumes you are proficient with Unity and have a virtual world you would like to add environmental feedback effects to. Provided with your control device is a Unity integration package. Import this into your Unity project as a custom package. A new folder will become available in your project under Assets/cyPIPES. Open Assets/cyPIPES/Prefabs and locate the cyPIPES prefab. Simply add this prefab to your scene's hierarchy. If you are using the VR plugin known as "SteamVR" your tracked space object is likely the "*[CameraRig]*" prefab. Select the cyPIPES object and in the public field "VR play space obj" located inside the cyPIPESparsePost component shown in the inspector drag "*[CameraRig]*" in as the reference. Now your EFD configuration that you created with the VR configuration application will be illustrated in the virtual tracked space. If you press play now and look at your scene view tab you will see lines much like the ones pictured in Figure 31.9.

What this view shows are the EFD assignments to invisible tiles that represent the six sides of your VR tracked space. Each EFD is assigned to these sides as individual members of each tile. The blue lines are raycasts from each EFD toward the center of the tracked space and the green lines are raycasts from each EFD away from the center. These raycasts from each EFD pass through at least one of the tiles (sides of the imaginary cube) and this is how each EFD is assigned to each tile.

The next step is to add virtual environmental effects to your virtual world to trigger your EFDs appropriately. In Assets/cyPIPES/Prefabs you will find environmental effects prefabs like "heat_fx_source_cyPIPES." There is an environmental effect source prefab for wind, heat, and "other" types of effects. Place one into your scene at an appropriate place. For example, if you have a virtual fire place a heat source prefab as a child of this

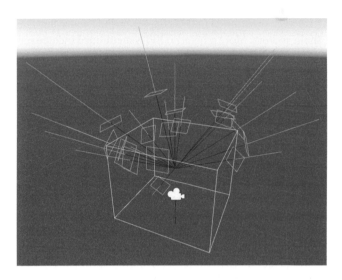

Figure 31.9

A screenshot from Unity where each virtual EFD is shown as a white square and a blue and green line is drawn from each (toward and away from the center, respectively).

fire object and reset its local position to 0,0,0. This should place the virtual heat effect at the pivot point of the fire object. Next select your heat source prefab and in the inspector change its range value to a number (in meters) reasonable for the effective range (for example 5 m). Make sure your VR headset is within the tracked space and preview your scene. As long as you are within the effective range of the virtual fire and you have a configured heat EFD in the direction of your virtual fire any heat EFDs in this direction should be actively providing heat.

You may place as many virtual environmental effects sources in your scene as you need. When wind environmental effects are used you can set their range and intensity. Intensities of 1–3 are supported where an intensity of 1 is a light ambient breeze which usually signals to a user they are "outside." An intensity of 2 is a light pulse much like it feels like when rough weather is forming and an intensity of 3 is fully on which is usually what it feels like to stand on a windy coastline or riding a motorcycle for example. These are all observations based on common house fans. Your results may vary if you choose to experiment with very large fans like industrial units or very small fans. You are making a sensorial display and the subjective "resolution" of this display is based on the EFDs chosen and the arrangement you design. Pictured in Figure 31.10 is what can be viewed in Unity's scene view tab during preview mode when you have many effects prefabs. Each effect raycasts a line toward the user and detects whether they are within range and if a tile has been intersected. These raycast checks will always follow the user. Animating or scripting movement of a virtual environmental effect source is supported. For example, if a virtual heat effect is scripted to move through the sky of a virtual environment corresponding with the movement of a virtual sun, the heat effect source direction will be perceived to move with the virtual sun's movement-assuming heat EFDs are installed in the VR system.

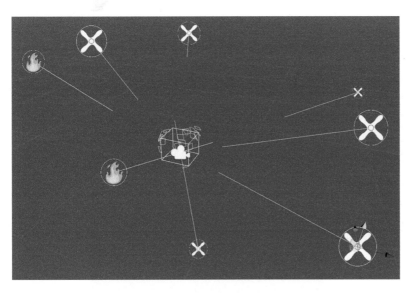

Figure 31.10

Screenshot from Unity's scene view showing virtual environmental effects around the user's tracked space.

Here are a few tips on how to use the plugin in some clever ways. A typical example might be something like having a dragon that blows fire at a user, whereby you could attach a heat effect prefab to the dragon's mouth and script the prefab's active state with Unity's commonly used "GameObject.SetActive(true)" or false to expose the effect only when the dragon blows fire. A trickier case is when you want wind effect prefabs to appear as a suction event. For example, an airlock opens on a spacecraft and you want the air to seem like it is rushing out. For this sensation you can place a wind effect prefab at the airlock where the air is going out and set its intensity to a negative value like "−3" and the control system will activate the fans that are located opposite of the side between the user and the airlock creating the suction effect.

In certain cases, you might want to manually change the behavior of an individual channel on a specific control device. Located in Assets\cyPIPES\Examples\ManualControl is a prefab object named "exampleManualfx.prefab." Place this prefab in your hierarchy, and then start preview mode. In preview mode you will notice in the inspector with this prefab selected each control device and each channel is exposed within new components named "cyPIPES_ManualControl". Pictured in Figure 31.11 is the inspector view of the prefab showing three control devices attached. You can individually toggle on and off each channel with the check boxes next to each channel. These check boxes help you find the specific EFD that you are trying to control. Once you find it make a note of the seven digit "unit ID" number.

Next shut off preview mode and open the script component named "exampleManualControlScript". This script is shown in Listing 31.1. The purpose of this script is to demonstrate boilerplate code that turns channel 2 on and off by pressing the spacebar.

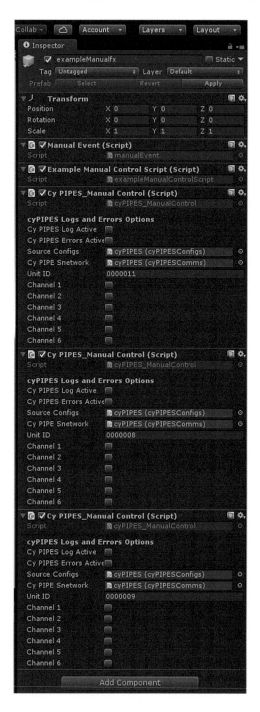

Figure 31.11

The Unity inspector view of the cyPIPES_ManualControl prefab.

Line 7 creates the "manualEvent" object that is assigned on line 12. Lines 21 and 24 show how an individual channel on a specific control device is targeted.

Listing 31.1. A Unity code class example for scripting manual channel states in cy.PIPES™ devices.

```
using System.Collections;
using System.Collections.Generic;
using UnityEngine;

public class exampleManualControlScript : MonoBehaviour {

    manualEvent fxEvent;

    // Use this for initialization
    void Start () {

        fxEvent = gameObject.GetComponent<manualEvent> ();

    }

    // Update is called once per frame
    void Update () {

        //Use the spacebar to manually trigger channel 2 on unit "0000011"
        if (Input.GetKeyDown (KeyCode.Space)) {
            fxEvent.onUnit ["0000011"].ch2 = 1;
        }
        if (Input.GetKeyUp (KeyCode.Space)) {
            fxEvent.onUnit ["0000011"].ch2 = 0;
        }

    }

}
```

Manually scripting the behavior of channels comes in handy when working with input devices that should trigger effects. For example, if a VR user is equipped with a virtual flame thrower the flame thrower could be triggered by a handset button press event and in this case a specific heat EFD could also be triggered with this button press so that the virtual flame is felt as ambient heat.

31.7 Custom Environmental Feedback Effects

The previous sections have covered how to setup commonly acquired EFDs like fans or heat lamps. An exciting area of multimodal VR is the innovation of new EFDs. The most sought after custom EFD is a scent emitter. There are many ways to design a system to emit scents. One way is by using compressed air over vials filled with liquid scents perpendicularly connected to air lines. A control device channel can trigger a solenoid valve rated for 120-V AC current to turn the air flow on and off. The illustration in Figure 31.12 shows this configuration.

Each airline can deliver a single scent by terminating into a manifold with a constantly running fan blowing through it. Figure 31.13 shows a user behind an example scent

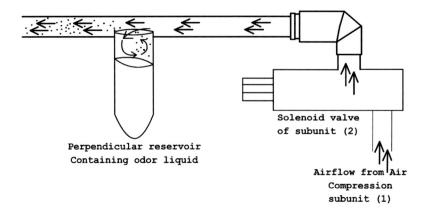

Perpendicular reservoir
Containing odor liquid

Solenoid valve
of subunit (2)

Airflow from Air
Compression
subunit (1)

Figure 31.12

The configuration of a custom scent emitter EFD.

Figure 31.13

A user seated behind a custom scent emitter EFD.

manifold made from PVC piping and a small desk fan is attached to the back wafting the scents toward the user.

Scent emitters are typically complicated systems like this, but other effects are relatively simple. To create a shake motor you only need to source an electric motor rated for AC power and securely attach a small weight to one side of the drive shaft. Attach this motor securely to the floor or a chair and connect to a control device channel to generate a simple shaking effect. For example, this effect has been used to simulate what a WWI biplane cockpit feels like when the defensive machine gun is fired during a VR flight simulation (Figure 13.14).

Figure 31.14

A user standing under an incandescent heat lamp feeling warmth coming from a simulated hot air balloon blast valve. Fans surrounding the user provide breezes to simulate the wind conditions as the balloon's elevation changes. (Pictured in the bottom right corner is the user's perspective of the hot air balloon blast valve in the virtual environment.)

31.8 Concluding Thoughts

Extending modern day VR systems for environmental feedback is fertile ground for innovation. VR developers need only to experiment with arranging and controlling EFDs to find new ways to tell better stories, train better technicians, and share educational experiences that allow users to feel like they are somewhere real. Multimodal VR should be more prevalent and hopefully you now feel empowered to engage.

References

[Cyutil 2017]

cy.PIPES™. Commercial Website. CYUTIL llc. URL: http://cyutil.io/

[DMX 2017]

DMX-512. 2017. Web. 1 Oct. 2017. URL: http://dmx-512.com/.

[Deligiannidis and Jacob, 2006]

Deligiannidis, Leonidas and Robert J. K. Jacob. The VR scooter: Wind and tactile feedback improve user performance. *3D User Interfaces, 2006. 3DUI 2006. IEEE Symposium on Proceedings of 3D User Interfaces*, Alexandria, VA: IEEE. 2006.

[Frend 2016]

Frend, Chauncey E. (2016). *Piazza d'Oro: A VR 4D Tour.* YouTube online video clip, 8 Jan. 2016. URL: https://youtu.be/c389W_IDSrg.

[Frend 2017]

Frend, Chauncey E. (2017). CYUTIL/cyPIPES-UnityIntegration-SteamVR. GitHub. CYUTIL, 01 Oct. 2017. Web. 01 Oct. 2017. URL: https://github.com/CYUTIL/cyPIPES-UnityIntegration-SteamVR.

[Hans 1959]

Hans, Laube. *Motion pictures with synchronized odor emission.* U.S. Patent No. 2,905,049. 22 Sep. 1959.

[Heilig 1962]

Heilig, Morton L. (1962). *Sensorama simulator.* U.S. Patent No. 3,050,870. 28 Aug. 1962.

[Hülsmann et al., 2013]

Hülsmann, Felix, Julia Fröhlich, Nikita Mattar, and Ipke Wachsmuth (2013). Wind and warmth in virtual reality: Requirements and chances. *Proceedings of the Workshop Virtuelle & Erweiterte Realität*, Würzburg, Germany. 2013.

[Moseley 2016]

Moseley, Doobie. DCA interviews: The stories behind the original California Adventure - Page 4 of 6. https://www.laughingplace.com/w/featured/2016/02/05/dca-interviews-stories-behind-original-california-adventure/, 06 Feb. 2016. Web. 01 Oct. 2017.

[Yanagida et al., 2003]

Yanagida, Yasuyuki, Shinjiro Kawato, Haruo Noma, Nobuji Tetsutani, and Akira Tomono (2003). A nose-tracked, personal olfactory display. *ACM SIGGRAPH 2003 Sketches & Applications*, San Diego, CA: ACM. 2003.

SECTION X
Building the Infrastructure of VR

32

Virtual Reality System Concepts Illustrated Using OSVR

Russell M. Taylor II
ReliaSolve LLC
UNC Chapel Hill Computer Science

The immersive nature of virtual and augmented reality systems engages the human visual system in ways that require wider field of view and lower latency than other 3D computer graphics systems to provide artifact-free rendering that avoids inducing fatigue and discomfort in viewers. The need to construct consistent transformations between multiple objects in the system (head, hands, and/or screens) requires a common space. The need to precisely match the viewing direction requires off-axis projection matrices that are carefully matched to the relative positions of the viewer's eyes and screens. System lens designs often induce chromatic aberration and nonlinear distortions of the screen images that depend on the location of the viewer's eyes with respect to the lenses and the location of the lenses with respect to the screens. The temporal sampling apertures of tracking systems and the finite times required to render and scan out the images, together with operating-system-induced delays, introduce latency between the viewer's head pose and the images being displayed at a given moment in time.

Virtual Reality (VR) systems have developed a set of approaches to addressing these issues. The result of applying these concepts is a geometric rendering state that describes to the application how to render each eye. As the visual sense is the primary perceptual channel exploited by virtual reality systems, that is the focus of this chapter—getting the visual aspects correct is paramount.

This chapter introduces each of these issues, presenting both theoretical descriptions and example implementations in the Open-Source VR system (OSVR.org). OSVR is a universal open source VR ecosystem for technologies across different brands and companies pioneered and led by Yuval Boger with a core development team at Sensics including Ryan Pavlik, Jeremy Bell, Greg Aring, Georgiy Frolov, and Kevin Godby. Chapter author Russ Taylor provided consulting support including developing the *RenderManager* rendering kit that implements many of the functions described herein. Many others from the growing OSVR community have contributed to its development. The Apache 2 open-source and open-hardware licensing for OSVR makes it an effective base for building both research and commercial solutions.

32.1 Common Space

To enable proper rendering, the viewer's head (and sometimes eyes) are tracked. Because of the need to interact with the virtual world, their hands are also often tracked; indeed, to enable a feeling of presence, some systems track a whole-body skeleton. In head-mounted systems the screens are attached to the viewer's head, in CAVE-like systems they are located in the real world, and in projection-based systems they are projected onto objects located in the real world. This section describes the spaces needed to support viewing and interacting with the virtual world.

As seen in Figure 32.1, VR systems often involve separate devices at different locations. The computational loads involved, the need for physical separation between cameras and

Figure 32.1

This shows three versions of the *Nanomanipulator* system that enabled a viewer to see and touch real atoms and molecules using a scanned-probe microscope [Taylor et al. 1993]. The left image shows a non-VR mode of operation using standard 3D graphics and a force display pen where only the hand is tracked. The center image shows a magnetically-tracked head-mounted display system co-registered with a mechanical force-feedback hand-tracking system (the image seen in one eye is displayed on the screen for collaborators). The right image shows optically tracked glasses with the viewer looking at a stereo display and using a force-feedback hand-tracking system.

the objects they are tracking, and the fact that different vendors provide different tracking systems means that often more than one device is used to perform tracking. An inertial measurement unit augmented by an external camera may be used to track the head while a depth camera is used to determine the whole-body skeleton. For screen-based systems, the screens are necessarily at different fixed locations in the room while the viewer's head is tracked separately. A force-feedback device may be used to track the hand and interact with the world while a camera-based system is used to track the viewer's head.

Consistent display and interaction requires determining the transformations between each tracked object in the same coordinate system. Figure 32.2 follows the model in [Robinett and Holloway1992], which calls this coordinate system *Room* space, a space that is rigidly attached to the physical room or vehicle where the viewer is located. *Room* space is connected to the *Virtual World* space in which the application object lives by a transformation that enables the entire VR system to move as a unit in the world. Depending on the system, displays live in either *Room* space (fishtank VR, CAVE-like systems) or *Head* space (head-mounted displays). The locations of various tracker bases live in room space and measure sensors that are attached with an offset and rotation to head, hand, and any other tracked space. Because the application may want to draw things in these spaces (hand models, indication of camera location), the VR system must make its spaces available to the application.

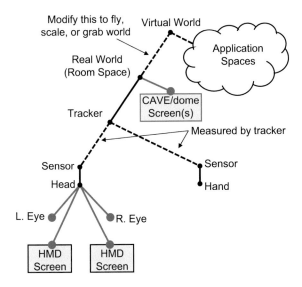

Figure 32.2

This VR space diagram, reworked from [Robinett and Holloway 1992], shows the spaces managed by a VR system. Solid lines are determined during system calibration; dashed lines are updated during viewing (with the application managing its own set of spaces, which it can modify at will). The large-dot blue transforms (eyes and screens) are used together to determine the projection and viewing transformations. On some systems, the eyes may also be tracked, but the transformations described in this chapter ignore this tracking.

32.1.1 Implementation of Spaces Within OSVR

OSVR is separated into *server* and *client* portions, with servers managing devices and keeping track of semantic paths that provide meaningful names (for example, mapping/ xbox/button/0 to /me/hands/left/fingerTrigger) and that describe how transformations are nested to provide VR-relevant transformations (for example, mapping /myExternalOculus/ tracker/0 to /me/head).

OSVR is also separated into subsystems: *Core* and *RenderManager* are the two that will be referenced here. *Core* manages devices, transformations, configuration, and message passing. *RenderManager* implements advanced rendering techniques for a number of rendering systems (*OpenGL*, *Direct3D*, *GLES*).

OSVR_Core manages the common spaces within OSVR using one or more *osvr_server* processes. Client applications connect to these servers to find out about devices and events. OSVR uses *interfaces* to provide access to spaces and other devices, which are accessed by named paths as shown in Listing 32.1:

Listing 32.1. Getting an interface to head space.

```
OSVR_ClientContext m_context;
m_context = osvrClientInit("com.osvr.renderManager");
std::string headSpaceName = "/me/head";
OSVR_ClientInterface m_roomFromHeadInterface;
OSVR_PoseState m_roomFromHead; ///< Transform to use for head space
osvrClientGetInterface(m_context, headSpaceName.c_str(), &m_roomFromHeadInterface);
```

Once configured, the client context can be updated. Each call to update reads all messages from the server and updates the state of all interfaces. This state is only updated when requested, so that a consistent set of interface states can be used for rendering to all eyes. Once the context has been updated for a frame, the application can read the state of any interfaces along with the time at which the state was valid as shown in Listing 32.2:

Listing 32.2. Reading the head pose state.

```
osvrClientUpdate(m_context);
OSVR_TimeValue timestamp;
osvrGetPoseState(m_roomFromHeadInterface, &timestamp, &m_roomFromHead);
```

For trackers that provide them, velocity and acceleration information is also available in the interface state, supporting predictive tracking.

32.2 Projection and Viewing Transformations

This section describes projection transformation and the portions of the viewing transformation required to set the viewpoint. It is adapted from [OSVRView 2016]. It assumes planar rectangular screens. See the ***Distortion Correction*** section below for how to convert distorted systems (non-ideal lenses, non-planar display surfaces) into the planar model used here.

This discussion ignores the effects of eye tracking, and it also ignores the fact that the center of projection of the eye is not the same as its center of rotation. (The center of projection is always along the viewing direction in front of the center of rotation, so the approximation is slight.) With eye tracking the only change is to move each eye's position from the center of rotation of the eye to the tracked center of its entrance pupil.

32.2.1 Overview

The purpose of the combined projection and viewing transformations are to provide a geometric description of how to properly project 3D points onto one or more rectangular planar screens that the viewer is looking at in such a way that they appear to remain fixed in space as the viewer's head moves and rotates.

When dealing with fixed-screen displays (head-tracked stereo on a monitor, CAVE displays, or VR desk designs), the screen remain fixed in room space and the eyes move around. When dealing with head-mounted displays, each screen moves along with the eyes and remains at the same location in head space. Although this affects how these locations are determined, it does not affect the basic mathematics involved or the approach to determining the viewing transformations.

To make the discussion easier to illustrate and understand, it is presented initially for the 2D case and then extended into 3D.

32.2.2 Without Lenses

Figure 32.3 shows the situation without lenses. This matches the case for fixed-screen displays, but is an approximation for head-mounted configurations. (The case with lenses will be discussed next.) The transformations can be computed in physical-world units, for example, meters; they do not depend on the window size in pixels. The location and size of each screen and all eye positions are all that is needed to determine the projection and viewing transformations. Methods for determining these locations are described in the **Implementation** section.

32.2.2.1 Projection Transformation

The result of projection is a 2D image on a planar projection surface. To appear correctly when drawn on the screen, this projection surface needs to be parallel to the physical

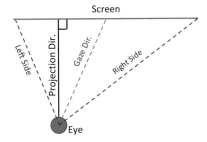

Figure 32.3

Top view of the projection transformation parameters without lenses. In general, the projection direction is not the same as the gaze direction towards the center of the screen (off-axis projection).

screen and it must subtend the same region on the retina. It can be moved closer to or further from the eye, but then must be scaled so that its edges are at the same projected locations as the real screen. This is easiest to think about in terms of angles and a viewing direction, which are independent of depth.

It is tempting to project along the presumed *gaze direction*, which is towards the center of the screen. However, doing so would project onto a planar surface that is not parallel to the screen. To make the two parallel, the *projection direction* must be perpendicular to the screen, along its normal vector. Note that this will make the center of projection lie outside the screen if the gaze direction is sufficiently off center. (Another term for this case, where the gaze and projection vectors differ, is *off-axis projection*.) Given this unique projection direction, two angles can be specified, one for each edge of the screen. One rotates the projection direction to point towards the left edge of the screen (a slight positive rotation in Figure 32.3) and the other to point to the right edge of the screen (a large negative rotation in Figure 32.3). Chapter 33 provides details of constructing an off-axis projection matrix [Kooima 2019].

32.2.2.2 Viewing Transformation

The job of the viewing transformation is to place the center of projection at the location of the eye in *Virtual World* space (where the graphical objects to be rendered are defined). This placement requires translating the origin in *Eye* space to its location in world space and rotating it so that the negative Z axis in eye space is looking along the projection direction in world space. Together with the projection transformation, this operation takes 3D points in world space and projects them onto a virtual screen that is consistent with the pose of the physical screen compared to the center of the physical viewer's eye location.

32.2.3 Going to 3D

Going from the 2D-to-1D projection example above to a 3D-to-2D projection requires another translation to set the vertical location of the eye with respect to the screen. It also requires two more rotations. These rotate the world so that the X axis in eye space is parallel to the X axis in screen space (from left to right) and the Y axis is parallel to the Y axis in screen space (from bottom to top). Together with the Z rotation, this aligns the four corners of the virtual screen with the corners of the physical screen.

32.2.4 Implementation

The projection and viewing transformations must ultimately be implemented in the graphics library being used to display the world. These libraries (*OpenGL*, *Direct 3D*, *Unreal*, *Unity*, *Vulkan*, and others) each have their own coordinate systems. Some of the them are right-handed, and some left-handed. Some have the origin at the upper-left corner of the screen and some at the lower left. Some have specified world-space units (meters, centimeters) and some do not.

The coordinate system used in this chapter matches the OSVR internal coordinate system. As with many toolkits, OSVR includes utility adapters to convert its internal representations of viewing and projection matrices to the formats used by various rendering libraries.

32.2.4.1 Finding Eye Space

In OSVR, *Head* space is defined with its origin halfway between the center of rotation of the viewer's eyes, with its X axis pointing towards the right eye, its Y axis pointing up out the top of the viewer's head, and its Z axis pointing out the back of the head. Getting from room space to head space is the job of the tracking and interaction systems as described elsewhere. Getting from head space to eye space for each eye is a matter of translating along the X axis by half of the inter-pupillary distance (IPD) in +X for the right eye and -X for the left.

32.2.4.2 Determining Screen Edges

For head-mounted displays without eye tracking, the screen edges are fixed in eye space. This means that the projection transformation remains fixed for a given eye as the viewer's head moves around the environment so that only the viewing transformation requires updating.

For fixed-screen displays, the location of each screen must be measured or constructed such that the locations of its edges are known in room space. The relative position and orientation of each eye relative to each screen changes between each rendered frame, so both the viewing and projection transformations must be updated. This is also required for eye-tracked head-mounted display (HMD) systems.

Because the screens in the HMD are too close for most viewers to focus on, HMD displays employ lenses to turn the physical screen into a virtual image. The impact of this is described in the next section.

32.2.5 With Ideal Lenses

An ideal lens uniformly magnifies or minifies all objects behind it, scaling their size and distance consistently. As shown in Figure 32.4, this enlarges the screen and moves it further away, producing an *image of the screen* that is parallel to the actual screen but located behind it. Note that the rays through the lens bend, causing the image to appear larger than a direct projection would be, yielding a wider field of view.

The algorithm for determining the projection and viewing transforms remains the same as above, but now all measurements are made from the image of the screen rather than the physical screen. This is not theoretically challenging, but it is a practical challenge to determine when the lens parameters are not known because the edges of the screen may not be visible through the lens. Assuming the lens characteristics and the physical size and

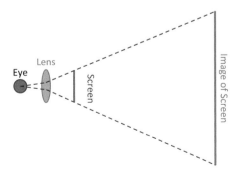

Figure 32.4

An ideal lens magnifies the physical screen and produces a virtual image of the screen that appears to be much further from the eye. An ideal lens produces a flat, undistorted screen.

location of the screen with respect to the lens are known, the location of the image can be computed. If not, calibration is needed.

32.2.5.1 Adjustable Lenses

Some head-mounted displays, such as the *OSVR HDK 1.2*, let the user adjust the location of the lenses to make room to insert eyeglasses into the display and to adjust the width so that their pupils stay within the *exit pupil* of the lens (the region where it behaves like an ideal lens, sometimes referred to as the *eye box*).

For an HMD where the lenses can be moved with respect to the screens, the position and size of the image of the screen move with respect to the eye. As the lens is moved closer to the screen (further from the eye), the image of the screen appears to get larger, producing a larger field of view. As the lens is moved to the left, the image of the screen appears to move to the right. When the lens remains stationary and the eye is moved within the exit pupil of the lens, the image of the screen appears to remain the same. (When the eye is moved outside the lens' exit pupil, additional distortion is seen.)

So long as the viewer's pupil remains in the exit pupil of the lens, the projection and viewing transformations should be based on the actual center of projection of the eye (based on the IPD) rather than based on the nominal center of the exit pupil for the lens and based on the virtual image of the screen. If the viewer's pupil goes beyond the exit pupil of the lens, causing distortion, then the HMD lens locations should be adjusted and the system recalibrated.

32.2.5.2 Specification of the Screen

The following describes a compact general description of a screen, for a description of how to specify these parameters in OSVR configuration files, see the **Specifying the screen** subsection of the **Distortion Correction** section below.

Fixed Rectangular Screen: The specification of a rectangular fixed-screen systems can be done by specifying the room-space coordinates of the lower-left, lower-right, and upper-left corners in meters. Because this allows a non-rectangular result, in the case where the vectors from the lower-left corner to the lower-right and upper-left corners are not orthogonal, the projection of the upper-left coordinate onto the plane perpendicular to the vector from the lower-left to lower-right corner will be used as the upper-left corner (which will reduce the screen height).

Head-Mounted Displays (HMDs): The screens in a head-mounted display may be mounted at any angle with respect to each other and with respect to the device and the viewer's relative eye positions. The lack of a standard for fiducials on head-mounted displays and the fact that some can be individually adjusted means that no coordinate system can be defined with respect to the HMD itself that will be correct in all circumstances.

A general solution describes the location of the corners of the image of the screen with respect to *Head* space, which has its origin halfway between the center of rotation of the eyes, its X axis pointing towards the right eye, its Y axis pointing up, and its Z axis pointing towards the back of the head. There is a separate definition for each screen. Although the viewing and projection matrices will depend on the viewer's IPD, the screen location depends only on the lens locations (presuming that the viewer's eyes lie within the exit pupils for each lens). As with the fixed rectangular screen each screen is specified by providing three sets of 3D coordinates: the image of the screen's lower-left corner, its lower-right corner, and its upper-left corner. These corners are the locations of the image of the screen even if those locations are not visible to the viewer through the lenses (this can make calibration challenging). As for fixed rectangular screens, in the case where the vectors from the lower-left corner to the lower-right and upper-left corners are not orthogonal, the projection of the upper-left coordinate onto the plane perpendicular to the vector from the lower-left to lower-right corner will be used as the upper-left corner (Figure 32.5).

Specification for HMDs whose lenses introduce distortion, along with fixed curved screens is described in the **Distortion Correction** section below. The basic approach is for the distortion correction to map pixels from the physical display onto an appropriately-defined rectangular screen that this chapter will refer to a "*canonical screen*" and then to specify three corners of this canonical screen (whose corners may or may not be visible) as described above.

A note on field of view (FOV) calculations: As seen in Figure 32.6, the viewport width is proportional to the tangent of half of the horizontal field of view, and the height to half that of the vertical field of view. This means that for non-square aspect ratios, the ratio of the window width/height is not directly proportional to the ratio of the HFOV/VFOV. This means that *you cannot multiply the horizontal field of view by the ratio of the display size in pixels to compute the vertical field of view.*

For example, the horizontal field of view on the *OSVR HDK 1.2* is 90° and it covers half of the screen (1920/2). It is *incorrect* to compute the vertical field of view using 90 / ((1920/2) / 1080) = 101.25°. The correct calculation is *atanDegrees((tanDegrees(90/2) / ((1920/2) / 1080))) * 2 = 96.73°.* The diagonal field of view uses the screen diagonal size in pixels (1,445) rather than 1920/2 to get a diagonal field of view of 112.8°.

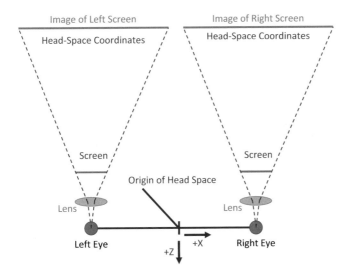

Figure 32.5

The corners of the screens are specified in *Head* space, whose origin is halfway between the two eyes with the –Z axis facing forward and the +X axis pointing from the left eye towards the right.

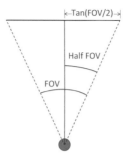

Half FOV

Tan(FOV/2)

FOV

Figure 32.6

The relationship between the field of view and the display size or pixel count involves twice the tangent of the half angle. This must be taken into account when converting from horizontal to vertical or diagonal fields of view.

32.3 Distortion Correction

This section adapts [OSVRDistort 2016] and describes how to remove the effects of distortion caused by curved screens and lenses. Although it is possible to construct lens systems that do not introduce distortion, weight and cost constraints on HMDs often lead to the use of lenses that do cause distortion. Removing this distortion can be handled as part of rendering.

The basic function of distortion correction is to map locations from a rectangular, planar so-called *canonical screen* that is defined by the distortion-correction algorithm onto coordinates within a physical display being viewed through a lens that causes distortion. This same approach can be used to undistort pixels that are presented on a non-rectangular or non-planar display (such as a curved TV or a projection that includes keystone or that is onto a non-planar surface). Note that this transformation can be specified in fractional screen coordinates in a similar manner to texture coordinates and does not depend on display resolution—the distortion remains the same even when the number of pixels being displayed changes.

In the overall rendering process, the projection and viewing transformations take points in 3D model space and project them onto the rectangular and planar canonical screen, and then distortion correction adjusts the resulting image to undo the nonlinear effects of lenses or curved screens used to view it, mapping each point from its canonical location back into its physical location.

32.3.1 Approach

The distortion correction is free to select any rectangle as the canonical screen to be projected on, so long as it properly undistorts images rendered onto that rectangle. We shall see that the canonical screen should lie in depth within the range of the virtual image of the real screen to reduce shift in distortion as the eye rotates to look in different directions.

Two special cases of distortion correction are presented and then a more general solution is described.

32.3.1.1 Case 1: Curved Screen

Figure 32.7 shows an example of a curved display (like the currently-available OLED TVs) viewed without a lens from a viewpoint in the middle of the screen along the screen's normal at that location. The center of the figure shows a top-down 1D view of the scene and a first-person view of the screen from the eye's point of view. Note that the distortion correction for a curved screen depends on the viewer's eye position. The more curved the screen, then more pronounced the effect. This is also true for other forms of distortion.

In Figure 32.7a, the blue screen is the (distorted) screen that would be seen and the green rectangle is one possible choice for an undistorted canonical screen. We are free to choose any depth for the canonical screen so long as we adjust its projected size to match the extents seen in the 2D view—it could be brought closer and scaled down or pushed back further and scaled up. This particular canonical screen is smaller than the physical screen—there are locations on the physical screen that are outside the canonical screen.

32.3.1.1.1 Overfill There are some locations on the physical screen shown in Figure 32.7a that do not correspond to any location on the chosen canonical screen. This means that there is no image to be moved to that location. To avoid this, the canonical screen (green) can be selected so that it completely includes the physical screen, which will provide a mapping for every point on the physical display (but will also necessarily provide "wasted" mappings for some points outside the physical display). This example is shown in Figure 32.7b.

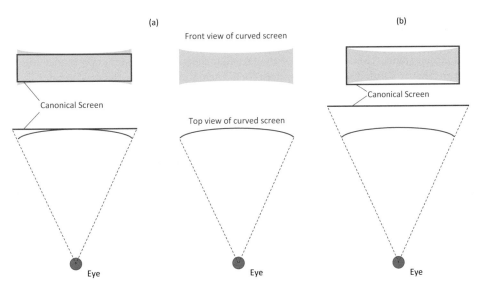

Figure 32.7

Two potential **canonical** screens for a curved-screen display viewed straight on. (a) The canonical screen is tangent to the physical screen and covers only a subset of the screen's surface (it misses the corner regions). (b) The canonical screen is behind the physical screen and covers the entire screen and a region beyond it.

This overfill is also required for other distortions, including radially-symmetric distortions. This is because any non-linear distortion will turn the rectangular boundary of the screen into a set of curves.

(In Figure 32.7b, the canonical screen is behind the real screen, which will cause the distortion correction to depend more strongly on eye position. A better solution would place the canonical screen somewhere within the depths covered by the physical screen, rendering into offscreen regions as in Figure 32.7b.)

32.3.1.1.2 Correcting the Distortion   Figure 32.8 shows two potential approaches to undistorting cylindrical projection and describes some reasons that might lead to choosing one over the other.

Pre-distortion and its deficits: Figure 32.8(b) shows an approach that might be taken, which is to pre-distort the original scene geometry by the inverse of the optical distortion that will be done by the cylindrical projection so that the resulting rendered image can be directly drawn on the (blue) physical screen and have the correct projected image. This requires applying an arbitrary nonlinear mapping to the geometry, which is not easily done and which the graphics hardware would piecewise-linearly interpolate across triangles. Another way to do this same pre-distortion is to do a standard rendering pass and then do a second pass where the original (green) canonical texture generated in the first pass is rendered onto distorted geometry that projects onto the appropriate location on the (blue) screen. Either approach produces an image that includes a non-linear warping of the geometry, resulting in an image that cannot be translated or rotated to handle temporal corrections because of head rotation (see the ***Time Warp*** section below).

Post-undistortion: Figure 32.8(a) shows another approach, which is to determine which point on the canonical screen (green) corresponds to each point on the distorted real screen (blue). This makes use of the fact that the graphics system can render into a texture that is handed to the VR system for presentation. During the final render pass, the texture coordinates for each point are adjusted to read each visible pixel from its corresponding location in the green texture. This undistortion can be done in the graphics library's *vertex shader* by producing a dense mesh that has adjusted texture coordinates per color or in the *pixel shader* either by applying a function to the texture coordinates or using a texture map to provide the new texture coordinate per color to map to the proper location on the screen. This approach has the benefit that the image sent to the

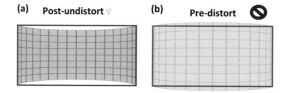

Figure 32.8

Two approaches to distortion correction. (a) Construct a map from every point in the real screen (blue) to corresponding locations within the canonical (green) texture and use this to pull the correct pixel in the shader. (b) Render pre-distorted geometry texture mapped with the canonical (green) image into the display (blue), pushing each pixel to its correct location.

final rendering pass is still a linear projection, enabling it to work with other techniques described later, such as time warping.

32.3.1.2 Case 2: Per-color Radial Distortion

Many lenses have *chromatic aberration* (a different magnification for each wavelength of light), resulting in three different distorted images, one per primary color. This distortion happens in addition to the desired behavior of the lens, which is to magnify the physical display and to move its virtual image further from the eye so that the viewer can focus on it. It is possible to make lens systems that are achromatic and produce the same per-color distortion, but it is also possible to correct for this chromatic distortion within the rendering system.

Although the position of the virtual image of the screen for an ideal lens does not depend on the position of the user's eye (so long as the eye is in the exit pupil for the lens), radial distortion does depend on the location of the viewer's eye. This means that completely correcting for radial distortion requires accounting for the location of each of the viewer's eyes relative to its lens as well as knowing the location of each lens with respect to its screen.

The following parameterization provides one approach (the one used by OSVR) to specifying this type of distortion:

- **Center of projection:** This provides the coordinates for the location on the virtual image of the screen where the ray from the center of the viewer's eye through the center of projection of the lens intersects it. This is a fractional coordinate from 0–1 in each axis, with the lower-left corner of the screen being (0,0) and the upper-right being (1,1).
- **Distance scales:** Because distortion correction depends on both the lens geometry and the screen geometry and may not be directly related to the viewport size or aspect ratio (for lenses that expand more in one direction than the other), one must specify not only the radial distortion polynomial coefficients (which scale powers of the distance from the center of projection to the point), but also the space in which this is measured. This is specified as the number of unit radii in the space the parameters are defined in that span the texture coordinates, which range from 0 to 1. This can be different for X and Y, as the viewport may be non-square and the lens system may make yet a different aspect ratio. There are separate D components for width (D_X) and height (D_Y).
- **Per-color coefficients:** A set of polynomial coefficients can be provided for each color. The coefficients can specify the new radial displacement from the center of projection as a function that scales the original displacement. The first coefficient in each polynomial is a constant factor (multiplied by offset^0, or 1), the second is the linear factor, the third is quadratic, and so forth. There can be as many coefficients as desired.
- The coefficients for R, G, and B; the Distances for X and Y; and the center of projection (COP) may be specified in any consistent space that is desired (scaling all of them linearly will have no impact on the result), but the lower-left corner of the space (as viewed on the canonical screen) must be at (0,0) and upper-right must be at (D_X,D_Y).

The parameters for each color specify the new radial displacement from the center of projection as a function of the original displacement. Listing 32.3 shows how to calculate the distorted location based on an original location and the above parameterization:

Listing 32.3. Calculating radial distortion.

```
// Orig is the (x,y) coordinate specified with X in (0..Dx) and Y in (0..Dy)
// COP is the center of projection specified in normalized screen coordinates (0..1) for X and Y
// D is (Dx,Dy) as described above
// Final is the radially-distorted coordinate
Offset = Orig - COP*D; // Vector, component-wise multiplication
OffsetMag = sqrt(Offset.length() * Offset.length());        // Scalar
NormOffset = Offset / OffsetMag;                            // Vector
Final = COP*D + (a0 + a1*OffsetMag + a2*OffsetMag*OffsetMag + ...) * NormOffset; // Location
```

Examples: (1) For a display 10 pixels wide by 8 pixels high that has square pixels whose center of projection is in the middle of the image, we would get: D = (10, 8); COP = (0.5, 0.5); parameters specified in pixel-unit offsets. (2) For a display that is 6 units wide by 12 units high, but whose optics stretch the view horizontally to produce a square viewing image with pixels that are stretched in X, we could have: D = (12, 12); COP = (0.5, 0.5); parameters specified in vertical pixel-sized units **or** D = (6,6); COP = (0.5, 0.5); parameters specified in horizontal pixel-sized units.

32.3.1.3 More General Solution: Using a Screen-Point-to-Angles Table

Suppose that either through direct measurement with a camera or through ray-tracing in the optical design for a head-mounted display, you produce a mapping between physical points on the display screen and angles from the center of the eye, for a given IPD. This mapping can be arbitrary, so long as it is a mathematical function (does not contain folds) and it may be an unordered set of points. Assume that angles are specified in degrees from views looking along the -Z axis in head space (straight forward) and the positions on the display are specified as distances in millimeters from the point on the display that corresponds to the point that would be see at angle (0,0). Further, assume that the focal distance to the virtual image of the real screen is around 2 m (some portions being closer, and some further). An example of this is shown in Figure 32.9.

32.3.1.3.1 Step 1: Determine a Canonical Screen that Spans the Physical Screen The *eye-space location* of each point is computing using polar coordinates, using the 2-m focus estimate as the radius. The longitudinal angle is assumed to have positive spin around the Y axis with 0 facing forward along the –Z axis and the latitudinal angle is assumed to be positive when rotating up towards the +Y axis.

The X *screen-space extents* are defined by the lines perpendicular to the Y axis passing through:

- **Left:** the point location whose reprojection into the Y = 0 plane has the most-positive angle (note that this may not be the point with the largest longitudinal coordinate, because of the impact of changing latitude on X-Z position).

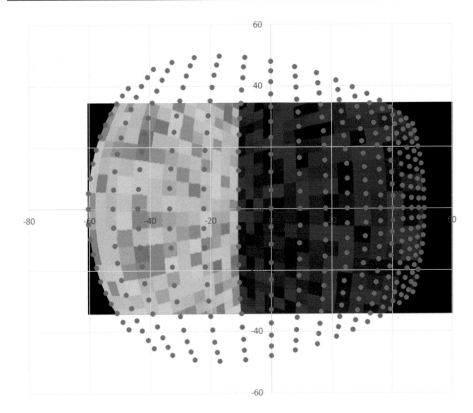

Figure 32.9

A mapping from real-world angles to physical-display locations drawn on top of a rectangular physical display on which is drawn an image distorted by its inverse so that it will look correct when viewed through the lens. Each blue dot represents one sample of the mapping. Dots that lie outside the rectangle will not be visible on the display. Black areas in the display are outside the mapped region so either are not visible through the lenses or must have their distortions extrapolated from dots within the region.

- **Right:** the point location whose reprojection into the $Y = 0$ plane has the most-negative angle (note that this may not be the point with the smallest longitudinal coordinate, because of the impact of changing latitude on X-Z position).

The *Y screen-space extents* are assumed to be symmetric and correspond to the lines parallel to the screen X axis that are within the plane of the X line specifying the axis extents at the largest magnitude angle up or down from the horizontal. This is the point with the largest-magnitude Y value when it is projected into the plane of the screen as determined by the X screen-space extents.

Because the projections of all points in the set will lie within these screen-space extents, no points from outside this region correspond to any point on the physical screen. If the mapping provides angles for each point on the physical screen, there will be a point on the canonical screen to map to. If not all points on the physical screen have mappings, it may be necessary to overfill the render region to provide them (see the ***Overfill*** section below).

Note: The approach described above will only work for displays whose fields of view do not extend 90° from forward in either the nasal or distal orientation. (Planar projection in general will only work for displays whose monocular horizontal field of view is less than 180°. Displays with larger fields of views will need to be rendered using multiple projections that are stitched together.) For displays that have fields of views less than 180° but which extend beyond 90° distal, the reprojection must be done not on the Y = 0 plane but on a plane rotated away from the nose such that all displayed angles pass through it. A similar rotation vertically could be used to handle displays that are asymmetric about the X axis.

32.3.1.3.2 Step 2: Mapping from Physical Screen Coordinates Given points in the physical screen, the distortion map provides the coordinates of the corresponding point on the canonical screen. This determines the appropriate point to display at this location on the screen. This is calculated in two steps:

- **Step 2A:** Map from physical-display coordinate to angle using the provided table.
- **Step 2B:** Map from angle to canonical-screen coordinate by projecting the ray from the eye onto the plane of the canonical screen. Then determine the screen-space X and Y coordinates (X = 0 at left and 1 at the right, Y = 0 at the bottom and 1 at the top).

Doing this mapping for points other than those specified in the table requires interpolation for display points between those specified and extrapolation for points outside their convex hull.

32.3.1.3.3 Implementation of Distortion Calibration within OSVR The above procedure is implemented in the *angles_to_config* program in the OSVR *Distortionizer* project [OSVRAngles 2017]. Additional details (described below) are needed to describe the general results above in a manner usable by OSVR.

Specifying the screen in the server configuration file The current OSVR display description includes the specification of a *horizontal field of view*, a *vertical field of view*, a *center of projection* (which is the normalized location on the screen where the line through the eye point perpendicular to the screen pierces the screen) and a *percent overlap* (which is related to the rotation of the screens around the Y axis).

Figure 32.10 shows some of the relevant parameters. Following it, the entries in the OSVR server configuration file are specified, along with a description of how to compute each of their values.

- **display/hmd/field_of_view/monocular_horizontal:** This value is computed as if the screen is being viewed by an eyepoint located along the line perpendicular to the center of the screen. We determine it using the half-screen width and the perpendicular distance from the origin to the plane of the screen.
- **display/hmd/field_of_view/monocular_vertical:** This value is computed as if the screen is being viewed by an eyepoint located along the line perpendicular to the center of the screen. We determine it using the half-screen height and the perpendicular distance from the origin to the plane of the screen.

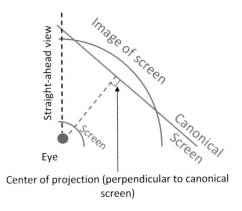

Center of projection (perpendicular to canonical screen)

Figure 32.10

Configuration of an HMD with a curved screen that is rotated to provide a larger distal field of view. The eye location is not in the center of the screen, resulting in an off-center projection. The angle between the projection and the straight-ahead view is specified in the *overlap_percent* parameter in the OSVR configuration file.

- **display/hmd/field_of_view/overlap_percent:** This percentage is computed as if the screen is being viewed by an eyepoint located along the line perpendicular to the center of the screen and as if both eyes were co-located (IPD = 0). (Note; the resulting viewing transform does not make this assumption, just the current algorithm to map from *overlap_percent* to angle.)
- **display/hmd/eyes[0]/center_proj_x:** This location is computed as the fraction of the distance from the left side of the screen to the right side where the line through the eye perpendicular to the screen crosses the screen. This value subtracted from 1 is used in eyes[1]/center_proj_x.
- **display/hmd/eyes[0]/center_proj_y:** Because there is currently no way to specify screens that are tilted up and down with respect to the Y = 0 plane, this value is always 0. The value of eyes[1]/center_proj_y is also 0.

Producing the distortion map in the server configuration file   The configuration file format allows the specification of a variety of distortions, identified by the *display/hmd/distortion/type* variable. If the red, green, and blue components of the distortion are all the same, the type *mono_point_samples* can be used. This means that we need to specify just one distortion mesh, which maps from normalized (X,Y) coordinates in a the physical display ([0,0] at the lower-left corner, [1,1] at the upper right) into normalized coordinates in the canonical screen.

We compute the input normalized coordinates for the mesh by normalizing the table's display coordinates to convert them from millimeters to screen fractions, subtracting the coordinates of the lower-left corner of the screen and dividing each axis by the screen dimension. We compute the output coordinates as described in Step 2.

We then store the unordered set of points into the *display/hmd/distortion/mono_point_samples* array, which has a vector of elements, each of which has two elements, the first of which is the 2D coordinates in normalized physical-screen coordinates and the second of which is the 2D coordinates in the canonical-screen coordinates.

An example output, which is a partial description of an HMD, is shown in Listing 32.4. It provides the identity mapping.

Listing 32.4. HMD general distortion configuration file example.

```
{
 "display": {
  "hmd": {
   "distortion": {
    "type": "mono_point_samples",
    "mono_point_samples": [
     [ [0,0], [0,0] ],
     [ [1,0], [1,0] ],
     [ [0,1], [0,1] ],
     [ [1,1], [1,1] ]
    ]
   }
  }
 }
}
```

The **OSVR RenderManager** uses this set of unordered point samples to compute a mesh by using a bilinear fit to the nearest 3 non-colinear points to determine each of the coordinates for each point in space that must be sampled to produce a mesh with the specified number of points.

32.3.1.3.4 Implementation of Distortion Correction within OSVR As shown in Figure 32.11, distortion correction is implemented within the *Sensics OSVR-RenderManager* component [OSVRRenderManager 2017] by storing a set of texture coordinates for each color with each vertex in the mesh that describes the virtual screen rectangle as shown in Listing 32.5:

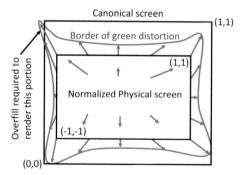

Figure 32.11

OSVR uses a regular mesh to describe the mapping from normalized physical-screen coordinates to texture coordinates within or beyond the Canonical screen. The green map is shown here; there are separate maps for red and blue. The green arrows show the mapping from original (base) to distorted (arrow end) for a subset of the points on a mesh; the curved line shows the mapping for the border of the mesh.

Listing 32.5. Distortion mesh structure.

```
/// 2D float data, like a texture coordinate for example.
using Float2 = std::array<float, 2>;
/// Describes a vertex 2D position plus three 2D texture coordinates.
class DistortionMeshVertex {
public:
    DistortionMeshVertex(Float2 const& pos,
                         Float2 const& texRed,
                         Float2 const& texGreen,
                         Float2 const& texBlue)
        : m_pos(pos), m_texRed(texRed), m_texGreen(texGreen), m_texBlue(texBlue) {}

    // Flips a texture coordinate that is in the range 0..1 so that
    //   it is inverted about 0.5 to be in the range 1..0.  Useful for
    //   flipping OpenGL Y coordinates into Direct3D ones.
    static float flipTexCoord(float c) { return 1.0f - c; }

    Float2 m_pos;               //< X,Y
    Float2 m_texRed;            //< U,V
    Float2 m_texGreen;          //< U,V
    Float2 m_texBlue;           //< U,V
};

class DistortionMesh {
public:
    std::vector<DistortionMeshVertex> vertices;
    std::vector<uint16_t> indices;
};
```

The (X,Y) coordinates describe the normalized physical-screen-space location of vertices that span the range −1 to 1 in X and Y; four vertices are sufficient to describe a linear transformation but more are needed to describe distortion. The (U,V) texture coordinates describe the relative location within or beyond the canonical screen to look up the color associated with that vertex location in the physical screen and they are linearly interpolated by the graphics library between the vertices. The lower-left corner of the canonical screen is at (0,0) and the upper-right is at (1,1). See the ***Overfill*** section for how points outside this range are handled.

Each rendering library (*OpenGL, Direct3D, etc.*) implemented in OSVR passes these coordinates to its vertex shader, where they are used to look up the location within the texture map associated with each eye. The OpenGL GLSL vertex shader program to perform this lookup (along with the projections used to handle projection, viewing, and time warp) as shown in Listing 32.6:

Listing 32.6. GLSL Vertex Shader implementing distortion correction and timewarp.

```
#version 100
attribute vec4 position;              //< Homogeneous coordinates for a canonical screen vertex
attribute vec2 textureCoordinateR;    //< Distorted red texture coordinates for this vertex
attribute vec2 textureCoordinateG;    //< Distorted green texture coordinates for this vertex
attribute vec2 textureCoordinateB;    //< Distorted blue texture coordinates for this vertex
uniform mat4 projectionMatrix;        //< Used to correct for overfill
uniform mat4 modelViewMatrix;         //< Used to handle display scan-out orientation, Y inversion
```

```
uniform mat4 textureMatrix;              //< Used to implement time warp
varying vec2 warpedCoordinateR;          //< Transformed red texture coordinate for fragment shader
varying vec2 warpedCoordinateG;          //< Transformed green texture coordinate for fragment shader
varying vec2 warpedCoordinateB;          //< Transformed blue texture coordinate for fragment shader
void main()
{
    gl_Position = projectionMatrix * modelViewMatrix * position;
    warpedCoordinateR = vec2(textureMatrix * vec4(textureCoordinateR,0,1));
    warpedCoordinateG = vec2(textureMatrix * vec4(textureCoordinateG,0,1));
    warpedCoordinateB = vec2(textureMatrix * vec4(textureCoordinateB,0,1));
}
```

The corresponding fragment shader is shown in Listing 32.7:

Listing 32.7. GLSL Fragment Shader implementing distortion correction and timewarp.

```
#version 100
precision mediump float;             //< Sets floating-point precision used
uniform sampler2D tex;               //< Texture map with image from canonical screen
varying vec2 warpedCoordinateR;      //< Warped texture coordinate for red channel
varying vec2 warpedCoordinateG;      //< Warped texture coordinate for green channel
varying vec2 warpedCoordinateB;      //< Warped texture coordinate for blue channel
void main()
{
    gl_FragColor.r = texture2D(tex, warpedCoordinateR).r;
    gl_FragColor.g = texture2D(tex, warpedCoordinateG).g;
    gl_FragColor.b = texture2D(tex, warpedCoordinateB).b;
}
```

The *tex* sampler is the texture passed by the application that represents the eye being rendered. The red, green, and blue coordinates are independently warped by their respective distortion meshes and then reassembled into the fragment color.

32.4 Handling Latency and Jitter

Many system latencies combine to produce "motion to photon" delay: tracker sensor delays, tracker finite sampling rates, transmission delays, and synchronization delays on the input side; finite rendering time, O/S and driver buffering delays, reformatting delays, and scan-out delays on the output side. Because of these delays, the poses available to construct the projection and viewing transforms when initiating rendering for a frame differ from the poses that each eye will have when display scan-out happens for that frame. Additionally, for some displays (e.g., HMDs that scan out in portrait mode), the delay for the right eye is different from that for the left eye.

Holloway showed in [Holloway 1995] that for normal head motions when observing an object of interest at a distance of around 1 m, each 1ms of total system delay produces about 1mm of offset error in physical space—in a calibrated system errors caused by latency far outweigh all other sources of alignment error. Furthermore, this delay causes motion-dependent "swimming" of the world, which is a major source of discomfort for viewers. During the ~16 ms scan out of a screen at 60 Hz, objects move approximately 1.6 cm; typical graphics pipelines not designed for VR add up to two additional frames of latency, causing objects to move considerably, and the world to swim uncomfortably, when this is not dealt with.

Furthermore, this delay is not constant: unless steps are taken to synchronize the tracker sampling and rendering to the actual image scan-out, the delays shift over time and cause the scene to appear to jitter back and forth. An extreme form of jitter is when the graphics update rate does not keep up with the display refresh rate. All jitter is perceived as doubled images, which is quite distracting.

VR systems employ several techniques to deal with this latency and jitter, including *Frame Sync*, *Predictive Tracking*, *Time Warp (synchronous and asynchronous)*, and *Direct Rendering*. Each of these is described below. Not all techniques are employed in every system, but they can be combined to provide a superior experience.

32.5 Frame Sync

The underlying rendering and display scan-out circuitry usually runs at a fixed refresh rate, somewhere between 60 and 90 Hz. The currently available frame is scanned out whether or not there is a new image to be displayed, and independent of the rendering initiation or completion time. Thus, for long renders an old image may be repeatedly displayed. This section describes how to synchronize rendering with scan-out.

In the case of a single shared buffer between the rendering and scan-out circuitry, so-called *single buffering*, this can result in tearing artifacts when the rendering system clears and then updates the shared buffer while scan-out is occurring—causing neighboring scan lines to be rendered from different frames (a temporal discontinuity—or tear between scanlines). To avoid this tearing in single-buffered mode one must ensure that all buffer clearing and rendering take place during the vertical blanking time at the end of each frame.

A more robust approach to avoiding tearing is to used *double buffering* (or triple buffering), in which case the rendering system is drawing to one buffer while the previously-rendered buffer is being scanned out. Once the renderer completes a frame, it swaps which buffer is to be displayed at the next scan-out and then gets to work rendering the next frame. Double buffering greatly increases the amount of time available for rendering a frame; rather than the small fraction of a frame within the vertical blanking, it can now take an entire frame (or more) to render an image without causing tearing. It also enables seamless decoupling between the rendering loop and the display loop—so long as the rendering does not get more than one frame ahead it will never cause tearing because the frames are swapped out during vertical retrace. The frame-display portions of graphics libraries often provide a way for the application to stall when it would be two frames ahead, waiting until the current frame has finished scanning out before swapping the buffers and returning.

To remove the jitter caused by a variation in the relative timing of render start and the next display scan-out, the application or VR library needs to know when the next scan-out is coming. One approach is to always render ahead so that the graphics library always stalls before returning a new buffer. This approach has the deficit that it starts the new rendering a whole frame before that frame will be scanned out, rendering it with pose information that will be a whole frame behind when scan-out starts. It also does not apply in cases where the application's frame rate cannot keep up with the display frame rate.

Another approach is to use an operating-system-dependent barrier or timing-request function to find out when the next vertical retrace is going to happen, or to find out when the last one has happened (and with the knowledge of the refresh rate compute when the next scan will happen). The application can thus schedule rendering onset such that it will complete just before the next frame is ready to scan out. In this case, double buffering does not add latency because the buffers are being swapped immediately before being scanned out.

There is a subtle remaining issue that is discussed further in the section on **Time Warp**; different parts of the display scan out at different times. To support intra-frame time warp, the time that the line in the center of the display scans out should be chosen for each eye.

32.5.1 Implementation in OSVR

Frame sync behavior is implemented in the *Sensics OSVR-RenderManager* [OSVRRenderManager 2017] using different approaches for different situations. The OpenGL and Direct3D11 native code paths are currently implemented using the Simple Directmedia Library (SDL) [SDL 2017] to obtain windows, and it calls *SDL_GL_SetSwapInterval(1)* to enable vertical sync, which causes frame presentation to block until vertical sync before returning. (The user can also supply their own windowing library in place of SDL2, and an example using Qt is provided in the source code.)

On its *direct rendering* display paths, OSVR uses either vendor-provided routines or observes when vertical syncs happen using OS hardware queries and informs the application of this timing information by providing a timing function that returns the structure shown in Listing 32.8:

Listing 32.8. Render timing information structure.

```
typedef struct {
    /// Time between refresh of display device
    OSVR_TimeValue hardwareDisplayInterval;

    /// Time since the last retrace ended (the last presentation)
    OSVR_TimeValue timeSincelastVerticalRetrace;

    /// How long until the app must send images to RenderManager
    ///   to display before the next frame is presented.
    OSVR_TimeValue timeUntilNextPresentRequired;
} RenderTimingInfo;
```

The application can then busy-wait on this value until it has sufficient time to complete rendering before querying the current tracking pose and initiating the render. At least under the Windows 10 operating system, busy waiting must be performed rather than sleeping because the operating system does not reliably return with a granularity of less than 10 milliseconds. Because each eye may have different timing, the query includes a parameter telling which eye is being rendered. Listing 32.11 in the *time warp* discussion shows the implementation for waiting for render completion.

32.6 Predictive Tracking

The *inertial measurement units* included in many VR tracking systems provide direct measurements of positional and (acceleration and rate of rotation). The *Kalman* and other *optimal estimation filters* used to perform *sensor fusion* on the tracking systems can also estimate these derivative estimates along with the location and orientation. The resulting *state vector* can be used to estimate a *pose* (location and orientation) at points in time other than the present, such as the expected future time when the next frame to be rendered will be displayed. Ron Azuma showed that such predictions can improve tracking for delays of up to about 80 ms [Azuma 1995]. This section describes how to harness predictive tracking to reduce perceived latency.

This estimation is done by standard physics-based double integration of acceleration and single integration of orientation changes over the time difference between the start of rendering and the expected scan-out. This estimation should be done separately for each eye because scan-out often does not start at the same time for each. Because of finite display scan-out time, it is advisable to calculate the delay to the center of the scanned-out image rather than to its beginning.

The prediction interval can be made very accurate with respect to the system *input* latencies when all data is properly time-stamped from a consistent, system-wide (cross-component), frame of reference for time. If the system is using frame sync, either by querying for the upcoming scan out time or by always commencing rendering just after a scan out, then the prediction interval can also be made very accurate with respect to the *output* latencies. (Because the rendering latencies usually dominate the end-to-end system latencies, and because only the rendering system has access to up-to-date frame sync information, predictive tracking should be done in the rendering portion of the VR system using state vectors passed from earlier stages when frame sync is being used.)

Because portrait-mode display scan-out (where both eyes are on the same display) sequentially scans one eye out and then the other, the prediction time for the right eye may be half a frame time ahead or behind the left eye.

32.6.1 Implementation of Predictive Tracking within OSVR

OSVR implements predictive tracking inside the code that provides the application with rendering state information (viewport, modelview & projection matrix). It bases this prediction on the sum of three quantities: (1) the time since the most-recent state vector was constructed (the previous tracker report time) (2) the time until the next vertical retrace; and (3) a per-eye value that depends on the hardware being used and includes the sum of the uncompensated tracker latency with the fixed rendering latencies (O/S and driver buffering delays, reformatting delays, and scan-out delays). See [RMPredictFuturePose 2017;RMPredictiveTracking 2017] for the complete implementation. This code (shown in Listing 32.9) makes use of the Eigen library:

Listing 32.9. Predictive Tracking.

```
// Function called below that performs dead-reckoning orientation estimation.
inline Eigen::Quaterniond applyQuatDeadReckoning(
        Eigen::Quaterniond const& initialOrientation, double angVelDt,
        Eigen::Quaterniond const& velocityDeltaQuat, double predictionDistance) {
    Eigen::Quaterniond ret = initialOrientation;
    // Determine the number of integer multiples of our deltaquat needed.
    int multiples = static_cast<int>(predictionDistance / angVelDt);
```

```
        // Determine the fractional (slerp) portion to apply after that.
        auto predictionRemainder = predictionDistance - (multiples * angVelDt);
        auto remainderAsFractionOfDt = predictionRemainder / angVelDt;

        Eigen::Quaterniond fractionalDeltaQuat =
            Eigen::Quaterniond::Identity().slerp(remainderAsFractionOfDt, velocityDeltaQuat);

        // Actually perform the application of the prediction.
        for (int i = 0; i < multiples; ++i) {
            ret = velocityDeltaQuat * ret;
        }
        ret = fractionalDeltaQuat * ret;
        return ret;
    }

    // Function called below that predicts a future position and orientation.
    static void PredictFuturePose(
        const OSVR_PoseState &poseIn,
        const OSVR_VelocityState &vel,
        double predictionIntervalSec,
        OSVR_PoseState &poseOut) {

        // Make a copy of the pose state so that we can handle the
        //  case where the out and in pose are the same.
        OSVR_PoseState out = poseIn;

        // If we have a change in orientation, make it.
        if (vel.angularVelocityValid) {
            Eigen::Quaterniond newRotation =
                osvr::util::applyQuatDeadReckoning(
                    osvr::util::eigen_interop::map(poseIn.rotation), vel.angularVelocity.dt,
                    osvr::util::eigen_interop::map(vel.angularVelocity.incrementalRotation),
                    predictionIntervalSec);
            osvr::util::eigen_interop::map(out.rotation) = newRotation;
        }

        // If we have a linear velocity, apply it.
        if (vel.linearVelocityValid) {
            out.translation.data[0] += vel.linearVelocity.data[0] * predictionIntervalSec;
            out.translation.data[1] += vel.linearVelocity.data[1] * predictionIntervalSec;
            out.translation.data[2] += vel.linearVelocity.data[2] * predictionIntervalSec;
        }

        // Copy the resulting pose.
        poseOut = out;
    }

    ///===========================================================
    /// Inline code starts here, calling the above functions.
    /// Use the state interface to read the most-recent
    ///   location of the head.  It will have been updated
    ///   by the most-recent call to update() on the context.
    /// DO NOT update the client here, so that we're using the
    ///   same state for all eyes.
    OSVR_TimeValue timestamp;
    if (!m_headPoseCache || !m_headPoseCache->getLastReport(timestamp, m_roomFromHead)) {
        // This is not an error -- they may have put in an invalid
        //   state name for the head; we just ignore that case.
    }

    // Do prediction of where this eye will be when it is presented
```

```
                // if client-side prediction is enabled.
                if (m_params.m_clientPredictionEnabled) {
                    // Get information about how long we have until the next present.
                    // If we can't get timing info, we just set its offset to 0.
                    float msUntilPresent = 0;
                    RenderTimingInfo timing;
                    if (GetTimingInfo(whichEye, timing)) {
                        msUntilPresent +=
                            (timing.timeUntilNextPresentRequired.seconds * 1e3f) +
                            (timing.timeUntilNextPresentRequired.microseconds / 1e3f);
                    }

                    // Find out how long ago this tracker info was found.
                    float msSinceTrackerReport = 0;
                    OSVR_TimeValue now;
                    osvrTimeValueGetNow(&now);
                    msSinceTrackerReport = static_cast<float>(
                                        osvrTimeValueDurationSeconds(&now, &timestamp) * 1e3f);

                    // The delay before rendering for each eye will be different because
                    //  they are at different delays past the next vsync.
                    // The static delay common to both eyes has already been added into their offset.
                    float predictionIntervalms = msSinceTrackerReport + msUntilPresent;
                    if (whichEye < m_params.m_eyeDelaysMS.size()) {
                        predictionIntervalms += m_params.m_eyeDelaysMS[whichEye];
                    }
                    float predictionIntervalSec = predictionIntervalms / 1e3f;

                    // Find out the pose velocity information, if available.
                    // Set the valid flags to false so that if to call to get
                    //   velocity fails, we will not try and use the info.
                    OSVR_VelocityState vel;
                    vel.linearVelocityValid = false;
                    vel.angularVelocityValid = false;
                    if (osvrGetVelocityState(m_roomFromHeadInterface, &timestamp, &vel) !=
                        OSVR_RETURN_SUCCESS) {
                        // We're okay with failure here, we just use a zero velocity to predict.
                        // Using normal get state calls here because we're effectively
                        //   throwing away the returned timestamp for this data.
                    }

                    // Predict the future pose of the head based on the velocity
                    //   information and how long we should predict.  Check the
                    //   linear and angular velocity terms to see if we should be
                    //   using each.  Replace the pose with the predicted pose.
                    PredictFuturePose(m_roomFromHead, vel, predictionIntervalSec, m_roomFromHead);
                }
```

32.7 Time Warp

Because rendering a scene takes time, and because there can be a delay between the end of rendering and the start of display scan-out, the image produced using the head pose that was available when rendering began is not perfectly matched to the pose when that image is presented to the viewer. A solution is to reproject—warp—the original image based on the inverse difference between the original pose and the new pose calculated for the newly estimated time of presentation. The rendered image is thus adjusted to more closely match what should have been rendered had the future pose been known a priori. This section

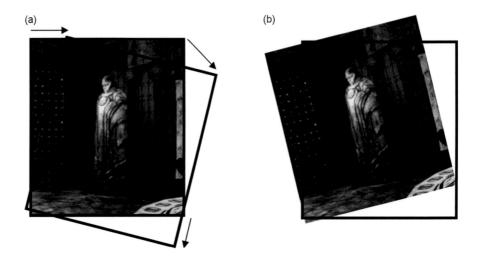

(a) (b)

Figure 32.12

(a) *Unity Sun Temple* demo frame drawn for the canonical screen pose at start of rendering and outline of where the canonical screen pose is after head rotation during rendering. (b) Canonical screen shown from the viewer's perspective (its motion follows the head, so remains axis aligned) and the rendered image after being time warped by the inverse relative transformation to remain stable in the 3D world.

describes how to reduce the impact by re-warping the temporally out-of-date images—time warping (Figure 32.12).

Fully accurate reprojection of each pixel in the image requires knowledge of its depth because the relative locations of pixels change as the center of projection translates and as the orientation of the projection surface changes. However, much of the viewer's rapid head motion only involves rotation around the center of projection, so a good approximation can be made by projecting the rendered image onto a rectangle in space and then altering that rectangle.

For rotations around the viewing direction, this reprojection is exactly correct. For other rotations and for translations, the quality of the reprojection depends on the distance between the projection plane and the objects in the scene. Reprojections of planar objects aligned with the screen at the same distance used for reprojection will be exactly correct, and objects with other orientations and distances will exhibit some variability; this variability is typically less than the error of the original image, so is still an improvement over using the original, unwarped image. Of course, the less time between rendering start and presentation the less distortion.

To avoid an extra rendering pass, this reprojection can be done by adjusting the transformation used during the distortion correction rendering pass.

32.7.1 Implementation of Time Warp within OSVR

OSVR adjusts the texture transformation within its vertex shader to enable time warping to be done in the same rendering pass used for the distortion correction (this the reason for inclusion of the separate *textureMatrix* variable in that shader). OSVR keeps track of the rendering poses used to generate each image and reprojects them for each eye using an oversized (see ***Overfill and Oversampling below)*** screen-aligned rectangle projected 2 m in front of that eye. This transformation is suitable for direct use within OpenGL; for D3D, OSVR adjusts the resulting transformation by inverting Y in two places and transposing the matrix.

The reprojection calculation assumes that it is starting in a texture-coordinate space that has (0,0) at the lower left corner of the image and (1,1) at the upper-right corner of the image, with +Z pointing out of the image. It constructs a transformation from the space used to render into the current-pose space. Next, it moves the points from texture space into world space by scaling and translating them to match a viewport at a given distance in Z from the eyepoint. The points are now in projection space.

The ModelView matrix is then inverted from the last position and applied, moving the points back into world space. The process is then reversed, using the ModelView matrix from the current location (all other matrices are the same) to bring the points back into texture space. It is up to the caller to bring the texture coordinates to and from the space described above (see the ***Overfill and Oversampling*** section for how this is done).

The following code relies on the Eigen library [Eigen 2017] to do its processing (some error checking has been removed for readability; see [RMATW 2017] for the complete implementation) as shown in Listing 32.10. This code includes the "*just-in-timewarp*" described below.

Listing 32.10. Computing Time Warps for each eye.

```
/// @param [in] usedRenderInfo Rendering info used to construct the
///    textures we're going to present.
/// @param [in] currentRenderInfo Rendering info to warp to.
/// @param [in] assumedDepth Depth at which the virtual projected
///    window should be location (defaults to 2 meters)
/// Note that this function is used to compute both synchronous and
///    asynchronous time warps, only the currentRenderInfo changes.
bool RenderManager::ComputeAsynchronousTimeWarps(
        std::vector<RenderInfo> usedRenderInfo,
        std::vector<RenderInfo> currentRenderInfo, float assumedDepth) {

    // See if we're using a D3D11 rendering library.  If so, we need
    //    to scale some Y values by -1 and transpose the result. The standard
    //    approach works for OpenGL.
    float flipYScale = 1.0f;
    bool doTranspose = false;
    if (dynamic_cast<RenderManagerD3D11Base*>(this)) {
        flipYScale = -1.0f;
        doTranspose = true;
    }

    // Empty out the time warp vector until we fill it again below.
    m_asynchronousTimeWarps.clear();

    size_t numEyes = GetNumEyes();
    if (assumedDepth <= 0) {
        return false;
    }
```

```
if ((currentRenderInfo.size() < numEyes) ||
    (usedRenderInfo.size() < numEyes)) {
    return false;
}

for (size_t eye = 0; eye < numEyes; eye++) {
    // Compute the scale to use during forward transform.
    // Scale the coordinates in X and Y so that they match the width and
    //   height of a window at the specified distance from the origin.
    // We divide by the near clip distance to make the result match that
    //   at a unit distance and then multiply by the assumed depth.
    float xScale = static_cast<float>(
        (usedRenderInfo[eye].projection.right -
         usedRenderInfo[eye].projection.left) /
        usedRenderInfo[eye].projection.nearClip * assumedDepth);
    float yScale = static_cast<float>(
        (usedRenderInfo[eye].projection.top -
         usedRenderInfo[eye].projection.bottom) /
        usedRenderInfo[eye].projection.nearClip * assumedDepth);

    // Compute the translation to use during forward transform.
    // Translate the points so that their center lies in the middle of
    //   the view frustum pushed out to the specified distance from the origin.
    // We take the mean coordinate of the two edges as the center that
    //   is to be moved to, and we move the space origin to there.
    // We divide by the near clip distance to make the result match that
    //   at a unit distance and then multiply by the assumed depth.
    // This assumes the default r texture coordinate of 0.
    float xTrans = static_cast<float>(
        (usedRenderInfo[eye].projection.right +
         usedRenderInfo[eye].projection.left) /
        2.0 / usedRenderInfo[eye].projection.nearClip * assumedDepth);
    float yTrans = static_cast<float>(
        (usedRenderInfo[eye].projection.top +
         usedRenderInfo[eye].projection.bottom) /
        2.0 / usedRenderInfo[eye].projection.nearClip * assumedDepth);
    float zTrans = static_cast<float>(-assumedDepth);

    // NOTE: These operations occur from the right to the left, so later
    //   actions on the list actually occur first because we're post-multiplying.

    // Translate the points back to a coordinate system with the center at (0,0);
    const Eigen::Isometry3f postTranslation(Eigen::Translation3f(0.5f, 0.5f, 0.0f));

    // Determine the impact of just-in-timewarp in the coordinate system
    //   with the center of the screen at the origin and unit width and
    //   height.  We only do this if just-in-timewarp is enabled; otherwise,
    //   we set this to the identity matrix.
    Eigen::Matrix<float, 4, 4> justInTimeWarp;
    justInTimeWarp.setIdentity();
    if (m_params.m_justInTimeWarp) {
        std::array<float, 4> coeffs = ComputeJustInTimeWarp();
        const float &xScale = coeffs[0];
        const float &yScale = coeffs[1];
        const float &xShearWithY = coeffs[2];
        const float &yShearWithX = coeffs[3];
        justInTimeWarp(0, 0) = xScale;
        justInTimeWarp(1, 1) = yScale;
        justInTimeWarp(0, 1) = xShearWithY;
        justInTimeWarp(1, 0) = yShearWithX * flipYScale;
    }
```

```
/// Scale the points so that they will fit into the range (-0.5,-0.5)
///   to (0.5,0.5) (the inverse of the scale below).
const Eigen::Affine3f postScale(
    Eigen::Scaling(1.0f / xScale, flipYScale / yScale, 1.0f));

/// Translate the points so that the projection center will lie on
///   the -Z axis (inverse of the translation below).
const Eigen::Isometry3f postProjectionTranslate(
    Eigen::Translation3f(-xTrans, -yTrans, -zTrans));

/// Compute the forward last ModelView matrix.
const Eigen::Isometry3f lastModelView = osvr::util::eigen_interop::map(
    usedRenderInfo[eye].pose).transform().cast<float>();
Eigen::Isometry3f lastModelViewTransform(lastModelView);

/// Compute the inverse of the current ModelView matrix.
const Eigen::Isometry3f currentModelViewInverseTransform =
    osvr::util::eigen_interop::map(
    currentRenderInfo[eye].pose).transform().cast<float>().inverse();

/// Translate the origin to the center of the projected rectangle
Eigen::Isometry3f preProjectionTranslate(
    Eigen::Translation3f(xTrans, yTrans, zTrans));

/// Scale from (-0.5,-0.5)/(0.5,0.5) to the actual frustum size
Eigen::Affine3f preScale(Eigen::Scaling(xScale, flipYScale * yScale, 1.0f));

// Translate the points from a coordinate system that has (0.5,0.5)
//   as the origin to one that has (0,0) as the origin.
Eigen::Isometry3f preTranslation(Eigen::Translation3f(-0.5f, -0.5f, 0.0f));

/// Compute the full matrix by multiplying the parts.
Eigen::Projective3f full =
    postTranslation * justInTimeWarp * postScale * postProjectionTranslate *
    lastModelViewTransform * currentModelViewInverseTransform *
    preProjectionTranslate * preScale * preTranslation;

// Store the result, transposing if we're using D3D.
matrix16 timeWarp;
if (doTranspose) {
    Eigen::Matrix4f::Map(timeWarp.data) = full.matrix().transpose();
} else {
    Eigen::Matrix4f::Map(timeWarp.data) = full.matrix();
}
m_asynchronousTimeWarps.push_back(timeWarp);
}
return true;
}
```

32.7.2 Asynchronous Time Warp (ATW)

Due to scene complexity, O/S interrupts, or other causes the rendering process sometimes takes more time than a single scan out interval. For non-immersive displays, this can introduce jerkiness in playback; in immersive VR it also introduces a doubled image when the viewer's head pose is changing. To avoid these artifacts, the VR system can re-warp and re-display the previously presented image based on updated tracking information at the time the next frame needs to be displayed.

The warping function is the same as for standard time warp and does the same adjustment based on the difference between the viewer's pose at the time the image began rendering and the current pose.

To ensure that a new warped image is available each frame, asynchronous time warp must use *frame sync* and it must launch a separate rewarping thread that keeps the most recently presented image and use that to warp and present just ahead of display scan-out. This thread should have real-time priority in both the operating system and on the GPU. (To enable interruption of long-running renders, it must make use of vendor-specific APIs to enable pre-emptive rendering.) On operating systems such as Windows 10 with coarse sleep-return temporal granularity (e.g., 10ms or more), it may be necessary to busy-wait on the time before refresh to avoid missing updates.

To ensure that basic scene rendering has fully completed prior to attempting the last-millisecond final rendering pass, the application thread must use a rendering-library-specific call to ensure that all operations are complete and the texture is ready for use before handing it to the rewarping thread.

Because the rewarping thread must always have a texture containing the basic scene ready, it must either make a copy of the texture presented by the application or the application must use double buffering and not modify the texture that was most recently presented; it must only modify a texture after presenting a different texture for display.

(Note that asynchronous time warp is only correct for non-moving objects in the scene. Moving objects will have shifted positions between the beginning and end of rendering, and applying this time warp to them will produce artifacts like those produced by jitter to those objects, similar to how this happens to the entire scene when rendered without frame sync.)

32.7.3 Implementation of Asynchronous Time Warp within OSVR

Asynchronous time warp is implemented in the *Sensics OSVR-RenderManager's* ATW renderer [OSVRRenderManager 2017]. As of March 2018, it is implemented only for *direct mode* interfaces using the *Direct 3D* graphics library because these are the only ones that currently support frame sync but it on Windows it is wrapped using the OpenGL Interop libraries to provide ATW for OpenGL as well.

OSVR constructs a completion-query event when the renderer is opened and uses it to ensure that rendering to the texture completes before passing it to the rewarping thread (see [OSVRRMD3Dbase 2017] for the complete implementation) as shown in Listing 32.11:

Listing 32.11. Ensuring rendering completion.

```
// Constructed during initialization and re-used during rendering
D3D11_QUERY_DESC desc = {};
desc.Query = D3D11_QUERY_EVENT;
m_D3D11device->CreateQuery(&desc, &m_completionQuery);

// Using the query each time through the rendering loop
```

```
m_D3D11Context->End(m_completionQuery);
m_D3D11Context->Flush();
while (S_FALSE == m_D3D11Context->GetData(m_completionQuery, nullptr, 0, 0)) {
    // We don't want to miss the completion because Windows has
    //   swapped us out, so we busy-wait here on the completion event.
}
```

A rewarping thread in the ATW RenderManager class uses a second RenderManager to do the actual rendering. It internally keeps track of either copying buffers or locking shared buffers before handing them to the rendering thread.

As of March 2018, pre-emptive GPU scheduling is only available within OSVR on nVidia Pascal-series cards (eg. GeForce 1080), and only with GeForce driver version 372.54 or later. In other cases, ATW cannot pre-empt a long-running render thread. This means that a long-running rendering thread will block access to the GPU and prevent the rendering thread from gaining access, causing it to miss frames.

32.7.4 Just In Time Warp (AKA Beam Racing, Just-In-Time Pixels, Intra-Frame Warp)

Many head-mounted displays scan the visible pixels from one end of the display to the other, thus pixels at the bottom line are rendered almost a full cycle behind the pixels at the top. Because the images produced by the application are rendered at a single point in time, head motion during the frame causes spatial misalignment between what should be seen and the rendered scene. For example, the image of a cube rendered in a frame where the viewer's head is rapidly rotating from the left to the right should show the lower portions of the cube to the left of the higher portions because the head has moved since the upper pixels were displayed, yet with standard rendering are directly below them. This makes the perceived object seem to be slanted towards the left.

Noting that "The ideal way to generate an image [...] would be to recalculate for each pixel the position and orientation of the camera and the position and orientation of the scene's objects, based upon the time of display of that pixel" Olano et al. propose "*Just-in-time-pixels*" [Olano et al. 1995]. Because of the expense of re-rendering each scene, they propose an approximation of determining the correct transformation for the first and last scan lines in an image and using linear interpolation for object locations in the scan lines between them. Figure 32.13 shows this implementation in action on a simple test scene.

32.7.5 Implementation of Intra-frame Time Warp within OSVR

Observing that the largest distortion due to head motion is often caused by rotation of the head in the vertical or horizontal planes and further noting that affine transformations can be readily applied during the rendering pass (the time warp implementation already includes a general 4×4 matrix multiplication), OSVR-RenderManager can easily approximate the impact of these transformations at negligible increased rendering cost by adding anisotropic scaling and shearing to the time-warp texture reprojection matrix. OSVR predicts the viewing time for each eye in the center of the viewing area and distorts other image regions based on linear horizontal and vertical rotational velocity estimates. As is the case with regular time warp of planar-projected images, these transformations are approximations that work better for small temporal differences.

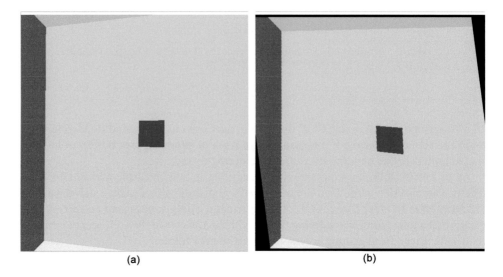

(a)   (b)

Figure 32.13

(a) An image of a small dark blue cube within a colored cube room taken with the head held still shows the cube to be square. (b) A just-in-time rendering of this same scene with the head rapidly moving shows shearing in X and a scale reduction in Y to compensate for changes in location of the scan lines during scan-out. Note that the still image is deceiving because when you look at it on paper it's entirely "rendered" at the same time and your head isn't moving—when viewed from within the moving HMD, the scene appears normal; without just-in-time rendering, the cube appears to be stretched in Y and sheared in the opposite direction. (As for the black regions, see the section on **Overfill and Oversampling** below.)

The case where the display scans out from top to bottom and the viewer's head is rotating from right to left and slightly downwards matches the case shown in Figure 32.13, where the lower portion of the square must be offset to the right with respect to the center of the image so that it will be drawn at a location in physical space that is directly below its top (it is drawn later, and the head has rotated to the left). The distortion is compensated for by adding shearing to the texture reprojection matrix which causes it to sample texture locations increasingly to the right as the image is scanned out from top to bottom. The amount of shear is selected that causes a vertical line drawn at the center of the image to appear to remain vertical in the presence of the estimated rotational speed.

Figure 32.13 also shows the case where the display scans out from top to bottom and the viewer's head is rotating downward causes the bottom of the cube to appear to be drawn lower in physical space, causing it to appear to stretch vertically. To offset this, an anisotropic scaling is performed in the vertical direction, where X coordinates are left unchanged but Y coordinates are adjusted to compensate for the perceived stretching by shrinking the cube vertically. For upwards head rotation, the Y coordinates are stretched. The scaling factor is selected that results in no vertical stretching or squashing for a pixel located at the center of the image.

The two transformations are orthogonal for small motions, so can be safely applied independently of one another.

For an HMD whose screen is mounted upside down (at a display rotation of 180°), the distortions described above are inverted—downward head motion causes apparent squashing and upward motion causes apparent stretching. This case can be handled by inverting the change in X and Y positions. For the case of displays that scan out from right to left and left to right, the shearing and stretching operations are swapped. The general case can be treated as a rotation about the +Z axis (which comes out of the image), transforming from the (X,Y) coordinate system to a (shear, scale) coordinate system with the signs of the scaling and shearing factors determined by the rotation. Because the display orientation in the operating system and the display scan-out may not be related, a configuration-file entry declares from which border of the HMD screen scan-out commences.

Listing 32.10 included the construction of the shearing and stretching transformations, which rely on the function shown in Listing 32.12 to compute the appropriate amount and orientation of the shear and anisotropic scaling.

Listing 32.12. Determining Just In Time Warp coefficients.

```
/// This function computes the coefficients of nonuniform scaling
///    and shearing required to implement just-in-timewarp in a space
///    where (0,0) is the center of the screen and the screen width and
///    height are both 1 (dimensions go from -0.5 to 0.5 in each axis).
/// It first computes the velocity, then based on that and the rotation
///    of the scan-out with respect to the image produces the four values.
/// It does not check to see whether just-in-timewarp is enabled.
/// @return Four doubles, indicating:
///            0th = the scaling of the image in the X direction,
///            1st = the scaling of the image in the Y direction,
///            2nd = the shear in X coordinate as Y varies,
///            3rd = the shear in the Y coordinate as X varies.
///        At most one of the scalings and
///            at most one of the shear transformations will be active
///            at a time; which ones are active depends on the orientation.
std::array<float, 4> RenderManager::ComputeJustInTimeWarp() {
    // We initialize the values with ones that won't cause any
    //    change. We will override them as we find reason.
    std::array<float, 4> ret = { 1, 1, 0, 0 };

    // Figure out which edge of the display scan-out starts at based
    //    on the just-in-time rotation. This describes which edge will
    //    be rotated to point "up" when the display is rotated about the
    //    +Z axis (out of the screen) and it starts at the canonical orientation
    //    with X to the right and Y up. The four results are 0 = top, 1 = right,
    //    2 = bottom, 3 = left. The code rounds to the nearest one.
    int edgeUp = static_cast<int>(
        floor((m_params.m_justInTimeWarpRotation + 44.9999) / 90));
    if (edgeUp < 0) { edgeUp += 4 * static_cast<int>(1 - edgeUp / 4); }
    edgeUp = edgeUp % 4;

    // Find out the timing information, which will let us know the
    //    duration of a full-screen scan-out. If we are scanning out
    //    from left to right or right to left, divide this by the number
    //    of eyes per display to find the per-eye scan-out duration.
    RenderTimingInfo timing;
    if (!GetTimingInfo(0, timing)) {
        // If we have no timing information, then we have nothing to use
```

```
        //   to predict so we return the do-nothing result.
        return ret;
    }
    double screenScanTime = (timing.hardwareDisplayInterval.seconds +
        timing.hardwareDisplayInterval.microseconds / 1e6);
    if (edgeUp % 2 == 1) {
        screenScanTime /= GetNumEyesPerDisplay();
    }

    // Find out the pose velocity information, if available.
    // Set the valid flags to false so that if to call to get
    //   velocity fails, we will not try and use the info.
    OSVR_TimeValue timestamp;
    OSVR_VelocityState vel;
    vel.linearVelocityValid = false;
    vel.angularVelocityValid = false;
    if (osvrGetVelocityState(m_roomFromHeadInterface,&timestamp,&vel)!=OSVR_RETURN_SUCCESS) {
        // No velocity information available, so we return the do-nothing result.
        return ret;
    }

    // Convert the incremental orientation change in world space back
    //    into (local) head space by transforming it by the inverse of the
    //    current head pose.
    //  Handle a non-Identity room-from-world transform in the OSVR-Core
    //    room-to-world transform (as opposed to the RenderManager one, which is
    //    already handled because we apply that transformation ourselves). We
    //    do this by getting and applying the room-to-world transform from Core
    //    here. Again, we can ignore the RenderManager room-to-world that was
    //    passed in as RenderParam because all of our differential transform
    //    work here takes place below it.
    OSVR_PoseState pose;
    if (osvrGetPoseState(m_roomFromHeadInterface,&timestamp, &pose) != OSVR_RETURN_SUCCESS) {
        // No pose information available, so we return the do-nothing result.
        return ret;
    }
    osvr::common::Transform xform(ei::map(pose).matrix(), ei::map(pose).matrix().inverse());
    xform.transform(m_context->getRoomToWorldTransform());
    Eigen::Quaterniond localRot = xform.transformDerivative(
        ei::map(vel.angularVelocity.incrementalRotation));
    // Turn incremental rotation into Euler rotation rates in radians/second.
    // Do this by converting the Quaternion into Euler and then dividing by the
    //    delta time.  We do this twice, once with the X axis being defined as the
    //    last axis to be rotated around and once with the Y axis as the last. (The
    //    last axis is the first listed in right-to-left multiplication.)  If we
    //    use the same Euler set for more than one angle, sometimes we get flips by
    //    Pi around the axes.
    const double &dt = vel.angularVelocity.dt;
    Eigen::Vector3d euler = localRot.toRotationMatrix().eulerAngles(0, 1, 2);
    if (euler[0] > boost::math::double_constants::pi / 2) {
        // Rotation around first axis is always positive when returned from eulerAngles; switch
        //   the second quadrant into the fourth so that we get symmetry around 0.
        euler[0] -= boost::math::double_constants::pi;
    }
    double rX = euler[0] / dt;
    euler = localRot.toRotationMatrix().eulerAngles(1, 2, 0);
    if (euler[0] > boost::math::double_constants::pi / 2) {
        // Rotation around first axis is always positive when returned from eulerAngles; switch
        //   the second quadrant into the fourth so that we get symmetry around 0.
        euler[0] -= boost::math::double_constants::pi;
    }
```

```
                double rY = euler[0] / dt;

                // Determine the amount of rotation around the X axis in degrees that takes
                //   place during the eye scan-out time.  Do the same for Y.
                double xRotationDegrees = screenScanTime * osvr::common::radiansToDegrees(rX);
                double yRotationDegrees = screenScanTime * osvr::common::radiansToDegrees(rY);

                /// Determine the fraction of the display width in angles in X that will be
                ///   covered by this rotation around Y over the course of the frame.  Do the same
                ///   for the fraction of the height in angles in Y that will be covered by rotation
                ///   about X.  Leave these signed, so that we know whether to rotate in the positive
                ///   or negative direction.
                float xRotationNormalized = static_cast<float>(xRotationDegrees /
                    osvr::util::getDegrees(m_params.m_displayConfiguration->getHorizontalFOV())
                );
                float yRotationNormalized = static_cast<float>(yRotationDegrees /
                    osvr::util::getDegrees(m_params.m_displayConfiguration->getVerticalFOV())
                );

                // Based on the scan-out direction, adjust the relevant output parameters to
                //   indicate the amount of scaling and shearing that will take place over
                //   an eye scan-out time.
                switch (edgeUp) {
                case 0: // Top up.
                    // As the head rotates around +X, we get stretching in Y.
                    // To compensate, we need to scale Y down when rotating in +X.
                    ret[1] = 1 - xRotationNormalized;

                    // As the head rotates around +Y, we get shearing in +X with increasing Y.
                    // To compensate, we need to shear in X based on -Y.
                    ret[2] = -yRotationNormalized;
                    break;

                case 1: // Right up
                    // As the head rotates around -Y, we get stretching in X.
                    // To compensate, we need to scale X down when rotating in +Y.
                    ret[0] = 1 + yRotationNormalized;

                    // As the head rotates around +X, we get shearing in -Y with increasing X.
                    // To compensate, we need to shear in Y based on X.
                    ret[3] = xRotationNormalized;
                    break;

                case 2: // Bottom up
                    // As the head rotates around +X, we get compression in Y.
                    // To compensate, we need to scale Y up when rotating in +X.
                    ret[1] = 1 + xRotationNormalized;

                    // As the head rotates around +Y, we get shearing in -X with increasing Y.
                    // To compensate, we need to shear in X based on Y.
                    ret[2] = yRotationNormalized;
                    break;

                case 3: // Left up
                    // As the head rotates around Y, we get stretching in X.
                    // To compensate, we need to scale X up when rotating in +Y.
                    ret[0] = 1 - yRotationNormalized;

                    // As the head rotates around +X, we get shearing in Y with increasing X.
                    // To compensate, we need to shear in Y based on -X.
                    ret[3] = -xRotationNormalized;
                    break;
```

```
        }

    return ret;
}
```

32.8 Direct Rendering (aka Direct Mode, Direct-to-Display)

To support transparent borders and other user-interface effects, some operating systems store each rendered frame before compositing it onto the display, which adds a frame of latency. To improve throughput, some graphics-card drivers keep two or more frames in the pipeline, with CPU rendering completing more than a frame sooner than the image will be presented to the display. Both approaches add to the end-to-end latency for VR systems. This section describes how to avoid these delays using direct rendering.

Vendor-specific APIs have been provided by nVidia and AMD to bypass the operating system and render directly to the display device. (A vendor-independent approach is being implemented within a new Microsoft API as well.) Each of these approaches also offers control over the number of buffers and their presentation to the display surface, enabling either frame asynchronous or frame synchronous swapping of buffers and determination of the time at which vertical retrace happens. This enables front-buffer rendering, but also double-buffer rendering where the buffers are swapped just before vertical retrace, thus providing the combined benefit of extended render times together with low-latency presentation.

32.8.1 Within-Display Buffering

A similar effect can happen inside the display devices themselves. Many devices will support taking images in either landscape or portrait mode and support flipping the scan-out upside down in either mode. Of course, these displays natively scan out in only one particular direction (often portrait mode, starting at the right side of the display as mounted in an HMD) so to flip the image they must first internally buffer a whole frame before starting scan out.

Determining which orientation is preferred requires reading manufacturer specifications or careful testing with a sensitive latency meter. Once determined, best performance is achieved by driving the display in the native mode and doing any required frame flipping within the VR system's final rendering pass.

32.8.2 Graphics-Language Interoperability

On Windows 10, Direct Rendering is only available for the Direct3D graphics library and not for OpenGL. On upcoming Linux interfaces, it may be available only on Vulkan. Accessing these capabilities from OpenGL or other languages requires sharing image buffers between graphics libraries, either using the nVidia NV_DX_ interop interface [nVidia 2010], using shared handles or using Khronos EGL buffers [Khronos 2017].

In these cases, rendering is performed in one rendering library and then the buffers are shared with the Direct-Rendering-capable library and it presents them to the display. These approaches require an additional flushing of the graphics commands to GPU before passing control of the buffers between libraries to ensure that all rendering dependencies are met.

Note that different graphics libraries have different coordinate systems (or different defaults that are used by their communities). For example, OpenGL and Direct3D use different origins for texture coordinates, with OpenGL using the lower left corner and Direct3D the upper left. This requires adjustments to be made when sharing buffers between libraries.

32.8.3 Implementation of Direct Rendering within OSVR

Because the individual vendor APIs are only available under nondisclosure agreements, the *Sensics OSVR-RenderManager* library implements *RenderManager* interfaces for them and distributes them with OSVR-built DLLs but cannot release the source code for these drivers. To maximize the portion of the code using open source, all techniques using DirectMode: *Asynchronous Time Warp, OpenGL Interoperability, Frame Sync*, and even the interface that applications use to control *Direct Rendering* are implemented by either harnessing a Direct Rendering RenderManager or are implemented within it using the same RenderManager interface used by the open-source drivers.

OSVR-RenderManager uses OpenGL Interop to share buffers between an application OpenGL context (Legacy or Core) and the Direct3D context used for display. It handles the buffer flipping and coordinate transformations needed to translate images, distortion correction, and time warps between the systems. It does this by providing a *RenderManagerD3DOpenGL* class [RMD3DOpenGL 2016].

OSVR-RenderManager also handles the image flipping required to avoid **Within-Display Buffering**, as well as providing the option to drive portrait or landscape displays mounted at any orientation. It provides transformations to the application so that it can render the images as if they were right-side-up (enabling text, sprites, and other pixel-aligned techniques to work properly) and then re-orienting the image as needed to meet display needs [RMRotateViewport 2017; RMConstructModelView 2017].

32.9 Overfill and Oversampling

Time warp reprojects an image from a different viewpoint. Normally, the original image could be rendered to exactly cover the canonical screen; however, reprojection causes the new viewpoint to see past those original borders. This produces black borders creeping in from the edges. Distortion correction can produce a similar effect when the canonical screen does not completely fill the display, resulting in similar borders. Both issues can be addressed using *Overfill—i.e.* rendering an image that goes beyond the edges of the canonical screen. This section describes how to use these approaches to remove rendering artifacts (Figure 32.14).

Overfill requires adjustment of both the projection transformation (making the projection region wider) and the graphics viewport size in pixels (providing a place to store the extra pixels); the viewing transformation remains the same. The size of overfill needed

(a)   (b)

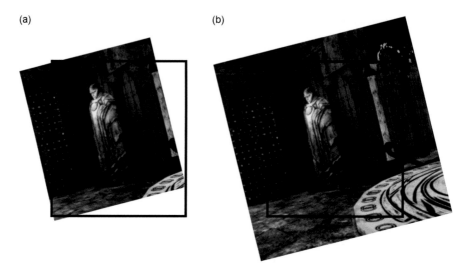

Figure 32.14

(a) Time-warped frame from *Unity Sun Temple* demo reveals borders around the image that were not rendered. (b) By rendering past the borders of the canonical screen, there is now enough image to cover the entire new viewport.

to hide the borders depends on the distortion correction being done, on the length of time between rendering and warping, and on the speed of rotation of the viewer's head: faster rotation reveals more border per unit time.

Distortion correction will, by definition, increase the visible size of some regions on the canonical screen and decrease the size of others. If the rendered image has as many texture elements as there are pixels on the display, then some regions will be expanded such that there are more physical display pixels than available texture elements, producing images that sacrifice the potential sharpness of the display. This can be addressed using *Oversampling—i.e.,* rendering an image that has more texture elements than the display has pixels.

Oversampling requires adjustment of only the pixel size of the graphics viewport; the viewing and projection transformations remain the same. The amount of oversampling required depends on the largest magnification caused by distortion correction.

Oversampling can also be used in the opposite direction, reducing the number of texture elements compared to the number of display pixels, to increase the rendering rate for applications that have large amount of per-pixel processing. This trades off reduced image resolution for increased rendering speed.

32.9.1 Implementation of Overfill and Oversampling within OSVR

The *Sensics OSVR-RenderManager* library implements both overfill and oversampling, taking them into account when generating the projection transformation and when generating the viewport description. Overfill is handled in the projection transformation by specifying a fractional increase in size, which is then used to expand the projection as shown in Listing 32.13:

Listing 32.13. Overfill handling in projection transformation calculation.

```
double xMargin = width / 2 * (m_params.m_renderOverfillFactor - 1);
double yMargin = height / 2 * (m_params.m_renderOverfillFactor - 1);
left -= xMargin;
right += xMargin;
top += yMargin;
bottom -= yMargin;
```

This expansion must be inverted in the code that renders to the graphics library so that only the correct fraction of the image is visible within the resulting displayed frame. This is handled in the OpenGL code path by adjusting the *projectionMatrix* entry in the vertex shader shown in Listing 32.14:

Listing 32.14. Overfill handling in vertex shader projection.

```
m_projectionUniformId = glGetUniformLocation(m_programId, "projectionMatrix");

GLfloat myScale = m_params.m_renderOverfillFactor;
GLfloat scaleProj[16] = { myScale,0,0,0,  0,myScale,0,0,  0,0,1,0,  0,0,0,1 };
glUniformMatrix4fv(m_projectionUniformId, 1, GL_FALSE, scaleProj);
```

Along with oversampling, overfill is used to expand the viewport size as shown in Listing 32.15:

Listing 32.15. Overfill handling in viewport calculation.

```
viewport.width = xFactor * m_displayWidth * m_params.m_renderOverfillFactor
                         * m_params.m_renderOversampleFactor;
viewport.height = yFactor * m_displayHeight * m_params.m_renderOverfillFactor
                         * m_params.m_renderOversampleFactor;
```

The expansion in viewport must be taken into account in the code that handles time warp and distortion correction so that it maps the standard texture coordinate range (0,0)–(1,1) into the portion of the texture that represents the canonical screen. This approach supports the expansion of the range within the overfilled viewport [RMCorrectCoord 2017] as shown in Listing 32.16:

Listing 32.16. Overfill support in Distortion Correction.

```
/// Takes a texture coordinate that is specified in the coordinate system of
///   a Presented texture for a given eye, which has (0,0) at the lower left
///   and (1,1) at the upper right.  The lower left and upper right are at the
///   boundaries specified by the overfill rectangle, which are not visible
```

```
///   for overfill factors > 1.
/// @param eye eye to get coordinates for
/// @param inCoords coordinates to modify
/// @param distort distortion parameters
/// @param color red=0, green=1, blue=2
/// @param overfillFactor scaling factor to allow for timewarp
/// @param interpolators list of unstructured mesh interpolators
using Float2 = std::array<float, 2>;
inline Float2 OSVR_RENDERMANAGER_EXPORT DistortionCorrectTextureCoordinate(
        const size_t eye, Float2 const& inCoords,
        const DistortionParameters& distort, const size_t color,
        const float overfillFactor,
        const std::vector< std::unique_ptr<UnstructuredMeshInterpolator> >& interpolators) {
    // Check for invalid parameters
    if (color > 2) {
        return inCoords;
    }

    // Convert from coordinates in the overfilled texture to coordinates
    //   that will cover the range (0,0) to (1,1) on the screen.  This is
    //   done by scaling around (0.5,0.5) to push the edges of the screen
    //   out to the (0,0) and (1,1) boundaries.
    using Eigen::Vector2f;
    using Eigen::Map;
    const auto inMap = Map<const Vector2f>(inCoords.data());

    Vector2f xyN = (inMap - Vector2f::Constant(0.5f)) * overfillFactor
                    + Vector2f::Constant(0.5f);
    const float xN = xyN.x();
    const float yN = xyN.y();

    const auto normalized_inCoords = Float2{xN, yN};

    Float2 ret = DistortionCorrectNormalizedTextureCoordinate(
        eye, normalized_inCoords, distort, color, interpolators);
    // Convert from unit (normalized) space back into overfill space.
    ret[0] = (ret[0] - 0.5f) / overfillFactor + 0.5f;
    ret[1] = (ret[1] - 0.5f) / overfillFactor + 0.5f;

    return ret;
}
```

32.10 Rendering State

VR systems take time-varying, linear, and nonlinear geometric descriptions of the relative locations and orientations of objects in space and produce descriptions suitable for implementation in the linear geometric operations available in graphics libraries. This section describes how to manage this state across graphics libraries.

The resulting linear operations can be implemented in various rendering systems, including basic graphics libraries (OpenGL, Direct3D, GLES, Vulkan, etc.), game engines (Unreal, Unity, Blender, etc.), and others (VTK, OpenCV, etc.). These systems have a variety of distance units (meters, mm, pixels, etc.) and coordinate systems (right-handed vs. left-handed, screen lower-left vs. upper-left, etc.). This means that no single internal representation can be used within a VR system that is to be implemented across multiple rendering systems. It also means that all aspects of the coordinate system must be carefully described because they will be unfamiliar to users of some of the rendering systems.

The variety of coordinate systems requires that for a VR system to be easily adapted between rendering systems it must either provide adapters for each rendering system or use conditional compilation or wrappers to behave differently when used with different systems.

32.10.1 Time

The proper spatial alignment of rendered viewpoints with objects that remain stationary in the real world is required to prevent "swimming" of the virtual world around the viewer. This is even more important in augmented reality systems, where overlaid virtual objects must remain aligned with their real-world counterparts.

This alignment requires a level of timing accuracy that is beyond the needs of most non-immersive 3D graphics displays. Combining multiple devices, and sometimes multiple computers, in the collection of tracking data (and sometimes video data to integrate the real world) can make accurate timing difficult. The Network Time Protocol (NTP) [NTP 2017] can be tuned to achieve submillisecond agreement among a small number of computers on the same network. Properly aligned, submillisecond-precise clocks between processes have recently become common on some operating systems and compilers.

USB interfaces, video cameras, network drivers, and other drivers within an operating system often enable high throughput and offload work from the CPU by providing buffering and a separation of fast kernel-level drivers from slower user-level drivers. This can introduce both latency and jitter in the time between a physical measurement on a device and the presentation of that measurement to the system. Reducing this can require adjustment of system scheduling intervals, tuning parameters on network connections, raising the priority of processes that handle devices, and busy-waiting on inputs rather than letting the operating system release data to the system at its usual intervals [Taylor et al. 2001]. It can also require back-dating the time associated with measurements based on the known capture and transmission time [Taylor et al. 2001].

To enable consistency between all portions of a VR system, each event and measurement should be time stamped. This enables comparison and proper relative dating of all measurements within the system, producing a common frame of reference.

32.10.2 Implementation of Rendering State within OSVR

OSVR-Core associates timing information with all system events and measurements and uses busy-waiting on actively-used devices to ensure low-latency measurement and data transport. Its internal end-to-end latencies for device measurement, estimation, and reporting are considerably submillisecond. When compiled using Visual Studio 2015 or higher on Windows, and on all other operating systems, it provides submillisecond-accurate consistent clocks across processes on a single computer; it relies on NTP to maintain accuracy between computers.

The *Sensics OSVR-RenderManager* provides graphics-language-specific (OpenGL, Direct3D, Unity, Unreal) conversion functions to describe the number and size of required textures, viewports, projection and ModelView matrices needed to configure rendering for scenes [RMGLD3D 2016; RMGLGL 2016]. The RenderManager receives all viewports and textures in their canonical (viewer up is texture up) orientation and internally maps everything to the correct orientation, enabling the use of bitmap fonts and other rendering effects that require canonical orientation. An optional, callback-based rendering path provides these transformations for arbitrary OSVR spaces (head space, hand space, room space, etc.).

The *Sensics OSVR-RenderManager* manages the display-orientation remapping using *Modelview* matrices within the vertex shaders for each of its rendering paths. It internally keeps track of any rotation required by the display and any flipping required by the rendering library compared to the OSVR internal coordinate system. The following routine uses this information to produce a generic matrix that each rendering path then copies into the matrix used by its shader as shown in Listing 32.17:

Listing 32.17. Display-Orientation remapping.

```cpp
bool RenderManager::ComputeDisplayOrientationMatrix(
        float rotateDegrees, //< Rotation in degrees around Z
        bool flipInY,        //< Flip in Y after rotating?
        matrix16& outMatrix  //< Matrix to use.
        ) {

    /// Scale the points to flip the Y axis if that is called for.
    float yScale = 1;
    if (flipInY) { yScale = -1; }
    Eigen::Affine3f preScale(Eigen::Scaling(1.0f, yScale, 1.0f));

    // Rotate by the specified number of degrees.
    Eigen::Vector3f zAxis(0, 0, 1);
    float rotateRadians = static_cast<float>(rotateDegrees * M_PI / 180.0f);
    Eigen::Affine3f rotate(Eigen::AngleAxisf(rotateRadians, zAxis));

    /// Compute the full matrix by multiplying the parts.
    Eigen::Projective3f full = rotate * preScale;

    // Store the result.
    memcpy(outMatrix.data, full.matrix().data(), sizeof(outMatrix.data));

    return true;
}
```

32.11 Conclusion

The geometry-critical and time-critical rendering needs in virtual reality require the concerted use of a suite of techniques beyond those applied in non-immersive interactive computer graphics systems. This chapter describes each of those needs and provides example code to implement them based on the OSVR system, which itself is an open-source solution that implements all of them working together.

References

[Azuma 1995]

Azuma, Ronald Tadao (1995). *Predictive tracking for augmented reality. PhD thesis*, Computer Science. Chapel Hill, The University of North Carolina. http://cs.unc.edu/techreports/95-007.pdf

[Eigen 2017]

Eigen C++ template library for linear algebra (2017). http://eigen.tuxfamily.org

[Holloway 1995]

Holloway, Richard Lee (1995). *Registration errors in augmented reality systems. PhD thesis,* Computer Science. Chapel Hill, The University of North Carolina. http://cs.unc.edu/techreports/95-016.pdf

[Kooima 2019]

Kooima, Robert (2019). Perspective projection for VR. In Sherman, W. R. editor, *VR Developer Gems*, Chapter 33. Boca Raton, FL: CRC Press.

[Khronos 2017]

Khronos EGL (nee Embedded-System Graphics Library) specification (2017). https://khronos.org/egl/

[NTP 2017]

NTP Network Time Foundation (2017). http://ntp.org/

[nVidia 2010]

nVidia OpenGL-DirectX interoperability extension (2010). http://developer.download.nvidia.com/opengl/specs/WGL_NV_DX_interop.txt

[Olano et al. 1995]

Olano, Marc, Jon Cohen, Mark Mine, and Gary Bishop (1995). Combatting rendering latency, *Proceedings of the 1995 Symposium on Interactive 3D Graphics (I3D'95),* Monterey, California. pp. 19–24.

[OSVRAngles 2017]

OSVR Distortion Calibration Angles (2017). https://github.com/OSVR/distortionizer/tree/master/angles_to_config

[OSVRDistort 2016]

OSVR Distortion Correction (2016). https://github.com/OSVR/OSVR-Docs/blob/master/Configuring/distortion.md

[OSVRRenderManager 2017]

OSVR RenderManager (2017). https://github.com/ReliaSolve/OSVR-RenderManager

[OSVRRMD3Dbase 2017]

OSVR Rendering completeness check source code (2017). https://github.com/ReliaSolve/OSVR-RenderManager/blob/master/osvr/RenderKit/RenderManagerD3DBase.cpp

[OSVRView 2016]

OSVR Viewing transformations (2016). https://github.com/OSVR/OSVR-Docs/blob/master/Configuring/projectionAndViewMatrices.md

[RMATW 2017]

OSVR Asycrhonous Time Warp computation source code (2017). https://github.com/ReliaSolve/OSVR-RenderManager/blob/3458fb7ac8948215026ac416a3aa6cec4320e6af/osvr/RenderKit/RenderManagerBase.cpp#L1630

[RMConstructModelView 2017]

OSVR RenderManager ConstructModelView souce code (2017). https://github.com/sensics/OSVR-RenderManager/blob/397e4374ca7a04f7113edef680b39241bb3e0101/osvr/RenderKit/RenderManager.h#L975

[RMCorrectCoord 2017]

OSVR Texture coordinates distortion correction source code (2017). https://github.com/ReliaSolve/OSVR-RenderManager/blob/75318eabd698bf1c42f64fd5ded77587215e1eb0/osvr/RenderKit/DistortionCorrectTextureCoordinate.h

[RMD3DOpenGL 2016]

OSVR OpenGL over Direct3D rendering interface source code (2016). https://github.com/ReliaSolve/OSVR-RenderManager/blob/master/osvr/RenderKit/RenderManagerD3DOpenGL.cpp

[RMGLD3D 2016]

OSVR Direct3D callback interface source code (2016). https://github.com/ReliaSolve/OSVR-RenderManager/blob/75318eabd698bf1c42f64fd5ded77587215e1eb0/osvr/RenderKit/GraphicsLibraryD3D11.h

[RMGLGL 2016]

OSVR OpenGL callback interface source code (2016). https://github.com/ReliaSolve/OSVR-RenderManager/blob/75318eabd698bf1c42f64fd5ded77587215e1eb0/osvr/RenderKit/GraphicsLibraryOpenGL.h

[RMPredictFuturePose 2017]

OSVR Velocity-based pose prediction source code (2017). https://github.com/ReliaSolve/OSVR-RenderManager/blob/3458fb7ac8948215026ac416a3aa6cec4320e6af/osvr/RenderKit/RenderManagerBase.cpp#L118

[RMPredictiveTracking 2017]

OSVR source code to acquire more recent tracking pose (2017). https://github.com/ReliaSolve/OSVR-RenderManager/blob/3458fb7ac8948215026ac416a3aa6cec4320e6af/osvr/RenderKit/RenderManagerBase.cpp#L1503

[RMRotateViewport 2017]

OSVR source code for altering the viewport based on new head rotation (2017). https://github.com/ReliaSolve/OSVR-RenderManager/blob/3458fb7ac8948215026ac416a3aa6cec4320e6af/osvr/RenderKit/RenderManagerBase.cpp#L1317

[Robinett and Holloway 1992]

Robinett, Warren, and Richard Holloway (1992). Implementation of flying, scaling, and grabbing in virtual worlds. *Proceedings of the ACM Symposium on Interactive 3D Graphics*, Cambridge, MA, ACM SIGGRAPH.

[SDL 2017]

Simple DirectMedia Layer cross-platform development library (2017). https://libsdl.org

[Taylor et al. 1993]

Taylor II, Russell M., Warren Robinett, Vernon L. Chi, Frederick P. Brooks Jr., William V. Wright, R. Stanley Williams, and Erik J. Snyder (1993). The Nanomanipulator: A virtual-reality interface for a scanning tunneling microscope, *Computer Graphics: Proceedings of SIGGRAPH' 93*, Anaheim, CA, pp. 127–134.

[Taylor et al. 2001]

Taylor II, Russell M., Thomas C. Hudson, Adam Seeger, Hans Weber, Jeffrey Juliano, and Aron T. Helser (2001). VRPN: A device-independent, network-transparent VR peripheral system. *Proceedings of the ACM Symposium on Virtual Reality Software & Technology*, VRST, Banff Centre, Canada.

33

Perspective Projection for VR

Robert Kooima
Chicago, IL, USA

33.1 Introduction

Perspective projection is a well-understood aspect of 3D graphics. It is not something that 3D programmers spend much time thinking about. Most OpenGL applications simply select a field of view, specify near and far clipping plane distances, and call `gluPerspective` or `glFrustum`. These functions suffice in the vast majority of cases.

But there are a few assumptions implicit in these. `gluPerspective` assumes that the user is positioned directly in front of the screen, facing perpendicular to it, and looking at the center of it. `glFrustum` generalizes the position of the view point, but still assumes a perspective rooted at the origin and a screen lying in the *XY* plane.

The configuration of the user and the screen seldom satisfy these criteria, but perspective projection remains believable in spite of this. Leonardo's *The Last Supper* uses perspective, but still appears to be a painting of a room full of people regardless of the position from which you view it. Likewise, one can still enjoy a movie even when sitting off to the side of the theater.

33.2 Motivation

The field of Virtual Reality (VR) introduces circumstances under which these assumptions fail and the resulting inaccuracy is not tolerable. VR involves a number of complicating aspects: first-person motion-tracked perspective, stereoscopic viewing, and multi-screen, non-planar display surfaces. For example, Figure 33.1 shows the Varrier™ [Sandin et al. 2005].

This technology was invented at the Electronic Visualization Laboratory (EVL) at the University of Illinois at Chicago. The Varrier installation pictured here was created at Calit2 on the campus of the University of California at San Diego. It is a 12 × 5 array of LCD screens arranged in a 180° arc, 10 ft in diameter. Each LCD displays 1,600 × 1,200 pixels, with a parallax barrier affixed to the front, giving autostereoscopic viewing—3D stereo viewing without specialized 3D glasses. The display as a whole is driven by a cluster of 16 Linux PCs, each with two GPUs, driving four displays connected to each cluster node.

As is common in VR systems, a motion tracking system senses the position and orientation of the user's head. This allows the 3D spatial position of each eye to be computed relative to the position of the display, which leads to the first-person tracked perspective aspect of VR. Figure 33.2 shows a top-down view of the 60-panel Varrier indicating the coordinate system of the motion tracker.

In the case of the Varrier, the origin of the tracker coordinate system is on the floor at the center of the arc, the X axis points to the right, Y points up (out of the figure), and Z

Figure 33.1

The Varrier autostereoscopic virtual reality display.

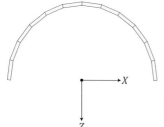

Figure 33.2

The user coordinate system, with the Y. off-axis pointing up (out of the page).

points back. In Figure 33.1, I'm standing a bit right of center, and I'm 5′10″, so my tracked head position is around $(2.0, 5.8, 0.0)$.

To display a single coherent virtual environment, all 60 screens must define their projections in a common frame of reference. For convenience, we simply reuse the motion tracker's coordinate system for this purpose, and the positions of the corners of all 60 screens have been measured or calculated in this space. Given these positions, plus the tracked position and orientation of the user's head, we can compute the positions of the user's eyes, and thus the 120 distinct perspective projections necessary to render one scene consistently across the entire cluster. We call this common coordinate system the *user coordinate system*.

Now, because the user is free to move about the space, the view position does not remain centered upon any of the screens and the gluPerspective function fails. Because the display wraps around the user, most screens do not lie in the XY plane and the glFrustum function fails. We must therefore formulate a more generalized perspective projection.

In the coming sections we will build up such a formulation from basic principles, mathematically, in stages. Our ultimate degree of generality will surpass even the needs of the Varrier. Following that, we will see the implementation of this more general approach to perspective projection in C using OpenGL. Finally, we will play with a very simple example which uses the generalized projection to render crossed-eye stereo pairs suitable for viewing on a normal 2D display.

33.3 Formulation

The perspective projection is determined separately for each screen-eye pair, so we need only consider a single screen being viewed by a single eye. In Figure 33.3 we see one display screen. The important characteristics are the screen corners p_a at the lower left, p_b at the lower right, and p_c at the upper left. Together, these points encode the size of the screen, its aspect ratio, and its position and orientation relative to the user.

We can use these three points to compute an orthonormal basis for the screen's local coordinate system. Recall from linear algebra class that an orthonormal basis for a 3D coordinate system is a set of three vectors, each of which is perpendicular to the others, and all of which have a length of one. In screen space, we refer to these vectors as v_r, the vector toward the right, v_u, the vector pointing up, and v_n, the vector normal to the screen (pointing directly out of it.) See Figure 33.4.

Just as the standard axes X, Y, and Z give us an orthonormal basis for describing points relative to the origin of 3D Cartesian space, the screen-local axes v_r, v_u, and v_n give us a

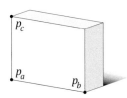

Figure 33.3

The measured or calculated positions of the corners of the screen, in the user coordinate system.

Figure 33.4

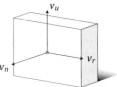

basis for describing points relative to the screen. We compute these from the screen corners as follows:

$$v_r = \frac{p_b - p_a}{\left\|p_b - p_a\right\|} \quad v_u = \frac{p_c - p_a}{\left\|p_c - p_a\right\|} \quad v_n = \frac{v_r \times v_u}{\left\|v_r \times v_u\right\|}$$

33.3.1 On-axis Perspective

Now we begin to consider the position (specifically, the 3D location) of the user's eye, p_e, relative to the screen, as in Figure 33.5.

In this specific example, the eye is centered on the screen. The line drawn perpendicular to the screen along v_n strikes it directly in the middle. We refer that point of intersection as the *screen-space origin*. This coincides with the origin of the screen-space vector basis depicted above.

Also in this example, the pyramid-shaped volume, or "frustum," having the screen as its base and the eye as its apex is perfectly symmetric. This is exactly the type of perspective projection producted by `gluPerspective`.

33.3.2 Off-axis Perspective

If we move the eye position away from the center of the screen, then we find ourselves in a situation like Figure 33.6. The frustum is no longer symmetric, and the line from the eye drawn along v_n no longer strikes the screen in the middle. We defined the screen-space origin to be this point of intersection, and we continue to do so, thus we see that when the user moves then the screen-space origin moves with him.

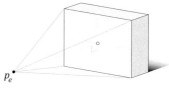

Figure 33.5

Eye position (location) for on-axis perspective projection.

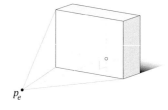

Figure 33.6

Eye position for off-axis perspective projection.

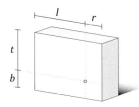

Figure 33.7

The parameters of the off-axis perspective function `glFrustum`.

This is where `glFrustum` comes in. As documented in the OpenGL specification (versions 1 and 2) this function takes parameters giving the left, right, bottom, and top frustum extents, plus distances to the near and far clipping planes. We will refer to these as variables l, r, b, t, n, and f respectively. The first four frustum extent variables may be understood as user-space distances from the screen-space origin to the respective edges of the screen, as in Figure 33.7.

In this example, l and b are negative numbers, while r and t are positive numbers, but this need not be the case. If the user moves far to the side of the screen, then the screen space origin may not fall within the screen at all, and any of these parameters may be positive or negative. In the opposite extreme, an on-axis perspective like Figure 33.5 will have $l = r$ and $b = t$.

33.3.3 Determining Frustum Extents

Before we may use these values, we must compute them. As an intermediate step, we will need to know the vectors from the eye position p_e to the screen corners, shown in Figure 33.8. These vectors are trivially computed as follows.

$$v_a = p_a - p_e \quad v_b = p_b - p_e \quad v_c = p_c - p_e$$

It is also useful to know a bit more about the screen-space origin. In particular, let d be the distance from the eye position p_e to the screen-space origin. This also happens to be the length of the shortest path from the eye to the plane of the screen. This value may be computed by taking the dot product of the screen normal v_n with any of the screen vectors. Because these vectors point in opposite directions, the value must be negated.

$$d = -(v_n \cdot v_a)$$

Given this, frustum extents may be computed. Take the frustum right extent r for example. When we take the dot product of the unit vector v_r (which points from the screen origin toward the right) with the non-unit vector v_b (which points from the eye to the right-most point on the screen) the result is a scalar value telling us how far to the right of the screen origin the right-most point on the screen is.

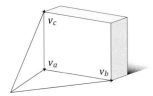

Figure 33.8

The screen corner vectors.

Because frustum extents are specified at the near plane, we use similar triangles to scale this distance back from its value at the screen, d units away, to its value at the near clipping plane, n units away.

$$l = (v_r \cdot v_a)n/d \qquad r = (v_r \cdot v_b)n/d$$
$$b = (v_u \cdot v_a)n/d \qquad t = (v_u \cdot v_c)n/d$$

The OpenGL function `glFrustum` inserts these values into the standard 3D perspective projection matrix using this definition:

$$P = \begin{bmatrix} \dfrac{2n}{r-l} & 0 & \dfrac{r+l}{r-l} & 0 \\ 0 & \dfrac{2n}{t-b} & \dfrac{t+b}{t-b} & 0 \\ 0 & 0 & -\dfrac{f+n}{f-n} & -\dfrac{2fn}{f-n} \\ 0 & 0 & -1 & 0 \end{bmatrix}$$

This matrix is clever, and it is worth examining in order to form an intuitive understanding of its function. Perspective projection involves foreshortening. The greater the distance to an object, the smaller that object must be scaled. To accomplish this, the x and y components of a vertex are divided by its z component.

This division is implemented using homogeneous coordinates. A homogeneous 3D vector has four components, (x, y, z, w), where w defaults to 1. This implicitly defines the 3D vector $(x/w, y/w, z/w)$. Notice the third component of the bottom row of P is -1. When P is multiplied by a homogeneous vector, this -1 has the effect of moving the vector's (negated) z value into the resulting homogeneous vector's w component. Later, when this homogeneous vector is collapsed down to its equivalent 3D vector, the division by z implicitly occurs. This trick is the very basis of 3D computer graphics, and its importance cannot be overstated.

Unfortunately, this formulation means that the foreshortening effect, and thus perspective projection, only works when the view position is at the origin, looking down the negative Z axis, with the view plane aligned with the XY plane. The foreshortening scaling occurs radially about the Z axis. It is useful to understand these limitations and their source, as we'll need to work past all three.

33.3.4 Take a Deep Breath

Let's take a step back and see where we are. We've started with basic constants defining the position of a screen in space p_a, p_b, and p_c along with the position of an eye in space p_e. We've developed formulas allowing us to use them to compute the parameters of a standard 3D perspective projection matrix l, r, b, and t.

It's a good start, and it's useful when developing single-screen applications with user-centered perspective. But we haven't seen anything more powerful than `glFrustum` yet.

While we have the ability to create a frustum for an arbitrary screen viewed by an arbitrary eye, the base of that frustum still lies in the XY plane. If we applied this amount of knowledge to the Varrier, then all 60 screens would display nearly the same limited view of the virtual scene. We need two more capabilities: first, we need to rotate the screen to orient it in the motion tracker's coordinate system, and second, we need to correctly position it relative to the user.

33.3.5 Projection Plane Orientation

We would like to rotate our XY-aligned frustum within the user coordinate system. We may do this with a simple matrix multiplication. It is more intuitive if we consider happening backwards—rotating the user space to be aligned with the XY plane.

Let's review a bit more linear algebra. Define a 4×4 linear transformation matrix M using the screen space basis vectors v_r, v_u, and v_n as columns, like so:

$$
M = \begin{bmatrix}
v_{rx} & v_{ux} & v_{nx} & 0 \\
v_{ry} & v_{uy} & v_{ny} & 0 \\
v_{rz} & v_{uz} & v_{nz} & 0 \\
0 & 0 & 0 & 1
\end{bmatrix}
$$

This is the transformation matrix for screen-local coordinates. It maps the Cartesian coordinate system onto the screen space coordinate system, transforming the standard axes X, Y, and Z into the basis vectors v_r, v_u, and v_n. If something is lying in the XY plane, then this transformation matrix M will realign it to lie in the plane of the screen.

$$
v_r = M \cdot \begin{bmatrix} 1 \\ 0 \\ 0 \\ 0 \end{bmatrix} \qquad v_u = M \cdot \begin{bmatrix} 0 \\ 1 \\ 0 \\ 0 \end{bmatrix} \qquad v_n = M \cdot \begin{bmatrix} 0 \\ 0 \\ 1 \\ 0 \end{bmatrix}
$$

This is extremely useful in 3D graphics. A 3D model is created by an artist in its own coordinate system, with its own local orientation. To position such an object in a scene, a transformation such as this M is used. The column basis construction allows the programmer to orient the object in terms of the concepts "to the right," "up," and "backward" instead of fumbling with Euler angles, pitch, roll, and yaw.

Unfortunately, this is the exact opposite of what we want. We want something lying in the plane of the screen to be realigned to lie in the XY plane, so that we may apply the standard perspective projection to it. We need this mapping:

$$
\begin{bmatrix} 1 \\ 0 \\ 0 \\ 0 \end{bmatrix} = M \cdot v_r \qquad \begin{bmatrix} 0 \\ 1 \\ 0 \\ 0 \end{bmatrix} = M \cdot v_u \qquad \begin{bmatrix} 0 \\ 0 \\ 1 \\ 0 \end{bmatrix} = M \cdot v_n
$$

This mapping is produced by the inverse of M. Fortunately, M is an orthogonal rotation, so its inverse is simply its transpose, and we can produce the desired transform simply by loading the screen space basis vectors into M as rows instead of as columns.

$$M^T = \begin{bmatrix} v_{rx} & v_{ry} & v_{rz} & 0 \\ v_{ux} & v_{uy} & v_{uz} & 0 \\ v_{nx} & v_{ny} & v_{nz} & 0 \\ 0 & 0 & 0 & 1 \end{bmatrix}$$

We compose the perspective projection matrix P defined above with this matrix M^T and we finally have something more powerful than glFrustum. We have a perspective projection that relaxes the projection plane alignment requirement. But we're not quite finished yet.

33.3.6 View Point Offset

The nature of the camera is one of the fundamentally confusing aspects of 3D computer graphics. Consider camera motion. While we would like to imagine that we are free to move the camera freely about 3D space, the mathematics of perspective projection as defined by matrix P disallow this. (Recall, above, the nature of the foreshortening division by z.)

The camera is forever trapped at the origin. If we wish to move the camera five units to the left, we must instead move the entire world five units to the right. If we wish to rotate the camera clockwise, we must instead rotate the world counterclockwise.

Above, when we wanted to rotate our frustum to align it within our user space, we instead rotated our user space backwards to align it with our frustum. Similarly now, we want to move our frustum to position the apex upon the motion-tracked eye position, so we instead must translate our tracked eye position to the apex of the frustum. The apex of the perspective frustum is necessarily at zero, thus we translate along the vector from the eye.

This can be accomplished using the OpenGL function glTranslatef, which applies the standard 3D transformation matrix:

$$T = \begin{bmatrix} 1 & 0 & 0 & -p_{ex} \\ 0 & 1 & 0 & -p_{ey} \\ 0 & 0 & 1 & -p_{ez} \\ 0 & 0 & 0 & 1 \end{bmatrix}$$

33.3.7 The Composition of Everything

That covers everything we need. We can compose these three matrices giving a single projection matrix, sufficiently general to accomplish all of our goals.

$$P' = PM^T T$$

Beginning with constant screen corners p_a, p_b, p_c, and varying eye position p_e, we can straightforwardly produce a projection matrix that will work under all circumstances. Most significantly, an arbitrary number of arbitrarily-oriented screens may be defined together in a common coordinate system, and the resulting projection matrices will present these disjointed screens as a single, coherent view into a virtual environment.

33.4 Implementation

The following C function (Listing 33.1) computes this perspective matrix and applies it to the OpenGL projection matrix stack. It takes four float vectors, p_a, p_b, p_c, p_e, which are the screen corner positions and the eye position as defined above, plus n and f which are the near and far plane distances, identical to those passed to gluPerspective or glFrustum.

This function uses four vector operations: subtract, dotProduct, crossProduct, and normalize, which are not listed here. In all likelihood, you already have a library containing functions performing the same tasks.

All variables defined in this function have the same names as in the description above. Note that this function is not optimized. The screen space basis vectors, v_r, v_u, and v_n may be precomputed and stored per screen, as may be the screen-space basis matrix M which uses them.

Listing 33.1. Perspective matrix calculation.

```
void projection(const float *pa,     // Lower-left screen corner
                const float *pb,     // Lower-right screen corner
                const float *pc,     // Upper-left screen corner
                const float *pe,     // Eye position
                float n, float f)    // Near and far clipping distances
{
    float va[3], vb[3], vc[3];
    float vr[3], vu[3], vn[3];

    float l, r, b, t, d, M[16];
    // Compute an orthonormal basis for the screen.
    subtract(vr, pb, pa);
    subtract(vu, pc, pa);

    normalize(vr);
    normalize(vu);
    crossProduct(vn, vr, vu);
    normalize(vn);

    // Compute the screen corner vectors.
    subtract(va, pa, pe);
    subtract(vb, pb, pe);
    subtract(vc, pc, pe);

    // Find the distance from the eye to screen plane.
    d = -dotProduct(va, vn);

    // Find the extent of the perpendicular projection.
    l = dotProduct(vr, va) * n / d;
    r = dotProduct(vr, vb) * n / d;
```

```
    b = dotProduct(vu, va) * n / d;
    t = dotProduct(vu, vc) * n / d;

    // Load the perpendicular projection.
    glMatrixMode(GL_PROJECTION);
    glLoadIdentity();
    glFrustum(l, r, b, t, n, f);

    // Rotate the projection to be non-perpendicular.
    memset(M, 0, 16 * sizeof(float));

    M[0] = vr[0]; M[4] = vr[1]; M[ 8] = vr[2];
    M[1] = vu[0]; M[5] = vu[1]; M[ 9] = vu[2];
    M[2] = vn[0]; M[6] = vn[1]; M[10] = vn[2];

    M[15] = 1.0f;

    glMultMatrixf(M);

    // Move the apex of the frustum to the origin.
    glTranslatef(-pe[0], -pe[1], -pe[2]);

    glMatrixMode(GL_MODELVIEW);
}
```

Some may wonder why I've applied the `glMultMatrixf` and `glTranslatef` to the OpenGL projection matrix rather than the model-view matrix. It would work either way. I feel the use of the projection matrix lends the implementation better encapsulation. Applications may use it as a drop-in replacement for the standard perspective functions without worrying about smashing a valuable model-view stack with a later `glLoadIdentity`, as is a very common practice.

This distinction is even wider when you consider the OpenGL 3.0 forward compatible and OpenGL ES 2.0 programming models. Both of these APIs do away with the matrix stacks entirely. Applications that use them must construct their projection matrices on the CPU and upload them to vertex shader uniforms on the GPU. By composing the screen-space orientation and eye position translation matrices with the perspective projection on the CPU, the vertex shader need not concern itself with the nature of the projection.

33.5 Example

To make this discussion as concrete as possible, we look at a specific example. A full-fledged multi-screen implementation like the Varrier would be beyond the scope of this document, given that a great deal of supporting software is necessary before we can even begin. For this reason, we consider a simple stereo pair renderer.

Figure 33.9 shows the example output. To view this image properly, cross your eyes such that your right eye focuses upon the left image, and your left eye focuses upon the right image. If the image is scaled so that each of the two rectangles is 3″ wide, and viewed from a distance of 18″, then the image of the teapot should appear to hover 2″ in front of the paper.

Stereo rendering is an excellent application of this projection function, because many stereo application implementors do it wrong. Some applications offset the eyes

Figure 33.9

A crossed-eye stereoscopic rendering of a teapot.

horizontally but leave the view axes parallel. Some introduce a simple "toe-in" rotation without accounting for the off-axis perspectives. Both of these approaches cause the left-eye and right-eye viewports to differ in user space, which results in *edge violation*, a condition which is uncomfortable (and potentially nauseating) for the viewer, and leads to image discontinuities in tiled stereoscopic display systems.

The generalized perspective projection formulation allows you to do it correctly and automatically. You need only select one set of screen corners and a pair of eye positions, and the projection function produces a correctly skewed projection matrix.

Figure 33.10 shows a top-down view of the virtual scene depicted by the Figure 33.9. The eyes are positioned near the origin, offset using an average interocular distance of 2.5″. The teapot model is positioned at $z = -16″$, and the screen is at $z = -18″$. The image plane is defined to be 3″ wide and 1.5″ high. In summary, the screen corners are

$$
p_a = \begin{bmatrix} -1.5 \\ -0.75 \\ -18.0 \end{bmatrix} \quad p_b = \begin{bmatrix} 1.5 \\ -0.75 \\ -18.0 \end{bmatrix} \quad p_c = \begin{bmatrix} -1.5 \\ 0.75 \\ -18.0 \end{bmatrix}
$$

The left and right eye positions are

$$
p_L = \begin{bmatrix} -1.25 \\ 0.0 \\ 0.0 \end{bmatrix} \quad p_R = \begin{bmatrix} 1.25 \\ 0.0 \\ 0.0 \end{bmatrix}
$$

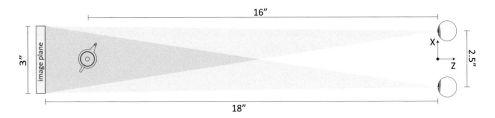

Figure 33.10

An overhead view of the teapot scene, its viewer, and its display.

33.6 Extended Capabilities

As suggested in the motivation, this perspective function has generality beyond what is commonly needed. In particular, screens may have arbitrary orientation. They may even be rotated, installed upside down, laid flat on the floor, or hung from the ceiling. This makes the approach applicable to CAVE-like projector-based installations [Cruz-Neira et al. 1993]. The only requirement is that because screens can be rotated in non-standard directions, p_a should contain the position of the screen's *logical* lower left corner, i.e., the first pixel of the last row of pixels, rather its *spatially measured* lowest, leftmost corner. (And so with p_b and p_c.)

Also note that the ostensibly rectangular screen is configured using only three points. The position of the fourth point is implicit. The formulation discussion refers to the screen-space basis (v_r, v_u, v_n) as "orthonormal," and the implementation does normalize it, but does not orthonormalize it. Thus, the configuration is free to introduce a skew transform, in addition to the screen-orientating rotation transform. I have never seen a circumstance where this is useful. If you ever find a rhombic display, let me know!

33.7 Conclusion

This has been a rather lengthy description of a fairly brief bit of code. By discussing it in detail, I hope to convey a thorough understanding of its function, correctness, and usefulness. This code has found use in several virtual reality research projects at the Electronic Visualization Lab (EVL) at the University of Illinois at Chicago, where the Varrier and CAVE systems were invented, and elsewhere. Its value to us has been great. I hope you find it useful as well.

References

[Sandin et al. 2005]

Sandin, Daniel J., Todd Margolis, Jinghua Ge, Javier Girado, Tom Peterka, and Thomas A. DeFanti. The Varrier™ autostereoscopic virtual reality display. *ACM Transactions on Graphics (TOG)*, 24(3): 894–903, 2005. ACM.

[Cruz-Neira et al. 1993]

Cruz-Neira, Carolina, Daniel J. Sandin, and Thomas A. DeFanti. Surround-screen projection-based virtual reality: the design and implementation of the CAVE. In *Proceedings of the 20th Annual Conference on Computer Graphics and Interactive Techniques*, pp. 135–142. ACM, 1993.

Fast and Easy Collision Detection for Rigid and Deformable Objects

Rene Weller and Gabriel Zachmann
University of Bremen

In this chapter, we present two methods for collision detection in virtual environments. The first method relies on a data structure called the *Inner Sphere Tree (IST)*. ISTs are suitable for rigid objects and they are the first data structure that is able to compute the *penetration volume* between a pair of colliding objects at haptic rendering rates. This new contact information guarantees physically-plausible and continuous forces and torques for the collision responses that are essential for stable physically-based simulations and haptic rendering. ISTs do rely on a bounding volume hierarchy that requires a time-consuming pre-processing that becomes invalid in case of deformations. Consequently, for deformable objects, we propose another algorithm (we call it *kDet*) that does not need any pre-processing. kDet works completely on the GPU and has a constant running time for practically all relevant objects.

34.1 Introduction

An immersive experience in interactive virtual environments requires not only realistic sounds, graphics, and interaction metaphors, but also a plausible behavior of the objects with which we interact. For instance, if objects in the real world interact, i.e., if they collide, they may, depending on properties such as rigidity, (1) bounce off each other or

(2) possibly break into pieces or (3) deform. Naturally, we expect a similar behavior in computer simulated environments.

However, in a computer-generated world, objects are usually represented as an abstract geometric model. Commonly, we approximate their surfaces with polygons. Such abstract representations have no physical properties per se. In fact, they would simply float through each other. Therefore, we have to algorithmically add an appropriate handling of contacts.

In detail, we first have to *find* contacts between moving objects. This process is called *collision detection*. In a second step, we have to *resolve* these collisions in a physically plausible manner. We call this the *collision response*.

In order to compute physically plausible collision responses, some kind of contact data is required that must be delivered by the collision detection algorithm. Basically, there exist four different kinds of contact information that can be used by different collision response solvers: we can either (1) track the *minimum distances* between pairs of objects, (2) determine the exact *time of impact*, (3) define a minimum translational vector to separate the objects, the so-called *penetration depth*, or (4) compute the *penetration volume* (see Figure 34.1).

According to [Fisher and Lin, 2001, Section 5.1], the *penetration volume* is "the most complicated yet accurate method" to define the extent of intersection. In Section 34.2 we present the first data structure, the so-called *Inner Sphere Trees (ISTs)*, that yields an approximation of the penetration volume for objects consisting of hundreds of thousands of polygons.

However, ISTs are not an all-in-one solution suitable for every purpose. They also have drawbacks; e.g., they are, thus far, restricted to watertight objects. Moreover, they rely on

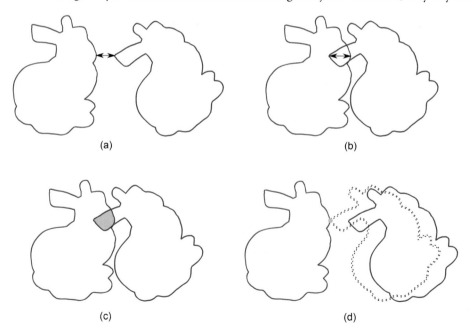

(a)

(b)

(c)

(d)

Figure 34.1

Different penetration measures (a) Minimum distance, (b) Penetration depth, (c) Penetration volume, (d) Time of Impact.

a clever data structure, a special kind of bounding volume hierarchy, that quickly culls non-colliding parts of the object. This data structure is built in a time-consuming pre-processing step. Unfortunately, if the objects are not rigid, i.e., they deform over time, then this pre-computed data structure becomes invalid and must be re-computed or updated.

Hence, for deformable objects, we propose another collision detection algorithm we call *kDet*. This algorithm does not require a pre-processing step and is suitable for deformable and even fracturing simulations. Moreover, it supports adding or removing polygons during runtime. kDet runs completely on the GPU and it has a constant parallel running time for almost all relevant objects.

34.2 Inner Sphere Trees

Here, we introduce our Inner Sphere Tree data structure that:

- provides hierarchical bounding volumes from the *inside* of an object;
- utilizes a proposed clustering algorithm to construct a sphere hierarchy;
- uses a unified algorithm based on the ISTs of a pair of objects computing both an approximate minimal distance and the approximate penetration volume; without the application knowing in advance the current relationship between the pair of objects; and
- has a collision response scheme based on the penetration volume to compute *stable* and *continuous* forces and torques, in both direction and value.

The ISTs and, consequently, the collision detection algorithm are independent of geometric complexity; they depend only on the approximation error.

34.2.1 Basic Idea

The main idea of the ISTs is that we do not build an (outer) hierarchy based on the polygons on the boundary of an object. Instead, we fill the interior of the model with a set of non-overlapping simple volumes that closely approximate the object's volume. In our implementation, we use spheres for the sake of simplicity, but the idea of using inner bounding volumes (BVs) for lower bounds instead of outer BVs for upper bounds can be extended analogously to all kinds of sub-volumes. On top of these inner BVs, we build a hierarchy for fast computation to approximate proximity and *penetration volume* [Weller and Zachmann, 2009a, b].

The "penetration volume" corresponds to the (virtual) water displacement of the overlapping portions of the objects and, thus, leads to a physically motivated and continuous repulsion force and torques.

Our data structure can support a variety of object representations, such as polygon meshes or NURBS surfaces. The only precondition is that they be watertight. In order to build the hierarchy on the inner spheres, we utilize a recently proposed clustering algorithm. A parallel version of this clustering algorithm runs completely on modern GPUs.

34.2.2 Sphere Packing

In this section, we present the *Protosphere* algorithm, which computes space-filling polydisperse sphere-packings for arbitrary objects [Weller and Zachmann, 2010].

The basic idea is simple and related to prototype-based approaches known from machine learning. Furthermore, this prototype-based approach directly leads to the parallel version of our algorithm. It is independent of the object's representation (polygonal, NURBS, CSG, etc.); the only precondition is that it must be possible to compute the distance from any point to the surface of the object. Moreover, our algorithm is not restricted to 3D but can be easily extended to higher dimensions.

34.2.2.1 Apollonian Sphere Packings for Arbitrary Objects

A simple algorithm to fill an object with a set of non-overlapping spheres is the following greedy method. For a given object we start with the largest sphere that fits into the object. Iteratively, we insert new spheres, under the constraints that:

1. they must not intersect the already existing spheres; and
2. that they have to be completely contained inside the object.

The resulting sphere packing is called an "Apollonian sphere packing" [Borkovec et al., 1994]. One important property of Apollonian packings is that they are known to be space filling. There exist efficient algorithms to compute Apollonian diagrams for very simple geometrical shapes like cubes or spheres, but they are very difficult to generalize to arbitrary objects, let alone their computation time. Hence, in order to transfer the idea of Apollonian sphere packings to arbitrary objects, we have to make further considerations.

We start with a classic 3D Voronoi diagram. Let P denote the surface of a closed, simple object in 3D. Consider the largest sphere s inside P. Obviously, s touches at least four points of P (otherwise, it would not be the largest sphere), and there are no points of P inside s (see Figure 34.2). This implies that the center of s is a Voronoi node (VN) of P.

Figure 34.2

The largest sphere that fits into an object, touches at least three points in 2D, and four points in 3D, respectively.

34. Fast and Easy Collision Detection for Rigid and Deformable Objects

Consequently, it is possible to formulate the greedy space filling as an iterative computation of a generalized Voronoi diagram (VD) of P plus the set of all spheres existing so far (see Figure 34.3).

This basic idea has a major drawback: many algorithms have been devised for the calculation of the classic VD and for its many generalizations. However, there are relatively few methods dedicated to the construction of VDs for spheres in 3D and, to our knowledge, there is no algorithm available that supports the computation of VDs for a mixed set of triangles and spheres, let alone a fast and stable implementation.

Fortunately, a closer look at the simple algorithm we proposed above shows that we do not need the whole *Voronoi diagram*, but only the *Voronoi nodes*. Hence the core idea of

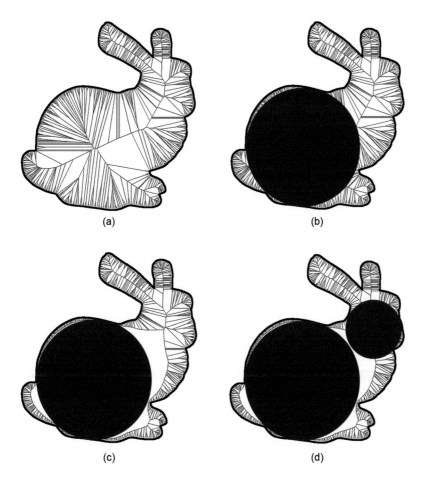

(a) (b)

(c) (d)

Figure 34.3

The basic idea of our Protosphere algorithm: (a) compute a Voronoi diagram for the object, (b) place the largest sphere, i.e. we use the Voronoi node with the largest distance to the surface as the center and the radius is defined by the respective length of the edges, (c) re-compute Voronoi diagram for the object and the new sphere, and (d) place largest sphere in the new Voronoi diagram etc.

our novel algorithm is to find the VNs directly and approximately. Again, the basic algorithm is very simple: we let a single point, the *prototype*, iteratively move towards one of the VNs (see Algorithm 1).

Algorithm 1: Prototype p convergePrototype(object O)

---

place **point** p randomly inside object O
while p has not converged **do**
    // set q_c as that point on the surface with minimum distance from p
    $q_c = \arg\min \left\{ \| p - q \| \ : \ q \in \text{surface of } O \right\}$
    choose $\varepsilon(t) \in [0,1]$
    $p = p + \varepsilon(t) \cdot (p - q_c)$
return p

The last line of the loop in Algorithm 1 guarantees that, after each single step, p is still inside the object, because the entire sphere around p with radius $\| p - q_c \|$ is inside the object.

Moreover, moving p away from the border into the direction $(p - q_c)$ leads potentially to bigger spheres in the next iteration (see Figure 34.4 for a visualization of our algorithm). Usually, $\varepsilon(t)$ is not a constant or chosen randomly, but a cooling function that allows large movements in early iterations and only small changes in the later steps. A cooling function allows large movements of the prototypes in the first iterations in order to move very quickly towards the maximum. In the later iterations, when we have almost arrived at the maximum, the function slows down to small movements for a fine tuning.

The accuracy of the approximated VN depends on the choice of the cooling function and on the number of iterations. We choose, as our cooling function, the following variation of a Gaussian function to meet these requirements:

$$\varepsilon(t) = 1 - e^{-0.5\left(\frac{|t - t_{\max}|}{0.5 t_{\max}}\right)^c} \tag{34.1}$$

where t is a counter for the iterations and $t_{\max}$ denotes the maximum number of iterations. The cooling factor c controls the steepness of the cooling function.

The overall sphere packing algorithm is described in Algorithm 2.

Algorithm 2: spherePacking(object O)

---

while *user-defined number of spheres is not met* **do**
    $p = \text{convergePrototype}(O)$
    $s = \text{new }$ **sphere** at position p
    $O = O \bigcup s$

---

            34. Fast and Easy Collision Detection for Rigid and Deformable Objects

Figure 34.4

The prototype convergence algorithm: (a) Place prototype P randomly inside the object. (b) Compute minimum distance d from the prototype P to the surface. (c) Move prototype P into the opposite direction, away from the surface P. (d) Continue until the prototype converges.

34.2.2.2 Parallelization

Performing these algorithms on a single prototype does not guarantee finding the global optimum (which is the sought-after VN), because the algorithms presented in the previous section depend on the starting position of the prototype and can end up in a local maximum (see Figure 34.5). Hence, we use a set of independently moving prototypes instead of only a single one. This can be easily parallelized, if the prototypes are allowed to move independently. However, a naïve implementation has its drawbacks: many prototypes converge to the same end position (see Figure 34.5). Consequently, we get a lot of similar and thus redundant computations. Obviously, this is not very efficient, even in parallel computing.

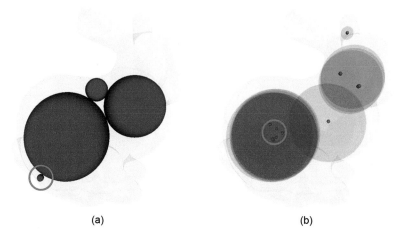

(a)   (b)

Figure 34.5

Depending on the prototype's start position, it can run into a local maximum instead of finding the global maximum: in the left image, a much larger sphere would fit, e.g. into the head of of bunny but due to the start position, the prototype converged to the green encircled position (a). If we start with several prototypes simultaneously to avoid local maxima, some of these prototypes converge to the same end position that is encircled in green (b).

Therefore, we use a slightly different approach based on a uniform distribution of the prototypes. Actually, we compute a uniform grid and start with a prototype in each cell within the object. During the movement step of Algorithm 1 the prototypes are confined to their cells. This results in a uniform density of the prototypes, and moreover, the grid can be used to speed up the distance computations. For the latter we additionally compute the discrete distance from each cell to the surface (the *distance field*). For further acceleration, we remove those prototypes from the computation that show the same closest point in two consecutive iterations and thus are clamped twice to the same position. Obviously, those prototypes cannot be Voronoi nodes.

Algorithm 3 shows the pseudo-code of the complete parallelized version. Figure 34.6 shows a visualization of the main steps.

Algorithm 3: parallelSpherePacking(object O)

In parallel: Initialize discrete distance field
while *user-defined number of spheres is not met* **do**
    In parallel: Place p_i randomly inside grid cell c_i
    In parallel: $p_i = $ convergePrototype($O \cup$ inserted spheres)
    In parallel: Find VN $p_m \in \{p_i\}$ with max distance d_m
    Insert **sphere** at position p_m with radius d_m
    In parallel: Update discrete distance field

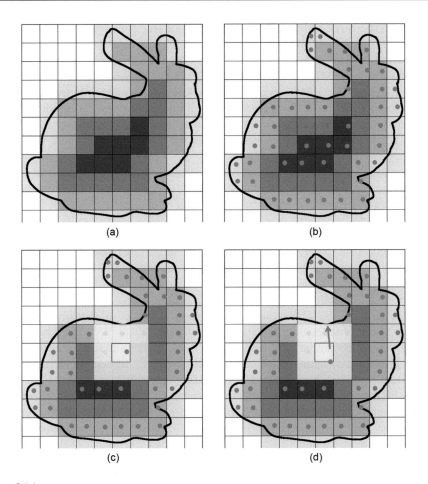

Figure 34.6

The parallel Protosphere algorithm: using a discrete distance field. (a) The discrete distance to the surface is colour coded. (b) We place a prototype (P_i) in each cell (c_i) of the distance field. (c) We use the discrete distance only to define a region in which we have to look for closest objects for each prototype. (d) During the convergence step we clamp the prototypes to their cells.

Our algorithm extends Apollonian sphere packings to arbitrary objects. This is the reason for the space filling property of our algorithm.

34.2.3 Hierarchy Creation

Based on the sphere packing, we create an *inner* bounding volume hierarchy. *Bounding Volume Hierarchies (BVHs)* are widely used to accelerate geometric intersection queries like ray tracing, visibility computations, or collision detection. The basic idea is simple: instead of calculating slow and complex geometric intersection tests between all geometric primitives, we wrap them recursively into simple *bounding volumes (BVs)* that allow faster intersection tests. This generates a tree data structure with a single, large BV at the root position that encloses all geometric primitives. Obviously, the geometric primitives are the leaves of such a BVH. We use a top-down *wrapped hierarchy* approach according to the notion of [Agarwal et al., 2004], where inner nodes are tight bounding volumes for all their leaves, but they do not necessarily bound their direct children (see Figure 34.7). Compared to layered hierarchies, the big advantage is that the inner BVs are tighter. We use a top-down approach to create our hierarchy, i.e., we start at the root node that covers all inner spheres and divide these into several subsets.

The partitioning of the inner spheres has significant influence on the performance during runtime. Previous methods for constructing BVHs, like the surface area heuristic, produce hierarchies that can accelerate ray-tracing dramatically. However, for penetration computations, taking the objects' volume into account produces much better BVHs [Weller et al., 2006]. Algorithms for building the classical *outer* sphere trees work well if the spheres constitute a *covering* of the object and have similar size, but in our scenario, we use disjoint inner spheres that exhibit a large variation in size.

34.2.4 Batch Neural Gas Hierarchy Clustering

For the clustering of the spheres, we chose the *batch neural gas* algorithm (BNG), which is popular in machine learning research [Cottrell et al., 2006]. BNG is a robust clustering algorithm which can be formulated as stochastic gradient descent with a cost function closely connected to quantization error. Like *k-means*, the cost function minimizes the mean squared Euclidean distance of each data point to its nearest center. But unlike k-means, BNG exhibits very robust behavior with respect to the initial cluster center positions (the *prototypes*): they can be chosen arbitrarily without affecting the convergence. Moreover, BNG can be extended to allow the specification of the *importance* of each data point; here, we describe how this can be used to increase the quality of the ISTs [Weller et al., 2014].

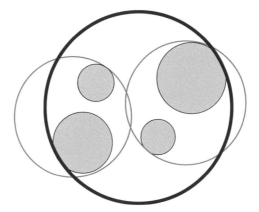

Figure 34.7

In a wrapped hierarchy, the parent sphere covers all its leaf nodes, but not necessarily its direct children.

34. Fast and Easy Collision Detection for Rigid and Deformable Objects

In the following, we give a quick recap of the basic batch neural gas followed by a description of our extensions and application to build the inner sphere tree.

Given points $x_j \in \mathbb{R}^d$, $j = 0,\ldots,m$ and prototypes $w_i \in \mathbb{R}^d$, $i = 0,\ldots,n$ initialized randomly, we set the rank for every prototype w_i with respect to every data point x_j as

$$k_{ij} := \left|\left\{ w_k : d\left(x_j, w_k\right) < d\left(x_j, w_i\right)\right\}\right| \in \{0,\ldots,n\} \tag{34.2}$$

In other words, we sort the prototypes with respect to every data point. After the computation of the ranks, we compute the new positions for the prototypes:

$$w_i := \frac{\sum_{j=0}^{m} h_\lambda\left(k_{ij}\right) x_j}{\sum_{j=0}^{m} h_\lambda\left(k_{ij}\right)} \tag{34.3}$$

These two steps are repeated until a stop criterion is met. In the original publication by [Cottrell et al., 2006], a fixed number of iterations is proposed. Indeed, after a certain number of iteration steps, which depends on the number of data points, there is no further improvement. We propose to use an adaptive version and stop the iteration if the movement of the prototypes is smaller than some ε. In our examples, we choose $\varepsilon \approx 10^{-5} \times \text{BoundingBoxSize}$, without any differences in the hierarchy compared to the non-adaptive, exhaustive approach. This improvement speeds up the creation of the hierarchy significantly.

The convergence rate is controlled by a monotonically decreasing "neighborhood" function $h_\lambda(k) > 0$ that decreases with the number of iterations t, with λ specifying the "neighborhood range." We use the function proposed in the original publication [Cottrell et al., 2006]: $h_\lambda(k) = e^{-\frac{k}{\lambda}}$ with initial value $\lambda_0 = \frac{n}{2}$, and reduction $\lambda(t) = \lambda_0 \left(\frac{0.01}{\lambda_0}\right)^{\frac{t}{t_{max}}}$, where t_{max} is the maximum number of iterations. These values are taken according to [Martinetz et al., 1993].

Obviously, the number of prototypes defines the arity of the tree. If it is too big, then the resulting trees are very inefficient. On the other hand, if it is too small, the trees become overly deep and with many levels containing big spheres that do not approximate the object very well. Experiments with our data structure have shown that a branching factor of four produces the best results. Additionally, this has the benefit that we can use the full capacity of SIMD units in modern CPUs during the traversal.

34.2.4.1 Magnification Control

In our experience, the regular BNG as presented so far already produces much better results than other, simpler heuristics, such as greedily choosing the biggest spheres or the spheres with the largest number of neighbors. However, it only utilizes the location of the centers of the spheres; it does not yet take the size of the spheres into account. This is because neural gas uses only the number of data points and not their importance. As a consequence, the prototypes tend to avoid regions that are covered with a very large sphere, i.e., centers of big spheres are treated as outliers and they are thus placed on deep levels in the hierarchy. Indeed, it is better to place big spheres at higher levels of the hierarchy in order to get early lower bounds during distance traversal (see Section 34.2.5.1 for details).

Therefore, we use an extended version of the classical batch neural gas that takes the size of the spheres into account. Our extension is based on an idea of [Hammer et al., 2006], where *magnification control* is introduced. The idea is to add weighting factors in order to "artificially" increase the density of the space in some areas.

With weighting factors $v(x_j)$, Equation 34.3 becomes:

$$w_i := \frac{\sum_{j=0}^{m} h_\lambda(k_{ij}) v(x_j) x_j}{\sum_{j=0}^{m} h_\lambda(k_{ij}) v(x_j)} \tag{34.4}$$

Where $v(x_j)$ identifies a control parameter to address the importance. In [Hammer et al., 2006], a function of density is used to control the magnification. In our scenario, we already know the density, because our spheres are disjoint. Thus, we can directly use the volumes of our spheres to let $v(x_j) = \frac{4}{3}\pi r^3$.

Summing up the hierarchy creation algorithm: we first compute a bounding sphere for all inner spheres (at the leaves), which becomes the root node of the hierarchy. To do so, we use the fast and stable smallest enclosing sphere algorithm proposed in [Gärtner, 1999]. Then, we divide the set of inner spheres into subsets in order to create the children. To do that, we apply the extended version of batch neural gas with magnification control mentioned above. We repeat this scheme recursively (see Figure 34.8 for some clustering results).

In the following, we will call the spheres in the hierarchy that are not leaves *hierarchy spheres*. Spheres at the leaves, which were computed by one of the sphere packing algorithms from Section 34.2.2, will be called *inner spheres*. Note that hierarchy spheres are not necessarily contained completely within the object.

34.2.4.2 Parallel Hierarchical Batch Neural Gas

The Batch Neural Gas algorithm produces a very good partitioning of the inner spheres, but as a drawback, it is very time-consuming. Specifically, it executes $\mathcal{O}(n)$ BNG calls – one for each hierarchy sphere—where n denotes the number of inner spheres. In case of a balanced tree with height $\mathcal{O}(\log n)$, we have an overall running-time of $\mathcal{O}(n \log n)$, but with a relatively high hidden constant factor that results from the number of iteration steps.

However, BNG in its pure form, as well as the hierarchical BNG calls of our BVH creation, are perfectly suited for parallelization. Assuming $\mathcal{O}(n)$ processors, we are able to reduce the asymptotic running-time to $\mathcal{O}(\log^2 n)$. In the following, we will sketch the details of this parallel hierarchical BNG implementation using the GPU.

Figure 34.8

This figure shows the results of our hierarchy building algorithm based on batch neural gas clustering with magnification control. All of those inner spheres that share the same color are assigned to the same bounding sphere. The left image shows the clustering result of the root sphere, the right images the partitioning of its four children.

Obviously, on the first level of our hierarchy, the ordering k_{ij} and, consequently, also $h_\lambda(k_{ij})v(x_j)x_j$ can be computed independently for each sphere x_j. Summing up all those values can be implemented in parallel too, by using a parallel scan algorithm [Sengupta et al., 2008]. Also; the parallel assignment of spheres to prototypes is straight forward: we simply have to compute the distances of each sphere to the prototypes. Please note, that each sphere is assigned to exactly one prototype.

In the next level of the BVH creation, we have to add four new prototypes for each prototype from the previous level (in case of a branching factor of four). However, triggering an own parallel process for each sub-set of spheres would forgo the advantages of parallel computing, especially on the deeper hierarchy levels. Therefore, we chose an alternative. In the following we will describe its technical details.

First, we sort the spheres with respect to the prototype that the spheres were assigned to (see Figure 34.9). This can be done in parallel by using a parallel sorting algorithm [Satish et al., 2009]. This technical detail allows us later to use fast parallel prefix-sum computations. However, after the sorting we virtually insert four new prototypes for each prototype from the previous hierarchy level. The fact that each sphere has been assigned to exactly one prototype in the previous level allows us to compute the values that are required for BNG (in particular, k_{ij} and h_lambda) in parallel for each sphere. We simply have to ensure that these values are computed for the *right new* prototypes (see Figure 34.10).

Finally, we have to sum the individual values to get the new prototype positions; this means we have to compute $\sum_{j=0}^{m} h_\lambda(k_{ij})v(x_j)x_j$ and $\sum_{j=0}^{m} h_\lambda(k_{ij})v(x_j)$. Surprisingly, we can directly re-use the parallel prefix-sum from above [Sengupta et al., 2008], even if

we now need the sums for each new prototype individually: we simply have to subtract the values at the borders of our sorted prototype array (see Figure 34.11).

Algorithm 4 summarizes our complete parallel hierarchical BNG implementation.

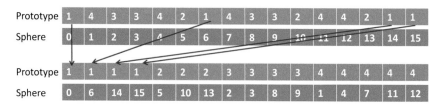

Figure 34.9

The top array stores the indices of the prototype to which the sphere in the array below has been assigned after the initial BNG clustering. In a first step, we sort the spheres with respect to their prototype index (the two lower arrays). Note, that each sphere is assigned to exactly one prototype.

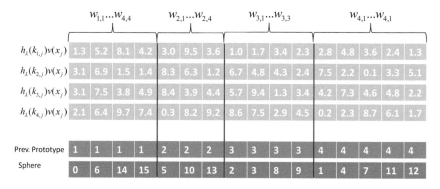

Figure 34.10

An example for the second level of the hierarchical BNG. According to Figure 34.9, each sphere has been assigned to a prototype. We insert 16 new prototypes, $(w_{1,1},...,w_{4,4})$, four for each prototype $(w_1,...,w_4)$ from the previous level and compute the values that are required by BNG, e.g., $h_\lambda(k_{ij})v(x_j)$. Please note that we need not allocate new memory or copy any values from CPU to GPU. We can simply re-use the memory from the previous level because each sphere was assigned to exactly one prototype. Consequently, we get a constant memory consumption for each level.

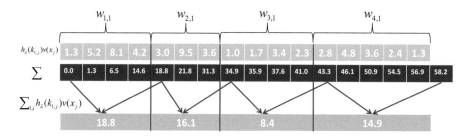

Figure 34.11

In order to compute the new position of the prototypes for the next iteration, we must determine $\sum h_\lambda(k_{ij})v(x_j)x_j$. Therefore, we compute the prefix sum (brown array) for each of the four prototype arrays from Figure 34.10. The differences between the values at the borders directly deliver us the individual sum for each prototype.

34. Fast and Easy Collision Detection for Rigid and Deformable Objects

---

Algorithm 4: Parallel hierarchical BNG

---

while *Not on inner sphere level* **do**
    iteration = 0
    while *iteration < maxNumberIterations* **do**
        iteration++
        In parallel Sort prototype array
        In parallel forall *Spheres* **do**
          compute $h_\lambda\left(k_{ij}\right)v\left(x_j\right)x_j$
          and $h_\lambda\left(k_{ij}\right)v\left(x_j\right)$
        In parallel Compute prefix sum
        In parallel forall *Prototypes* **in** *level* **do**
          Compute new position
    read back prototype positions

The prefix sum and the sorting of the prototypes for n inner spheres can be computed in parallel using $\mathcal{O}(n)$ processors in $\mathcal{O}(\log n)$. Basically, both algorithms are based on an implicit balanced binary tree structure (see [Satish et al., 2009] and [Sengupta et al., 2008] for more details). The "per sphere" steps of Algorithm 4 have a complexity of $\mathcal{O}(1)$, obviously. If the tree is balanced, the outer while-loop is called $\mathcal{O}(\log n)$ times. Overall, we get a parallel time complexity of $\mathcal{O}(\log^2 n)$. The memory consumption is $\mathcal{O}(n)$.

In practice, it is essential that there is not too much traffic between the memories of the CPU and the GPU. In our implementation there is almost no traffic required. We only have to save the positions of the prototypes from the last iteration in the outer loop of Algorithm 4[*]. We only need to allocate memory for the prototypes once. This memory can be re-used for all iterations. In our prototypical naïve implementation using CUDA without further optimizations, we get an overall speed-up by a factor of ten compared to the sequential hierarchy computation.

34.2.5 Traversal Algorithms

Our data structure supports almost all kinds of collision queries; namely, (1) *proximity queries*, which report the separation distance between a pair of objects, (2) *penetration volume queries*, which report the common volume covered by both objects and, moreover, it supports (3) *continuous collision detection queries*, which report the exact time of impact when two objects collide. Obviously, the traversal can be easily modified in order to also provide boolean answers that simply report whether the objects collide or not.

As a by-product, the proximity query can return a witness realizing the distance, the penetration volume algorithm can return a partial list of intersecting polygons, and the continuous collision detection query can return the first pair of colliding spheres.

---

[*] However, even this is not really necessary. In the future, we plan to also move the smallest enclosing sphere computation to the GPU. Then, we only have to read back the whole hierarchy once.

We start with a separate discussion of the distance and penetration volume queries in order to point out their specific requirements. In Section 34.2.5.4, we describe how to combine these traversal schemes to a unified algorithm that is able to provide distance and penetration volume information, without the user needing to know in advance, whether the objects overlap or not. Furthermore, we will describe a time-critical extension of both algorithms that allows an approximation of the appropriate contact information, distance and penetration volume, respectively, when a pre-defined time-budget is not exceeded.

Finally, we will describe an algorithm that uses our new data structure to compute the time of impact. In fact, the main focus during the design of our ISTs was the computation of a continuous penetration measure, the penetration volume, at haptic rates. But it turns out that ISTs also have some nice implications on continuous collision detection.

34.2.5.1 Distances

Our proximity query algorithm works like most other classical BVH traversal algorithms: we check whether two bounding volumes overlap or not. If this is the case, then we recursively step through their children. In order to compute lower bounds for the distance, we simply have to add an appropriate distance test at the right place. This has to be done when we reach a pair of inner spheres (i.e., the leaves of the ISTs) during traversal (see Algorithm 5). These inner spheres are located completely inside the object and thus, provide a lower bound on the sought-after distance. During traversal there is no need to visit branches of the bounding volume test tree that are farther apart than the current minimum distance because of the bounding property. This guarantees a high culling efficiency.

Algorithm 5: checkDistance(A, B, minDist)

---

input : A, B = spheres in the inner sphere tree
in/out : minDist = overall minimum distance seen so far
if A *and* B *are leaves* **then**
    // end of recursion
    $\text{minDist} = \min\{\text{distance}(A, B), \text{minDist}\}$
else
    // recursion step
    forall *children* a[i] **of** A **do**
        forall *children* b[j] **of** B **do**
            if $\text{distance}(a[i], b[j]) < \text{minDist}$ **then**
                checkDistance(a[i], b[j], minDist)

34.2.5.2 Penetration Volume

In addition to proximity queries, our data structure also supports a new kind of penetration query, namely the *penetration volume*. This is the volume of the intersection of the two objects, which can be interpreted directly as the amount of the repulsion force if it is considered as the amount of water being displaced.

The algorithm that computes the penetration volume (see Algorithm 6) does not differ very much from the proximity query: we simply have to replace the distance test by an overlap test and maintain an accumulated overlap volume during the traversal. The overlap volume of a pair of spheres can be easily derived by adding the volumes of the spherical caps.

Due to the non-overlapping constraint of the inner spheres, the accumulated overlap volumes provide a lower bound on the real overlap volume of the objects.

Algorithm 6: computeVolume (A, B, totalOverlap)

---

input : A, B = spheres in the inner sphere tree
in/out : totalOverlap = overall volume of intersection
if A *and* B *are leaves* **then**
    // end of recursion
    totalOverlap += overlapVolume(A, B)
else
    // recursion step
    forall *children* a[i] **of** A **do**
        forall *children* b[j] **of** B **do**
            if $\mathrm{overlap}\left(a[i], b[j]\right) > 0$ **then**
                computeVolume(a[i], b[j], totalOverlap)

34.2.5.3 Intersection Volume of Spheres

The main challenge during the traversal is the computation of the penetration volume between a pair of spheres. According to [Weisstein, 2012], this can be expressed in a closed formula. Basically, the intersection volume of two intersecting spheres is a lens built of two spherical caps. Without loss of generality we assume that one sphere is centered at the origin and the second sphere is displaced by a distance d on the x-axis (see Figure 34.12 for the setting). The equations of the spheres can be expressed as

$$x^2 + y^2 + z^2 = r_1^2 \tag{34.5}$$

and

$$(x-d)^2 + y^2 + z^2 = r_2^2 \text{ , respectively} \tag{34.6}$$

Consequently, the intersection is:

$$(x-d)^2 - x^2 = r_2^2 - r_1^2 \tag{34.7}$$

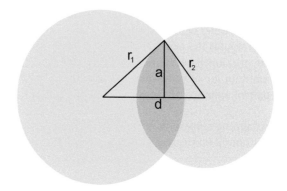

Figure 34.12

Penetration volume of two spheres with radius r_1 and r_2, respectively. a denotes the radius of the circle of the two spherical caps that build the intersection volume.

In order to compute the intersection volume, we can simply add the volumes of the two spherical caps with distances $d_1 = x$ for the first sphere and $d_2 = x - d$ for the second sphere. The heights of the spherical caps are:

$$h_1 = r_1 - d_1 = \frac{(r_2 - r_1 + d)(r_2 + r_1 - d)}{2d} \tag{34.8}$$

and

$$h_2 = r_2 - d_2 = \frac{(r_1 - r_2 + d)(r_1 + r_2 - d)}{2d} \tag{34.9}$$

In common, the volume of a spherical cap of height h for a sphere with radius r can be expressed by (see e.g., [Weisstein, 2012] for more details.):

$$V(R,h) = \frac{1}{3}\pi h^2 (3r - h) \tag{34.10}$$

Consequently, we get for the total intersection volume V for two spheres:

$$V = V(r_1, h_1) + V(r_2, h_2)$$

$$= \frac{\pi(r_1 + r_2 - d)^2 (d^2 + 2dr_2 - 3r_2^2 + 2dr_1 + 6r_1r_2 - 3r_1^2)}{12d} \tag{34.11}$$

Summarizing, Equation 34.11 allows us to compute the overlap between a pair of spheres efficiently during the traversal.

34. Fast and Easy Collision Detection for Rigid and Deformable Objects

34.2.5.4 Unified Algorithm for Distance and Volume Queries

In the previous sections, we introduced the proximity and the penetration volume computation separately. However, it is quite easy to combine both algorithms. This yields a unified algorithm that can compute both the distance and the penetration volume, without the user having to know in advance whether the objects overlap or not.

We start with the distance traversal. If we find the first pair of intersecting inner spheres, then we simply switch to the penetration volume computation.

The correctness is based on the fact that all pairs of inner spheres we visited so far during distance traversal do not overlap and thus do not extend the penetration volume. Thus, we do not have to visit them again and can continue with the traversal of the rest of the hierarchies using the penetration volume algorithm. If we do not meet an intersecting pair of inner spheres, the unified algorithm still reports the minimal separating distance.

34.2.6 Continuous Volumetric Collision Response

To maintain stable 6-DOF haptic rendering from a physically based rigid body simulation, we explore how to use the penetration volume to compute continuous forces and torques.

Mainly, there are three different approaches to resolve collisions: (1) the penalty-based method, (2) the constraint-based method and (3) the impulse-based method. The constraint-based approach computes constraint forces that are designed to cancel any external acceleration that would result in interpenetrations. Unfortunately, this method has at least quadratic complexity in the number of contact points. The impulse-based method resolves contacts between objects by a series of impulses in order to prevent interpenetrations. It is applicable to real-time simulations but the forces may not be valid for bodies in resting contact.

So, we decided to use the penalty-based method, that computes penalty forces based on the interpenetration of a pair of objects. The main advantages are its computational simplicity, which makes it applicable for haptic rendering and its ability to simulate a variety of surface characteristics. Moreover, the use of the penetration volume eliminates inconsistent states that may occur when only a penetration depth (i.e., a minimum translational vector) is used.

Obviously, the amount of overlap can be directly used to define the *amount* of repelling forces. However, in order to apply such penalty forces in haptic environments or physically-based simulations, the *direction* of the force is required in addition to its amount.

A simple heuristic would be to consider all overlapping pairs of spheres (R_i, S_j) separately. Let $\mathbf{c}_i, \mathbf{c}_j$ be their sphere centers and $\mathbf{n}_{ij} = \mathbf{c}_i - \mathbf{c}_j$. Then, we compute the overall direction of the penalty force as the weighted sum $\mathbf{n} = \sum_{i,j} \mathrm{Vol}(R_i \cap S_j) \cdot \mathbf{n}_{ij}$ (see Figure 34.13).

Obviously, this direction is continuous, provided the path of the objects is continuous. However, this simple heuristic also has its drawbacks: in case of deep penetrations it is possible that some internal intersections point into the false direction. As a result, the

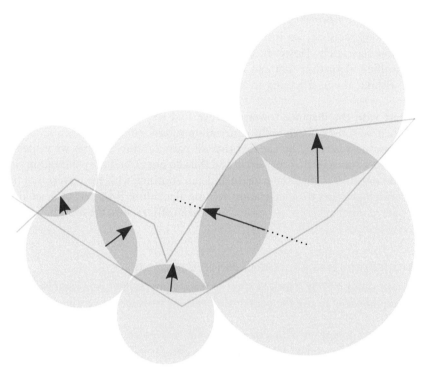

Figure 34.13

The direction of the penalty force can be derived from the weighted average of all vectors between the centers of colliding pairs of spheres, weighted by their overlap.

objects will be sucked up into each other. Therefore, it can be necessary to flip some of the directions $\mathbf{n}_{ij}$.

In the following, we will present an extension based on normal cones for all spheres throughout the hierarchy that can help to identify these pairs. Moreover, we will show how our ISTs can also provide continuous torques.

34.2.6.1 Contact Forces

Algorithm 6 and its time-critical derivative return a set of overlapping spheres or potentially overlapping spheres, respectively. We compute a force for each of these pairs of spheres (R_i, S_j) by:

$$\mathbf{f}(R_i) = k_c \operatorname{Vol}(R_i \cap S_j)\mathbf{n}_{(R_i)} \tag{34.12}$$

where k_c is the contact stiffness, $\operatorname{Vol}(R_i \cap S_j)$ is the overlap volume, and $\mathbf{n}_{(R_i)}$ is the contact normal.

Summing up all pairwise forces gives the total penalty force:

$$f(R) = \sum_{R_i \cap S_i \neq \emptyset} f(R_i)$$ (34.13)

In order to compute normals for each pair of spheres, we augment the construction process of the ISTs: in addition to storing the distance to the object's surface, we store a pointer to the triangle that realizes this minimum distance. While creating the inner spheres by merging several voxels, we accumulate a list of triangles for every inner sphere. We use the normals of these triangles to compute normal cones which are defined by an axis and an angle. They tightly enclose the normals of the triangles that are stored in the list of each inner sphere.

During force computation, the axes of the normal cones C_R and C_S are used as the directions of the force since they will bring the penetrating spheres outside the other object in the direction of the surface normals (see Figure 34.14). Note that $\mathbf{f}(R_i) \neq \mathbf{f}(S_j)$.

If the cone angle is too large (i. e. $\alpha \approx \pi$), we simply use the vector between the two centers of the spheres as in the naive approach.

Obviously, this force is continuous in both cases, because the movement of the axes of the normal cones as well as the movement of the centers of the spheres are continuous, provided the path of the objects is continuous.

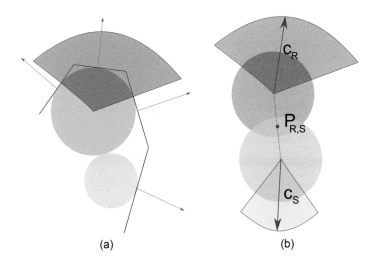

(a)   (b)

Figure 34.14

(a) we compute a normal cone for each inner sphere. The cone a list of triangles that is associated with the sphere. Note that the spread angle of the normal cone can be 0 if the sphere is closest to a single triangle. (b) the axis of the normal cones $\mathbf{C}_R$ and $\mathbf{C}_S$ are used for the force direction. The center $P_{R,S}$ of the spherical cap defines the contact point.

34.2.6.2 Torques

In rigid body simulation, the torque τ is usually computed as $\tau = (P_c - C_m) \times \mathbf{f}$, where P_c is the point of collision, C_m is the center of mass of the object and $\mathbf{f}$ is the force acting at P_c. Like in the section before, we compute the torque separately for each pair (R_i, S_j) of intersecting inner spheres:

$$\tau(R_i) = (P_{(R_i, S_j)} - C_m) \times \mathbf{f}(R_i) \tag{34.14}$$

Again, we accumulate all pairwise torques to get the total torque:

$$\tau(R) = \sum_{R_i \cap S_j \neq \varnothing} \tau(R_i) \tag{34.15}$$

We define the point of collision $P_{(R_i, S_j)}$ simply as the center of the intersection volume of the two spheres (see Figure 34.14). Obviously, this point moves continuously if the objects move continuously. In combination with the continuous forces $\mathbf{f}(R_i)$, this results in a continuous torque.

34.3 kDet: Deformable Collision Detection with Hierarchical Grids on the GPU

ISTs work perfectly for watertight rigid objects. However, in case of deformations, the BVH becomes invalid. A complete rebuild would take too long, and until now it is an open question how to quickly update the hierarchy. Hence, for deformable objects we propose a polygon-based algorithm called *kDet* that additionally has the advantage that it runs completely on the GPU. kDet computes all intersecting pairs of polygons for a pair of polygonal objects. Consequently, traditional all-pairs collision response methods can be easily applied. It is possible to prove a worst-case running time for kDet that is independent of the number of polygons. Our algorithm is very well suited for deformable and even topology-changing objects, because it does not require any complex data structures or pre-processing.

34.3.1 Basic Idea

The main idea behind our kDet algorithm is based on a simple observation: when we want to check two objects A and B for collisions, we do not have to consider *all* polygon pairs; rather, it is sufficient to simply check each polygon of A against *larger* polygons of B and vice versa. Obviously, a naive implementation would result in a quadratic running time. The challenge is to reduce the number of potentially colliding triangles to a constant number for each polygon. In other words, we have to identify polygons in a certain neighborhood and we have to show that there are not overly many polygons in this neighborhood.

A widely used approach for neighbor searching are uniform grids. However, choosing an appropriate cell size is challenging: if the cell size is too large, there may be many polygons assigned to the same cell. On the other hand, if the cell size is chosen too small, large polygons occupy a large number of cells. Fortunately, in our case, we are not interested in finding *all* neighbors; we only need to find *larger* polygons. This means we can use a hierarchy of grids with different cell sizes and assign each polygon to the specific level in this hierarchy where it does not occupy too many cells.

34.3.2 Populating the Hierarchical Grid

Before performing a collision query, we must assign the polygons to their particular grid cells. To do that, we apply a simple rule: let A be a set of polygons. For each polygon $p_i \in A$ let d_i be the diameter of the circumcircle and let $d_{\min} = \min\{d_i\}$. We set the cell size of the finest grid in our hierarchy to $d_{\min}$. Coarser levels are derived by successively doubling the cell size. The hierarchy level l_i of each polygon p_i can be computed by

$$2^{l_i} \cdot d_{\min} \leq d_i < 2^{l_i+1} \cdot d_{\min}$$

In other words, each polygon is assigned to the level so that the cell size is at most the diameter of the circumcircle. Then we simply add the polygon to all cells in the level l_i that are intersected by that polygon (see Figure 34.15).

34.3.3 Collision Queries

If we want to check two objects A and B for collision, we simply test all polygons $p_i^A \in A$ against all *larger* polygons $p_j^B \in B$ and vice versa. In detail, for each $p_i^A \in A$ we compute its level l_i and all cells in B's hierarchical grid that are intersected by b_i at this level. For each of these cells we test all included polygons P_j^B with at least the size of the circumcircle, i.e.

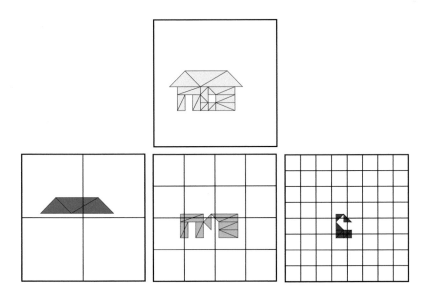

Figure 34.15

Three consecutive levels of the hierarchical grid with distributed polygons based on their circumcircle.

$c_i^A \leq c_j^B$. In order to check also larger triangles, we ascend in the hierarchy until we reach the maximum level and again, test P_i^A against all included polygons of B for an intersection (see Algorithms 7 and 8).

Algorithm 7: checkCollisions(object A, object B)

---

forall *polygons* $p_i \in A$ **do**
   checkCollisions(p_i, B)
forall *polygons* $p_j \in B$ **do**
   checkCollisions(p_j, A)

This algorithm guarantees that we find for each polygon $p_i \in A$ all intersecting polygons $p_j \in B$ with at least the same diameter of the circumcircle.

Overall, we will find *all* colliding pairs of polygons if we test A against B and vice versa, because either of the polygons has a larger circumcircle, assuming general position of the polygons. Obviously, for real-world tests we cannot assume general positions. Here, we avoid double checking polygon pairs by simply testing only strictly larger polygons in one direction.

Algorithm 8: checkCollisions(polygon p_i, object B)

Get hierarchy level l_i for p_i
forall *hierarchy levels:* $l_i \dots l_{\max}$ **do**
   forall *cells* $c_k \cap t_i \neq \varnothing$ **do**
      forall polygons $p_j \in c_k$ **do**
         polygonIntersection (p_i, p_j)

34.3.3.1 Parallelization

This algorithm can be easily parallelized. For the population of the hierarchical grid, we assign all polygons independently to their particular cells. Simple atomic operations avoid race conditions if two polygons are assigned to the same cell. During the queries, we can also check all polygons for each object in parallel. Algorithm 9 shows the complete parallel algorithm. It uses Algorithm 8 that will be executed as the kernel for the collision check per polygon.

Algorithm 9: checkCollisionsParallel(object A, object B)

In Parallel forall *polygons* $p_i \in A$ **do**
   assignPolygonToGridcell(p_i)
In Parallel forall *polygons* $p_j \in B$ **do**
   checkCollisions(p_j, A)

In Parallel forall *polygons $p_j \in B$* **do**
   assignPolygonToGridcell(p_j)
In Parallel forall *polygons $p_j \in A$* **do**
   checkCollisions(p_i, B)

In case of rigid objects, the assignment to the grid cells does not have to be computed before each collision check, but it can be done once at the beginning of the simulation as a pre-processing step. However, even if the assignment is computed before each collision check, as it would be required for deformable objects, it does not affect the theoretical complexity of our algorithm.

34.3.4 Analysis

The construction of our hierarchical grid can be done in linear time in case of sequential processing and constant time in the parallel case: computing the level of each triangle takes $\mathcal{O}(1)$ time. Due to the choice of the level—the cell size is at least the diameter of the circumcircle of each polygon—the polygon can intersect only a constant number of cells on its level. Hence, it has to be inserted into at most a constant number of cells. More precisely, each polygon can intersect at most eight cells on its level. Overall, we get a linear time for the construction of the hierarchical grid.

The query time consists mainly of two factors: the height of the hierarchy and the maximum number of polygons in a cell.

First, we show that the height of the hierarchy is independent of the number of polygons. Actually, the height of the hierarchy depends only on the ratio between the largest and the smallest polygon of each individual object. Let $d_{min} = \min\{d_i\}$ and $d_{max} = \max\{d_i\}$ where $p_i \in A$ are the polygons of a set of polygons A and d_i is the diameter of the circumcircle of each polygon p_i. Then the height h of the hierarchy is $h = \log\left(\dfrac{d_{max}}{d_{min}}\right)$. Obviously, h is independent of the *number* of polygons in A, and it only depends on their size distribution.

It still remains to be shown that the number of polygons per cell is constant. Obviously, for specially constructed worst cases like the Chazelle polyhedron, this is not true (see Figure 34.16). The main reason is, that a polygon can be infinitesimally small: this might generate polygons with an infinite number of other polygons in their neighborhood. However, we can easily define a geometric predicate that limits the number of neighbors:

Definition 3.1

Let A be a polygon set and $k>0$ some constant. We call A k-free if for each sphere s with diameter d there are at most k larger polygons $p_i \in A$, $i=1,\ldots,k$ intersecting s. Larger means that the diameter d_i of the minimum enclosing sphere of p_i is larger than d.

For such k-free polygon sets, it is easy to prove a constant number of polygons per cell: Due to the construction of the hierarchy, the minimum diameter d of the circumcircle of any polygon inside a cell with length c is at most $\dfrac{c}{2}$. We can cover the complete cell

Figure 34.16

Specially constructed objects like Chazelle polyhedra (left) realize a quadratic number of intersecting pairs of polygons in the worst case.

with spheres of diameter $\frac{c}{4}$, for instance by overlaying two regular sphere packings (see Figure 34.17 for a 2D example). Obviously, the number of spheres is constant and independent of the particular cellsize, because the diameter of the spheres is a fraction of the length of the cell. This number can be improved by using a better sphere covering. If we have such a sphere covering and if the object is k-free, there can be at most k polygons intersecting such a sphere of diameter $\frac{c}{4}$ by definition. Summarizing, we have a constant number of spheres that are required to cover a cell and we have at most a constant number of polygons intersecting each of these spheres; consequently, the total number of polygons inside a cell is constant.

This restriction to k-free polygonal objects seems to limit the viability of our algorithm. In fact, we analyzed a large object database of more than 10,000 real-world 3D objects and the results show that our definition holds for all but a handful of pathological cases. For more details we refer the interested reader to [Weller et al., 2017].

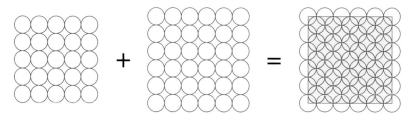

Figure 34.17

Covering of a cell in the uniform grid with two shifted regular circle lattices.

To summarize: in case of k-free sets of polygons, we get at most a constant number of polygons in each cell of the hierarchy, each polygon intersects at most a constant number of cells and the number of levels in the hierarchy is independent of the number of polygons. Overall, we get a running time of $\mathcal{O}\left(\log\left(\frac{d_{max}}{d_{min}}\right)n\right)$ for a collision query which is almost linear in the number of polygons.

In the parallel case, we process all polygons at the same time for both the hierarchy construction and the collision queries. The construction requires an atomic operation when inserting several polygons into the same cell. However, the number of polygons per cell is constant, and consequently, the number of atomic operations is also constant per cell. This means we get a constant running time for the construction. In the query algorithm, all steps are constant per polygon except the height of the hierarchy. Hence, we get a parallel running time of $\mathcal{O}\left(\log\left(\frac{d_{max}}{d_{min}}\right)\right)$ for the query which is independent of the polygon count and thus, almost constant. For both algorithms we need only a linear number of parallel processors.

The factor $\log\left(\frac{d_{max}}{d_{min}}\right)$ somewhat blemishes the analysis, and it is easy to construct artificial worst-case objects that would produce a linear height of the hierarchy. However, objects with such a wide spread in polygon sizes can be easily identified, in contrast to objects that produce a quadratic number of polygon intersections, and moreover, they are typically avoided in real-world scenarios.

In case of deformable (or fracturing) objects, $\frac{d_{max}}{d_{min}}$ could change due to the deformations. In our experiments, we did not observe such a behavior. We are positive that most deformation methods will not change $\frac{d_{max}}{d_{min}}$ much, because an extremely varying polygon size is usually unwanted, if only for reason of numerical stability and high-quality rendering. However, the theoretical proof of a constant $\frac{d_{max}}{d_{min}}$ for existing deformation schemes or the development of novel deformation schemes that keep this within certain bounds is an interesting question for future works.

34.3.5 Implementation Details

The high-level description of our algorithm from the previous section is useful to understand the underlying concepts and for the theoretical analysis. An actual implementation should also consider details of current computer architectures like memory consumption or the memory access of current massively parallel processors like GPUs.

34.3.5.1 Spatial Hashing

A major drawback of the naive algorithm is the high memory consumption that is required to maintain a hierarchy of uniform grids. Usually, most of the cells remain empty, even if we restrict the grids' extents to the bounding boxes. In order to overcome this drawback, we use hash tables instead of real grids.

Hash tables are a widely used data structure that already have been applied successfully to represent uniform grids in the past [Turk, 1989]. Hash tables achieve almost constant insertion and query time while reducing the memory overhead. The main challenge when using hash tables is to find an appropriate hash function. We investigated different hashing functions, such as DJB2 hashing [Eitz and Lixu, 2007], which spreads the triangles relatively uniformly in the hash table and, thus, minimizes hash collisions. Additionally, we tested 3D Morton codes [Morton, 1966] that generate locality-preserving hash values of the triangles that should help to maximize coalesced memory access in our GPU implementation. In order to further improve the memory access, we initially pre-sort the triangles with respect to the Morton codes and the hierarchy levels (for instance, one of the readily available sorting algorithms in the Thrust library can be used). However, we do this only once at the beginning of the simulation, rather than before each individual collision check. Consequently, this pre-processing heuristic does not affect the constant running time.

Another question that arises when using hash tables is the resolution of hash collisions that appear when several polygons have the same hash value. Closed hashing would result in extremely non-coalesced memory access. Open hashing, on the other hand, would require dynamic memory allocation if we would use lists for instance. Fortunately for our algorithm, we already know the maximum number of polygons per cell, which we could use to pre-allocate memory for the hash buckets, at least as long as there is only one grid cell assigned to each hash value. However, this constant factor is only an upper bound that is rarely met in real applications and, hence, simply using such a large number of entries for each bucket would result in an overly large memory footprint of the hash table. To overcome these drawbacks, we decided to use a hybrid hashing strategy: we reserve a certain, relatively small, number of entries for each bucket and in case of a bucket overflow, we simply search for an empty bucket and link it to the overflown bucket.

34.3.5.2 Further Improvements

It is possible to prove a parallel constant running time for kDet assuming a perfect PRAM machine, however, this requires a linear number of processors. Even if a linear number of processors is relatively small compared to a quadratic number of processors that a naive collision detection would need for a constant running time, the actual number of processors of current GPUs is limited to, at most, a few thousand. On the other hand, recent 3D scenes consist normally of hundreds of thousands of polygons. Hence, the polygons have to be processed in batches whose size depends on the number of processors. So, a reduction of the potential polygons is still useful.

Such a reduction can be easily integrated into our approach without affecting the constant running time. To do that, we rely on the simple observation that usually, only very small parts of the objects collide. Consequently, it is not necessary to insert *all* polygons into the hash table and to check all for collisions, but only those that are in potentially colliding areas. These areas can be easily identified: They have to be inside the overlap of the objects' bounding boxes. Hence, it is sufficient to compute the overlapping region of the bounding boxes, check which polygons are inside this area, and restrict our tests to this smaller number of polygons. The bounding boxes can be computed in parallel in constant time using atomic operations. Additionally, testing whether a polygon is inside the overlapping region can be performed in parallel constant time.

This heuristic can be easily applied whenever a collision detection between a pair of different objects is performed. However, in case of deformable objects, we can additionally use our algorithm to compute self-collisions between polygons of the same objects efficiently: We simply have to insert all polygons of the deformable object into the hash map and check it against itself. Our experiments have shown that in this case, the aforementioned pre-test usually requires more time than simply checking all polygons. Moreover, in practice, it turns out to be more efficient to simply add all polygons of all objects to the same hash map hierarchy, instead of keeping an individual hash map hierarchy for each object, and treat the inter- and intra- collision checks as a single self-collision check.

34.4 Conclusions and Future Works

We have presented a hierarchical data structure, the *Inner Sphere Trees*. The ISTs support different kinds of collision detection queries, including proximity queries and penetration volume computations with one unified algorithm. Distance and volume queries can be answered at rates of about 1 kHz (which makes the algorithm suitable for haptic rendering) even for very complex objects with several hundreds of thousands of polygons.

Another big advantage of our penetration volume algorithm, when utilized for penalty-based simulations, is that it yields continuous directions and magnitudes of the force and the torque, even in cases of deep penetrations. Moreover, our inner sphere trees are perfectly suited for SIMD acceleration techniques and allow algorithms to make heavy use of temporal and spatial coherence.

Last but not least, we have presented a method for partitioning geometric primitives into a hierarchical data structure based on the Batch Neural Gas clustering. Our approach considers the object's volume instead of restricting the partitioning to the surface, as most other algorithms do.

Additionally, we have presented a new algorithm, kDet, that is able to find all intersecting polygons in almost linear sequential time for all practically relevant objects. A parallel version can even achieve a constant worst-case running time. kDet is suitable for all kinds of polygon soups and can be applied to deformable and even topology-changing objects at no extra costs, because no complicated pre-processing steps or acceleration data structures are necessary.

34.4.1 Future Work

However, our approaches also open up several avenues for future work, starting with the partitioning of the geometric primitives: it would be interesting to apply our clustering approach also to classical *outer* BVHs. For the ISTs there is also room for improving the hierarchy. For example, in particular cases, false positives can be reduced in object to object intersection when the spheres of inner nodes are actually increased in size. Such cases occur when the curvature of the larger sphere better conforms to the actual shape of the object and thus reduces the excess volume that protrudes outside the volume of the actual object—the greater overall volume of the node is harmless as the rest resides within the object, and thus generates no false positives.

Another option could be investigation of inner volumes other than spheres. This could improve the quality of the volume covering because spheres do not fit well into some objects, especially if they have many sharp corners or thin ridges.

Moreover, we would like to explore other uses of *inner bounding volume hierarchies*, such as ray tracing or occlusion culling. Note that the type of bounding volume chosen for the "inner hierarchy" probably depends on its use.

A major drawback of the ISTs is their restriction to watertight objects. This is mainly, because we have to compute a sphere packing of the objects' interior. In real word applications, e.g., in virtual prototyping tasks in the automotive industry, thin sheets are widely modelled as a single polygon layer.

In the future we plan to extend our ISTs to such open geometries by defining a *quasi-volumetric penetration measure* for thin or non-closed objects. The basic idea is very simple. Instead of filling the object's interior with spheres, we fill the free space, or at least a certain region surrounding an object. At the edges we break these sphere packings into several connected components. During the traversal we just have to select the correct connected component to be checked.

kDet also opens up a lot of interesting avenues for future work: a natural next step would be the development of an algorithm that optimizes the constant factor for real-world objects by improving the meshing. Obviously, the height of the hash map hierarchy should also be considered for this optimization. We believe, our definition of -freedom could be also used to improve existing approaches. For instance, it can lead to new construction methods for optimized bounding volume hierarchies. The development of simulation methods that maintain the constant and the height of the hierarchy during deformations is another challenge.

References

[Agarwal et al., 2004]

Agarwal, Pankaj, Leonidas Guibas, An Nguyen, Daniel Russel, and Li Zhang (2004). Collision detection for deforming necklaces. *Computational Geometry: Theory and Applications*, 28: 137–163.

[Batcher, 1968]

Batcher, Kenneth E. (1968). Sorting networks and their applications. In Proceedings of the *April 30–May 2, 1968, Spring Joint Computer Conference, AFIPS '68 (Spring), pp. 307–314*. ACM, New York.

[Borkovec et al., 1994]

Borkovec, Micha, Walter De Paris, and Ronald Peikert (1994). The fractal dimension of the Apollonian sphere packing. *Fractals an Interdisciplinary Journal on the Complex Geometry of Nature*, 2(4): 521–526.

[Cottrell et al., 2006]

Cottrell, Marie, Barbara Hammer, Alexander Hasenfuss, and Thomas Villmann (2006). Batch and median neural gas. *Neural Networks*, 19: 762–771.

[Eitz and Lixu, 2007]

Eitz, Mathias, and Gu Lixu (2007). Hierarchical spatial hashing for real-time collision detection. In *IEEE International Conference on Shape Modeling and Applications, 2007, SMI '07*, Lyon, France, pp. 61–70.

[Fisher and Lin, 2001]

Fisher, Susan, and Ming C. Lin (2001). Fast penetration depth estimation for elastic bodies using deformed distance fields. In *Proceedings of the International Conference on Intelligent Robots and Systems (IROS)*, Maui, HI, USA, pp. 330–336.

[Gärtner, 1999]

Gärtner, Bernd (1999). Fast and robust smallest enclosing balls. In Nesetril, J., ed., *ESA. Lecture Notes in Computer Science*, vol. 1643, pp. 325–338. Springer, Berlin.

[Hammer et al., 2006]

Hammer, Barbara, Alexander Hasenfuss, and Thomas Villmann (2006). Magnification control for batch neural gas. In *ESANN, pp. 7–12*.

[Martinetz et al., 1993]

Martinetz, Thomas M., Stanislav G. Berkovich, and Klaus J. Schulten (1993). 'Neural-gas' network for vector quantization and its application to time-series prediction. *IEEE Transactions on Neural Networks*, 4(4): 558–569.

[Morton, 1966]

Morton, Guy M. (1966). A computer oriented geodetic data base; and a new technique in file sequencing. *Technical report*, IBM Ltd.

[Satish et al., 2009]

Satish, Nadathur, Mark Harris, and Michael Garland (2009). Designing efficient sorting algorithms for manycore GPUs. In *Proceedings of the 23rd IEEE International Parallel and Distributed Processing Symposium*, Rome, Italy.

[Sengupta et al., 2008]

Sengupta, Shubhabrata, Mark Harris, and Michael Garland (2008). Efficient parallel scan algorithms for GPUs. *Technical report NVR-2008-003*, NVIDIA Corporation.

[Turk, 1989]

Turk, Greg (1989). Interactive collision detection for molecular graphics. *Technical report*.

[Weisstein, 2012]

Weisstein, Eric W. (2012). *Sphere-sphere intersection*. Wolfram Research, Inc. URL: http://mathworld.wolfram.com/Sphere-SphereIntersection.html.

[Weller and Zachmann, 2009a]

Weller, René, and Gabriel Zachmann (2009). Inner sphere trees for proximity and penetration queries. In *Robotics: Science and Systems Conference (RSS)*, Seattle, WA, USA.

[Weller and Zachmann, 2009b]

Weller, René, and Gabriel Zachmann (2009). A unified approach for physically-based simulations and haptic rendering. In *Sandbox 2009: ACM SIGGRAPH Video Game Proceedings*, New Orleans, LA, USA. ACM Press.

[Weller and Zachmann, 2010]

Weller, René, and Gabriel Zachmann (2010). Protosphere: A GPU-assisted prototype guided sphere packing algorithm for arbitrary objects. In *ACM SIGGRAPH ASIA 2010 Sketches*, pp. 8:1–8:2. ACM, New York.

[Weller et al., 2006]

Weller, René, Jan Klein, and Gabriel Zachmann (2006). A Model for the Expected Running Time of Collision Detection using AABB Trees. In *12th Eurographics Symposium on Virtual Environments (EGVE)*, Lisbon, Portugal, May 8–10.

[Weller et al., 2014]

Weller, René, David Mainzer, Abhishek Srinivas, Matthias Teschner, and Gabriel Zachmann (2014). Massively parallel batch neural gas for bounding volume hierarchy construction. In *Virtual Reality Interactions and Physical Simulations (VRIPhys)*, Bremen, Germany. Eurographics Association.

[Weller et al., 2017]

Weller, René, Nicole Debowski, and Gabriel Zachmann (2017). kDet: Parallel constant time collision detection for polygonal objects. *Computer Graphics Forum*, 36(2): 131–141.

Index